THAI LEGAL HISTORY

This is the first book to provide a broad coverage of Thai legal history in the English language. It deals with pre-modern law, the civil law reforms of the late nineteenth and early twentieth centuries, and the constitutional developments post-1932. It reveals outstanding scholarship by both Thai and international scholars, and will be of interest to anyone interested in Thailand and its history, providing an indispensable introduction to Thai law and the legal system. The civil law reforms are a notable focus of the book, which provides material of interest to comparative lawyers, especially those interested in the diffusion of the civil law.

Andrew Harding is a leading scholar in Asian legal studies, who has worked extensively on Thai and Southeast Asian constitutional law. He is co-author of *The Constitutional System of Thailand: A Contextual Analysis* (2011), and is co-founding-editor of the series of 'Constitutional Systems of the World' (Hart/Bloomsbury). He is a former Head of the Law School, SOAS, University of London, former Director of the Centre for Asian Legal Studies at the National University of Singapore, former Director of the Asian Law Institute, and former Chief Editor of the *Asian Journal of Comparative Law*. His latest book is *Constitutional Courts in Asia* (2018).

Munin Pongsapan is Associate Professor and Dean of the Law Faculty, Thammasat University, where he teaches contract law, the law of obligations, civil law systems, and legal history. He received his LLB from Thammasat University, LLM from the University of Cambridge, and PhD in law from the University of Edinburgh. He is a contributor of Volumes I, III, IV, and V of the 'Studies in the Contract Laws of Asia' project.

T0370704

This painted manuscript shows a procession in an annual festival called 'Chak Pra' held in the Southern part of Thailand. At first glance, the painting literally shows a chariot carrying the statue of Buddha with several groups of participants. In particular, the Chariot is pulled by indigenous peoples, while very few of them were actually near the Buddha on the chariot. Women and a child followed behind the chariot. A Khaek (literally means guest but commonly refers to Muslim, Indian subcontinent, and Indo-Malayan) and a Chinese hawker join as an observer within the procession. Also, this could be interpreted as the metaphors of hierarchy and other within Siamese/ Thai society under the realm of Hindu-Buddhist cosmological order.

Thai Legal History

FROM TRADITIONAL TO MODERN LAW

Edited by

ANDREW HARDING

National University of Singapore

MUNIN PONGSAPAN

Thammasat University

CAMBRIDGE
UNIVERSITY PRESS

Shaftesbury Road, Cambridge CB2 8EA, United Kingdom

One Liberty Plaza, 20th Floor, New York, NY 10006, USA

477 Williamstown Road, Port Melbourne, VIC 3207, Australia

314–321, 3rd Floor, Plot 3, Splendor Forum, Jasola District Centre, New Delhi – 110025, India

103 Penang Road, #05–06/07, Visioncrest Commercial, Singapore 238467

Cambridge University Press is part of Cambridge University Press & Assessment, a department of the University of Cambridge.

We share the University's mission to contribute to society through the pursuit of education, learning and research at the highest international levels of excellence.

www.cambridge.org
Information on this title: www.cambridge.org/9781108829861

DOI: 10.1017/9781108914369

© Cambridge University Press & Assessment 2021

This publication is in copyright. Subject to statutory exception and to the provisions of relevant collective licensing agreements, no reproduction of any part may take place without the written permission of Cambridge University Press & Assessment.

First published 2021
First paperback edition 2023

A catalogue record for this publication is available from the British Library

Library of Congress Cataloging-in-Publication data
NAMES: Harding, Andrew, 1950– editor. | Pongsapan, Munin, editor.
TITLE: Thai legal history : from traditional to modern law / edited by Andrew Harding, National University of Singapore; Munin Pongsapan, Thammasat University, Thailand.
DESCRIPTION: Cambridge, United Kingdom ; New York, NY : Cambridge University Press, 2021. | Includes bibliographical references and index.
IDENTIFIERS: LCCN 2020030253 (print) | LCCN 2020030254 (ebook) | ISBN 9781108830874 (hardback) | ISBN 9781108914369 (ebook)
SUBJECTS: LCSH: Law – Thailand – History.
CLASSIFICATION: LCC KPT120 .T428 2021 (print) | LCC KPT120 (ebook) | DDC 349.593–dc23
LC record available at https://lccn.loc.gov/2020030253
LC ebook record available at https://lccn.loc.gov/2020030254

ISBN 978-1-108-83087-4 Hardback
ISBN 978-1-108-82986-1 Paperback

Cambridge University Press & Assessment has no responsibility for the persistence or accuracy of URLs for external or third-party internet websites referred to in this publication and does not guarantee that any content on such websites is, or will remain, accurate or appropriate.

Contents

Tables

Contributors

Apinop Atipiboonsin is a lecturer at the Faculty of Law, Thammasat University. His primary areas of research include comparative constitutional law, administrative law, and family law. He graduated with an LLM from Columbia Law School, New York, as a Harlan Fiske Stone Scholar in 2016, and is currently an SJD candidate at the University of Virginia School of Law.

Chris Baker and Pasuk Phongpaichit are leading scholars in Thai studies. They met at the University of Cambridge in the late 1970s and have been resident in Thailand since 1980. Pasuk is Professor of Economics at Chulalongkorn University. Together they have written on Thailand's political economy, history, and literature including *A History of Ayutthaya: Siam in the Early Modern World* (Cambridge University Press, 2017), *The Palace Law of Ayutthaya and the Thammasat: Law and Kingship in Siam* (Cornell University, 2016), and *Unequal Thailand: Aspects of Income, Wealth and Power* (NUS Press, 2015). In 2017 they were jointly awarded the Fukuoka Grand Prize.

David Engel is SUNY Distinguished Service Professor Emeritus at the State University of New York, Buffalo. He is a leading scholar on Thai law and law and society studies, and is co-author with his Thai wife Jaruwan Engel of *Tort, Custom, and Karma: Globalization and Legal Consciousness in Thailand* (Stanford University Press, 2010) (Recipient of Jacob Book Prize Honorable Mention); *Code and Custom in a Thai Provincial Court: The Interaction of Formal and Informal Systems of Justice* (University of Arizona Press, Association for Asian Studies Monograph Series, 1978); and *Law and Kingship in Thailand during the Reign of King Chulalongkorn* (University of Michigan Center for South and Southeast Asian Studies, 1975).

Henning Glaser is the Founding Director of the German-Southeast Asian Center of Excellence for Public Policy and Good Governance, an academic institute and provider of training and consultancy services at Thammasat University's Faculty of Law. There, he has taught public and comparative law since 2007. He also is the Executive Director of the Asian Governance Foundation and advises governmental and non-governmental institutions on various issues of constitutional politics. His research focus includes the historical foundations and deep structure of constitutional law and politics in Asia.

Tyrell Haberkorn is an associate professor of Southeast Asian Studies in the Department of Asian Languages and Cultures at the University of Wisconsin-Madison. Her work is primarily focused on state violence and dissident cultural politics in Thailand. She is the author of *Revolution Interrupted: Farmers, Students, Law and Violence in Northern Thailand* (University of Wisconsin Press, 2011), and *In Plain Sight: Impunity and Human Rights in*

Thailand (University of Wisconsin Press, 2018), a new history of post-absolutist Thailand written through the lens of impunity.

Andrew Harding is a leading scholar in Asian legal studies, who has worked extensively on Thai and South East Asian constitutional law. He is co-author of *The Constitutional System of Thailand: A Contextual Analysis* (Hart, 2011), and is co-founding editor of the series of which that book is part, 'Constitutional Systems of the World', with Hart/Bloomsbury. He is a former Head of the Law School, SOAS, University of London, former Director of the Centre for Asian Legal Studies at the National University of Singapore, former Director of the Asian Law Institute, and former Chief Editor of the *Asian Journal of Comparative Law*. His latest book is *Constitutional Courts in Asia* (Cambridge University Press, 2018).

Kanaphon Chanhom is associate professor of law at Chulalongkorn University and an assistant to the University President. He earned his PhD degree from the University of Washington in 2010. His areas of interest are criminal law and legal history. He has written several books on criminal law and the history of criminal law in Thailand.

Khemthong Tonsakulrungruang is an early career scholar at Chulalongkorn University's Law Faculty, who recently completed his doctorate at Bristol University. He has published widely on constitutional law in Thailand, especially on the Constitutional Court. His doctoral thesis is on the influence of Buddhism on the Thai legal system.

Kongsatja Suwanapech is an early career scholar teaching at Thammasat University's Faculty of Law. He has a LLM degree from Edinburgh University and has research interests in the history of the Ayutthaya Period and modern Thai law.

Krisdakorn Wongwuthikun is Assistant Professor, Graduate School of Law, National Institute of Development and Administration (NIDA); he has an LLB from Thammasat University; an LLM in Global Environmental and Climate Change from the University of Edinburgh; and a PhD in Law from the University of Dundee.

Peter Leyland is Professor of Public Law at SOAS, University of London, and Emeritus Professor of London Metropolitan University. His research interests focus on UK and Thai public law and comparative public law, with a particular focus on devolution. Publications include: volumes on the *Constitution of the United Kingdom* (3rd ed., 2016) and the *Constitutional System of Thailand* (with Andrew Harding, 2011). Professor Leyland is joint founding editor of Hart series 'Constitutional Systems of the World'.

Duncan McCargo is a leading scholar in Thai studies. Currently he is Director of the Nordic Institute for Asian Studies and Professor of political science at the University of Copenhagen as well as Visiting Professor of political science at Columbia University. He has published widely on the politics of Thailand, including on the Thai judiciary and legal profession. McCargo's book, *Fighting for Virtue: Justice and Politics in Thailand*, was published by Cornell University Press in 2019. His latest book (with Anyarat Chattharakul) is Future Forward: The Rise and Fall of a Thai Political Party (NIAS Press 2020).

Eugénie Mérieau studied Law, Political Science, and Oriental Languages and Civilizations at the Universities of Sorbonne, Sciences Po, and the National Institute for Oriental Languages and Civilizations in Paris. In 2017, she completed her PhD on 'Thai Constitutionalism and Legal Transplants: a study of Kingship'. She has held various teaching and research positions, including researcher for the King Prajadhipok's Institute under the

Thai Parliament, and consultant for the Asia-Pacific Office of the International Commission of Jurists. She is currently a postdoctoral fellow in Law at the National University of Singapore.

Munin Pongsapan is Associate Professor and Dean of the Law Faculty, Thammasat University, where he teaches contract law, the law of obligations, civil law systems, and legal history. He received his LLB from Thammasat University, LLM from the University of Cambridge, and PhD in law from the University of Edinburgh. He is a contributor of Volumes I, III, IV, and V of the 'Studies in the Contract Laws of Asia' project published by Oxford University Press.

Naporn Popattanachai is Assistant Professor, Faculty of Law, Thammasat University. He has an LLB from Thammasat University; an LLM in European Legal Studies from the University of Bristol; an LLM in Environmental Law and Policy from University College London; and a PhD in Law, Nottingham Law School, Nottingham Trent University.

Narun Popattanachai is a lawyer at the Office of the Council of State, Thailand. His research interests span capital market regulation, securities regulation, and corporate governance. He holds a doctorate in law from Columbia University. He obtained his LLB and LLM degrees from University College London and a second LLM from Columbia. Since 2013 he has been a member of the New York Bar Association.

Rawin Leelapatana recently completed his doctorate at Bristol University on the history of Thai constitutionalism, and teaches at Chulalongkorn University, Faculty of Law. He has published a number of articles on constitutional law, including a co-authored article with Andrew Harding, published in the *Chinese Journal of Comparative Law*.

Adam Reekie obtained an MA from Queen's College, Oxford and is a solicitor (England & Wales, non-practising); he obtained an LLM from Thammasat University, where he now lectures in law.

Surutchada Reekie obtained her LLB, LLM, and PhD from University College London, and is Lecturer in the Faculty of Law, Chulalongkorn University. Her research is mainly on comparative private law, but she has worked on Thai tort law as well as legal history.

Preface

The main motivating factor in developing this book project was a realisation that there was little material in English on Thai legal history as such, but that, on the other hand, there was amongst Thai scholars a discernible enthusiasm for the subject as well as considerable achievement in terms of published work in the Thai language. A brief review of the literature in the English, Thai, and French languages appears before Chapter 1. Unlike the situation in most other jurisdictions, law schools in Thailand generally offer a compulsory course on legal history, and Thai lawyers and legal scholars seem to be generally very well versed in the subject, as well as very keen to talk and write about it. In most cases it seemed as though a concern with contemporary issues had led these scholars, including those contributing to this book, in an historical direction. This is hardly surprising when these issues would usually require an understanding of the reception of civil law in Siam, and/or an understanding of the underlying legal culture as the background on which the civil law was painted, so to speak. These matters are indeed extensively discussed in every chapter of this book.

The editors were aware that a number of younger scholars had completed a doctoral thesis in some aspect of Thai legal history: our youngest contributor was at the time of writing twenty-seven years old, and some others had recently completed a doctorate or were in the course of doing so. In addition, although Thai legal history has not attracted a great deal of legal scholarship amongst international scholars, a fair number of such scholars from other disciplines such as history, anthropology, and political science, as well as law, have written very insightfully on topics that form part of this subject or have distinct bearing upon it.

Accordingly, we were both surprised and pleased that our proposal for this book encountered more or less instant and enthusiastic commitment from so many scholars of both varieties, almost indeed from everyone who was invited; so much so that our viability benchmark of twelve chapters was rapidly outstripped by both responses and excellent suggestions as to other possible contributors. We are able to offer as a result no less than seventeen chapters in this book, covering most periods of Thai legal history and most legal topics. The book does not seek to be a textbook on the subject. Nor does it seek to be completely comprehensive in coverage or to provide a running narrative of events and issues. Rather it presents a set of reflective chapters that also, as it happens, between them set out most of the relevant historical/legal facts. We consider that taken together these chapters offer, in spite of our disavowal of comprehensiveness, a fairly full picture of Thai legal history.

This means that this book is the first in English (as is mentioned above, there are several in Thai) to offer a reasonably comprehensive overview and coverage of the topic. This is not to take away anything from previous publications that have contributed signally to our understanding of the subject. The literature is discussed further in outline in a Note following Chapter 1.

The truly fascinating story of legal development in Siam/Thailand from pre-modern times through modernisation and its many consequences up to the present day, well developed and widely understood in the Thai imagination, has therefore only been partially told in English or to an international audience. Accordingly, the present collection of essays attempts to draw on the considerable expertise and current research of both Thai and international scholars to provide both an overview and some in-depth studies of Thai legal history, both pre-modern and modern, from the Ayutthaya period through the Bangkok encounters with the West and the nineteenth to twentieth century reforms, up to the present century. The story also covers many, indeed almost all, major areas of both private and public law, and addresses a very wide range of both themes and perspectives.

Most of the chapters were discussed in draft form at a symposium at Thammasat University's Faculty of Law on 27 and 28 September 2019. This event provided an opportunity to discuss the drafts and suggest improvements as well as fuller integration of the content and opening to different perspectives and issues raised in the discussion. There is nonetheless, we feel, plenty of room for further research on the topics dealt with as well as the topics that are not dealt with, or not dealt with exhaustively, in this volume. There is no doubt, as we discussed at the symposium, much more work to be done, but we hope that this book will be a natural starting point for those who carry this work forward in the future.

In setting out and discussing this history in both length and depth, we hope that this book will add to understanding not just of legal history but of the legal present. It is striking that many chapters in the book take the legal history more or less up to date, and view legal history through the lens of current issues in Thai law. Accordingly, the division of the chapters into three groups should be taken in the light of this fact. We believe therefore that this book will add considerable depth not just to the understanding of Thai legal history, but to contemporary debates and discourses around legality and law reform in Thailand.

For the sake of clarity and authenticity, we refer to pre-1939 Thailand and Thai as 'Siam' and 'Siamese', but otherwise as Thailand from 1939 onwards. Thai terms are set out in a Glossary and have been standardised spelling-wise across the various chapters.

Finally, we wish to thank the contributors for their support, hard work, suggestions, and enthusiasm for the project; Joe Ng and Cambridge University Press for their support and their legendary professionalism in publishing the book; the staff of Thammasat University for their assistance with the symposium; William Roth, Adam Reekie, and Lasse Schuldt of Thammasat University for their sterling help with the work of subediting and formatting, and in one or two cases rewriting; Rawin Leelapatana of Chulalongkorn University for his help with the Chronology and the Glossary; and the Faculty of Law, Thammasat University, for funding the symposium and providing student assistance. We also thank the *Asian Journal of Law and Society* for granting permission to reproduce, with some changes, David Engel's article on the Blood Curse Ritual.

Chronology

12th century	– emergence of the Tai Kingdom
13th century	– appearance of the first copy of *Dhammasastra*
1238	– Sukhothai Kingdom
1351 to 1767	– Ayutthaya Kingdom
c.1400	– idea of *Thammasat* was known in Siam
1651	– creation of the *Manusara dhammasattha*
1687	– Treaty of Commerce between France and Siam
1767	– fall of Ayutthaya
1767 to 1782	– Thonburi Kingdom
1782 to present	– Bangkok (*Rattanakosin*) Kingdom
1789	– completion of conquest of four Muslim provinces by the Siamese
1805	– promulgation of the Three Seals Code by King Rama I
1826	– Burney Treaty of Friendship and Commerce between Siam and Great Britain
1851 to 1868	– King Mongkut (King Rama IV)
1855	– Bowring (Anglo-Siamese) Treaty
1868 to 1910	– King Chulalongkorn (King Rama V)
1874 and 1883	– Treaties regarding jurisdiction over British subjects
1892	– Gustave Rolin-Jaequemyns recruited by the Siamese government to reform the Thai legal system
1894	– judicial function assigned to the Court of Justice under the Ministry of Justice
1896	– establishment of the Judicial Reform Committee
1897	– establishment of the Law School, Ministry of Justice
1898	– conclusion of the Japanese-Siamese Protocol
1901	– commencement of individual land ownership
1907	– Treaty with France concerning jurisdiction over French-Asiatic subjects
1908	– enactment of the first Penal Code
	– beginning of function of the Supreme Court
1909	– extension of International Court's jurisdiction to the whole country
1910 to 1923	– King Vajiravudh (King Rama VI)
1912	– Palace Revolt – Thai-ness made state ideology

1925 to 1935	– King Prajadhipok (King Rama VII)
1925	– promulgation of the Civil and Commercial Code
1932	– Revolution on 24 June establishing constitutional monarchy – promulgation of first Interim Constitution on 27 June – promulgation of first Permanent Constitution on 10 December – Robert Lingat's first edition of *History of Thai Law* published
1933	– Law School of the Ministry of Justice transferred to Chulalongkorn University – promulgation of the Council of State Act 1933
1934	– Law School of the Ministry of Justice was transferred to Thammasat University
1935 to 1946	– King Ananda (King Rama VIII)
1935	– completion of the Civil and Commercial Code (Book V) and the enactment of the Civil and Criminal Procedure Codes – abdication of King Prajadhipok
1939	– final termination of unequal treaties – Siam becomes Thailand
1946	– King Ananda mysteriously found dead on 9 June
1946 to 2016	– King Bhumibol (King Rama IX)
1947	– coup restoring Thai-ness; promulgation of the 1947 Constitution aimed at restoring royal hegemony
1956	– promulgation of the current Criminal Code
1957	– coup staged by Field Marshal Sarit Thanarat, overthrowing Field Marshal Plaek Phibunsongkhram, in September
1958	– further coup staged by Field Marshal Sarit Thanarat, restoring royal hegemony, in October
1959	– promulgation of Constitutional Charter of 1959
1973	– '14th October uprising', popular uprising overthrowing the government led by Field Marshal Thanom Kittikachorn
1976	– '6th October massacre' at Thammasat University, and coup on 6 October
1978	– promulgation of 1978 Constitution establishing semi-liberal democracy on 22 December – establishment of the Judicial Service of the Courts of Justice
1991	– coup overthrowing General Chatchai Choonhavan in February – August 1991 to September 1992: judicial crisis
1992	– promulgation of the Act amending the First book of the Civil and Commercial Code on 31 March – 'Black May' incident
1997	– promulgation of the 1997 Constitution on 11 October – establishment of the Constitutional Court on 11 October
2001	– Thaksin Shinawatra becomes Prime Minister on 9 February – Administrative Court begins to function on 9 March
2006	– rally of PAD and coup overthrowing Thaksin Shinwatra on 19 September
2007	– promulgation of the 2007 Constitution on 24 August

2008	– PAD protest – Samak Sundaravej and Somchai Wongsawat ousted as Prime Ministers by Constitutional Court – Abhisit Vejjajiva becomes Prime Minister
2009	– 'Bloody Songkran' incident, UDD protest
2010	– 'Savage May' incident', UDD protest
2013	– proposal for Amnesty Bill; protest by the PDRC
2014	– coup staged by General Prayuth Chan-ocha ousting Prime Minister Yingluck Shinawatra – promulgation of 2014 Interim Constitution, allowing the Prime Minister to wield emergency powers under Section 44, on 22 July
2016 to present	– King Vajiralongkorn (King Rama X)
2017	– coming into force of 2017 Constitution on Chakri day (6 April)

Table of Cases

BRITAIN

Laurie and Morewood *v.* Dudin Brothers [1926] 1 KB 233

THAILAND

Appeal Court Decision Black Case No 2196/2558
Appeal Court Decision Red Case No 18002/2558
Constitutional Court Ruling No 18–22/2555
Constitutional Court Ruling No 28–29/2555
Constitutional Court Ruling No 1/2557
Constitutional Court Ruling No 7/2559
Criminal Court Order Black Case O. 1805/2558
Supreme Administrative Court Black Case No 326/2552
Supreme Administrative Court Black Case No 992/2556
Supreme Administrative Court Judgment No D5/2006
Supreme Administrative Court Judgment No D118/2007
Supreme Administrative Court Judgment No D33/2553
Supreme Administrative Court Judgment No 49/2554
Supreme Administrative Court Red Case No 33/2557
Supreme Administrative Court Red Case No 921/2560
Supreme Court Decision No 615/2451
Supreme Court Decision No 946/2451
Supreme Court Decision No 390/2463
Supreme Court Decision No 575/2465
Supreme Court Decision No 494–495/2473
Supreme Court Decision No 1229/2473
Supreme Court Decision No 563/2474
Supreme Court Decision No 719/2475
Supreme Court Decision No 208/2477
Supreme Court Decision No 810/2478
Supreme Court Decision No 871/2478
Supreme Court Decision No 56/2479
Supreme Court Decision No 507–508/2480

Legislation, Constitutional Provisions, and Treaties

BRAZIL

Civil Code
  Article 956

ENGLAND

British Consular Court (The HBM Court) Order in the Council
  Article 4
Seditious Libel Act

FRANCE

Civil Code (Code Civil) of 1804
Draft Penal Code of 1934
Penal Code of 1810
  Article 64

GERMANY

Civil Code (Bürgerliches Gesetzbuch) 1900
  s 194
  s 241
  s 249
  s 250
  s 251
  s 271
  s 275
  s 280
  s 284
  s 285
  s 286
  s 325

INDIA

INTERNATIONAL LAW

ITALY

JAPAN

PRUSSIA

SWITZERLAND

THAILAND

Abbreviations

ADR	alternative dispute resolution
APA	Administrative Procedure Act (1996)
BGB	German Civil Code (Bürgerliches Gesetzbuch)
CDC	Constitution Drafting Commission
CDD	Committee on Developing Democracy
DRKH	the Democratic Regime with the King as Head of the State
HBM Court	His Britannic Majesty's Court
JCC	Japanese Civil Code
KTSD	Three-Seals Law Code (kotmai tra sam duang)
NARC	National Administrative Reform Council
NCPO	National Council for Peace and Order
NGOs	non-governmental organisations
NIDA	National Institute of Development Administration
NPKC	National Peace Keeping Council
PAD	People's Alliance for Democracy
PCD	Pollution Control Department
PDRC	People's Democratic Reform Committee
REITs	Real Estate Investment Trusts
SEA	Securities and Exchange Act B.E. 2535 (1992)
SEC	Thai Securities and Exchange Commission
TC	Thai Constitution
TCCC	Thai Civil and Commercial Code
THB	Thai baht
TSD	Thai-style democracy
UDD	United Front for Democracy Against Dictatorship
UK	United Kingdom
VOC	Dutch East India Company (Vereenigde Oostindische Compagnie)

1

Introduction

Andrew Harding

1.1 PAST, PRESENT AND FUTURE

The starting point for much research and speculation on Thai law is that the framing and understanding of contemporary issues is so much rooted in the past. This much should be true of legal history, or even for that matter of history in general, anywhere. As we see from the contributions to this volume, however, it seems truer of Thai law than one might expect, given the enormous changes over the last one and a half centuries.

But why exactly do we study legal history? Is it in order to gain a more complete understanding of law in the past, which contributes to our understanding of history and how we got where we are; or a more complete and intelligent understanding of law in the present? In the implicit view of the contributors to this volume, each of these reasons appears to be both adequate and compelling. Not many of our contributors can be described as pure historians, and in almost all cases their work displays as much interest in the present as it does in the past. At least they do not describe a static legal world, but rather a dynamic one where both change and continuity are essential parts of the stories they tell. While legal scholars, historians and political scientists may have slightly different reasons for studying legal history, the joining of these three modes of scholarship in this volume offers welcome triangulation and counterpoint. Importantly, the past is seen here as something of value and integrity in its own right, not just as a prelude to the present. In this vision, law and the past are both implicated in the *volksgeist*;[1] there is probably no clearer example of this than Thailand. The essays presented here have in general a Savigny-like assumption as to the relation between law and society, and the following words of Savigny seem very apt to a study of Thai legal history:

> this organic connection of the law with the essence and character of a people manifests itself also over time, and here also it is to be compared to language. As with language, so too the law does not stand absolutely still for even an instant, but undergoes the same movement and evolution, is subject to the same law of internal necessity as every earlier development, therefore, the law grows forward with a people, constitutes itself out of them, and finally becomes extinct as a people lose their individuality.[2]

[1] Friedrich Karl von Savigny, *Vom Beruf unserer Zeit für Gesetzgebung und Rechtswissenschaft* (Goldbach: Keip, 1997) 8–9, translated by E. Donald Elliott in 'The Evolutionary Tradition in Jurisprudence' (1985) 85 *Columbia Law Review* 38.

[2] Ibid., 42. I am grateful to Munin Pongsapan for this reference.

The melding of past and present (and, by implication of course, the future too – some chapters – 11, for example, on the law of trusts – discuss or imply current or possible law-reform issues) is present throughout the volume. It is taken to a logical conclusion in Peter Leyland's Chapter 13 on administrative law, to which the label 'holographic' was attached during discussion at the symposium at Thammasat University[3] in which the chapters were discussed. This adjective could also be applied to several other chapters. In Chapter 13 various tropes in administrative law are examined conceptually rather than chronologically, narrative dissolving almost entirely into conceptual analysis. A similar tendency is seen in Khemthong Tonsakulrungruang's Chapter 5 on the influence of Buddhism, and in Eugénie Mérieau's (Chapter 6) on the law of lèse-majesté through the ages. However, some other chapters either adopt a more conventionally diachronic approach, or seek to pinpoint a particular significant moment or series of moments in history. Examples are David Engel's Chapter 7 on the blood curse, in which one can see traditional Lanna history and culture captured within intense recent constitutional conflict in Bangkok; and Chapter 17, by Duncan McCargo, exploring an episode in executive-judiciary relations in the early 1990s. Even these chapters have an eye to both what went before and what came after such moments.

The complex interactions of law and society in different periods of history are present throughout this book, so that one could, in line with what is said above about Savigny, view it as being as much about law and society as it is about legal history, notwithstanding the technical tenor and concern of some of the material, especially that relating to the reform period set out in Part II. This law-and-society approach is another (I suggest inevitable) consequence of a multi-disciplinary approach to legal history.

Another axis of comparison that the various chapters indicate is that of the lens through which history and law are being viewed, and here geography and comparison become important. The chapter by Krisdakorn Wongwuthikun and Naporn Popattanachai (Chapter 14), for example, starts from the perspective of international law by looking at the standard of 'civilisation' in the nineteenth century, a matter of close concern to Siam, as it led to the treaties of extraterritoriality and then the civil-law reforms, which are discussed further in several of the other chapters.[4] Certain chapters also see historical connections between Siam/Thailand and a broader geography encompassing, for example, Buddhist Southeast Asia (Chris Baker and Pasuk Phongpaichit, Chapter 3, and Khemthong Tonsakulrungruang, Chapter 5); Lanna (David Engel, Chapter 7); Britain (Adam Reekie and Surutchada Reekie, Chapter 8; and Surutchada Reekie and Narun Popattanachai, Chapter 11); Germany and Japan (Munin Pongsapan, Chapter 9); and France and Germany (Apinop Atipiboonsin, Chapter 12). As with many legal history stories in Southeast Asia, legal transplantation is a constant factor, and not just in respect of modernisation in the nineteenth to twentieth centuries, but even before that in the context of Buddhist law.[5]

[3] Faculty of Law, Thammasat University, 27–8 September 2019.

[4] See Chapters 7, 10, this volume; David M. Engel, *Law and Kingship in Thailand during the Reign of King Chulalongkorn* (Ann Arbor: University of Michigan Center for South and Southeast Asian Studies, 1975); M. B. Hooker, 'The "Europeanisation" of Siam's Law 1855–1908' in M. B. Hooker (ed.), *Laws of South-East Asia, vol 2* (Singapore: Butterworths, 1988), 531–607; A. J. Harding, 'The Eclipse of the Astrologers: King Mongkut, His Successors and the Reformation of the Thai Legal System', in S. Biddulph and P. Nicholson (eds.), *Examining Practice, Interrogating Theory: Comparative Legal Studies in Asia* (Leiden; Boston: Martinus Nijhoff Publishers, 2008).

[5] Andrew Huxley (ed.), *Thai Law, Buddhist Law: Essays on the Legal History of Thailand, Laos and Burma* (Chiang Mai: White Orchid Press, 1996).

All this of course indicates that with regard to any given legal issue the present cannot be properly understood without reference to the past, and both cannot be understood without reference to society, culture and to those factors Montesquieu described, in relation to the highly resonant theme of legal transplantation, as having an environmental nature.[6] If this seems an obvious point, it is probably even truer in Thailand than it might be elsewhere. The reason for this is that, as is heavily implicit or even explicit in many of these chapters, the gap between law and society often seems unusually wide, so that one struggles to map the legitimacy, reach and even sometimes the very definition, of law. Many of the chapters address this gap explicitly, explaining its nature and consequences over time.

1.2 THE STRUCTURE OF THE BOOK AND THE TYPOLOGIES OF LAW

Before proceeding further, we need to consider a question relevant to many chapters in this book, and also the structure of the book – what is the meaning of 'legal' in 'legal history'? While the contributors do not appear to sense a need for exactitude, the reader might need this matter explained.

It will be rare these days to find scholars who define law solely by reference to *lex scripta* (written law), as opposed to *lex tradita* (traditional law). Legal pluralism has taught us that law has many sources, both in the epistemological sense (how and where do we find it and prove it – 'written on the wall of the universe in characters the size of elephants', or 'in the government gazette in characters the size of ants'[7]?) and in the history-of-ideas sense (conceptually or metaphysically, where does it come from? From the unmoderated nature of the universe or the sovereignty of the ruler?). Although the state is the pre-eminent source of legislation, it cannot create out of nothing by sheer will a body of law in the wider sense of rules and institutions extending to a comprehensive conceptual apparatus for resolving disputes and ordering of all public and private relations. In almost all systems this dual nature of law is present. Indeed, in Chapters 3 and 5 in particular (but see also Chapters 15 and 16), the balance between the two conceptions of law is examined specifically and in some depth.

This only of course partly resolves the problem of what counts as 'law/legal', because we still need to know in relation to *lex tradita*, given that many things can be handed down to successive generations, what is counted as 'lex'. There is no easy resolution of this, and in an important way the implicit approach taken in the chapters that follow is that it should not matter that there is a penumbra of ambiguity surrounding this question. We should be content for the purposes of legal history, in a society where custom and religion have meant so much, with an understanding that whatever a community as a whole (not just legislators, lawyers or judges) considers as normative, that is, as regulating and ordering society's internal structures and relationships, can be considered as legal.[8] For example, where Kongsatja Suwanapech in Chapter 4 discusses initial royal commands, it seems irrelevant to ask if these are law, because they shed so much light on legal imagination. We do not even need to call in aid an Austinian theory of law as a set of commands to appreciate this point. Traditionally, in Siam, royal commands of any kind were considered to be binding for the future as general rules, and are therefore more than entitled in the Thai context to be

[6] C. Montesquieu, *The Spirit of Laws*, vol. 1 (New York: Nugent T tr., Colonial Press, 1899), 6 ff.
[7] Harding, 'The Eclipse of the Astrologers', 314.
[8] B. Z. Tamanaha, 'Understanding Legal Pluralism: Past to Present, Global to Local' (2008) 30 *Sydney Law Review* 375, 392 ff.

called 'law', even though it is their ultimate theoretical impact, not their legal enforceability, that is significant.

The material presented in this book sees Thai legal history as falling naturally into three parts that are defined ultimately by the process of modernisation in which the law and the legal system were changed beyond recognition during the late nineteenth and early twentieth centuries, as discussed in detail in Part II. This period represents a kind of centre of gravity for most Thai legal-history studies, or a fulcrum balancing the ancient and the modern; and the reform period features extensively, one way or another, in discussion even in the other two Parts of the book that deal principally with what went before, and what came after, the reform period. Part I looks at the pre-modern period, with an emphasis on sources in the dual sense indicated above; Part II is mainly concerned with private law; while Part III looks at public law and the constitutional struggles of the post-reform period to date.

This division seems a conventional one, and was not disputed as a suitable arrangement by the chapter authors when they met in Bangkok in September 2019 to discuss the chapters in draft. However, almost all of the chapters also break easily the bounds that such a division seems to impose – again by treating past, present and future as essentially one. Eugénie Mérieau's Chapter 6, for example, on the concept of lèse-majesté, deals historically with an idea that has both deep roots in the past and is very much for many people a defining element of Thai law as it is today. For Rawin Leelapatana (Chapter 15), the idea of *dhammaraj* is as relevant now as it was in the pre-modern period. More than this, the vector of reform, once instantiated more than 100 years ago, is still far from spent, as all of the chapters in Part II recognise as they move beyond the reform period into more recent times with discussion of long-term consequences and further reforms. Thus, the division of Thai legal history into these three parts should be taken as a convenient arrangement to facilitate clarity of exposition, not as a rigid, confining or comprehensively explanatory, distinction.

It may be helpful here, in order to understand more carefully the nature of this tripartite division of the material, and referring back to the problem of defining 'law', to recall Ugo Mattei's creatively destructive attempt to demolish the concept of legal families by substituting three basic types of law that may be seen in different configurations in a given national legal system. These types, each based on the social activity giving rise to it, are traditional law, professional lawyers' law and the law of politics.[9] The three Parts of this volume correspond essentially to these three types, but it should be seen that all three are still present (as, one would argue, elsewhere) in the legal system of Thailand, quite consistently with Mattei's analysis. If one can discern layers of law here, the layers do not always simply displace lower layers, but may still be seen, much as geological layers of rock may be seen in a canyon.[10]

This conception of legal typology explains the resistance of the material discussed in this volume to being parcelled easily into distinct periods. The legal families approach to analysing legal systems, much elaborated by earlier comparative law scholarship, in the case of legal systems like that of Thailand, would have us see Thailand as a 'civil law' country.[11] Such description defies historical analysis, since the civil law reforms were only finally completed less than a century ago (in 1935), as well as defying sociocultural analysis

9 Ugo Mattei, 'Three Patterns of Law: Taxonomy and Change in the World's Legal Systems' (1997) 45(1) *American Journal of Comparative Law* 5, 13 et seq.

10 Andrew Harding, 'Comparative Law and Legal Transplantation in South East Asia: Making Sense of the "Nomic Din"', ch. 9 of D. Nelken and J. Feest (eds.), *Adapting Legal Cultures* (Oxford: Hart Publishing, 2001) 208.

11 For a detailed analysis of what this means in practice, see Prachoom Chomchai, *Gleanings of Thai Private Law in a Roman and Anglo-Saxon Setting* (Bangkok: Faculty of Law, Thammasat University, 2015).

based on analysis of legal culture, religion and politics.[12] This is very apparent, for example, in Rawin Leelapatana's Chapter 15 on Thai-style democracy. It is striking that even the chapters concerned with the civil law reforms do not confine themselves to purely technical lawyers' analysis of the issues, as one would expect with a system seem as falling entirely within a civil law 'family'; Munin Pongsapan's Chapter 9 on contract law is a narrow exception here, showing that even a purely civilian comparative discussion can be revealing about the technology of lawyers' reform processes.

1.3 PART I

Part I discusses, or at least begins the discussion, with traditional Siamese law that predates the period of modernisation, but with an eye also to the later and even contemporary relevance of traditional legal culture and conceptions of law. Three of the six chapters in this part (Chapters 3, 4 and 6) are concerned mainly with the Thai concept of kingship. The other two chapters relate to Buddhism (Chapter 5), and legal culture (Chapter 7). Thus, three critical and historic elements that enliven any discussion of law in Thailand (monarchy, religion and culture),[13] are central to a consideration of the traditional law but also shed light on contemporary legal issues in the twenty-first century. These three traditional elements reappear throughout the book, even in those chapters (Chapters 15 by Rawin Leelapatana, 16 by Henning Glaser and 18 by Tyrell Haberkorn) concerned with the most recent events. These chapters discuss the sources of traditional authority and legitimacy in monarchy, religion and Thai culture.[14]

For the pre-modern period, the main problem is epistemological, and this is due to a lack of unarguable and helpful sources for the ascertainment of law, the notable exception to this being the Three Seals Code which dates from 1805. Chris Baker and Pasuk Phongphaichit's Chapter 3 is groundbreaking in overturning our long-standing, major assumptions about law in the pre-Bangkok era. These assumptions are based on Lingat's well known assertion that the major source of law was the *thammasat*, with royal legislation, the *rajasat*, being merely interstitial and resting on its consistency with the *thammasat* for its very validity, as if, in Prince Dhani Nivat's words, 'it can almost be said that in the past the *thammasat* was a constitution that placed limits on the king's legislative power'.[15] Lingat drew a sharp distinction between Western and Eastern concepts of law, where the former depended on the will of the sovereign and the latter on the primacy of tradition. As we have seen, and contrary to the legal-families approach, this distinction reflects a broader understanding of the ambiguity surrounding sources of law more generally, across all societies. Chapter 3 argues that Lingat's theory lacks supporting evidence in respect both of the primacy of the *thammasat* and of the absence of royal promulgation of law. The evidence presented suggests that the idea of royal promulgation should be taken in light of the traditions of the Ayutthaya era, continued in the Bangkok era up to at least the mid-nineteenth century, under which the King gave judgment in matters disputed before him, or reviewed earlier decisions, and then

[12] Pridi Kasemsup, 'Reception of Law in Thailand – A Buddhist Society' in M. Chiba (ed.), *Asian Indigenous Law: In Interaction with Received Law* (Bangkok: KPI, 1986).

[13] F. E. Reynolds, 'Dhamma in Dispute: The Interactions of Religion and Law in Thailand' (1994) 28 *Law and Society Review* 433.

[14] See, further, C. Baker and Pasuk Phongpaichit (translated and edited), *The Palace Law of Ayutthaya and the Thammasat* (Ithaca, NY: Cornell Southeast Asia Program Publications, 2016).

[15] Prince Dhani Nivat, 'Rueang borommarachaphisek' [On the coronation] (1946) 4 *Warasan haeng sayam samokhom chabap phasa thai* [*Journal of the Siam Society*] [Thai edition] 10–11.

gave instructions for them to be expressed as general laws in royal decrees. From (inter alia) the discovery of parts of the Three Seals Code in provincial locations, we can conclude that it was used throughout the kingdom and formed the basis for administration of justice until its replacement by the civil law reforms. It seems to have been a notable culmination of a traditional process of updating the laws at the beginning of a reign, incorporating those laws and decisions from the previous reign that were considered part of the general law. As the authors state: 'The text [of the Three Seals Code] attempts to bridge the contradiction between the "natural" origin of the *thammasat*, and the royal origin of the laws, by stating that the kings studied the *thammasat*, and then adapted and elaborated its content into the royal law-making.'

Accordingly, by collecting, verifying and indexing the law, the Three Seals Code, in spite of its variegated sources, is actually good evidence of law going back at least to the sixteenth century, not just law as stated in 1805. Contrary to the nineteenth-century view of Siam's legal system, observed by foreigners, as barbaric and chaotic – lacking in what were called 'civilised' standards (for which see Chapter 14) – earlier travellers to Siam in the seventeenth and eighteenth centuries seem to have had a favourable view of Siamese law. They praised the ordering of Siamese society as being very much based on written legal sources and the court system and the King for enforcing the law with reason and consistency. Perhaps what had changed by the nineteenth century was not Siam's legal system but the Western legal systems by whose standards Siam's was then assessed.

Enlarging on the theme of royal power in the context of high symbolism, Kongsatja Suwanapech's Chapter 4 uses the initial royal commands at each King's coronation through time as evidence of the changing nature and concept of monarchy. The wording of these commands indicates subtle changes of emphasis reflecting changes in society. Earlier commands provide evidence of ultimate royal ownership of all land; whereas later commands from King Mongkut onwards emphasise the sovereignty of the King as the people's representative. The change is striking, and occurred over a short period of half a century between the Three Seals Code, designed to cure the pollution of the *thammasat* via corrupt human agency, and the embracing of positive law as the expression of human will through the exercise of royal prerogative. Critical in Kongsatja's analysis is the Buddhist notion of the King as the *Mahasommutiraj* or Great Elected, which enabled King Mongkut to assert human power over the law. Interestingly enough, the author cites King Chulalongkorn's brother, Prince Phichit Preechakorn's, skilful blending of religion, custom and British utilitarian ideas (Jeremy Bentham was a close friend of Sir John Bowring,[16] which might explain the connection) in justifying an extensive royal power to legislate. There have in fact only been two initial royal commands during the era of constitutional monarchy, those of King Bhumipol and recently King Vajiralongkorn. These, as one would expect, reflect the constitutional nature of the monarchy, which sits better with the idea of the King as the 'Great Elected' than it does with the King as subject to the *thammasat*.

The other main aspect of pre-modern law is of course Buddhism, which has impacted heavily as a formulant on Thai law throughout its development. In his Chapter 5, Khemthong Tonsakulrungruang discusses this impact from the earliest times up to the present century – another example of the holographic nature of the discussion of Thai legal history. From this diachronic and conceptual discussion we can see the development of a body of Buddhist law in Southeast Asia from the teachings of Buddha in the *Tipitaka*, the concept of *dhamma* as

[16] Bowring was the author of the treaty of 1855, for which see, further, Chapter 14.

the ultimate truth of the universe, with *karma* as the enforcement of this truth; and the *vinaya* as the disciplinary code for monks.

Although the author accepts the finding in Chapter 3 that man-made law, the *rajasat*, had pre-eminence over the *dhamma* as a source of law in the Ayutthaya period, he nonetheless stresses the ultimate power, even up to the present day, of *dhamma* in providing a higher moral content for the positive law. The contribution of *vinaya* lies in providing a concept of fair procedure and legalism to the Buddhist tradition, but it is the *Thammasat* as a code of law that provides the basis of traditional law in Siam, as elsewhere in Southeast Asia. In the Siamese version, we find *dhamma*, *vinaya* and local custom amalgamated. It was this tradition that was found by King Rama I to have been corrupted or polluted by subsequent judgments. Being disturbed by an appeal case where the judges had granted a divorce to a faultful woman against her faultless husband, he ordered a restatement of the traditional law that became the Three Seals Code. It was this law that in turn was eclipsed by the civil law reforms later in that century. However, the author traces the complex and contested relationship between the received, secular, civil law legislated by the King and the traditional notion of law, so that the idea of dhamma-over-law remained and remains influential in Thai jurisprudence to this day. As Khemthong Tonsakulrungruang puts it succinctly, '[t]he Three Seals Code was replaced by modern legal codes, but the idea of *dhamma* as higher law was not'. Much the same can presumably also be said of the many constitutions since 1932 (see Chapters 15, 16 and 18).

What appears to emerge from this process is an unlikely but nonetheless successful phenomenon of syncretism, the origins of which can be traced back to the great monk-legislator King Mongkut, who laid the foundations of the reform process in the 1850s. As an example of this we can see the process of training judges, in which the values of *dhamma* are used to inculcate judicial virtues such as the absence of fear, favour, anger and ignorance. Ultimately, Thai jurisprudence by this process has filled the gap between the (necessary) positive law and (equally necessary) idea of substantive justice by using traditional legal/moral concepts.

As with the other chapters in Part I, Eugénie Mérieau's Chapter 6 on the law of lèse-majesté moves smoothly from the deeply traditional to the very modern. Indeed, this law is seen by many as a defining feature of Thai law, whether they argue for it or against it. This chapter yet again explores the persistence of tradition, while also noting the ways in which this law responded to foreign concepts as well as traditional ones during the reform period. This remarkable story has deep roots in Buddhist kingship and Thai legal consciousness reaching right up to the present day (see her discussion of recent Constitutional Court cases), and at almost every juncture marks off Thai from European law, not least in the context of constitutional struggles.

Finally in Part I, Chapter 7, by David Engel, deals with an unusual but illuminating topic: the blood-curse ritual performed by red-shirt protesters from Northern and Northeastern Thailand in Bangkok during the political disturbances of 2010. The origins of this ritual are found in Lanna culture and indicate a very different legal consciousness in those areas of Thailand from the metropolitan legal culture of Bangkok, where the blood-curse ritual was regarded with dismay and seen as typical of people from uncivilised regions of Thailand. As Engel shows, this ritual was an expression of outrage at the exclusion of those regions from the equal citizenship guaranteed by successive constitutions, and is based on traditional legal culture that is deeply rooted in the Lanna region, which had its own legal history originating in the code of King Mangraisat. The geographical divide in Thailand is also attributed to legal history in that Bangkok's imposition on Lanna of the civil-law reforms under King Rama V was seen as another attempt to impose the power of Bangkok and obliterate the culture and autonomy of Lanna. The story of the blood curse shows also that Lanna legal culture is remarkably persistent in its view of justice, rights and wrongs, in spite of its being overwhelmed by the Thai state during the reform period. Justice in Lanna is seen as occurring between the parties to a dispute not as being given by a judge. It would be interesting to know how widespread this aspect of legal culture is in Thailand, and hopefully more attempts will be made in the future to look at law from a non-metropolitan viewpoint.

1.4 PART II

Part II examines the crucial half-century or so of legal reforms 1885–1935 inspired by King Chulalongkorn the Great (Rama V), with chapters devoted to various aspects of the creation of the modern legal system following the Bowring Treaty of 1855 with Britain and other treaties with Western states creating a regime of extraterritoriality, in which foreigners on Siamese soil were subject to their own rather than Siamese law.

In doing so, this Part examines the origins, dimensions and consequences of professional lawyers' law, and it is – as one might expect – the most legal-technical part of the discussion of Thai legal history. This part covers all major areas of law: contract law (Chapter 9 by Munin Pongsapan), criminal law (Chapter 10, by Kanaphon Chanhom), the law of trusts (Chapter 11 by Surutchada Reekie and Narun Popattanachai), family law (Chapter 12 by Apinop Atipiboonsin), and administrative law (Chapter 13 by Peter Leyland). Two chapters (Chapter 8 by Surutchada Reekie and Adam Reekie, and Chapter 14 by Krisdakorn Wongwuthikun and Naporn Popattanachai) are devoted to the influence on Siam of international law and foreign lawyers. The main emphasis in this part (Chapters 10 and 13 excepted) is on private law, and here the discussion turns from general issues of monarchy, religion and culture (these are never far away, however, as we have seen) to the more technical matters that are characteristic of law reform. These discussions of the reform period, as indicated above, also take the discussion right up to the present century. Chapter 11 on the law of trusts, for example, makes it clear that the problem of trusts is by no means resolved even in 2020, after about 160 years of discussion and development since the first trust was created in Siam in 1861.

Original research in the Supreme Court archives forms the basis for Chapter 8 by Surutchada Reekie and Adam Reekie on the role of British judges in the Siamese Supreme Court between 1910 and 1940. This chapter provides a counterpoint to the substantive law coverage of the other chapters in Part II by looking at an interesting aspect of the judicial branch.[17] It is of course surprising, paradoxical even, to find British judges, trained in the common law, sitting in the apex court in a system in the process of converting from traditional to civil law, especially when Siam had recruited most of its legal advisers from civil law countries such as France, Belgium and Japan. Moreover, there was no treaty obligation to appoint British judges, as opposed to having European legal advisers sign off on decisions of the first instance and appeal courts, but not the Supreme Court. Yet, their presence was by no means simply diplomatic or ornamental, as they participated in well over 1,000 decisions over an extended period in which the Supreme Court (established in 1910) found its feet in the newly reformed legal system. The cases were not necessarily ones involving foreigners or

[17] For a study of the judiciary in more recent times, see Chapter 17, this volume.

commercial interests, but represented rather the full range of legal issues and parties. They appear also to have decided more cases than other foreign judges. Over time, these British judges themselves became acclimatised to the civil law basis of the Siamese legal system, although there is some evidence of use of common-law reasoning techniques during the earlier part of this period. Taken with the chapter on the law of trusts (Chapter 11), this chapter gives some credence to the idea that the modern Thai legal system owes at least something to the common law as well as to the civil law, despite Part II's predominant emphasis on civil law.

Chapter 9 by Munin Pongsapan is a study of the drafting of contract provisions on non-performance and damages in the Thai Civil and Commercial Code (TCCC). This drafting process compels us to reflect on the process of legal transplantation in Siam and more generally. While transplant theory focuses on the conflict between existing and foreign law, the study shows that a bare transplantation of legal text, where there is in effect no previous equivalent law, is unproblematical in itself: in pre-reform Siam, contractual obligations were seen as moral rather than legally enforceable, and there being no distinction between contractual and other civil or criminal wrongs, there was in effect no commercial law. The problem lies rather in the interpretation of the provisions adopted, having regard to their historical origins and theory within the 'donee' system, which gives rise to the potentially difficult second stage of transplantation – the transplantation of theory. The study finds that, in the drafting process, insufficient attention was paid to proper use of comparative law and legal history, as opposed to the use of felicitous language in drafting the provisions.

After seventeen years of drafting provisions of the TCCC based on the French Code civil, the French model was in effect replaced by (what was erroneously considered to be) the model adopted in the Japanese Civil Code, thought to be a virtual copy of the German *Bürgerliches Gesetzbuch*. The main Siamese draftsman, in reviewing civil law models, mistakenly assumed the identical nature of the two codes, whereas in fact the Japanese code was drawn from different sources. Of the five members of the drafting committee, three were English-educated Thai lawyers, and the other two were French lawyers, so that none of the committee was actually expert in German law, English sources being in use to ascertain what German law said. Accordingly, while the study supports Watson's idea of the ease of transplantation, it also finds that, contrary to Watson's idea, a systematic knowledge of the relevant law is essential to avoid uncertainty arising from the transplant.[18]

Similar issues of sourcing of law reform arose with criminal law, discussed by Kanaphon Chanhom in Chapter 10. The chapter provides a brief survey of pre-reform Siamese criminal law. It explains how Siamese custom was integrated with the imported *thammasat*. There was, however, no clear distinction between civil and criminal law, a distinction that was introduced in the reform process, which began with the drafting of the Penal Code of 1908, regarded as not just successful but as a template for other areas of law reform. Extraterritoriality was introduced primarily for criminal law purposes, so that criminal law reform was seen by King Chulalongkorn as an important basis for Siam's further development and reform. As with the TCCC, a mixed cast of characters, Siamese, Japanese and European, sat on the drafting committees, but it was the French lawyer Padoux, relying on Italian and Japanese precedents as well as existing customs and the Indian Penal Code (there is more evidence of common law influence here) who eventually pulled it all together. The codification of criminal law went hand in hand with judicial efforts; thus, the defence of insanity was

[18] See, for example, Alan Watson, 'Legal Transplants and Law Reform' (1976) 92 *Law Quarterly Review* 79, 140.

carefully provided for in the Code, while the defence of mistake was inserted into the law by judicial decision. The chapter concludes with discussion of further criminal law reforms undertaken during the mid-twentieth century. In 1956, the Thai Criminal Code replaced the Penal Code, making some changes to defences but retaining most of the principles established in the 1908 Code. The process of reforming criminal law was thereby completed and seen generally as a success, attributed to wise leadership, good drafting and flexible adjustment by judges and scholars.

The topic explored by Surutchada Reekie and Narun Popattanachai in Chapter 11 is wholly unexpected in the history of a civil law country – the law of trusts. The chapter not only details a surprisingly long history of the equitable trust under common law going back to 1861, but finishes with speculation about the future development of this area in light of current legislative process. One of the interesting points about this chapter is that it illustrates extremely well the hybrid rather than purely civilian origins of Thai law. The trust was originally introduced to deal with the estates of deceased British residents following the Bowring Treaty of 1855. During the reform period, English law could be used to fill gaps in the existing law. When the TCCC was finally given effect in 1925, section 1686 prohibited the trust. From then until 2007, when this section was amended to allow specific cases of the trust to be provided by law, trusts were not recognised, but of course this did not affect existing trusts, of which there must have been many; the authors record forty cases going to the Supreme Court on trusts during this period. Finally in the present century, Thailand is moving towards wider recognition of the economic and social value of the trust as an instrument for asset management.

Apart from this, the story of the trust is a fascinating case for those interested in legal transplants. The incorporation of the trust in the Thai civil-law system has not been easy, and one is drawn to think of Teubner's 'legal irritant'[19] as a way of describing this process. Teubner views the legal irritant as provoking gradual accommodation as the host system adjusts to the irritant. Chapter 11 describes just such a process of accommodation taking place over a period of 160 years and even by now not nearly completed.

One would expect that family law, being the area of law most related to social values and cultural issues, would be the most difficult area to change. Apinop Atipiboonsin's Chapter 12 on this subject fulfils this expectation and is directed principally to the issue of gender relations in family law. As with other chapters in this Part, this chapter traces the issues leading to reform, the reform process, and the ongoing effects of the reform debate and process.

Ever since the divorce case of *Amdaeng Pom* leading to the Three Seals Code in 1805, the position and status of women has been an important issue in Thai law. Ultimately, at the very end of the reform process, the issue of marriage had to be dealt with, the introduction of legal monogamy being effected in the final part of the reforms enacted in 1935. A knot of ambiguities is presented in this chapter. In ancient times, Thai women were amongst few in Asia living in a matrilineal, matrifocal society. Yet, their rights were very limited. The legal position of women has been remarkably improved since 1935; but on the other hand, the actual social impacts of this improvement have been less than might be imagined, and the law still contains some issues of inequality, such as with bride price and adultery.

[19] G. Teubner, 'Legal Irritants: Good Faith in British Law or How Unifying Law Ends Up in New Differences' (1998) 61 *Modern Law Review* 11.

Peter Leyland's Chapter 13 on administrative justice adopts a genealogical approach, finding the origins of the current system in the past and defining a line connecting the two. The essential condition for administrative justice was of course a centralised administrative state, and so the inquiry begins in the late nineteenth century when modern Thailand with its powerful centralised bureaucracy was in the process of being defined geographically and its administrative structure reformed. Apart from the structural development of administrative law, Leyland discusses the increasingly important and related area of judicial review of administrative actions, starting with the emplacement of the administrative court system in 1997. The number of cases in this system now numbers over 10,000 per year, and this system is reckoned to be a success story amongst the 1997 reforms. In particular, the external element (always present in this volume) in the form of the concepts of legitimate expectation and proportionality, deriving from German law, is discussed. The chapter draws attention to the increasing use of middle-class/activist-driven environmental litigation in more recent times. Although, as Leyland points out, the intention in reforming administrative law in the reform period was not to create a liberal-democratic order but rather a strong centralised state, the outcome has been to create some effective remedies against administrative acts. As with other topics, we see here a complex layering of law where the legal logic takes on, to some extent, a life of its own.

In Chapter 14, Krisdakorn Wongwuthikun and Naporn Popattanachai draw the lens wider to look at the reform process in the context of international law and the 'standard of civilisation'. This chapter discusses the unequal treaties Siam concluded with foreign states from 1855, embodying the principle of extraterritoriality. This concept is discussed further in Chapter 8 and forms background to, and explanation of, the reform process and how it was designed to slough off the poor reputation of Siamese law.

As Thongchai Winichakul has explained, the encounter with international law was a highly disruptive moment in the development of the Thai state.[20] International law necessitated many internal changes and a humbling acceptance of a lower, semi-colonised, status within its structure of rules. This chapter traces the origins and the concept of civilised status as formulated by international lawyers and applied to Siam between 1855 and 1938, by which time all the unequal treaties had been revoked and Thailand was able to take its place as fully equal to other states, a status it had gradually been attaining since the late nineteenth century. By confronting international law and its institutions in a positive way, Thailand was able ultimately to counter the threat of colonisation which lurked behind Bowring's insistence on the treaty of 1855. One interesting feature of this story is that Siam has not always been treated as uncivilised; indeed before the nineteenth century it had been treated on an equal basis. This changed when Western powers asserted their power in the region, basing the concept of civilisation squarely on the characteristics of a Christian state, thereby serving their own interests.

The importance of international law in the shaping of Thai law as we know it now can hardly be overstated. As we have seen in other chapters, it not only sparked the reform process but continues to exercise some influence over the development of law in modern Thailand.

1.5 PART III

Part III of the book examines the seemingly perennial problem of constitutional struggle from the fall of the absolute monarchy in 1932 to the drafting of the 2017 Constitution. In so doing,

20 Thongchai Winichakul, *Siam Mapped: A History of the Geo-Body of a Nation* (Honolulu: University of Hawai'i Press, 1997), ch. 1.

this Part examines the underlying political nature of law, or the foundations of law, in Thailand.

In this period, the attempt by King Chulalongkorn to separate the reform of private law from public law went awry as Thailand experimented with as many as twenty constitutions from 1932, in a state of seemingly permanent provisional constitutionalism punctured by several military coups, the latest being in 2006 and 2014. The cyclical nature of constitutionalism in Thailand again refers back to legal culture, the role of the monarchy, and also the rather newer element of militarism, first present in the coup of 1932 but continually present over the following nine decades. Following the latest coup in 2014, only in 2019 were elections held and a civilian government restored under the 2017 Constitution.

In the view of the authors presented here, the contemporary condition of law in Thailand is incomprehensible without an understanding of the legal history set out in Parts I and II, and amounts to a crisis of legality that is still being played out as we move to Part III.

The theme of constitutional struggle was introduced in David Engel's Chapter 7 on the blood-curse ritual. Two chapters opening Part III of the book, Rawin Leelapatana's Chapter 15 and Henning Glaser's Chapter 16 analyse in depth the nature and history of this conflict over the nature of democracy and constitutionalism in the constitutional (post-1932) period. Chapter 15 deals with the pre-1997 period, while Chapter 16 deals with the post-1997 period. The authors present an historic struggle between two conceptions of constitutionalism, based on what Rawin Leelapatana calls the *dhammaraja* tradition of Thai-style democracy that looks to royal power and traditional political values, and a liberal-democratic conception of the constitution. Rawin Leelapatana traces the contradictory development of these two conceptions leading to what he terms a 'binary-star' system in which neither conception has been able to escape fully the gravitational pull of the other, explaining the apparently eternal cycle of coups and democratic constitutions (referred to as constitutional *samsara*) that commenced with the coup against the absolute monarchy in 1932. The narrative presents an almost schizophrenic constitutional system, with constitutional, civilian government giving way periodically to military government established by overthrow of the established constitution. The contribution of this chapter to an understanding of legal history (and indeed legal present) lies in its explanation of Thai-style democracy. This is likened to 'Weber's patrimonialism, in that it is a product of a traditional belief in a stratified authority rather than in individualism and humanism', linking, in King Vajiravudh's formulation, nation, religion and monarchy in an official state ideology. Tracing the persistent conflict between two conceptions of the constitution (never itself, interestingly, part of the official ideology), the chapter concludes that

> coups and martial law were convenient means for the traditional elites and the military to parry and resolve what they deemed to be threats to the *Thai-ness* tradition. However, and secondly, the more the military strove to prolong the TSD [Thai-style democracy], the more it had to struggle against mass demands for constitutionalism and liberalisation and risked further losing their legitimacy. This development forced the conservative camp after 1973 to refrain from maintaining a permanent military rule, and instead to accommodate, or more precisely, to co-opt a greater space for liberalism.

Taking up the story with the 'people's constitution' of 1997, Henning Glaser's chapter, searching for basic structure in Thai constitutionalism, discerns a different approach to constitutionalism in the post-1997 period compared to the earlier periods discussed in the previous chapter. This period, he argues, is

> characterised by a new form of constitutionalism in which the Constitution figures as a more *legally* conceived rule-book with much more reach and impact than before, while the polity is ultimately still governed by unwritten normative references. This is the constitutional era of the new DRKH [democratic regime with the King as head of state], whose fate reflects that of the political system at large.

The 1997 Constitution introduced 'a stunning range of new or significantly upgraded institutions as watchdog bodies over electoral politics', replacing 'the formerly predominant political mode of constitutionalism' with a form of 'tight legalism' in which the 'Constitution and the concretizing organic laws created a differentiated regime of highly rigid anti-electoral regulations reinforced by an apparatus of draconic sanctions'. The basic structure is found in the DRKH, rendered immovable by the Constitution's own provisions. In due course, the rising conflict of 'colour-coded [red-yellow] politics' following Thaksin Shinawatra's assumption of office as Prime Minister was seen as setting electoral politics against the DRKH, precipitating yet further actions and reactions resulting in the coups of 2006 and 2014 and their corresponding constitutions, interim and permanent. As a result, constitutional developments since 2006 have bound the system more firmly to its DRKH basic structure, a cultural constitution still at odds (as during previous periods, discussed in Chapter 15) with the legalism implicit in constitutional government.

Duncan McCargo in Chapter 17 tells the interesting story of a signal attempt to preserve judicial independence in the 1990s. Judicial independence was compromised when the government attempted to interfere with the process of high-level judicial appointments. Although the judicial crisis was ultimately resolved, it was also partly a result of division over personalities within the judiciary. McCargo warns:

> The 1991–92 judicial crisis was partly about interference in the Thai judiciary by politicians. While today's judges have extracted from the story the simple moral that politicians must not be allowed to meddle in judicial appointments and decisions, there was much more to the crisis than that. The story was also about a prominent judge [Pramarn Chansue] who became in effect a politician in his own right, polarising the judiciary from within.

This chapter offers a unique window into the underlying realities of relations and processes within the judiciary and between the judiciary and executive powers. Such divisions within the judiciary are not unusual, and obviously undermine public trust and judicial standing. Happily, despite the complexity of the issues this episode had to deal with, the eventual outcome is positive for judicial independence, and the episode is an important one in Thai legal history.

A question about Thai law that is frequently raised is why there have been so many coups d'état and why nobody is ever punished for an act of what looks very much like treason. Tyrell Haberkorn's Chapter 18 on coup-amnesty provisions provides part of the explanation, and is another example (like Kongsatja Suwanapech's discussion of initial royal commands in Chapter 4) of how examination of texts repeated over time (albeit with some changes) can be revealing. In respect of the twelve coups that have occurred since 1932, '[i]mpunity has been secured in eight coups by stand-alone laws, in two coups by articles in post-coup constitutions, in one coup by both a constitutional article and a stand-alone law, and in only one case with no special legal measure promulgated. Each amnesty article or law has retroactively legalised the coup in question and protected the coup-makers from possible prosecution or other sanction'. Such amnesty provisions have proved in an important sense determinative of Thai constitutionalism and how we should conceive it.

In offering a hopeful conclusion that accountability for a military coup can be conceived in future, Tyrell Haberkorn illustrates the fact that, if long-standing legal history is to be changed, we need to trace it, understand it and see how it can be reversed.

1.6 CONCLUSION

A study of legal history recognises above all that there is no neat dividing line between past, present and future. In the imagination of the authors, the present appears to be almost an arbitrary dividing line between the past and the future. They recognise, as they peer into the future, that law has always in the past been a site of struggle, whether over constitutionalism, freedom of expression, property and economic justice, the rule of law, or military/royal prerogative, and it will no doubt continue to be so. Whereas in the past these struggles were within the drafting group and the government, we now see that they take place in the public forum of politics where we see different visions being set out.

In illuminating the past, the chapters in this book have outlined the shape and the trajectory of law in Thailand, as evidenced in many fields of endeavour. The authors recognise too that there are many questions still to be answered before a complete picture of Thai legal history can be presented. Despite encompassing eighteen chapters, this volume does not cover all areas of law, and there is without doubt much more to be said about the areas that are covered. It is to be hoped that this wide-ranging collection offers groundwork for the future, both in scholarship and in law reform. Each chapter implicitly or explicitly suggests that there is more we need to know, and that different perspectives may be brought to bear on the subject than those evident in this volume.

It is fervently to be hoped that scholars of several disciplines, not just legal scholars, will contribute to an understanding of Thai legal history, which we hope at least to have outlined usefully in our endeavours in putting together this volume. The comparative youth of most of our contributors offers strong expectation of an outstanding future for this subject. In discussing Thai legal history, we hope also to have contributed to the understanding of legal history across Asia and beyond.

2

Thai Legal History

A Brief Literature Review

Rawin Leelapana, Andrew Harding, and Eugénie Mérieau

It will be useful before we proceed further to orientate the reader briefly as to the existing literature on Thai legal history. It should be stressed that this subject has a rich literature, but it is spread over the last 300 years and is in at least three languages (Thai, English, and French). This review contains only the major items and is not intended as a complete list, but rather as a starting point for further research.

2.1 THAI LANGUAGE LITERATURE

บวรศักดิ์ อุวรรณโณ [Borwornsak Uwanno], กฎหมายมหาชน เล่ม 2: การแบ่งแยกกฎหมายมหาชน-เอกชน และพัฒนาการกฎหมายมหาชนในประเทศไทย [*Public law II: The Separation Between Public and Private Law and the Development of Thai Public Law*] (5th ed., Bangkok: Chulalongkorn University Press, 2007)

This book narrates the history of Thai public law, in particular the role of the monarchy as the embodiment of the constituent power, and the making of the 1997 Constitution. However, like Sawaeng Boonchalermvipas' book, mentioned below, Borwornsak does not provide an in-depth assessment of the interface between 'modern' and 'ancient' legal traditions in contemporary Thailand.

ร. แลงกาต์ [Robert Lingat], ประวัติศาสตร์กฎหมายไทย [*Thai Legal History*] (Bangkok: Thammasat University Press, 2010)

This book assesses the sources of Thai ancient laws as well as the history of tort, contract, and land laws in Thailand. However, the book leaves several gaps to be filled, in particular, the history of Thai criminal and public law.

มุนินทร์ พงศาปาน [Munin Pongsapan], ระบบกฎหมายซีวิลลอว์: จากกฎหมายสิบสองโต๊ะสู่ประมวลกฎหมายแพ่งและพาณิชย์ [*The Civil Law System: From Law of the Twelve Tables to the Civil and Commercial Code*] (3rd ed., Bangkok: Winyuchon, 2020)

Munin Pongsapan's book traces the development of the Thai Civil and Commercial Code through the lens of the history of the civil law system. It provides a sophisticated analysis on how foreign private law is received in Thailand. However, like Lingat's book, the aim of this monograph limits its focus to private law.

เสน่ห์ จามริก [Saneh Chamarik], การเมืองไทยกับการพัฒนารัฐธรรมนูญ [*Thai Politics and Constitutional Development*] (3rd ed., Bangkok: Foundation for the Promotion of Social Sciences and Humanities Textbooks Project, 2006)

According to Saneh, constitutional law should not be taken as synonymous with liberal constitutionalism, according to which a written constitution is understood as a mechanism for limiting state authority. Instead, he sees 'constitution' as a product of history, that is, as the interface between different forces within a political entity. However, having adopted a historical, rather than doctrinal, research approach, Saneh examined constitutional provisions and doctrines only in few pages of this book.

แสวง บุญเฉลิมวิภาส [Sawaeng Boonchalermvipas], ประวัติศาสตร์กฎหมายไทย [*Thai Legal History*] (19th ed., Bangkok: Winyuchon, 2020)

Sawaeng Boonchalermvipas's work is a compulsory reading for first year law students. It includes the influence of English and continental laws upon contemporary Thai criminal, civil and commercial, and procedural laws. Yet it does not assess the vestiges of ancient Thai law, in particular, its influence upon the application of contemporary law.

ธงชัย วินิจจะกูล [Thongchai Winichakul], เมื่อสยามพลิกผัน [*When Siam Changed*] (Nonthaburi: Samesky, 2019)

Thongchai's monograph is perhaps the most critical amongst all of those listed. The author comprehensively assesses how 'traditional Thai legal culture' (especially criminal and procedural law) has influenced the process of modernisation, summing up by proposing the new concept of 'patrimonial rule of law' – the rule of law based on social stratification. However, Thongchai does not examine how demands for modern, Western-style laws struggle against the traditional notion of authority.

2.2 ENGLISH LANGUAGE LITERATURE

Dhani Nivat, 'The Old Siamese Conception of the Monarchy' (1947) 36 *Journal of the Siam Society* 91; Chris Baker and Pasuk Phongpaichit, *The Palace Law of Ayutthaya and the Thammasat: Law and Kingship in Siam* (Ithaca, New York: Cornell University Press, 2016)

In his article, Prince Dhani explained the key features pertaining to the ancient Siamese conception of the monarchy. He argued that like the Western idea of the rule of law, the Siamese royal prerogative was limited by the principle of the Dhammaraja (the Buddhist righteous king) enshrined by the ancient constitution – the Thammasat. However, in *The Palace Law of Ayutthaya and the Thammasat*, Baker and Pasuk question Dhani's argument that Thammasat had long functioned as the basis of royal authority given that lawmaking had a large and hitherto unappreciated role in the premodern Thai state. For Baker and Pasuk (see Chapter 3 of this volume), Dhani underestimated the absolute power of the Siamese monarch in law-making.

Andrew Harding and Peter Leyland, *The Constitutional System of Thailand: A Contextual Analysis* (Oxford: Hart Publishing, 2011)

The book primarily focuses on the effort to implement a Western-style democratic government in post-1932 Thailand and how/why it has been compromised by the repeated cycle of coups. It provides a general yet very comprehensive background of Thailand's constitutional system, especially for those not familiar with the subject. However, finalised in 2011, the book requires an update to include an assessment on the effects of the 2014 coup – an attempt to turn the clock back to the semi-democracy period in the 1980s – on the country's twenty-first century constitutional landscape.

Andrew Harding, 'The Eclipse of the Astrologers: King Mongkut, his Successors, and the Reformation of Law in Thailand' in Penelope (Pip) Nicholson and Sarah Biddulph (eds.), *Examining Practice, Interrogating Theory: Comparative Legal Studies in Asia* (The Hague: Martinus Nijhoff 2008); David Engel, *Law and Kingship in Thailand during the Reign of King Chulalongkorn* (Ann Arbor: University of Michigan, 1975)

The two sources are prequel (Harding) and sequel (Engel). Harding and Engel assess the modernisation of the Thai legal system beginning in the mid-nineteenth century by illustrating the two competing worldviews adopted by the two kings, Mongkut and Chulalongkorn. Both kings were enlightened modernisers, yet, were also conservatives who regarded excessive adoption of 'Western traditions' as a menace to Thai-ness. The two items significantly provide a basic understanding for those unfamiliar with the between 'local' and 'Western' ideals in modern Thailand.

M. B. Hooker, 'The "Europeanisation" of Siam's Law 1855–1908' in M. B. Hooker (ed.), *Laws of South-East Asia, vol 2* (Singapore: Butterworths, 1986), 531–607

This piece looks at Siam's legal response to the treaties of extraterritoriality, from the Bowring Treaty up to the completion of major legal reforms in 1908.

Andrew Huxley (ed.), *Thai Law, Buddhist Law: Essays on the Legal History of Thailand, Laos and Burma* (Chiang Mai: White Orchid Press, 1996)

This collection covers an area greater than Siam, but is a valuable discussion of Buddhist law during and immediately after the Ayutthaya period.

Kanaphon Chanhom, 'Codification in Thailand during the 19th and 20th Centuries: A Study of the Causes, Process and Consequences of Drafting the Penal Code of 1908' (University of Washington, 2010)

The thesis assesses causes, process, and consequences regarding the making of the Siamese Penal Code of 1908. Against the argument that such law is defective, it praises the longevity and huge influence of such law over the current Criminal Code of 1957. It ultimately suggests the Commission responsible for the future amendment of the current Penal Code to consider factors which enable the longevity of its predecessor, notably the expertise of the drafters and the balanced mix between Thai and Western legal principles.

Khemthong Tonsakulrungruang, 'Toward A New Buddhist Constitutionalism: Law and Religion in the Kingdom of Thailand' (University of Bristol, 2020)

The thesis applies the clash between liberal democratic constitutionalism and Buddhist-infused justice to suggest a New Buddhist Constitutionalism. This clash precipitates a conflict not only within different sectors of Buddhism itself but also between Buddhism and other religions. The thesis ultimately suggests how legal mechanisms can provide new forms of reconciliation.

Tamara Loos, *Subject Siam: Family, Law, and Colonial Modernity in Thailand* (Ithaca, NY: Cornell University Press, 2006)

This book provides insightful information regarding the underlying struggle behind Thailand's family law. Here, Loos comprehensively assesses how the tension between 'tradition' Siamese jurisprudence and the transplantation of Western legal doctrines has influenced modern-day family law, especially the idea of monogamous marriage. Her account that 'Siam's sovereignty was fundamentally a gender and legal issue as much as it was a political and economic one .... Siam would not be free of burdensome extraterritoriality clauses until it "modernized" its legal system, which ultimately meant adopting a 'modern' family law on monogamous marriage' (pp. 101–2) is worth examined in future studies.

Munin Pongsapan, 'Reception of foreign private law in Thailand in 1925: a case study of specific performance' (University of Edinburgh, 2013)

The thesis assesses the drafting process of Thailand's Civil and Commercial Code in 1925. It ultimately provides an intriguing argument that without a proper understanding towards legal transplantation and legal history, lawyers can misunderstand the true underlying features of Thailand's own legal rules and concepts.

H. G. Quaritch Wales, *Ancient Siamese Government and Administration* (London: Bernard Quaritch, 1934)

A classic and invaluable source for the study of government in pre-modern times, this work tells us a great deal about traditional legal culture and administration.

Rawin Leelapatana, 'The Kelsen-Schmitt debate and the use of emergency powers in political crises in Thailand' (University of Bristol, 2019)

The thesis applies the debate between Hans Kelsen and Carl Schmitt on the use of emergency powers in political crises to the political struggle between the pro-democracy and the nationalist-royalist faction in post-1932 Thailand. It provides a picture regarding the legal history of such struggle. Thai legal history is ultimately used to suggest the novel *binary-star conception of emergency powers* which reflects the pull of gravity between liberal and conservative views towards emergency powers.

Michael Vickery, *The Constitution of Ayutthaya: An Investigation into the Three Seals Code* (London: SOAS, 1993)

This book is a detailed discussion of the Three Seals Code. Another piece by Vickery on the Constitution of Ayutthaya appears as a chapter in Huxley's book, referred to above.

2.3 FRENCH LANGUAGE LITERATURE

Georges Coédès, *Recueil des inscriptions du Siam* [*Collection of Siamese inscriptions*] (Bangkok: Bangkok Times Press, 1924)

Georges Coédès offers an erudite commented translation of the Siamese inscriptions from the times of the Kingdom of Dvaravati to the Bangkok era. They are relevant in so far as they include many inscriptions with dispositions of a legislative character, most notably from the Sukhothai kingdom.

René Guyon, *L'œuvre de codification au Siam* [*The work of codification in Siam*] (Paris: Imprimerie Nationale, 1919)

This short book provides an analysis of the various legal codes (civil and commercial, criminal code, criminal and civil procedure), and offers some background on their respective geneses.

Robert Lingat, *L'Esclavage privé dans le vieux droit siamois* [*Private Slavery in Old Siamese Law*] (Paris: Domat-Montchrestien, 1931)

This is one of the most important works ever written on slavery laws in the early nineteenth century. Lingat analyses slavery laws as part of contract law, and shows to which extent Thai slavery laws are derived from Hindu Laws, and how they were indigenised.

Robert Lingat, *Le Régime des biens entre époux en Thaïlande* [*The Community of Property between Spouses in Thailand*] (Hanoi: Imprimerie d'Extrême-Orient, 1943)

In this volume, Lingat analyses the peculiarity of the 'community of property' regime for spouses in Siam (and the rest of Indochina), a peculiarity he holds as proof that there is a distinctive Indochinese law, differing from both Chinese and Hindu law.

Eugénie Mérieau, *Le constitutionnalisme thaïlandais à la lumière de ses emprunts étrangers, une étude de la fonction royale* [*Thai Constitutionalism and Legal Transplants, A study of Kingship*] (Paris: Presses de l'Institut Universitaire Varenne, 2018)

This book provides a fresh analysis of Thai constitutional history, from the late nineteenth century to the early twenty-first century. Its originality lies in its analysis of Thai constitutional history in light of transplants interpreted on the basis of shifting local doctrines.

Georges Padoux, *Code pénal du Royaume de Siam. Promulgué le 1er juin 1908 entré en vigueur le 22 Septembre 1908.Version française avec une introduction et des notes* [*Penal Code of the Kingdom of Siam Promulgated on June 1st, 1908 and Entered into Force on September 22, 1908, French version with an introduction and notes*] (Paris: Imprimerie Nationale, 1909).

In this volume, Georges Padoux, the key drafter of the 1908 Penal Code, gives his views on the Code and reflects on its drafting process. Each article of the Code comes with notes indicating the foreign codes used as sources of inspiration.

Thapanan Nipithakul, *Les sources du droit et du pouvoir politique au traverses anciens textes thaïɒlandais* [*The sources of Law and Political Power Through Ancient Thai texts*] (Toulouse : Presses de l'Université de Toulouse, 2007)

This book examines the influence of the Hindu Code of Manu on traditional Siamese Law as well as on the administration of justice. It includes a translation of the Siamese Phrathammasat.

PART I

Traditional Law and its Modern Resonances

3

Thammasat, *Custom, and Royal Authority in Siam's Legal History*

Chris Baker and Pasuk Phongpaichit

พระมหากษัตริย์มิได้ทรงบัญญัติกฎหมายขึ้นอย่างแท้จริง[*]

Le roi ne légifère pas.

A ruler has no power to enact law.[1]

In his pioneering and magisterial history of Thai law written in the 1930s, Robert Lingat argued that Thai kings could not make laws but only enforce laws that conformed to tradition and a universal moral code, the *dharmaśāstra* or *thammasat*.[2] He argued that this formulation had spread from India throughout Southeast Asia, and stood in contrast to Europe where kings were legislators who created 'positive law' reflecting their own will. In a famous essay from 1946 to 1947, Prince Dhani Nivat cited Lingat's proposition to support his argument that a Thai monarch was a 'King of Righteousness' who obeyed moral laws. Prince Dhani's essay became a foundation text of the Bangkok Ninth Reign (1946–2016). Lingat's interpretation of Thai legal history became more or less sacrosanct. To this day, legal historians place the *dharmaśāstra* or *thammasat* at the core of the traditional legal system, and reproduce Lingat's argument.

Yet in the history of Siam, there is only one *thammasat* that is securely known as a document. That is the *Thammasat* that stands at the head of the Three Seals Code, the collection of law texts assembled in 1805. By contrast, hundreds of *dhammasattha* manuscripts have been found in Burma, and significant numbers in other parts of Southeast Asia. These codes might be sponsored by kings but were compiled by monks and legal experts, and were used by elders, headmen, and others settling disputes, not by royal courts. While these *dhammasattha* contain long lists of moral principles and legal rulings, the *Thammasat* of 1805 has nothing similar, only a short passage on the importance of judges making fair decisions free of bias.[3]

* Thanks to Andrew Harding and Munin Pongsapan for initiating this project; to Prachoom Chomchai for an elegant comment; to Eugénie Mérieau for help on sources; and to Christian Lammerts for his pioneering research and his help.

1 R. Lingat, *Prawatisat kotmai thai* [History of Thai Law], 2 vols. (Bangkok: Foundation for the Promotion of Social Sciences and Humanities Textbooks, 1983 [1935]), vol. 1, 44; R. Lingat, *L'Influence Indoue dans l'ancien Droit siamois*, Etudes de sociologie et d'ethnologie juridiques, XXV (Paris: Ed. Domat-Montchrestien, 1937), 21; R. Lingat, 'Evolution of the Conception of Law in Burma and Siam' (1950) 38(1) *Journal of the Siam Society* 9.

2 The documents are spelled in several ways in the sources, depending on language and author. Here, the Indian texts are given as *dharmaśāstra*, the Mon and Burmese as *dhammasattha*, the Thai as *thammasat*, and the text at the head of the Three Seals Code as the *Thammasat*.

3 For an English translation of the 1805 *Thammasat*, with commentary, see Chris Baker and Pasuk Phongpaichit, *The Ayutthaya Palace Law and the Thammasat: Law and Kingship in Siam* (Ithaca, NY: Cornell SEAP, 2016).

In contrast, there is strong historical evidence of royal lawmaking in Siam. Old law codes from Tai communities were named after kings and derived their authority from his name. Foreign visitors to the old capital of Ayutthaya commented on the dominant royal role in the legal system. The texts assembled in the Three Seals Code show that kings made laws by ruling and decree, preserved them in the royal archive, titled them as 'royal' laws and edicts to give them authority, and vigorously propagated their use in an elaborate system of courts headed by the king.

The status of Lingat as a scholar and pioneer, and the political adoption of his ideas, has complicated any reappraisal of his legal history of Siam. Here we argue that royal lawmaking was a major function of Siamese kingship in the Ayutthaya era, and that the *thammasat*, rather than being the fount and origin of Siam's legal tradition, was adopted into the royal lawmaking tradition rather late in the history. First, we sketch Lingat's history and its adoption by Prince Dhani Nivat. Second, we trace the development of royal lawmaking in Siam. Third, we examine the *Thammasat* which heads the Three Seals Code of 1805.

3.1 ROBERT LINGAT, PRINCE DHANI NIVAT, AND THE *THAMMASAT*

Robert Lingat (1892–1972) studied Pali, Sanskrit, and Thai in Paris and served as an interpreter for the Siamese troops sent to France in the First World War. In 1923, he was appointed legal adviser to the government of King Vajiravudh. From 1930, he began work on editing the Three Seals Code for the canonical edition published by Thammasat University in 1938–9, and also authored several research articles on Thai law and history. In 1931, he was awarded *docteur en droit* from Paris for a thesis on 'L'esclavage privé dans le vieux droit siamois'. After the foundation of Thammasat University in 1934, Pridi Banomyong invited Lingat to teach a master's course on the history of Thai law. His *Prawatisat kotmai thai* (History of Thai Law) emerged from this course and was published in three volumes (1935, 1939, 1948). After the conflict between Siam and France in 1940, Lingat left Siam and lived mainly in Indochina until 1955, and Paris thereafter.[4]

3.1.1 *Lingat's History of Thai Law*

In the first volume of *Prawatisat kotmai thai*, Lingat constructed the early history of Thai law as follows.[5] In ancient Hindu India, adepts who could communicate with the gods learnt the universal moral principles, which were written down in codes called *dharmaśāstra* and used to guide legal judgments. This practice spread to the Mon who were a culturally dominant civilisation in early Mainland Southeast Asia. As the Mon were Buddhist, they stripped out the Hindu aspects of the *dharmaśāstra*, and inserted a story where an adept found the moral code written on the wall of the universe and brought it back for the benefit of humanity. *Dhammasattha* codes in Mon and Burmese have survived from thirteenth-century Pagan onwards. Gradually Buddhist ethics were incorporated into these codes, especially from the *vinaya*, the monastic code of discipline.

4 Roland Drago, 'Robert Lingat (1892–1972)' (1972) 24(3) *Revue internationale de droit compare* 702–4; Eric Leon, *Robert Lingat (1892–1972), Professeur de droit orientaliste* (Bordeaux: Université de Bordeaux, 2017); Charnvit Kasetsiri and Wigal Pongpanitanont, 'R. Laengka kap prawatisat kotmai thai' [R. Lingat and the history of Thai law] in Lingat, *Prawatisat kotmai thai*, vol. 1 (1983). Lingat was appointed a judge at the court of appeal around 1930; on this practice, see Chapter 8, this volume.

5 R. Lingat, 1 *Prawatisat kotmai thai* 14–19, 33–49. The same argument is found in his *L'Influence Indoue*.

From the Mon, Lingat continued, this practice spread elsewhere in Southeast Asia. The preface to the Thai *Thammasat* of 1805 states that the document came from the Mon country. Lingat argued that this transfer happened at a very early date, prior to the foundation of Ayutthaya, and that the *thammasat* was present in Sukhothai, as shown by an inscription found in 1930.[6] He assumed that a *thammasat* was in use in the Ayutthaya era and proposed that the Sukhothai version, Ayutthaya version, and the 1805 document were all the same text.[7] He admitted this proposal was speculative but this passage seems to betray his ideal version of the history.

In Siam, Lingat continued, the legal history developed slightly differently from Burma. In executing their duty to uphold and enforce the law, kings made legal rulings and issued edicts which were written down, but these were temporary assertions of authority by the current king and hence lapsed at a change of reign. Since some were of lasting use, a system was created whereby these rulings were scrutinised and those found to conform with the *thammasat* were incorporated into a permanent code. Later Lingat wrote, 'such a procedure [of scrutiny] was actually followed during the Ayuthia period at every change in the reign, when it was entrusted to members of the High Court of Justice, composed principally of Brahmins versed in the science of law'.[8] In Lingat's view, King Rama I's action in 1805, assembling and scrutinising all legal texts surviving from the Ayutthaya era, thus creating the Three Seals Code, was in keeping with this practice.

3.1.2 *'The King Could Not Truly Legislate'*

Lingat belonged to the same generation and same intellectual orientation as the great historian, Georges Coèdes.[9] Both were impressed by the impact of Indian culture on early Southeast Asia, and both sought to make sweeping region-wide generalisations about this impact. Coèdes pictured Indian statecraft and institutions shaping the political history of Southeast Asia. Lingat ascribed an analogous role to Indian law:

> Hindu law is the basic origin of the Mon *dhammasatham* texts, and thus is the origin of Thai law as well . . . Hindu law is like a common system that relates old Thai law with the laws of other countries that received direct or indirect influence from Indian civilisation, in the same way that Roman Law did for the laws of various countries in the west.[10]

He concluded that Roman Law, which encoded the will of the ruler, and Hindu Law, based on tradition and morality, resulted in completely different systems, and completely different implications for kingship:

> In Thailand in the past, the king could not truly legislate . . . He was the ultimate judge and had the power to hand down punishments and edicts . . . but such actions were only the outer surface of the law or the administration of the law. He could not make the rules which had to be respected and followed because, at that time, law was considered totally the province of

6 It is now known as Inscription 38 and dated around 1400. See Alexander B. Griswold and Prasert na Nagara, 'A Law Promulgated by the King of Ayudhyā in 1397 A.D. Epigraphic and Historical Studies, No. 4' (1969) 57(1) *Journal of the Siam Society* 109.

7 Lingat, 1 *Prawatisat kotmai thai* 37.

8 R. Lingat, *The Classical Law of India*, trans. J. Duncan M. Derrett (Berkeley: University of California Press, 1973) 270.

9 Coèdes recognised their affinity, see Georges Coèdes, 'Robert Lingat: L'esclavage privé dans le vieux droit siamois' (1931) 31 *Bulletin de l'Ecole Francaise d'Extreme-orient* 528–9.

10 Lingat, 1 *Prawatisat kotmai thai* 41.

> custom and the *thammasat* . . . The king had full freedom to make judgments or edicts that contravened the *thammasat* or existing custom, but such judgments and rulings had power only in their immediate application, not as law. Only when royal rulings were in conformity with judicial principle, that is, in line with the *thammasat*, could they be called *rachasat* and have the same power as the *thammasat*.[11]

Lingat developed this theory in the 1930s and repeated it many times without modification, even in an appendix to his 1967 *magnum opus* on India.[12]

3.1.3 *Prince Dhani Nivat and the Non-absolute Monarchy*

On 24 March 1946, Prince Dhani Nivat[13] delivered a lecture in English at the Siam Society attended by King Rama VIII, the future King Rama IX, and the Princess Mother. Subsequently, he translated the text into Thai, printed in December 1946, and expanded part of this talk into an English-language article on 'The old Siamese conception of the monarchy', published in 1947.[14] This essay aimed to recast 'the theory of the Siamese Monarchy' for an era in which absolute monarchy had been abolished.

Dhani argued that 'divine kingship' (*devaraja*) of Khmer origins was only of fleeting importance in the distant past. In Thai tradition, the ideal ruler was a 'King of Righteousness', who was bound by moral laws, including the Ten Virtues of Kingship, the description of a wheel-rolling emperor in the Three Worlds cosmology, and most particularly the *thammasat*. In the Thai version of the article, he reflected Lingat's argument that the king could not legislate: 'It seems that the king did not have the power to legislate outside the *thammasat* in any way. In present-day language it can almost be said that in the past the *thammasat* was a constitution that placed limits on the king's legislative power'.[15] In the published English version, Dhani expanded this point, referring to Lingat as 'a distinguished legal historian', and drawing very closely on Lingat's account of the legal history.[16]

> As has been said by scholars of legal history, the function of the king was not to legislate but to protect the people and preserve the sacred law. It might have been true in many cases that by promulgating ordinances the king could bend and entirely contravert the *Thammasat* to suit his end; and yet he could not hope to give his decisions the lasting form and authority of the latter; imposed as it was by superior agency.[17]

[11] Lingat, 1 *Prawatisat kotmai thai* 44.

[12] Lingat, *Classical Law of India*, 270.

[13] A grandson of King Mongkut, Prince Dhani Nivat Sonakul was brought up in the palace, studied Pali and Sanskrit at Oxford, and rose to be Minister of Education shortly before the 1932 revolution. Subsequently, he published several historical and literary studies, and served as President of the Siam Society for twenty-six years. In 1950, King Bhumibol appointed him as a Privy Councillor and bestowed the status of *phra-ong jao* and the title of Phraworawongthoe Krommuen Bidyalabh Bridhyakon.

[14] Prince Dhani Nivat, 'The Old Siamese Conception of the Monarchy' (1947) 36(2) *Journal of the Siam Society* 91.

[15] Prince Dhani Nivat, 'Rueang borommarachaphisek' [On the coronation], *Warasan haeng sayam samokhom chabap phasa thai* (1946) 4 *Journal of the Siam Society* [Thai edition] 10–11.

[16] Dhani, 'Old Siamese conception', esp. 97. Dhani cites Lingat's, *L'Influence Indoue*.

[17] Dhani, 'Old Siamese conception', 99. On this passage, Dhani has a footnote, not to Lingat but to H. G. Quaritch Wales, *Ancient Siamese Government and Administration* (London: Bernard Quaritch, 1934), 170. There Wales wrote, 'The function of the king, in the legal system, was not to legislate, but to protect his people and preserve the sacred law . . . [T]he king, though by the absolute nature of his power he could bend and even entirely controvert the *Dharmasāṭra* according to his will, could not hope to give his decisions the lasting force and authority of the sacred *Dharmasāṭra*, imposed as it was by a superior agency'. Wales's argument, published in 1934 *before* Lingat's *Prawatisat*, follows Lingat's exposition in *Prawatisat*, sentence by sentence, for about a page. Wales has no footnote but acknowledges Lingat (and Burnay) at the start of the chapter. Lingat had stated the key points of his

Lingat returned to Thailand to give a lecture at the Siam Society in March 1949, when Prince Dhani was President of the Society. The lecture on 'The evolution of the conception of law in Burma and Siam' included an elegant, abbreviated translation of the core passage from *Prawatisat kotmai thai*:

> This [Western] notion of law is entirely foreign to the traditions of the peoples in the Far East . . . A ruler had no power to enact law . . . As he was invested with absolute power, his judgments were final, but they were mere orders, namely personal and accidental injuctions [sic], having nothing of a general and permanent rule such as our law has.[18]

After the 1932 Revolution, the Siamese monarch was no longer absolute but under a constitution. Prince Dhani's recasting as a 'King of Righteousness' or *thammaraja* endowed the monarch with an alternative and potentially rival source of authority. Over the following decades, Prince Dhani's recasting gained in strength.[19] In parallel, Lingat's interpretation of the role of the *thammasat* in Thai law and kingship became sacrosanct. In 2006, sixty years after Prince Dhani's article, the Faculty of Law of Chulalongkorn University published a bilingual book on *Ten Principles of a Righteous King and the King of Thailand*,[20] using Dhani's vocabulary, while articles published to mark two centuries of the Three Seals Code reproduced Lingat's argument almost word-for-word.[21]

3.2 KINGS MAKING LAWS IN SIAM

Lingat wrote his *Prawatisat* at a time when source material on Thai history was very sparse. His account of the origin and development of Thai law had only one footnote[22] and a couple of casual references to other works. The question of when the *thammasat* was passed from Mon to Thai sparked a debate to which Prince Damrong, W. A. R. Wood, Andrew Huxley, and several others contributed, with estimates spanning over a millennium from the Dvaravati era to 1805. The wide difference in these estimates was a function of the lack of evidence.

argument in 'Commentaire des lois sur les epoux, par le Pha:ja Vĩnăĩsŭnthon', (1930) 24(2) *Journal of the Siam Society* 211, but Wales may have seen a fuller draft.

18 Lingat, 'Evolution', 9.

19 Prince Dhani's essay is one of two texts through which the royal intellectuals of the pre-1932 regime hoped to revive the monarchy. The other text is Prince Damrong Rajanubhab, *Phra prawat somdet phra naresuan maharat* [A biography of King Naresuan the Great] (Bangkok: Fine Arts Department, 1950), which he wrote for the education of the future King Rama VIII. Both texts seem to have succeeded. King Rama IX shaped a new image of the Thai king as *thammaraja*, while King Naresuan supplied a martial dimension, projected in writing, image, and film. For some consequences, see Chapter 6 in this volume: Eugénie Mérieau, 'A History of the Thai Lèse-Majesté Law'.

20 Eugénie Mérieau, 'Buddhist Constitutionalism in Thailand: When Rājadhammā Supersedes the Constitution' (2018) 13(2) *Asian Journal of Comparative Law* 283.

21 See for instance Channarong Bunnun, 'Phra Thammasat', in Winai Pongsripian and Wirawan Ngamsantikun (eds.), *Nitipratya thai: prakat phraratcha prarop lak inthaphat phra thammasat lae On the Laws of Mu'ung Thai or Siam* [Thai Legal Philosophy: The Preface, Tenets of Indra, Thammasat, and *On the Laws of Mu'ung Thai or Siam*] (Bangkok: Thailand Research Fund, 2006), especially the excerpt quoted in the conclusion below. See also Surasak Likasitwatanakul and Kannika Chansang, *R. Laenga kap thai sueksa: ruam bot khwam plae lae botkhwam sueksa phonngam* [R. Lingat and Thai studies: Collected articles in translation and studies] (Bangkok: Thammasat University Press, 2005); and Winai Pongsripian (ed.), *Kotmai tra sam duang: waen song sangkhom thai* [Three Seals Law: Mirror of Thai Society], 2 vols. (Bangkok: Thailand Research Fund, 2004).

22 To Forchhammer, who claimed in 1885 to have found 'the oldest law-book as yet found in Burma', and who linked it directly to the Indian *dharmaśāstra* tradition. These claims are now considered 'incredible'. See D. Christian Lammerts, *Buddhist Law in Burma: A History of Dhammasattha Texts and Jurisprudence, 1250–1850* (Honolulu: University of Hawai'i Press, 2018) 105–7.

3.2.1 *The Elusive* Thammasat

The journey of the Sanskrit word *dharmaśāstra* to Burmese *dhammasattha* and Thai *thammasat* has created a tempting trail for the historian to follow. But recent work shows that this trail was not as straightforward as it once seemed.

Christian Lammerts cautions that evidence on the production and use of *dhammasattha* in Burma prior to the seventeenth century is scant. There are several bibliographies, mostly compiled in the nineteenth century, which list many old *dhammasattha* texts by name, but few have been identified among surviving texts today. The oldest surviving manuscripts of *dhammasattha* in Burmese language date from the mid-eighteenth century. The *Manusāra dhammasattha*, which survives in several manuscript versions, has a preface dating its original creation to 1651 with details that match other historical records. The *Dhammavilāsa dhammasattha* text may be pre-1628, but the evidence is shakier. Lammerts argues that, on current knowledge, these two may be the oldest surviving Myanmar *dhammasattha*.[23] Several other texts lay claims to much earlier origins but these claims lack substantiation and in many cases are patently false. Earlier scholars (including Lingat) often accepted these claims without sufficient scrutiny.[24] Fewer texts in Mon have survived, and Nai Pan Hla suspects that only one (in two versions) dates earlier than 1757.[25]

Lammerts also argues that there is little evidence of Sanskrit scholarship in early Burma. The *dhammasattha* developed in a context of Pali scholarship, and drew on Buddhist literature. There is no simple descent from Indian *dharmaśāstra* to Mon and Burmese *dhammasattha*.[26]

There is also no evidence of an early passage from Mon/Myanmar to Siam. Sukhothai Inscription 38, which Lingat mentioned, records a law principally about the abduction of slaves. The dating and authorship are vexed but it was probably inscribed around 1400.[27] The text repeatedly states that offenders against its various clauses will be punished 'in accordance with the rules of the Rājāśāstra and the Dharmaśāstra',[28] and in one place it uses the same phrase about rewarding cooperative witnesses.[29] This inscription is clear proof that the idea of a *thammasat* was known in Siam around 1400, but the repeated use of the phrase 'in accordance with the rules of the Rājāśāstra and the Dharmaśāstra' seems like a formula, meaning 'in accordance with law'. Two other references in the law to Rājāśāstra alone give a sense of referring to a document (specifying punishments), but there is no secure sighting of a *thammasat* as a document.

This inscription is the only reference to a *thammasat* in Siam prior to the Three Seals Code of 1805. Given the large number of *dhammasattha* manuscripts found in Burma, and the

23 D. Christian Lammerts, 'Buddhism and written law: Dhammasattha manuscripts and texts in premodern Burma', Ph.D dissertation, Cornell University (2010), esp. 29, 52–3; Lammerts, *Buddhist Law*, chapter 3.

24 Starting with Forchammer's *King Wagaru's Manu Dhammasattham*, published in 1892.

25 Nai Pan Hla, *Eleven Mon Dhammasāt Texts*, collected and translated in collaboration with Ryuji Okudaira (Tokyo: The Centre for East Asian Cultural Studies for UNESCO and the Toyo Bunko, 1992), xxvii.

26 Lammerts, *Buddhist Law*, 22–32, 43–5.

27 Griswold and Prasert na Nagara argued the law was promulgated by a king of Ayutthaya in 1397. Others have suggested that the date was later, and the author was a king of Sukhothai. See Griswold and Prasert na Nagara, 'Law promulgated by the King of Ayudhyā'; Vickery, 'Guide through some recent Sukhothai historiography', 230–3; Phiset Jiajanphong, *Sasana lae kan mueang nai prawatisat sukhothai-ayutthaya* [Religion and politics in the history of Sukhothai and Ayutthaya] (Bangkok: Sinlapa Watthanatham, 2002).

28 ในขนาดในราชศาสตรธรรมศาสตร, *nai khanat nai ratchasat thammasat*; for Griswold and Prasert's gloss on ขนาด *khanat*, see Griswold and Prasert na Nagara, 'Law promulgated by the King of Ayudhyā', 133, n. 30.

29 Griswold and Prasert na Nagara, 'Law promulgated by the King of Ayudhyā', 120–45.

smaller but significant caches from Lanna and Lanchang,[30] this absence is striking. Recent searches have found hundreds of legal texts in Thai provincial archives but not a single pre-Bangkok *thammasat*.[31]

Nor are there any indirect sightings of *thammasat* in other sources. In Siam, there is a tradition of royal panegyrics, beginning in the inscriptions of Ramkhamhaeng and Lithai of Sukhothai and continuing with poems in praise of King Trailokanath (1448–88), King Prasat Thong (1629–36), and King Narai (1656–88). One standard part of these panegyrics vaunts the king's broad knowledge of many disciplines and subjects including warfare, religion, history, and literary arts. None of these panegyrics mentions knowledge of the *thammasat*, in contrast to similar panegyrics from Cambodia, Champa, and Java.[32] The Thai royal chronicles mention revisions of several important texts including the Tipiṭaka, Manual of Victorious Warfare, and Jataka tales. If kings had ordered revisions of the *thammasat* at the start of a reign, as Lingat and other scholars have suggested, then these might have appeared in the chronicles in the same way.

3.2.2 *Kings and Laws*

The evidence for the presence of *thammasat* in Siam is very weak. In contrast, the evidence for kings making laws is very strong.

Early law codes are known from Tai-speaking communities, including several versions of the *Mangraisat*, attributed to the founder king of Chiang Mai.[33] These various texts share three characteristics. First, the authority behind these codes is a king. Second there is no mention of a *thammasat*, though some codes have the word in their title as if it meant simply 'law code'. Third, these codes are eminently practical. They have no theoretical reasoning. Some are clearly shaped by Buddhist ethics but others are not. They deal with the topics that cause dispute in most societies – sexual and marital relations, property and theft, unwarranted violence.

The foreign visitors who left the first detailed accounts of Siam in the seventeenth century noted the importance of law and particularly of the written law. Joost Schouten, a Dutch VOC officer resident in Ayutthaya for six years in the 1630s, wrote: 'The King thus soveraignly disposing of all things, does notwithstanding nothing without some appearance of reason, and

30 Aroonrut Wichienkeeo, 'Lanna customary law' in A. Huxley (ed.), *Thai Law: Buddhist Law. Essays on the Legal History of Thailand, Laos and Burma* (Bangkok: White Orchid Press, 1996) 31–42; and Yoneo Ishii, 'The Thai Thammasat (with a note on the Lao Thammasat)' in M. B. Hooker (ed.), *The Laws of South-East Asia* (Singapore: Butterworths, 1986), vol. 1, 198–9.

31 From research in over thirty provinces, Pitinai Chaisaengsukkul found 683 legal manuscripts with over 30,000 pages. Most are excerpts from the Three Seals Code, especially laws on procedure and common causes of disputes (slavery, marriage, debt). Not one is a *thammasat*. See Pitinai Chaisaengsukkul, *Kotmai haeng anajak sayam: wijai phuen than* [Law of the Siamese kingdom: Basic research] (Bangkok: Samcharoenphanit, 1994). Sarup Ritchu found the same in the south, 'Legal manuscripts from southern Thailand' in Huxley, *Thai Law: Buddhist Law*, 61–72. See also Jakkrit Uttho, 'Khwam samphan khong kotmai tra sam duang kap kotmai chabab chaloeisak thi phop nai hua mueang tang tang' [Relationship between the Three Seals Law and local codes found in provincial centres] in Winai, *Kotmai tra sam duang*, vol. 1, 61–116.

32 There are inscriptions dating back to 667 CE in Cambodia, 875 CE in Champa, and Java in the ninth century which vaunt the king's knowledge of *dharmaśāstra* or similar terms; see Lammerts, 'Buddhism and written law', 189–97.

33 Mayoury Ngaosyvathn, 'An introduction to the laws of Khun Borom', in Huxley, *Thai Law: Buddhist Law*, 73–80; Aroonrut, 'Lanna customary law'; Aroonrut and Gehan Wijeyewardene (ed. and tr.), *The Laws of King Mangrai* (Canberra: Australian National University, 1986); Prasert na Nagara, *Mangraisat* (Bangkok: Liangchiangjongjaroen, 1974).

conformity to the Laws of the Kingdom. . . . The ordinary Justice, both Criminal and Civil, is admitted through the Kingdom according to their ancient Customes and Laws, by Officers purposely appointed'.[34]

Jeremias Van Vliet in the 1630s commented: 'In the whole kingdom there are law courts of mandarins to administer criminal and civil cases and the written laws after the old fashion'.[35] Simon de la Loubère, a lawyer by training who visited Siam in the 1680s, left a long account of the organisation of the judiciary in both the capital and provinces, described court process in detail, commented on the range of punishments, and attempted to gain access to the written laws, without success.[36] The scribe of an Iranian embassy in 1685–6 left a more dismissive account of Siam's legal system, emphasising the tendency to delay and the extraction of fees by judicial officers, but confirmed the general importance of the law and the overriding power of the king.[37]

Schouten commented on the role of the king in making law:

> The Sovereignty and Government of *Siam* is in the King . . . . He maketh Laws without any advice or consent of his Council or Lords, his will being the rule he walks by, unless his goodness descend sometimes to counsel with his Mandoryns, them of his Council; these sometimes deliberate upon his Majesties propositions, and present their result to him by way of humble supplications, which he confirms, changes or rejects, as he thinks good.[38]

3.2.3 *Internal Evidence of the Three Seals Code*

The main evidence for royal lawmaking is found in the Three Seals Code, a collection of texts assembled in 1805 when King Rama I ordered a scrutiny of the 'royal decrees and laws in the palace library'.[39] There are twenty-seven or forty-two texts in the Code, depending on how they are enumerated.[40] Although most have a preface with a date and title of the reigning king, Vickery cautions that many dates are clearly faulty and the identification of the king is often ambiguous.[41] The earliest dates fall in the mid-fourteenth century at the very start of the Ayutthaya era, but the first reference to the laws in an external source (the royal chronicles) is in 1548.

In Ayutthaya Siam, laws were not created by legislation (drafting, scrutiny, proclamation) but by the accumulation of court judgments and royal edicts. The king was the chief judge and all judgments were theoretically delivered in his name. Many clauses in the Three Seals laws appear to originate from particular court judgments. In the older codes, such as those on marriage and theft, this origin is clear as there has been little editing. Other clauses came from royal edicts. The Palace Law (clause 118) specifies that the king's words become law: 'If the King speaks on any government matter connected with law or custom, it is considered

34 François Caron and Joost Schouten, *A True Description of the Mighty Kingdoms of Japan and Siam* (Bangkok: Siam Society, 1986 [1671]), 126, 131.

35 Chris Baker et al. (eds.), *Van Vliet's Siam* (Chiang Mai: Silkworm Books, 2005) 153.

36 Simon de La Loubère, *A New Historical Relation of the Kingdom of Siam*, trans. A. P. Gen (London, 1793) 81–8.

37 Muhammad Rabi' ibn Muhammad Ibrahim, *The Ship of Suleiman*, tr. John O'Kane (London: Routledge, 1972) 121–7.

38 Caron and Schouten, *Mighty Kingdoms*, 125–6.

39 *Kotmai tra sam duang* [Three Seals Code, hereinafter *KTSD*] (Bangkok: Khurusapha, 1994), vol. 1, 4–5.

40 See the table in Baker and Pasuk, *The Ayutthaya Palace Law*, 4–5.

41 Michael Vickery, 'Prolegomena to Methods for Using the Ayutthayan Laws as Historical Source Material' (1984) 72 *Journal of the Siam Society* 37.

a ruling to be followed'.[42] In the epic poem, *The Tale of Khun Chang Khun Phaen*, there is a vignette of such a ruling being made. When Khun Chang wades out into the river to present a petition to the king, 'The king then issued an edict. "Henceforth from today, should anyone on guard duty neglect their government service by allowing people into the vicinity, that person shall be liable to punishment of seven grades including execution, under this edict for the protection of the king". He disembarked and entered the palace'.[43]

In the Surabha Jātaka, one of the non-canonical *jātaka* tales known only in Siam and its neighbours, a king makes a series of judicial rulings after each of which 'he orders high officials to inscribe the ruling as a royal decree for governing the realm from now on'.[44] The prefaces of several laws in the Three Seals Code frame the process of lawmaking in this form: the king proceeded to the audience hall, where certain named officials attended, and 'gave a royal command to draw up the royal edicts and decrees as follows'.[45] This procedure of lawmaking continued to the mid-nineteenth century. King Mongkut judged or reviewed court cases, and then generalised the decisions as decrees.[46]

At intervals, these collected rulings seem to have been sifted, edited into the form of a general rule rather than a specific judgment, sorted according to type (*laksana*), and written into codes with titles like *phra aiyakan laksana phua mia*, the 'sacred rulings of the type for husband and wife', namely the law on marriage. In early times, this editing process was rather rough and ready. In some laws which seem of early vintage, such as the law on marriage, clauses in different segments of the law offer contradictory rulings on the same issue. In later years, the process may have become more sophisticated. There is a trace in the preface to the Thirty-Six Laws which states that the king commanded two councils consisting of sixteen officials to review forty-eight rulings and royal orders, resulting in thirty-six clauses issued as law.[47] The Old Royal Decrees, which mostly date from the early to mid-eighteenth century, show the process explicitly: some decrees begin with a description of an original court case and ruling, followed by the decision drafted in the form of a law. Mongkut's legal edicts were similar in form.[48]

The laws were collected into codes that were updated from time to time. On his accession in 1548 King Chakkraphat consulted the laws to determine the rewards to be given to those nobles who had assisted his coup. The officials showed him the '*Phra thammanun* from the royal library'.[49] From his visit in 1687–8, Simon de la Loubère reported:

> The Publick Law of *Siam* is written in three Volumes. The first is called the *Pra Tam Ra*, and contains the names, functions, and prerogatives of all the Offices. The second is intituled, *Pra*

42 Baker and Pasuk, *The Ayutthaya Palace Law*, 103. The following clauses make provision for appealing against such rulings.

43 Chris Baker and Pasuk Phongpaichit (tr. and ed.), *The Tale of Khun Chang Khun Phaen* (Chiang Mai: Silkworm Books, 2010) 789–90.

44 *Panyat chadok* [*The Fifty Jātaka*] (Bangkok: Government Savings Bank Foundation, 2011), vol. 3, 272–4.

45 For example, *KTSD*, vol. 2, 331.

46 See *Prachum prakat ratchakan thi 4* [*Collected proclamations of King Mongkut*], ed. Charnvit Kasetsiri (Bangkok: Toyota Thailand Foundation and the Foundation for the Promotion of Social Sciences and Humanities Textbooks Project, 2004). For a famous example, see 495–7.

47 Thirty-Six Laws, *KTSD*, vol. 4, 229–30. This law is not dated but may be early eighteenth century, as the first of these laws is about the control of manpower, a focus of dispute and legislation from the late seventeenth century onwards.

48 *KTSD*, vol. 4, 293–354; vol. 5, 1–192.

49 *Phraratcha phongsawadan krung si ayutthaya chabap phan janthanumat (joem)* [*Royal Chronicles of Ayutthaya, Phan Janthanumat Edition*] (Bangkok: Si Panya, 2010) 37; Richard D. Cushman (trans.), *The Royal Chronicles of Ayutthaya* (Bangkok: Siam Society, 2000) 26.

Tam Non, and is a Collection of the Enactments of the Ancient Kings; and the third is the *Pra Rajya Cammanot*, wherein are the Enactments of the now reigning King's Father.[50]

The *Phra tamra* perhaps contained the Civil and Military Lists, or was a collection of the laws on procedure. The *Phra thammanun* seems to have contained the laws edited and classified by subject, while the *Phraratcha kamnot* contained royal decrees not yet sorted by subject. By 1805, *Phra thammanun* had become the title for a text on the court system, and the *Phraratcha kamnot kao* (old royal decrees) contained laws dating from 1707 onwards, suggesting that the version seen by La Loubère had been sorted and a new version begun in the early eighteenth century.

Kings not only made laws but gave them royal authority and propagated their use. The term *aiyakan*, which appears in the titles of most of the laws, means 'business of the lord/ruler', emphasising the royal origin.[51] At several places in the Three Seals Code, there are clauses requiring people to use the official system of courts for settling disputes. Crimes against Government states: 'From this time forward', in cases of theft or abduction, 'do not take revenge but bring charges at the appropriate court of the city governor'; and in cases over debt and slavery, 'make a complaint, bring charges, or make petition at the appropriate department to be examined by the magistrate. Anyone not following this law, but taking the case into his own hands', faced punishment by caning.[52] There is a similar passage in the Law on Theft demanding that aggrieved parties bring cases to court and prescribing penalties for those who seek restitution through force.[53] There are similar instructions in the *Phra thammanun*.

The use of these codes was not confined to the capital. Extracts from the laws in the Three Seals Code have been found in many provincial archives. While most of these date to the nineteenth century, Jakkrit Uttho surmises that the *yokkrabat*, officers who acted as royal emissaries to the provinces from the seventeenth century onwards, may have carried parts of the laws in their toolkit. Many of the texts were found in *wat* libraries, hinting that monks and abbots acquired them to help in settling local disputes.[54]

In 1847, James Low published a study of Thai law based on several manuscripts he had collected in provincial Siam. One manuscript had been sent to the 'Raja of Ligore for his guidance' in a year that seems to be 1740. Another had been copied for a Chaophraya Inthawong 'when he went in 1596 … as General of the Army sent against Tenasserim'.[55] Low describes these manuscripts as 'digests' with extracts from several laws, 'rather confusedly jumbled', and 'numerous cases and precedents to guide both judges and those who may come, or be brought before them'. The dates, royal titles, and other aspects of these texts confirm Low's impression that these manuscripts dated to the Ayutthaya era.[56] One passage

[50] Meaning King Prasat Thong, father of King Narai. The French term 'constitutions' is here translated as 'enactments' (in place of Gen's 'constitutions'), following Jacq-Hergoualc'h's gloss on the French edition of the text: 'un recueil d'actes, de décret, de lois et de règlements'. La Loubère, *New Historical Relation*, 81; Michel Jacq-Hergoualc'h, *Etude historique et critique du livre de Simon de La Loubère 'Du royaume de Siam,' Paris, 1691* (Paris: Editions Recherche sur les civilisations, 1987) 304, fn. 7.

[51] Winai Pongsripian, 'Khwam samkhan khong "Kotmai tra sam duang: waen song sangkhom thai"' [The importance of "Three Seals Law: Reflection of Thai society"] in Winai (ed.), *Kotmai tra sam duang*, 12.

[52] *Phra aiyakan aya luang*, clause 102, *KTSD*, vol. 4, 75–6.

[53] *Phra aiyakan lakkhana jon*, clause 66, *KTSD*, vol. 3, 253–4; see also *Phra thammanun*, clause 1, *KTSD*, vol. 1, 161.

[54] Jakkrit Uttho, 'Khwam samphan', 42–9.

[55] These dates are credible. In the 1590s, King Naresuan sent an army which captured Tenasserim, and subsequently appointed several officers to administer the city, including a *yokkrabat*; see Cushman, *Royal Chronicles*, 138–9.

[56] See James Low, 'On the law of Mu'ung Thai or Siam' (1847) 1 *Journal of the Indian Archipelago and Eastern Asia* 327, facsimile in Winai, *Nitipratya thai*.

tells that a king was dismayed to find that judicial officers were ignorant of the law, and thus, 'The King orders copies [of the laws] to be given to his officers, and it is through these officers that the people procure copies'.[57]

Ayutthaya kings made laws, gave their name to them as a source of authority, preserved them in archives, and promoted their use.

3.3 THE *THAMMASAT* OF 1805

The *Thammasat* stands at the head of the Three Seals Code of 1805. What relationship does this text have to the tradition of *dhammasattha* in Burma? The preface states that the document was translated from a Mon version:

> Throughout time, the treatise that has been of benefit to the beings of the world is that called the *Thammasat* which the rishi Manosāra first expressed in the Māgadhī language [Pali], and which ancient teachers have passed down in the Ramañña [Mon] country in the Ramañña language. At this time, those who are judicial officers in the Siam country have difficulty in understanding this, hence I will compose this *Thammasat* in the Siam language.[58]

Scholars have argued fervently over when this document crossed over the Tanaosri Range and from one language to another. But a close examination of the *Thammasat* shows that the story is more complicated.

The *dhammasattha* in Mon or Burmese tradition generally had three main parts: an account of the origin of the text, brought back from the wall of the universe; a discourse on the importance of fair judgment, often illustrated with stories on the origin and consequences of good and bad judgments; and lists of legal principles and legal provisions, usually categorised under eighteen 'root matters' and an unlimited number of subordinate 'branch matters'. This third part generally occupied nine-tenths of the text.[59]

The Thai *Thammasat* of 1805 is partly similar and partly different. Here we will examine the *Thammasat* section by section,[60] looking at the content, and the possible origins in texts from Mon and Burmese.

3.3.1 Section 1. *Introduction*

After a standard invocation of the Buddha, the author explains that this *Thammasat* came from the Mon country and is here translated into Thai (see translation above).

3.3.2 Sections 2–3. *Mahāsammata*

This section begins with a summary of the geography of the human world from the Three Worlds cosmology, followed by a summary of the origins of society and kingship, and finally the expansion of human society from the four sons of King Mahāsammata to 101 countries with different customs and languages. This passage locates the text in Buddhist history and cosmology.

57 Ibid., 395.

58 Baker and Pasuk, *The Ayutthaya Palace Law*, 33–4; *KTSD*, vol. 1, 8.

59 See for example, D. Christian Lammerts, 'The Dhammavilāsa Dhammathat: A critical historiography, analysis, and translation of the text', M.A. dissertation, Cornell University (2005).

60 For the full English translation, see Baker and Pasuk, *The Ayutthaya Palace Law*, 33–49. The section numbers do not appear in the original but have been added in all printed editions. We have added the subheadings.

Origins: such summaries are found in many documents. The passage on the origins of society and kingship is found in the second part of the Aggañña Sutta.[61] The passage on the expansion of human society is found in two Mon *dhammasattha* texts, varying only slightly in the last few lines.[62]

3.3.3 Section 4a. *Discovery of the* Thammasat

Brahmādeva is an official of King Mahāsammata who goes off to become a rishi and sires two sons with a *kinnari*, a mythical bird-human hybrid. Both sons become rishi. The first son Bhadra travels to the wall of the universe and returns with knowledge from the Vedas. Both sons enter royal service. After making a bad judgment, the second son Manosāra again travels to the wall of the universe and returns with the *thammasat* with which he instructs King Mahāsammata.

Origins: in the Burmese *Manusāra dhammasattha*, the story is the same except that the two brothers make only one joint trip to the wall of the universe. The Burmese telling is also lengthier.

3.3.4 Section 4b. *The Gourd Field*

In between the brothers' two visits, Manosāra is employed by King Mahāsammata as a judicial official. He makes a bad judgment in a case concerning two adjacent fields of gourds. Remorse over this judgment prompts his second trip to discover the *thammasat*.

Origins: a very similar version of the tale of the gourd field is found in the Burmese *Dhammavilāsa dhammasattha*.[63]

3.3.5 Section 4c. *The Conduct of the King*

The passage describes an ideal routine for part of the king's day from evening through to audience on the following morning.

Origins: such passages can be found in the Indian *arthaśastra* texts, in the Mon-Myanmar *dhammasattha*, and in the Ayutthaya Palace Law. The passage here follows one in the Burmese *Manusāra dhammasattha*, almost clause by clause, including a distinctive description of the king cleaning his teeth, and differs only slightly towards the end. Some Mon texts also have the same passage, but with several differences in detail.[64]

3.3.6 Section 5. *The Four Wrong Courses*

The passage exhorts magistrates to avoid the Four Wrong Courses (*agati*) of greed, hatred, anger, and fear. Magistrates who do so will find their wealth and repute increase like the waxing moon, while those who fail will find their wealth and repute shrink like a waning

61 Steven Collins, 'The discourse on what is primary (Aggañña Sutta), an annotated translation' (1993) 21 *Journal of Indian Philosophy* 301.

62 Nai Pan Hla, *Eleven Mon Dhammasat Texts*, 593–4 (MDT IV and MDT VII).

63 Lammerts, 'The Dhammavilāsa Dhammathat', 108–9. Nai Pan Hla states that this story does not appear in any Mon text, see *Eleven Mon Dhammasāt Texts*, xxii.

64 Lammerts, 'Buddhism and written law', 468; Nai Pan Hla, *Eleven Mon Dhammmasāt Texts*, 594–5 (MDT IV and MDT VII).

moon. Magistrates who accept bribes are cursed to be consigned to torments in hell and be reborn with deformities for many lifetimes.

Origins: such passages are standard in Mon and Burmese texts. The version in the Burmese *Manusāra dhammasattha* is very close, including a distinctive image of a bribe-taker encumbered with hands like a spade or hoe, and forced to eat his own body.[65]

3.3.7 Section 6. *Twenty-Four Concerns for Magistrates*

This section lists twenty-four topics of judicial procedure, from origination of cases through to judgment, grouped under eight headings, each with three topics.

Origins: the topics presented in Sections 6, 7, and 8 are relevant to a formal, court-based process of law. There are no similar passages in Mon-Burmese *dhammasattha* texts.

3.3.8 Section 7. *Root and Branch Matters*

This section is an introduction to the framework of root and branch matters in the next two sections.

3.3.9 Section 8. *Root Matters for Judges and Magistrates*

This section and the next are indexes to the laws in the Three Seals Code. This section covers matters of judicial procedure (see Table 3.1). For each of the ten, there is a Pali couplet with translation. On punishment, for example, the passage runs:

On the law titled on punishment, there is Pali as follows '*daṇḍābhipattikāraṇaṃ yaṃ sabbesaṃ parājīnaṃ / tampi patitadaṇḍaṃ daṇḍo nāmā ti kittitaṃ*' (translation: 'The application of punishments including any fines and compensation for anyone who loses a case are stated by Manosāra the teacher under the title of punishment').

The same couplet and translation are reproduced at the head of the respective law: 'Here will be stated root matters for judges called *phrommathan* or *phrommasak* on punishment

TABLE 3.1 *Root matters for judges and magistrates*

	List in Section 8 of the Thammasat	Law or section in the Three Seals Code	Pali in preface compared to Pali in Thammasat
1	Tenets of Indra	Tenets of Indra	different
2	Phra Thammanun	Phra Thammanun	same
3	witnesses	Witnesses	same
4	rejection of witnesses	Acceptance of Cases (part)	same
5	substitution	Acceptance of Cases (part)	same
6	exclusion	Acceptance of Cases (part)	same
7	acceptance of cases	Acceptance of Cases (part)	same
8	delay	Acceptance of Cases (part)	same
9	punishment	Phrommasak (part)	same
10	dismissal of cases	Acceptance of Cases (part)	same

65 Lammerts, 'Buddhism and written law', 462–3.

according to the Pali in the *Thammasat* stating: *daṇḍābhipattikāraṇaṃ* ... [as above]' (translation: The application ... [as above]).[66]

3.3.10 Section 9. *Root Matters of Dispute*

This section is an index into the substantive laws in the code (see Table 3.2). For each of twenty-nine 'causes of dispute', the *Thammasat* gives a Pali title followed by a translation, for instance: '*jāyampatīkassa vipattibhedā* namely, disputes of the type about matters of husband and wife'. In the preamble to most of the laws, there is a back-reference in a standard form, in this case: 'This law on husband and wife has Pali in the *Thammasat* saying *jāyampatīkassa vipattibhedā* meaning the various origins of disputes between husband and wife.'[67]

Lingat stated, 'Siamese laws generally begin with a preamble setting forth the fundamental rules, that is, *dhammasattham* rules, sometimes in their pali [sic] version, and next they give, in a succession of *mātrās* or sections, the prescriptions derived from them in course of time'.[68] This is misleading. The Pali in the preface of each of these laws is a descriptive title of the law alone. There are no rules or statements of principle in Pali in the prefaces.

Sections 8 and 9 are a table of contents for the Three Seals Code, with back-references in the prefaces of the laws. Although the various laws appeared over several centuries, these back-references are in a standard form, suggesting this framework was a late insertion in the code. In ten laws the preface ends: 'Here are the branch matters in royal legislation that ancient kings conceived in accordance with the Phra *Thammasat* and set out at clauses as follows'.[69] The wording is almost identical in each law, again suggesting a late insertion.

When was this cross-referencing constructed between the *Thammasat* and the preambles of the various laws in the code? Possibly at the revision of the Three Seals Code in 1805, but that is unlikely because of several discrepancies. First, some laws listed in section 9 of the *Thammasat* do not appear in the 1805 code. Second, several laws which are grouped in the 1805 code appear separately in the *Thammasat*'s list (for example, Revolt and Warfare merged as a single law, and six laws grouped under Miscellaneous Laws). Third, in a few cases the Pali back-reference in the preamble to the law differs from the Pali in the *Thammasat* (see Table 3.2).[70]

3.3.11 Section 10. *Branch Matters*

In this section, the 'branch matters', which in the Mon-Burmese *dhammasattha* means the lists of rules and principles that form the bulk of these texts, are equated with 'the royal proclamations, laws, and royal legislation which are all royal law-making', namely, the content of the remainder of the Three Seals Code. Through this equation, the Thai *Thammasat* becomes totally different from the Mon-Myanmar *dhammasattha* and the Indian *dharmaśāstra*, guides for judges and arbitrators, created and used outside the scope of royal command.

66 *Phrommasak* clause 11, *KTSD*, vol. 1, 208.
67 Law on marriage, preface, *KTSD*, vol. 2, 205.
68 Lingat, 'Evolution', 28.
69 See for example, Acceptance of Cases, *KTSD*, vol. 2, 261.
70 Of the ten laws indexed in Section 8, the verse quoted in the preamble is the same except in the case of the Tenets of Indra. Of the twenty-nine topics listed in Section 9, twenty-four match to a law or part-law in the code, and eighteen have the same Pali title, while two have a different Pali title (4 and 6 in table), and three make no back-reference (2, 6, and 17).

TABLE 3.2 *Root matters of dispute in the* Thammasat

	Pali title in Section 9 of the *Thammasat*	Thai translation in Section 9 of the *Thammasat*	Linked law	Pali in preface compared to Pali in *Thammasat*
1	*iṇṇaṃ dhanañca*	credit and debt	Debt	same
2	*rañño dhanacorahāraṃ*	misappropriation of royal property		
3	*adhammadāyajjavibhattabhāgaṃ*	partition of inheritance	Inheritance	same
4	*parassa dānaṃ gahaṇaṃ puneva*	gift and return of property	Miscellaneous (part)	different: *sinehato . . . suddhāya*
5	*bhattikā ca*	hired and unpaid labour	Miscellaneous (part)	none
6	*akkhappaticāradhūtā ca*	gambling	Miscellaneous (part)	different: *abbhutalakkhaña*
7	*bhaṇḍañca keyyāvikayañca*	purchase and sale		
8	*avahārañca*	theft	Theft	same
9	*khettādithānañca*	house land and paddy field	Miscellaneous (part)	same
10	*ārāmavanādithānañca*	upland field, garden, and forest	Miscellaneous (part)	same
11	*dāsīdāsañca*	debt slaves and war slaves	Slavery	same
12	*paharañca khuṃsā*	assault, abuse, and insult	Assault etc.	same
13	*jāyampatīkassa vipattibhedā*	husband and wife	Marriage	same
14	*saṅgāmadosā pi ca*	warfare	Revolt and Warfare (part)	same
15	*rājaduṭṭhoca*	treason	Revolt and Warfare (part)	same
16	*rājāṇañca*	violating royal legislation		
17	*suṅkādivivādapatto ca*	royal taxes and market dues		
18	*parampaseyho pi ca atta āṇam*	threats and intimidation	Against People	same
19	*ītīyakāro*	invective and cursing	Miscellaneous (part)	same, and more
20	*thānāvitikkamma balākarena*	trespass		
21	*puttādiādāgamanā saheva*	taking children	Abduction	same
22	*hetumpaṭicca adhikāraṅaṃ va*	just cause	Miscellaneous (part)	same
23	*agghāpanāyū ca*	valuation by age	Phrommasak (part)	same
24	*dhanūpanikkhā*	mortgage	Miscellaneous (part)	same
25	*āthabbanikā pi ca*	magic and spirits	Miscellaneous (part)	same
26	*bhaṇḍadeyyaṃ ca*	rental	Miscellaneous (part)	same
27	*tāvakāsīkañca*	lending and borrowing	Miscellaneous (part)	same
28	*gaṇīvibhāgañca*	division of subordinates	Division of Persons	same
29	*pañcūdarantaṃ*	appeal	Appeal	different[1]

[1] The law on appeal has a six-line verse in Pali, not found in the *Thammasat*, but it is simply a description of the law, defining five different types of appeal (*KTSD*, vol. 2, 184–5).

The text attempts to bridge the contradiction between the 'natural' origin of the *Thammasat*, and the royal origin of the laws, by stating that the kings studied the *Thammasat* and then adapted and elaborated its content into the royal lawmaking. Throughout the *Thammasat* and similar texts, the translation and exposition in Thai often strays from the Pali at the head of the section. In this section, the divergence is greater than usual:

> Pali, translation:[71] The various divisions [of law] that go by the name of branch [laws] were established in the *dhammasattha* to serve as a measure, in conformity with wisdom, by the former king Narinda-rāmādhipati, a possessor of excellent merit who comprehended human conduct and made great effort to increase the prosperity of his kingdom.
>
> Thai: The various kinds of branch matters ... are many, namely the royal proclamations, laws, and royal legislation which are all royal law-making. All the branch matters described here [were created by] past kings ... through a succession of reigns. With the desire to support and benefit all the populace, the kings endeavoured to consider matters according to the *Thammasat*, and to have royal legislation to adapt and elaborate [its content] as royal proclamations and laws with many articles, through a succession of reigns down to today.

The Thai modifies and extends the Pali in several ways. Most notably it changes 'the former king Narinda-rāmādhipati'[72] into 'past kings ... through a succession of reigns', and specifically identifies the branch matters with 'the royal proclamations, laws, and royal legislation which are all royal lawmaking'. The link between the *Thammasat* and royal lawmaking is made in the Thai, not the Pali.

Prince Dhani recognised that this section undermined the traditional view on the *thammasat*. He argued that this section 'is obviously an interpolation', and criticised the Pali and the translation.[73]

3.3.12 Section 11. *Conclusion*

This section is a reminder to magistrates to study the *Thammasat* and avoid the Four Wrong Courses, so that they deliver correct and socially useful judgments.

3.3.13 *Appraisal of the 1805* Thammasat

The 1805 *Thammasat* is an assemblage of texts that differ in style, content, and origin.[74] The early part (sections 2–5 above) closely replicates material found in passages from various Mon and Burmese *dhammasattha*. These passages might have been assembled into one text in Burma, as such bricolage was common, but no such text is known. Alternatively, the bits were put together in Siam.

The middle part (sections 6–9) departs from Mon-Burmese tradition and clearly reflects the distinctive legal history of Siam. It uses the vocabulary of root and branch matters but fills

[71] With thanks to Christian Lammerts.

[72] Several possibilities: 1. A reference to the founder of Ayutthaya (a claim to antiquity); 2. 'Rama the ruler', meaning Rama, king of Ayodhya in the Ramayana, and, by allusion, any king of Ayutthaya; 3. King Prasat Thong who appears in some sources as Ramathibet.

[73] Dhani, 'Old Siamese conception', 98.

[74] The usage of Pali differs across sections. Sections 1, 5, 10, 11 start with a Pali verse followed by translation and exposition in nissaya style. Sections 2, 3, 4 have no Pali. Sections 6, 7, 8, 9 have Pali headers followed by translations.

that framework very differently. The number of root matters is not the standard eighteen but thirty-nine. This total is subdivided, with the first ten on judicial procedures for a court-based judicial system, and the remaining twenty-nine forming a table of contents for the whole Three Seals Code. The branch matters, the moral principles, and legal rulings which occupy the largest amount of space in the Mon-Burmese texts, are completely absent.

The conclusion (sections 10–11) attempts to marry Siam's royal-made law with the idea of a moral law, a *thammasat*. When was this done? As noted above, probably not in 1805 as there are discrepancies between the index in the *Thammasat* and the contents of the Three Seals Code. There is a hint on the possible timing in the law on slavery. This law was updated, probably in the early eighteenth century when conflict arose over the control of slaves and other dependents. The reference to the *thammasat* in the preamble to this law is more elaborate than the formulaic version found elsewhere: '[The king] proceeded to the flower-baldachin throne in the eastern wing of the Maha Phaichon audience hall, gave thought to the sacred *thammasat*, then, speaking with the voice of a lion, pronounced the royal legislation as follows.'[75]

In addition, this preface refers to the 'seven types of slave in the sacred *thammasat*'. Such lists are common in the Mon and Burmese *dhammasattha*, but this is one of very few such appearances in the Three Seals Code.[76] Perhaps the adoption of the *thammasat* dates to this time as part of a project to remodel Siamese kingship with Buddhist principles – a project that flourished in the reign of King Borommakot (r. 1733–58).[77]

By an irony of history, at the time when there was an attempt to bridge royal law to the *Thammasat* in Siam, in Burma the trend was the exact opposite. From the eighteenth century, Buddhist scholars and their patrons in Burma worried that the story of the *dhammasatha* being found on the wall of the universe, and thus being a natural and universal law, was in breach of the Buddhist scriptures. Around 1810, a scholar was commissioned to investigate. He pronounced that the story had no scriptural basis. Law was thus a human construction, susceptible to change, and liable to be judged against Buddhist ethics.[78]

3.4 CONCLUSION

As Prachoom Chomchai observed,[79] a historian and a lawyer will write the history of law in different ways.

In the 1930s, Robert Lingat compiled a pioneering history of Thai law. In keeping with the orientalist intellectual milieu of the time, he made his Thai history part of a larger Asian story dominated by the cultural influence of India. He was keen to 'tie old Siamese legislation with a great juridical tradition',[80] and to draw a sharp contrast between east and west. In his scheme, Asian law stemmed from a universal moral code not the will of a ruler. At the time, few sources were available for compiling Thai history. Like other contemporaries, Lingat compensated

75 *KTSD*, vol. 2, 287. Lingat repeatedly referenced this preface as if it were typical of the whole code (e.g., *L'Influence Indoue*, 23), whereas it is unique.

76 Thanks to the Center for Integrated Area Studies, Kyoto University, which maintains the searchable database of the Three Seals Code at app.cias.kyoto-u.ac.jp/infolib/meta_pub/G0000003ktsd.

77 See Chris Baker and Pasuk Phongpaichit, *A History of Ayutthaya: Siam in the Early Modern World* (Cambridge: Cambridge University Press, 2017) 246–8.

78 Lammers, *Buddhist Law in Burma*, chapter 5.

79 In a comment on an earlier version of this chapter on 27 September 2019.

80 R. Lingat, *L'esclavage privé dans l'ancien droit siamois (avec une traduction des anciennes lois siamoises sur l'esclavage)* (Paris: Ed. Domat-Montchrestien, 1931) 27.

through ingenuity, imagination, and drawing on regional parallels.[81] At key points, Lingat misrepresented the evidence: in particular, he claimed that there were legal principles in Pali in the prefaces of laws in the Three Seals Code, and that there was a process of scrutinising new legislation against the *thammasat* at the start of each Ayutthaya reign.[82] Also like other contemporaries, he pushed the story far back into the past to give Siam a long tradition.

Lingat's work has special status because of his role as a pioneer and his wide-ranging scholarship. Thai legal scholars have been comfortable with the idea that Siam's legal tradition has a deep history and a philosophical base. In addition, in the 1940s, Lingat's legal history became part of the theoretical underpinning of a theory of Thai kingship for a new era in which monarchy was no longer absolute. As this recast kingship prospered, the theoretical underpinning escaped challenge. An essay published as part of the celebration of two centuries of the Three Seals Law in 2005 recapitulated Lingat's theory almost word for word:

> The *Thammasat* in the Three Seals Code allowed the king freedom to draft royal laws (*rachasat*) to a limited extent; that is, in drafting legislation the king had to 'think according to the *Thammasat*' . . . . Kings [of Ayutthaya] did not confuse their royal power with the sacred power of law. A king had the absolute power to do whatever he liked, but a king's rulings remained mere royal orders; they could not change the law that Manu revealed and could not gain permanence as immortal law.[83]

Today many more sources are available for writing Thai history, while some sources that Lingat used are now seen as questionable. There is limited evidence for the *thammasat* playing a prominent role in Siam's history. There is only one ambiguous siting of a *thammasat* before 1805. By contrast, the evidence for a tradition of royal lawmaking is very substantial. The early law codes of Thai communities, the observations of Siam by foreign visitors from the seventeenth century, vignettes from old Thai literature, and the internal evidence of the Three Seals Code all show the leading role of kings in making, preserving, and propagating law. In later Ayutthaya, the amount of legislation, the number of courts, and the pressure for people to use them all expanded in parallel with the king's absolutist power.

Rather than being the fount of legal tradition in Siam, the *thammasat* was a late adoption into a tradition of royal lawmaking, perhaps as part of a project, begun in the eighteenth century, and reprised in the mid-twentieth, to suffuse Thai kingship with Buddhist morality.

This does not mean there is no Buddhist influence on the Thai legal tradition. Simply because Buddhism has so deeply influenced thinking and social organisation in Siam since at least the fourteenth century, Buddhist ideas of what is right and just are woven into the weft and warp of the Siamese laws. As Khemthong Tonsakulrungruang shows (Chapter 5 in this volume), the study of this influence is broader than the pursuit of an elusive Thai *thammasat*.

In old Siam, the king was a legislator, and royal legislation was a key institution of the Siamese state in the pre-modern era.

81 Andrew Huxley generalised the history of the *thammasat* by brilliantly using regional parallels; see especially 'Thai, Mon and Burmese Dhammathats: Who influenced whom?' in Huxley (ed.), *Thai Law: Buddhist Law* 81; and 'Pali Buddhist Law in Southeast Asia' in Rebecca R. French and Mark A. Nathan (eds.), *Buddhism and Law* (Cambridge: Cambridge University Press, 2014) 16 7.

82 The scrutiny procedure appears only in the preface of the Thirty-Six Laws (*KTSD*, vol. 4, 229–30), and there is no evidence of it being used at any other time, let alone at every change of reign.

83 Channarong Bunnun, 'Phra Thammasat', 91, 93.

4

The History of the Initial Royal Command

A Reflection on the Legal and Political Contexts of Kingship and the Modern State in Siam

Kongsatja Suwanapech

When a Siamese or, since 1939, Thai king is officially crowned, he normally pledges his initial royal command (the 'Command'), known as *'Phra Phathom Borom Ratcha Ong-kan'*. Although the Command is mainly given for a ceremonial purpose, it indicates to some extent the status of kingship, the interrelation between kingship and law, the relationship between the state and individuals in terms of property ownership, and the evolution of the modern state and the political system. Since 1932, the *'Phra Phathom Boromma Ratcha Ong-kan'* has broadly been cited to justify the position of the Siamese/Thai monarchy in compliance with the constitutional regime. However, little academic attention has been paid to the symbolic meanings and historical development of this Command. Moreover, most studies on kingship tend to focus on the *'Dhammaraja* doctrine' which underpins the Command but often neglect its historical layers and dynamic contexts. This chapter seeks to examine the historical development, significance, and relevance of this concept.

The chapter will begin by exploring the origin and importance of the coronation ceremony and the Command. This will be followed by a discussion of the development of the Command from the late Ayutthaya era to the ninth reign of the Chakri Dynasty. Some critical analysis will also be provided of the adjustments of words and phrases in the Command throughout history with regard to kingship, legal concepts, and the relationship between the state and individuals in terms of property ownership, particularly from the age of Westernisation and reformation from the reign of King Mongkut onwards. In the final part, it will critique the role of the Command in a contemporary context.

4.1 MEANING AND SIGNIFICANCE OF THE INITIAL ROYAL COMMAND

Customarily, after being fully crowned as king and receiving all regalia, the Siamese or Thai monarch may pledge his coronation oath known as *'Phra Phathom Boromma Ratcha Ong-kan'* in order to affirm his divine right to the throne. *'Ong-kan'*, deriving from Sanskrit, means a divine word or command which can only be used to refer to a Hindu God's order.[1] This etymological root signifies the Hindu political concept of *'Devaraja'* (God King) behind the ceremony. To briefly give a picture of the ceremonial procedure, after the anointment, the Hindu High Priest would chant to invite the Hindu Gods and offer the royal regalia to

[1] Pleung Na Nakorn, 'พจนานุกรมแปล ไทย-ไทย (Thai Dictionary)' https://dictionary.sanook.com/search/dict-th-th-pleang/โองการ (accessed 1 April 2019).

the monarch. Then, as it was believed that the Brahmin could ritually transmit messages from the immortal to the mortal world, the Command had to be received initially by the High Brahmin only.[2] Therefore, Brahmins were trusted by the crown as sages and played a significant part in the coronation ceremony by offering the right over the kingdom and the regalia, and hearing the Command before the king; ordinary people were customarily not allowed to do this.[3] After that, the monarch would pour the holy water which relates to the Command. The act of pouring water was regarded in Hindu-Buddhist beliefs as the ratification of an oath that had just been taken.[4] In particular, once the word had slipped through His Majesty's lips, he had to act according to the very words of the oath.[5]

In terms of formality the Command also marked the royal prerogative of the king to rightfully enact a royal command which used to be regarded as a law in the legal system. The Command would not be called '*Ong-kan*' unless the heir to the throne had held the coronation ceremony and pledged the Command.[6] After the ceremony, the Command could be called '*Ong-kan*' since the person who was crowned symbolically transformed into the state of a fictional deity as 'the incarnation of celestial gods'[7] and had to be followed by mortals.[8] Therefore, the coronation ceremony was regarded as an essential rite to justify the state of kingship.

4.1.1 *Historical Development of the Initial Royal Command: from Late Ayutthaya to the Bangkok Era*

The royal protocol of coronation which is currently adopted is highly influenced by that of Ayutthaya Kingdom. From late Ayutthaya to the first coronation ceremony of King Chulalongkorn, the Commands were pledged in the same pattern, as 'Greenery, aqua and all items in this Kingdom without owners belong to the priests and people'.[9] A noticeable change appeared in the second coronation of King Chulalongkorn. After reaching the age of majority and regaining his ruling power from the regency, he held a second coronation. At the ceremony, he stated:

> On this occasion that all the people honouring me as the ruler and for me to receive the purification bathing which marks my kingship over Siam, the celebrated Kingdom of people, I, through the tradition of *Dhammikkaracha*, will grant the greenery and aqua in this Kingdom left unprotected for the usage of respected priests, brahmins and common people.[10]

2 Paphatsaun Thianpanya, 'Siamese Cosmology: A Study of Political and Legal Authorities in the Three Seals Law' (DPhil Thesis, Thammasat University, 2008) 204.

3 King Chulalongkorn, *พระราชวิจารณ์เรื่องพงศาวดารกับเรื่องพระราชประเพณีการตั้งพระมหาอุปราช* [*Critiques on Chronicles and Royal Customs of appointing Phra Maha Upparat*] (Bangkok: Phra Chan Press, 1973) 21.

4 H. G. Quaritch Wales, *Siamese State Ceremonies* (Sudhisak Palpho tr., Bangkok: River Books, 2019) 87–8.

5 Interview with พระมหาราชครูพิธีศรีวิสุทธิคุณ [Brahmin Chawin Ransibrahmanakul], the Senior Brahmin, Devasathan Brahmin Shrines (30 May 2019); See also ibid., 87; Dhani Nivat, 'The Coronation of His Majesty Prajadhipok King of Siam', *ประชุมพระนิพนธ์ของพระวรวงศ์เธอ กรมหมื่นพิทยลาภพฤฒิยากร* [*Collected Works of Prince Dhani Nivat*] (Bangkok: Phra Chan Press, 1974) 72.

6 Damrong Rajanubhab, 'พระราชพิธีบรมราชาภิเษก รัชกาลที่ 2 [The Coronation Ceremony of King Rama II]' in The Fine Arts Department (ed.), *ประมวลบทความพระราชพิธีบรมราชาภิเษก* [*The Compilations of Articles regarding the Coronation Ceremonies*] (Bangkok: The Fine Arts Department, 2018) 93.

7 Dhani Nivat, 'Coronation of His Majesty Prajadhipok', 72.

8 Paphatsaun Thianpanya, 'Siamese Cosmology', 204.

9 Kum Bunnag, *พระราชพงศาวดารกรุงรัตนโกสินทร์* [*The Royal Chronicles of Krung Rattanakosin*] (Bangkok: Sripanya Publishing House, 2012) 133.

10 Nontaporn Youmangmee, *เสวยราชสมบัติกษัตรา* [*The Succession to the Throne of the Monarchy*] (Bangkok: Matichon Publishing House, 2019) 107.

After the reign of King Chulalongkorn, King Vajiravudh, and King Prajadhipok, who were King Chulalongkorn's sons, succeeded in turn to the Siamese throne. King Vajiravudh in his Command changed the phrase into

> Behold, my fellow Brahmins. Now, we hold a royal duty in ruling the Kingdom by Dhamma for the ease and the greatest benefit of my people. I have bestowed my kingship upon you and prosperity. I will be the guide and also will govern, guard and defend fairly from now on. May all my people lay their trust and live in harmony.[11]

The Command of King Prajadhipok, the last absolute monarch of Siam, was in line with that of his brother. After the Siamese Revolution in 1932 the coronation did not take place until the ninth reign of King Bhumibol Adulyadej, who succeeded his brother King Ananda Mahidol.[12] When King Bhumibol was crowned, his Command was, 'I will rule the Kingdom by Dharma for the greatest benefit of Siamese people'.[13]

Regarding the classification of the historical development of the Command, the establishment of democracy has been commonly applied to categorising it into two periods, namely the pre-constitutional and constitutional periods. It is claimed that the significant adjustment was during King Bhumibol Adulyadej's coronation,[14] as he was the first constitutional monarch who held a coronation ceremony. According to Laosinwatthana, as the king no longer had ruling power in the democratic state, the words in the Command had to be adjusted in accordance with the new regime.[15] However, changes before the revolution in 1932 have been overlooked, as it is clear that there have been changes in the phrases over time since the reign of King Chulalongkorn.

4.2 ANALYSIS OF THE COMMAND

4.2.1 *Reclassifying the Commands*

Although the criterion of classification referred to above is attributed to an attempt to indicate the difference between pre-constitutional and first constitutional Commands, this classification seems to be problematic, in that one is likely to neglect the changes in the Commands throughout history even before the 1932 revolution. Moreover, it also overlooks the analysis of the theories of kingship and royal authority behind the phrases of the Commands. Hence, it leaves open the question of whether the first constitutional Commands were truly constitutional or democratic. In other words, the typical classification seems to justify the conformity of the modern monarchy to constitutionalism and democracy, regardless of legal and political contexts. To understand the legal and political concepts behind these changes, developments in the Commands should be reexamined and reclassified.

11 Ibid., 107–10.

12 Despite the fact that the Siamese Revolution occurred in 1932 during the reign of King Prajadhipok, the King's coronation was held before the revolution. Moreover, there was no coronation ceremony in the reign of King Ananda Mahidol, King Bhumibol's brother because of his sudden death on 9 June 1946.

13 Nontaporn Youmangmee, *Succession to the Throne*, 110.

14 Sangsoon Ladawan, *พระราชพิธีบรมราชาภิเษกกรุงรัตนโกสินทร์* [*The Coronation Ceremonies in Rattanakosin Era*] (The Secretariat of The Prime Minister, 1983) 17; See also Napaporn Laosinwatthana, *การเสด็จขึ้นครองราชย์ พระราชพิธี คติ ความหมาย และสัญลักษณ์แห่ง 'สมมติเทวราช'* [*Succession, Royal Ceremony, Principles, Meaning, and Symbols of 'God-King'*] (Bangkok: Museum Press, 2006) 44.

15 Napaporn Laosinwatthana, *Succession, Royal Ceremony*, 44.

4.2.2 *Theories of Kingship in the Commands*

To create the institutions of government and the justice system, there needs to be a consensual agreement to allow the ruler to organise those institutions. Theories of kingship in Siam have been similarly premised on this agreement to legitimise the right of the monarchy to rule and enact royal decrees. To achieve this, the tales and myths of the origins of society, ruler, and law based on Hindu and Buddhist doctrines, for instance, were created to depict a social agreement. The initial royal commands could be instruments to reflect on different theories of kingship of the Siamese or Thai monarchy behind the phrases in different contexts.

4.2.2.1 Source of All Property in the Kingdom

The Commands of late Ayutthaya and early Bangkok kings indicate that all subjects enjoy the right to use property under the king's entitlement. It is observed that the contents reflect another theory of kingship which is the unique characteristic of pre-modern Thai monarchy, diverging from Hindu-Indian kingship and law. Among several royal titles in the law of Three Seals Code symbolising Hindu gods, *Kshatriyas*, Buddha, and others, there is one referring to the king as '*Phra Chao Phaen Din*' which does not have its roots in the theory of kingship from India.[16] In fact, the traditional concept rooted in the region regards the king as the lord of all lands and lives to justify his power to the hierarchical social system within the kingdom through land and labour sources.[17] This regional concept in Siamese traditional law which appears in the Command could reflect the relationship between the state and individuals in terms of property ownership in Thai traditional law.

Although the phrase of the Command recognises the rights of individuals to enjoy ownerless things, it appears that the rightful owner of all properties, particularly the land, still was the king. It has been pointed out that the phrase is regarded as the oath of the king to own everything upon the land, as the king is the lord of both living and non-living things.[18] Section 41 of *Phra Ayakarn Laksana Bet Set* ('Miscellanous Law') states that 'Any places in Krungthep-Mahanakhorn-Sriayutthaya-mahadilok-Phopnoppharat-Ratchathani-Burirom belong to His Majesty the King'.[19] The land will belong to the citizens only when he grants it to them. According to the French ambassador who visited the royal court of Ayutthaya in the seventeenth century, the Siamese people had no rightful ownership; therefore, they had no attachment to any property which could be called back by the king or his royal servants.[20]

Regarding the individuals' use of the land, people were allowed to use the land as a reward for their contribution of labour to the state.[21] Despite this, the king still reserved a privilege and power to distribute the land to his subjects. To affirm that this privilege was well preserved for the king, no one was entitled to transfer the land. According to section 42 of the Miscellaneous Law, 'in one section, the land outside the capital city which belongs to Ayutthaya and is not people's property is prohibited from being purchased and should not

16 Paphatsaun Thianpanya, 'Siamese Cosmology', 158–61.

17 Akin Rabibhana, *The Organisation of Thai Society in the Early Bangkok Period 1782–1873* (Kob Fai Publishing Project, 2017) 94.

18 Quaritch Wales, *Siamese State Ceremonies* 87.

19 Section 41 of *Phra Ayakarn Laksana Bet Set* (Miscellaneous Law), the Three Seals Code 1805.

20 Simon de la Loubère, *Du Royaume de Siam* (San T. Komolbutr tr., 4th ed., Bangkok: Sri Panya Publishing House, 2014) 320.

21 H. Q. Quaritch Wales, *การ ปกครอง และ บริหาร ของ ไทย สมัย โบราณ* [*Ancient Siamese Government and Administration*] (Bangkok: Charoenvit Publishing, 1975) 187.

be left unattended'.[22] Lingat notes that the legal policy of the legislation outlaws the transfer of land plots between private individuals because the action would violate the privilege of the king to authorise the use of land plots for his subjects.[23] As it tends to symbolise the grandeur of royal authority over the kingdom, the traditional legal view could not differentiate between private ownership of land and royal authority.[24] This could be similarly compared to the feudal patrimonial theory in which state power arises from the ruler's ownership of land.[25] Therefore, it is likely that landholding was rather attached to the rulers' power or kingship. In principle, the rightful owner of all land plots in the kingdom was still the state in the name of the king, whereby private ownership of land was not recognised. Yet, it is worth mentioning that, in practice, later legislation recognised land sale agreements, land plots as marriage properties, and land plots as inheritance, but the practices were not prevalent.[26]

Nevertheless, it appears that the concept of '*Phra Chao Phaen Din*' is distinctive to the Hindu and Buddhist legal doctrines which were the framework of traditional Thai law. Traditional Hindu law recognises private ownership of land which is separate from the king's right. According to the law of Manu, for instance, the law justifies seven methods to acquire land. Moreover, the law also prohibits the king from expropriating the land from Brahma, while His Majesty is entitled to call the land back from other castes under certain conditions.[27] Similarly, a Buddhist doctrine also recognises the private right to own land plots. The Buddhist text *Akkanyasutra* shows the evolution of private property through the stories of the creation of the world and human society. According to the text, as rice was in short supply, humans sought a benevolent person to distribute rations to them. Yet, before that, they solved the shortage by sharing the rice and acting 'to demarcate the land'.[28] Kosananan points out that this event could be seen as the evolution of private property.[29] In this regard, it may be additionally observed that Buddhist doctrine recognised the private ownership of land even before the advent of a ruler or king. Lingat notes that even after the evolution of kingship, it appears from the texts that humans never confer the right to own the land to the king but only share their products with the ruler.[30] Even Mon and Burmese laws, which are said to be the framework of Ayutthaya and Bangkok traditional laws, also follow their Indian legal roots.[31] Furthermore, there is no etymological connection between '*Phra Chao Phaen Din*' and Pali and Sanskrit languages in India.[32] Despite adopting the Indian *Thammasat* and Hindu-Buddhist doctrines as legal models, Siam still preserved its indigenous legal concepts. Similarly, being concealed by the divine ceremony of Hindu Devaraja, the Commands from late Ayutthaya until King Rama Chulalongkorn's reign implicitly hide a royal right over land of individuals in pre-modern Siam.

22 Section 42 of *Phra Ayakarn Laksana Bet Set* (Miscellaneous Law), the Three Seals Code.
23 Robert Lingat, ประวัติศาสตร์กฎหมายไทย [*Thai Legal History*] (Bangkok: Thammasat University Press, 2010) 378.
24 Ibid., 359.
25 Worachet Pakeerut, คำสอนว่าด้วย รัฐและหลักกฎหมายมหาชน [*Textbook of State and Principles of Public Law*] (Textbook and Course Materials Project of Faculty of Law Thammasat University, 2012) 48.
26 Lingat, *Thai Legal History*, 380.
27 Law of Manu, cited in John W. Spellman, *Political Theory of Ancient India: A Study of Kingship from the Earliest Times* (Oxford: Clarendon Press, 1964) 203.
28 *Akkanyasutra*, *Tripitaka*.
29 Jaran Kosananan, ปรัชญากฎหมายไทย [*Thai Legal Philosophy*] (Bangkok: Rakhamhaeng University Press, 1998) 86.
30 Lingat, *Thai Legal History*, 358–9.
31 Ibid., 359.
32 Dhani Nivat, 'The Old Siamese Conception of Monarchy', ประชุมพระนิพนธ์ของพระวรวงศ์เธอ กรมหมื่นพิทยลาภพฤฒิยากร [*Collected Literary Works of Prince Dhani Nivat*] (Bangkok: Phra Chan Press, 1974) 102.

In the nineteenth century, during the modernisation of Siam, the concept of '*Phra Chao Phaen Din*' would be redefined. At the beginning of the change, the separation of royal power in the public law sphere from private ownership of land would be more clearly divided. King Mongkut seemed to acknowledge the separation between public power and private rights over land. According to his royal command regarding compensation on expropriation, he states that 'Despite the fact that the King is the lord of all land, allowing his subjects to enjoy the use of land is the same as if he provides it to his subjects'.[33] Therefore the king decided to grant compensation when the state called land plots back without a public purpose.[34] In this regard, the king acknowledged and valued private rights over land, even though they were not officially recognised as private ownership at that time.

As a result of the social and economic changes following the signing of the treaty of friendship and commerce with the British in 1855, there was a substantial increase in the export of rice. There was high demand for exchanges of land for agriculture, and the number of disputes over land plots rose. From 1901 onwards, title deeds were officially issued to confirm individual land ownership.[35] Yet the concept of '*Phra Chao Phaen Din*' was not dissolved, but reinterpreted to conform with the modern context. In Prince Rabi's[36] lecture on land law, he acknowledged the existence of title deeds which constituted evidence of ownership, but this did not debar royal power over the land. Prince Rabi further claimed that citizens could only claim against individuals but were not entitled to assert ownership of land against the king.

> The official books on the land are not considered the violation to His Majesty's power or the loss of the king's power to anyone. This proves to be true when there is a banishment from one's land. This can happen with or without the red official book. The term 'people's right' means the right among citizens but not to the king's power.[37]

In this regard, it could be seen that the prince attempted to separate royal power over the land from ownership of land by regarding the former as public power and the latter as a private right. Ownership of land could be recognised, while kingship can still be preserved in the sphere of public power. In other words, public power can still be superior to claims of a private right.[38] Yet by the time of King Chulalongkorn, the concept which defines kingship in a modern state would not be ownership of land, but the concept of sovereignty which entitles the king to legislate and rule over Siamese territory instead.

4.3 THE GREAT ELECTED: THE FOUNDATION OF MODERN SOVEREIGNTY

During the time of changes and colonial pressure in nineteenth to twentieth century Siam, it was necessary for the king to legislate and administer the law in accordance with the social and economic context. The theories of kingship had to be remodelled in response to the

33 พระบรมราชโองการเรื่องพระราชกำหนดว่าด้วยการพระราชทานที่บ้านเรือน, นา, สวน [The Royal Command regarding the Royal Grants of Houses, Crops, and Plantations] cited in Nipaporn Ratchataphatthanakun, *Khong Klang, Khong Luang, Khong Satharana: Expropriation for Public Use in Siam from 1874 to 1920*, (Bangkok: Thammasat University Press 2017) 17.

34 Ibid.

35 Sawang Boonchalermvipas, *ประวัติศาสตร์กฎหมายไทย* [*Thai Legal History*] (Bangkok: Winyouchon 2012) 179–80.

36 Prince Rabi Bhadhanasakdi, son of King Chulalongkorn was educated in law at the University of Oxford during the period of Westernisation in Siam in the nineteenth century. After his studies overseas, he came back and was appointed as Minister of Justice and the principal of law school of the Ministry of Justice.

37 Rabi Bhadhanasakdi, *ว่าด้วยที่ดิน* [*Regarding Land Law*] (Bangkok: Lahutod Publishing House, 1909) 2.

38 Worachet Pakeerut, *Principles of Public Law*, 141.

winds of change. The Command of King Chulalongkorn during his second coronation may be seen as evidence of the reformation in Siam. This appears to be a significant change in the Command, since his predecessors had never pledged that they were elected by all. Therefore, the question of why the Command was modified at that time arises.

Before the reign of King Mongkut, law and kingship were premised in the law of *Thammasat*, apart from other Hindu-Buddhist theories of kingship. Regarding the justification of kingship, in theory, the king had no capability to create new law, but only to issue a royal command in accordance with the principles of *Thammasat*.[39] To replace the idea of the protector of immutable law, the Buddhist theory of *Mahasommutiraj*, which simply means the 'Great Elected,' was selected and emphasised to entitle the Siamese monarchy to legislate and rule during the time of modernisation. However, *Mahasommutiraj* had been recognised by Indianised Siamese society for centuries and was also referred to in the preface of the Thai *Thammasat*. This theory was originally rooted in a Buddhist text called *Akkhanya Sutta*.[40] According to the text, after conflicts and violence, humans gathered and decided to elect 'who was the most handsome, the best favoured, the most attractive, the most capable'[41] to exercise justice and allocate rations to society (or to rule). Then, the humans would in return share the rice with the Great Elected.[42] As the *Mahasommutiraj* was elected a judge, it shows that the concept is connected with the interrelation between kingship and law. From the reign of King Mongkut onwards, while *Mahasommutiraj* would be adopted and emphasised, the premise of kingship and royal power would also depart from the natural and immutable law of *Thammasat* in order to formulate the concept of sovereignty in a modern state.

It was King Mongkut who selected and reinterpreted the concept of *Mahasommutiraj*. First, he separated the theory from the story of the origin of the *Thammasat*, attempting to disclaim the mystical origin. In his writing *Nana Thamma Vijarini* (A critique on Dhamma), he states that the concept of *Mahasommutiraj* originates from India while the *Thammasat* in Siam originated from the Mon.[43] Moreover, King Mongkut began to humanise the state of the Great Elected. He simply states that 'At the time, people chose one particular person blessed with a sharp mind. He wished for the happiness of his people so they agreed to be under his power. That person was named "His prosperous the great"'.[44]

After his coronation ceremony, the king adopted his royal name '*Mahachonnikorn Samoson Sommot*'[45] which means 'Elected by the Consensus of All'. On the occasion of his sixtieth birthday, he asserted: 'Although I reign on my throne by your acceptance and blessings, I would not take this throne for granted and for myself. My only wish is to serve the country and to make ends meet for the governors who are the main force in ruling the country for the greatest benefit of the people.'[46]

39 David M. Engel, *Law and Kingship in the Reign of Chulalongkorn* (Ann Arbor: Center for South and Southeast Asian Studies, University of Michigan, 1975) 4; See also Chapter 1, this volume.

40 Chris Baker and Pasuk Phongpaichit, *A History of Ayuddhaya: Siam in the Early Modern World* (Cambridge: Cambridge University Press, 2017) 108.

41 C. A. F. Rhys David and T. W. Rhys David, *Dialogues of Buddha, Part III, Sacred Books of the Buddhists, vol.4* (Pali Text Society, 1965) 88 cited in Baker and Phongpaichit, *History of Ayuddhaya*, 108.

42 *Akkanyasutra, Tripitaka.*

43 King Mongkut, 'นานาธรรมวิจาริณี (Critique on Justice)' *Collected of Literary Works by the King* (Bangkok: Maha Makut Buddhist University Press, 1969) 133.

44 Ibid., 131.

45 Kasidit Ananthanathorn, *A Life of Thai Constitutional Regime* (LLM thesis, Thammasat University, 2017) 135.

46 National Archive of Thailand, *Rama IV* 99/3 *พระบรมราโชวาทรัชกาลที่ 4 ในงานเฉลิมพระชนมพรรษาครบ* 60 ปี [The royal guidance of King Rama IV on his 60th birthday] cited in Naruemon Theerawat, *Political Thought of King Mongkut* (MA Thesis, Chulalongkorn University, 1982) 202.

By separating the royal legitimacy from the law of *Thammasat*, it seems to be the initiation of formulating the concept of sovereignty to enact a new law, in accordance with the development of society. The king attempted to connect the foundation of the monarchy with political entities by adopting *Mahasommutiraj*, since it would justify the duties of the ruler and his people to contribute to the progress of the kingdom.[47] As a consequence, his justification to enact legislation for state affairs had no more dependence on the fundamental law of *Thammasat*.[48] An example was *Pra Kat Phraratchabanyat Phua Khai Mia* [Announcement on the Law Regarding Husbands Trafficking Wives], regarding which King Mongkut stated:

> His Majesty is not familiar with the former law but it was rightfully dictated. Once His Majesty analysed the law thoroughly, he realised that the law in itself is unfair, women were treated unequally as if cattle while men were treated with the dignity of men. Consequently, His Majesty has dictated to the judge and jury that from that moment on, the former law is now dysfunctional and can no longer be applied.[49]

In this regard, it is noticed that when the king amended the statutes, he did not claim legitimacy from *Thammasat* as his predecessors' legal protocol. Instead, he asserted the power to amend the law on a basis of his royal prerogative.[50] The king directly critiqued the injustice of the old legislation and exercised a royal prerogative to abolish and enact a new legal policy to achieve justice. This shows that his understanding of kingship and legal theory was completely different from the time when Rama I, the founder of Bangkok, revised and enacted the Law of the Three Seals Code, as the king stated that 'these royal decrees and royal laws were very defective, faulty, and contradictory because covetous people with no shame over sin had amended them for their own liking'.[51] According to Preechasilapakul, King Rama I's view indicates the traditional legal theory that the law was not intrinsically unjust, but was modified by 'covetous people'. The changes during King Mongkut's reign, on the contrary, marked the start of legal positivist paradigm which views that law can be made and altered by human will in Siam/Thailand.[52]

King Chulalongkorn, as a legitimate and moral heir of King Mongkut, succeeded to his father's throne and was crowned at the age of fifteen. Like his father, the king attempted to strengthen the bond between monarchy and people by asserting himself as the source of progress and justice, since the monarchy's political power was deprived by the court nobles during the period running from King Mongkut to early in King Chulalongkorn's reign.[53] In his second coronation, after reaching the age of majority, King Chulalongkorn did not neglect to affirm the theory of the Great Elected, established and reinterpreted by his father,

47 Nakarin Mektrairat, *ความคิด ความรู้ และอำนาจการเมืองในการปฏิวัติสยาม* 2475 [*Thoughts, Knowledge, and Political Power in Siamese Revolution* 1932] (2nd ed., Bangkok: Same Sky Publishing House, 2003) 84.

48 Attajak Sattayanurak, *การเปลี่ยนแปลงโลกทัศน์ของชนชั้นผู้นำไทยตั้งแต่รัชกาลที่* 4 *ถึงพุทธศักราช* 2475 [*The Changes of Visions of the Thai Elites from the Fourth Reign to* 1932] (3rd ed., Bangkok: Chulalongkorn University Press, 2012) 40.

49 *ประกาศพระราชบัญญัติผัวขายเมียบิดามารดาขายบุตร* [*Announcement on the Law Regarding Husbands Trafficking Wives and Parents Trafficking Children*] https://vajirayana.org/ประชุมประกาศรัชกาลที่-๔-ภาค-๗/๒๗๘-ประกาศพระราชบัญญัติเรื่องผัวขายเมียบิดามารดาขายบุตร (accessed 24 April 2019).

50 Somchai Preechasilpakul, *ความย้อนแย้งในประวัติศาสตร์ของ บิดากฎหมายไทย* [*The Paradoxes of the History of the Father of Thai law*] (Bangkok: Winyouchon, 2003) 32.

51 Chris Baker and Pasuk Phongpaichit (eds.) and (trs.), *The Palace Law of Ayutthaya and the Thammasat: Law and Kingship in Siam* (Ithaca: Cornell Southeast Asia Program Publications, 2016) 1.

52 Somchai Preechasilpakul, *Paradoxes*, 32.

53 Kullada Kesboonchoo Mead, *ระบอบสมบูรณาญาสิทธิราชย์: วิวัฒนาการรัฐไทย* [*The Rise and Decline of Thai Absolutism*] (Arthid Jaemrattanyou tr., Bangkok: Samesky Publishing House, 2019) 178–9.

in his Command. On that occasion, he also issued a royal ordinance to abolish the custom of crawling during the royal audience.[54] He stated: 'In the Kingdom of Siam, there is still the existence of the tradition of oppression and injustice. I have to reduce these problems but we cannot change the longstanding tradition at once. The changing process must be gradual and perfect timing is vital. This is for the progressive prosperity of the Kingdom'.

These two events could be seen as the declarations of King Chulalongkorn's idea of kingship. The claim for his kingship legitimately derived from the consensual agreement of all. As a ruler over the kingdom, he was not bound by any set of rules beyond human will and was enabled to abolish any unjust legal norms and enact new legislation in order to promote the progress of the country. This Great Elected theory, later known as '*Anekchonnikorn Samoson Sommot*', would play a significant part in bringing the justification of the monarchy into conformity with the democratic regime after Siamese Revolution in 1932.

4.4 ESTABLISHMENT OF SOVEREIGNTY OF THE MODERN STATE AND THE ABSOLUTE MONARCHY

During the transitional period of reformation in King Chulalongkorn's reign, Siamese elites were attempting to reconcile traditional and modern concepts of kingship. Prince Phichit Preechakorn, King Chulalongkorn's brother and advisor, expresses his views on law, justice, and kingship in his article called '*Dhammasan Vinitchai*' (A Consideration of Justice) which was published in 1885.[55] He asserts that it is justifiable for the king to enact law in the realm of four *Dhammasan* doctrines which came from accepted customs of people in order to achieve stability and the greatest benefit of people.[56] It is observed that the prince still stands on the religious doctrine of *Dhamma* in order to justify royal authority. The prince's legal conception is closely connected to the Indian concept of *Dhamma*, despite having adopted some newer ideas.[57] Yet, *Dhamma* in *Thammasat* was broader and more conceptual than *Dhamma* in the eye of the prince which summarises the boundary of *Dhamma* or *Dhammasan* into four points. Moreover, it is suggested that the prominent point of '*Dhammasan Vinitchai*' is that people are central to these four points of *Dhamma*, as they are the sources and bases of the *Dhamma*.[58]

Notwithstanding referring to the traditional doctrine, it seems that the prince's 'newer ideas' were highly influenced by Western utilitarian thought in the nineteenth century, pioneered by earlier elites. Prokati points out that the four points of *Dhamma* were similar to Bentham's explanation on happiness which consists of subsistence, abundance, equality, and security. He further assumes that the Siamese elites and Prince Phichit might have experienced Bentham's idea through Sir John Bowring, a close friend and an editor of Bentham's work who visited Thailand in 1855.[59] Additionally, there is also evidence showing that King Mongkut ordered collections of books from Bowring which potentially included Bentham's work.[60]

54 Somchai Preechasilpakul, *Paradoxes*, 36.

55 Pichit Preechakorn, 'ธรรมสารวินิจฉัย (Critique on Justice)' in the Royal Society (ed.), *ประชุมพระนิพนธ์* [*Collected literary works*] (Bangkok: Office of National of Thailand, 1929).

56 Ibid., 45–9; Engel, *Law and Kingship*, 10; Kittisak Prokati, *การปฏิรูปกฎหมายไทยภายใต้อิทธิพลยุโรป* [*Law Reform under European Influence*] (3rd ed., Bangkok: Winyuchon, 2010) 58–60.

57 Engel, *Law and Kingship*, 9.

58 Jaran Kosananan, *Thai Legal Philosophy*, 384.

59 Kittisak Prokati, *Law Reform*, 58; See also Jeremy Bentham, 'The Theory of Legislation' (C. K. Ogden ed, London: Routledge & Kegan Paul, 1931) 96.

60 Michael Wright, 'ความทรงรู้โลกภายนอกก่อนรัชกาลที่ ๕ (๒) [External Knowledge before the Fifth Reign (2)]' (Matichon Weekly 28 May–3 June 2004) 91 cited in Phra Kaen Kao, 'The Greatest Benefit of People' (Enlightened Jurists, 25 March 2011) www.enlightened-jurists.com/page/195 (accessed 19 January 2019).

Despite this, the unique characteristic of '*Dhammasan Vinitchai*' is how Prince Phichit Preechakorn tries to centre royal authority as a source of both law and justice. Moreover, any legislation enacted by the king seems to be just, in accordance with *Dhammasan*. When the prince examined the meaning of *Dhammasan*, he asserted that four points of *Dhammasan* can be achieved by legislation enacted by 'the graciously merciful king'. Then, regarding the topic 'what is law?', he explains that once the king as the source of four *Dhammasan* points has enacted the law by declaring it to the public, all people must follow. Not knowing the law is not a ground for an excuse to reject the law.[61] In this regard, it seems that the prince firmly believed that royal authority, in any case, could create a just law to provide the greatest benefit to people. In other words, both the law as it ought to be and the law as it is can be made by royal authority in the name of justice or *Dhammasan*.

Nevertheless, this view of the prince on law is somewhat to be distinguished from Bentham's ideas. First, Bentham made the distinction between law as it ought to be and law as it is.[62] Second, Bentham suggests that the compatibility of law as it is to utilitarian principles has to be measured by law as it ought to be. On the other hand, Pichit Preechakorn jumped to the conclusion that not only could royal authority create effective law as it is but also achieve *Dhammasan* which, according to the prince's view is similar to law as it ought to be to provide the greatest benefit to people. Moreover, the prince did not urge the readers to measure the royal decrees enacted by the king and see whether they are in accordance with *Dhammasan* or utilitarian principles as Bentham suggested. Thus, there seems to be a compromise between traditional and Western concepts regarding royal authority. It is likely that the prince attempted to affirm the legislative power of the king; meanwhile, he was still able to connect the royal power to traditional *Dhamma* doctrines. Engel points out that the prince's essay 'was a conscious attempt to formulate a system of natural law, implying some form of social compact between the modern King and his subjects based upon the ancient concept of Dhamma'.[63]

King Chulalongkorn also took part in strengthening his royal authority and shaping modern kingship, but went further than what his brother had suggested. Despite the fact that administrative and legal reforms proceeded throughout his reign, the king was not likely to sacrifice his absolute power after justifying his kingship for modern sovereignty. Moreover, his assertion about sovereignty does not seem to be dependent on any premises. In 1885,[64] Prince Prisdang and other nobles submitted a petition which proposed legal, administrative, and political reforms in Siam in response to the concerns of the king and the elites regarding the intrusion of imperial power. To promote external trust in the justice and efficiency of Siam, a constitutional monarchy and the cabinet system, therefore, were introduced by the petitioners.[65] Even though a critic pointed out that this petition did not refer to the participation

61 Pichit Preechakorn, 'Critique on Justice', 52.

62 Worachet Pakeerut, *ประวัติศาสตร์ความคิดนิติปรัชญา* [*Intellectual History of Legal Philosophy*] (Bangkok: Read Publishing House, 2018) 385–6.

63 Engel, *Law and Kingship*, 9.

64 Prior to 1941 (2484 BE), Thai New Year was in April. However, in September 1940 (2483 BE), the Thai Parliament set 1 January 1941 (2484 BE) as the start of the year 1941 (2484 BE).

65 Prisdang Jumsai, 'เจ้านายและข้าราชการกราบบังคมทูลความเห็นเปลี่ยนแปลงราชการแผ่นดิน ร.ศ.๑๐๓ (The Petition of Royal Families and Officials for Reforming State Affairs R.E. 103)' in Prasob Chulaket (ed.), *เจ้านายและข้าราชการกราบบังคมทูลความเห็นเปลี่ยนแปลงราชการแผ่นดิน ร.ศ.๑๐๓ และ พระราชดำรัสในพระบาทสมเด็จพระจุลจอมเกล้าเจ้าอยู่หัวทรงแถลงพระบรมราชาธิบายแก้ไขการปกครองแผ่นดิน* [*The Petition of Royal Families and Officials for Reforming State Affairs R.E. 103 and Royal Speech of Phra Baht Som Dej Phra Chula Chom Klao Chao You Hua regarding the Royal Policies of State Reforms*] (Bangkok: Excise Department Publishing House, 1967) 21–9.

of people in the political system,[66] the suggestion of reforms was still too progressive for the king. With regard to the king's response to the petitioners, despite conceding the importance of legal and administrative reforms, he wisely acknowledged the petition, but finally declined the proposals providing two main reasons. Firstly, he asserted the conservative ministers' disqualification for supporting the reformation. The second reason was that the professional human resources were not adequate to achieve the project of legal reform.[67]

In 1888, he gave a speech called 'a royal explanation on the governmental reforms' which may be seen as a counter-reaction to the critiques on his reform policies. In the statement where he explained the existing judicial system, he referred to the law of *Thammasat* not as immutable law, but as the law which was transplanted from another region, like his father's explanation. The king also justifies royal authority for enacting royal decrees in accordance with social changes, while Brahmins, he explained, who had expertise in *Thammasat* law were merely appointed by royal prerogative to work as the judiciary.[68] Siamese kingship, in the eyes of King Chulalongkorn, is absolute and cannot be restrained by any law. Interestingly, the king acknowledged the Western idea of limited monarchy which is restrained by 'law' and did not object to such system. Yet such system was not suitable to Siam since the European peoples were not pleased with their despotic monarchy. On the other hand, the Siamese trusted in their monarch as the source of justice and benefits of his people.[69] The king seemed to create a new theory of kingship; yet, the idea tends to be a combination between Western utilitarianism and the Buddhist theory of elective kingship.

In the late 1880s, the king and his advisors prepared 'the draft of the first royal decree regarding Siamese royal customs'.[70] The draft clearly shows the scope of his kingship and royal authority in the king's view. Section 2 states the supremacy of kingship which cannot be restrained by any premises and Section 3 affirms the legality of the proclaimed royal guidance. By the end of King Chulalongkorn's reign, the theory of kingship and royal authority reached its peak. The king, not being restrained by any law or any religious doctrines, wholly held state power which entitled him to establish or adjust his own state organs.[71] Regarding the role in law making, the king, as absolute monarch, legitimately enacts law without restraints. Prince Rabi confirms the concept in his lecture that 'Law is the enforcement of the authority figure in the society and those who violate it must be punished. The term "The authority figure" which is described in the legal term definition must be clearly explained that the highest authority figure in the government is His Majesty the King of Thailand'.[72]

This explanation nullified the sacred status of the law of *Thammasat* and justified the royal authority for the administrative, judicial reforms and codification in Siam. The introduction of the Penal Code to Siam was remarkable evidence of modern views on kingship and law. The

66 Piyabutr Saengkanokkul, *ประวัติศาสตร์ ข้อความ คิด อำนาจ สถาปนา และ การเปลี่ยนผ่าน* [*Conceptual History Constituent Power Transition*] (Bangkok: Samesky Publishing House, 2016) 16.

67 Engel, *Law and Kingship*, 15.

68 King Chulalongkorn, 'พระราชดำรัสในพระบาทสมเด็จพระจุลจอมเกล้าเจ้าอยู่หัวทรงแถลงพระบรมราชาธิบายแก้ไขการปกครองแผ่นดิน [*Royal Speech of Phra Baht Som Dej Phra Chula Chom Klao Chao You Hua regarding the Royal Policies of State Reforms*]' in Prasob Chulaket (ed.), *เจ้านายและข้าราชการกราบบังคมทูลความเห็นเปลี่ยนแปลงราชการแผ่นดิน ร.ศ.๑๐๓ และ พระราชดำรัสในพระบาทสมเด็จพระจุลจอมเกล้าเจ้าอยู่หัวทรงแถลงพระบรมราชาธิบายแก้ไขการปกครองแผ่นดิน* [*The Petition of Royal Families and Officials for Reforming State Affairs R.E. 103 and Royal Speech of Phra Baht Som Dej Phra Chula Chom Klao Chao You Hua regarding the Royal Policies of State Reforms*] (Bangkok: Excise Department Publishing House 1967) 73–4.

69 Ibid., 106.

70 ร่างพระราชกฤษฎีกาที่ 1 [The Draft of the First Royal Decree] cited in Tida Saraya, *พระบาทสมเด็จพระจุลจอมเกล้าเจ้าแผ่นดินสยาม* [*Phra Baht Chula Chom Klao the King of Siam*] (Mueng Boran Press, 2018) 350.

71 Worachet Pakeerut, *Principles of Public Law*, 44–5.

72 Rabi Bhanasakdi, *เลคเชอร์* [*Lecture*] (Sobhon Bhibanakorn Publishing House, 1925) 1,106.

law of *Thammasat* was seen as inapplicable and outdated despite generations of royal amendments. The king, therefore, decided to replace the old law with a code which was drafted by chosen legal experts, while the revision and approval were still under his royal prerogative.[73]

At King Vajiravudh's coronation, the king did not emphasise that he was elected by the consensus of all anymore in his Command, but still stated his duties to ensure the ease and the greatest benefit of his people. This is probably because King Vajiravudh chose instead to emphasise his legitimacy as an appointed heir of royal succession. There is evidence for this in part of King Vajiravudh and King Prajadhipok's royal titles after their coronations. The former's title was '*Borommachanakka Disorn Sommot*' (the Elected by the Great Father) and the latter's was '*Borommachetta Sothorn Sommot*'[74] (the Elected by the Great Brother of Full Blood). This change was also the legacy of King Chulalongkorn's restoration of power which secured the royal succession by establishing the title of 'Siamese Crown Prince' for an heir to solve the prior problem of conflicts during the transitional period.[75] Moreover, from the later part of King Chulalongkorn's reign to King Prajadhipok's, the expansion of the reformed governmental system run by newly educated professionals finally led to the decline in the Siamese absolute monarchy.[76] The existent theory of the Great Elected which connected the monarch to people was not adequate to justify the monarchy. Instead, King Vajiravudh, educated in England and influenced by Western secularism, transformed and further developed the monarch from the Great Elected into the representative of the nation.[77]

However, it is observed that the royal duties, kingship, and royal prerogative emphasised by King Vajiravudh and King Prajadhipok were still rooted in theories of kingship and law established by King Mongkut and King Chulalongkorn. The monarchy adjusted and emphasised the traditional Buddhist elective theory by connecting themselves to the people and then justified their absolute sovereignty over a state, empowering themselves in order to establish a modern form of administration and a Western legal tradition. As such, the Siamese modern monarchy could still tackle the advent of concepts such as constitutionalism, the parliamentary system, and democracy which they categorised as 'Western', whereas they could selectively Westernise the state functions as long as the changes were suitable to Siam in their eyes. In other words, Western political and legal concepts were translated into Siamese versions.[78] The developments of the Commands from late Ayutthaya until King Prajadhipok were relatively accordant with the developments of kingship and royal authority from pre-modern to modern Siam.

4.5 THE ROLE OF THE COMMAND IN A CONTEMPORARY CONTEXT

4.5.1 *Positioning the Command in the New Regime*

In 1932, a group of civilian and military members called '*Khanarassadorn*' (People's Party) decided to abolish the absolute monarchy and constitute democracy in Siam. The event is

73 The Penal Code for the Kingdom of Siam R.E. 127.

74 'ประกาศเฉลิมพระปรมาภิไธย', ราชกิจจานุเบกษา เล่ม 33 น่า 213 วันที่ 11 พฤศจิกายน 2459 ['Announcement of the Royal Title' Royal Gazette No.33 Page 213 11 November 1917]; คำถวายพระพรชัยมงคลและพระราชดำรัสตอบในการพระราชพิธีบรมราชาภิเษก พ.ศ. 2468, ราชกิจจานุเบกษา เล่ม 42 ตอนพิเศษ วันที่ 3 มีนาคม 2468 [Message and Royal Respondance on the Occasion of the Coronation Ceremony Special Royal Gazette No.42 3 March 1925], 99 cited in Kasidit, *Thai Constitutional Regime*, 136.

75 Kullada Kesboonchoo Mead, *Rise and Decline*, 178–9.

76 See ibid., 177–232.

77 Ibid., 252.

78 Thongchai Winichakul, 'บททดลองเสนอ : อภิสิทธิ์ปลอดความผิด (impunity) และความเข้าใจสิทธิมนุษยชนในนิติรัฐแบบไทยๆ (Proposal: Impunity and Perception on the Rule of Law in Thai Style)' (2017) ฟ้าเดียวกัน (ฉบับพิเศษ 40 ปี 6 ตุลา) (Samesky: Special Edition 40th Anniversary 6 October 1975) 191.

well known as '*Karn Abhivat Siam*' (The Siamese Revolution). The monarchy survived this revolution; however, it had to be repositioned under the constitution, in accordance with the new political system. Throughout the political history of Thailand after 1932, there have been tensions between traditionalist and constitutional theorists. The issue about the status and contents of the Command is one of the examples which shows the controversies over kingship and royal prerogative in modern Thailand.

Regarding the status of the Command, not long after the revolution, the question as to whether the king should take an oath to protect the constitution arose during the discussion on the draft permanent 1932 constitution of Siam. Pridi Banomyong, civilian leader of the People's Party, made a note of the discussion with King Prajadhipok in his writings.[79] While the king referred to the oath of office of the United States, he suggested that, in Siam, the monarch need not pledge an oath to protect the constitution. The first reason was because the king has already 'handed over' the constitution; this is equivalent to the royal oath to protect the constitution. Apart from that, according to royal custom, the king has to pledge an oath at the coronation ceremony. After the king's explanation, Pridi asked whether the king would adjust the phrases of the Command. Instead of answering Pridi's request, the king further commented that the preface of the constitution, drafted and written by King Prajadhipok himself, had already called on the royal families to follow and preserve the constitution.[80] This clearly indicates the duty of royal successors to preserve the constitution.[81] Then, the king showed the special gazette edition regarding his Command at the coronation ceremony[82] and cited the act of pouring holy water from the ceremonial gold bottle in order to insist on the status of the Command as an oath to guard the constitution.

This matter was raised again when Nguan Thongprasert, one of the members of the Constitution Drafting Commission (CDC), asked during the conference whether the monarch ought to swear an oath to protect the constitution if the MPs ought to do so.[83] However, other members of committee suggested that there has already been a royal custom, so there is no need to over-lengthen the constitution by adding the royal oath. On the contrary, Nguan argued that such royal custom was not a provision and there has never before been an oath to protect the constitution. Facing opponents who saw no necessity to affirm the duty in the written constitution, he then called for a vote among the committee. Pridi records as follows:

> I hereby declare to the assembly which regards the appeal of Mr. Nguan Jongprasert toward the requirement that His Majesty must perform a vow. Even though the act is not written down formally, His Majesty must perform a vow when ascending to the throne. The act of not writing down does not mean that His Majesty is not required to perform a vow. This statement must be recorded in the report.

It is noted that Pridi appears to have been convinced by King Prajadhipok to regard the Command as an oath to protect the constitution during his audience with the king. Before the vote, Jaroon Suepsang argues that he acknowledges the royal tradition, but sees incorporation

79 Pridi Banomyong, *จงพิทักษ์เจตนารมย์ประชาธิปไตย* [*Keep Protecting the Spirit of Democracy*] (Bangkok: Winyouchon, 2000) 66–8.

80 Ibid., 57–8.

81 The preface of the Constitution of Siam 1932 states that 'May the members of the royal family, governors, military personnel and commoners unite harmoniously to protect and sustain the constitution of the Kingdom of Siam in order for it to exist eternally in our country as His Majesty wishes'.

82 Special Royal Gazette No.42, 3 March 1925.

83 Thai Parliament, Minutes of the Draft of the Constitution of Siam 1932 (Noraniti Setabutr ed., King Prajadhipok's Institute, 2009) 57–60.

in the constitution as highly significant; merely making a record in the minutes is inadequate, and the next monarch might not vow to protect the constitution. However, in the end, the resolution was forty-eight to seven not to constitutionalise the duty for succeeding monarchs to swear the oath.

Eighteen years after the revolution, King Bhumibol held a coronation and pledged his notable Command. This remarkable Command has often been cited to justify the conformity of the monarchy to the constitution and democracy. For instance, according to the conservative legal scholar Krea-ngam, in the democratic system, the king was no longer the owner of greenery, aqua and all items; as such, the king would state, in different phrases, 'I will rule the Kingdom by *Dhamma* for the greatest benefit of Siamese people'.[84] In response to Nitirat's proposal on the oath, Kittisak Prokati, a law professor from Thammasat University, posted a message publicly on Facebook liked and shared by hundreds of peoples that

> On the occasion that His Majesty has ascended to the throne through the principle of 'Anekchonnikorn Samoson Sommot' as inscribed in the book of Dharma and ancient tradition, the present-day monarch has voiced his first royal declaration which states that 'I will rule the kingdom by Dharma for the greatest benefit of Siamese people'. This manifesto is more than just a declaration to the public but instead in front of the ceremonial assembly. If we keep this tradition, why we must require him to make a vow for the parliament?[85]

Even the Command before 1932 was asserted in order to claim that the monarch has ensured the freedom of individuals for centuries. The phrase which confirms the king as the owner of greenery, aqua, and all items was cited to generalise the character of the Command before the 1932 revolution. Krea-ngam claims that despite being the lord of all land, the king had already allowed his subjects to enjoy the use of properties since the first day he crowned.[86] Kesemsri, a famous Thai historian, points out in his lecture on 'Analysis on Thai Historical Studies: The Monarchy in the Thai Social Context' that the phrase is regarded as a social contract between the king and his subjects to confer rights to properties.[87]

4.5.2 *Deconstructing the Myths*

4.5.2.1 The Status of the Command

The aforementioned assertions seem to overlook the history of the Command in its prior contexts. First of all, regarding the status of the Command, the religious root of the coronation ceremony must not be forgotten, as pledging the Command is rather the depiction of the transformation from a human into the mythical status of the God King which is entitled to issue an '*Ong-kan*' or law. Therefore, the form of the procedure seems traditionally to signify the supremacy of the monarchy and the prerogative to enact law over other political entities.

Moreover, even if we admit that the Command is an oath, there is still the question of to whom the monarch swears the oath and for what purpose. King Chulalongkorn clearly states that the Command has to be received by the Brahmin only. Moreover, regarding the purpose of the Command, Prince Dhani Nivat claims that the traditional Command's phrase is

84 Wissanu Krea-ngam, 'สถาบัน พระ มหา กษัตริย์ ใน ประวัติศาสตร์ ไทย (2) (Thai Monarchy in Thai History)' (ThaiPublica, 10 November 2018 <https://thaipublica.org/2015/12/wissanu-krea-ngam-2/> (accessed 13 September 2020).

85 Kittisak Prokati, <www.facebook.com/kittisak.prokati/posts/10151217575550484> accessed 27 January 2012.

86 Wissanu Krea-ngam, 'Thai Monarchy'.

87 Supawat Kasemsri, *การศึกษาประวัติศาสตร์ไทยเชิงวิเคราะห์: สถาบันพระมหากษัตริย์ในปริบทสังคมไทย* [*Analytical Studies of Thai History: the Monarchy in Thai Context*] (Discourse on Sirindhorn, Bangkok, February 2013) 20.

regarded as the royal oath to own all things as lords of lives.[88] This claim and evidence that the Siamese traditional law preserves the king's prerogative to allocate and call back resources, of course, are contradictory to the social contract to confer rights to property as Kasemsri asserted. Having observed the evidence, it can be seen that before 1932 there was no royal tradition which required a king to give an oath to protect the constitution as King Prajadhipok and others including Pridi claimed. It is not convincing to conclude that the Command is a vow to all people at a ceremony with few participants.

4.5.2.2 Theories of Kingship

It is observed that asserting the existent royal custom as an oath to protect the constitution depicts the myth of continuity between the old and new regimes. It initially allowed '*rajaprapheni*' (royal customs) including theories of kingship which are intangible to be defined and incorporated into the new regime.[89] Indeed, such royal customs were likely to be myths overshadowing the importance of democracy and constitutionalism.

The first misleading myth which is a typically claimed to justify the conformity of ancient Thai monarchy with democracy is the Great Elected theory, known as '*Anekchonnikorn Samoson Sommot*'. During the conference on the draft 1932 constitution this theory, adapted by King Mongkut, was revived in order to reconcile the premise of the monarchy and the new regime. When the subject matter arose regarding an oath to protect the constitution during the royal accession, the president of CDC also claimed that this was not a new theory, but rooted in a traditional theory called '*Anekchonnikorn Samoson Sommot*'. This theory, according to the president, holds that kingship emanates from the invitation of people, not from divinity, like other countries.[90] Since 1932, there have been reproductions of this idea led by educated elites such as Prince Dhani Niwat, Prince Wan Waithayakorn, and Seni Pramoj,[91] which still echo in the Thai academic world of law and politics. For instance, regarding the role of King Mongkut in framing the theory in modern Siam, Chaiyaporn claims that Mongkut has combined Eastern and Western concepts, *Anekchonnikorn Samoson Sommot* and popular sovereignty respectively.[92] Indeed, as mentioned above, the theory was even cited by Prokati to assert the legitimacy of the Command as an oath to protect the constitution.

These views seem to jump to the conclusion that this theory is similar to democracy while overlooking its historical context. Having examined the historical context of the Command throughout the period, it is true that the modern monarchy claims its justification from the Buddhist text of *Akkanyasutra* which is the root of *Mahasommutiraj*, or the Great Elected theory. Yet, it should be noted that the modern monarchy tends to gradually reinterpret and adjust traditional theories to justify its absolute power in the name of the people. In other words, *Anekchonnikorn Samoson Sommot* is different from *Akkanyasutra*. The first piece of evidence is King Mongkut's attempt to separate *Thammasat* from *Akkanyasutra* by tracing their origins. Next, it can be seen that '*Anekchonnikorn Samoson Sommot*' emphasises only some parts of *Akkanyasutra* to justify kingship, but neglects the condition between the ruler

88 Quaritch Wales, *Siamese State Ceremonies*, 87–8; However, this view was disputed by Wales in his book on the basis that the custom was traditionally an oath of loyalty to Brahmin in ancient India.

89 Eugénie Mérieau, 'Buddhist Constitutionalism in Thailand: When Rājadhammā Supersedes the Constitution' (2018) 13(2) *Asian Journal of Comparative Law* 9.

90 Thai Parliament, *Minutes of the Draft of the Constitution of Siam 1932*, 57.

91 Nakarin Mektrairat, *Thoughts, Knowledge and Political Power*, 82–102.

92 Chaiyan Chaiyaporn, *คาสว่างกับรัชกาลที่ 4* [*Enlightenment with King Rama IV*] (Bangkok: Matichon Publishing House, 2017) 153–9.

and the rules. In this regard, the adjusted theory neglects the conditional agreement between the Great Elected and the people. When the people decided to seek the Great Elected, not only did they confer the power to allocate rice to the Great Elected but also shared the grains with him. Niphitkul points out that the act of sharing the grains symbolises a contractual relationship between the ruler and the ruled. Therefore, if the ruler breached the contract, the ruled may cease to provide the grains to the ruler. However, the newer theory, adjusted by King Mongkut, seems to emphasise only the basis of royal authority rather than the contractual relationship.[93]

Furthermore, while popular sovereignty focuses on the procedure of elections and participation in decisions on state affairs, the consensual agreement of *Anekchonnikorn Samoson Sommot* is rather conceptual without any concrete electoral popular participation. Regarding the royal succession in pre-modern Siam until King Chulalongkorn's reign, the monarchs were elected by few participants; as Prince Prisdang points out, the ancient monarchs were selected by a few monks and court nobles.[94] Moreover, during the Siamese reformation, although there were pieces of legislation enacted by King Chulalongkorn regarding individuals' rights to fair treatment by the modern judicial system and freedom of speech, Siamese citizens had no direct or indirect participation in electing their king or even mandating their legislators.[95] In the royal command which established the '*Ratthamontri Sabha*' (Council of Ministers), the king decided to cut the phrase which states that people could participate in this sort of organisation as soon as they were adequately educated, even though the phrase is far from handing over a popular mandate.[96] In fact, it was after the Siamese revolution in 1932 that *Mahasommutiraj* in the Buddhist text was to some extent actualised in the modern world through the parliamentary system, and the people's representatives were also entitled to participate in the process for making a king.[97]

It is paradoxical that Siamese elites could claim their legitimacy from the mandate of people, while also resist democratic concepts from the West by a claim about suitability to Siamese society. Although the benevolent merit of the Great Elected (the most handsome, the best favoured, the most attractive, the most capable) is not likely to comply with individualism and equality, the idea of a popular mandate is to some extent rooted in the Eastern Buddhist text. The assertion of the theory of *Anekchonnikorn Somoson Sommot* seems to be selectively distorted and chosen to justify the sovereignty of the king and the exercise of royal prerogative rather than to promote the role of the people in their political entities. Thus, it is misleading to claim that Thai kingship is premised in the popular mandate, regardless of the historical context. As Preechasilpakul comments, the assertion, incredibly, attempts to depict the continuity of two completely distinctive systems and the traditional and the new rules of royal succession respectively.[98]

Another influential myth which must be deconstructed is the emphasis on the kingship theory of *Dhammaraja*, as it appears that King Bhumibol's Command to rule by *Dhamma*

93 Enlightened Jurists, 'Seminar on Coup D'etat and Constitutionalism' (Prachatai 1 October /2012) https://prachatai.com/journal/2012/10/42914 (accessed 14 February 2019).

94 Prisdang Jumsai, 'Petition of Royal Families', 22.

95 Engel, *Law and Kingship*, 113–14.

96 Kullada Kesboonchoo Mead, *Rise and Decline*, 191.

97 Yet it is worth noting that after 1991 this statement was no longer convincing. From the Constitution of Thailand 1991 BE, the parliament is merely entitled to acknowledge the succession.

98 Somchai Preechasilpakul, *นี่คือปณิธานที่หาญมุ่ง: ข้อถกเถียงว่าด้วยสถาบันพระมหากษัตริย์ในองค์กรจัดทำรัฐธรรมนูญของไทย ตั้งแต่ พ.ศ.2475–2550* [*This Is an Aspiration We Aim For: Controversies over Monarchy of the Draft Constitution Committee from 1932–2007*] (Bangkok: Samesky Publishing House, 2019) 185.

has often been cited to affirm the status of the righteous king and compliance with democracy and a constitutional monarchy. *Dhammaraja* has been defined through the doctrines of ten royal virtues and the law of *Thammasat*. For instance, in a textbook called '*Phra Mahakasat Thai Nai Rabobprachatipa Tai*' (Thai Monarchy in a Democratic System) published by one of king's privy councillors, the author cited King Bhumibol's Command and claimed that the ten royal virtues and other *Dhamma* principles have restrained royal power for centuries since the Kingdom of Sukhothai.[99] Bowornsak Uwanno, a legal scholar, asserts that Western absolute monarchy has never happened in Siam since the king adopted the Hindu-Buddhist doctrine of *Dhammaraja*.[100] He even justified the royal prerogative to veto a bill by adopting the ten royal virtues as a constitutional convention to justify the veto.[101]

This assertion also seems to neglect the development of theories of kingship throughout history. From the history of the Command, it is observed that ruling by *Dhamma*, the tradition of *Dhammikkaracha*, appeared in the Commands from the reigns of King Chulalongkorn to that of King Bhumibol. With respect to the assertion of immutable *Dhamma* to control royal power throughout history, there seems to be no systematic state institutions to check the concordance between the religious doctrine and the exercise of royal power and challenge royal authority, as it appears that not only did the Siamese monarchy adopt the ten royal virtues but also the theory of *Devaraja*, which enhanced royal absolutism, to enact and apply law.[102] For example, some royal decrees of the Three Seals Code which allow and obligate court officers to expostulate about an unjust royal decision before the final decision were often claimed as evidence for the role of *Dhamma* in deterring the royal prerogative.[103] Meanwhile, it appears that the code also affirms that the status of the royal command is equivalent to the god's command.[104] Moreover, *Dhamma* was relatively dynamic in accordance with social and political changes. It can be seen that the doctrines were reinterpreted over time, such as Prince Phichit Preechakorn's assertion of *Thammasat* during the transitional period of modernisation. This could be regarded as a newer version of *Dhamma* by combining Occidental utilitarian ideas and the indigenous concept of *Dhamma* during the transitional period of modernisation. Afterwards, royal sovereignty could finally be established with no interdependence between *Dhamma* and the king's sovereignty, but the former could occasionally be referred to whenever the king wanted to reject what he called 'Western limited monarchy'. Thus, when King Prajadhipok pledged his Command, he was merely repeating the modernised concepts of kingship and royal prerogative framed by his royal predecessors with no place for constitutionalism and democracy.

With respect to King Bhumibol's Command,[105] although it did not state kingship as the owner of all property and land or as the ruling monarch who was fully responsible for

99 Tanin Kraivixien, *พระ มหา กษัตริย์ ไทย ใน ระบอบ ประชาธิปไตย* [*Thai Monarchy in a Democratic System*] (Bangkok: Khurusapha Publishing House, 1976) 32.

100 Bowonsak Uwanno, *กฎหมายมหาชน เล่ม 2 การแบ่งแยกกฎหมายมหาชน-เอกชน และพัฒนาการกฎหมายมหาชนในประเทศไทย* [*Public Law Vol.2 The Distinction between Public and Private Law and the Development of Thai Public Law*] (Bangkok: Chulalongkorn University Press, 2007) 147.

101 Bowonsak Uwanno, 'ทศ พิ ธรา ช ธรรม: ธรรมเนียม ปฏิบัติ ทาง รัฐธรรมนูญ [The Ten Royal Virtues: the Convention of the Constitution]' (2010) *The Secretariat of Cabinet Journal* 3.

102 Jaran Kosananan, *Thai Legal Philosophy*, 232–4.

103 Section 106 of the Palace Law of Ayutthaya, the Three Seals Code.

104 Jaran Kosananan, *Thai Legal Philosophy*, 163.

105 King Vajiralongkorn also pledged his Command in similar terms to that of his father, but announced it publicly in the royal gazette without any countersign. He states that 'I will continue, preserve, build upon the royal legacy, and rule by *Dhamma* for the greatest benefit of people forever'; See also ประกาศพระปฐมบรมราชโองการ ใน พระ ราช พิธี บรม ราชาภิเษก พุทธศักราช ๒๕๖๒ (The Announcement of the Initial Royal Command in the

governmental affairs, most claims tend to neglect the development of *Dhamma* through legal and political contexts over time and overgeneralise that *Dhamma* covers only the ten royal virtues and other Buddhist doctrines. In fact, the dynamic of *Dhamma*, as observed, shows the adaptability of Siamese monarchy. They could adopt Western legal positivism, sovereignty, and absolute monarchy; meanwhile, their absolutism was still justified under the realm of the *Dhammaraja* custom, as they selectively filtered Western ideas and combined them with their traditional bases of kingship.[106] As Mérieau points out, 'the King does not swear an oath to the constitution, but to Dhamma, when he accedes to the throne'.[107] Those who claim for *Dharmaraja*, without reluctance, exploit this religious doctrine to create their own 'Thai style of democracy' by neglecting to define or analyse the extensive senses of *Dhammaraja* which, in the realm of Siamese elites, not only comprises moral obligations, but also the justification for the exercise of power.[108]

As such, one of the biggest challenges of Thailand's political development is that theories of kingship and religious doctrines seem to devalue and overshadow the consciousness of democracy and constitutionalism. Arbitrary power, regardless of the rule of law, can be justifiable power as long as it has been exercised in the realm of *Dhamma*, *Khwam Dee Ngam* (Virtue), or *Kwarm pen Dham* (Justice). Some Thai legal experts have blamed Western legal positivism for creating narrow-minded lawyers who justify law enacted by despotic rulers and neglect the Thai traditional values.[109] In fact, it can be seen that the justification for unrestrained power was rooted in Thai culture. As Winichakul argues, Western ideas about the acceptance of the ruler's power were not the whole cause of the acceptance of the ruler's power in Thailand, but the cause was rather rooted in the harmonisation between Western ideas and Thai legal culture which justifies the power of righteous rulers.[110]

4.6 CONCLUSION

The history of the Commands has shown the historical developments of kingship, sovereignty and legal theory. Hindu–Buddhist and regional theories of kingship, which have been blended and adjusted over time, were adopted to justify royal legitimacy and prerogative of the Siamese monarchy from the Ayutthaya era to that of Bangkok. In particular, during the advent of Western colonial influences from the nineteenth to the twentieth centuries, the Siamese elites had to reconcile traditional and Western values to reform the monarchy in modern Siam. In fact, there is no pre-democratic or democratic Command, since the Command has no indication of either democracy or rule of law, but rather it is a restatement of pre-modern and modern monarchy. In the present, it is still used to justify the righteous status of the monarchy in the contemporary regime and the political system, and to supersede the significance of democracy, the rule of law and constitutionalism which

Coronation Ceremony 2563 B.E.), ราชกิจจานุเบกษา (Royal Gazette) www.ratchakitcha.soc.go.th/DATA/PDF/2562/B/014/T_0001.PDF (accessed 1 May 2019).

106 For the literary work on the positioning between Western and local ideas of the Siamese Elites, see Taweesak Pueksom, *หยด เลือด จารึก และ แท่น พิมพ์: ว่า ด้วย ความ รู้/ ความ จริง ของ ชนชั้น นำ สยาม พ. ศ. 2325–2411* [*Blood Drop, Manuscript, and Printing Press: the Management of Knowledge and Truth of the Siamese Elites*] (Bangkok: Illumination Editions, 2018).

107 Eugénie Mérieau, 'Buddhist Constitutionalism in Thailand: When Rājadhammā Supersedes the Constitution', 16.

108 Anek Makanan, *จักรพรรดิราช คติอำนาจเบื้องหลังชนชั้นนำไทย* [*Chakkravatin: Ideology of Power of the Thai Elites*] (Bangkok: Matichon Publishing House, 2018) 34–6.

109 Sawang Boonchalermvipas, *Thai Legal History*, 186–8, 244–5; Kittisak Prokati, *Law Reform*, 141.

110 Thongchai Winichakul, 'Impunity and Perception', 207.

are called 'Western ideas' by those justifying it. The paradigm clash between so-called traditional and Western values are struggles in which Thais may face contemporary political conflicts. This chapter would not opine on whether the king should swear an oath to protect the constitution instead of pledging the Command but rather point out that the myths of 'traditional values' versus 'Western ideas' should be revised and deconstructed carefully. Perhaps, the obstacles to Thai constitutional and political development may be rooted in the understanding of the Thai values in its own political and legal culture.

5

Buddhist Influence on the Ancient Siamese Legal System, from Ayutthaya to the Twenty-First Century

Khemthong Tonsakulrungruang

A discussion of Buddhism and law is notably absent among law and religion scholars. Although the false impression of Buddhism as an ascetic religion has been debunked, it remains the river less travelled compared to Christianity, Islam, Judaism, or even Hinduism and Confucianism.[1] Very little is known about the Buddhist legal tradition and its influence on the laws of Far East Asia.

Buddhism, however, offers very perplexing images regarding law. Buddha never promulgated a legal code, an equivalent of Shariah, to his lay disciples, but he left a well-developed code of conduct which made monastic life highly legalistic. Surprisingly, this legalistic tradition never produced a renowned lawyer on a par with Augustin, Aquinas, or Bartholus in Christianity. In India and China, the two largest sources of Asian civilisation, Buddhism's influence was obscured by Hindu and Confucian legal thought.[2] Elsewhere, the Islamic legal tradition featured more prominently. Only in mainland Southeast Asia, the stronghold of the Theravada Buddhism tradition, did the Buddhist legal tradition flourish. Located at the crossroads between India and China, Southeast Asia has been an important trade route since premodern times. Waves of traders, and later priests, from India arrived and some settled, spreading Indic beliefs among local inhabitants. By the beginning of the second millennium, Buddhism was well established. When Tai kingdoms emerged in the eleventh century CE, they embraced Buddhism as part of their belief system. Then, Buddhism permeated into every aspect of life, from literature to artwork, to the political structure and to law. Still, very little research has been done on this subject, in particular among Thai legal scholars.[3] They uncritically agree that Buddhism paid some contribution to the ancient law of Siam, but how did it do so? Since R. Lingat's seminal work on *dhammasastra*,[4] there has been little development of thinking on this. In fact, the question has never been seriously addressed.

[1] Rex Ahdar, 'Navigating Law and Religion: Familiar Waterways, Rivers Less Travelled, and Uncharted Seas' in Rex Ahdar (ed.), *Research Handbook on Law and Religion* (Cheltenham: Edward-Elgar, 2018) 6.

[2] H. Patrick Glenn, *Legal Traditions of the World* (Oxford: Oxford University Press, 5th ed., 2014) 289, 330–2.

[3] There is very little discussion about the role of Buddhism in shaping Siam's ancient law. See Sawaeng Boonchalermvipas and Atiruj Tanboonjareon, *ประวัติศาสตร์กฎหมายไทย* [*Thai Legal History*] (Bangkok: Winyuchon, 8th ed., 2019); Chachapon Jayapon, *ประวัติศาสตร์กฎหมายไทย ภาคก่อนปฏิรูป* [*Thai Legal History: Pre-reform*] (Bangkok: Winyuchon, 2018). See also Sompong Sucharitkul, 'Thai Law and Buddhist Law' (1998) 46 *American Journal of Comparative Law* 667.

[4] See Robert Lingat, 'Evolution of the Concept of Law in Burma and Siam' (1950) 38 *Journal of the Siam Society* 9; Robert Lingat, *ประวัติศาสตร์กฎหมายไทย เล่ม 1–2* [*Thai Legal History Book 1–2*] (Bangkok: The Foundation for the Promotion of Social Sciences and Humanities Texbooks Projects, 1935, reprinted 1983).

This chapter's objective is thus to continue a discussion on Buddhism and law from the work of the late Andrew Huxley, a Buddhist law expert who once boldly likened Buddhism's contribution to the Asian legal tradition to that of Roman *ius civile* to the European legal tradition.[5] It begins by asking a simple question: what is law in Thai Buddhism? To answer the question, it explores the many layers of law in the Buddhist universe. Law, from the Buddhist perspective, refers to different sets of norms, with different natures and hierarchy. How these laws are related and interacted is little understood. By understanding the idea of these laws, we can then understand what is Buddhist in the traditional legal system.

More importantly, this chapter asks a second question, whether the Buddhist legal tradition is still relevant to us today. The ancient Buddhist kingdoms in Southeast Asia ceased to exist with the arrival of the British and French empires, which forced the kingdoms to modernise their legal systems. However, a handful of social-science scholars suspect that the residue of Buddhist legal thought remains influential; unfortunately, lawyers often focus on the technical aspect of legal study and tend to ignore the cultural factor of legal implementation.[6] This chapter wishes to address these concerns.

5.1 *DHAMMAVINYA*: LAWS FROM THE BUDDHIST CANON

Known as *Tipitaka*, the Buddhist canon is a collection of Buddha's teaching first compiled by his disciples immediately after Buddha's death.[7] *Tipitaka* is comprised of two components: *dhamma* and *vinya*, both of which can be translated as 'law', but in very different senses.

5.1.1 Dhamma: *the True Law*

Dhamma is the core of Buddhism. The term denotes several meanings including the teaching of Buddha, truth, nature, and law.[8] Throughout his life, Buddha preached *dhamma* to the world and that is the most common understanding of *dhamma*: that it is Buddha's teaching.[9] But what precisely did Buddha teach? Prince Sitthata was on the quest to learn about the truth of life and became Buddha when he understood *dhamma*. He realised what he claimed to be the truth of the world, about the natural state of everything, all beings as well as objects.[10] In this instance, *dhamma* is the truth.[11] This truth is also the law: the rule of cause and effect, the impermanence of things, and suffering – the third meaning of *dhamma*.[12] Prayer describes this law as constant and eternal, operating independently from time, place, or person.[13] Even non-Buddhists would face suffering and impermanence and the law of *kamma*. *Kamma* is a very important concept in Buddhism. It is the law of cause and effect.

5 Andrew Huxley, 'Buddhist Law' in Herbert M. Kritzer, et al. (eds.), *Legal Systems of the World: A Political, Social, and Cultural Encyclopedia* (Santa Barbara: ABC–CLIO, 2002) 205–6.

6 Thongchai Winichakul, 'บททดลองเสนอ: อภิสิทธิ์ปลอดความผิด (impunity) และความเข้าใจสิทธิมนุษยชนในนิติรัฐแบบไทยๆ' [Proposing Experiment: Impunity Privilege and the Understanding of Human Rights in Thai-Style Legal State] (2016) 14 *Same Sky Book* 191, 205–7.

7 Rupert Gethin, *The Foundations of Buddhism* (Oxford: Oxford University Press, 1998) 40.

8 Prayudh Payutto, *พจนานุกรม พุทธ ศาสน์ ฉบับ ประมวล ศัพท์* [*Buddhist Dictionary: vocabulary*] (Nakhorn Pathom: Wat Nyanaves, 31st ed., 2018) 156–7.

9 Rupert Gethin, 'He Who Sees Dhamma Sees Dhammas: Dhamma in Early Buddhism' (2004) 32 *Journal of Indian Philosophy* 513, 516.

10 Prayudh Payutto, *นิติศาสตร์แนวพุทธ* [*Buddhist Jurisprudence*] (Nakhorn Pathom: Wat Nyayaves, 16th ed., 2010) 12–13.

11 Gethin, 'He Who See Dhamma', 517–18.

12 Ibid., 519.

13 Gethin, *The Foundations of Buddhism*, 36.

A good deed produces joyful consequences, moving a person closer to *nirvana*, while a bad deed leads to suffering, binding a sentient being in an endless cycle of rebirth.[14] This law has no maker. It is the natural law of the world. Buddha never claimed to invent *dhamma*. He only discovered it through meditation. The last meaning of *dhamma* is of something proper.[15] A person shall live according to the proper path of *dhamma*. Suffering can be lessened or gone entirely if a person understands *dhamma*, or, better, practises it. Conversely, ignorance of *dhamma* only increases suffering, trapping that being in the endless cycle of rebirth.

Taking all meanings of *dhamma* into consideration, *dhamma* as law is the law of the highest order.[16] It is the truth of the universe, so no living creature can escape from it. Things come and go according to *dhamma*. Although it does not have an enforcing mechanism, consequence will befall everyone sooner or later. It is, therefore, proper behaviour – even a duty – to observe *dhamma*.

The content of *Tipitaka* is expansive, containing forty-five years' worth of Buddha's teaching. Mainly, Buddha focuses on the Four Noble Truths: about the nature of sufferance and the cessation of it.[17] People may end sufferance if they achieve right minds and behaviours through studying and practising *dhamma*.

But Buddhism is not only about *Tipitaka*. Over time and vast landscapes, learned monks everywhere composed a number of commentaries and local treatises. In pre-modern Southeast Asia, Buddhism fulfilled not only the ethical and spiritual, but also political, cosmological, as well as cultural roles. There emerged literature that was inspired by Buddhism but was distinct enough to merit its own genre. King Lithai of Sukhothai (c. BE 1890–1911, CE 1347–1368) was inspired by Buddhism to compose *Trai Phum Phra Ruang* (The Three Worlds according to King Ruang) which described the Buddhist cosmology where deities, men, and animals were placed according to their *kamma*.[18] *Trai Phum Phra Ruang* justified the stratification of the socio-political pyramid in Siam.[19] The cult of *Jataka*, which told stories of Buddha's past lives when he was born in various forms and endeavoured, through several missions, to attain Buddhahood, helped legitimise the idea of the Buddhist kingship, in which the king was regarded as the most meritorious man in the kingdom and the centre of the universe.[20] These expansions can also be regarded as parts of *dhamma*. Before the Mongkut-Chulalongkorn Buddhist reform in the early twentieth century, few monks were able to read the canon; they were more familiar with non-canonical literature.[21]

14 Peter Harvey, *An Introduction to Buddhist Ethics: Foundations, Values, and Issues* (Cambridge: Cambridge University Press, 2015) 14–19.

15 Gethin, 'He Who See Dhamma', 516–17.

16 See Rebecca R. French and Mark A. Nathan, 'Introducing Buddhism and Law' in Rebecca R. French and Mark A. Nathan (eds.), *Buddhism and Law* (New York: Cambridge University Press, 2014) 4–5; Prayudh Payutto, *Buddhist Jurisprudence*, 20–1.

17 Gethin, *The Foundations of Buddhism*, 59–60.

18 Craig J. Reynolds, 'Buddhist Cosmography in Thai History, with Special Reference to Nineteenth-Century Culture Change' (1976) 35(2) *The Journal of Asian Studies* 203, 204–7.

19 Chai-anan Samudavanija and Sombat Thamrongthanyawong, *ความคิดทางการเมืองและสังคมไทย* [*Thai Political and Social Ideas*] (Bangkok: Bannakij, 1980) 90–105; Cholthira Klud-U, 'ไตรภูมิพระร่วง รากฐานของอุดมการการเมืองไทย' [Trai Phum Phra Ruang: The Foundation of Thai Political Ideology] (1974) 4 *Thammasat Journal* 106, 115–21.

20 See Patrick Jory, *Thailand's Theory of Monarchy: The Vessantara Jataka and the Idea of the Perfect Man* (Albany: State University of New York Press, 2016).

21 Yoneo Ishii, *Sangha, State, and Society: Thai Buddhism in History* (trans. Peter Hawkes) (Honolulu: The University of Hawaii Press, 1986) 76–7. See Barrend Jan Terweil, *Monks and Magic* (Copenhagen: NIAS Press, 4th ed., 2012) 16–20.

The association of *dhamma* and law is evident in Siam's first textbook for children, the *Story of Phra Chai Suriya* (BE 2383–2385, CE 1840–1842).[22] The rhyme tells the story of a kingdom where the king fails to prevent corruption among his judges. Once justice fails, the people do not rebel against the ruler but a natural disaster in the form of a huge flood kills all corrupt people. Only a benevolent Prince, Chai Suriya, and his wife survive. They are later rescued by the god Indra. The story vividly depicts the importance of justice in upholding not only the political order, but also the natural harmony, and the interconnectedness of both orders.

Dhamma, or *tham* in Thai, is closely associated with the concept of law and justice. *Dhamma* thus confers a norm higher than a normal man-made rule. *Kwam-pen-tham* is fairness and another similar word, *Yu-ti-tham*, is justice. Another regularly encountered term is *nititham*, which is a Thai translation of 'the rule of law'. *Niti* is law, hence the *dhamma* of law, and *dhamma* of law users too.[23] Another term coined recently is good governance or *Thammapiban*.[24] In summary, the Thai legal mind is heavily influenced by *dhamma*, in all senses described above. It is the true, natural, and proper goal that judges must strive to achieve and the right procedures to follow. Dhammic law is an ideal-type that man-made law must try to imitate.

5.1.2 Vinaya: *Monastic Derivative of* Dhamma

Vinaya, or discipline, is the other half of Buddha's teaching. *Dhamma* is Buddha's revelation of truth and *vinaya* is his law. The Book of Vinaya (*Vinaya Pitaka*) forms one of the three Books of Buddha's Teaching. As a monastic code for the gathering of monks, known as the *sangha*, it resembles modern positive law.

In the early years of Buddhism, the *sangha* was small and no law was needed for this close-knit community.[25] Every recruit was said to be an *Arahat*, an enlightened one, so he already knew right from wrong and behaved accordingly.[26] *Vinaya* became necessary only after the *sangha* expanded. Non-*arahat* monks showed erroneous behaviour, leading to complaints to which Buddha responded by issuing a rule. Throughout his lifetime, Buddha legislated one *vinaya* after another in a piecemeal manner. One prohibition at a time, *vinaya* was built in this way and is thus a compilation of case law.[27] The number of offences varies according to the tradition. In the Theravada tradition, *vinaya* comprises 227 offences for male monks and 314 for female monks. *Vinya* is not applicable to a lay Buddhist.

But is *vinaya* another eternal law? On one hand, it seems like a response to social reality. When the community grew larger and less homogenous, a written rule was necessary. It was made by Buddha, responding to specific circumstances, a conflict, or a dispute. It is generally

22 Chosita Maneesai, 'พินิจภาพย์พระไชยสุริยาของสุนทรภู่' [Analysis of Sunthorn Phu's Phra Chai Suriya] (2012) 37 *Journal of Royal Institute* 59.

23 See Thanin Kraivixien, *หลักนิติธรรม* [*The Rule of Law*] (Nonthaburi: Office of Civil Service Commission, 2nd ed., 2009).

24 See Eugénie Mérieau, 'Buddhist Constitutionalism in Thailand: When Rajadhamma Supersedes the Constitution' (2018) 13 *Asian Journal of Comparative Law* 283, 292–3.

25 Oskar Von Hinuber, 'Buddhist Law According to the Theravada-Vinaya: A Survey of Theory and Practice' (1995) 18 *Journal of the International Association of Buddhist Studies* 7,7.

26 Pluem Chotetisatayangkur, *คำอธิบายกฎหมายพระสงฆ์* [*Lecture on Law of the Sangha*] (Bangkok: Mahachulalongkorn Rajwittayalai, 2nd ed., 2010) 19–21; Rupert Gethin, 'Keeping the Buddha's Rules: The View from Sutta Pitaka' in French and Nathan (eds.), *Buddhism and Law*, 66.

27 Petra Kieffer-Pultz, 'What the Vinayas Can Tell Us About Law' in French and Nathan (eds.), *Buddhism and Law*, 47.

accepted that Buddha would have laid down more *vinaya* should he have lived longer and faced more societal changes.[28] Buddha seemed to realise the incompleteness of his *vinaya* as he gave permission to alter some minor points after his death.[29] In this sense, *vinaya* should not be understood as a sacred or eternal law.

However, many Buddhists argue that *vinaya* is a derivative of *dhamma*, the actual implementation of the abstract principle into a written rule. Although *vinaya* is not perfect, it is an essential part of living in the *sangha*, which they regard as the ideal community. The rationale of *vinaya* is that it helps the *sangha* community to stay united and appear respectable to outsiders.[30] Buddha claimed that his religion would survive far longer than that of preceding Buddhas, because his monks were disciplined by *vinaya*.[31] *Vinaya* holds the community together. The orderly *sangha* brings it respect from lay communities. *Vinaya* is necessary training to enhance a monk's mindfulness. For many Thais, therefore, it is sacred. Even with Buddha's permission for making a minor alteration, they would prefer not to do so. They would not risk amending the rules, which might disintegrate the community. The *sangha* could not agree on which point was minor so they decided to maintain all of them in the same way.[32] They agreed not to add or withdraw any *vinaya*. Later, according to a well-known story, in the Second Recension – roughly a century after Buddha's death – a dispute arose. Some monks wished to amend some *vinaya*: those who refused became Theravada, the followers of the word of elders, to whose lineage Thai monks belong.[33] It is common for Thai Buddhists to evaluate good or bad monks by their strictness in observing *vinaya*. When Prince Mongkut founded a new sect of *Thammayuttikanikaya*, his emphasis was not on orthodoxy, but orthopraxy. He wished to establish a sect that was subject to a stricter interpretation of *vinaya*, not of *dhamma*.[34]

Vinaya comprises two main parts: substantive and procedural. Offences are ranked from the most serious to the lightest crimes. A monk who commits *parajika*, the most serious, automatically has his monkhood invalidated, whereas a less serious crime results in confinement, probation, and penitence.[35] Some *vinaya*, especially serious ones, overlap with secular law – for example, manslaughter or theft – but many prescribe social manners necessary for the *sangha*'s harmony and integrity, for example, prohibition on running, toilet manners, or table etiquette.[36] Each *vinaya* begins with the story of why Buddha had to prohibit such action. It then continues with cases in the same category. Thus, *vinaya* is organised into a list of rules.

A list of 227 *vinaya* seems long, but some of them are just redundant. Quite often a *vinaya* goes into ridiculously minute detail. For example, a series of offences concerns what type of medicine one could take for certain illnesses. One by one, Buddha gave rules on animal fat, plant roots, bitter juice, fruit, sap, salt, powder, raw meat, eyedropper, stone grinder, etc., until all were satisfied.[37] Another vivid example is on sexual conduct. When Buddha prohibited

28 Pluem Chotetisatayangkur, *Law of the Sangha*, 23.

29 Vinaya Pitaka vol. 7, Vinaya. Culla 2, 308.

30 Prayudh Payutto, *Buddhist Dictionary*, 402. Gethin, *The Foundations of Buddhism*, 91–4.

31 Vinaya Pitaka vol. 1, Vinaya. Mahāvi (1), 1–18.

32 Vinaya Pitaka vol. 7, Vinaya. Culla 2, 310–12.

33 Prayudh Payutto, *Thai Buddhism in the Buddhist World* (Bangkok: Pra Buddha Mingmongkol Foundation, 9th ed., 2008) 42–3. A different account is given in Gethin, *The Foundations of Buddhism*, 49–58.

34 Stanley J. Tambiah, *World Conqueror and World Renouncer* (Cambridge: Cambridge University Press, 1976) 209–12.

35 Kieffer-Pultz, 'What the Vinayas Can Tell Us', 49; Hinuber, 'Buddhist Law', 10–15.

36 See the summary of Vinaya Pitaka in Hinuber, 'Buddhist Law'.

37 Vinaya Pitaka vol. 5, Vinaya. Mahāvagga (2).

sexual intercourse with other human genitalia, monks experimented with other body parts, for example, corpses, animals, and objects. Instead of plainly ruling out sexual misconduct, Buddha went after one incident after another until no sexual conduct could be allowed.[38] Obsession with such detail is a point of ridicule in the eyes of critics of Buddhism.[39]

Notwithstanding the obsession with detail on the substantive side, *vinaya* is quite advanced when it comes to procedure. It demonstrates understanding of fairness and natural justice, shared by modern legal thought. The first offender was spared because Buddha had not yet prohibited such action. Inapplicability of *vinaya* to the first trouble-making monk is similar to *nullum crimen nulla poena sine lege* in modern criminal law.[40] Disciplinary action must be conducted before the whole community of monks.[41] There are rules on admissibility of witnesses. Intentional and negligent acts receive different punishments.[42] Mental illness is a legitimate defence,[43] and the accused has the right to defend himself. A certain monk is assigned as an investigator, a specialist in interpreting and applying *vinaya*, known as *Vinayasathara*.[44] He must consider facts, relevant rules, and commentary. This legal culture makes the *sangha* community very legalistic. Ancient Lankan kings even acknowledged some monks as legal experts whose monastic rulings could be applied to secular disputes.[45]

Interestingly, Theravada's obsession with *vinaya* has an exception. That is the monarchical exercise of power over the *sangha*. Buddha allows the *sangha* community to withdraw some *vinaya*, should the king wish it.[46] Despite the vow not to amend, the *sangha* generally accepts monarchical control of the *sangha* as a fact of life. *Vinaya* is inadequate to deal with social changes, so the king, in the quest to take care of the *sangha*, may issue more rules to govern them.[47] This juxtaposition provides the justification for the temporal rulers to intervene in the *sangha*'s business under their jurisdiction. If necessary, that intervention includes a temporal ruler exercising his power to punish a monk, usually considered a holy man.

Intended for monastic life, *vinaya*'s influence eventually reached a wider audience. When Buddhism was introduced into Southeast Asia, local rulers must have been delighted to find a well-developed legal code that they could adopt into their premodern societies. Offences were systematically listed and segmented into details, and procedures were much more structured. Besides, it came with rich commentaries from Indian and Lankan scholar-monks. It thus became a prototype for the ancient legal codes of many Southeast Asian kingdoms. An indirect contribution was the way in which *vinaya* helped train a young man who would later choose a legal profession. A life in the *sangha*, which was heavily occupied by discussion about monastic rules, groomed lawyers through its legalistic culture.

38 Vinaya Pitaka vol. 1, Vinaya. Mahāvi (1).

39 Mookhom Wongdesa, เปิดทองหน้าพระ [Gold Flake on the Face of Buddha] (2015) *Read Journal* 69; Shravasti Dhammika, *Broken Buddha: Critical Reflections on Theravada and a Plea for a New Buddhism*, available at www.bhantedhammika.net/the-broken-buddha.

40 Kieffer-Pultz, 'What the Vinayas Can Tell Us', 53.

41 Ibid., 50; Huxley, 'Buddhist Law', 206–7.

42 Kieffer-Pultz, 'What the Vinayas Can Tell Us', 54.

43 Ibid., 53.

44 Hinuber, 'Buddhist Law', 22.

45 Ibid., 25–6, 28.

46 Kieffer-Pultz, 'What the Vinayas Can Tell Us', 55–6.

47 Ibid., Pluem Chotetisatayangkur, *Law of the Sangha*, 30.

5.2 *DHAMMASASTRA*: THE ANCIENT BUDDHIST CODE

The *Dhammasastra* is Southeast Asia's own product, a common heritage of Thais, Burmese, Laotians, and Cambodians. Buddhism bred this unique genre of Buddhist-inspired law which, until the nineteenth century CE, was spread from the Bay of Bengal in the west to the Cambodian empire in the east, as far north as Assam and Southern China, and to the Upper Malay Peninsula in the south.[48] The name is very telling as '*dhamma*' is never used to refer to secular law in the Indian context.[49] Even Sri Lanka, Thailand's Theravada Buddhist compatriot country, did not have an equivalent of it.[50] It first emerged as a legal code in the Mon Kingdom in what is today's Southwest Myanmar, the ancient centre of Southeast Asian Buddhism.[51] *Dhammasastra* may have originated from the Law of Manu, the Hindu code, but the Mon had 'buddhi-ised' as well as 'indigenised' it into the local form.[52] The first copy appeared in the thirteenth century CE, although some experts believed that the law may have existed much earlier, around the late first millennium.[53]

Dhammasastra refers not to a single specific book of law and there is no original copy. It is better understood as a regional cult. Ancient kingdoms of Southeast Asia produced a number of *dhammasastra*. Unsurprisingly, given its widespread adoption, it inspired countless local variations. Huxley proposes three subcategorisations: Western, Eastern, and Northern *dhammasastra*. Western refers to the area along the eastern coast of the Bay of Bengal where today is Myanmar, the ancient home of the kingdoms of Mon, Ava, and Burma. Western *dhammasastra* was developed mainly by specialised lawyers, focusing on case law, hence Huxley's term 'common law Buddhist'.[54] Eastern *dhammasastra* was centred in the central basin of the Chao Praya River, where the Kingdom of Ayuthaya was located, and spread eastward to Laos and Cambodia. Huxley calls the Eastern subtype the state-centred *dhammasastra* because of the dominant role of the king and his legal peers.[55] Northern *dhammasastra* is the landlocked area to the north of Myanmar and certain other parts of Southern China. Perhaps because these Tai kingdoms were constantly attacked from all sides by warring superpowers, their kings played a limited role in developing *dhammasastra*. Their *dhammasatra* development was led by monks, who authored the text as well as tried cases.[56]

Huxley refers to *dhammasastra* as Buddhist law, but what is Buddhist about *dhammasastra*? Is it *dhamma* or *vinaya*? The answer is not straightforward. *Dhammasastra* is more complicated than a secularised version of *vinaya*. It is an amalgamation of *dhamma*, *vinaya*, and local customs, but each *dhammasastra* shows varying influence from each source. It generally begins with the story of Manu's quest for perfect justice. In Hinduism's *Manusamastri*, Manu is the first human, the ancestor of all men, but in Buddhism's *dhammasastra*, he is a judge in the court of Mahasamata, the first king of the world according to *Agganyasutta*.[57]

48 Andrew Huxley, 'Pali Buddhist Law in Southeast Asia' in French and Nathan (eds.), *Buddhism and Law*, 168–9.

49 Frank Reynolds, 'Buddhism and Law – Preface' (1995) 18 *Journal of the International Association of Buddhist Studies* 1, 3.

50 Christian Lammerts, 'Genres and Jurisdictions: Laws Governing Monastic Inheritance in Seventeenth-Century Burma' in French and Nathan (eds.), *Buddhism and Law*, 191.

51 Lingat, *Evolution of the Concept of Law*, 12–13.

52 Ibid., 13–15.

53 Andrew Huxley, 'Studying Theravada Legal Literature' (1997) 20 *Journal of the International Association of Buddhist Studies* 63, 69.

54 Ibid., 71–2.

55 Ibid.

56 Ibid.

57 Lingat, *Evolution of the Concept of Law*, 15.

Agganyasutta is a scripture that tells the story of how the world is created and the first king is crowned. When greed triggers people to fight over resources, they gather to select the fairest among them to be the king.[58] The first duty of the king is to deliver justice and maintain order.[59] Thus, a Buddhist king is not a warrior but a judge. Manu was upset by his own incompetence so he travelled to the end of the universe, where he discovered the text of *dhammasastra* written on the wall of the universe. After learning the text, he flew back to the palace and composed the law called *dhammasastra*.[60] Details of the story may differ but the essence remains the same.[61] *Dhammasastra*, similar to *dhamma*, was discovered and then revealed to the populace. It has no author.

Regarding the content, *dhammasastra* is organised into lists of various topics. After the opening story, it goes on to types of manslaughter, types of debt, types of theft, types of wives, and types of prejudice that judges had to avoid, amongst other lists.[62] These lists are drawn from several sources. Lists from *vinaya* probably contributed to the law on crimes, property, and theft, while *dhamma* came in the form of stories of Buddha's incarnations and the role of the king and judges.[63] Others, such as family and estate laws, were said to be derived from local norms.[64] At least in Northern Thailand, the story of Mahosodha became a hypothetical precedent for pre-modern lawyers. In this story, when Buddha was born a genius young man named Mahosadha used his wit and wisdom to judge justly.[65]

Thus, *dhammasastra* is another category of sacred law in ancient Southeast Asia. Monks were bound by *vinaya*, but lay persons by *dhammsastra*.[66] *Dhammasastra* bridges a gap between *dhamma* and the king's law. When a Buddhist commits a crime, should *kamma* punish him or will the king? *Dhammasastra* offers a punishment according to *dhamma*, the true law, handed down by the worldly ruler.[67] A description of punishments in the Siamese *dhammasastra* mirrors those in hell: a criminal may have his skull pierced open and burned with hot iron, or his skin peeled, his lips and tongue hooked, his torso buried in the ground or he may be burned alive, eaten alive by hungry dogs, or deep-fried alive before fed his own flesh.[68] It is doubtful that any listed punishment had ever been implemented, but symbolically it resembles the description of hell in the ancient stories that described the Buddhist cosmology.[69]

58 Somboon Suksamran, 'Buddhism, Political Authority, and Legitimacy in Thailand and Cambodia' in Trevor Ling (ed.), *Buddhist Trends in Southeast Asia* (Singapore: Institute of Southeast Asia Studies, 1993) 104.

59 Tambiah, *World Conqueror and World Renouncer* 14; Chai-anan Samudavanija and Sombat, *Thai Political and Social Ideas*, 36–9.

60 Lingat, *Evolution of the Concept of Law*, 15.

61 See Burmese legal tradition, ibid., 17–18.

62 See Chris Baker and Pasuk Phongpaichit, *The Palace Law of Ayutthaya and the Thammasat* (Ithaca: Cornell University Press, 2016) 19–26.

63 Huxley, 'Studying Legal Literature', 70.

64 Ibid.

65 Andrew Huxley, 'The Tradition of Mahosadha: Legal Reasoning from Northern Thailand' (1997) 60 *Bulletin of the School of Oriental and African Studies, University of London* 315.

66 Huxley, 'Pali Buddhist Law in Southeast Asia', 168.

67 Huxley, 'Buddhist Law', 208.

68 Sawaeng Boonchalermvipas, *ประวัติศาสตร์กฎหมายไทย* [*The Thai Legal History*] (Bangkok: Winyuchon, 15th ed., 2016) 99–100.

69 Cholthira, 'Trai Phum Phra Ruang', 112–14; Craig J. Reynolds, 'Buddhist Cosmography in Thai History, with Special Reference to Nineteenth-Century Culture Change' (1976) 35 *Journal of Asian Studies* 203, 205; Jana Igunma, 'A Buddhist Monk's Journeys to Heaven and Hell' (2013) 6 *Journal of the International Association of Buddhist Universities* 65. Personal communication from the author to historian Chris Baker (28 September 2019).

However, despite Huxley's extensive work on the subject, he could not satisfactorily answer how Buddhist is the Buddhist law. There is no direct link between *dhammasastra* and *dhamma* from the canon. Only recently Christian Lammerts was able to show that in seventeenth century Burma monastic commentators labelled *dhammasastra* as a heterodox literature.[70] They were not convinced that the law came from the wall of the universe. Still, their acceptance of *dhammasastra* as law was rooted in the understanding that all the Buddhist kings, from the Great Elect and other kings in Jatakas, legislated rules that were harmonious with *dhamma*.[71] It seems that the idea of *dhamma* as a true law is more important than the actual scripture. What makes *dhammasastra* a Buddhist law is the understanding that it is promulgated by a Buddhist king. This notion is further exemplified in the case of Ayutthaya where monarchs actively took over the legislative role, as is now explained.

Dhammasastra was not the only source of law in these Buddhist kingdoms. Another type of law, *Rajsastra*, was sometimes mentioned. *Rajsastra* is king-made law. Although in principle the king may not rewrite the sacred *dhammasastra*, he was the ultimate ruler and judge. By exercising his administrative and judicial power, he could issue a decree provided it was not contrary to the *dhammasastra*.[72] A subject dissatisfied by the court's ruling might try to appeal a case before him. That case turned into a legal precedent to be recorded and collected.[73] Therefore, the king can make law too. This collection of case law is thought to be supplementary to *dhammasastra*. However, a distinction between the two types of law is not always clear-cut. In reality, rulers often tried to share the sacred aura of *dhammasastra* with their orders. Several *dhammasastra* contained the name of a specific king as the author, or titled as the royal *dhammasastra*, blurring the line.[74] In the case of Siam, evidence from Chris Baker and Pasuk Phongphaichit suggests that *rajsastra* succeeded in overtaking *dhammasastra*.[75] This finding matches Huxley's description of Ayutthaya's *dhammasastra* as 'king-led', meaning that the Siamese monarchs played a much greater role in legal business than those in Burma. Actually, Baker and Pasuk suggest that *dhammasastra* might have arrived in Siam significantly later than Lingat and Huxley had believed.[76] The name '*dhammasastra*' was mentioned in the inscription from the fourteenth century CE, but Baker and Pasuk find no concrete evidence of *dhammasastra* anywhere.[77] Therefore, the importance of *dhammasastra* might be overstated.

Many of the documents from the Ayutthaya era were lost when the city fell to the Burmese army in the seventeenth century CE. Knowledge about Ayutthaya relies on that of the early Bangkok period, an assumption of validity that some scholars question.[78] After the fall of Ayutthaya, King Taksin (BE 2310–2325, CE 1767–1782) founded the Thonburi dynasty, but it lasted only fifteen years. Taksin was succeeded by his general, Chakri (BE 2325, CE 1782), who founded Bangkok and crowned himself King Rama I. When King Rama I heard an appeal on divorce, he realised that the law that allowed a divorce without cause was absurd.

70 Christian Lammerts, 'Narratives of Buddhist Legislation: Textual Authority and Legal Heterodoxy in Seventeenth Through Nineteenth-century Burma' (2013) 44 *Journal of Southeast Asian Studies* 118, 139.

71 Ibid., 140–1.

72 Prince Dhani Nivat, 'The Old Siamese Concept of the Monarchy' (1946) 36 *Journal of Siam Society* 91, 98–100; Lingat *Evolution of the Concept of Law*, 26.

73 Lingat, *Evolution of the Concept of Law*, 26.

74 Huxley, 'Studying Theravada Legal Literature', 75–6.

75 Baker and Pasuk Phongpaichit, *The Palace Law of Ayutthaya*, 26–7; Lingat, *Evolution of the Concept of Law*, 27–8.

76 See Chapter 3 of this volume.

77 Ibid.

78 See Nidhi Eowsriwong, ปากไก่และใบเรือ [*Pen and Sail*] (Nonthaburi: Same Sky Books, 4th ed., 2012).

Although he followed that law in order to uphold legal certainty, he complained that the vacuum after Ayutthaya's downfall allowed greedy shameless jurists to corrupt *dhammasastra* for their personal gain.[79] He declared law reform as his next mission after the recension of *Tipitaka*. This statement was very telling as it showed a connection between *dhamma* and law as two necessary pillars to hold the kingdom together. He thus ordered the law recension in 1805. As the King of a new dynasty, this recension provided him with a good opportunity to insert his rules into the sacred book.[80] Nevertheless, he was careful not to proclaim the new code – known as the 'Three Seals Code' – as his legislative product. He insisted that it was a mere correction of an old lost law. Nonetheless, in comparison with Burmese *dhammasastra*, the Three Seals Code contained more lists from king-made law.[81] Only the first chapter which related the story of Manu was called *dhammasastra*.

Over a millennium, however, *dhammasatra* had served as the main source of law for any disputes above village level. Within the kingdom of Siam, copies of the Three Seals Code and other older *dhammasastra* have been retrieved throughout the country, suggesting that the law must have often been consulted by local rulers when the local custom failed to settle a dispute. But it was kept out of the hands of peasants. King Rama III confiscated Three Seals Code copies, reasoning that this knowledge, if it got into the wrong hands, could be harmful.[82] This prohibition reflected the notion of *dhammasastra* as a sacred law that was only accessible by meritorious elites.

Along with the idea of law came legal personnel. The highly legalistic monastic culture produced premodern legal specialists who were trained to interpret law, reason a case, and write a commentary. Some of these learned men went on to be secular judges. This culture was more prevalent in the pre-colonial Burma, where the role of lawyers was most prominent. Some even had their names recognised as authorities.[83] By contrast, legal training in Siam, where the monarch had greater influence over *dhammasastra*, was never robust enough to the point of producing authoritative legal scholars. The titles of premodern judges suggest that judgeship was often assigned to *brahmins*, who acted as servants of the court. Ayutthaya had inherited the *brahmin* cult from the Khmer Empire in the fifteenth century CE. Furthermore, a bureaucrat was often assigned both judicial and administrative functions.[84] There was no independent judiciary. Such structure prevented professionalisation and specialisation of legal careers.

The years of *dhammasastra* had gone, but this amalgamation of law and religion still left an imprint in the consciousness of Thais. When the People's Party founded a university specialising in legal study after 1932, they named the institution Thammasat University.

5.3 THE ARRIVAL OF MODERN POSITIVE LAW

Nidhi Eowsriwong, a historian, argues that, since the beginning, Bangkok's legal conscience was different from that of Ayutthaya.[85] King Rama I asserted his authority as a Buddhist king to depart from *dhammasastra* and made law himself. For example, he issued the ten laws which regulated monks' behaviour supplementary to the *Tipitaka*. The *Kod Mai Phra Song*, as it

79 *กฎหมายตรา ๓ ดวง เล่ม ๑* [*Three Seals Code, Volume 1*] (Bangkok: Pridi Banomyong Foundation, 2005) 2–3.

80 Baker and Pasuk Phongpaichit, *The Palace Law of Ayutthaya*, 1–2.

81 Lingat, *Evolution of the Concept of Law*, 27–8; Baker and Pasuk Phongpaichit, Chapter 3 in this volume, xxx–xxx.

82 Sawaeng Boonchalermvipas, *The Thai Legal History*, 128–9.

83 Huxley, 'Pali Buddhist Law in Southeast Asia', 170–81.

84 Ibid., 60–2.

85 See Nidhi Eowsriwong, *Pen and Sail*, chapters 2 and 4.

became known, was not part of *dhammasastra* but a separate law.[86] But the real wave of change arrived by the mid-nineteenth century CE. Partly the change came from within: the Three Seals Code had fallen behind the advancement of the society so King Rama IV asserted royal legislative power more heavily. Mongkut had spent three decades as a Buddhist monk while having regular communication with Christian missionaries whose criticism of the traditional society must have influenced the prince-monk.[87] Although he was an ardent Buddhist, his thinking was influenced significantly by humanist liberal ideas. Throughout his reign, Mongkut issued a large amount of dispositions. Some were long and law-like.[88] Others were shorter and read more like complaints.[89] Some decrees merely asked for cooperation. Topics ranged from trivial personalised issues of the choice of words to be used with the King himself, to concern over sanitation, tax, or interaction with foreign merchants and dignitaries.[90] But one thing is obvious: Mongkut was the lawmaker. More remarkable was the way he decreed these laws; they were written in an easy to understand vernacular tongue and accompanied by reasons.[91] Moreover, he tried to make his law appear more rationalistic and compassionate. His method was to convince rather than coerce his subjects. He decreed with reason. When he prohibited the sale of a wife, he complained that such barbaric practice was unfair to women.[92] He spoke openly of which behaviour he liked or disliked. He blessed and thanked those who complied and ill-wished those disobedient few.[93] His style reflected how he perceived himself. He portrayed himself as an original version of a Buddhist king according to the text, ruling by compassion and *dhamma*, not violence, the product of the two world-views he had learned.

Another initiative of Mongkut was the Royal Gazette publication to circulate his law. Mongkut's law was no longer the elites' secret. It had to be announced according to a protocol in order to be in effect. Mongkut even permitted the Three Seals Code to be commercially available to the general public.[94] The notion of law shifted from the sacred natural order, known only to the meritorious ruling class, to legislation that all subjects had a right to know. The Royal Gazette continues to today.

The pressure from colonialism played a role, too. For an outsider, Siam's legal system must have appeared barbaric.[95] *Dhammasastra* was an entanglement of law and religion, whereas there was no training institution which could produce legal specialists who would implement the law professionally. In the 1850s King Mongkut's Siam had entered into trade treaties with twelve Western nations plus Japan. The deal forced Siam to submit to extraterritorial rights, meaning that subjects of these thirteen nations were no longer under the Siamese courts' jurisdiction.[96] This legal arrangement was due to disdain of Siam's archaic legal system.

86 Ibid., 418–21; Pluem Chotetisatayangkur, *Law of the Sangha*, 25–30.

87 Thanet Aphornsuvan, 'The West and Siam's Quest for Modernity: Siamese Responses to Nineteenth Century American Missionaries' (2009) 17 *South East Asia Research* 401, 408–11; Ishii, *Sangha, State, and Society*, 157–60.

88 ประกาศพระราชบัญญัติฝ่ายพระบวรราชวังเรื่องเล่นเบี้ยในพระบวรราชวัง [Palace Announcement on Gambling in Palace Premise] in Chanvit Kasetsiri, et al. (eds.), *ประชุมประกาศรัชกาลที่* 4 [*Collected Proclamations of the King Mongkut*] (Bangkok: Thailand Text Book Foundation, 2004) 27–31.

89 ประกาศเรื่องเรียกกะปิ น้ำปลา ว่าเยื่อเคย น้ำเคย (ฉบับที่ ๑) [Announcement on How to Call Shrimp Paste and Fish Source (1st ver.), Ibid., 22.

90 Ibid., 97–104, 121.

91 Seni Pramoj, *คิงมงกุฎในฐานะนักนิติศาสตร์* [*King Mongkut the Jurist*] (Bangkok: Winyuchon, 2015) 80–2.

92 Chanvit Kasetsiri et al. (eds.), *Proclamations of King Mongkut*, 496.

93 Ibid., 217.

94 Sawaeng Boonchalermvipas, *The Thai Legal History*, 129.

95 See, further, Krisdakorn Wongwuthikun and Naporn Popattanachai, Chapter 15 of this volume.

96 David Wyatt, *Thailand: A Short History* (New Haven: Yale University Press, 2nd ed., 2003) 168–73; Tamara Loos, *Subject Siam: Family, Law, and Colonial Modernity in Thailand* (Ithaca: Cornell University Press, 2005) 42–3.

Rationality was not the strong point of *dhammasastra*. The law was not publicly accessible, there was no separation between criminal and civil laws and procedure was also confusing.[97] Trial was by ordeal and punishment was cruel. Judges were incompetent and corrupt. In summary, the Three Seals Code was ill-equipped for a more cosmopolitan Siam. The system of extraterritoriality extended to cover not only Europeans but also their colonial subjects, that are Chinese, Indians, and Malays. Chinese, Indians, and Malays. Soon, hundreds walked streets of Bangkok with special protection granted by their consuls.[98] This privilege contrasted sharply with local Thais, and this concern prompted the authorities to consider legal reform.

Mongkut's successor, King Chulalongkorn, continued the reform in the quest to regain Siam's sovereignty. Chulalongkorn's administration felt more keenly than ever the necessity of having a more modern legal system. Burma, Indochina, and Malaya, Siam's neighbours and former tributary states, all fell to British and French powers that claimed to bring civilisation to the backward nations.[99] Buddhism in Siam was challenged as a backward, mythical, religion, so Siamese aristocrats then replaced the traditional with a Western, more scientific and secular, paradigm. The concept of Buddhist law seemed to be abandoned, too. In 1896, Chulalongkorn ordered the Judicial Reform Committee of foreign experts, mostly European, along with his trusted ministers, to draft Thailand's law codes.[100]

The Judicial Reform Committee looked at codes from various European nations and India, as well as Japan.[101] First came the Penal Code in 1908 and then the Civil and Commercial Code was promulgated in 1932.[102] One by one, chapters of the Civil and Commercial Code replaced sections of the Three Seals Code. By 1935, the last codes on civil and criminal procedure were in place, terminating the service of the Three Seals Code for good. The codification was no small task for it took over thirty years and four kings to complete. By that time, Siam was able to renegotiate treaties to abolish the unfair extraterritorial rights provisions.[103]

Codification was only part of Chulalongkorn's larger judicial reform. Prior to the reform, the judicial was considered part of the administrative function. Each department had its own court, which it regarded as a good source of income.[104] Jurisdictions often overlapped with one another.[105] In provinces the backlog was huge.[106] A dissatisfied party would often try to appeal the decision to the king. In 1894, the judicial function was reassigned to the Court of Justice, which was under the new Ministry of Justice.[107] It had the Supreme Court (created in 1908) as the final arbiter so no one could appeal to the king. Judicial staff were professional lawyers, trained and tested for the job, and this new system was carried out by Chulalongkorn's son, Prince Ratchburi.

Prince Ratchburi had been sent to study law in the United Kingdom.[108] Upon his return, he was then appointed the Minister of Justice. He also founded the first Western-style law

97 Engel, *Law and Kingship*, 60–2.

98 Loos, *Subject Siam*, 43–4; Frank C. Darling, 'The Evolution of Law in Thailand' (1970) 32 *Review of Politics* 197, 203–4.

99 Engel, *Law and Kingship*, 12.

100 See Loos, *Subject Siam*, 47–71.

101 See Chapter 10, this volume.

102 Darling, 'The Evolution of Law in Thailand', 209; see, further, Part II of this volume, discussing the civil law reforms.

103 Chris Baker and Pasuk Phongpaichit, *A History of Thailand* (Cambridge: Cambridge University Press, 3rd ed., 2014) 122.

104 Engel, *Law and Kingship*, 60.

105 Ibid., 60–1.

106 Walter E. J. Tips, *Gustav Rolin-Jaequemyns and the Making of Modern Siam* (Bangkok: White Lotus, 1996) 247.

107 Ibid., 248. Engel, *Law and Kingship*, 66–9.

108 Nikorn Tassaro, *พระเจ้า บรม วงศ์ เธอ พระองค์ เจ้า รพี พัฒน ศักดิ์ กรม หลวง ราชบุรี ดิเรก ฤทธิ์: พระ บิดา แห่ง กฎหมาย ไทย* [*Prince Raphi Phatthanasak, Prince of Ratchaburi: Father of Thai Law*] (Bangkok: Nanmee Books, 2006) 86.

school, where he lectured, wrote textbooks, and examined students who would later become judges and attorneys.[109] Thus a law school and professional lawyers were created. Prince Ratchburi's lectures had a profound effect on how these early lawyers understood law. He warned his students not to confuse law with justice. Law could only be an order from the sovereign, regardless of its morality.[110] His positivistic teaching contrasted sharply with the religious view of the old regime. Later, more Thais were sent abroad to the West – to Britain and continental Europe – to study law. Prince Ratchburi's half-brother, Vajiravuth, was a law graduate from Oxford who composed a few books on international law.[111]

The third wave of modernisation came in 1932, when the People's Party, progressive revolutionaries, ended the absolute monarchy and introduced democracy to Siam. A written constitution formally replaced the traditional political order with democratic liberal ideals. Gone was the era of the king as the law-maker. Although permanent democratic consolidation never happened, at least parliamentary legislative procedure was installed. A law becomes a law when it is approved by the Parliament, where representatives of the people convene. The democratic protocol steered the legal system further away from the traditional notion of law.

5.4 BUDDHISM AND LAW IN TWENTY-FIRST CENTURY THAILAND

Chulalongkorn's legal reform upended the concept of law in Thailand. The ancient law was the derivative of the higher norm of *dhamma*: sacred, eternal, and constant. It came from a mythical source and was enforced by *kamma*. Its legitimation rested on supra-natural characteristics. To the contrary, post-reform law has been understood as an order of the sovereign, legislated by mortal commoners according to a prescribed procedure.[112] Hence, law is man-made. Its content is not a temporal imitation of Buddhist truth, but prepared by experts to respond to political, economic, or social needs. Therefore, the content is ever changing. It is enforced by professional judges who are trained in the Western legal tradition. Its enforceability comes from legal sanction, for example, imprisonment and fines, not *kamma*. The question is whether Buddhism still plays any role in the modern world of law. Is Buddhist legal thought truly a relic of the past?

Chulalongkorn's transformation did not produce an entirely secular society. Natural science may have replaced Buddhism's legends of the birth of the world and of mankind, but in Thailand a secular worldview has never superseded Buddhist morality and conscience.[113] *Dhamma* remains the ultimate truth of the Thai universe. The Three Seals Code was replaced by modern legal codes, but the idea of *dhamma* as higher law was not. On one hand, a modern law offers certainty, rationality, and effectiveness. It is a written rule accessible by the public. A change is known in advance and stakeholders may voice their concern in the process. On other hand, Western law has no religious aura; it is simply the will of the ruler and it can be changed at will. Therefore, it is artificial. Its origin, by transplant, points out that it is alien to Thailand. Thais suppose that the content of modern law must conform with *dhamma*. While legal text is borrowed from the Western legal tradition, the

109 Ibid., 107–10.

110 Thanin Kraivixien, *กฎหมายกับความยุติธรรม* [*Law and Justice*] (Bangkok: Office of the Court of Justice, 2004) 10.

111 King Rama VI, *กฎหมาย ทะเล (จาก สมุทร สาร)* [*Law of the Sea (From Samutara Sarn*] (Bangkok: Chulalongkorn University Faculty of Law, 2009 reissue).

112 Yud Saeng-Uthai, *ความรู้เบื้องต้นเกี่ยวกับกฎหมายทั่วไป* [*General Introduction to Jurisprudence*] (Bangkok: Yud Saeng-Uthai Foundation, 15th ed., 2002) 45–64.

113 Nidhi Eowsriwong, *Pen and Sail*, 311–25.

objective of that law, and the manner in which it is used, are influenced by Buddhism. In other words, the Thai legal system is Western hardware with Buddhist software.

The notion of *dhamma*-over-law is clearly reflected in the work by P. A. Payutto, considered to be the leading authority on the topic of Buddhism and law, and the author of a well-known book of 'Buddhist jurisprudence'. He attacks Western law as lacking the wisdom to fully understand human nature, so it will never lead to an ideal life.[114] The concept of a person as a rights-holder is individualistic, so it can only teach people selfishness.[115] It emphasises consumerism, which is the wrong goal in life. He therefore sees law as a symptom of social illness.[116] The more laws there are, the worse the society has become.[117] His conclusion is that, by adopting Buddha's *dhamma*, one will no longer need law. Buddhist precepts are superior, finer, and more nuanced, better to build a perfect society, peaceful and harmonious.[118] Thus, Payutto is asserting the claim of Buddhist superiority over positive law, and urging positive law to imitate the right social order.

Payutto's animosity towards Western law reveals Thailand's ambivalence about modernisation. On one hand, Thailand is proud of itself for being able to adapt in time and safeguard its independence.[119] The modern legal system especially is the beacon of that pride. The legal code manifested Siam's civilisation so it later retrieved the lost judicial power from unfair treaties.[120] On the other hand, Thais are taught that that experience was bitter and painful. A conventional nationalistic narrative tells of Siam being bullied by Western superpowers.[121] Involuntarily, it severed the tie with the centuries-old custom and tradition, the precious oriental heritage, and was forced into the system of modern law. Surely no one missed the ancient law of caning and other barbaric practices. Still, it convinces many Thais that the Western transplant is in general foreign, and, therefore, incompatible with the Thai society.[122]

Evidence abounds of how *dhamma* has, however, captured positive law. The inferiority of positive law to *dhamma* is confirmed by an oft-cited speech by a man of the highest merit. King Bhumibol always reminded newly-graduated barristers that law (*kod-mai*) and justice (*kwam-yuti-tham*) were two different things. The former may or may not lead to the latter, so he encouraged young lawyers to use law for justice.[123] He explained that a law is only a tool and justice has wider meaning than law; it extends to morality.[124] In the 2007 Constitution, for the first time, drafters mandated, under the King's signature, that the judiciary must decide cases according to justice, the constitution, and laws.[125] Also, judges must be independent in deciding a case correctly, in timely fashion, and fairly.[126] The order of wording in this conservative constitution tells that justice (*kwam-yuti-tham*) came before even a constitution, the highest

114 Prayudh Payutto, *Buddhist Jurisprudence*, 46–7, 63–4, 91–4.
115 Ibid., 86.
116 Ibid., 79–82.
117 Ibid., 128–30.
118 Ibid., 72–9.
119 Thongchai Winichakul, *โฉมหน้าราชาชาตินิยม* [*The Face of Royalist Nationalism*] (Nonthaburi: Same Sky Books, 2016) 25–8.
120 For example, see Praphan Koonmee, 'เสียอธิปไตยทางศาล ก็คือเสียอธิปไตยเหนือดินแดน' [To Lose Judicial Sovereignty is to Lose Territorial Sovereignty] *Manager Online*, 20 January 2011, at https://mgronline.com/daily/detail/9540000008363 (accessed 27 November 2019).
121 Thongchai, *The Face of Royalist Nationalism*, 46–53.
122 In general, see discussion in chapter 2 of Thongchai Winichakul, *เมื่อ สยาม พลิก ผัน* [*When Siam Changes*] (Nonthaburi: Same Sky Books, 2019).
123 King Bhumibol's speech to inaugurate new judges on 29 October 1981.
124 Ibid.
125 Constitution BE 2550 (2007) (รัฐธรรมนูญแห่งราชอาณาจักรไทย พุทธศักราช 2550), s. 197 para 1.
126 Ibid., s. 197 para 2.

order of written laws. However, the justice clause was later dropped from the 2017 Constitution, although the fairness clause remained.[127]

Another example of *dhamma*-over-law is *Nititham*. *Nititham* is a Thai translation of the term 'rule of law'. Although the concept was originally introduced from the Western legal tradition, it has been indigenised by, most importantly, Thanin Kraivixien, the royalist conservative judge and Privy Councillor. Trained as an English barrister, Thanin is able to indigenise the Western concept to fit the local context. He is a regular speaker to judges on judicial morality. He argues that the Buddhist equivalent, the kingly virtue of uprightness (*avirodhana*), is superior to the original Western concept because, even in times of emergency when national security trumps the rule of law, Buddhism's *avirodhana* allows a ruler to always act rightly.[128] Thanin supported his argument by quoting King Bhumibol's speech that lawyers must be courageous to serve rightly, both by law and morality.[129] He recommended the government promote the rule of law by educating government agencies about *hiri-otappa* (shame over moral transgression) and the law of *kamma*.[130] Another leading voice is a French-educated scholar, Borwornsak Uwanno, who relentlessly advocated for better rule of law: supremacy of law, natural justice, and separation of powers.[131] However, he ultimately concluded that the rule of law concerns only the outward aspects of form, behaviour, and structure.[132] He proposes that *dhamma* must be brought in to fulfil the essence of democracy, '*dhamma* constitutional democracy'.[133]

Basically, both Thanin and Borwornsak are asserting *dhamma* over written law. But the idea that the law must command the rulers and the ruled to observe *dhamma* is, at best, very abstract, and at worst, an outright indoctrination, verging on theocracy. Notwithstanding the extremeness, their idea is highly influential. Their writing and public lectures are widely circulated among judicial personnel and civil servants. The 2007 Constitution, for the first time, dictated that all state apparatus must act according to *nititham* (the rule of law).[134] *Nititham* has its contender, *Nitirat* (*droit état*), but the 2007 drafters chose *nititham* because Thais are more familiar with *tham* (*dhamma*).[135] The choice added a religious overtone to the concept, allowing Buddhism's dominance over positive law. The Constitutional Court, in a series of judicial reviews since 2006, has cited *nititham* to impose scrutiny upon elected politicians.[136] Some of the decisions, however, prompted criticism of judicial overstep. Eventually, '*dhamma* constitutional democracy' became the moral justification of the authoritarian regime and the destruction of liberal democracy.

127 Constitution of Thailand BE 2560 (2017), (รัฐธรรมนูญแห่งราชอาณาจักรไทย พุทธศักราช 2560) s. 188.
128 Thanin Kraivixien, *Rule of Law*, 9–10, 28–9.
129 Ibid., 38–9.
130 Ibid., 48.
131 Borwornsak Uwanno, 'หลักนิติธรรมกับการปกครองในระบอบประชาธิปไตย' [Rule of Law and Democracy] *Rabhi Memorial'51* (Bangkok: Thai Bar Association 2008) 30–3.
132 Borwornsak Uwanno, 'หลัก นิติธรรม ประชาธิปไตย และ ธรรมาธิปไตย' [Rule of Law, Democracy, and Dhammacracy] (Individual Study Paper, The Rule of Law and Democracy Course, The Constitutional Court, 2016) 30.
133 Ibid., 68–76.
134 2007 Constitution, s. 3.
135 Thanin Kraivixien, *Rule of Law*, 18.
136 Khemthong Tonsakulrungruang, 'Constitutional Amendment in Thailand: Amending in the Spectre of Parliamentary Dictatorship' (2019) 14 *Journal of Comparative Law* 173; Khemthong Tonsakulrungruang, 'The Constitutional Court of Thailand: From Activism to Arbitrariness' in Albert H. Y. Chen and Andrew Harding (eds.). *Constitutional Courts in Asia: A Comparative Perspective* (Cambridge: Cambridge University Press, 2018); Khemthong Tonsakulrungruang, 'Entrenching the Minority: The Constitutional Court in Thailand's Political Conflict' (2017) 26 *Washington International Law Journal* 247.

At ground level, *dhamma* is the main theme in judicial personnel training. All new judges must undergo a month-long training programme, during which they learn how to proceed with a trial as well as how to behave as a good judge. Here, the only residue from the *dhammasastra* era is reiterated by generations of lawyers.[137] The four prejudices (*aggati*), the answer to Manu's quest to provide justice, is still guidance for young judges' impartiality. A judge can decide a case rightly and justly only if his mind is absent of fear, favour, anger, and ignorance. This old wisdom can help a young judge through deciding the matter of life and death. Actually, death presents an awkward problem of how a Buddhist judge should deal with capital punishment. An answer from the famous Buddhadasa is often quoted: that a judge, if doing his duty without biases, is only the agent of *kamma*, he is not harming a convict out of his own intention so he is not implicated in the cycle of cause and effect, of harm and revenge.[138] By invoking an exception on the state of mind, this is a clever compromise with the principle of non-violence that Buddhism holds dear. The view is widely accepted by the judiciary. This shows how the Thai judiciary picks some versions of *dhamma* to overcome a moral problem.

Dhamma also provides guidance for a judge's life outside the courtroom. Getting rid of the four prejudices means one has to be mindful of one's action and mind. A judge is urged to practise *dhamma*.[139] In the Code of Judicial Conduct, a judge must 'behave morally, live in solitude, live a simple life, be polite, have good manners, be amicable, and also behave in a trustworthy way to general public.'[140] Although behaving morally is said not to follow any particular religion, living in solitude is elaborated by teaching from the *Sangha Raja*, the Supreme Patriarch of the Thai Buddhist order. Solitude refers to *santosa* in Buddhism, which is explained as an ideal judge must be content with what he honestly earns.[141] Moreover, he must be humble and frugal.[142] A judge must stay clear from worldly temptation (*apayamukha*).[143] Strikingly, the ideal life of a judge is an ascetic one, resembling that of a monk. This similarity is confirmed by several role-model judges, including Thanin Kraivixien himself, whose biographies display many Buddhist virtues.[144] Actually, it seems that religiosity, not professionalism, is what defines the judicial career.

5.5 CONCLUSION

Dhamma and *vinaya*, both of which are law in themselves, had limited influence on the shaping of the traditional legal system of Siam. *Dhammasastra* did not refer to a specific passage of *dhamma* and, at least in the cases of Ayutthaya and Bangkok, paid little attention to lists of offences in the *vinaya*. What matters is the idea of *dhamma* as law. But the belief in a Buddhist kingship assumes that the king is a giver and protector of law, justice, and order,

137 For example, Kajorn Havanond, 'จรรยาบรรณตุลาการ' [Judicial Ethics] (1985) 32 *Dullapaha* 2.

138 Buddhadasa, 'ตุลาการตามอุดมคติแห่งพระพุทธศาสนา' [Judges According to Buddhist Ideals] in *Rabhi Memorial'51* (Thai Bar Association, 2011) 38–9.

139 Sanya Thammasak, 'รวม โอวาท สำหรับ ตุลาการ' [Compiled Teaching for Judges] (1991) 38 *Dullapaha* 88; Somdej Phra Yannasangvorn, 'ตุลาการ ใน อุดมคติ ของ พระพุทธ ศาสนา' [Judges in Buddhist Ideal] (1988) 35 *Ministry of Justice Journal* 4.

140 The Judicial Code of Ethics, (ประมวลจริยธรรมข้าราชการตุลาการ), s. 35.

141 *ประมวลจริยธรรมข้าราชการตุลาการ* [*The Judicial Code of Ethics*] (Bangkok: Office of the Court of Justice, 2009) 82–5.

142 Ibid., 85.

143 Duncan McCargo, 'Reading on Thai Justice: A Review Essay' (2015) 39 *Asian Studies Review* 23, 28–9.

144 Kitpatchara Somanawat, 'Constructing the Identity of the Thai Judge: Virtues, Status, and Power' (2018) 5 *Asian Journal of Law and Society* 91.

and therefore his decrees are deemed inherently in accordance with *dhamma*. The mythical and sacred *dhammasastra* could then provide natural justice to subjects of the Siamese kings.

The influence of Buddhism in Thai law remains strong despite the modernisation of the system. *Dhammasastra* and *vinaya* may no longer have relevance to modern legal conscience, but *dhamma* as the true source of law reigns supreme. It is part of Thai jurisprudence. *Dhamma* becomes the ultimate goal of law, fairness, justice, and the rule of law. Modern legal codes might provide a functional and effective set of rules, but people still expect legislators, lawyers, and judges to write and enact modern law according to *dhamma*. Regrettably, most legal scholars seem unaware of the influence of Buddhism. The main focus of most studies of Thai legal history is on the choice between common and civil law. In a larger picture, lawyers are interested in the juridical science of arguing and reasoning according to the two traditions. They overlook the cultural influence of Buddhism.

This chapter shows that Buddhism provides the morality of law in Thailand. *Dhamma* acts as a compass for judges and lawyers to navigate the legal vessel. As the goal of *dhamma* is to foster peace and order, Buddhist morality should be welcomed. The only caveat is that *dhamma* and law are not one and the same. As observed by a growing number of scholars, the idea of *dhamma* over positive law has recently been captured and abused to undermine universal values, such as democracy, human rights, equality, and legal certainty.[145] *Dhamma* should be best understood as supplementary. The topic of Buddhism and law should earn greater attention from the community of Thai legal scholars. Remaining ignorant of the intrinsic link between *dhamma* and law is a key factor in allowing Thailand's political crisis to continue. Only by learning about the historical role of Buddhism in shaping modern legal thought, will one finally understand the root of the current conflict and how Thailand might avoid being haunted by the past.

[145] David Streckfuss, *Truth on Trial in Thailand: Defamation, treason, and lese-majeste* (New York: Routledge 2011); Björn Dressel, 'Thailand's Traditional Trinity and the Rule of Law: Can They Coexist?' (2018) 42 *Asian Studies Review* 268; Eugénie Mérieau, 'Buddhist Constitutionalism in Thailand: When Rājadhammā Supersedes the Constitution' (2018) 13 *Asian Journal of Comparative Law* 283.

6

A History of the Thai Lèse-Majesté Law

Eugénie Mérieau[*]

The Thai lèse-majesté law is known to be one of the harshest in the world. It states: "Whoever defames [*minpramat*], insults [*dumin*], or threatens [*sadeng khwam-akhathamat-rai*] the King, the Queen, the Heir to the Throne, or the Regent, will be punished with a jail sentence between three and fifteen years."[1] The formulation and uses of the Thai law of lèse-majesté have fluctuated throughout the years in relation with the "sacredness" of the king, itself reflected in Article 8 of the Constitution, which states: "The King shall be enthroned in a position of revered worship and shall not be violated."[2] However, a more accurate translation would be: "The person of the King is sacred [*sakkara*] and inviolable [*lameut mi day*]."[3] The second paragraph resonates with the law of lèse-majesté: "No person shall expose the King to any sort of accusation or action."

Its premodern antecedents, backed by a monarchy deified on the Hindu model, organized a space of absolute speech interdiction in the presence of and regarding the person of the king. From the nineteenth century onward, Siamese "modernizing monarchs" engaged in a process of de-Hinduization/Europeanization of kingship and reformed Siamese laws of lèse-majesté on the model of European authoritarian monarchies. The 1932 revolutionaries enacted a constitution providing for the trial of the king in case of high treason: the monarchy was desacralized and the king discredited. King Prajadhipok abdicated in 1935, followed by a ten-year-long regency. The law of lèse-majesté almost fell into oblivion.

The accession to the throne of Bhumibol Adulyadej in 1946 followed by the 1947 "royalist coup" revamped the lèse-majesté law while introducing the second paragraph to Article 8 of the Constitution.[4] In the 1960s, the military redrafted Article 112 and used it to build the king's charisma, a use of the lèse-majesté law that ultimately proved successful. By the mid-1970s, the monarch, Bhumibol Adulyadej, enjoyed an unprecedented popularity, backed by a reinvented "sacredness." At the height of "hyperroyalism,"[5] the 2005–2014 political crisis

[1] The same wording is used to protect the supreme patriarch, head of the Buddhist clergy: "Whoever defames [*minpramat*], insults [*dumin*], or threatens [*sadeng khwam-akhathamat-rai*] the Supreme Patriarch, will be punished with a jail sentence not exceeding a year, or a fine of 20,000 Thai baht, or both"; Article 44 of the 1962 Sangha Law, revised in 1992. The same wording also applies to foreign kings, queens, heads of state, and ambassadors (Articles 133 and 134 of the Penal Code).

[2] Article 8, translation by the Council of State.

[3] Article 8, Constitution BE 2540 (1997).

[4] The 1949 Constitution adds Article 6 "No person shall expose the King to any sort of accusation or action" to Article 5 "The person of the King is sacred [*sakkara*] and inviolable [*lameut mi day*]."

[5] Thongchai Winnichakul, *Thailand's Hyperroyalism, its Past Success and Present Predicament* (Singapore: ISEAS, 2016).

saw a surge in the number of lèse-majesté cases. Yet, since 2018, roughly one year after a new king, Vajiralongkorn, acceded the throne, the law is subject to a de facto moratorium.

In their contemporary interpretations, Article 112 of the Thai Penal Code and Article 8 of the Constitution build on ancient Siamese traditions.

6.1 THE BUILDING OF A *DEVARĀJA* (KING-GOD/KING OF GODS) ON THE HINDU MODEL

Hindu-Buddhist principles erected the king as a character whose figure was virtuous and divine (*dharmarāja* and *devarāja*).[6] A specific vocabulary was built to speak of and to the king. This distinct language, formed using the language of Buddhism, Pāli, as well as Sanskrit and Khmer, gave the king special sanctity. Words thus created were prefixed with the word *phra*, a mark of religious respect used for monks. The Palace Law, dated from the fifteenth century codified the use of royal vocabulary in its Articles 204 to 211. For example, Article 210 stated: "To answer the King, use 'khahraphuttachao'; to address the King, use 'kha phraphuttachao khothun'; in a conversation [in the third person], use 'phraongchao tratsang tratchai'."[7]

While *phraongchao* refers to "the Lord," *khaphraphuttachao* means "slave of your Lord." The king is also called *phrachaoyuhua* or "Lord above [our] heads." The monosyllabic word *chao* contains the same semantic ambiguities as the English word "Lord" – it was used in the spoken language as early as the Ayutthaya period to make the king a "Lord of Life" (*chao chiwit*) and "Lord of Land" (*chao phaendin*). To refer to the king, the dedicated expression is *phrabatsomdetphrachaoyuhua* or "the sacred feet of the Lord above my head." This expression finds its material application in the attitude of prostration that accompanies it. The head of the commoner, a sacred part of the body, is thus below the foot of the king, the body part considered the least sacred. The introductory formula to an address to the king is as follows: *khodecha falaong thuliphrabatbokklaobokkramom*, which means: "May the power of the dust under the dust of the soles of your sacred feet protect the top of my head." The royal vocabulary (*ratchasap*) bears with it the idea that the king is a *devarāja*, but also a *bodhisattva*. The words that compose the royal vocabulary are mostly religious words from the Pāli and Sanskrit; royal vocabulary is thus linked to Buddhism.

The Palace Law also provided for very severe sanctions toward whoever dared to disrespect the king. Article 87 states: "Whoever meets the King's eye ... will be sentenced to the punishment of the crime of sedition."[8] The crime of sedition was punished by having the perpetrator chained or put to death.[9] This clause bears resonance to Article 6 of Chapter VII of the Hindu Manu Code, which deified the king[10] and according to which, "Like the Sun, [the King] burns eyes and hearts, and nobody on earth can look him in the eyes."[11] The Palace

6 "Rāja" means "king" in Sanskrit. A *Dharmarāja* is one who reigns according to the dharma – the law, the truth, justice, thus a lawful king. As such, he is a bodhisattva, a future Buddha. A *Devarāja* is a divinized king.

7 Article 210, translation by Pasuk Phongpaichit and Chris Baker, *The Palace Law of Ayutthaya and the Thammasat: Law and Kingship in Siam* (Ithaca: Cornell University Press, 2016), 233.

8 Article 87, Palace Law, Pasuk and Baker translation, 99.

9 Article 85, Palace Law, Pasuk and Baker translation, 98.

10 Legal historians state that, as early as the thirteenth century, during the early Sukhothai period (1238–1347), the Kingdom of Siam did adopt laws inspired by the Hindu Manu Code. In 1767, these laws were destroyed in a fire set by the Burmese during the war that ended the Ayutthaya Kingdom. In the early nineteenth century, Rama I (r. 1782–1809) ordered the collection and compilation of the ancient laws of Ayutthaya.

11 "For, when these creatures, being without a king, through fear dispersed in all directions, the Lord created a king for the protection of this whole [creation], taking [for that purpose] eternal particles of Indra, of the Wind, of Yama, of the Sun, of Fire, of Varuna, of the Moon, and of the Lord of Wealth [Kubera]. Because a king has been

Law stated that during royal audiences, any whispering was punished with a death sentence.[12] The simple act of raising one's eye toward the king was punishable by death, the act of touching him and members of the royal family as well. When members of the royal family fell from royal barges into the water, they were not saved from drowning, owing to the prohibition against touching them, and could die. According to Article 25 of the Palace Law

> If the [primary Queen's] royal barge sinks, the boat staff swims away; anyone who stays with the boat is condemned to death. If the royal barge sinks or capsizes; and [the Queen] is swimming and near death, the retainers and boat staff extend battering rams and throw coconuts for her to cling to, if possible; but if not possible, do not take hold of her, if they take hold and bring her up to survive, they are condemned to death; if they throw coconuts that enable her to survive, reward of ten *tamlueng* of silver and one golden bowl; if the royal barge sinks and other people seem to throw coconuts, and bring her up to survive they are condemned to severe punishment of death for their whole clan.[13]

In his description of Siam at the end of the seventeenth century, the Jesuit missionary Nicolas Gervaise wrote:

> There is no State in the Indies that is more monarchical than that of Siam. Kings which have governed it until now have had honours that seem to only belong to God ... This freedom that everybody gives himself in Europe to speak about the Prince and His conduct, is to them a State crime; from there it comes that the name of the King is never known by the people during their lifetime; out of fear, as they say, that he would be profaned by the indifferent language of some impious subject.[14]

Describing his impressions of the Kingdom of Siam under the reign of Mongkut in the middle of the nineteenth century, the missionary Jean-Baptiste Pallegoix spoke about a "despotism in all the force of the term," notably regarding the prohibition to look at the king.

> The government of Siam is despotism in all the force of the term; the King is feared and respected almost like a god; nobody dares to look him in the eyes; courtiers, when they assist to the audience, stay prostrated on the knees and elbows; when His Majesty is passing somewhere, everybody jumps down to earth, and those who would not do it would risk to have their eyes slit by archmen who precede [the procession] and who so skillfully throw balls of dirt with the bow they always keep drawn.[15]

During the nineteenth century, in order to avoid colonization, the monarchy engaged in a process of "conservative modernization" of its law, including the introduction of lèse-majesté on the European model.

6.2 THE DE-HINDUIZATION AND EUROPEANIZATION OF KINGSHIP

In 1805, the ancient laws of Siam that had accumulated over the centuries were compiled in a code called the Three Seals Code. This code recycled in its entirety the Palace Law of the

formed of particles of those lords of the gods, he therefore surpasses all created beings in lustre; and, like the sun, he burns eyes and hearts; nor can anybody on earth even gaze on him; through his [supernatural] power he is Fire and Wind, he Sun and Moon, he the Lord of Justice [Yama], he Kubera, he Varuna, he great Indra"; trans. George Bühler, book 7, art. 3–7.

12 Article 57, Palace Law.

13 Article 25, para. 2, Palace Law, Pasuk and Baker translation, 87.

14 Nicolas Gervaise, *Histoire politique et naturelle du royaume de Siam* (Paris: Claude Barbin, 1688).

15 Jean-Baptiste Pallegoix, *Description du royaume thaï ou Siam* (Paris: Mission de Siam, 1854), 259.

fifteenth century, along with more recent laws. Article 7 of the section on crimes against the king (*phra ayakan luang*)[16] provided for sentences more severe than for lèse-majesté:

> Whoever dares, without fear or embarrassment, speak (*thanong ong at*) about the King, his acts, edicts and ordinances, is guilty of violating royal laws and will be punished with [one or more of] the eight following means: beheading and seizure of the house, fission of the mouth, amputation of ears, hands and feet, 25 or 30 lashes, imprisonment for one month and forced labour, three fines and slavery, two fines, one fine, or pardon on the promise of good behaviour.

Article 72, on the crime of propagating rumors about the king, stated: "Whoever propagates diverse rumours (*titien nintha*) about the king, will be punished with [one or more of] the following means: first, beheading and confiscation of property, second, forced labour, and finally, 50 lashes." Later, under the reigns of Rama III (r. 1824–1851) and Rama IV (r. 1851–1868), in the context of the diffusion of printing, and the intensification of commerce with European nations, Rama V (r. 1868–1910) revised the lèse-majesté law on the European model. In 1900, he promulgated a decree on "defamation by print" inspired by the lèse-majesté laws in force in Prussia.[17] Article 4 stated: "Whoever defames (*minpramat*) the King or a royal person, whether provincial prince or the son of the King, by words uttered or written under any form in public or in reunion, shall be imprisoned for no more than three years or pay a fine of 1,500 Thai Baht or both."

Penalties were thus "modernized" with the suppression of physical punishments and their replacement with prison sentences and fines delimitated by the law, breaking with the system still in force at the time of the Three Seals Code. New lèse-majesté sentences were comparable to the system then in force in Prussia (two months to five years in prison).[18] Initiating this trend of modernization of the royal institution, under the previous reign of Rama IV (King Mongkut), the prohibition against watching royal processions was abolished,[19] as well as the prohibition against referring to the king by his name.[20] Rama V (Chulalongkorn) then abolished prostration, following the example of Japan, China, Vietnam, and India.[21]

Meanwhile, the Three Seals Code was replaced by new codes drafted with the help of European and Japanese legal advisers. In 1908, the new Penal Code, doubled the maximum

16 David Streckfuss, *Truth on Trial in Thailand: Defamation, Treason, and Lèse-Majesté* (London: Routledge, 2010), 61.

17 David Streckfuss, "The Intricacies of Lese Majesty: A Comparative Study of Imperial Germany and Modern Thailand," in *Saying the Unsayable: Monarchy and Democracy in Thailand*, ed. Søren Ivarsson and Lotte Isager (Copenhagen: Nordic Institute of Asian Studies, 2010), 124. One could also adopt the hypothesis that the 1900 decree was a Japanese inspiration, owing to the admiration that the Siamese had for the Japanese modernization process, both Westernized and also unique to imperial Japan.

18 Article 75 of the Prussian Penal Code of 1851 provides for penalties of two months to five years in jail: "§75 [Majestätsbeleidigung] Wer durch Wort, Schrift, Druck, Zeichen, bildliche oder andere Darstellung die Ehrfurcht gegen den König verletzt, wird mit Gefängniß von zwei Monaten bis zu fünf Jahren bestraft," Preußisches Strafgesetzbuch von 1851. Article 95 of the Penal Code of the German Empire of 1871 provided for the same penalties: "95. (1) Wer den Kaiser, seinen Landesherrn oder während seines Aufenthalts in einem Bundesstaate dessen Landesherrn beleidigt, wird mit Gefängnis nicht unter zwei Monaten oder mit Festungshaft bis zu fünf Jahren bestraft."

19 Wales H. G. Quaritch, *Siamese State Ceremonies: Their History and Function* (London: Bernard Quaritch Ltd, 1931) 35–39; Tambiah J. Stanley, *World Conqueror and World Renouncer: A Study of Buddhism and Polity in Thailand against a Historical Background* (Cambridge: Cambridge University Press, 1976) 226.

20 Wales, *State ceremonies*, 35–39. See also Kullada Kesboonchoo-Mead, *The Rise and Decline of Thai Absolutism* (London: Routledge, 2004), 44.

21 Decree on new practices, 12th Moon of the 12th month, 1873.

penalty for lèse-majesté, up to seven years.[22] Article 98 and 100 created separate regimes of defamation for the king, the queen, the heir to the throne, and the regent on the one hand, and princes and princesses of royal blood on the other hand. "Whoever defames (*thanong ong at*) or threatens (*sadeng khwam-akhatamat-rai*) the King, the Queen, the Heir to the Throne, or the Regent while performing duties toward the King, will be punished by imprisonment not exceeding seven years or a fine not exceeding 5,000 baht, or both."

The dispositions of the new Code expanded the field of its protection over the preceding versions. Besides these crimes, Title 2 of the Penal Code concerning crimes of treason addressed disloyalty to the monarchy. Article 104 stated that: "Whoever, by any means, [acts] with the intention to induce the following effects: weaken loyalty toward the king, [or] defame (*khwamdumin*) the king, the government, or the administration, will be punished with imprisonment not exceeding three years and a fine not exceeding 1,000 THB." In an authoritative commentary on the Code published the same year, a Thai jurist referred for the first time to the Roman word *lèse-majesté*.[23]

Meanwhile, "whispering" in presence of the king and improperly using the royal vocabulary were no longer listed as crimes. Toward the end of his reign, in 1922, Rama VI promulgated (r. 1910–1925), in 1922, a decree on books, documents, and journals. In its Article 5, it introduced criminal liability for lèse-majesté for owners, editors, or writers of journals, and imposed "a jail sentence not exceeding five years, a fine not exceeding 5,000 THB or both."[24] "The teaching of political and economic theories aiming to create a resentment and defamation toward the king or social classes, is a crime subject to imprisonment not exceeding 10 years, or a fine not exceeding 5,000 THB, or both."

In 1927, Rama VII promulgated a new decree characterizing those who commit the crime of lèse-majesté as enemies of the nation. Article 6(5) defined the enemy of the nation as such: "Whoever aims, through direct or indirect, induction or suggestion, through direct words or comparisons, implicitly or through other means, to create a resentment and defamation toward the king, the government, or the administration." Five years later, the absolute monarchy was overthrown.

6.3 REVOLUTION AND THE DESACRALIZATION OF THE MONARCHY

The June 1932 revolution took place without blood being spilled. Once the revolutionaries were in possession of places of power, they reached a compromise with the king; provided the king accepted to become a constitutional monarch, they would preserve him as a figure of

22 According to Chitti Tingsabadh, article 98 had been "copied" from the British Seditious Libel Act. See Jaran Kosananan, "Khwamrungreng heng thot thi mai pen tham le kanpitkan khwamching nai matra 112 heng pramuon kotmai aya" [The violence of an unjust sentence and the covering of the truth according to article 112 of the Penal Code] *Fa Diao Kan* 7 (2009): 81. However the commentary provided by Georges Padoux, key drafter of the 1908 Penal Code, does note the influence of the British Libel Act as modified in its version for the Indian colony, but on another disposition, not on article 98–100. Georges Padoux, *Le Code Pénal du Royaume de Siam, Version française avec une introduction et des notes* (Paris: Imprimerie nationale, 1909), 24.

23 Ammatho Phrainthra-Pricha, *Kham athibai laksana aya* [Handbook of Criminal Law] (Bangkok : Sophanaphiphatanakan, 1908), 525. He cites "crimen laesae majestatis omnia alia criminal excedit quoad poenam."

24 His younger brother, Rama VII modified Article 104 to preempt the perceived threat of republicanism and communism - within a few years, monarchies in Portugal (1910), China (1912), Russia (1917), and Germany (1918) had been overthrown. Siamese elites in the 1920s were well aware of the revolutionary danger.

national unity. Yet the Constitution of 27 June 1932, drafted by the leader of People's Committee, Pridi Banomyong, did not include any article proclaiming the sacred character of the king. Instead, the first constitutional draft allowed the monarch to be impeached by the National Assembly and judged. The People's Committee also attempted, just like at the time of the French Revolution, to substitute the crime of "lèse-constitution" for that of "lèse-majesté."[25] Revolutionaries passed a law of "defence of the constitution," which punished all conspiracy against the constitution as high treason. The initial project of the revolutionaries who had brought down the constitutional monarchy had republican accents, unveiled the day after they seized power in 1932.[26]

The king was displeased with the Constitution and obtained that a new Constitution-drafting assembly be appointed under his supervision to write a new charter.[27] During the drafting process, assembly members proposed to add an article on the sacred character of the king. They chose the word *sakkara* ("to revere"), instead of *saksit* ("sacred"). The president of the Constitution-drafting committee stated:

> In Article 3 one reads that "the person of the king is sacred and inviolable." This means that the king is the chief of the nation and the entire people and that he occupies a position that makes him out of reach to any criticism whatsoever. That is why all countries where the regime is monarchical and which have adopted a constitution have adopted similar clauses.[28]

According to him, Article 3 was a translation from Japanese itself perhaps translated from German. It established the king as a sacred figure.[29]

Yet in 1933, King Prajadhipok was the object of a defamation lawsuit filed by Thawatt Ridet, the general secretary of the Workers' Association of the Tramway Society of Bangkok. Thawatt claimed that a document signed by Prajadhipok wrongly accused him of organizing a strike movement, not to further workers' interests but for personal gain (to create a trade

25 George Armstrong Kelly, "From Lèse-Majesté to Lèse-Nation: Treason in Eighteenth-Century France," *Journal of the History of Ideas* 42 (1981), 269–286. The two crimes coexisted for some time. Jean-Christophe Gaven, *Le crime de lèse-nation: Histoire d'une invention juridique et politique (1789–1791)* (Paris: Presses Universitaires de Sciences-Po, 2016), 19. Nonetheless, they did not abolish the lèse-majesté law, and nowhere have historians found an intention or even a willingness to do so, demonstrating that they thought that the law would fall into oblivion by itself, following what had happened to similar laws in European constitutional monarchies.

26 The republicanism of the 1932 revolution is contested. However, it is clearly spelled out in the First announcement of the People's Committee: "When this King succeeded his elder brother, the people first hoped that he would be governing with moderation, but its hopes were disavowed. The King still reigns above the law as it has done in the past. . . . Dear people, it is time to understand that our country belongs to the people, not to the King, as we have always been told . . . As for the Head of State, the People's Committee has no desire to steal the throne. Consequently, we are inviting the King to keep his title. However, he must govern the country under the Constitution, and will not do anything without the consent of the People's Representatives Assembly. The People's Committee already informed the King and is now waiting for an answer. If the King refuses, or if he does not reply within the said timeframe, for the selfish reason that he would see his power diminished, we will consider this act as an act of treason, and it will be necessary for the country to adopt a democratic form of government." The afore-mentioned "democratic form of government" refers to parliamentary republic. Indeed, the People's Committee explained further: "A democratic form of government means that the Head of State will be a commoner elected by parliament for a limited term." First announcement of the People's Committee, 24 June 1932.

27 See Eugénie Mérieau, "The 1932 Compromise Constitution, Matrix of Thailand's Constitutional Instability," in *Constitutional Foundings in Southeast Asia*, edited by Kevin Tan and Bui Ngoc Son (Singapore: Hart Publishing, 2019), 297–317.

28 Assembly of Representatives, 35/2475, 25 November 1932, *Documents*, p. 30.

29 Ibid.

union, appoint himself secretary general, and thus obtain a salary).[30] The government presented the case to the Assembly of Representatives, which decided that neither the tribunals nor the Assembly itself were competent to deal with a trial launched against the person of the king. Consequently, without further debate, the lawsuit was dropped. But it was fully agreed that Thawatt had exercised his rights, not that he had committed an act of lèse-majesté. The next year, Article 104(1) of the Penal Code was revised in the following terms:

> Whoever commits the following actions as words, uttered, written, or printed or any other means (1) defamation against the King or the government or the administration ... This person shall be liable to imprisonment not exceeding seven years and a fine not exceeding 2,000 THB. But if this speech, writings, or printed documents are in conformity with the constitution, are made for public good, or are the expression of opinions expressed in good faith or harmless remarks, they will not be considered as a violation of the law.

The new formulation of the lesè-majesté law placed the common good above the reputation of the king.[31] The appreciation of "good faith" came to moderate the broadness of the law. This situation did not last long. The Second World War broke out, and the 1932 revolutionaries were progressively marginalized. A committee to revise the Penal Code was nominated. It concluded in its final report that the 1946 dispositions relative to the crimes violating the safety of the state had to be "entirely re-modelled to be both more exhaustive and more in conformity with modern ideas."[32] Yu Saeng-Uthai, a prominent jurist, was accused of lèse-majesté for having explained on radio the legal status of the king, most notably the signification of inviolability mentioned in the constitution. Ultimately, he was never judged.[33] In 1946, the young king Ananda Mahidol was found dead in his bedchamber, and his younger brother, Bhumibol Adulyadej, was proclaimed king the same day.

6.4 THE MILITARY AND THE RESACRALIZATION OF MONARCHY

In 1947, the military seized power in a "royalist" coup against the Pridi faction.[34] The 1948–1949 Constitution-drafting committee designed a royalist constitution, providing for a King's Privy Council and a Senate appointed by the king. Committee members also engaged in intense debates on the issue of the inviolability of the king. They sought to expand the scope of then-Article 5 on the king's inviolability. They added another article, which read: "the King cannot be subjected to any accusation or action of any sort." The 1949 version of the Article was never modified.

Ten years later, a new Penal Code was promulgated. The former Article 98, which had become Article 112 of the new Penal Code, appeared in the section on crimes against the

30 Somsak Jiemteerasakul, "Koroni Thawat Ridet Fong Phrapokklao" [The Case of Thawat Ridet's Lawsuit against Prajadhipok], *Silapawattanatham* (2004) 26: 101–120. The document dealt with the economic plan of Pridi Phanomyong, then prime minister, suspected of communist leanings.

31 See footnote 17.

32 Quoted in Streckfuss, *Truth on Trial*, 103.

33 see Streckfuss, *Truth on Trial*, 181. Yut had a reading of the Monarchy close to the practice of European monarchies. Besides voicing doubts about Article 8, he was critical of the institution of the Privy Council. His thoughts on the Monarchy are compiled in Yut Saeng Uthai, *Khamatibai rattathamanun khong rachaanachak 2511 lae thamanun khanpokkrong 2515 wa duei phramahakasat* [Handbook of 1968 and 1972 Constitutions concerning the Monarchy], (Bangkok: Winyuchon, 2008 (1972)).

34 The royalist coup was led by General Phin Choonhavan, overthrowing the government of Thawan Thamrong Nawasawat and installing the civilian Khuang Aphaiwong in power. Thawan Thamrong Nawasawat was an ally of Pridi Panomyong, the leader of the 1932 revolution.

safety of the state. The article suppressed the exoneration clauses and substantially modified the content of the law as follows: "Article 112: Whoever defames (*minpramat*), insults (*dumin*), or threatens (*sadeng khwamakatamatrai*) the King, the Queen, the Heir to the Throne, or the Regent will be punished by imprisonment not exceeding seven years." Thus, the term "insult" (*dumin*) was added to "defamation" and "threat." The addition of this term enabled the application of the law to expand to acts that would not have been punished under the previous versions.[35] The lèse-majesté law targeted accusations according to which King Ananda were to have been killed, either accidentally or intentionally, by his younger brother.[36]

In 1957, the military once again seized power in a coup. It expanded the scope of application of the lèse-majesté law through "Decree 17." The decree stated that the revolutionary committee had the power to prohibit, seize, or destroy any written article and to order the revocation of the license of the printer, the editor, or the owner of any articles discussing the king, or articles that were defamatory toward the queen, the heir, or the regent.[37] Books on the monarchy were banned due to lèse-majesté.[38] Public speculation about the processes of royal succession could also have been specifically targeted.[39]

In 1976, allegations of lèse-majesté provoked both a massacre and a coup in Bangkok. Ultra-royalist militias took offense at a theatre play staged by students at Thammasat University in which a man bearing a resemblance to Prince Vajiralongkorn was hanged; the militias assaulted the students, who had been protesting government instability. Following the massacre, the military seized power to "preserve monarchy from the communist threat": "A group of people has defamed the prince, what amounts to an offence to the heart of the entire Thai nation, an intention to harm the monarchy."[40] Following the 1976 coup, the military ordered lèse-majesté cases to be transferred to the martial courts.[41] A year later, the authors of the 1976 coup enacted the "Order 42,"[42] and amended the Penal Code, although acts qualified as "insults," "defamations," and "threats" were not legally defined. "Whoever defames (*minpramat*), insults (*dumin*), or threatens (*sadeng khwam-akatamat-rai*) the King, the Queen, the Heir to the Throne, or the Regent will be punished with imprisonment of between three and fifteen years." This formulation remains unchanged until today. More books were banned due to lèse-majesté.[43]

Meanwhile, Article 8 of the Constitution on the inviolability of the king also remained unchanged. During the drafting of the 1997 Constitution, the second paragraph of Article 8 however raised many questions. Did it refer only to an action or accusation before tribunals,

35 Streckfuss, *Truth on Trial*, 103.

36 In 1960, Kosai Mungjaroen was found guilty of lèse-majesté for having said that the death of King Ananda in 1946 involved his younger brother, Bhumibol. The tribunal of first instance judged that, owing to the fact that Kosai's words were intentional, he was guilty. Kosai argued that he was being sincere and acting in good faith, and he appealed to the Supreme Court. He was sentenced to a three-year jail term, reduced to two years due to his confession. Thus, in this case, judges interpreted the law leniently by imposing a sentence substantially less than the maximum possible sentence, which was seven years. Streckfuss, *Truth on Trial*, 191.

37 Streckfuss, *Truth on Trial*, 104.

38 The book *The Devil's Discuss* by Rayne Kruger discussing the investigation into the death of Ananda Mahidol was banned in 1964.

39 In 1972, King Bhumibol appointed his son Vajiralongkorn, then twenty years of age, Crown Prince.

40 Announcement of the National Reform Council, 6 October 1976, Royal Gazette, vol. 93, issue 120, at 1.

41 According to Article 7 of the Martial Law, the military can order the transfer of specific cases from the civilian court to the martial court : "Those who have the power to declare a state of Martial Law also have the authority to declare that the military court consider and pass judgments on criminal cases occurring where Martial Law has been declared and which have occurred during the time when a state of Martial Law has been declared."

42 It was repealed in 1991.

43 The anonymous *The Nine Reigns of the Chakri Dynasty* was banned in the early 1980s. It postulated the extinction of the dynasty after the ninth reign was banned. Raktham Rakthai, *Rachakan haeng Rachawong* [The nine reigns of the Chakri dynasty] (Raktham Rakthai: Bangkok, 1983).

or to any sort of accusation, substantiated or unsubstantiated, concerning the king? During the drafting, members of the Constituent Assembly proposed to clarify the matter by adding an explicit mention of lèse-majesté in Article 8. The draft article read as follows: "The person of the King is inviolable and sacred. He cannot be exposed to any accusation, lèse-majesté [*du min*] or criminal proceedings."[44] The proposal was rejected, on the grounds that lèse-majesté was already implicit in Article 8. The drafters decided to leave Article 8 as it was, saying that the Constitutional Court would eventually solve the question if it was raised.[45]

6.5 THE 2012 INTERPRETATION OF LÈSE-MAJESTÉ BY THE CONSTITUTIONAL COURT

In 2012, the Constitutional Court was petitioned to interpret Article 8 of the Constitution in relation to Article 112 of the Penal Code.[46] It was asked to rule on the constitutionality of the lèse-majesté law based on two petitions submitted by the criminal court in the course of the trials of democracy activists Somyot Phreuksakasemsuk and Ekkachai Hongkaiwan.[47] In its decision rendered on October 10, 2012, the court confirmed the constitutionality of the lèse-majesté law, arguing that it "gave effectivity" to Article 8 of the constitution according to which "the King is sacred (*sakkara*) and inviolable (*lameut mi day*). Nobody can expose the King to any accusation or action of any sort." In doing so, it clarified the meaning of Article 8. First, the court referred to *the faith* of the Thai people in their king and the royal institution:

> Concerning the point to know whether Article 112 of the Penal Code violates the dispositions of Article 8 of the Constitution ... The Thai Monarchy is the heart and the inviolable soul of Thai people. The King has reigned according to the ten royal virtues and accomplished his royal duties for the happiness of his people; in particular, King Bhumibol Adulyadej, the current Head of State, upholder of the entire nation and father of compassion toward his subjects, whom he visits and to whom he has given development projects, projects he himself conceived to alleviate their suffering and solve their problems; ... [The people] have faith (*sattha*) and are loyal (*chongrakphakdi*) toward the King and the institution of the monarchy, and this in a constant manner. Thai people have respected and admired the monarchy for very long; this is a particularity of Thailand that no other country knows.

44 Proposal by Kanchana Siwiroj, 1997 *Constitution drafting assembly*, 9 June 1997.

45 Members of the constitution-drafting committee discussed this topic in 1997. *Suchit Boonbongkan*: I would like to ask Professor Bowornsak [Uwanno] if the word "inviolable" also includes lèse-majesté. If it is the case, then there is no need to add it. *Secretary General*: I don't know. The second paragraph refers to any action, whether accusations or lawsuits; in the case of lèse-majesté or defamation, it is a violation [of the person of the King] ... *Pravit Chaenwiranan*: Mister President ... I would like to ask if criticism is a violation of inviolability or not; because criticism sometimes is not only animated of an intention to violate inviolability. I am asking this question because I think that this already happened in Thailand. In the future, will criticism be considered as a violation of the person of the King or not? I am asking experts, thank you. *Thongthong Chantarasu*: I think that the word "violate" here has a very broad definition. It is not only the legal signification of the civil code or the usual definition of the dictionary but also a definition complementing the word "inviolable" of the first sentence. Constitution-Drafting Committee Minutes, June 9, 1997.

46 The court was asked to verify the constitutionality of Article 112 with regard to Articles 3 (the sovereignty of the people), 8 (the king's inviolability), 29 (limits to rights and liberties to be only imposed based on strict necessity), and 45 (freedom of expression).

47 Somyot Phreuksakasemsuk, a human rights defender, was arrested in 2011 for lèse-majesté, as the owner of a magazine entitled *Voice of Taksin* in which two articles had been signaled for lèse-majesté. In 2012, in first instance, then in 2013, in appeal, Somyot was sentenced to ten years in jail, five years per article. Meanwhile, the author of these articles remained unidentified. Ekkachai Hongkaiwan was arrested in 2011 for selling copies of a TV documentary on the royal family. He was convicted in 2013.

The court, then, argued further: lèse-majesté is constitutional because the constitution enshrines the sacred character of the monarch.

> Article 8 of the Constitution belongs to Title 2 concerning royalty. In the first paragraph, it states that the King is sacred and inviolable, and in paragraph 2, it states that nobody can accuse or sue him. These dispositions recognise the status of the King as someone sacred. The King is the Head of State and a fundamental institution for the country, and consequently the State must guarantee that nobody can violate, accuse, or sue the King in any possible manner. Article 112 states that whoever defames, insults, or threatens the King, the Queen, the Heir, or the Regent is punishable by three to fifteen years of imprisonment; this article is in conformity with the Constitution, giving Article 8 its true legal force. Thus, there is no reason to say that Article 112 violates Article 8 of the Constitution.[48]

Further down, the court adopted similar reasoning: the king being the heart of national unity and the object of adoration among his subjects, a criminal law punishing any insult toward him is appropriate, in order not to hurt the feelings of the other "believers." "The King as Head of State is the main institution in the country; defamation, insults, or threats toward the King are actions affecting the heart of Thais, who respect and revere the King and the institution of royalty; [these acts] give birth to anger among the people."[49]

The court also alluded to the idea that the implementation of the lèse-majesté law preserved the morality of society,[50] while discarding the question of proportionality (*satsuon*), which was actually the argument of the plaintiffs, based on global standards of constitutional jurisprudence.[51] Instead, the court stated that the sentence was "appropriate" (*mosom*): "Besides this, the determination of the penalty contained in Article 112 is strictly necessary and appropriate to the characteristics of action in defamation, insults or threats to the King, the Queen, or the Regent."[52] By voting unanimously for the constitutionality of Article 112, judges conformed to the doctrinal interpretation of lèse-majesté as part of a wider trend of Royalist-Buddhist readings of Thai Constitutionalism.[53] Architects of such readings have associated the constitutionally entrenched sacred character of the king with both the Buddhist religion and Article 112 of the Penal Code. Bowornsak Uwanno, a renowned jurist, wrote: "In Thai society, the lèse-majesté offence has its basis not only in the principles of international law or constitutional law but also in Thai ethics, culture, and Buddhist principles, which are unique to Thai society."[54] He also stated:

> The bond between the Thai monarchy and the Thai people is unique. It is not one between the Head of State as a political institution and the people as holders of sovereign power. It is a special relationship with certain characteristics that may be difficult for foreigners to

48 Decision 28–29/2555, October 10, 2012, 9–10.

49 Decision 28–29/2555, October 10, 2012, 11.

50 Decision 28–29/2555, October 10, 2012, 13.

51 Anne Peters, "Proportionality as a Global Constitutional Principle" in *Handbook on Global Constitutionalism*, eds. Anthony F. Lang Jr., Antje Wiener (Cheltenham: Edward Elgar, 2017) 248–264.

52 Decision 28–29/2555, October 10, 2012, 13.

53 For an account of Buddhist readings of the Constitution, see Eugénie Mérieau, "Buddhist Constitutionalism in Thailand: When Rājadhammā Supersedes the Constitution", *Asian Journal of Comparative Law* 10 (2018), 1–23. For an account of royalist readings of the Constitution, see Eugénie Mérieau, 'Thailand's Deep State, Royal Power and the Constitutional Court', *Journal of Contemporary Asia* 46 (2016): 445–466.

54 Bowornsak Uwanno, *Lèse majesté: A Distinctive Character of Thai Democracy amidst the Global Democratic Movement* (Nonthaburi: KPI Press, 2009) 33.

> appreciate. . . . This is the basis of a provision which appears in every Thai constitution – that "the person of the King shall be enthroned in a position of revered worship and shall not be violated. No person shall expose the King to any sort of accusation or action" (Section 8 of the present Thai Constitution). This provision is the "effect" of Thai culture and ethics, not the "cause" which coerces Thai people to respect the King as alleged by some.[55]

Thus, Article 8, although inspired by the imperial Constitution of Japan, was deemed to be an "effect" of Thai culture. Bowornsak explained that the king cannot be considered a "semi-God" in accordance with the Hindu tradition, but mostly as a "father." However, his advocacy in favor of the lèse-majesté law still relies on a comparison with the crime of blasphemy:

> This culture of paternalistic governance also explains a phenomenon which may not take place anywhere else. When the Thai King is unfairly criticized, most Thais feel like their own parent is being attacked and cannot accept it – much in the same way that Thais do not accept anyone demeaning the Buddha or even statues that represent him.[56]

Bowornsak also compared notions of the king and the father of the nation to justify the severity of the law as being compatible with the legal tradition according to which crimes against parents are more severely punished than against other persons. "In Thai society, parricide is, based on its religious and ethical norms, an unforgivable sin and the gravest act of ingratitude."[57] This tradition bears some resonance with the Buddhist principles of Anantarika-Karma, which places parricide and matricide as two of the five grave offences with immediate karmic retribution. Bowornsak goes on:

> [The restrictions posed to freedom of expression by the lèse-majesté law] are not dissimilar to the limitation on freedom of expression as regards criticism of God and the Prophet in Muslim countries, which is not understood by some Westerners, who ridicule the Muslim prophet revered by all Muslims, thereby creating a controversy that almost leads to worldwide violence.[58]

In its report submitted to the framework of the UN Human Rights Council Universal Periodic Review in February 2016, the Thai government utilized the following argument, which associates lèse-majesté with blasphemy to justify its use of the law: "Thailand fully respects freedom of opinion and expression and freedom of assembly as they form the basic foundation of a democratic society. However, freedom of expression shall be exercised in a constructive manner that does not insult any faith or belief system, be they religions or main institutions."[59]

Since the 2000s, a derogatory system of law applied to lèse-majesté offenders, who were denied the presumption of innocence, the right to bail pending trial, and the acceptance of truth as a mitigating circumstance.[60] Sentences were always heavy under the civilian government of Yingluck Shinawatra, beyond "reason": a twenty-year

55 Bowornsak Uwanno, *Lèse majesté*, 33.
56 Bowornsak, *Lèse-majesté*, 34. See also Peter Skilling, "Ideology and Law. The Three Seals Code on Crimes Related to Relics, Images and Bodhi-trees", *Buddhism, Law & Society* (2015–16), 69–104.
57 Bowornsak, *Lèse-majesté*, 24.
58 Ibid.
59 National Report, Universal Periodic Review, February 2016, para. 116.
60 Eugénie Mérieau, On Blasphemy in a Buddhist Kingdom, Buddhism, Law & Society (2019), 53–92.

sentence was handed down to a man for sending private text messages mocking the queen in 2011.[61] After the 2014 coup, the military junta led by Prayuth Chan-Ocha ordered the transfer of all cases of lese-majeste law to the jurisdiction of the military courts. Since then, in a prominent case, a young activist, Pai Daodin, was prosecuted in 2016 for having shared a BBC biography of King Vajiralongkorn on his Facebook profile and sentenced to a two-and-a-half year jail sentence, but was released early after being granted a royal pardon. Since the promulgation of the 2017 Constitution, there has been a de facto moratorium on the use of the lèse-majesté law.[62]

The lèse-majesté law is not to be understood as a stand-alone piece of criminal legislation, but is considered in Thailand to be the very implementation of the constitutional status of the head of state, namely, his sacredness.

[61] Amporn Tangnoppakhun or Akong, also known as "Uncle SMS," died in prison on May 8, 2012.

[62] Eugénie Mérieau, Military Dictatorship under Royal Command, Southeast Asian Affairs (2019).

7

Blood Curse and Belonging in Thailand

Law, Buddhism, and Legal Consciousness

David M. Engel

7.1 INTRODUCTION: THE BLOOD-CURSE RITUAL

In March 2010, tens of thousands of protesters filled the streets of Bangkok. Most of them wore red shirts to signify their loyalty to the ousted Prime Minister, populist billionaire Thaksin Shinawatra. The protestors carried signs demanding the restoration of free elections and what they considered true democracy rather than control by the military and the traditional ruling elites. They were mostly country people, farmers and laborers who had travelled to Bangkok from Thailand's two most populous regions – the north and northeast. These were not the first mass rallies to choke Bangkok's streets, and they would not be the last. But this time things would end very badly. There would be a military crackdown. There would be shootings, explosions, and the mysterious torching of a large upscale shopping plaza. Nearly one hundred people would die.

Before the crackdown, however, the so-called 'red shirts' who gathered in the heart of Bangkok were still spirited and exuberant. They were determined to remind urban residents of their overwhelming electoral strength, and they wanted to protest what they considered their legal disenfranchisement. They chose an extraordinary way to do it, leaving most observers stunned and appalled. The red shirts performed a blood-curse ritual to denounce and disempower what they considered an illegitimate Thai government.

Following instructions from their leaders, approximately 70,000 supporters lined up to have small amounts of their blood extracted by a team of volunteer doctors and nurses. The blood, about 300 litres altogether, was combined in makeshift containers. Then the demonstrators marched, led by a statue of the Buddha and a Brahmin officiant in white robes. They ceremonially splashed blood on the four gates of the Government House where the Prime Minister had his office, at his private residence, and at other official sites in Bangkok and elsewhere.[1] The curse was directed at the government itself, at those who had ousted Thaksin from power, at the army, and at the Constitutional Court for disbanding the red shirt's political party on the grounds of electoral fraud and for barring their leaders from politics for five years. As well, the demonstrators were cursing the election of Prime Minister Abhisit Vejjajiva, the young Eton and Oxford educated leader of the Democrat Party, whom they believed would not have prevailed in a fair head-to-head contest with Thaksin. They were

[1] See generally, Erik Cohen, 'Contesting Discourses of Blood in the "Red Shirts" Protests in Bangkok' (2012) 43 *Journal of Southeast Asian Studies* 216–33, and Salisa Yuktanan, 'Ritualising Identity-Based Political Movement: Challenging Thailand's Political Legitimacy through Blood-Sacrificing Rituals' (2012) 2 *Michigan Journal of Asian Studies* 89–110.

cursing the Supreme Court for the recent decision to strip Thaksin's family of $1.4 billion obtained by corruption. In short, the blood curse was aimed at the entire Bangkok establishment for time and again acting in ways they interpreted as disempowerment of the rural masses.

What was the meaning of this ritual? What did it signify for the clash between the followers of Thaksin and their opponents? Did the blood curse have anything to do with the law – or with Thai legal history?

In one sense, this incident could be viewed as simply one more link in the chain of events constituting the political history of Thailand in the early years of the twenty-first century. Thaksin had resoundingly won elections in 2001 and 2005. In 2006, the royalist People's Alliance for Democracy staged demonstrations, the Constitutional Court declared a snap election victory by Thaksin invalid, and the military staged a coup while Thaksin was out of the country. In 2007, Thaksin's political party was dissolved, and he remained in exile, yet his proxies won re-election. In 2008, the courts once again dissolved the pro-Thaksin party, found Thaksin guilty of corrupt dealings, and removed two of his allies, Prime Minister Samak Sundaravej and his successor, Prime Minister Somchai Wongsawat, from office, opening the way for Parliament to elect an opposition leader, the Democrat Party's Abhisit Vejjajiva, as Prime Minister. In 2009 and 2010, it was the red shirts' turn to stage anti-government demonstrations, including the blood-curse ritual that is the subject of this chapter. New elections in 2011 led to another landslide victory by Thaksin's party, which installed his sister, Yingluck Shinawatra, as Prime Minister. More anti-red shirt court rulings and more street demonstrations by the yellow shirts eventually culminated in a military coup in May 2014 and the end of elections and most other political activities until 2019.[2]

This brief timeline of Thailand's political history at the beginning of the new century suggests the turbulence of the era and the role that the court system rather frequently played. The purpose of this chapter, however, is not to offer yet another discussion of Thailand's troubled political struggles. Rather, this analysis will focus on one event – the blood-curse ritual in 2010 – and will explore its deeper roots in the history of Thai law and religion. In doing so, it will offer a perspective on Thai legal history that differs in certain important respects from conventional Bangkok-centred accounts and will propose instead a multicentred view of the origins, the impact, and the intent behind the modern Thai legal system itself.

The broader subject of this essay is the multilayered meanings of modernity for different people and groups in the Thai nation state. As Talal Asad has observed, modernity is not a state of being, not a stage in social evolution, but rather a 'project' that is promoted by particular influential people at a particular time for a particular purpose: 'Modernity is a *project* – or rather, a series of interlinked projects – that certain people in power seek to achieve. The project aims at institutionalising a number of (sometimes conflicting, often evolving) principles: constitutionalism, moral autonomy, democracy, human rights, civil equality, industry, consumerism, freedom of the market – and secularism'.[3]

In Thailand, the project of modernity entailed a transformation of both law and Buddhism – indeed, the two transformations were inextricably linked. And the result, to cite Asad once more, is a legal and a religious culture that is simultaneously modern and nonmodern, secular and sacred, and a society that is populated by 'hybrid selves' whose worldviews are fluid, fragmented, and continually emerging:

[2] See Chapters 16, 18, this volume.

[3] Talal Asad, *Formations of the Secular: Christianity, Islam, Modernity* (Stanford: Stanford University Press, 2003) 13.

> We should look, therefore, at *the politics* of national progress – including the politics of secularism – that flow from the multifaceted concept of modernity exemplified by 'the West' . . . But should we not also inquire about the politics of the contrary view? What politics are promoted by the notion that the world is *not* divided into modern and nonmodern, into West and non-West? What practical options are opened up or closed by the notion that the world has *no* significant binary features, that it is, on the contrary, divided into overlapping, fragmented cultures, hybrid selves, continuously dissolving and emerging social states?[4]

The imagery of hybrid selves in a fragmented Thai culture at the turn of the twenty-first century aptly characterises the participants in the blood-curse ritual that is the theme of this chapter. But the roots of this situation extend far back into the history of Thai law. In exploring these roots, this chapter draws on research conducted over a number of years in the North, the region of Thailand known as Lanna (literally, 'a million rice fields'). It focuses on the modernity project in Lanna, particularly as it led to a clash between fundamentally different understandings of Buddhism and law – one urban, cosmopolitan, 'rational', and state-sponsored; the other rural, localised, arguably 'irrational', and historically opposed by the state. It suggests that the blood-curse ritual of 2010 reflects not only the more obvious contemporary debates over constitutionalism and the rule of law in Thailand, but also certain less obvious legal and religious strains that were probably not apparent even to the participants.

7.2 RELIGION, MODERNITY, AND LEGAL CONSCIOUSNESS

There can be little doubt that the historical connections between law and Buddhism for many centuries have shaped the *legal consciousness* of Thai people – a term that refers to the ways in which ordinary men and women think about, use, avoid, or reject the law. Studies of legal consciousness explore not only how law becomes active in people's thoughts and actions, but also why, in some situations, the law never enters their minds at all. In Thailand, as in most societies, state law sometimes influences ideas and behaviour in direct and highly visible ways, offering a language and a set of institutional procedures that enable people to achieve a goal or status that would otherwise be difficult to attain. But at other times state law may appear distant, threatening to a way of life, and even disempowering, despite its promise of equality and fairness. Moreover, customary norms and non-state legal systems can offer important alternatives to state law and can affect legal consciousness in a variety of ways. As we shall see, non-state legal traditions in northern Thailand have deep roots in the local culture and have close connections to religious beliefs and practices that are familiar to many residents of the region. Buddhism and non-Buddhist religious traditions in Thailand are quite clearly relevant to legal consciousness in all of its various forms.[5]

This article, however, does not begin with the 'modern' assumption that church and state occupy – or should occupy – separate spheres and that the role of law is – or should be – maintenance of the boundary between the two. The conceptual splitting of law from religion – and the related idea of secularism – may be an aspiration of those who promote modernity, but it is not necessarily valid descriptively. Rather, this chapter interrogates what Fitzpatrick calls the 'mythology of modern law'[6] and asks to what extent the idealised binaries

4 Ibid., 15.

5 See generally, David M. Engel and Jaruwan S. Engel, *Tort, Custom, and Karma: Globalization and Legal Consciousness in Thailand* (Stanford: Stanford University Press, 2010).

6 Peter Fitzpatrick, *The Mythology of Modern Law* (New York: Routledge, 1992).

of modernity correspond to empirical reality. It asks when, how, and to what extent the conceptual framework of modernity becomes significant for Thai law and legal consciousness. Does religion in fact represent a separate domain in the thoughts and actions of Thai people as they engage with the state and with legal and political issues of the day? At what point in Thailand's history did the 'politics of secularism', to borrow Asad's terminology, become salient, and who promoted them? If we join Asad in rejecting a simplistic dichotomous view of law and religion in contemporary Thai society – modern versus nonmodern – and if we accept the possibility that Thai people experience 'overlapping, fragmented cultures, [and] hybrid selves', we may gain a more realistic understanding of Buddhism itself as well as the critically important role that religion continues to play in a seemingly modern polity.

Both law and religion are ways of 'imagining the real',[7] and their relationship has a history that should be critically examined in any society. It is not helpful simply to accept the law's own concepts and categories regarding religion and to use them as a framework for sociolegal analysis. Those concepts and categories should be the *objects* rather than the tools of analysis. The law may adopt a resolutely secular perspective, yet religious perspectives and practices may remain integral to popular views of dispute resolution and of justice itself. The tension between law and religion on the books and 'in action', moreover, resolves itself differently in different locations within the state and in different historical moments.

In this analysis of the blood-curse ritual, then, we begin by asking how the ideas of modernity and secularism arrived in Thailand. What were the critical terms and discourses concerning law and religion that came to be associated with the modern Thai state? Who promoted the 'project' of modernity in Thailand and for what purpose? What have the consequences been for different people and groups and for the political and social crisis of the early twenty-first century? In short, this article offers at least a partial response to three highly pertinent questions about law, religion, modernity, and secularism recently posed by Winnifred Fallers Sullivan and her co-authors: '(H)ow did law become secular, what are the phenomenology and social and individual experience of legal secularism, and what are the challenges that taking into account religious formations poses for modern law's self-understanding?'[8]

7.3 THE HISTORICAL CONTEXT

What Asad calls the project of modernity was promoted comprehensively under King Rama V, who, at the turn of the twentieth century, asserted unprecedented control over semi-autonomous principalities in regions such as Lanna that were distant from the capital in Bangkok. Rama V's aim was to form a new kind of polity fashioned after the European nation-state. The establishment of European-style courts and law codes was a central part of this project as was the imposition of a centralised, rationalised form of Buddhism. In 1932, Thailand became a constitutional monarchy. From that date to the present time, rule of law and basic constitutional principles have specified inclusion and equality for all Thai citizens in every region of the country, including many who previously considered themselves outside the Thai state. In theory, at least, all were now integrated into what became

[7] Clifford Geertz, *Local Knowledge: Further Essays in Interpretive Anthropology* (New York: Basic Books, 1983).

[8] Winnifred Fallers Sullivan, Robert A. Yelle, and Mateo Taussig-Rubbo, eds., *After Secular Law* (Stanford: Stanford Law Books, 2011) 2.

known in 1939 as 'Thailand' on equal terms under law,[9] and their religious freedom was guaranteed.[10]

Although Thailand's Civil and Commercial Code and its Penal Code appear strictly secular and do not feature religion as a source of legal norms or as a framework for dispute resolution, Thai constitutions have consistently reserved a special place for Buddhism. For example, the 2017 Constitution, specifies that the king must be a Buddhist;[11] and it singles out Buddhism as the religion of the 'majority of the Thai people for a long period of time', mandating that the State must support and protect Buddhism as well as 'other religions' and should 'promote and support education and dissemination of dharmic principles of Theravada Buddhism for the development of mind and wisdom development, and shall have measures and mechanisms to prevent Buddhism from being undermined in any form'.[12] Thus, despite its limited role in the Thai law codes, religion is very much present in Thai constitutional law. Moreover, it permeates Thai legal consciousness in countless ways.

Although Buddhism is enshrined in the Constitution and centrally administered by the Thai state, its forms and practices vary across the Thai social landscape, producing strikingly different forms of legal consciousness in different sectors of Thai society. The vast majority of the population self-identifies as Buddhist, yet significant religious differences exist among urban and rural Thais and among central Thais and those in the north, south, and northeast. For this reason, when modern law and constitutionalism were established as hallmarks of the emergent Thai state, its guarantees of equality and religious freedom contained hidden contradictions. The very process of inclusion – purporting to make the residents of the entire geopolitical space of the new Thai state into 'citizens' bearing equal rights and legal status – tended to produce a lasting sense of exclusion among those who suddenly found themselves absorbed into a culturally unfamiliar national entity and who were regarded as socially or culturally inferior. The remainder of this chapter will attempt to explain this paradox of inclusion and exclusion with respect to Lanna and its manifestation in the blood-curse ritual of 2010.

7.4 THE BLOOD CURSE AND LEGAL CONSCIOUSNESS

The Thai nation unites the blood and flesh of all Thai people.

Thai National Anthem

The blood-curse ritual had very different meanings for the red-shirt demonstrators and for most urban middle-class onlookers. In the eyes of the red shirts' Bangkok-based opponents, the ritual was bizarre and outrageous. It confirmed the red shirts' irrational, primitive, and unhygienic qualities. Because they came primarily from the North and Northeast, they were viewed as upcountry bumpkins, unsophisticated, uneducated, and stupid. Some even dismissed the demonstrators as *khwai*, water buffalo – a label portraying men and women as dirty and ignorant labourers. Performing the blood-curse ritual played directly into these prejudices. How could people who would do such a thing ever participate as equals in civil

9 For example, Section 4 of the recent 2017 Constitution guarantees the Thai people's 'human dignity, rights, liberty, and equality' and provides that all Thais 'shall enjoy equal protection under this Constitution'.

10 2017 Constitution, Sections 27 and 31.

11 Ibid., Section 7.

12 Ibid., Section 67.

discourse? They didn't even speak standard dialect,[13] and they followed what were considered deviant cultural and religious practices.

But for the red-shirt demonstrators, the blood-curse ritual had entirely different meanings. Since they viewed the political power structure as biased in favour of privilege and status, they felt that ordinary people had nothing but their votes and their very blood to support their position. As Yuktanan points out, blood has a sacred quality that expresses both patriotism and Thai-ness.[14] A reference to blood appears in the opening line of the Thai national anthem.[15] For the demonstrators, the blood-curse ritual represented a way for social outsiders to claim membership in the Thai nation. It signified their patriotism and their willingness to make a fundamental sacrifice for their country. It also indicated a sense of collective identity. Thousands of people merged their individual essence to create a community literally based on common blood. For them, as Yuktanan wrote, this ritual spoke a 'sacred language as well as the language of blood to not only invent a collective identity but to also sacralise their demands for democracy'.[16]

But, as we have seen, the blood-curse ritual was not intended only to affirm collective identity, patriotism, and Thai-ness. It was also used to put a curse on the government and its leaders.[17] One of the Democrat leaders, Suthep Thaugsuban, fully understood this dimension of the ritual. Speaking for the government, this opponent of the red shirts commented sarcastically, 'The world sees some people in Thailand as believers in black magic and as uncivilised'.[18] The red shirts may have viewed the curse as a weapon of the weak, a weapon used by people who were outside the establishment. But non-red shirts viewed it as just another confirmation of social inferiority, as proof that the red shirts were primitive and barbaric.

The use of a curse in conflict situations is actually well known in Lanna, although the organiser of this particular ritual may not have come from the North or Northeast – there is some uncertainty about who was responsible for planning this dramatic display. Nonetheless, the curse carried out by the demonstrators was readily understandable within Lanna legal culture. Rosalind Morris, for example, discusses a traditional northern cursing ritual – *phithii saab chaeng* – performed in Chiangmai in 1992 to protest insulting statements about Lanna voters made by General Suchinda in Bangkok.[19] That ritual involved burning dried hot chili peppers and salt rather than scattering blood, but it was considered very efficacious. The same type of ceremony was used seven years later by Chiangmai farmers who became angry with a group of university professors. The farmers felt that the professors had unfairly sided with highland communities in a conflict over water rights, so they burned the chilies and salt and cursed the relatively privileged and high-status scholars.[20]

13 See Saowanee T. Alexander and Duncan McCargo, 'Diglossia and Identity in Northeast Thailand: Linguistic, Social, and Political Hierarchy' (2014) 18 *Journal of Sociolinguistics* 60–86.

14 Salisa Yuktanan, 'Ritualising Identity-Based Political Movement: Challenging Thailand's Political Legitimacy through Blood-Sacrificing Rituals' (2012) 2 *Michigan Journal of Asian Studies* 89–110.

15 Ibid., 103.

16 Ibid., 99.

17 Erik Cohen, 'Contesting Discourses of Blood in the "Red Shirts" Protests in Bangkok' (2012) 43 *Journal of Southeast Asian Studies* 216–33, 230.

18 Ibid., 227.

19 Rosalind C. Morris, *In the Place of Origins: Modernity and Its Mediums in Northern Thailand* (Durham, NC: Duke University Press, 2000) 262–6.

20 Ananda Rajah, 'Political Assassination by Other Means: Public Protest, Sorcery and Morality in Thailand' (2005) 36 *Journal of Southeast Asian Studies* 111–29.

The author is familiar with a Karen village in the highlands far from the city of Chiangmai, where a sign marks a sacred forest in which the family of each new-born baby ties a bamboo container containing the infant's umbilical cord to a tree they have selected. The sign warns that cutting down any tree in this forest is a violation of the law, but that violators will also be cursed by the community. Local leaders tell visitors that people fear the curse much more than the possibility that the government will fine or imprison them. Certainly, cursing rituals are found elsewhere in Thailand, but they have particularly strong roots in Lanna culture.[21] They are a means of stepping outside the law – and outside orthodox Buddhism – to enforce customary norms. They also give marginalised people a chance to exercise power over those with higher social status.

The blood-curse ritual of the red shirts on the streets of Bangkok was, in this sense, an attempt by the demonstrators to project local-level legal consciousness onto the national stage. It carried with it a distinctive understanding of identity, group affiliation, and legality. The red shirts believed they had lost their judicial contests and had their electoral victories taken from them, so the curse was all they had left. If the law could not deliver them justice, the curse might. It simultaneously empowered the demonstrators and disempowered them by reinscribing their inferiority, irrationality, and backwardness in the eyes of others.

In short, the use of the cursing ritual made sense to the demonstrators because it represented an explicit invocation of the sacred to bring justice to Thailand's legal and political institutions. But the very conception of the sacred for Lanna residents differed from that of the Bangkok onlookers, who saw the beliefs and practices of the demonstrators as primitive and misguided. Lanna legal consciousness has deep historical roots in law and religion that extend back for many centuries, and the conflict with what we might call Bangkok legal consciousness can best be understood in terms of a much longer history involving the central Thai kingdom and the outlying regions it sought to control.

7.5 BANGKOK AND LANNA LEGALITIES

There was, of course, no Thai nation state until the late nineteenth or early twentieth century. Separated by more than four hundred miles, travel and communication between the central kingdom[22] and Lanna were difficult and the exercise of power was tenuous. At times, Lanna was governed directly or indirectly by neighbouring Burma. At other times, Lanna paid tribute to the kingdoms of central Thailand while still manoeuvring to protect its autonomy.[23] Lanna had its own distinctive language and culture, its own brand of Buddhism, and its own legal tradition.

Lanna legal and religious traditions trace their origins to the reign of King Mangrai, who founded the northern kingdom more than seven hundred years ago. Lanna's premodern law texts, known as *Mangraisat* – the *sastras* of King Mangrai – were organically connected to

[21] Ibid., 113: 'Although consciously linked to assertions of Northern Thai culture and identity in this instance, *sayasaat* and *phithii saap chaeng* are more generally embedded in Thai folk religion, an amalgam of animist and Buddhist beliefs. In Northern Thailand, these beliefs have been important aspects of purification and protective rites at the household and village levels involving the expulsion of inauspicious spirits. Historically such rites have also been performed at the level of the *müang* (walled city, principality or premodern polity), of which Chiang Mai was arguably the exemplary centre in the North'.

[22] 'Central kingdom' here refers to the kingdom of Ayutthaya from 1351 to 1767 and, after Ayutthaya's destruction by the Burmese in the late eighteenth century, to the short-lived Thonburi Dynasty (1767–82) and the current Chakri Dynasty founded in Bangkok in 1782.

[23] Sarassawadee Ongsakul. *History of Lan Na*, (trans.) Chitraporn Tanratanakul (Chiangmai: Silkworm Press, 2005).

village-level customs and practices and to Lanna-style Buddhism. Thus, understandings of law and justice from the village to the palace – the legal consciousness of ordinary people and the ruling elite – had a distinctive Lanna flavour.[24] Pre-modern Lanna legal consciousness had three important characteristics, particularly with respect to the law of wrongs:

1. *Connection of law to spirits and the supernatural.* Lanna religion was an amalgam of traditional Buddhism and the worship of local spirits. 'Villagers' Buddhism' in Lanna was even more syncretic in this regard than in central Thailand.[25] Locality spirits and ancestral spirits articulated and enforced legal norms. Wrongful acts were expressed in terms of their offensiveness to the spirits – they had a supernatural aspect that could be understood only with reference to Lanna conceptions of the sacred. Wrongful acts were identified not by judges as we might understand them but by spirit mediums or by local princes endowed with religious authority. Legal remedies involved sacred rituals to appease the spirits.
2. *Connection of law to place.* The locality where improper conduct occurred could determine both the nature of the offense and the injurer's obligations. Conduct that was considered harmless in one locale could place villagers at risk if it occurred elsewhere, because there it offended that locality's spirits and required ritual propitiation. Legal norms were not universal. They were not, that is, applicable to all persons in all locations. The sacred geography of Lanna was also a map of the law, with multiple centres of varying norms and potency.
3. *Law's roots in collective identity.* The legal subject was not highly individuated. Wrongs to individuals and groups were typically framed in terms of harm to their *khwan*, or spiritual essence, not just their bodies or property.[26] But the *khwan* of villagers were linked to one another and could be nourished or strengthened through collective ceremonies. Moreover, fields, forests, mountains, and dams also had *khwan*, thus connecting human communities to their natural surroundings. Wrongful acts, therefore, harmed the *khwan* of social groups and their environment, not just individuals. Wrongdoers had an obligation to restore order in the community, not just compensate the individual victim's loss.

These three characteristics of the Lanna legal consciousness remain important even today. But now they are contained within a very different legal framework. How did this come about?

After a particularly bloody and destructive battle with the Burmese, the Siamese people of central Thailand regrouped and eventually founded the current Chakri dynasty in Bangkok in 1782. The newly installed king, Rama I, as he attempted to consolidate his kingdom and his power, ordered a new compilation of prior laws to purge impurities and imperfections that had arisen over the years. The resulting legal code, known as the Three Seals Code, was

[24] David M. Engel, '"The Spirits Were Always Watching": Buddhism, Secular Law, and Social Change in Thailand,' in *After Secular Law*, eds. Winnifred Fallers Sullivan, Robert A. Yelle, and Mateo Taussig-Rubbo (Stanford: Stanford University Press, 2011).

[25] Shalardchai Ramitanon, *Phi jao nai* [*Spirits of the nobility*], 2nd ed. (Chiangmai: Ming Müang Press, 2002).

[26] Charles F. Keyes defines and describes *khwan* in the following passage: 'This "vital essence" exists in plural forms, occupying 32 parts of the human body, according to the Thai belief. ... In practice, villagers throughout the region think of the 'vital essence' as a unity. The 'vital essence' must be in the body of the human, the rice, or the animal lest the human or animal suffer misfortune and eventually die or the rice be deprived of its nutrient quality and its fertility. Thus, periodic rites are performed in order to secure the "vital essence" to the body, such rites for humans occurring on such occasions as a radical change in status, a shift of residence, or a serious accident or disease'. Charles F. Keyes, *The Golden Peninsula: Culture and Adaptation in Mainland Southeast Asia* (New York: Macmillan, 1977) 116.

closely connected to Rama I's broader effort to reform Thai religion. Indeed, some provisions of the new law code spoke directly to the deviant regional religious practices that Bangkok sought to root out by declaring them unlawful. In this conception, law and religion were inseparable. The king had a responsibility to preserve and protect both law and religion. He could demonstrate his legitimacy by maintaining their purity, and he could thereby construct his identity as *thammaracha* – literally a 'dharma king'.[27] By this means, the King could establish his *barami*, or moral perfection and charismatic authority.[28] Rama I's successors in the Chakri dynasty, for the same reason, engaged in similar purification efforts. By the time Rama V ascended the throne in 1868, his reforms of Thai law and religion adhered to a pattern established by the *thammaracha* kings who came before him.

Even though Rama V's 'modernising' reforms followed a centuries-old premodern pattern of moral purification, his reform endeavours had a strongly European flavour. Rama V, in his effort to construct a modern nation-state, enacted a Western-style 'rational' legal system, with courts and law codes fashioned after French and German models. He then imposed this entire framework on Lanna and other regions of Thailand. His actions were no doubt read in Lanna as yet another effort by Bangkok to take over their region – a perception supported by substantial evidence. Bangkok leaders believed they could successfully annex the north by forcing Lanna's cultural and political arrangements to conform to a centralised model administered from Bangkok. Terms like 'purification' or 'rationalisation', from the perspective of the people of Lanna, carried an implication of disempowerment or even colonisation. They signified an intention to purge Lanna religion of its involvement with local spirits, to weaken traditional forms of legitimation in Lanna, and to bring local religious and political leaders under the control of the central government.

Thus, the arrival of this alien-appearing legal system in Lanna coincided with political annexation by Bangkok and eventual integration into the emergent nation-state. The transformation of Lanna's legal system was part of Bangkok's broader strategy to transform Lanna's religious, cultural, political, and social arrangements. Legal change was not separable from the reform of culture and religion but was integral to them. The most conspicuous feature of the new European-style legal system was not that it was modern, rational, or secular, but that it was extraordinarily powerful. Lanna residents resisted all of these reforms, but their leaders, institutions, and many of their traditions were simply overwhelmed.

Modern Thai law opposed each of the three characteristics of Lanna-style law and legal consciousness enumerated above. The European-style law codes aimed to sever any connection between law and spirits or the supernatural and were framed almost entirely in secular terms. Law was no longer variable according to location but was uniform across all the spaces of the nation state.[29] Collective identity was foreign to modern injury law, which typically constructs each person as a separate and autonomous individual.[30] The concept of *khwan* was no longer used to determine harm (though the term *kha tham khwan* – payment for the *khwan* – is still used colloquially to refer to damages paid by an injurer to the victim). It is no accident that each of these three developments also reinforced Bangkok's efforts to bring

[27] S. J. Tambiah, *World Conqueror and World Renouncer: A Study of Buddhism and Polity in Thailand Against A Historical Background* (Cambridge: Cambridge University Press, 1976) 187.

[28] Patrick Jory, 'The *Vessantara Jataka*, *Barami*, and the *Bodhisatta*-Kings: The Origin and Spread of a Thai Concept of Power' (2002) 16 *Crossroads* 36–78.

[29] Benedict Anderson, *Imagined Communities: Reflections on the Origin and Spread of Nationalism* (London: Verso, 1991) 19: 'In the modern conception, state sovereignty is fully, flatly, and evenly operative over each square centimeter of a legally demarcated territory'.

[30] My research over the years in Lanna has focused primarily on injuries and the law of wrongs.

greater "rationality" to Thai Buddhism and purge Lanna religion of its connections to locality spirits and other supernatural beings. Secular law and rational religion were two sides of the same coin, and both were aimed, at least in part, at cultural transformation of the hinterlands.

What remained of traditional Lanna legal culture by the mid-to-late twentieth century? Modernity in the form of Rama V's new legal system dealt the Lanna justice concept a powerful blow, but Lanna-style legal consciousness did not simply disappear. Throughout much of the twentieth century, Lanna justice concepts persisted in a parallel universe outside the formal legal system. Far from the new courthouses of the Thai state, village mediators continued to resolve conflicts through compromise rather than through the adjudication of legal rights. Spirit mediums continued to voice the concerns and commands of locality spirits. Wrongdoers were still required to provide rituals to appease the spirits and restore the *khwan*.

Occasionally the mechanisms of traditional justice broke down or were unavailable to handle certain kinds of claims. When that happened, some disputants filed lawsuits to bring pressure on their adversaries and compel them to come to terms. The aim of most plaintiffs in these legal actions, however, was not to vindicate legal rights but to enforce traditional customary norms. Lanna legal consciousness lived on in the interstices of modern law.

By the end of the twentieth century, however, economic, technological, and demographic changes weakened Lanna cultural institutions. As villagers moved to urban settings and village life became less important in their lives, locality spirits lost their authority and collective identities began to fade. People no longer saw themselves as part of village communities with strong and coherent customary legal norms and procedures. They began to forget their customs and legal traditions.

In the place of traditional Lanna justice, interviewees said that the people of the north generally responded to injuries with generosity and forgiveness. Justice is attained by reconciling the disputants, not by winner-take-all adjudication. Justice, in other words, is intersubjective. Bancha, a Chiangmai resident, characterised Lanna legal culture this way: 'You must give each other justice', not receive it from a judge. It does not matter so much who is right and who is wrong – justice in Lanna is not about right and wrong. As he put it, 'Both sides should be able to understand each other. Justice should give equally to both of them'. Therefore, Lanna residents do not expect the courts or the legal system to provide justice. As Phakdi, another Lanna resident, stated, 'Justice can't be the result of a legal decision. Rights are fixed and defined by the law, but justice isn't based on a verdict. We can't tell what justice will be. It depends on the feelings of satisfaction of the two parties'.

Most of the interviewees understood Buddhist teachings to counsel against the aggressive pursuit of their own individual rights, and they rejected the invocation of law to resolve interpersonal dealings or disputes. Rights-based claims were viewed as selfish and materialistic, since they no longer represented the interests of an entire community. These interviewees feared that pursuing legal claims would violate Buddhist teachings and create more bad karma. In the end, secular legalism would lead to further suffering and misfortune for them and for members of their family, and it would not produce justice in the Lanna sense of the word.[31] Rights are part of the legal-religious-cultural package that was aimed in some senses at the elimination and not the protection of Lanna as a distinctive cultural entity. Rights can be a Trojan horse that smuggles alien ideologies into Lanna and hastens its destruction.[32]

[31] David M. Engel and Jaruwan S. Engel, *Tort, Custom, and Karma: Globalisation and Legal Consciousness in Thailand* (Stanford: Stanford University Press, 2010).

[32] Raimundo Panikkar, 'Is the Notion of Human Rights a Western Concept?' (1982) 120 *Diogenes* 75–102.

7.6 CONCLUSION

The blood-curse ritual was an attempt by the red-shirt demonstrators to reconcile two ultimately irreconcilable forms of legal consciousness. First, they wanted to express a belief that their basic constitutional rights of equality and democratic participation had been violated. They contended that the liberal principles of the so-called People's Constitution of 1997 and its successors had never been fully realised. A century of integration into the Thai legal and political system had, in their view, resulted in their exclusion and subordination rather than inclusion and equality. Their rights had been denied. Second, they wanted to step outside the rule-of-law framework itself and participate in an entirely different type of discourse about justice. The traditional principles of law, sacrality, and community could not be adequately expressed through judicial decisions or debates about rights but could, they believed, be more fully communicated through a ritual that had no place in the framework of legal modernity.

The red shirts and their supporters have from time to time used the language and the principles of 'modern' legalism, which originated in the program of nation-building and centralisation initiated from Bangkok by King Rama V in the late nineteenth century. They sometimes speak the language of rights. They have scored some legal victories, and by invoking the tropes of electoral democracy and majority rule they have won support both inside Thailand and in the international community. But, on the whole, the red shirts and their leaders have not fared well in legal battles, and they do not regard the Thai legal system as their friend. Moreover, criminality and corruption among the red shirts have undercut their efforts to claim the legal high ground.

Unlike the Thai judicial system, the blood-curse ritual spoke a culturally intelligible language for the red shirts and their supporters. Cursing rituals maintain the premodern legal culture of Lanna in inverted form. The spirits are asked to harm an adversary rather than help a relative or friend. But, as Rosalind Morris observes, asking the spirits to inflict this injury on an outsider can actually produce *justice* for the community, 'because it will correct an imbalance in the moral order'.[33] The curse is the dark side of traditional Lanna law, but it rests on the same foundation of legality, sacrality, and collective identity, expressed now in a patriotic and nationalist ideology.

Viewing the incident of March 2010 through the lens of law, history, and religion makes it legible and connects it to the long and sometimes conflicted history of Lanna and Bangkok. It makes an otherwise bizarre behaviour intelligible in terms of what Asad might call a hybrid legal consciousness. It also explains why the outcome of the blood- curse ritual was not what the demonstrators intended. It did not empower them or offer them a way out of their unproductive relationship with the modern Thai legal or constitutional systems. Instead, it reconfirmed their identity as primitive, irrational, and atavistic elements whose traces needed, quite literally, to be swept from the streets in the name of modernity.

33 Rosalind C. Morris, *In the Place of Origins: Modernity and Its Mediums in Northern Thailand* (Durham, NC: Duke University Press, 2000) 265.

PART II

Foreign Influence and the Reform Period

8

British Judges in the Supreme Court of Siam

Surutchada Reekie and Adam Reekie[*]

8.1 INTRODUCTION

From 1856 CE until the late 1930s CE, Siam's legal system operated within the constraints of extraterritoriality.[1] Under a succession of unequal treaties signed with predominantly Western powers, Siam ceded the jurisdiction of its courts over subjects of the treaty partners in favour of the jurisdiction of consular courts, which applied their own laws.[2] By the first years of the twentieth century, Siam was successful in achieving a measure of release from this system under the provisions of further treaties, albeit with certain protections for the subjects of the treaty partners.[3] These included that European legal advisers, who were already employed by the Siamese Ministry of Justice in connection with the ongoing programme of Siam's legal modernisation, had to be present in court and sign off on judgments in cases concerning foreign subjects.[4] The role and influence of foreign legal advisers on the drafting of the Siamese legal codes produced in this era has been noted elsewhere in academic literature.[5] However, throughout this period and beyond, British lawyers sat on the Committee of the Supreme Court, a role equivalent to modern day Thai Supreme Court judges. Their role, and their impact on the development of the Thai legal system, has not hitherto been analysed in scholarship.

* The authors would like to thank Peter Reekie, Panupong Phectsuwan, the Court Museum of Thailand, and the Supreme Court Library for their kind assistance.

1 Extraterritoriality was first imposed in relation to Britain in the Treaty of Friendship and Commerce between Siam and Britain, 1855 CE, in force 1856 CE, Britain and Foreign State Papers vol. 46, 138 (the 'Bowring Treaty'). Complete judicial autonomy was returned to Thailand through a series of international instruments agreed in 1937 and 1938 CE, following the completion of the kingdom's major legal codes.

2 See, for example, Article II of the Bowring Treaty, discussed further in Section 8.2 below.

3 For example, in relation to Britain, The Anglo–Siamese Treaty, 10 March CE 1909, ratified 9 July CE 1909, British and Foreign State Papers vol. 102, 126 (the '1909 Treaty') discussed further in Section 8.2 below.

4 See, for example, Section 4 of the Protocol concerning the Jurisdiction applicable in the Kingdom of Siam to British subjects annexed to the 1909 Treaty, discussed in Section 8.2 below.

5 See, for example, Tamara Loos, *Subject Siam: Family, Law, and Colonial Modernity in Thailand* (Chiang Mai: Silkworm Books, 2002) 59–63; Department of Legal Studies in Society, Philosophy and History, *Record of an Interview with Phraya Manavorarajasevi on 12 September B.E. 2523* (A Thai language manuscript of an interview with one of the Thai drafters of the Civil and Commercial Code, Thammasat University Library) 37–47; Andrew J. Harding, 'The Eclipse of the Astrologers: King Mongkut, His Successors, and the Reformation of Law in Thailand' in Penelope Nicholson and Sarah Biddulph (eds.), *Examining Practice, Interrogating Theory: Comparative Legal Studies in Asia* (Leiden: Martinus Nijhoff, 2008) 320–1.

Other chapters in this volume address this period through focusing, at a high level, on the pressure put on Siam by the unequal treaties and Siam's modernisation efforts in response,[6] and, through a more detailed lens, at the contemporary codification projects, with one Chapter dedicated to the drafting process of the Civil and Commercial Code[7] and one which includes discussion of the drafting process of the Penal Code.[8] This Chapter takes a different approach, in an attempt to investigate a hitherto unrecognised potential factor of influence in the development of the law of Siam/Thailand at the start of the twentieth century, operating alongside the project of modernisation through codification: that of British lawyers sitting in the highest court in the Kingdom.

This Chapter presents research into four British lawyers who sat on the Committee of the Supreme Court during the period from 1910 CE to 1941 CE. During this time, the Siamese (and from 1939 CE, the Thai[9]) Government employed a number of British lawyers in the role of Judicial Adviser, which included a seat on the Committee. The four British judges, selected and employed by the Siamese Government directly, were Sir Skinner Turner (1910–15 CE), Mr Marston Frank Buszard (1915–32 CE), Sir Robert Erskine Holland (1933–6 CE), and Mr Alexander Frank Noel Thavenot (1936–41 CE). It is important at the outset to note the limitations to the research presented in this Chapter. Whilst the authors have uncovered a body of new materials and information which will shed light onto a virtually unexplored issue of legal history in Siam, there are some missing pieces.[10] It is hoped that further research will uncover more data to draw additional conclusions concerning the extent of the influence of their judgments on the Thai legal system.

Section 8.2 of this Chapter will provide context for the consideration of the roles and the importance of British judges on the Supreme Court, set within the evolution of the jurisdiction of the Siamese and Thai courts over foreigners and the presence of foreign legal advisers in the kingdom. Section 8.3 presents and considers the taxonomy of the cases in which British judges sat in the Committee of the Supreme Court demonstrating the extent of their involvement in the interpretation of the evolving law. Section 8.4 will consider selected cases which reveal some interesting dynamics in relation to these British judges, trained in common law, as they sat on the highest court of Siam/Thailand during a crucial period in which the kingdom became a code-based civil law jurisdiction. Section 8.5 will offer some conclusions based on the research presented.

6 See Krisdakorn Wongwuthikun and Naporn Popattanachai, this volume.

7 See Munin Pongsapan, this volume.

8 See Kanaphon Chanhom, this volume.

9 The name of the kingdom was changed from Siam to Thailand in 1939 CE. This Chapter will therefore use Siam and Thailand, and the adjectives Siamese and Thai, as applicable to the period.

10 Firstly, the documents in relation to the employment of foreign legal advisers kept at the Archive of the Court Museum of Thailand were not complete, hence the authors found personal files of only two out of the four British judges. Secondly, the publicly accessible database of cases of the Supreme Court of Thailand only contains selected cases. Moreover, it is currently only dated back to 1920 CE, a number of years after two British judges, Skinner Turner and Marston Buszard, started, and in Turner's case finished, their role as Supreme Court judges. Thirdly, in an attempt to create a more complete picture, the authors had secured limited access to the non-publicly accessible archive of the Supreme Court Library via the library staff who have authority to handle the case reports directly, and with their kind assistance found additional cases of these two judges. However, this, again, was incomplete, as some yearbooks of case reports were not in sufficiently good physical condition to be viewed by the staff.

8.2 THE BOWRING TREATY, THE SIAMESE COURTS' JURISDICTION OVER FOREIGNERS, AND THE ROLES OF EUROPEAN LEGAL AND JUDICIAL ADVISORS

In CE 1855 Siam signed the first of fifteen unequal treaties with Western powers.[11] The Bowring Treaty, between Siam and Britain, was the result of many years during which Siam came under pressure to open up international trade with foreign countries.[12] Together with a supplementary agreement concluded in the following year,[13] this treaty granted extraterritorial jurisdiction over all British subjects in Siam to the British consul in Bangkok.[14] Under Article II of the Bowring Treaty, all cases, criminal or civil, in which a British subject was involved would be tried and determined by the British consul according to English law.[15] This was a complete denial of the Siamese courts' jurisdiction over British subjects. For example, for Siamese authorities to arrest a British subject on suspicion of a crime, they would need to first approach the British consul and convince him to grant a warrant.

At first, the impact of this was limited due the small number of the British subjects in Siam at the time, and practical problems were limited by the fact that these British subjects were generally confined to Bangkok and the surrounding areas.[16] However, in the latter part of the nineteenth century, the increase in trade between Siamese and British subjects in the northwest, who now included Burmese, Mon, and Shan after the expansion of British power in Burma, created logistical problems since the British consul was based in Bangkok.[17] Furthermore, such problems were exacerbated by claims of the local authorities that the Bowring Treaty did not apply to Chiang Mai or any of the Laos tributary kingdoms.[18] These factors necessitated a new approach.

11 The list of the countries which signed unequal treaties with Siam, and the year of the signing, are as follows: the United Kingdom (1855 CE), the United States (1856 CE), France (1856 CE), Denmark (1858 CE), Portugal (1859 CE), the Netherlands (1860 CE), Germany (1862 CE), Sweden (1868 CE), Norway (1868 CE), Belgium (1868 CE), Italy (1868 CE), Austria–Hungary (1869 CE), Spain (1870 CE), Japan (1898 CE) and, Russia (1899 CE). James C. Ingram, *Economic Change in Thailand 1855–1970* (Stanford: Stanford University Press, 1971) 33–5.

12 M. B. Hooker, 'The "Europeanisation" of Siam's Law 1855–1908' in M. B. Hooker (ed.), *Laws of South-East Asia* (Singapore: Butterworths, 1986) 531.

13 On 13 May 1856 CE the British Government sent Harry Parkes to conclude a supplementary agreement to clarify the terms of the Bowring Treaty. The supplementary agreement detailed methods of procedure but retained the essence of the Bowring Treaty.

14 The circumstances concerning this treaty, the justifications of the inequalities of such treaties from the point of view of Western nations, and the impetus created for legal change in Siam are addressed in Krisdakorn Wongwuthikun and Naporn Popattanachai, this volume.

15 Article II of the Bowring Treaty provides as follows: 'The interests of all British subjects coming to Siam shall be placed under the regulation and control of a Consul, who will be appointed to reside at Bangkok. Any disputes arising between Siamese and British subjects shall be heard and determined by the Consul, in conjunction with the Siamese officers; and criminal offences will be punished, in the case of British offenders, by the Consul, according to English laws, and in case of Siamese offenders, by their own laws, through the Siamese authorities. But the Consul shall not interfere with any matters referring solely to Siamese, neither will the Siamese authorities interfere in questions which only concern the subjects of Her Britannic Majesty'.

16 Akiko Iijma, 'The "International Court" System in the Colonial History of Siam' (2008) 5(1) *Taiwan Journal of Southeast Asian Studies* 31, 34.

17 Rong Syamananda, *A History of Thailand* (Bangkok: Kurasapha Ladprao Press, 1971) 142–3; Iijma, '"International Court" System', 43.

18 In 1860 CE, Schomburgh, the British consult at Bangkok, on his first visit to Chiang Mai, drew the local prince's attention to the fact that British subjects were not being treated in accordance with the provisions of the treaty. The response was that the treaty only referred to Siam, that is the Bangkok-based central kingdom, and could not be applied to Chiang Mai or any of the Laos tributary kingdoms. See Nigel Brailey, *The Origins of the Siamese Forward Movement in Western Laos 1850–92* (PhD dissertation, University of London, 1968) 127; Iijma, '"International Court" System', 43.

As a part of a new phase of engagement with the northern territories,[19] and under the provisions of new treaties agreed in 1874 CE and 1883 CE, King Rama V appointed judges with jurisdiction over British subjects in that part of the Kingdom.[20] The court became known as the International Court.[21] In spite of this name, it was presided over by judges appointed by the Siamese Government, applied Siamese law, and operated in the Siamese language.[22] Jurisdiction of the court was subject to a right to evocation under the 1883 CE treaty, whereby the British consul had the power to evoke a case before the International Court had given judgment and transfer it to the consular court in Chiang Mai.[23] Appeals from judgments would be heard by the Appeal Court in Bangkok.[24]

By the mid-1890s CE, the International Court was considered by British consular reports to be very successful.[25] In 1909 CE, a new treaty expanded its jurisdiction from the northern territories to cover the whole country in respect of British subjects registered before the date of the treaty.[26] The 1909 Treaty was intended to pave the way towards ending extraterritoriality, since British subjects registered after the date of this treaty would be subject to the jurisdiction of the ordinary Siamese courts.[27] However, there were a number of safeguards in favour of British subjects. In addition to preserving the right of evocation by the British consul, the treaty specified that European legal advisers must be present in cases involving British subjects and add their signatures to judgments.[28] Judgments on appeal had to be signed by two European legal advisers, though appeals on points of law lay to the Supreme Court.[29]

19 Chris Baker and Pasuk Phongpaichit, *A History of Thailand* (Cambridge: Cambridge University Press, 2014) 53; Syamananda, *History of Thailand*, 142.

20 Treaty of 14 January 1874 between the Governments of Siam and India, British and Foreign State Papers vol. 66, 537; Treaty of 3 September 1883, British and Foreign State Papers vol. 74, 78.

21 Josiah Crosby, *Siam* (London: HM Stationary Office, 1920) 6; Iijma, '"International Court" System', 51–2.

22 P. W. Thornely, *The History of a Transition* (Bangkok: Siam Observer Press Ltd, 1923) 199–201; Iijma, '"International Court" System', 52.

23 In respect of the operation of the court under these treaties, see generally, Thornely, *History of a Transition*, 199–201; Rungsaeng Kittayapong, *The Origins of Thailand's Modern Ministry of Justice and its Early Development* (PhD Thesis, University of Bristol, 1990) 73–8.

24 In respect of appeals from the International Court, the Appeal Court in Bangkok was a mixed court in which the final decision rested with a Siamese judgment where the defendant was Siamese, and with a British judge where the defendant was British. See Thornely, *History of a Transition*, 200; Francis Bowes Sayre, 'The Passing of Extraterritoriality in Siam' (1928) 22(1) *American Journal of International Law* 70, 76.

25 The consular report for the year 1899 CE gave a positive assessment of the court, as being 'advantageous' for British subjects, the use of the local language, and the applicable law being those most familiar to the parties engaged in the disputes, which were usually between Burmese or Shans registered as British subjects, and Siamese and concerned the timber trade. Indeed, the report praises the incumbent Siamese judge, who it states had been educated in Edinburgh, and, unlike 'old-fashioned' judges, was imbued with 'modern ideas' and happy to receive, and be guided by, reasonable suggestions of the British consul, who was entitled to be present at trials in accordance with treaty provisions. See Iijma, '"International Court" System', 56.

26 The 1909 Treaty, see n. 3 above.

27 In this respect, the British treaty continued the direction of the 1907 CE Franco–Siamese Treaty, which similarly extended the jurisdiction of the International Courts to all cases involving French Asiatic subjects and proteges throughout Siam, pending promulgation and enforcement of the Siamese Codes. The extension of the jurisdiction of the International Courts was granted in exchange for Siam's release of claims to territories in the south and northeast respectively. See Sayre, 'Passing of Extraterritoriality', 79.

28 Indeed, the treaty specified that in the case of non-Asiatic British subjects, the opinion of the European legal adviser in the relevant Court of First Instance would prevail – 1909 Treaty, Protocol concerning the Jurisdiction applicable in the Kingdom of Siam to British subjects, s. 4.

29 Although two European judges had to sign appeal judgments, a practice arose whereby they did not need to agree with the judgment of the majority. Where one or both European judges disagreed, they could annex a dissenting opinion. Therefore it appears that the presence of the European judges on the appeal court was a safeguard in that the decision-making procedure had been overseen by European judges, but it did not mean that the European judges' opinion necessarily prevailed over subjects of the treaty powers. This interpretation of the treaty was

Under the treaty, these safeguards also applied to the ordinary Siamese courts in cases involving British subjects. Although the jurisdiction of the International Court was set to end with the coming into force of the Siamese Codes,[30] the treaty contained no end date for the role of the European legal advisers sitting in the ordinary Siamese courts.[31]

European legal advisers had been present in the kingdom since the first European General Advisor, Gustave Rolin-Jaequemyns, started recruiting them after his arrival in 1892 CE.[32] The role of the Legal Adviser and the Assistant Legal Advisers, whom he oversaw,[33] was twofold: they sat on the codification committee, preparing Thailand's new legal codes, and also were each appointed to one of the newly organised courts to help the Siamese judges apply the new laws.[34] Their presence was not initially required by any treaty provision; however, the 1909 Treaty, along with similar treaties with other Western powers, formalised their role and transformed them from being advisers to Siamese judges to being judges themselves, as a safeguard, from their point of view, for Western subjects.[35]

In 1902 CE, following the death of Rolin-Jaequemyns, an English lawyer, Mr Stewart Black, entered the service of the Siamese Government as the first Judicial Adviser, or 'Adviser to the Ministry of Justice' – a direct translation of the name of the position in Thai.[36] In a memorandum written in 1907 CE, Black explained that the role of Judicial Adviser included being a judge of the Supreme Court and in control of the other European legal advisers attached to the Ministry of Justice. He stated that all cases in which foreigners were concerned were brought to him and he had the 'last say' in such cases.[37] Whether or not his claim was true, it was suggested that Prince Rapee, the Minister of Justice, owing to focusing his activities at the time on the law school, left several aspects of administration in Black's hands.[38] Indeed, it seems that Black was seen to abuse this position and overstep his authority, misrepresenting his draft of overly British-friendly regulations relating to the 1909 Treaty as having been approved by Prince Rapee, leading to his dismissal in 1910 CE.[39]

The recruitment of Black as Siam's first British Judicial Adviser marked the beginning of a long line of British lawyers who served in various positions in Siam during the country's period of legal reform.[40] This chapter focuses on four British barristers who were appointed to

endorsed by the Supreme Court and agreed to by the British Legation and the Siamese Foreign Office. See Thornely, *History of a Transition*, 208–9.

30 The Penal Code, the Civil and Commercial Code, the Codes of Procedure, and the Laws on the Organization of the Courts.

31 Sayre, 'Passing of Extraterritoriality', 80–1.

32 Christian de Saint-Hubert, 'Rolin-Jaequemyns (Chao Phya Aphay Raja) and the Belgian Legal Advisors in Siam at the Turn of the Century' (1965) 53 *Journal of the Siam Society* 181, 188–9; Syamananda, *History of Thailand*, 138–9.

33 In CE 1900, the Legal Adviser and nine out of the eleven Assistant Legal Advisers were, like Gustave Rolin-Jaequemyns, Belgians. The remaining two Assistant Legal Advisers were Dutch and Japanese, the latter being Tokichi Masao who later became influential in the drafting of the Penal Code. See de Saint-Hubert 'Rolin-Jaequemyns', 188.

34 de Saint-Hubert, 'Rolin-Jaequemyns', 188; Loos, *Subject Siam*, 59.

35 Thornely, *History of a Transition*, 206.

36 Rungsaeng Kittayapong, *Origins*, 262; 'Roster of Foreigners employed by the ministry of Justice as Legal Advisors' Archive of the Court Museum of Thailand, the Office of the Courts of Justice, Ratchadaphisek Road, Bangkok. (Thai language. Translation by Surutchada Reekie) (the 'Roster').

37 Beckett, British Charge d'Affairs in Bangkok to Sir Edward Grey, Foreign Secretary 17 October CE 1907, enclosure No 1, PRO FO 422/61.

38 Rungsaeng Kittayapong, *Origins*, 262.

39 Ibid., 263–5.

40 Documents obtained from the Archive of the Court Museum of Thailand show that there were twenty-three British lawyers hired by the Ministry of Justice during the years 1902–41 CE in such roles as 'assistant to the Department of Public Prosecutors', 'Assistant Legal Adviser', 'Adviser to the Ministry of Justice', 'Legal Adviser to

the honourable position of 'Members of the Committee of the Supreme Court'. The role of these British Supreme Court judges would continue until the eve of the Japanese invasion of Thailand in 1941 CE. Indeed, their employment continues both after the abolition of the requirement for European advisers to sign off on judgments involving British subjects in 1926 CE, and after the last vestiges of extraterritoriality were abolished in the wake of the completion of the last of the legal codes, through a round of fresh international instruments negotiated with Western powers in 1937 CE and 1938 CE.[41]

8.3 FOUR BRITISH BARRISTERS WHO BECAME SIAM'S SUPREME COURT JUDGES

This section explores the personal backgrounds of the four British barristers who sat alongside Siamese, and occasional French, judges on the Supreme Court panel, usually of three or five judges. Along with their backgrounds, this section presents a short taxonomy of the cases that they adjudicated, to give a high-level view of their activities on the bench. The four barristers will be considered in the chronological order of their appointment to the Supreme Court. Together, there was always a British judge in the Supreme Court of Siam during the years 1910 CE to 1941 CE.

8.3.1 *Sir Skinner Turner (Member of the Committee of the Supreme Court 1910–1915 CE)*

Skinner Turner was born on 2 June 1868 CE near Tonbridge, Kent. Educated at King's College School and London University, he was admitted to Middle Temple on 15 November 1887 CE.[42] Following his call to the Bar on 18 June 1890 CE, he practised on the Western Circuit and the Hampshire Sessions before joining the Foreign Office in 1900 CE.[43]

Turner had an extensive background as a judge in a number of territories throughout the British Empire.[44] For the first five years of his career he acted as Registrar to HM Court for East Africa, then as Acting Legal Vice-Consul in Uganda from October 1901 CE to February 1902 CE, and as a Town Magistrate in Mombasa for a brief period in the same year. He then moved to Zanzibar where he remained until 1905 CE as Acting Assistant Judge, then as Second Assistant Judge, then as Senior Assistant Judge from 1904 CE. At this time, he was a Member of the Court of Appeal for Eastern Africa. In 1905 CE, he moved to Siam to assume

the Criminal Court', 'Legal Adviser to the Northern County Court', 'Professor at the Bar Council', and 'Member of the Supreme Court Committee' (the Roster, n. 36 above).

41 After the end of WW I, Siam successfully negotiated a treaty with the United States that removed extraterritoriality, subject to a right of consular evocation which would persist until five years following the completion of Siam's legal codes, and without the requirement for foreign legal advisers in Siam's courts. Britain, reluctant to lose the influence of its legal advisers given the large value of British interests in the kingdom, was finally persuaded to sign a treaty on similar terms to that with the United States, ratified in 1926 CE. The process of codification would, however, still take nearly a decade to complete. The rights of consular evocation were abolished through a round of fresh international instruments negotiated with Western powers in 1937 and 1938 CE. See Sayre, 'Passing of Extraterritoriality', 82–8; Tanin Kraivixien, 'Thai Legal History' (1963) 49 *Women Lawyers Journal* 6, 16.

42 Register of Admissions, Middle Temple, 664, http://archive.middletemple.org.uk/Shared%20Documents/MTAR/updated/1886–1909.pdf accessed 12 June 2019.

43 Arnold Wright, *Twentieth Century Impressions of Siam: its history, people, commerce, industries and resources* (London: Lloyd's Greater Britain Pub Co, 1908) 95.

44 Information concerning Sir Skinner Turner's employment with the British Foreign Office is drawn from that provided in the Foreign Office List, 1917–38 (London: Harrison).

the position of a judge of the His Britannic Majesty's Court (the 'HBM Court for Siam'), newly established in 1903 CE by a British Order in Council.[45]

The role of this court, as it evolved through a further British Order in Council in 1906 CE, was to act, together with the district consular courts, as the first instance consular court for British subjects in Siam. Appeals from the court were initially to the Supreme Court of the Straits Settlement, but after 1906 CE, the HBM Court for Siam acted also as the appeal court for cases in Siam in which it had jurisdiction, which duty required the full court constituting a Judge sitting with one or more Assistant Judges.[46] Further appeals would ultimately be heard by the Privy Council.

Following the abolition of the HBM Court for Siam's jurisdiction under the 1909 Treaty, Skinner Turner immediately entered the service of the Siamese government – the records show that he was first appointed as Judicial Adviser to the Ministry of Justice on 9 July 1909 CE.[47] He was later promoted to the position of a Member of the Committee of the Supreme Court, and served in this position until 1915 CE, when he left the kingdom to take up a post as Assistant Judge of HM Supreme Court of China the following year. He retired in 1927 CE having been promoted to be Judge of the Supreme Court of China and appointed as a Member of the Full Court of Hong Kong. He received the honour of a knighthood from the British Crown and First Class of the Order of the Crown of Siam in recognition of his services.

8.3.1.1 Taxonomy of Cases Adjudicated in the Supreme Court

The publicly accessible database of Supreme Court cases of Thailand does not contain information dated back to the time in which Turner sat as a Supreme Court Judge. However, the authors' access to the non-publicly accessible archive of the Supreme Court Library revealed, from the case reports that were in sufficiently good physical condition and hence were allowed to be accessed, four Supreme Court cases, all from the year 1914 CE, in which he sat as a member of the panel of judges. The main issues[48] in these cases were general principles of civil law (one case, which involved trespass and a claim for damages),[49] property law (one case),[50] and criminal law (two cases, both theft).[51] None of these cases involved foreign subjects.

8.3.2 *Marston Buszard (Member of the Committee of the Supreme Court 1915–1932 CE)*

Marston Frank Buszard was born 28 March 1872 CE in Northamptonshire, England. Following education at Trinity College, Cambridge, he was admitted to Inner Temple on 7 November 1892 CE and called to the Bar on 29 April 1896 CE.[52] He was appointed as

45 Wright, *Impressions of Siam*, 95.
46 For detail on the powers, administration and operation of this court, see Thornely, *History of a Transition*, 200–1.
47 Roster, above n. 36.
48 Cases are classified in accordance with the authors' interpretation of the legal classification of the main issue addressed in each case. In a number of cases, several provisions are referred to by the Court. Such cases are considered to only address one issue for the purpose of the analysis here. As a result, the areas of law touched on by the Court are likely to be even more numerous and wide-ranging than revealed by this analysis.
49 Dika Number 788/2457.
50 Dika Number 688/2457.
51 Dika Numbers 691/2457 and 694/2457.
52 Inner Temple Admissions Database, www.innertemplearchives.org.uk/detail.asp?id=20046 accessed 12 June 2019.

Assistant Judge of the Court of Zanzibar on 4 July 1906 CE before taking up the post of Acting Assistant Judge in Siam on 11 October 1908 CE.[53] He was therefore the Acting Assistant Judge, junior to Turner, for the last year of the HBM Court for Siam. On 9 July 1909 CE, like Turner, he entered the service of the Siamese Government on the abolition of HBM Court for Siam, being the thirteenth foreigner ever employed by the Ministry of Justice.[54]

Whereas Turner initially held the position of Judicial Adviser and occupied a seat on the Supreme Court, Buszard began at the lower position of Legal Adviser. As an interesting aside, Buszard was assisted at this time by Phraya Manavarajasevi who acted as an interpreter early in his career,[55] before returning to play a crucial role in the drafting of the Civil and Commercial Code as discussed in another Chapter in this volume.[56] However, after Turner left Siam to accept a post on the Supreme Court in China, Buszard assumed the role of Judicial Adviser and sat on the Supreme Court. Overall he served twenty-four years in Siam until his retirement at the end of 1932 CE.[57] He was decorated for his services to the Siamese Government, receiving Third Class of the Siamese Order of the White Elephant and First Class of the Order of the Crown of Siam.

8.3.2.1 Taxonomy of Cases Adjudicated in the Supreme Court

The exact number of Supreme Court cases that Buszard sat as a judge is difficult to ascertain. Buszard served as a member of the Committee of the Supreme Court from the year 1915 CE. However, the publicly accessible and searchable online database only contains selected cases from the year 1920 CE. In an attempt to find cases during the period of 1915–19 CE, the authors have received limited access to the non-publicly accessible archive of the Supreme Court Library through the kind assistance of the library staff who directly handled the manuscripts and found, from the case reports that were in sufficiently good physical condition, two additional cases where Buszard sat as a Supreme Court judge. In total, covering his full tenure as a member of the Committee of the Supreme Court, the authors have identified 226 cases which involved Buszard, and in 104 of these cases, his name appeared first as the judge who was directly assigned the case.

From these 226 cases, 51 cases were identified – through it being clearly stated in the heading, or concluded from the facts of the case, or from other related cases – as involving British subjects, either as the parties to the case or victims of the crime.[58] A further forty-one cases involved other foreign nationals, who were Norwegian, French, American, Italian, Portuguese, Danish, Dutch, or Chinese.[59] However, some of these cases simply stated that the

53 Information concerning Marston Buszard's employment with the British Foreign Office is drawn from that provided in the Foreign Office List, 1917–38 (London: Harrison).

54 Roster, above n. 36.

55 Srimana Suriya, *Phrayamanavorarajasevi* (BE 2546) 33(2) Thammasat Law Journal 441, 442 (Thai language).

56 See Munin Pongsapan, this volume, at XXX.

57 http://eresources.nlb.gov.sg/newspapers/Digitised/Article/straitstimes19330103-1.2.72 accessed 12 June 2019.

58 Dika Numbers 135/2461, 222/2461, 251/2461, 392–93/2461, 443/2461, 1068/2462, 1095/2462, 1347/2462, 1585/2462, 199/2463, 329/2463, 443/2463, 1050/2463, 1056/2463, 69/2464, 631/2464, 682/2464, 734/2465, 1042/2465, 936/2465, 134/2466, 1041/2466, 412/2467, 518/2467, 854/2467, 194/2469, 385/2469, 713/2469, 737/2469, 851/2469, 859/2469, 478/2470, 531/2470, 550/2470, 592/2470, 40/2471, 139/2471, 609/2471, 659/2471, 891/2471, 798/2472, 902/2472, 157/2472, 1106/2473, 897/2474, 898/2474, 508/2475, 516/2475, 696/2475, 697–699/2475, 721/2475.

59 Dika Numbers 721/2457, 135/2461, 221/2461, 241/2461, 328/2461, 389/2461, 392–93/2461, 527–28/2461, 838/2461, 1137/2462, 1202/2462, 1403–04/2462, 1577/2462, 1585/2462, 1586/2462, 1589–90/2462, 114/2463, 194–195/2463, 199/2463, 235/2463, 1028/2463, 575/2465, 937/2465, 903/2465, 61/2467, 517/2467, 929/2467, 841–842/2469, 592/2470, 505/2471, 915/2471, 958/2471, 805/2472, 123/2473, 1079/2473, 1149/2473, 1165/2473, 1199/2473, 900/2474, 927/2474, 712–713/2475.

parties were foreigners of unidentified nationalities and therefore it is possible that there were more cases that involved British subjects than the fifty-one cases mentioned. In total, there were eighty-nine cases that involved foreigners of any nationalities.[60] The nature of legal disputes in these cases represents a wide range of main issues. Eighty-six of the cases are civil cases, involving general principles of civil law (eleven cases), obligations (twenty-two cases), specific contracts (twenty-eight cases), property (fourteen cases), family law (one case), and succession and inheritance (ten cases, one of which concerned a trust). In addition, there are criminal cases (forty-three cases), cases concerning procedural issues (sixty-six cases), cases concerning the jurisdiction and organisation of the courts (four cases), bankruptcy cases (ten cases), cases on issues relating to treaties (four cases), maritime law (one case), and other cases relating to specific Acts or regulations (twelve cases). Notably, Buszard had sat on the Supreme Court before many of the main Codes were enacted, therefore the legal issues involved a variety of written laws, including old Acts which were later replaced by the Codes (such as the Bankruptcy Act of R.S. 130 (1911 CE), the Partnership and Companies Act of R.S. 130 (1911 CE)), as well as the newly enacted Codes and Acts.

8.3.3 *Sir Robert Erskine Holland (Member of the Committee of the Supreme Court 1933–1936 CE)*

Robert Erskine Holland was born in Victoria, Westminster, London on 29 June 1873 CE, educated at Winchester College and attended university at Oriel College, Oxford.[61] He was admitted to Lincoln's Inn and called to the Bar on 14 November 1927 CE, having by this point already pursued an extensive career in foreign service.[62] Between 1895 and 1925 CE he served mainly in the political department as secretary to the Board of Revenue in Madras and later as British consul in Muscat. After service in WWI, he was the chief commissioner of the northwest Indian province of Ajmer-Merwara, then appointed as agent to the governor general in Rajputana and was a member of the secretary of state's Council of India. After leaving this post, he practised law until he was appointed as Judicial Adviser to the Government of Siam and Judge of the Supreme Court in 1933 CE, taking over the post from Marston Buszard.[63] From his personal file from the Archive of Court Museum, his salary was listed as 2,000 Baht, an extraordinarily high sum considering that Prince Rapee, when he started off as the Minister of Justice, received the salary of 240 Baht.[64] After remaining in the post for less than three years, he left Siam either in 1935 CE or early in

60 Four cases involved both British and other foreign subjects: Dika Numbers 135/2461, 392–93/2461, 1585/2462, 199/2463, 592/2470. An additional two cases appear to involve foreign subjects due to the names of the parties, although the nationalities are not stated: Dika Numbers 579/2463, 1149/2463.

61 In addition to records of his employment with the British Foreign office from the Foreign Office List, 1917–38 (London: Harrison) Sir Robert Erskine Holland has a short biography in J. F. Bosher, *Imperial Vancouver Island: Who Was Who, 1850–1950*, (USA: Xlibris Corporation, 2010) 360–1, from which this information is drawn.

62 Lincoln's Inn Admissions Registers Vol. 3, 1894–1956, 205, https://archive.org/stream/VOL318941956/VOL%203%201894–1956#page/n207/mode/2up accessed 12 June 2019.

63 His contract as legal advisor is dated 19 February 1933 CE, and his appointment as Member of the Committee of the Supreme Court was on 18 April 1933 CE. Source: 'Profile of Government Officials of the Ministry of Justice: Robert Erskin Holland', Archive of the Court Museum of Thailand, the Office of the Courts of Justice, Ratchadaphisek Road, Bangkok (Thai language. Translation by Surutchada Reekie).

64 Suthichai Theptrairat, 'Roles of Foreign Lawyers in the Age of Law Reform and the Thai Judiciary' (2017) 5 *Journal of the Courts of Justice* 5 (Thai language).

1936 CE,[65] after his contract was not renewed. He received the decoration of The Knight Grand Cross (First Class) of the Most Noble Order of the Crown of Siam for his services.[66]

From confidential British foreign office correspondence between the British Legation and Anthony Eden, at that time British Foreign Secretary,[67] it appears that Robert Holland's contract was not renewed since the Siamese Cabinet preferred to appoint Alexander Thavenot, then the British Judge in the Court of Appeal, to replace him. The underlying reasons for this, according to the British correspondent, were the Siamese authorities' dissatisfaction that Holland did not adjudicate a sufficient number of cases, combined with their wish to promote Thavenot from the Court of Appeal to match the promotion of a French judge who was Thavenot's junior.[68] The British Legation suggested agreeing to this request on the basis that Thavenot was well suited to the position of Supreme Court judge, given his long residence and experience of adjudicating cases in Siam, also noting with approval his good relationship with the British Legation.[69]

8.3.3.1 Taxonomy of Cases Adjudicated in the Supreme Court

The authors found fifty-six cases in which Holland sat as a Supreme Court judge, dated from 1934 to 1935 CE. In seventeen of these cases, Holland's name appeared first, indicating that the cases were assigned directly to him and were under his responsibility in term of case administration. Thirty-three of the fifty-six cases involved British parties or victims;[70] thirteen cases involved other foreign parties;[71] and one further case involved a party who was a foreigner but was not listed as a foreign subject, perhaps due to a mistake in the record.[72] Accordingly, nine out of the fifty-six cases in which Holland acted as Supreme Court judge involved only Siamese parties, arguing mostly over Siamese laws, with the exception of one case which involved a trust.[73]

The nature of legal disputes in these cases represented a wide range of main issues. Twenty-two of the cases are civil cases, involving general principles of civil law (one case), obligations (two cases), specific contracts (seven cases), property (four cases), succession and inheritance

65 Holland's contract officially ended on 30 January 1936 CE. There is a discrepancy in the sources as to his date of departure: the Siamese records state that he returned to England on 28 March 1935 CE, however correspondence from the British legation indicates that he was still in Siam in February 1936 CE, awaiting a decision as to whether or not his contract would be renewed. See the Roster, above n. 36, and Bangkok and Foreign Office Correspondence 1922–1940, FO371/20297 No 63 (71/3/36) from the British Legation, Bangkok to the Right Hon. Anthony Eden dated 10 February 1936 CE.

66 Granted on 26 December 1935 CE. Source: 'Profile of Government Officials of the Ministry of Justice: Robert Erskine Holland', Archive of the Court Museum of Thailand, the Office of the Courts of Justice, Ratchadaphisek Road, Bangkok (Thai language. Translation by Surutchada Reekie).

67 Foreign Office Correspondence 1922–1940, FO371/20297 No 63 (71/3/36) from the British Legation, Bangkok to the Right Hon. Anthony Eden dated 10 February 1936 CE.

68 Ibid., 192.

69 Ibid., 194–5.

70 Dika Numbers 159/2477, 214/2477, 329/2477, 362/2477, 363/2477, 364/2477, 457/2477, 493/2477, 516/2477, 591–592/2477, 838/2477, 924/2477, 942/2477, 987/2477, 1087/2477, 1135/2477, 1170/2477, 196/2478, 255/2478, 259/2478, 360/2478, 374/2478, 377/2478, 383/2478, 389/2478, 495/2478, 756–757/2478, 861/2478, 862/2478, 871/2478, 877/2478, 878/2478, and 879/2478.

71 Dika Numbers 117/2477, 622/2477, 656/2477, 852/2477, 1088/2477, 1104/2477, 1144/2477, 378/2478, 408/2478, 462/2478, 465/2478, 804/2478, and 872/2478.

72 Dika Number 1039/2477, which involved a dispute over a mining certificate. The defendant was one William Buchanan Houston, listed in a Singaporean newspaper as an engineer but with no further information as to nationality. See http://eresources.nlb.gov.sg/newspapers/digitised/issue/singfreepressb19170825-1 accessed 1 June 2019.

73 Dika Number 208/2477.

(four cases), and business organisations (four cases). There are also criminal cases (ten cases), procedural cases (ten cases), cases concerning other specific Acts (twelve cases) and cases concerning the law of evidence (two cases). These cases required the application and knowledge of Siam's newly enacted Codes, as well as other laws such as mining law, evidence law, tax law, printing law, and trade mark law.

8.3.4 *Alexander Frank Noel Thavenot (Member of the Committee of the Supreme Court 1936–1941 CE)*

Alexander Thavenot was born on 21 December 1883 CE in Port of Spain, Trinidad in the British West Indies. He was admitted to Gray's Inn on 12 September 1902 CE and called to the Bar on 5 July 1905 CE.[74] He took over the post of judicial adviser and occupied a seat on the Supreme Court in 1936 CE following Robert Holland's departure. However, he had been in Siam for many years before this appointment, having originally arrived in 1909 CE.[75] He was first employed by the Siamese Government on 17 April of that year as an Assistant Legal Adviser, with an initial salary of 175 Baht per month.[76]

His personal file kept at the Archive of the Court Museum[77] shows that, as Assistant Legal Advisor, Thavenot moved between a number of different courts, assigned to the International Court on 4 July 1910 CE, the International Court in Lampang province on 1 April 1911 CE, the Insolvency Division on 30 January 1913 CE, the Civil Court on 1 August 1914 CE, and the International Court in Nakhon Sri Thammarat province in 1915 CE. Some twelve years later, on 1 October 1927 CE, he was promoted to Legal Advisor and assigned to the Northern County Court, and was subsequently moved to the County Court of Nakhon Sri Thammarat, on 15 May 1930 CE, and then to the International Court the following year, on 31 September 1931 CE. He was promoted to the position of Judge of the Court of Appeal on 2 November 1931 CE, by which time his salary had risen to 1,700 Baht. He was appointed as Judicial Adviser on 8 January 1936 CE, after Holland's departure, with a salary of 2,000 Baht.

Thavenot left Siam in May of 1941 CE, having resigned in April following warnings from the British Legation regarding the coming Japanese invasion.[78] He received a pension of 800 Baht per month, which the Ministry sent to the Thai Embassy in London to pay him at the rate of 880 pounds per year.[79] In total, he received eight Siamese decorations for his services, the highest being Knight Commander (Second Class) of the Most Exalted Order of the White Elephant on 20 June 1940 CE.[80] He also received a British honour, appointed Commander of the British Empire on 8 June 1939 CE.

74 Gray's Inn Admissions Register, 1902 CE.

75 A transcript of a lecture Thavenot gave to the Royal Central Asian Society on 14 January 1942 CE, which contains some biographical information, was published in the Journal of the Royal Central Asian Society: A. F. Thavenot, 'Thailand and the Japanese Invasion' (1942) 29(2) *Journal of The Royal Central Asian Society* 111–19.

76 'Profile of Government Officials of the Ministry of Justice: A. F. Thavenot', Archive of the Court Museum of Thailand, the Office of the Courts of Justice, Ratchadaphisek Road, Bangkok. (Thai language. Translation by Surutchada Reekie).

77 Ibid.

78 Thavenot, 'Japanese Invasion', 114.

79 'Profile of Government Officials of the Ministry of Justice: A. F. Thavenot', Archive of the Court Museum of Thailand, the Office of the Courts of Justice, Ratchadaphisek Road, Bangkok. (Thai language. Translation by Surutchada Reekie).

80 Ibid.

8.3.4.1 Taxonomy of Cases Adjudicated in the Supreme Court

In the six years in which Thavenot sat as a Supreme Court judge (1936–41 CE), he heard an incredible 773 cases. In 183 of these, he was directly assigned the case and his name appeared first in the three-judge panel. The last case which he was directly assigned was in CE 1939,[81] and for the last two years of service as a member of the Committee of the Supreme Court his name only appeared as a panel member.

Focusing on the 183 cases in which Thavenot took the leading role, only twenty cases were known to have involved British subjects as parties to the case, either because they were clearly listed as British, or listed in another case as British, or not listed but were said to be British in the facts.[82] One case involved an American,[83] and four further cases involved foreigners of unknown nationalities,[84] and therefore it is possible that the number of cases that involved British subjects was more than the twenty cases mentioned. In total, there were only twenty-five cases which involved foreign subjects. However, the legal issues in all these twenty-five cases revolved around Siamese or Thai laws and newly enacted Codes.

When considering the nature of legal disputes in the cases Thavenot adjudicated, it can be seen that the cases covered a range of main issues. Of the 183 for which Thavenot was directly responsible, thirty-six concerned civil law issues, comprising general principles of civil law (two cases), obligations (three cases), specific contracts (nine cases), property (nine cases), family (four cases), succession and inheritance (three cases), loans and security (five cases), and wrongful acts (one case). The remaining cases are divided between criminal cases (seventy-five cases), procedural issues (forty-one cases), cases concerning the jurisdiction and organisation of the courts (one case), bankruptcy (one case), issues concerning treaties (two cases), cases concerning specific Acts or regulations (fifteen cases), the law of evidence (three cases), tax (six cases), and intellectual property (three cases). All but one of the 183 cases involved issues concerning Thai law only, the exception being the case Dika Number 507–508/2480 which involved English trust law. This case will be considered further below in Part 8.4.

8.3.5 *Observations*

Some observations may be made at this point. The research summarised above has identified 1,059 Supreme Court cases in which the four British judges sat, covering the period of three decades from 1910 to 1941 CE. Indeed, the true number of cases they adjudicated is likely to exceed this, given the incomplete nature of the information available as explained at the start of this Chapter. This fact is in itself remarkable. Moreover, when considering the volume of cases, the breadth of the different of areas of law concerned, and the period of time covered, it can be seen that all these factors point towards an enduring influence of these British individuals on the early development of the Siamese legal system. It is understandable that Siam would employ foreign experts to assist their judges in interpreting and applying the law, since the programme of legal modernisation was proceeding upon a path of borrowing from foreign sources, as discussed in detail elsewhere in this volume by

[81] Dika Number 1538/2482.

[82] Dika Numbers 143/2479, 1640/2479, 157/2480, 292/2480, 304/2480, 416/2480, 548/2480, 658/2480, 669/2480, 1290/2480, 74/2481, 183/2481, 218/2481, 324/2481, 432/2481, 698/2481, 925/2481, 68/2482, 405/2482, and 764–765/2482.

[83] Dika Number 364/2481.

[84] Dika Numbers 1149/2479 (William Buchanan Houston); 1161–1162/2481 (E. L. Mile or Mill); 457/2482 (James Hicks Salem); 497/2482 (Khrisna Sami).

Munin Pongsapan.[85] However, these four foreign experts were trained in English law, a common law system, when civil law models had been selected for the country's legal codes. The four British barristers had no more experience of interpreting and applying a civil law code than the Siamese judges with whom they were sitting. Furthermore, Siam was not obliged by any treaty provisions to employ British lawyers in the Supreme Court. The 1909 Treaty required European legal advisers to sign off on judgments at first instance and Court of Appeal level, but not at the level of the Supreme Court, whose jurisdiction in relation to cases involving British subjects was to determine appeals on points of law only.

The presence of British judges on the bench of the Supreme Court may perhaps best be explained by two factors. First, there arose a practice at the end of the nineteenth century, recognised by the Siamese government, of Siamese judges using English law in commercial cases where Siamese law was silent or obsolete on an issue.[86] With such practice, the recruitment of an English legal adviser at the Supreme Court level is understandable. Second, this accords with Siam's policy of balancing the interests of foreign powers exerting pressure on Siam.[87] French legal advisers, influential in the codification process, seem to have been balanced by the presence of a judicial adviser who sat on the Supreme Court, with an 'understanding' that he would be a British lawyer.[88] While some French legal advisers sat on the Supreme Court also,[89] the records suggest that the combined number of cases on which they sat was significantly fewer than those of the British judges.[90]

The quiet influence of the British judges may be further observed from the nature of their cases. It might have been anticipated that the British judges were only assigned cases where foreigners, or aspects of foreign law, were involved, in order to give comfort to Western treaty powers that justice had been done over their subjects to a Western-approved standard. However, this was not the case. The taxonomy of the cases discussed above reveals that the vast majority of the cases heard by the four British judges involved parties who were Siamese or Thai, and concerned Siamese and Thai laws only. Therefore, it may be speculated here that these British judges were profoundly entrusted and respected by the Siamese legal community, and perhaps increasingly so over time since the last British judge – Thavenot – heard more than 100 cases each year, the majority of which involved Siamese or Thai parties only.

These British judges must be considered to have played an integral part in the kingdom's developing legal system in its formative years, during the production and implementation of major legal codes. The evidence demonstrates that they were accepted into the Supreme Court and, given the volume of cases which they adjudicated, became vital to its operations.

8.4 BRITISH LEGAL INFLUENCE IN SIAM'S HIGHEST COURT?

Out of the 1059 cases reviewed by the authors, a small number stood out as indicating, explicitly or implicitly, an English law influence in the decisions of the court. This Chapter

85 See Munin Pongsapan, this volume.

86 Thornely, *History of a Transition*, 220; Preedee Kasemsup, 'Reception of Law in Thailand – A Buddhist Society' in Masaji Chiba (ed.), *Asian Indigenous Law: In Interaction with Received Law* (London: KPI, 1986) 292–3.

87 Syamananda, *History of Thailand*, 140–50.

88 Thornely, *History of a Transition*, 220.

89 The roster of foreigners employed by the Ministry of Justice of Siam, kept at the Archive of the Court Museum of Thailand, listed only two Frenchmen as judges on the Supreme Court: Clemont Niel and L. Duplatre (see Roster above n. 36). A search of the publicly accessible database showed a record of another French judge, Rene Guyon.

90 In total the authors found seventy Supreme Court cases from the publicly accessible database which involved French judges: Guyon (six cases) Duplatre (fifty-three cases) Niel (eleven cases).

separates them into two categories. The first category includes cases which reveal an attitude towards previous cases, which is distinctive of English legal reasoning. The second category concerns cases relating to trusts, a legal concept unfamiliar to the Siamese or Thai legal system. However, integral to the following analysis are also a number of cases involving a British judge that demonstrate arguably opposite characteristics, that is, examples of cases involving a British judge that appear untouched by the influences of English law identified elsewhere. The analysis of the cases therefore demonstrates a complex dynamic of Siamese and British legal influences in Siam's highest court during the first half of the twentieth century.

8.4.1 *The Use of Legal Precedents*

Considering three Supreme Court cases,[91] one for each of the first three British judges, it is possible to identify an attitude towards previous judgments which is characteristic of English common law legal reasoning. The Siamese or Thai Supreme Court frequently refers to previous decisions when giving a judgment. However, the style in which it does so is rather different to that found in English court judgments. The Siamese or Thai Supreme Court generally cites previous decisions as a legal source, a point of reference, or a support for their conclusion, usually without detailed discussion of their material facts and underlying rationales. By contrast, in these three cases, the judgment uses the common law style of comparing the material facts of the present case to those of cited precedents in concluding that the legal principle laid down in the previous case should apply.

Two of the three cases deserve closer consideration. The first is the case Dika Number 737/2469 of the year 1926 CE, which was directly assigned to Buszard. This case is extraordinary in that the judgment, alone of all cases reviewed by the authors, explicitly cites an earlier English case as the legal source for a decision, without referring to any Siamese legal principle.

The case involved a dispute over a contract for the sale of 1,400 sacks of rice. The buyer paid the defendant seller for the rice by cheque. The seller then issued a delivery order stating that the holder may claim the rice kept in his warehouse. The buyer sold the delivery order to the claimant, who duly paid for it. Later, the bank refused to cash the buyer's cheque, and therefore the seller refused to deliver the rice. The issue for the court was whether legal title to the rice had been transferred to the holder of the delivery order. On this issue, the Supreme Court ruled as follows:

> When the defendant [seller] was not duly paid for the goods, but the goods were still in his possession, he had the right to the goods under a lien. This was the case even if it appeared that the defendant acted with the intention to transfer the ownership of the goods. See Laurie and Morewood v Dudin Brothers 1 KD 1926 page 233.[92]

The English case cited here is *Laurie & Morewood* v. *Dudin & Sons*,[93] and involved constructive delivery of goods, with material facts similar to this Siamese Supreme Court case. This is remarkable for two reasons. First, the court is using an English case as a source of law for deciding a case in Siam. This apparent willingness to use English law where Siamese

[91] Dika Numbers 788/2457 (Turner); 737/2469 (Buszard); 208/2477 (Holland).

[92] Dika Number 737/2469, last paragraph (Thai language – translation by Surutchada Reekie).

[93] (1926) 1 KB 223. The discrepancies in the defendant's name and page number found in the Supreme Court judgment were perhaps due to typographical errors.

law was considered either absent, obsolete, or unclear,[94] points to the influence of English law at this early stage of Siam's legal reform on the highest court of the land. Secondly, the date of this case is significant. The first two books of the Civil and Commercial Code came into effect on 1 January 1926 CE, which included provisions covering the issue in the case. However, the court chose to use a legal principle from an English case, rather than the provisions of the Civil and Commercial Code, on which to base its decision.

This raises two possibilities. One is that the facts of the dispute may have occurred before the entry into force of the Civil and Commercial Code, in which case the Supreme Court were unwilling to apply the Code retrospectively. Instead, they applied an English case which, itself, would likely also have been decided after the facts of the dispute. However, the Court may have considered it to be evidence of a legal principle already laid down in the English legal system, and thus suitable to be applied to a Siamese case. The other possibility is that the Court chose to use the English case as a guide to applying the provisions of the Civil and Commercial Code. In either alternative, the influence of English law on the Court in this case is striking.

The second case, Dika Number 208/2477 of the year 1934 CE, was directly assigned to Holland. This case concerned a dispute over a trust of land established by a Siamese testator. The issue of the establishment and enforcement of common law trusts in a civil law country will be discussed further below. However this case also clearly demonstrates the application of legal precedents in the common law fashion, as can be seen from the wording of the judgment. In referring to a previous judgment, the Supreme Court first established its *ratio decidendi*, in accordance with common law approach: 'the Supreme Court was of the opinion that Dika Number 443/2463 laid down the following principle . . .'.[95] The Court then considered the material facts and concluded: 'and in this case when the defendant demanded the disputed land for her sole ownership, it can be said that she failed to properly execute her duties as trustee. The cited Dika case therefore directly applied to this case'.[96] This level of attention paid to the principle of law from a previous case being applicable to the present case through analogy of the material facts is characteristic of a common law style, and not in keeping with the general practice of the Siamese or Thai Supreme Court.

Contrary to these examples, there exists a vast number of judgments by a British judge that demonstrate the use of previous Supreme Court decisions in the typical Siamese or Thai Supreme Court style of citing a previous decision as a legal source, a point of reference, or as support for the conclusion. For instance, in the case Dika Number 575/2465 of the year 1922 CE, which was directly assigned to Buszard and which involved a dispute concerning a trust, the Supreme Court ruled, in relation of one of the three issues: 'When a legatee puts him or herself forward as a custodian of the assets of the deceased for other legatees as a trustee, the period of prescription for inheritance disputes of one year does not apply (Dika Number 804/126, 1455/2462, 390/2463)'.[97] This is a good illustration of a typical Siamese or Thai court's style of judgment and citation of previous cases – brief, factual and referring to previous cases as points of reference rather than engaging in a lengthy analysis of underlying legal rationales and principles laid now in precedents, typical in common law judgments.

Rather interestingly, although Thavenot sat in 773 cases, 183 of which the authors have accessed and reviewed – the highest number of cases compared to cases of the three other

94 Preedee Kasemsup, 'Reception', 292–3.
95 Para. 4 (Thai language – translation by Surutchada Reekie).
96 Ibid.
97 Para. 5 (Thai language – translation by Surutchada Reekie).

British judges by a far distance – the authors found no clear application of legal precedents in the common law style. In fact, when the cases of the four judges were considered as a whole, the influence of English law is distinctly less clear in Thavenot's cases. Rather, his cases bear all the characteristics of modern Thai Supreme Court judgments: on average they are short, factual, and rely mainly on the interpretation and application of the written laws, Codes or Acts, rather than the analysis and analogy of material facts, legal principles, and rationales from previous decisions. In seven of his cases, previous Supreme Court judgments are mentioned; however, they are cited in the style of the modern Thai Supreme Court judgments: a simple statement that a particular issue in the current case fits or does not fit with the remit of a previous decision.[98] The Court did not at any point, in any of these cases, mention what legal principles were laid down by the cited Supreme Court cases.

A good example is the case Dika Number 865/2481 in the year 1938 CE, in which two previous Supreme Court cases were cited. This was a criminal case brought by the public prosecutor of Chai-nat, a province in central Siam, against three men who were alleged to falsely report a crime. After briefly stating the facts and the decision of the Court of Appeal that found the defendants guilty of two out of three offences, the Supreme Court's ruling in full is as follows:

> The fact that the defendants colluded to create a false roster of buffaloes in the farm constituted the offence of falsifying documents under section 222(1). However, the argument that the roster constituted an important official document is rejected as the Local Administration Act did not specify that the village leader was the official responsible for rosters of farm animals, in accordance with case Dika Number 740/2474. Moreover, it was not a document which established ownership or obligation, or provided proof for a change of ownership in accordance with section 6(20) of the criminal law, and was not in accordance with case Dika Number 1320/2480. Therefore, it is held that the two defendants are found guilty under section 223 as well.[99]

This ruling demonstrates a marked difference from the common law judgment style such as that found in the above cases of Buszard or Holland. It also perfectly demonstrates the hallmark characteristics of modern Thai Supreme Court judgments. Where previous decisions were relied upon, they were cited only briefly, in a fashion that is markedly different from the use of legal precedents in English cases.

When the judgments are reviewed in relation to each judge, it is possible to acquire a sense of the character or style of each British judge on the Supreme Court of Siam. The cases of Turner and Holland, and the earlier cases of Buszard, are notably different from the later cases of Buszard in the early 1930s CE, and those of Thavenot's tenure in the late 1930s to early 1940s CE. By this time, the Thai Supreme Court had formulated its characteristic style of writing judgments, a style which remains in use today. From the four judges, Thavenot stands out: his cases are the most consistent with the style of a typical Siamese or Thai Supreme Court judgment. It seems likely that this Siamese/Thai characteristic of his judgments stemmed from the fact that he served in various lower courts in Siam for over twenty years before being promoted to the Supreme Court. Indeed, with his long service and expertise in Siamese/Thai laws, it is not surprising that he had developed such a style of judgment writing. As such, could it be said that he was more a 'Siamese' or 'Thai' judge, as a result of his long judicial training, than he was a 'British' judge by virtue of his nationality and education?

98 Dika Numbers 438/2481, 456–457/2481, 865/2481, 1152/2481, 1161–1162/2481, 1345/2481, 496/2481.

99 Thai language – translation by Surutchada Reekie.

8.4.2 *Trust Cases*

The second category of cases heard by British judges on the Supreme Court are those which concern trusts, a legal concept alien to the Siamese or Thai legal system. From the 951 cases reviewed, four involved trusts created for the purpose of managing inheritance or personal assets: Dika Numbers 575/2465 (Buszard), 880/2471 (Buszard), 208/2477 (Holland), and 507–508/2480 (Thavenot). It is argued elsewhere in this volume that a number of trusts were established in Siam in accordance with English law prior to a prohibition on the use of trusts introduced by Section 1686 in Book VI of the Civil and Commercial Code in 1935 CE.[100] For the purpose of the current discussion, these cases demonstrate the clear reception of an English legal principle, while citing no legal sources or previous Siamese Supreme Court cases in respect of the matter in dispute. This characteristic distinguishes them from case Dika Number 737/2469 of the year 1926 CE discussed above, which directly cited an English case.

In order to illustrate this point, relevant parts of the four judgments will be considered here. In case Dika Number 575/2465 of the year 1922 CE, one of the three issues was whether the existence of a trust could be proved from a contract between two legatees, stating that one legatee would hold the inheritance on behalf of other legates not parties to the contract. On this issue, the Supreme Court simply held that 'this contract can be accepted as evidence which supports the claimant's claim that the defendant held the assets as trustee'.[101] Without further explanation or reference to any legal source, the Supreme Court recognised the existence of a trust, and showed willingness to enforce it, if the party could prove that it was duly established.

In the second and third cases, the Supreme Court demonstrated a clear reception of the English trust law concept of a split in the legal and equitable titles of land, once again without citing any legal source, Siamese or English. In the two-paragraph judgment of the case Dika Number 880/2471 of the year 1928 CE, the Supreme Court's ruling in full is as follows:

> It appears that the claimant inherited the land, and never let go of her ownership of the land. The defendant and his wife were occupiers of the land instead of the claimant because, at the time of inheritance, the claimant was only 17 years old. Later the defendant and his wife asked to receive the land deed and put their names on the deed instead of the claimant's.
>
> The Supreme Court affirms the judgment of the Court of Appeal and reverses the judgment of the lower court, holding that the defendant was a trustee of the claimant's land, for the purpose of taking care of it on behalf of the claimant. The ownership of the land did not belong to the defendant.[102]

It can be seen that the Supreme Court recognised that the land's legal title as appeared in the land deed was separate from the equitable title, held by the beneficiary of a trust. A similar legal application can be seen in Holland's trust case: Dika Number 208/2477, discussed above in relation to the use of legal precedents. Without citing any English case, the Supreme Court's reception of the English trust law concept of a split in the legal and equitable titles of land was clear. In considering the issues of whether the defendant held the land on trust, and whether she duly exercised her duties as a trustee, the Supreme Court affirmed the decision of the lower court and, in so doing, cited a principle laid down in a previous Supreme Court

[100] See Adam Reekie and Naporn Popattanachai, this volume.
[101] Para. 5 (Thai language – translation by Surutchada Reekie).
[102] Thai language – translation by Surutchada Reekie.

case Dika Number 443/2463 of the year 1920 CE, that a land deed registration was not absolute proof of ownership of land. Accordingly, this allowed for the possibility that the person whose name appeared on the deed may be a trustee, and may be removed if she acted fraudulently or failed to execute her duties as a trustee.

The last case that involved a trust, Dika Number 507–508/2480 of the year 1937 CE, was adjudicated by Thavenot. It involved the issue of whether the transfer of a piece of land was an absolute gift to the third defendant, or resulted in a trust under which the third defendant held the land as a trustee for the benefit of the claimant. The Supreme Court concluded that the transfer was intended at the time to be a gift, and therefore the issue of whether the trust was set up in accordance with the required formalities under Siamese law regarding a transfer of land would not change the legal outcome. In just a few words, and without citing any clear legal source, the Supreme Court demonstrated its understanding of the differences between a trust and a gift, a subject of much discussion in common law systems. The judgment also showed the Court's ability and willingness to shift between English legal issues of trusts/gifts and Siamese legal issues regarding land conveyancing.

It can be seen that these four cases involve a variety of issues relating to trusts, and that the Supreme Court showed their acceptance of, as well as confidence in, the recognition and enforcement of trusts, an English law creation. The Supreme Court also demonstrated their willingness in applying a blend of legal principles from both English law and previous Siamese cases, which illustrates a combination of local Siamese law and English law influences. There seems to have been an attempt to administer the relevant English trust law principles within the evolving Siamese legal framework, including its written laws and court judgments.

8.5 CONCLUSION

Some further observations may be offered in conclusion of this chapter's investigation of the career of four British lawyers on the bench of the Supreme Court of Siam. The research for this Chapter started with a hypothesis that British lawyers in the Supreme Court of Siam, a civil law country, must have asserted a strong common law influence from the bench. Instead, the findings reveal a more complex interplay of different factors. Therefore, the term 'British Judges in the Supreme Court of Siam' accommodates at least two meanings.

The first meaning refers to Turner, Holland, and, to a lesser extent, Buszard, who were British by nationality and by their education and training as barristers. All three had travelled around the British Empire, deciding cases by applying English law in different locations and for many years before arriving in Siam. In the Supreme Court of Siam, they each exerted some clearly distinguishable British legal influence on judgments through the common law style of legal reasoning and use of precedents, even in disputes which involved Siamese code-based legal provisions.

Thavenot, by contrast, represents a second meaning for the term 'British Judges in the Supreme Court of Siam'. Whilst he was British by nationality and his legal background, Thavenot's long service in the Siamese judiciary seems to have moulded him into adopting what may be called a Siamese/Thai judicial style. If he were to be assessed based solely on the style of the judgments of cases he adjudicated, one may easily conclude that he was as much a 'Siamese' or 'Thai' judge, as the other judges on the panel. Indeed, if these cases were anonymised, it would be very difficult to recognise that there was a foreign judge on the bench, since they are virtually indistinguishable in their characteristics and style of writing from a typical Supreme Court case.

This leads to an intriguing third meaning, not explored in this chapter, of the many British educated judges of Siamese or Thai nationality. Are they more or less of a 'British' judge than Thavenot? Indeed, perhaps the nationality of a judge is less important than it may seem at a first glance. This investigation of British judges in the Supreme Court of Siam raises a caution against assumptions about the influence or style of reasoning of any particular judge based solely on their nationality. Judges in their career progression, like all individuals, are shaped and moulded by multiple factors including their background, education and life experience, and continue to develop as they gain further experience. The discussion here indicates a complex dynamic between the influences of common law and civil law cultures, personified in four representative judges. Indeed, moving beyond the scope of this Chapter, perhaps we could suggest that in this period, Thai law and the Thai legal system were similarly shaped by a complex and dynamic set of influences tied to culture, politics and the experience of history, rooted in the individuals who shaped its development. Therefore a thorough investigation of such influences can be instrumental in better understanding Thai law's path of evolution.

9

The Fundamental Misconception in the Drafting of the Thai Civil and Commercial Code of 1925

Munin Pongsapan

9.1 INTRODUCTION

The Thai Civil and Commercial Code (TCCC) of 1925, which has largely remained in place, emerged from a period in which Thailand was under threat from colonisation by Western powers. As a result of a number of unbalanced commercial treaties between the Thai and foreign governments, the jurisdictional sovereignty of the country had been eroded by consular jurisdiction and extraterritoriality. These treaties forced the Thai government to establish a modern legal system as part of its attempts to recover full judicial autonomy. The work of codification of civil and commercial law, which began in 1908 under the direction of French draftsmen, produced the desired result in 1925 only after Phraya Manavarajasevi (Plod na Songkhla) became involved. Plod was instrumental in replacing the French Civil Code of 1804 with the German Civil Code (BGB) of 1900 as the principal model and introducing the Japanese Civil Code (JCC) of 1898 and a copying method which he referred to as the 'Japanese method' to the new Thai-dominated drafting committee. The JCC and the Japanese method were chosen owing to Plod's conviction that the Japanese had established their civil code by copying the BGB. The drafting of the TCCC seems to well illustrate Alan Watson's theory of legal transplants. The draftsmen copied the wording of English translations of provisions of the BGB and the JCC without much concern about their conceptual foundations and finished their task within seven months. But Watson's contention that successful legal borrowing does not require 'a systematic knowledge of the law' must be approached with great caution. Plod was misled by a secondary source he consulted into believing that the JCC was practically a copy of the BGB. In reality, the Japanese Code was influenced by a variety of foreign laws, including German and French law. The drafting committee's lack of knowledge about the rules and concepts they borrowed and the method they adopted may have led to difficulties in interpreting the rules and concepts in question. This chapter will explore Plod's fundamental misconception in the drafting of the TCCC of 1925 and how it affects the interpretation of the transplanted rules of specific performance as a case study.

9.2 THE MAKING OF THE CIVIL AND COMMERCIAL CODE OF THAILAND IN 1925: HISTORICAL REFLECTIONS

Alan Watson believed that law changes mostly by borrowing, and thus for him:

> [Comparative Law] is the study of the relationship of one legal system and its rules with another. The nature of any such relationship, the reasons for the similarities and the

> differences, is discoverable only by a study of the history of the systems or of the rules; hence in the first place, Comparative Law is Legal History concerned with the relationship between systems.[1]

This approach to comparative law may be especially attractive to those who are studying Asian private law. Several modern Asian legal systems emerged from a period when countries were struggling against colonialism, which directly or indirectly resulting in the borrowing of foreign law. A good example is Thai private law, which was entirely founded on foreign private law, mainly German and Japanese law. The process of importing foreign private law in Thailand was not difficult and it did not cause conflicts between the old and the new legal systems. Traditional Thai contracts constituted moral rather than legal obligations and traditional Thai private law did not distinguish between civil and criminal disputes or between contracts and delicts; all of them were mixed. There was, unfortunately, no evidence of commercial law in pre-codification Thai society. Where a developed system of private law was absent, as in this case, superior foreign civil and commercial law was readily accepted. But the question remains as to whether an easy legal transplantation is always successful. Do legal transplants cause theoretical and practical problems with the interpretation of the transplanted rules?

For Watson, the JCC of 1898 is a typical example of a successful legal transplant. Watson believes that 'the first three books of the Code are virtually a translation of the *Bürgerliches Gesetzbuch*'.[2] Whether this view – a mirror of the mainstream perception of the reception of German law in Japan – is valid is crucial to our understanding of the making of the TCCC in general, and the adoption of foreign rules concerning specific performance and damages in Thai law in particular. The reason for this lies in the change of Thai policy in 1925 that involved replacing the French Code civil of 1804 with the BGB of 1900 as the principal model for a new Thai civil and commercial code. After the long, unsuccessful process of codification of private law modelled on the Code civil and directed by French draftsmen, the new drafting committee, with a Thai majority, agreed that the new code would be founded on the BGB and the JCC of 1898 by means of 'copying'. To follow the German Code was clearly the Thai draftsmen's ultimate aim, but the Japanese Code was also chosen because they believed that it was made by 'copying the BGB'.[3] Most of the provisions of the TCCC of 1925, especially Book II on Obligations, were thus copied from the BGB and the JCC of 1898, side by side, without any concern for their conceptual differences.[4]

The modern Thai codes emerged from a period in which the country was under threat from colonisation by Western powers. Thailand's jurisdictional sovereignty had been eroded by consular jurisdiction and the principle of extraterritoriality as a result of a number of unbalanced commercial treaties modelled on the Anglo–Siamese Treaty of 1855 (commonly known as the Bowring Treaty) between the Thai and foreign governments.[5] Increasing contact with the West also provided an opportunity for Thai people to assess their own

1 Alan Watson, *Legal Transplants: An Approach to Comparative Law* (Athens, GA: University of Georgia Press, 2nd ed., 1993) 6.

2 Ibid.

3 Phraya Manavarajasevi, บันทึกคำสัมภาษณ์พระยามานวราชเสวี (Transcript of the Interviews with Phraya Manavarajasevee) (Thammasat University, 1982) 4, 13, 23, 42.

4 For a detailed account of the making of the Civil and Commercial Code of Thailand in 1925, see Munin Pongsapan, 'The Reception of Foreign Private Law in Thailand in 1925: A Case Study of Specific Performance' (PhD Thesis, University of Edinburgh, 2013) 88–121.

5 Francis Bowes Sayre, 'The Passing of Extraterritoriality in Siam' (1928) 22 *American Journal of International Law* 70, 71–2.

weaknesses by comparing their traditional values and systems with what was perceived as Western 'modernity'.[6] Both external pressure and internal motivation accounted for the country's modernisation – a process which began in the second half of the nineteenth century.

Relying heavily on the assistance of foreign advisers, King Chulalongkorn (Rama V) introduced a variety of reforms.[7] Realising that negotiating the abolition of extraterritoriality required the establishment of a modern legal system, the King embarked on a process of judicial reform, beginning with the modernisation of the court system and sending royals and nobles to study law in England from the 1890s. These travelling students became instrumental in establishing modern Thai legal education based on the English system and, in so doing, ensuring the predominance of English law in Thai legal education for the next forty years. Although both the modern Thai courts and the Law School of the Ministry of Justice established in 1897 were dominated by concepts of English common law, King Chulalongkorn chose the civil law system as the model for modern Thai legislation. The codification of criminal law began in 1898 and was successfully concluded by a French-led drafting committee in 1907. The French influence increased when the work of codification of private law commenced in 1908, to the extent that the drafting of the civil and commercial code was from that time onwards completely in the hands of French draftsmen,[8] although their slow progress prompted King Vajiravudh (Rama VI) to add three English-educated Thai jurists to the drafting committee in 1916.

It was not until 1923 that the work of codification underwent a transformation. The drafting committee's composition changed, so that the Thai members outnumbered the French, and the BGB replaced the French Civil Code as the principal model for the TCCC of 1925. The Thai government tactfully rejected the French draft by promulgating it as the TCCC of 1923 but suspending it until it could be assessed by Thai legal professionals. As the government anticipated, the French-drafted Code was severely criticised for its incoherence and incomprehensibility, and this criticism paved the way for the drafting of a new civil and commercial code based on the BGB. All of these changes were masterminded by an English-educated Thai jurist, Phraya Manavarajasevi (Plod), who, while he was studying in England, had been inspired by the success enjoyed by the Japanese in establishing a civil code that was, as he believed, copied from the BGB.

The drafting committee, consisting of three Thais, including Plod, and two Frenchmen, began drafting the new Code in March 1925 and required only seven months to complete Books I and II, which were promulgated as the TCCC of 1925 in November of that year. The Code was first drafted in English before being translated into Thai. Insights into the drafting methods and materials used by the draftsmen of the Code of 1925 were provided by Plod more than fifty years after the Code came into effect when he was giving interviews to a group of academics from the Faculty of Law at Thammasat University in 1981 and 1982. In addition to an account of the manner in which the BGB and the JCC of 1898 took the place of the Code civil, Plod provided information on the sources of German and Japanese provisions upon which almost all of the Thai rules concerning the law of obligations, including the law of

6 Preedee Kasemsup, 'Reception of Law in Thailand – A Buddhist Society' in Masaji Chiba (ed.), *Asian Indigenous Law: In Interaction with Received Law* (Bangkok: King Prajadhipok's Institute, 1986) 291.

7 Chris Baker and Pasuk Phongpaichit, *A History of Thailand* (Cambridge: Cambridge University Press, 2nd ed., 2009) 68–9; M. B. Hooker, 'The "Europeanisation" of Siam's Law 1855–1908' in M. B. Hooker (ed.), *Laws of South-East Asia*, vol. 2 (Singapore: Butterworth, 1988) 552, 564.

8 René Guyon, *The Work of Codification in Siam* (Paris: Imprimerie Nationale 1919) 9–10.

contract, were based. The draftsmen looked at Chung Hui Wang's *The German Civil Code: Translated and Annotated* of 1907 and Ernst Schuster's *The Principles of German Civil Law* of 1907 for the English translation and commentary on the BGB provisions, respectively, while J. E. de Becker's *Annotated Civil Code of Japan* of 1909 and his *The Principles and Practice of the Civil Code of Japan* of 1921 were used as the sources of Japanese rules and their commentary, respectively. These English materials are pivotal in understanding the systems of non-performance and remedies for non-performance in Thai law, as all of the relevant Thai provisions were copied from them.

It is of vital importance to thoroughly examine De Becker's style of writing in his *Annotated Civil Code of Japan* volume II. Other than a brief commentary attached to each Japanese provision, perhaps one of the most outstanding features of this book is its referencing of local and foreign statues. For example, on article 399, the first provision of the Japanese Book of Obligations, De Becker wrote: 'Even a thing which cannot be valued (estimated) in money may be made the subject of an obligation. (In reference *vide* Arts. 90 and 537; also Art. 241 of the German Civil Code)'.[9]

The fact that, apart from the Japanese statutes, the BGB was the only foreign law to which this book made reference arouses much curiosity. To Plod, this information seemed conclusive proof that the JCC of 1898 was a copy of the BGB; he believed that De Becker's referencing derived from the Japanese draftsmen's official documents.[10] The predominance of the BGB by no means raised the Thai draftsman's suspicions and De Becker's perception of the reception of German law in the JCC will be authenticated in the next section.

The reason why the draftsmen of the TCCC of 1925 chose most of the German but only some of the Japanese provisions to serve as the non-performance rules lay in the method employed. The nature of the discussions in the meetings of the drafting committee reflected how the draftsmen imported foreign law.[11] According to the minutes of the meetings, the draftsmen principally relied on two foreign codes – the BGB and the JCC of 1898. They used the English drafts of Books I and II of the old TCCC of 1923 as the basis for Books I and II of the TCCC of 1925 and examined them article by article. They compared the drafts of the former Thai Code with the English translations of the BGB and JCC, written by Wang and De Becker respectively. Most of the TCCC rules were newly imported from the BGB and JCC. The old articles which were consistent with the German and Japanese Codes were preserved (although revised) while those that were inconsistent were removed. Some provisions, which were products of French jurisprudence, were kept when they were consistent with the German and Japanese rules, but the Thai draftsmen, who were critical of the French Code, avoided adopting any new French rules. When it came to a choice between German and Japanese provisions, whichever was linguistically superior prevailed. This drafting methodology resembles Watson's notion of legal borrowing, especially his view that the framing of a single basic code of private law is a relatively easy task[12] and that a successful transplant does not require 'a systematic knowledge of the law'.[13] The draftsmen of the TCCC of 1925 concentrated their attention on linguistics rather than on other aspects of the rules. They

9 J. E. de Becker, *Annotated Civil Code of Japan*, vol. 2 (London: Butterworth, 1909) 6.

10 Manavarajasevi, 'Interviews', 9, 23.

11 See National Archive of Thailand, Office of the Council of State Doc No 3, Book 4(2), 'รายงานการประชุมกรรมการร่างกฎหมาย ตั้งแต่ วัน ที่ 1 กันยายน ถึง 27 มีนาคม พ.ศ. 2467 (Minutes of the Meetings of the Committee of Legislation)' (1 September 1924–27 March 1925); Ibid., Doc No 3, Book 5(1), 'รายงานการประชุมกรรมการร่างกฎหมายตั้งแต่วันที่ 1 สิงหาคม ถึง 27 ตุลาคม พ.ศ. 2468 (Minutes of the Meetings of the Committee of Legislation)' (1 August–27 October 1925).

12 Alan Watson, *Legal Origins and Legal Change* (London: Hambledon Press, 1991) 100–1.

13 Alan Watson, 'Legal Transplants and Law Reform' (1976) 92 *Law Quarterly Review* 79, 79.

did not discuss, for example, the sources of the Japanese model's rules or how they had developed. They were often satisfied with the Thai rules provided that their wording was in line with those of the Japanese and German provisions.[14]

The draftsmen of the TCCC of 1925 seemed to follow the practice of De Becker's *Annotated Civil Code of Japan* by linking each Japanese provision to other provisions, which was mistaken by Plod for an official reference made by the Japanese draftsmen. Plod provided the names of the principal sources from which foreign provisions were copied and claimed to be the compiler of the list of statutes and materials which the draftsmen adopted as models for each provision of the Code of 1925 ('Plod's List of References').[15] Plod's List of References has usually been consulted by those who wish to trace the origin of Books I and II and has sometimes given the impression that the Code of 1925 is a proper product of comparative law. Relying on Plod's List of References, Naoyuki Isogawa, Professor of Civil Law at Kyushu University, remarked that 'TCCC [Thai Civil and Commercial Code of 1925] can more accurately than JCC [Japanese Civil Code of 1898] be characterized *as the genuine fruits of comparative jurisprudence*'.[16]

The prestige of the Japanese success in establishing a civil code may explain why the Thai draftsmen adopted the so-called copying method. If, however, one looks at the social and political climate of Thailand in the early twentieth century, other plausible explanations can be found. When the country was struggling with expanding consular jurisdictions, and to have modern codes would help regain full judicial autonomy, the Thai draftsmen had to resort to the most efficient method for drafting a code – that is, to copy foreign statutes. The French draftsmen's seventeen years of attempting to establish an original code proved to be a failure and the Thai government could not afford to wait any longer. Moreover, the British dominance in Thailand from the beginning of the modernisation process in the mid-nineteenth century meant that the language, culture, and education systems of Great Britain were more familiar to the Thai nobility than those of other Western countries. The primary destination of overseas legal education before 1923 was almost always England. The three Thai draftsmen of the TCCC of 1925 were all English barristers, and none of the draftsmen, including the two French draftsmen, were either educated in, or possessed a systematic knowledge of, German law. This explains why they relied heavily on English materials and could only copy English translations of the German and Japanese Codes.[17]

9.3 THE RECEPTION OF GERMAN LAW IN JAPAN: A MISCONCEPTION

Whether the JCC of 1898 was overwhelmingly influenced by the BGB is the key to our understanding of the TCCC of 1925, because the adoption of Japanese law in the Thai Code was founded on the mainstream conception of the reception of German law in Japan. This fact merits attention.

[14] Munin Pongsapan, 'Reception of Foreign Private Law', 117–21.

[15] See Phraya Manavarajasevi, *อุทาหรณ์สำหรับประมวลกฎหมายแพ่งและพาณิชย์บรรพ 1–2 ฉบับกรมร่างกฎหมาย และที่มาของกฎหมายในประมวลกฎหมายแพ่งและพาณิชย์ บรรพ 1–5* (Department of Legislative Drafting's Instances of Books I and II of the Civil and Commercial Code and Sources of the Provisions of Books I, II, II, IV, and V of the Civil and Commercial Code) (Bangkok University, 1990).

[16] Naoyuki Isogawa, 'The Japanese Civil Code in the World Legal Systems: Toward a Comparative Study of the Asian Civil Law' in Prachoom Chomchai (ed.), *Development of Legal Systems in Asia: Experiences of Japan and Thailand* (Bangkok: Thammasat University Press, 1998) 165. Emphasis added.

[17] For more details about explanations for the adopting of the copying method, see Munin Pongsapan, 'Reception of Foreign Private Law', 107–16

Until Eiichi Hoshino published a paper on the influence of French jurisprudence on the JCC of 1898 in the 1960s and Zentaro Kitagawa conducted extensive research on the reception of German law in Japan in the 1970s, it had long been widely believed that the JCC of 1898 was based predominantly on the BGB[18] and that 'the study of civil law in Japan generally had little relevance to French law'.[19] Despite Nobushige Huzumi and Kenjiro Ume, draftsmen of the JCC of 1898, from the very beginning insisting that the draftsmen 'could not agree to take the law of any one country as an exclusive model'[20] and that 'the new [Japanese] code is based on the French code and other codes of French origin at least as much as it is on the German code',[21] the influence of German law was overwhelming. Indeed, 'Because of the belief that the new Code was based on German Law, Japanese scholars and lawyers have worked hard to digest German civil law theories. The most common destination of Japanese academics studying abroad was Germany, especially before the Second World War'.[22]

Kitagawa reassessed the nature of the reception of German law in Japan before concluding that:

> Generally, [the] reception of foreign law may be divided into two processes: the process of [the] reception of foreign law(s) and the process of [the] assimilation of such law(s). Between these two processes, [the] historical significance and [the] role of the reception of German legal theory lies in the assimilation process which occurred subsequent to the enactment of the Japanese Civil Code. This assimilation process can be regarded as a process for developing Japan's domestic civil law system by casting the product of the mixed-type reception of foreign codes (ie [the] Japanese Civil Code) into a mould imported from a foreign country (ie German jurisprudence).[23]

This reinterpretation of the reception of civil law in Japan sheds new light on our understanding of the influence of German civil law on the JCC of 1898 and on Japanese legal science. It is also the key to the historical and doctrinal reinterpretation of the TCCC of 1925 and, more specifically, the rules concerning specific performance and damages. We can now understand that De Becker's *Annotated Civil Code of Japan* was most likely a product of the so-called 'reception of German legal theory' and this explains why the BGB was the only foreign statute to which this book referred. We can also discover that, because of De Becker's misleading reference, Plod erroneously believed that the JCC was a copy of the BGB.[24]

18 Even among Western scholars. For example, see Frederic William Maitland, 'The Making of the German Civil Code' in H. A. L. Fisher (ed.), *The Collected Papers of Frederic William Maitland*, vol. 3 (Cambridge: Cambridge University Press, 1911) 484–5; Watson, 'Legal Transplants and Law Reform', 83; K. Zweigert and H. K ötz, *An Introduction to Comparative Law* (Tony Weir trans.) (Oxford: Clarendon Press, 3rd ed., 1998) 298.

19 Taro Kogayu, 'French Law Research in the Study of Civil Law in Japan' in Zentaro Kitagawa and Karl Riesenhuber (eds.), *The Identity of German and Japanese Civil Law in Comparative Perspectives* (Berlin: De Gruyter Recht, 2007) 92.

20 Nobushige Huzumi, *The New Japanese Civil Code as Material for the Study of Comparative Jurisprudence* (Tokyo: Tokyo Printing, 1904) 10.

21 Kenjiro Ume's Speech at the French Civil Code Centenary Celebrations in 1904 at the Faculty of Law of the Imperial University of Tokyo, quoted in Yoshiyuki Noda, *Introduction to Japanese Law* (Anthony H. Angelo trans.) (Tokyo: University of Tokyo Press, 1976) 52.

22 Hiroshi Oda, *Japanese Law* (Oxford: Oxford University Press, 3rd ed., 2009) 666. See also Kenzo Takayanagi, 'Occidental Legal Ideas in Japan: Their Reception and Influence' (1930) 3 *Pacific Affairs* 740, 747.

23 Zentaro Kitagawa, 'Japanese Civil Law and German Law – From the Viewpoint of Comparative Law' in Zentaro Kitagawa and Karl Riesenhuber (eds.), *The Identity of German and Japanese Civil Law in Comparative Perspectives* (Berlin: De Gruyter Recht, 2007) 33–4.

24 For more details in the tracing of De Becker's *Annotated Civil Code of Japan* and an examination of Plod's perception of the reception of German law in Japan, see Munin Pongsapan, 'Reception of Foreign Private Law', 159–63.

9.4 LEGAL EDUCATION AND THE INTERPRETATION OF PRIVATE LAW IN THAILAND

Despite the adoption of the civilian system for the reform of legislation, the first thirty years of legal education in Thailand were dominated by English law. Established in 1897, the Law School of the Ministry of Justice was the first and only law school in Thailand before it was transferred briefly to Chulalongkorn University in 1933 and then permanently to Thammasat University in 1934. This law school was established and run by Thai jurists who had been educated in England in accordance with the English common law and undoubtedly its students, who became the first generations of judges and lawyers, received an English style legal education. Legal materials, which before the mid-nineteenth century were kept away from the public, were by no means sufficient for the resolution of the growing number of commercial disputes. The courts often applied English legal principles on a case by case basis.[25]

The administration of the Law School and its legal education programmes underwent a significant change in 1923 only after the French offered to relax the Franco–Siamese Treaty, including the extraterritorial term, in exchange for increasing the role of French legal advisors in the School's management, codification, and the administration of justice. This change, along with the progress in codification, forced the Thai government to prepare for the full enforcement of the modern codes. Accordingly, a small number of Thai students were sent to study law in France. One of them, Pridi Banomyong (1900–83), became the mastermind behind the Revolution of 1932, which confined the monarch to the constitution, and the founder of Thammasat University, which monopolised legal education until the early 1970s, when Thailand's second and third law schools emerged.[26] Pridi's admirers followed in his footsteps to receive their higher legal education in France.

At Thammasat University, French law was from the beginning predominant in the fields of private and public law. Most of the texts on private law, which are surprisingly small in number – especially the law of obligations and law of contract, were written in accordance with French jurisprudence. Until now, nothing in the Thai legal literature on the law of obligations has been primarily written in accordance with German and Japanese legal science in attempting to understand the Thai rules, despite the fact that Book II on Obligations of the TCCC was overwhelmingly influenced by the German and Japanese Civil Codes.[27] The early history of modern Thai private law is bizarrely mixed; the private law code based on German law was taught in accordance with French jurisprudence by professors trained in English law.

9.5 THE DRAFTING OF SPECIFIC PERFORMANCE PROVISIONS: A CASE STUDY

Close scrutiny of the drafting of provisions of the TCCC of 1925 may shed light on how the drafting committee employed the Japanese method and their fundamental misconception. The drafting of specific performance provisions is chosen as a case study.

The table above clearly shows that most of the draft provisions were simply replicas of their model rules. There are some linguistic alterations in section 213 TCCC (1925), a copy of De

[25] National Archive of Thailand, Ministry of Justice Doc No Yor 12 1/8, 'บันทึกนายยอร์ช ปาดูซ์ เรื่องข้อเสนอในการจัดทำประมวลกฎหมายแพ่งและพาณิชย์ (Georges Padoux's Proposal on the Drafting of the Civil and Commercial Code)' (20 July 1909) 15–16.

[26] Ramkamhaeng Open University Faculty of Law (1971) and Chulalongkorn University Faculty of Law (1972).

[27] For further details about legal education in Thailand, see Munin Pongsapan, 'Legal Studies at Thammasat University: A Microcosm of the Development of Thai Legal Education' in Andrew Harding, Jiaxiang Hu and Maartje de Visser (eds.), Legal Education in Asia: From Limitation to Innovation (Leiden: Brill Nijhoff 2017) 299–317.

Becker's translation of Article 415 JCC (1898), concerning compulsory performance, which does not change the literal meaning of the model provision, while section 215 TCCC (1925) is a partial copy of De Becker's translation of Article 415 JCC. The second part of Article 415 JCC relating to impossibility of performance was ignored since it was contained in separate provisions, namely sections 218 and 219 TCCC (1925), modelled on the BGB (1900). The draftsmen's discussion of the provisions in the table above reflects their general method for drafting the TCCC (1925): they focused more on the wordings of the model rules than their conceptual foundations. According to the meeting minutes, some typical words and phrases, for example, 'lengthy wording' and 'articulate wording', were used to show the draftsmen's judgement about the discussed model rules.[28] This illustrates the draftsmen's emphasis on the linguistic aspect of the model rules.

The draftsmen's discussion about the drafting of the provisions relating to the right to specific performance and compensation for damage at the drafting meeting on 24 August 1925 illustrates their adherence to the linguistic aspect of the rules. The meeting reviewed certain provisions of the old Civil and Commercial Code (TCCC 1923), namely sections 331 to 334 TCCC (1923),[29] which concern specific performance, in comparison with Article 414 JCC, Articles 956 and 957 of the Brazilian Civil Code, and sections 249 and 251 BGB. A Thai draftsman proposed that Article 414 JCC should be adopted since it was similar to the old Thai provisions (sections 331 to 334 of the TCCC (1923)), but that the word 'wilfully'[30] in the Japanese model seemed unnecessary and should be removed.[31] A French draftsman suggested that the phrase 'under the expense of the debtor' should be added to the draft of the new provision to clarify the wording. The meeting approved both proposals to draft a provision (section 213 TCCC (1925)) relating to specific performance modelled on Article 414 JCC with a few alterations, and agreed to drop sections 331 to 334 TCCC (1923).[32]

Other than these two proposals, there was no record of further discussion of the drafting of section 213 TCCC (1925) at the meeting on 24 August. However, at the meeting on 27 August, Plod, after reviewing the wording of the draft of section 213 TCCC (1925) of 24 August, suggested that the drafting committee should reconsider it. He proposed that, since in English law the term 'specific performance' used in the draft of 24 August had a narrow meaning, to cover the cases of restitution in kind as stated in sections 249 and 251 BGB, it

[28] National Archive of Thailand, Office of the Council of State Doc No 3(1) Books 5(1)(2), 'รายงานการประชุมกรรมการร่างกฎหมาย (The Minutes of the Meetings of the Committee of Legislation)' (3 March – 26 October 1925). The Minutes of the Meetings of the Committee of Legislation are, hereinafter, referred as 'Meeting Minutes'. See, for example, 'Meeting Minutes' (18 August 1925) 2–3.

[29] TCCC of 1923 [translations by Munin Pongsapan]; section 331: 'Where specific performance is possible and desirable the Court may at its discretion sanction the creditor's demand for specific performance'.
section 332: 'If the subject of the obligation is the doing of an act, the creditor may apply to the Court to have it done by a third person at the debtor's expense'.
TCCC of 1923, section 333: 'If the subject of the obligation is to do a juristic act or give a consent, the Court may appoint a third person to act on behalf of the debtor or a judgment may be substituted for a declaration of intention by the debtor'.
TCCC of 1923, section 334: 'If the subject of the obligation is the forbearance from an act, the Court may order that what has been done be removed at the expense of the debtor and impose proper measures adopted for the future'.

[30] This word does not exist in De Becker's translation of Article 414. In fact, De Becker used the term 'voluntarily'. It is more likely that the recorder of the meeting wrote down the wrong word or otherwise Chitr made a mistake in saying the wrong word.

[31] 'Meeting Minutes' (24 August 1925) 2.

[32] Ibid., 2–3.

should be replaced by the term 'compulsory performance' as used by De Becker in his translation of Article 414 JCC. He said:

> As I have examined the draft of s 20 [section 213 TCCC (1925)], I think that the term 'specific performance' according to English law has a too narrow meaning, and I therefore propose that we change it to 'compulsory performance' to accord with Art 414 of the Japanese Civil Code. Based on Sections 249 and 251 of the German Civil Code, this Japanese provision includes 'restitution in kind'.[33]

The meeting approved Plod's proposal. (See the comparison between section 213 TCCC (1925) and Article 414 JCC from the table above.) This proposal proves that Plod relied on De Becker's sources of Article 414 JCC, which referred to sections 249 and 251 BGB.

The draftsmen of the TCCC of 1925 not only borrowed the Japanese rule of specific performance (Article 414 JCC) but also copied the German provision, section 241 BGB, which lays the foundation of the concept of specific performance, word for word (see the comparison in the following table). This German provision was not adopted by the Japanese draftsmen who, instead, relied heavily on French law to establish the rule of specific performance in Article 414 JCC. A question arises as to how the two transplanted rules of specific performance were interpreted and whether they coordinate harmoniously in framing a theoretical understanding of specific performance in Thai law after the reception.

The meeting minutes of 18 August show that a Thai draftsman proposed that the first provision of Book II on obligations should be copied from section 241 BGB. Unfortunately, there was no record of discussion as to why he chose this German provision. There was, however, a debate over the choosing of a model. A French draftsman argued against copying section 241 BGB and suggested that the first article of the Thai obligations chapter should be better based on Article 399 JCC,[34] which is the first provision of its Book III on obligations. The majority of the draftsmen voted in favour of the Thai draftsman's proposal.[35] The reason for adopting section 241 BGB may be that the draftsmen needed a provision to define the term 'obligation', and this German provision seemed to meet the need. Unfortunately, the method of drafting deprived the draftsmen of the opportunity to explore the principles behind section 241 BGB as well as its implications on the concept of specific performance in German law. For this reason, we can guess the answer to the question above: that the draftsmen intended to use section 241 BGB simply as the definition of the term 'obligations' in the Code of 1925 and, therefore, never saw the underlying principles behind the words and the problem of having conflicting rules of specific performance in the same place, that is, section 241 BGB and Article 414 JCC.

9.6 THE THEORETICAL UNDERSTANDING OF THE TRANSPLANTED RULES OF SPECIFIC PERFORMANCE IN THAI LAW

Although their adherence to the BGB in drafting the provisions concerning non-performance seems to suggest that the draftsmen of the Code of 1925 intended to base the Thai system of

[33] Ibid., (27 August 1925) 3, translation by Munin Pongsapan.

[34] JCC of 1898, art. 399: 'Even a thing which cannot be valued (estimated) in money may be made the subject of an obligation' in De Becker, *Annotated Civil Code of Japan*, vol. 2, 6.

[35] 'Meeting Minutes' (18 August 1925) 2.

non-performance on German law, their adoption of the copying method deprived them of the chance to discuss the theoretical basis of the relevant provisions. This has some significant effects on the way Thai scholars and lawyers have understood the concept of specific performance afterwards. While the Japanese choose to systematise and explain its rules of non-performance and remedies for non-performance mainly according to German law, the academic interpretation of the borrowed rules of the same area of law in Thailand is disoriented and reflects diversity of the legal education backgrounds among the interpreters as well as their occasional disregard of historical and comparative approaches to researching the relevant rules.

The coexistence of sections 194 and 213 TCCC (1925) in the system of non-performance makes it difficult to identify the character of specific performance in Thai law because the former is a replica of a German provision, while the latter was copied from a Japanese provision which appears to be French in nature. This complexity leads to some undesirable results,[36] which include that the concept of specific performance has been explained and understood more within the scope of procedural law than of substantive law. Despite the fact that Thai scholars usually link section 194 TCCC (1925), which is a copy of section 241 BGB, with section 213 TCCC (1925), which is a copy of Article 414 JCC, they perceive specific performance as the *enforcement* of claims rather than 'a right conferred by substantive law', the latter being the common interpretation of the concept of specific performance in Germany.[37] This is not surprising since the wording of section 213 TCCC (1925) encourages interpreters to think that way and the model rule, Article 414 JCC, is similarly explained by Japanese scholars.[38] Furthermore, the phrase 'when the nature of an obligation does not permit of compulsory performance' always prompts interpreters to distinguish between obligations to do, not to do, and obligations to give to determine whether the creditor is entitled to the right to specific performance.

It is worth noting that in his *Annotated Civil Code of Japan*, De Becker linked Article 414 to Article 415 of the same Code, Articles 73 to 76 of the Japanese Code of Civil Procedure, and sections 249 and 251 of the BGB.[39] The BGB is the only foreign law to which De Becker referred; he mentioned none of provisions of the French Civil Code. However, having considered the texts of both Article 414 JCC, at least two noticeable features stand out. First, Article 414 JCC appears to be a procedural rather than a substantive rule. It prescribes *methods* for enforcing performance where the debtor does not perform his obligation. This feature certainly does not derive from the BGB, which deals with only the substantive aspect

36 The complexity of the system of remedies for non-performance in Thai law is reflected in Prachoom Chomchai's statement on a choice of remedies for non-performance that '[t]he uncertainty of the codified law is . . . such that one cannot be sure whether the foregoing depicts a genuine option or simply a scenario or sequence of proceedings to be observed'. Prachoom Chomchai, 'Introduction' in Prachoom Chomchai (ed.), *Development of Legal Systems in Asia: Experiences of Japan and Thailand* (Bangkok: Thammasat University Press, 1998) 80.

37 Florian Faust and Volker Wiese, 'Specific Performance: A German Perspective' in J. M. Smits and others (eds.), *Specific Performance in Contract Law: National and Other Perspectives* (Antwerp: Intersentia, 2008) 49.

38 See Kitagawa, 'Japanese Civil Law and German Law – From the Viewpoint of Comparative Law' in Zentaro Kitagawa and Karl R iesenhuber (eds.), *The Identity of German and Japanese Civil Law in Comparative Perspectives* (Berlin: De Gruyter Recht, 2007) 21–3. See also Kiyoshi Igarashi, *Einführung in das japanische Recht* (Darmstadt: Wissenschaftliche Buchgesellschaft, 1990) 5; Noda, *Introduction to Japanese Law*, 51.

39 JCC of 1898, Article 415 in De Becker, *Annotated Civil Code of Japan*, vol. 2, 25.

of specific performance. In fact, the provisions concerning the enforcement of performance are contained in the German Civil Procedure Code. Second, Article 414 JCC recognises the distinction between obligations to give and obligations to do and not to do, which is a main characteristic of the French law of obligations. The enforcement of performance in Article 414 appears to accord with this distinction. This feature is clearly not a main feature of the law of obligations in the BGB. These two features point to the conclusion that Articles 414 and 415 JCC were not mainly based on the BGB provisions that De Becker's book refers to (see Article 414 JCC in Table 9.1 above).

The following hypothetical may help illustrate the conflicting German and Japanese (French-based) approaches to specific performance. A hired B to clean her house. B did not perform his obligation within the time agreed. Does A have the right to demand specific performance from B? If this question is raised under the German Civil Code, German lawyers would agree that section 194 BGB gives A the right to demand specific performance from B regardless of being an obligation to do something. However, Japanese lawyers may be reluctant to reach the same conclusion as Article 414 JCC does not grant specific performance where the nature of obligation does not permit it and they generally agree that the nature of obligations to do something does not normally permit specific performance. What about the answer under Thai law? The existence of section 194 TCCC (1925), a copy of section 241 BGB, has not convinced Thai lawyers to adopt German jurisprudence to conceptualise specific performance fully, perhaps because the German provision is too abstract and its true meaning is only noticeable to those who have knowledge of German civil law. They mainly view section 194 TCCC (1925) as the definition of the term 'obligations'. The Thai answer seems to be in line with the Japanese one. This clearly illustrates that the borrowing of section 241 BGB did not bring its original meaning from German law to the new environment.

Since both Thailand and Japan separate their substantive and procedural codes of civil law, the German approach may offer a more systematic and sensible explanation for specific performance. From a perspective of substantive law, specific performance as the primary right or remedy for non-performance is always available to the creditor no matter whether it is an obligation to give something, an obligation to do something, or an obligation not to do something. Therefore, from the hypothetical above, A can always demand B to perform the obligation to clean the house. However, whether the court will permit A to enforce performance specifically is a question of procedural law and must be dealt with by the civil procedure code. Based on the German system of substantive law, the distinction between the natures of obligation is meaningless and thus section 213 TCCC (1925) and Article 414 JCC should not be included in the substantive law codes.

It is ironic that the Thai draftsmen, who were critical of French law, uncritically adopted the Japanese provision that was largely based on French legal concepts to establish section 213 TCCC (1925). Their use of the copying method for drafting the Thai rules on specific performance has left a legacy of theoretical disorientation: while many leading Thai jurists have German law in mind, their interpretation points the way towards French law. The position of the current system of remedies for non-performance, especially specific performance, seems to be ambiguous and unfortunate. The time is ripe for Thai academics and lawyers to explore the possibilities of reforming not only the system of specific performance, but also the entire system of the law of obligations in the Code of 1925 before it reaches its century in 2025.

TABLE 9.1 *Comparisons between TCCC of 1925 provisions and foreign models relating to non-performance and remedies for non-performance*

English drafts of the TCCC of 1925	Foreign models
s. 194 By virtue of an obligation the creditor is entitled to claim performance from the debtor. The performance may consist in a forbearance. (G.241)[1]	BGB (1900) s. 241 By virtue of an obligation the creditor is entitled to claim performance from the debtor. The performance may consist in a forbearance.[2]
s. 203 If a time for performance is neither fixed nor to be inferred from the circumstances, the creditor may demand the performance forthwith, and the debtor may perform this part forthwith. If a time is fixed it is to be presumed, in case of doubt, that the creditor may not demand the performance before that time; the debtor, however, may perform earlier. (G. 271)[3]	BGB (1900) s. 271 If a time for performance is neither fixed nor to be inferred from the circumstances, the creditor may demand the performance forthwith, and the debtor may performance his part forthwith. If a time is fixed it is to be presumed, in case of doubt, that the creditor may not demand performance before that time; the debtor, however, may perform earlier.[4]
s. 204 If the debtor does not perform after warning given by the creditor after maturity, he is in default through the warning. If a time by the calendar is fixed for the performance, the debtor is in default without warning if the does not perform at the fixed time. The same rule applies if a notice is required to precede the performance, and the time is fixed in such manner that it may be reckoned by the calendar from the time of notice. (C/P G.284; S.O. 102)[5]	BGB (1900) s. 284 If the debtor does not perform after warning given by the creditor after maturity, he is in default through the warning. Bringing and action for the performance and the service of an order for payment in hortatory process are equivalent to warning. If the time by the calendar is fixed for the performance, the debtor is in default without warning if he does not perform at the fixed time. The same rule applies if a notice is required to precede the performance, and the time is fixed in such manner that it may be reckoned by the calendar from the time of notice.[6]
s. 205 The debtor is not in default so long as the performance is not effected in consequence of a circumstance for which he is not responsible. (G.285)[7]	BGB (1900) s. 285 The debtor is not in default so long as the performance is not effected in consequence of a circumstance for which is not responsible.[8]

TABLE 9.1 *(Continued)*

English drafts of the TCCC of 1925	Foreign models
s. 213 If the debtor fails to perform his obligation, the creditor may make a demand to the Court for compulsory performance; except where the nature of the obligation does not permit it. When the nature of an obligation does not permit of compulsory performance, if the subject of the obligation is the doing of an act, the creditor may apply to the Court to have it done by a third person at the debtor's expense but if the subject of the obligation is the doing of a juristic act, a judgment may be substituted for a declaration of intention by the debtor. As to an obligation whose subject is the forbearance from an act, the creditor may demand the removal of what has been done at the expense of the debtor and have proper measures adopted for the future. The provisions of the foregoing paragraphs do not affect the right to claim damages. (C/P old text 331–334; C/P J.414; Restitution in kind G.249–251 included in this section).[9]	JCC (1898), Art. 414 When a debtor does not voluntarily perform the obligation, the creditor may make a demand for compulsory performance to the Court, unless the nature of the obligation does not permit it. When the nature of the obligation does not permit of compulsory performance, if the obligation has the performance of an act for its subject, the creditor may demand the Court to cause at a third person to do the same at the expense of the debtor; but with regard to an obligation which has a juristic act for its subject, a judgment may be substituted for an expression of intention by the debtor. With regard to an obligation which has a forbearance for its subject the creditor may demand the removal of what has been done at the expense of the debtor and have proper measures adopted for the future. The provisions of the preceding three Paragraphs do not affect a demand for compensation for damages [sic]. (In reference vide Art. 415 and the Code of Civil Procedure Art. 73–76; Also Arts. 249 and 251 of the German Civil Code.)[10]
s 215 When the debtor does not perform the obligation in accordance with the true intent and purpose of the same, the creditor may claim compensation for any damage caused there by. (C/P J.415)[11]	JCC (1898), Art. 415 When the debtor does not perform the obligation in accordance with the true intent and purpose of the same (*in forma specifica*), the creditor may demand compensation for accruing damage. The same applies when performance has become impossible owing to a cause attributable to the debtor. (In reference vide Art. 414; also Arts. 250, 286, and 325 of the German Civil Code.)[12]

s. 218 When the performance becomes impossible in consequence of a circumstance for which the debtor is responsible, the debtor shall compensate the creditor for any damage arising from the non-performance. In case of a partial impossibility the creditor may, by declining the still possible part of the performance, demand compensation for non-performance of the entire obligation, if the still possible part of performance is useless to him. (G.280)[13]	BGB (1900) s. 280 Where the performance becomes impossible in consequence of a circumstance for which the debtor is responsible, the debtor shall compensate the creditor for any damage arising from the non-performance. In case of partial impossibility the creditor may, by declining the still possible part of performance, demand compensation for non-performance of the entire obligation, if he has no interest in the partial performance. The provisions of 346 to 356 applicable to the contractual right of rescission apply mutatis mutandis *(f)*.[14]
s. 219 The debtor is relieved from his obligation to perform if the performance becomes impossible in consequence of a circumstance for which he is not responsible occurring after the creation of the obligation. If the debtor, after the creation of the obligation, becomes unable to perform, it is equivalent to a circumstance rendering the performance impossible. (G.275)[15]	BGB (1900) s. 275 The debtor is relieved from this obligation to perform if the performance becomes impossible in consequence of a circumstance for which he is not responsible *(z)* occurring after the creation of the obligation *(a)*. If the debtor, after the creation of the obligation, becomes unable to perform, it is equivalent to a circumstance rendering the performance impossible *(b)*.[16]

1 Office of the Council of State, Doc No 79, 'การตรวจแก้ร่างประมวลกฎหมายแพ่งและพาณิชย์ บรรพ 1 และ บรรพ 2 (The Book of the Revised Drafts)' (1925) 103.
2 Chung Hui Wang, *The German Civil Code: Translated and Annotated* (London: Stevens and Sons, 1907) 55.
3 'Book of the Revised Drafts', 106.
4 Wang, *German Civil Code*, 61.
5 'Book of the Revised Drafts', 106.
6 Wang, *German Civil Code*, 64–5.
7 'Book of the Revised Drafts', 107.
8 Wang, *German Civil Code*, 65.
9 'Book of the Revised Drafts', 109.
10 De Becker, *Annotated Civil Code of Japan*, vol. 2, 22.
11 'Book of the Revised Drafts', 109.
12 De Becker, *Annotated Civil Code of Japan*, vol. 2, 25.
13 'Book of the Revised Drafts', 110.
14 Wang, *German Civil Code*, 63–4.
15 'Book of the Revised Drafts', 111.
16 Wang, *German Civil Code*, 62.

TABLE 9.2 *Comparison between the English draft of section 194 TCCC (1925) and its foreign model*

English draft of section 194 TCCC (1925)	Wang's translation of section 241 BGB (1900)
By virtue of an obligation the creditor is entitled to claim performance from the debtor. The performance may consist in a forbearance. (G.241).[1]	By virtue of an obligation the creditor is entitled to claim performance from the debtor. The performance may consist in a forbearance.[2]

[1] 'Book of the Revised Drafts' 103.
[2] Wang, *German Civil Code* 55.

9.7 COMPARATIVE LAW AND LEGAL HISTORY

From the process of receiving foreign private law to the process of interpreting the law received in Thailand, there have always been problems with the use of comparative law.[40] If there were major failures in the making of the Code of 1925, an absence of a proper use of comparative law must be one of them. Plod himself admitted that the Code of 1925 was made mostly by copying and the draftsmen's claim that it was a product of comparative law was overstated.[41] It was unfortunate that during the time of codification comparative law was only a fledgling legal science. It did not enjoy the international academic attention it does today. However, this does not excuse ignoring careful comparisons, which means not only a careful scrutiny of the underlying principles of the rules to be adopted and their functions but also means being aware of their historical development. This chapter affirms that legal history is indispensable for those who make use of comparative law for the sake of borrowing. It proves that the flaws in the borrowing of foreign rules were caused by uncritically copying and by being unaware of misleading information in secondary sources. The problems therefore resulted from an absence of a proper use of comparative and historical methods. Had the draftsmen of the Code of 1925 traced the origin of the Japanese rules adopted they would have discovered that some of them did not derive from the BGB. Had they had a systematic knowledge of German private law they would have found that there is a distinction between the German and French concepts of specific performance. One can reasonably argue that the draftsmen could not always foresee the future theoretical and practical problems of the law they made and that interpretation varies depending on the interpreter's conception about the rule. It can hardly be denied that the draftsmen's sufficient knowledge of law would have prevented some potential problems which might arise from conflicting concepts.

[40] Andrew Harding viewed the problem of the use of comparative law as a common problem in Southeast Asia. According to Harding, '[t]he fundamental conceptual problem confronting those working on law in South East Asia is that the conventions of comparative law are often inadequate to convey South East Asian legal reality; what comparative law therefore lacks … is a suitably flexible and sophisticated grammar of the discourse'. Andrew Harding, 'Comparative Law and Legal Transplatation in South East Asia: Making Sense of the "Nomic Din"' in David Nelken and Johannes Feest (eds.), *Adapting Legal Cultures* (Oxford: Hart Publishing, 2001) 203.

[41] Phraya Manavarajasevi, 'คำรำลึกของพระยามานวราชเสวี (ปลอด วิเชียร ณ สงขลา) (Recollection of Phraya Manavarajasevi)' in The Council of State of Thailand (ed.), *ครบรอบ 48 ปี 2524 สำนักงานคณะกรรมการกฤษฎีกา* (48 Years of the Council of State (BE 2524)) (Council of State of Thailand 1981) 5.

9.8 CONCLUSION

On the surface, the making of the TCCC of 1925 seems to be an excellent example of Alan Watson's theory of legal transplants.[42] It matches many of his observations on legal change and does so better even than the reception of foreign civil law in Japan, one of his typical examples. Watson suggested that successful legal borrowing does not require 'a systematic knowledge of the law'[43] and that 'the transplanting of legal rules is socially easy ... [they] move easily and are accepted into the system without too great difficulty'.[44] This characterisation of legal change can be identified in the modernisation of Thai private law in 1925. While the Japanese took great interest when employing comparative methods in establishing their original code of law, the Thai draftsmen devoted their attention to copying the wording of foreign rules. Consequently, they neglected the historical and doctrinal foundations of the rules. The draftsmen of the TCCC of 1925 treated legal rules as if they were a substance which could be picked up and implanted very easily. It is clear that they understood the rules adopted mainly from their literal meaning and, as a result, some misconceptions occurred. It is hard to believe that a group of five draftsmen, three of whom were busy Thai officials who held top positions in the judiciary and in government departments, spent only approximately seven months drafting the first two books of the TCCC of 1925. However, with the help of the copy-and-paste method, codification happened quickly. On the one hand, it is fair and acceptable to acknowledge their success in establishing the Thai Civil and Commercial Code whose provisions have mostly remained intact. Book II on obligations, in particular, has remained completely unchanged. On the other hand, their fundamental misconception in the drafting process of the TCCC of 1925 has caused considerable difficulties in understanding and applying many of its rules and throws into doubt the success of the reception of foreign private law in Thailand.

42 See Harding, 'Comparative Law and Legal Transplantation in South East Asia' 213.

43 Watson, 'Legal Transplants and Law Reform', 79.

44 Watson, *Legal Transplants: An Approach to Comparative Law*, 99.

10

The Modernisation of Thai Criminal Law

From the 1908 Penal Code to the 1956 Criminal Code

Kanaphon Chanhom

The Siamese Penal Code is unique in its own way, and French, English, Siamese and Japanese influences have combined to produce a body of law, which it is hoped will suit the conditions of the country.[1]

This chapter discusses the modernisation process of criminal law in Thailand[2] from King Chulalongkorn's reign (1868–1910) to the current Criminal Code of 1956. During that time, several factors led Thailand to reform its law and administration, including pressure from foreign nations and the needs of the modern Thai society. Criminal law was the first area of law to be codified because it primarily affected an individual's fundamental rights. Committees were appointed to draft the Penal Code, the first systematic legal code in Thailand. Although there were many obstacles during the process of drafting, the Penal Code was finally promulgated and entered into force in 1908. This chapter argues that although the Penal Code of 1908 was not perfectly drafted, it was a steppingstone for modernisation of the Thai legal system, harmonised by Siamese legal and Western legal concepts to fit the new political, economic, and social conditions in the modernisation period, and later fulfilled by academic as well as court opinions, leading to further development of the current Criminal Code.

The chapter starts by exploring the pre-modern criminal law up to the first half of the nineteenth century. In this period, Indian law was incorporated with traditional law to fit the custom and beliefs of the Siamese people. It then discusses important factors that forced Thailand to modernise its law and administration of justice. Next, the chapter describes the drafting process of the 1908 Penal Code, the first systematic and modern legal code in Thailand, to reveal some problems during the drafting process. It further discusses the consequences of the Penal Code's drafting process, especially the fulfilment by scholars and courts of legal concepts to fit the new political and social conditions. Finally, the chapter discusses the drafting process of the 1956 Criminal Code.

10.1 PRE-MODERN CRIMINAL LAW

This chapter divides the pre-modern criminal law into three periods: pre-Sukhothai (before the thirteenth century); Sukhothai (thirteenth to fifteenth centuries); and Ayutthaya to Early Bangkok Periods (fourteenth to nineteenth centuries).

Like other legal systems, the pre-modern Siamese criminal law was not complex and began with the implementation of customary law, which was the most important source of law

[1] Ministry of Justice, *Report for the Year 125 (1906–07)* (Bangkok: Ministry of Justice, 1907) 9.

[2] Thailand was officially called 'Siam' until 1939.

developed from the pre-Sukhothai period.[3] Criminal policy during this period mainly focused on the protection of social interests. Therefore, merely harmful conduct against the society, but not against individuals, was considered criminal offences, especially treason, incest, and witchcraft.[4]

Customary law played an important role until the advent of Indian civilisation from the last century BCE. To enhance their dignity and empower themselves, the rulers in ancient Southeast Asia imported into their kingdoms Indian civilisation[5] led by Buddhist monks and Brahmins.[6] Indian legal science, together with the *dharmaśātra*, was brought into the kingdoms and adapted to local customs and beliefs. Being influenced by the Buddhist idea, a well-known empire, Dvaravati of the Mon (sixth to eleventh centuries), developed its legal system based on the *dharmaśāstra*. The new version of the *dharmaśāstra*, which was called *manudharmmasattham*,[7] was then spread over the territory of current Thailand.[8]

The Sukhothai Kingdom was founded in 1238 to be independent of the Khmer Empire. The sources of law in the Sukhothai Kingdom were the *dharmaśāstra*, and royal ordinances called the *rachaśāstra*.[9] A stone inscription made in the Sukhothai period referred to these two types of law. The primary purpose of this law was to place a duty on the people to help each other for the protection of their subordinates or property. The provisions stated that whoever did not assist his neighbours to arrest an abductor and robber would be punished or have to make compensation according to the *dharmaśāstra* and *rachaśāstra*.[10] However, other types of legal documents were not discovered. They might have been written on different kinds of material other than stone and damaged from time to time.

The Ayutthaya to the Early Bangkok Period was defined by its three capital cities: Ayutthaya (1350–1767), Thonburi (1767–82), and early Bangkok (1782–1855). Almost the same kinds of law were enforced and applied in these three capitals.

In addition to the *dharmaśāstra* written laws in this period were changed into the form of *rachaśāstra*. Under a more complicated society, the *rachaśāstra* concretely criminalised what kinds of action fulfilled the definitional elements of an offence and imposed penalties on the offender. Criminal offences in the *rachaśāstra* included both public and individual offences, such as insurrection, avoiding service, corruption, robbery, abduction, and quarrelling. Criminal law in this period was fairly comprehensive and useful. Many foreigners proved that the Thai pre-modern law, including criminal law, was humane and compatible with the nature and beliefs of local people under their social conditions.[11]

The content of the law was therefore quite static for hundreds of years. King Rama I (1782–1809), the founder of the Bangkok capital, ordered the reform of all kinds of laws in 1804. The law reform was merely purification of the statutes in the Ayutthaya Period in the form of the Three Seals Code. Criminal law and criminal justice were not changed as a result

3 Luang Sakonsattayathorn, 'Introduction to Criminology' (1932) 7 *Nitisarn* 740.
4 Ibid.
5 G. Cœdès, *People in Indo-China Peninsula* (Panya Borisoot tr., Bangkok: Thai Wattana Panich, 1982) 46.
6 Bang-orn Piyaphan, *History of South-East Asia* (Bangkok: Odian Store, 1994) 61–2.
7 R. Lingat, 'Evolution of the Concept of Law in Burman and Siam' (1950) 38 *Journal of the Siam Society* 15–16.
8 D. E. G. Hall, *A History of South-East Asia* (4th ed., London: Macmillan, 1981) 183.
9 For further discussion, see Chapter 3, this volume.
10 Fine Arts Department, *Stone Inscriptions in the Sukhothai Period* (Bangkok: Fine Art Department, 1984) 157–9.
11 See Jean-Baptiste Pallegoix, *Description of the Thai Kingdom or Siam: Thailand under King Mongkut* (Walter E. J. Tips, tr., Bangkok: White Lotus, 2000) 189; Walter E. J. Tips (tr) Karl Döhring, *The Country and People of Siam* (Bangkok: White Lotus, 1999) 34.

of this codification, and this led to the modernisation of criminal law and administration during King Chulalongkorn's reign (1868–1910).[12]

10.2 DRIVING FORCES IN THE MODERNISATION OF CRIMINAL LAW

The most important reason for the modernisation of criminal law by King Chulalongkorn was the foreign threat, leading to the Bowring Treaty (1855)[13] and other similar treaties[14] that were concluded during the reign of King Mongkut (1851–68), King Chulalongkorn's father.

Great Britain, after the successful expansion of its power in Southeast Asia, felt that the conditions in the first Anglo-Siamese treaty (the Burney Treaty) in 1826 were insufficient to secure British interests. It then tried to force Thailand to change its policy to freer trade.[15] Having seen the Burmese experience of fighting against Great Britain until it was eventually colonised, King Mongkut then signed the Bowring Treaty to maintain the sovereignty of Thailand. The last country that received the extraterritorial rights from Thailand was Japan by a protocol annexed to the Japanese Treaty of Friendship and Commerce in 1898.[16] These treaties essentially granted the foreign nations extraterritorial rights over their subjects in Thailand, including in criminal cases.

The grant of extraterritorial rights meant that Thai courts were unable to decide any criminal case in which the defendant was a subject of any of those countries. The government had to send such cases to the relevant consul to decide. For instance, the Bowring Treaty provided the extraterritorial clause that an English subject, as an offender, would be punished by the English consul under English law.[17] The clause stated:

> II. The interests of all British subjects coming to Siam shall be placed under the regulations and control of a consul, who will be appointed to reside [in] Bangkok. … Any dispute arising between Siamese and British subjects shall be heard and determined by the consul, in conjunction with proper Siamese officer; and criminal offenses will be punished, in the case of English offenders, by the consul, according to English laws, and in the case of Siamese offenders, by their own laws through the Siamese authorities. But the consul shall not interfere in any matters referring solely to Siamese, neither will the Siamese authorities interfere in questions which concern only the subjects of Her Britannic Majesty.[18]

12 Kanaphon Chanhom, *Foundation of Criminal Law* (2nd ed., Bangkok: Winyuchon, 2018) 111.

13 This was a treaty of amity and commerce between Thailand and Great Britain that reached trade and political aims. The Bowring treaty imposed a three per cent duty on all imports and British subjects were granted extraterritoriality.

14 United States of America (1856), France (1856), Denmark (1858), the Hanseatic Republic (1858), Portugal (1859), the Netherlands (1860), Prussia, and the States of the German Customs and Commercial Union and the Grand Duchies of Mecklenburg-Schwerin and Mecklenburg-Strelitz (1862), Sweden and Norway (1868), Belgium (1868), Italy (1868), Austria-Hungary (1869), Spain (1870), and Japan (1898).

15 Chusri Chamornmarn and Adisorn Muakpimai, *Nine Hundred Years of Thai Commerce* (Bangkok: Siam General Factoring, 1994) 172.

16 Georges Padoux, 'Law Reform in Siam' (1917) 2 *Chinese Social and Political Science Review* 3.

17 Kanaphon Chanhom, 'Codification in Thailand during the 19th and 20th Centuries: A Study of the Causes, Process and Consequences of Drafting the Penal Code of 1908' (PhD Thesis, University of Washington, 2010) 78–9.

18 *British and Foreign State Papers* 1855–1856, vol. 46 (London: William Ridgway, 1865) 139.
In addition, an agreement supplementary to the Bowring Treaty was agreed in 1856. By Article II of this agreement, it was provided:

At the beginning, the extraterritorial rights were not considered to be problematical.[19] As Francis B. Sayre, a former advisor for foreign affairs to the King of Siam, wrote: '[a]t the time when these [treaties] were adopted, no one dreamed that they could or would be used in future years to curb the domestic and foreign policy and handicap the future development of Siam'.[20]

The application of the treaties to 'subjects' was later extended to any protected persons ('*protégés*'), that is, persons from countries other than the party states. Moreover, the government found that the consuls did not decide such criminal cases seriously. An English consul admitted that he did not have enough legal knowledge, and let prisoners flee from their custody unless they were dangerous, or a newspaper referred to the case.[21]

In addition to the foreign threat, economic advancement after the Bowring Treaty led to a new structure of society as well as of the state and nation-building during King Chulalongkorn's reign. In the course of the transformation process a new form of administration was established and separated into twelve ministries, including the Ministry of Justice. The centralised judicial power was one of the most important stages of the judicial reform by the Ministry of Justice. Moreover, foreign advisors played a crucial role in driving the law reform process during King Chulalongkorn's reign. The most crucial foreign advisor was Gustave Rolin-Jaequemyns. He was a prominent Belgian international lawyer and recruited by the Thai government in 1892. Jaequemyns advised King Chulalongkorn to reform Thai law by codifying both private and criminal law in order to avoid the threat of imperialism.[22]

Another internal factor in modernising the law was the obsolescence of pre-modern law. As was mentioned above, the 1805 Three Seals Code merely purified the old law; it was not well equipped for the future situation of Siam. As a result, it was no longer able to support the country adequately during a time of intense political-socio-economic change. Punishment, such as cutting the criminal's mouth, ears, hands, and feet, was severe and unacceptable for some Westerners.[23] Also, there was no clear distinction between criminal and civil cases.

Consequently, the Thai government under King Chulalongkorn began to modernise the laws of the country. Foreign as well as Thai scholars who graduated from Europe introduced Western law into the draft of the new law. For example, the remission of punishment was adopted in the Royal Decree on Defamation of 1899,[24] the concept of criminal attempts into the Royal Decree on Rape of 1899,[25] and the principle of *nullum crimen, nulla poena, sine*

That all criminal cases in which both parties are British subjects, or in which the defendant is a British subject, shall be tried and determined by the British Consul alone . . .

That all civil cases in which both parties are British subjects, or in which the defendant is a British subject, shall be heard and determined by the British Consul alone . . .

That whenever a British subject has to complain against a Siamese, he must make his complaint through the British Consul, who will lay it before the proper Siamese authorities.

That in all cases in which British or Siamese subjects are interested, the Siamese authorities in the one case, and the British Consul in the other, shall be at liberty to attend at, and listen to, the investigation of the case; and copies of the proceedings will be furnished from time to time, or whenever desired, to the Consul or the Siamese authorities, until the case is concluded.

That although the Siamese may interfere so far with British subjects as to call upon the Consul . . . to punish grave offenses when committed by British subjects, it is agreed that, British subjects, their persons, houses, premises, lands, ships, or property of any kind, shall not be seized, injured or in any way interfered by the Siamese . . .

19 Kanaphon Chanhom, 'Codification in Thailand' 84.

20 Francis B. Sayre, 'The Passing of Extraterritoriality in Siam' (1928) 22 *American Journal of International Law* 71.

21 W. A. R. Wood, *Consul in Paradise: Sixty-Nine Years in Siam* (London: Souvenir Press, 1965) 32–3.

22 National Archives of Thailand, Recommendations of Gustave Rolin-Jaequemyns for Appointing the Legislative Council, Document No. Ror 5 O 1/6 8–10.

23 John Bowring, *The Kingdom and the People of Siam*, vol. 1 (London: John W. Parker & Son, 1857) 182.

24 See Royal Decree on Defamation of 1899, sections 5, 13.

25 See Royal Decree on Rape of 1899, section 6.

lege (no crime nor punishment without law) into the Fraud Act of 1900.[26] Those legal concepts and principles were later imported and incorporated into the General Part of the 1908 Penal Code.

10.3 THE DRAFTING PROCESS OF THE 1908 PENAL CODE

The policy to draft a series of legal codes began in 1898. King Chulalongkorn had a strong inspiration to enact such codes after his arrival from Europe in December 1897, and after the conclusion of the Japanese-Siamese Protocol in February 1898.[27] The first Codification Committee was then appointed.[28] The Committee later decided to adopt the civil law system as a model for the Code, but also considered legal principles derived from the Indian Penal Code of 1860, which incorporated the legal principles of the common law system.[29] The Committee examined Siamese and foreign laws, as well as judicial decisions, to find legal principles that were most suitable to be incorporated into the draft Penal Code.

In the beginning, the Committee worked very well and quickly. However, some critical problems later occurred due to the changes in the Committee's membership and the direction of the process of drafting the Penal Code. Regarding the changes of the Committee members, two Belgian members (Jaequemyns and Robert Kirkpatrick) moved back to their home country because of health problems.[30] Prince Rajburi had an excessive workload at the Ministry of Justice as the Minister and as a judge in the Court of Justice, so that he did not have enough time to participate in the drafting process.[31] Another member Dr. Tokichi Masao, a Japanese legal advisor who originally worked for the codification project, was then promoted as a judge in the Court of Appeals and later to the Supreme Court in 1902 after the project was discontinued.[32]

Concerning the direction to be taken in the drafting process, Corneille Schlesser, a Belgian lawyer who was assigned to work together with Masao, carefully reconsidered the first draft and found that it was not well organised. They decided to change the model from the Indian Penal Code to the European Penal Codes, the Italian Penal Code and the Draft Proposed Penal Code of Japan being the main models.[33] Schlesser later left for Belgium permanently and sent his second draft back to the Siamese government. These were the essential factors that delayed the Penal Code's drafting process and the project was temporarily discontinued from 1901 to 1903.

The second phase of this process began in 1903 when King Chulalongkorn desired to negotiate with France on the matter of extraterritoriality. After consulting with some ministers, he decided to continue with the Penal Code drafting. The King believed that codification could help establishing precise legal rules necessary for modernising the country and lead the way to the successful abolition of extraterritorial rights in Siam. In addition, the

26 See Fraud Act of 1900, section 7.
27 Kanaphon Chanhom, 'Codification in Thailand', 163.
28 The Committee's members consisted of: Prince Rajburi (Minister of Justice); Prince Bijit (former Minister of Justice); Phraya Prachakit Korachak (Chief Judge of the Civil Court); Gustave Rolin-Jaequemyns (General Advisor); Mr Robert Kirkpatrick (Legal Advisor); and Dr Tokichi Masao (Assistant Consultant of the Minister of Justice).
29 Walter E. J. Tips, *Gustave Rolin-Jaequemyns and the Making of Modern Siam* (Bangkok: White Lotus, 1992) 237.
30 Ibid., 166.
31 National Archives of Thailand, Letter from Prince Rajburi to King Chulalongkorn Relating to Supreme Court Cases, Law Drafting, and Routine Work in Ministry of Justice, Document No. Ror 5 Yor 10/16, April 28, 1902, 2–3.
32 Kanaphon Chanhom, 'Codification in Thailand', 174.
33 Ibid., 170–1.

codification process drafted by Schlesser and Masao was in any event nearly accomplished.[34] According to a request by France to have some French advisors, the Siamese government agreed in 1904 to hire a French lawyer, Georges Padoux, to continue the drafting process.[35]

An important event before the second phase of codification was continued was that Prince Rajburi, who played a crucial role in the first phase of the project, strongly disagreed that the project should continue. He argued that it was not an appropriate time for Siam to adopt legal codes. In his letter to King Chulalongkorn, Prince Rajburi argued that the codification was very difficult and the process spent a lot of time and budget.[36] Besides, the Siamese government officers would work in a stricter manner if Siam adopted legal codes.[37] On the contrary, Prince Damrong, King Chulalongkorn's younger brother and the Minister of Interior, suggested that there was no reason to delay the codification process. During the period of codification, government officers would be ready to work well under the provisions of legal codes.[38] King Chulalongkorn finally decided to continue the codification project and appointed Padoux as a legislative advisor.

Padoux's primary responsibility was to act as the chairman of the second Codification Committee.[39] His idea of drafting the Penal Code was to have a precise and systematic code which served the improvement and transformation of the country.[40] Based heavily on the research and draft of Masao and Schlesser, the Committee collected information about the existing laws and customs, as well as the decisions of the Siamese Supreme Court.[41] The Committee then compared them with the best modern Penal Codes and selected provisions which in their view were adaptable to the conditions and needs of the country.[42]

Padoux's process of drafting resembled that of the first draft but it was much faster because most information about existing laws and judgments had been collected by the first Committee before he continued the project, and the first draft was almost completed, specifically as a result of Masao and Schlesser's work.[43] Compared with the first draft, which was based heavily on the Indian Penal Code, Padoux's draft was based on Western penal codes, especially the Italian Penal Code of 1889.[44] For this reason, his draft was well structured and divided into two parts: the General Part and Specific Offences Part, while the first draft provided merely specific offences.

In 1907, the Committee proposed the new draft of the Penal Code to the Government and requested it to appoint a High Committee to examine it. The High Committee, consisting of experienced ministers and practitioners,[45] further revised the draft to respond to certain

34 Ibid., 178–9.

35 National Archives of Thailand, Agreement on Recruitment between Georges Padoux and the Thai Government, Document No. Yor Tor 3/10, 29 January 1902, 82.

36 National Archives of Thailand, Letter from Prince Rajburi to King Chulalongkorn on Codification for Thailand, Document No. Mor Ror 5 Yor/22 3–4.

37 Ibid., 4.

38 Ibid., 8.

39 The second committee consisted of: Georges Padoux; W. A. G. Tilleke (Acting Attorney General); Pra Athakarn Prasidhi (a judge in the Court of Foreign Cases); and Luang Sakon Satayathorn (a judge in the Civil Court).

40 Georges Padoux, *Report on the Proposed Penal Code for the Kingdom* (Bangkok: The American Presbyterian Mission Press, 1906) 5.

41 Padoux, 'Law Reform in Siam', 8; Padoux, *Report on the Proposed Penal Code for the Kingdom*, 5.

42 Padoux, 'Law Reform in Siam', 8.

43 Ministry of Justice, Report for the Year 125 (1906–07) 11.

44 Kanaphon Chanhom, *Textbook on Criminal Law: Specific Offences*, vol. 3 (Bangkok: Winyuchon, 2018) 25.

45 The High Committee was appointed and consisted of: Prince Damrong (Minister of Interior) as Chairman; Prince Devawongse (Minister of Foreign Affairs); Prince Nares (Head of Police Department); Prince Rajburi (Minister of Justice); Phra Atthakarn Prasidhi and Luang Sakon Sattayatorn as secretaries.

issues. In the course of examining the draft Penal Code, many questions were addressed by the High Committee, for example, whether Siam would abolish capital punishment, or whether adultery or embezzlement would be criminalised and put it into the code.[46] At the same time, Padoux sent the draft to all ministries for feedback, and met in person with ministers and head of departments, especially the Minister of the Interior and the Head of the Police Department, so that he could obtain an understanding of these departments' practical problems and ask whether the draft could solve those problems.

The revised version of the draft Penal Code was passed by the Cabinet in 1907. Signed by King Chulalongkorn, the Penal Code was promulgated on 1 June 1908 and came into force on 21 September 1908.[47] In addition to Thai and English versions, the Penal Code was officially translated into French by Padoux, and unofficially translated into Chinese by Chinese people who resided in Thailand.[48]

10.4 THE PENAL CODE IN ACTION

The Penal Code drafting was an essential factor for Siam to obtain the surrender of extraterritoriality from foreign powers. For example, the French Government in 1907 agreed to conclude a treaty with Siam to surrender its jurisdiction over specific categories of French Asiatic subjects due to the significant improvement in Siamese administration of law and justice.[49] The foreign powers further agreed that when Siam promulgated a Penal Code, a Civil Code, a Code of Criminal Procedure, a Code of Civil Procedure, and a law on the Organisation of Courts, the jurisdiction over every French Asiatic subject, or every British subject (Asiatic and non-Asiatic)[50] would be transferred to the Thai Courts.[51]

In addition to its effect on extraterritorial matter, the Penal Code of 1908 was widely accepted and admired by both Siamese and foreign scholars because it fitted the new political and social conditions in the modernisation period. King Chulalongkorn in a speech stated that it was the core beginning of legal reform and development in Siam.[52] P. W. Thornely, a former English judge in the Court of Appeals and legal advisor, observed that the Penal Code was an 'enormously successful piece of work, well suited to the needs of the country'.[53] The Penal Code was also the model for drafting other legal codes and acts, such as the provisional Code of Civil Procedure and the Civil Code.[54] In 1949, even after the Penal Code had been in force for more than forty years, Professor Dr. Yud Saeng U-Thai, a prominent professor and important drafter of the current Criminal Code, explained in a parliamentary meeting that the drafters worked very carefully on putting new and exciting concepts to the current Criminal Code because the court and legal experts accepted that the 1908 Penal Code enforcement achieved its goal and provided the basis for good law enforcement in the country.[55]

46 National Archives of Thailand, Appointing the High Committee to Examine the Draft Penal Code, Document No. Mor Ror 5 Yor /22, 9 October 1906, 16–20.

47 Penal Code of 1908, section 2.

48 Kanaphon Chanhom, 'Codification in Thailand', 195.

49 Padoux, 'Law Reform in Siam', 10.

50 See the Anglo-Siamese Treaty of 1909, Article 5.

51 Ibid., Article 11.

52 King Chulalongkorn, *Collection of King Chulalongkorn's Speech (1874–1910)* (Bangkok: Sophonphiphatthanakorn, 1915) 254–5.

53 P. W. Thornely, *The History of a Transition* (Bangkok: Siam Observer Press, 1923) 189.

54 Padoux, 'Law Reform in Siam', 8–9.

55 Memorandum on the Draft Criminal Code attached in Minutes of the House of Representative Meeting No. 19/2492 (1949), 1 September 1949, 1680.

Several factors contributed to the functional enforcement of the Penal Code 1908 during the modernisation period: the appropriate harmonisation of foreign and Siamese legal principles; the wisdom of King Chulalongkorn in law reform; and the knowledge and experiences of the drafters.[56] These will now be considered in turn.

With regards to the first reason, although some foreigners criticised Siamese law before modernisation as barbarous, because some provisions inflicted corporal punishment, such as whipping with the rattan stick,[57] foreigners who had resided in Siam longer disagreed with this criticism. Some stated that the ancient law was just and suitable for Thai people.[58] In addition to old law, the Penal Code drafters had imported modern legal principles that were harmonious with Siam's political, economic and social conditions, instead of merely transplanting foreign law into Siamese law.[59]

The drafters considered each principle by examining the old Siamese law, court decisions, and Western law to produce a new legal principle for the Penal Code. In a case of insanity, for example, the pre-modern law excused an insane person who committed an offence by the reason that he was unable to know whether his commission was right or wrong.[60] However, competent officers could detain him if he injured another person in a public area.[61] A Supreme Court decision extended this principle of criminal responsibility to semi-insane persons.[62] In this case, the defendant alleged that he was insane when he killed the victim. After being examined by a physician, the defendant was found to be partially liable on the ground that he was semi-insane.[63] After reviewing the law and decisions as well as various foreign legal codes,[64] the drafters incorporated these principles into Sections 46 and 47 of the Penal Code. Section 46 provided:

> [1] A person shall not be punished for any act done by him if at the time it is done he is prevented either by defective mental power or by any disease affecting his mind from appreciating the nature of illegality of his act, or from controlling his own conduct.
>
> [2] The Court may, if it thinks liberation dangerous for the public security, order such person to be put at the disposal of the Government for his detention in a lunatic asylum or other suitable place of safe custody.[65]

Section 47 also provided:

> Whenever a person, at the time of committing any offense, by reason of defective mental power or of any disease affecting his mind, is only partially able to control his conduct or to appreciate the nature or illegality of his act, the punishment provided for such offense shall be reduced at the discretion of the Court.[66]

56 Kanaphon Chanhom, 'Why Were Most Legal Principles in the 1908 Penal Code Still Existing through the Following Century?' in Kanaphon Chanhom (ed.), *The Penal Code for the Kingdom of Siam R.S. 127 (1908)*, (Bangkok: Chulalongkorn University Printing House, 2010) 2.

57 N. A. McDonald, *Siam: Its Government, Manners and Customs* (Philadelphia: Alfred Martien, 1871) 65–6.

58 Ernest Young, *The Kingdom of the Yellow Robe* (3rd ed., London: Archibald Constable & Co., 1907) 223.

59 Kanaphon Chanhom, 'Why Were Most Legal Principles in the 1908 Penal Code Still Existing through the Following Century?', 5–6.

60 Law of Quarrels of 1805, section 15.

61 Ibid.

62 Supreme Court's Decision No. 615/2451 (1908).

63 Praphat Ueychai, *Dissents from the General Meetings of the Supreme Court: A Hundred Years of Supreme Court Decisions in Criminal Law*, vol. 1 (Bangkok: National Council on Social Welfare of Thailand, 1994) 972–3.

64 For example, Article 64 of the French Penal Code of 1810 provided: 'If the person charged with the commission of a felony or misdemeanor was then insane . . ., no offence has been committed'.

65 Thai Penal Code of 1908, section 46.

66 Ibid., section 47.

Another example illustrating the drafters' meticulous work was the drafting of the offences against property. As admitted by Padoux, there were, before the Penal Code, 'a great many provisions concerning criminal matters',[67] but they were scattered in different laws and some provisions were 'obsolete or inconsistent with each other, and extremely intricate'.[68] For example, there existed sixteen criminal offences relating to property in the old Siamese criminal law; the offences were distinguished according to the place and nature of the commission of the offence. These were redundant and too detailed, because most of them related to the same thing, that is, the taking of property.[69] For instance, *chonplon* (โจรปล้น) was the case of house robbery committed by ten people or more; while *dassakorachon* (ทัศกรโจร) referred to people robbing a house and committing arson, causing damage a Buddha's statue, pagoda, Bhoti tree, monk's residence or temple. The penalty for the latter was more severe than that for the former.[70] After carefully reviewing all related materials, the drafters generalised, simplified, and transformed them in the Penal Code.

The second factor relates to King Chulalongkorn's wisdom and clear policy regarding the administration of justice and law reform. The King's policy direction was that Siamese legal principles should be considered together with foreign laws so that the modernised law would suit Siam's conditions during the transitional period.[71] The King had always paid attention to the Penal Code drafting since the beginning; he appointed competent Siamese and foreign drafters and examined the final revision himself.[72] The wisdom and courage of the King was admired by Masao, as stated at the beginning of his article 'The New Penal Code of Siam':

> The name of a great monarch often goes down to posterity in connection with some great law-book. That of the Emperor Justinian, who had been a great general, is handed down to us more in connection with his famous Codes than in connection with any of his great wars. Napoleon is now remembered equally well in connection with warfare as in connection with codification, but as time goes on, the glories of his famous wars will fade into obscurity and the time will come when, as in the case of Justinian, Napoleon's name will be remembered more in connection with his famous Codes than in connection with his famous wars. It may then be said that the recent promulgation of the Penal Code of the Kingdom of Siam was an event of no small significance to His Majesty, King Chulalongkorn of Siam. Indeed, anyone who reads His Majesty's preamble to the Penal Code cannot fail to be impressed with the deep appreciation His Majesty has of the importance of the steps His Majesty is taking in regard to the enactment of this Code and other Codes that are to follow.[73]

King Chulalongkorn's contributions to modernising his country were later recognised by the University of Cambridge. During the King's second visit to Europe, the University conferred the Doctor of Law *(honoris causa)* degree on him on 25 June 1907, at Devonshire House.[74] The English translation of the Vice-Chancellor's passage in Latin read:

> Of all the Kings of Siamese land he is the first to have made it a rule of life not merely to live for himself but to serve the interests of his whole people ... Then at last there arose a King

67 Padoux, *Report on the Proposed Penal Code for the Kingdom*, 4.

68 Ibid.

69 Kanaphon Chanhom, *Textbook on Criminal Law: Specific Offenses*, vol. 2 (4th ed., Bangkok: Winyuchon, 2019) 24–5.

70 Ibid., 25.

71 Kanaphon Chanhom, 'Why were Most Legal Principles in the 1908 Penal Code Still Existing through the Following Century?', 10.

72 Ibid., 13.

73 Tokichi Masao, 'The New Penal Code of Siam' (1908–9) 18 *Yale Law Journal* 85.

74 *Cambridge University Reporter* (Cambridge: Cambridge University Press, 1907) 1299.

> who immediately repressed the outrageousness of all those chiefs, utterly abolished depraved customs that had become inveterate, and stood further as nurturer, preserver, liberator and educator of his whole people; in whose reign, firstly, no one was born a slave, nor any later made a slave.[75]

The third reason contributing to the good quality of the Penal Code at the time of modernisation is the expertise and experience of the drafting committees' members. The committees were composed of both Siamese and foreigners; all of them were experts and experienced in criminal law and justice. Siamese committee members studied law either in Siam or England. Those educated in Siam included Prince Bijit (a former Minister of Justice) and Phraya Prachakit Korachak (a Chief Judge of the Civil Court). Prince Rajburi (a Minister of Justice at the time of codification), Pra Athakarn Prasidhi (a judge in the Court of Foreign Cases) and Luang Sakon Satayathorn (a judge in the Civil Court) studied English law at the University of Oxford; but they were also experts in Siamese law.[76]

The foreign committee members were from Belgium, France, and Japan. The most notable ones were Masao from Japan and Padoux from France. Masao did his thesis on Siamese ancient law[77] and received a Doctor of Civil Law degree from Yale University. After his graduation, Masao worked as an assistant at his university during 1896; but he needed to leave for Japan in 1897 due to the anti-Japanese movement in the United States. He was first invited to be acting chief editor of the Japan Times, the first English newspaper in Japan. At that time, Siam was going to accept Japanese extraterritoriality in the country and was offered to have a Japanese legal advisor for codification in Siam. Masao was a person who was well-qualified for this position because of his English language competency, legal expertise, and diplomatic ability.[78]

Padoux graduated from Paris University in 1889 and worked as an attaché in the French Foreign Office from 1890 to 1896. After that he became the Secretary-General of the Government of Tunis, codifying laws and sitting as a judge in French consular courts before leaving for Siam as legislative advisor in 1904.[79]

Years after the promulgation of the 1908 Penal Code, however, the code was found in some later cases to be unfit. It was because Padoux's intent to have a simple code for the court. For this reason, he did not incorporate legal concepts which might have been difficult to the court to understand and apply. For example, Padoux divided participation into two types (the principal and aider-and-abetter) instead of three types (the principal, instigator and aider-and-abetter).[80] Since some provisions of law were available for the deductive method, judges could apply and fulfil the provisions to fit cases in a proper way.[81] For example, a defendant shot at a policeman who was legally searching the defendant's house because he mistakenly understood that the policeman was a robber. The Supreme Court held that this case was about a mistake of fact, and such mistake could be a defence[82] even though this type of

75 Ibid., 1231.

76 Kanaphon Chanhom, 'Why Were Most Legal Principles in the 1908 Penal Code Still Existing through the Following Century?', 17.

77 See Tokichi Masao, 'The Sources of Ancient Siamese Law' (1905) 15 *Yale Law Journal* 28–32.

78 Junzo Iida, 'Japan's Relations with Independent Siam up to 1933: Prelude to Pan-Asian Solidarity' (PhD Thesis, University of Bristol, 1991) 114–16.

79 Kanaphon Chanhom, 'Codification in Thailand', 147–8.

80 Georges Padoux, *Code Pénal du Royaume de Siam* (Paris: Imprimerie Nationale, 1909) XLII–XLIII.

81 Kanaphon Chanhom, 'Why Were Most Legal Principles in the 1908 Penal Code Still Existing through the Following Century?', 26.

82 Supreme Court's Decision No. 810/2478 (1936).

defence was not provided in the 1908 Penal Code. Another case was about ignorance of facts, which was also a matter not stipulated in the Code. The defendant went hunting for food with the deceased. He saw a brow-antlered deer running into a patch of grass. He then shot at the deer but instead hit the deceased who subsequently died of his injuries. The Supreme Court, in this case, held that the defendant was not guilty of committing murder due to his ignorance of material facts.[83]

In addition to the judiciary, legal scholars helped in the understanding of most provisions of the Penal Code by proposing appropriate criminal law theories in support of the provisions. For instance, Section 44 of the Penal Code provided that a person who committed an offence by mistake or accident against a person other than the person whom he intended to injure would be criminally liable. This section did not elaborate on whether or not that person would be inflicted with aggravated penalty if the person injured by mistake, or intended to be injured, was one with whom the offender had a close relationship such as a parent or was one with special status, such as a policeman. In such circumstances, Professor Saeng U-Thai stated that the court should have decided the case in favour of the defendant. Therefore, if the defendant intended to kill his parent or a police officer, but by mistake committed murder against neither, he would not be held liable to the aggravated punishment.[84]

Political, economic and legal conditions improved considerably during the first half of the twentieth century, particularly after the 1932 Revolution during the reign of King Prajadhipok (1893–1941). The Penal Code provisions were changed to fit such conditions, such as offences against the security of the state, which were amended in order to serve the interests of democratic regime.[85] In addition, the level of imprisonment or fine was increased for some offences, including malfeasance in office, and offences relating to kidnapping and false evidence. Nevertheless, the main structure of the Penal Code was not much affected by these changes.[86]

10.5 THE DRAFTING OF THE CRIMINAL CODE

After several minor amendments to the Penal Code, a significant revision took place under Prime Minister Plaek Phibunsonkhram's government. With his strong intention to revise the 1908 Penal Code, the Prime Minister appointed the Committee on Drafting the Criminal Code in 1939 so that the new criminal code could be enacted to serve the new situation of Thailand The Committee consisted of foreign and Thai experts. The foreign legal advisor who played a crucial role in researching foreign law for the committee was René Guyon, a French jurist who had resided in Thailand for a long time and later changed his name to Thai, Pichan Boonyong. Thai experts included Professor Seni Pramoj[87] Professor Saeng U-Thai[88] and experienced judges as well as public prosecutors. Most importantly, Phibunsonkhram through his cabinet appointed Thawan Thamrongnawasawat, the Minister of Justice, as the Chairman in order to speed up the drafting process.[89]

83 Supreme Court's Decision No. 946/2451 (1908).

84 Yud Saeng U-Thai, *Textbook on the Penal Code of 1908* (6th ed., Bangkok: Winyuchon, 2005) 154–5.

85 Such as the additional title of the offences against the Prime Minister in 1939, but later repealed in 1944.

86 Kanaphon Chanhom, 'Codification in Thailand', 256–7.

87 Professor Seni Pramoj graduated from the University of Oxford and received the Barrister at Law from Gray's Inn. He was in office as the Prime Minister in 1976.

88 Professor Dr Yud Saeng U-Thai received his doctoral degree from University of Bonn, Germany. He was later the Secretary-General of the Council of State.

89 Minutes of the first meeting, Committee on Drafting the Criminal Code, 10 May 1939, 1.

At the beginning of the Criminal Code drafting, the government led by Phibunsongkhram merely wanted to revise certain provisions in the 1908 Penal Code. However, the Committee agreed to draft a completely new code so that it could reconstruct the whole parts of the Code. Professor Saeng U-Thai, who was in the Committee on Drafting the Criminal Code at the beginning to end, interestingly argued:

> [i]f the Committee amended the Penal Code article by article, it would be difficult to keep its original structure and to be well-done. It is analogous to bring fabric to patch a torn, old mosquito net. The superior way is to buy fabric and make a new mosquito net. The creator can design what style of net he wants to make.[90]

The Committee investigated the defects in the 1908 Penal Code provisions and observed new legal principles from foreign law.[91] Like the 1908 Penal Code drafters, the Committee on Drafting the Criminal Code refused to import new legal principles wholesale because it needed to consider whether such principles fitted the conditions of the country.[92] At the same time, they considered comments and feedback from the relevant departments and sought practical solutions to the issues raised. For example, some courts had an opinion that there should not have been a minimum penalty in provisions having at a penalty of at least three-years' imprisonment, because they found it difficult to impose a suitable penalty on the offender in some cases.[93] The reason why most offences had the minimum penalty was that Padoux wanted to minimise the discretion of the court at the first time of using a Western-style code so that it was more convenient and relaxed for the court than having only a maximum penalty.[94] The Committee agreed that only certain provisions should have the minimum penalty, as seen in the current Criminal Code of 1956.

The draft Criminal Code was under consideration by Parliament several times because political instability during that period delayed the process of enacting the new Code. Urged by Phibunsongkhram when he was in office as Prime Minister,[95] Parliament on several occasions appointed a parliamentary committee to consider the draft. Each parliamentary committee worked very hard, studying foreign laws that were developed during that time, and compared them with the Penal Code provisions before stipulating them in the Code. For example, the committee carefully considered the definition of the place of commission as that where the court had jurisdiction to punish the accused. The original provision of Section 5 drafted by the Committee on Drafting the Criminal Code extended the 'place of commission' to the place where the result took place (in Thailand, that is). The 1952 Parliamentary Committee agreed with the Committee on Drafting the Criminal Code to extend the application of the Criminal Code, but considered that the scope of the application in the draft was too broadly.[96] The Parliamentary Committee narrowed the provision in a redraft. As a result, the application of Criminal Code regarding territorial jurisdiction was extended to a case where the accused committed an offence outside, but the result took place inside, the territory of Thailand merely when the accused desired or foresaw such result, or where, by the

90 Yud Saeng U-Thai, *Textbook on the Criminal Code* (Bangkok: Saengdao, 1957) 194–5.
91 Yud Saeng U-Thai, 'The New Provisions in the Criminal Code' (1957) 7 *Dunlapha* 450.
92 Ibid.
93 Minutes of the first meeting, Committee on Drafting the Criminal Code, 10 May 1939, 4.
94 Padoux, *Report on the Proposed Penal Code for the Kingdom*, 23.
95 Phibunsongkhram was in office many times between 1938 and 1957.
96 Minutes of the 4th Meeting of 1952 the Parliamentary Committee, 9 October 1952, 1–5.

nature of the commission of the offence, the consequence would take place within that territory.[97]

The Parliamentary Committee also adopted some court decisions into the new Code. Comparing the Code with various foreign laws,[98] the Committee, for example, added provisions on the ignorance of facts[99] and mistake of facts[100] (discussed above in Section 10.4) to make the provisions of the Code clearer.

One of the essential tasks of the Parliamentary Committee was to add the provision for security measures under the prevention of crime concept. The measures consist of relegation of habitual offenders to restriction of movement, prohibition to enter a specified area, the requirement to execute a bond with security for keeping the peace, restraint in an institution of treatment, and prohibition to exercise certain occupations.[101] These measures are not punishments, but the Criminal Code makes them available for the court to protect society from the commission of criminal acts.[102] For example, when considering that the offender may commit the offence again if he/she continues to do the same occupation, the court may prohibit him/her to do that occupation after he/she is released from jail, for a period of up to five years.[103]

Many principles of the 1908 Penal Code were added or amended into the provisions of the current Criminal Code. All Committees carefully revised the draft and did not unreasonably add some new and exciting principles into the new Code because the 1908 Penal Code in use was effective enough in the eyes of the judges and scholars.[104] Also, Thai judges and lawyers were familiar with the Penal Code provisions. If the Committees put such new principles into the Code, the judges and lawyers would find it difficult to understand and work on the basis of those principles.[105] The Committees admitted that the 1908 Penal Code, especially the provisions on criminal responsibility, were fit for the lives of Thai people.[106] However, some provisions were amended, such as the provisions on insanity, necessity and duress, and self-defence, in accordance with modern legal concepts.[107]

10.6 CONCLUDING REMARKS

This chapter has discussed the development of pre-modern and modern criminal law in Thailand. Pre-modern law was influenced by the Indian *dharmaśāstra*, whereas modern

97 Section 5 Paragraph 1 of the current Criminal Code provides: 'Whenever any offence is even partially committed within the Kingdom, or the consequence of the commission of which, as intended by the offender, occurs within the Kingdom, or by the nature of the commission of which, the consequence resulting therefrom should occur within the Kingdom, or it could be foreseen that the consequence would occur within the Kingdom, it shall be deemed that such offence is committed within the Kingdom.'

98 Such as the Swiss Penal Code of 1937, the Italian Penal Code of 1933, the French Draft Penal Code of 1934, and the Japanese Penal Codes of 1907 and 1935.

99 Section 59, paragraph 3 of the current Criminal Code provides: 'If the doer does not know the facts constituting the elements of the offence, it cannot be deemed that the doer desired or could have foreseen the effect of such doing.'

100 Section 62, paragraph 1 of the current Criminal Code provides: 'Whenever any fact, if really existing, will cause the doing of any act not to be an offence, or the doer not to be punishable, or to receive less punishment, and even though such fact does not really exist, but the doer understands mistakenly that it really exists, the doer shall not be guilty, or shall be exempted from the punishment, or shall receive less punishment, as the case may be.'

101 Thai Criminal Code of 1956, section 39.

102 Saeng U-Thai, 'The New Provisions in the Criminal Code', 454.

103 Thai Criminal Code of 1956, section 50.

104 Memorandum on the Draft Criminal Code attached in Minutes of the House of Representative Meeting No. 19/2492 (1949), 1 September 1949, 1679.

105 Ibid., 1680.

106 Ibid., 1693.

107 Ibid.

law was influenced by Western law of the nineteenth century. However, Thailand has adopted foreign laws and blended them with its own domestic law and judicial decisions, so that the law fits its people and the conditions of the country in each period.

During the time of the threat from the Western powers, Siam reformed its law into the modern form in order to receive the surrender of extraterritoriality. Although it was in a hurry to enact a Penal Code, it did not merely translate Western codes and promulgate them immediately. On the contrary, Siam drafted the Penal Code carefully by comparing foreign laws with Siamese laws as well as court decisions to seek the most appropriate provisions and incorporate them into the code.

The 1908 Penal Code was said to be a successful piece of work during the time of legal modernisation and reformation of the administration of justice. Foreign countries later agreed to diminish the extraterritorial rights when the codification process was complete.[108] Thornley interestingly concluded:

> In drafting this Penal Code the commissioners studied numerous other Codes and produced a work which was intended to combine the main advantages of other systems and at the same time maintain the simplicity of arrangement and straightforwardness of language so desirable under the special circumstances of the case.[109]

The 1908 Penal Code was replaced by the current Criminal Code, which was also carefully drafted. Some principles of the Penal Code were amended to fit the new political, economic and social changes under the democratic regime.

Codification is a long process demanding much hard work. It requires many things apart from time and financial resource, especially legal expertise, and the leader's strong determination and clear policy direction. As may be seen in this chapter, most people who were involved in drafting the 1908 Penal Code and the 1956 Criminal Code were experienced. Foreign drafters collected information on laws from other countries for the purposes of comparison, while the Siamese/Thais considered them together with existing law and court decisions. They did not merely transplant foreign criminal law concepts and principles into the codes, but instead by consulting relevant people or departments they considered the conditions of the country before adopting any Western legal concepts. Without such competent drafters and drafting methods, the enforcement of such law might fail in practice and might require frequent redrafting of the law.[110]

Moreover, the strong determination of the leader to codify the law is one of the most important factors. There would no penal or criminal code if there had not been King Chulalongkorn and Prime Minister Phibunsongkhram's initiation and support. As has been discussed, King Chulalongkorn, while not interfering in the substance of the Penal Code, paid attention to the codification process by appointing foreign and Siamese experts, giving them the drafting policy and reviewing the draft Penal Code at the final stage. Phibunsongkhram pursued his goal of promulgation of the 1956 Criminal Code by appointing foreign and Thai scholars as well as practitioners, asking the Minister of Justice to preside over the Committee on the Criminal Code Drafting under his supervision, and urging the Parliament to consider the draft until the Criminal Code was in force.

108 For revocation of extraterritoriality, see further, Chapter 14, this volume.

109 Thornely, *The History of a Transition*, 189.

110 For example, Thailand experienced this kind of problem at the beginning of the Civil and Commercial Code drafting. For the drafting process of the Civil and Commercial Code, see Chapter 9, this volume.

As seen in this chapter, the perfection of law drafting never exists. Also, the successful enactment of law in one period of time does not guarantee that it will be successful in another period. As far as society changes, the law must be changed accordingly. Old law was not useless. It can be important sources and foundation of legal thought for policy makers and drafters to have a new law properly responding to social problems, as the pre-modern law and the 1908 Penal Code were for the current Criminal Code.

11

Thai Trust Law

A Legal Import Rooted in Pragmatism

Surutchada Reekie and Narun Popattanachai

11.1 INTRODUCTION

Against the conventional wisdom, Thailand despite having a civil law system is no stranger to trust instruments. There are records of trusts adopted and recognised under Thai law from as early as the late nineteenth century, predating many other leading Asian jurisdictions.[1] Yet, the implementation of trust law in the Thai legal system has not been plain sailing, and has thus far taken a number of different approaches since the essential features of the trust do not dovetail well with the country's legal infrastructure, either conceptually or practically.

The trust concept has its root in English law in medieval times as a way for affluent feudal landowners to mitigate land-based taxation and to diversify the range of dispositions of land which they could legally make on death. In addition, the English Court of Chancery played a significant role in imparting the ordinary meaning of the word 'trust' into legal terms. At its most fundamental level, trust is 'a confidence reposed in some other'.[2] Thus, to commit a breach of a trust is a serious matter, with detrimental repercussions readily sanctioned by the courts. As a result of the aforementioned historical evolution, a trust in the common law tradition refers to 'the duty or aggregate accumulation of obligations that rest upon a person called a trustee in reference to property under his control or held by him to administer in the manner prescribed by the trust instrument or in accordance with equitable principles'.[3] In the eye of the English law of trusts, therefore, it is possible for two exclusive ownership claims to exist simultaneously over the same asset – legal ownership by trustees and equitable ownership by beneficiaries.[4]

This separation of legal and equitable titles does not sit well with the Thai legal system, which can arguably trace its intellectual origin from the continental Roman-European legal family. Notably, one of its central dicta is the strict division between rights *in rem* and rights *in personam*. Correspondingly, the legal framework and the intellectual foundation of the Thai Civil and Commercial Code (TCCC) leave little room for equitable principles as required to

[1] In a Supreme Court Case Dika 728/2506 of the year 1963, it was stated that the trust central to the dispute was established approximately 100 years prior – around the year 1863. See also the Opinion Note of the Council of State regarding 'the request to inscribe the land title document with the name of the trustee, which is an issue concerning section 1686 of the Civil and Commercial Code' No. 56/2479.

[2] J. R. Long, 'The Definition of a Trust' (1922) 8 *Virginia Law Review* 426–33 at 427.

[3] Re Scott (1948) SASR 193 (Australia) at 196; *Lewin on Trusts*, 17th ed. (London: Sweet and Maxwell, 2000).

[4] J. Kim, 'Identity and the Hybridity of Modern Finance: How a Specifically Modern Concept of the Self Underlies the Modern Ownership of Property, Trusts and Finance' (2014) 38 *Cambridge Journal of Economics* 425–46 at 428.

establish a trust.[5] In addition to the conceptual incompatibility, the prevailing public policy consideration in Thailand goes so far as to expressly prohibit the creation of a trust or trust-like arrangement except when provided by specific legislation.[6]

This uneasy presence of trust law in the civilian tradition has been noted by international scholars in the East Asian context,[7] while Thai scholars have only recently begun to take notice of the struggle especially in relation to its commercial and other economic applications.[8] This chapter hopes to contribute to this growing body of literature by providing an analytical framework through which the history of trust law in Thailand should be appraised. It is argued that the development of trusts in Thailand ought to be viewed through the lens of legal pragmatism. Considered as part of critical legal studies, legal pragmatism proposes that in order to understand the actions of legal institutions, it is imperative that the investigator parse the ideological prevalence of classic legal doctrine and may, if necessary, reject legal formalism in order to try to understand the wider context in which the legal institutions under review are situated.[9] In other words, it is plausible to import a legal institution from Country A into Country B only to the extent that makes socio-economic sense by grafting certain aspects of such a legal institution onto the existing, more familiar domestic legal foundations, ignoring the lack of doctrinal integration created by the implanted alien legal concept. With this analytical framework in mind, it is possible to explain the entire history of trust law in Thailand as a coherent whole.

To substantiate this claim, the chapter tells the journey of trust law into the Thai legal rulebook, which runs in parallel with the expansion of international trade and industrial modernisation of the country from the nineteenth century onwards. For the sake of clarity, the journey may be observed in two legs mapping two episodes in which the question was posed of whether trust law should be introduced. The first venture came in the early period of the so-called 'Great Modernisation' when Siam experienced an influx of foreign laws, as discussed in detail elsewhere in this volume.[10] The second experiment was not undertaken until almost ninety-five years later with the introduction of the Trust for Transactions in the Capital Market Act BE 2550 (2007) and subsequently the Draft Bill on Trusts for the Purpose of Personal Asset Management, the latter having received cabinet approval in 2018 and, at the time of writing, undergoing the drafting procedure.[11] The two experimental periods were punctuated by an outright prohibition of trusts and trust-like instruments through the initial

5 Section 4 of TCCC stipulates that a law must be read according to its literal interpretation or purposive interpretation. If there is no clear interpretive principle established *ex ante*, the court may rely on local customs as interpretive guidance. If there is no relevant local custom, the court may draw an inference from other comparable bodies of law. If there is no comparable body of law to rely on, the court may rely on the general legal principles.

6 Section 1686 of TCCC.

7 Lionel Smith (ed.), *The Worlds of the Trust* (Cambridge: Cambridge University Press, 2013) 406; Lusina Ho and Rebecca Lee (eds.), *Trust Law in Asian Civil Law Jurisdictions: A Comparative Analysis* (Cambridge: Cambridge University Press) 10.

8 For instance: C. Sahachaiyunta, 'The Development on Trust Law in Thailand' (2018) 9(1) *Assumption University Law Journal* 197–210 (Thai language). See also Bunyat Sucheewa, 'Trust' (1962) 9(1) *Dulapaha* 18–49 (Thai language).

9 At its origin, legal pragmatism is an analytical framework adopted to explain how a law is interpreted, either by judges or other public officials responsible for its implementation and enforcement. See for instance, Ronald Dworkin, *Law's Empire* (Cambridge MA: Harvard University Press, 1986) at 50; Richard A. Posner, 'Legal Pragmatism Defended' (2004) 71 *The University of Chicago Law Review* 683–90 at 683–4; Charles L. Barzun, 'Three Forms of Legal Pragmatism' (2018) 95 *Washington University Law Review* 1003–34 at 1022.

10 See Munin Pongsapan, Chapter 9 of this volume.

11 Cabinet Resolution on the draft bill on trusts for the purpose of personal asset management (10 July 2018).

introduction of section 1686 of the TCCC in 1935. The following review of the history of trust law in Thailand will address these two developments in turn.

11.2 TRUST LAW PRIOR TO 2007

11.2.1 *Early Development of English Common Law Trusts in Siam*

Although no records of the establishment of the first English common law[12] trust in Siam have yet been found, it may be strongly conjectured that the reception of English trust law coincided with the introduction of extraterritoriality under the Bowring Treaty in 1855. Article II of the Treaty, read together with a Commercial Agreement signed in the following year,[13] effectively removed the exercise of legal jurisdiction over all British subjects from the Siamese judiciary to the British consul, as discussed in detail elsewhere in this volume.[14] In particular, the final sentence of the Article emphasised that Siamese authorities would not 'interfere in questions which only concern the Subjects of Her Britannic Majesty'.[15] Accordingly, under this arrangement a British subject would be able to establish a trust in accordance with English law in Siam. And whilst the detail of these trusts as well as the circumstances surrounding their establishment remain unknown – as trust instruments remain private documents – two things are clear. First, the British consulate exercised its supervising authority over these trusts; and second, in so doing, English trust law was applied. On the first assertion, evidence is ample. P. W. Thornely, in his meticulous account of historical legal development of Siam during the reform period, clearly stated that the British Court for Siam, referring to the His Britannic Majesty's Court (the 'HBM Court'),[16] had a continuing duty to: 'take charge of the estates of deceased pre-registered British subjects, and administers [*sic*] those estate itself or else appoints [*sic*] administrators. It also appoints trustees and guardians and can hold in trust or invest sums of money etc., all so long as no dispute arises between two or more persons'.[17]

Indeed, one British consul to Siam, who acted as Registrar and Judge of the HBM Court in the early twentieth century, stated that he was in charge of the estates of deceased British subjects and had a duty to invest,[18] alluding to the fact that he was a trustee as opposed to a mere administrator or guardian of the estate. These accounts are consistent with the findings of the Thai Supreme Court in many trust cases where the British Consul exercised a supervisory role over trusts established by British subjects in Siam. In the case Dika 1404–1405/2508 of the year 1965, it was stated that one of the trustees had resigned from his position with the permission of the British consular court.[19] Moreover, in the case Dika 1372/2498 of the year 1955, the settled facts of the case were that the trust deed central to the dispute was executed at the British Consular General in Bangkok.[20] Similarly, the facts of the case Dika 2676/2528 of the year 1985 revealed that the trust central to the dispute was established

12 Such trusts are referred to as 'common law' trusts in this chapter in order to distinguish them from trusts created by Thai statutes discussed in Section 11.2 below.

13 Commercial Agreement, supplementary to the Treaty between Great Britain and Siam, of 1855, signed at Bangkok, May 13, 1856.

14 See Part 1 of Reekie and Reekie, Chapter 8 of this volume.

15 Commercial Agreement of 1855, Article II.

16 See Chapter 8, this volume.

17 P. W. Thornely, *The History of a Transition* (Bangkok: Siam Observer Press Ltd, 1923) 213–14.

18 W. A. R. Wood, *Consul in Paradise* (London: Souvenir Press, 1965, reprint 2018) 37.

19 Para. 9.

20 Para. 14.

and duly registered with the British Consul some eighty years prior to the date of the hearing.[21] The second assertion that English trust law was applied may be supported on a general level by a reading of the Bowring Treaty as mentioned above, and more specifically by the case Dika 3148/2540 of the year 1997, which stated that the trust central to the dispute was established in accordance with English law.[22]

Accordingly, it can be understood that a number of trusts had been established in Siam by British subjects, either by will for the purpose of the management of the deceased's estate or by deed for the purpose of private asset management during the settlor's lifetime. The earliest record of a trust established by a British subject can be traced back to the year 1863, only eight years after the signing of the Bowring Treaty.[23] This initial reception of English trust law into Siam must have been noticed favourably by the Siamese, as evidence suggests that they welcomed this foreign legal instrument and started to vest their property into trusts. The first author's survey of Supreme Court rulings found twelve cases in which express trusts were successfully established by Siamese settlors prior to 1935: eight of these involved trusts established by will;[24] two involved *inter-vivos* trusts;[25] and in two cases the trusts central to the dispute were recognised by the Supreme Court as valid and enforceable, yet the facts were silent as to the circumstances surrounding their establishment.[26] Interestingly, in one case, Dika Case 575/2465 of the year 1922, the *inter-vivos* trust central to the dispute involved at least one French party. Whilst the ruling did not specify whether the claimant or the defendant, or both, was a French subject, it acknowledged that the case was decided in accordance with the Treaty between Siam and France, which allowed the French subjects who were parties to the case to appeal to the Siamese Supreme Court on the points of law only.[27] This case is the only piece of evidence which demonstrates that the popularity of English common law trusts in Siam extended beyond the British expatriate community, to the local Siamese and even further to the wider international community in Siam.

11.2.2 *Section 1686 of the TCCC and the Purported End of English 'Common Law' Trusts in Siam*

The final Book of the TCCC, Book VI on matters of succession and inheritance, was promulgated in the Government Gazette on 7 June 1935,[28] and came into force on 1 October of the same year. Book VI is divided into six titles in the following order: General Provisions, Statutory Right of Inheritance, Wills, Administration and Distribution of the Estate, Vacant Estate, and Prescription. Section 1686 is the first provision of Chapter IV

21 Para. 7.

22 Para. 7.

23 Dika Case 728/2506 of the year 1963.

24 Dika Cases 1229/2473 of the year 1930 (date of the will unknown, but prior to the time of dispute in 1930); 563/2474 of the year 1931 (date of the will unknown, but prior to the time of dispute in 1931); 136/2481 of the year 1938 (the will was dated in 1926); 176/2483 of the year 1940 (date of the will unknown, but presumably prior to 1935 as the Court recognised it as valid and not barred by section 1686 as will be discussed below); 1041/2484 of the year 1941 (date of the will unknown, but prior to the death of the settlor in 1927); 866/2487 of the year 1944 (the will was dated before 1924); 2587/2518 of the year 1975 (date of the will unknown but presumably prior to 1935); 3680/2535 of the year 1992 (the will was dated in 1926).

25 Dika Cases 661/2481 of the year 1938 (*inter-vivos* trust established in 1913); 494-495/2473 of the year 1930 (*inter-vivos* trust established prior to 1930).

26 Dika Cases 208/2477 of the year 1934 and 1483/2506 of the year 1963.

27 The Franco-Siamese Treaty of 13 February 1904.

28 The Act Announcing the Coming into Force of Book VI of the Civil and Commercial Code B.E. 2477, Government Gazette, vol. 52 p. 529 (7 June B.E. 2478) (Thai language).

'Legacies with Constitution of *Phu Pokrong Sap* (Guardianship)' of Title III 'Wills'. In its original version as submitted by the High Translating Committee prior to its promulgation in 1935, the provision reads: 'Trust created whether directly or indirectly by an act inter vivos or mortis causa shall have no effect whatever'.[29]

The provision was amended in 2007 by the Civil and Commercial Code Amendment (Number 17) Act of 2007, which added an exception that statutory trusts may be established by a law enacted for the specific purpose of creating such trusts. This paved the way for the introduction of the Trust for Transactions in the Capital Market Act of 2007 and the proposed Draft Bill on Trusts for the Purpose of Personal Asset Management, which, as discussed above, is at the time of writing undergoing legislative process.

The rationale behind the introduction of the statutory trusts exception, as will be explored in detail in Section 11.3 below, was not difficult to comprehend: it was a response to socio-economic considerations *vis-à-vis* the changing environment of the capital market. On the other hand, the logic behind the blanket ban of trusts in 1935 by virtue of Section 1686 is more intriguing. The discussion now turns to explore the development leading up to the promulgation of the provision and its effects on common law trusts in Siam.

According to René Guyon, who was appointed as a member of the Code Commission of Siam in 1908 and later, in 1916, Chief of the Drafting Committee of the Siamese Code of Law, the drafting of the proposed Civil and Commercial Code of Siam started in 1908, the year when the new Penal Code of Siam was promulgated.[30] The first draft of succession law, which was incorporated into a Book on Persons and Succession, was completed in 1911.[31] However, issues of succession were later separated from the law of persons, and the drafting of Book VI on Succession was not completed for over two decades.

In an enquiry note dated 23 August 1932, Guyon submitted a series of eighteen questions regarding the Siamese government's policy framework, which would inform the drafting of the succession and inheritance law.[32] The necessity of this enquiry was expounded in the prelude to the questions, that Book VI formed part of the civil law which had been traditionally governed by local customs, hence: 'It is deemed advisable, before completing the preliminary draft, to submit the most important points of policy in matter of Inheritance to the consideration of the Government in order to be given conclusive directions as to the general policy to be adopted in this country'.[33]

Question 17 concerned trusts, and should be reproduced here in full.

> Is the English practice of 'trust' to receive a statutory sanction in Siam? Under this practice, a person called 'trustee' is entrusted with certain property in order that he may deal with it in accordance with directions that are contained in a trust deed creating the trust. The beneficiary under a trust is called the 'cestui que trust'.
>
> A trust being likely to be considered as a real right, it should be permitted only by way of statutory provision because section 1298 of the TCCC reads, 'Real rights may be created only by virtue of this Code or other laws'.

[29] Archive of the Office of the Council of State, 'High Translating Committee (1935: Book VI: Civil and Commercial Code' (Document 133, Microfilm Roll 19, p.1340 of 2685).

[30] René Guyon, *L'Oeuvre de Codification au Siam* (Paris: Imprimerie Nationale, 1919) 17.

[31] Ibid., 25.

[32] Archive of the Office of the Council of State, 'Enquiry Concerning Book VI C.C.C. (Inheritance)' (Document 131/33, Microfilm Roll 19, p.978 of 2685). The note was submitted to the government by the Law Drafting Department, the current Office of the Council of State, in document number 30/231 of 25 August 1932.

[33] Ibid., 979.

> In this case as in the former case of 'entail' (dealt with hereabove in Question 14), attention is draft on the danger to tye-up [*sic*] real property (and contingently movable). Legislation must be cautious? to prevent the excesses of 'mortmain' and 'perpetuities'.

The government responded in a note from the President of the People Executive Committee, dated 6 September 1932, both in Thai and English versions.[34] The English version simply states: 'Question 17. – There shall be no statutory sanction for "Trust", except in cases concerning the administration of the property of a minor'.[35]

In contrast to this abrupt denial, the Thai version of the note answered the question in a different way: 'The matter of trust is very complicated and may have detrimental effects similar to the issue of substitution above'.[36]

The answer refers to the prior rejection of the English concept of substitution or estate-tail, which was also considered to be 'damaging to national interests' as it would enable valuable property to be tied down for the benefit of certain individuals.[37] This policy decision sheds important light on the perception of English trust law amongst Siamese executive elites, which was also echoed by the legal elites, as can be seen from the following minutes from a meeting of the Law Drafting Committee for the Revision of Book VI on 25 December 1934:

> Chapter 4 on wills that appoint a guardian of property: the meeting discussed the policy regarding whether principles of trusts should be adopted. Finally, the opinions became unanimous that principles of trusts, as originated from English law, are complicated and developed in piecemeal fashion. These were a true English invention, and not adopted elsewhere apart from those places that received English law. Moreover, the result of these trust principles would be directly contradictory to the free circulation of property.[38]

As can be seen, English trust law had not been well received by the decision-makers of Siam at this pivotal time of change. The prevailing view was that the trust, an equitable creature, was unique to the English legal system and unsuitable for Siam. An illuminating summary of the elites' opinions of English trust law may be found in the explanatory note accompanying a Thai version of the draft Book VI in 1932, in which the Drafting Committee decided to adopt the concept of guardianship of property instead of trusts for the purpose of managing inheritance of minor legatees:

> Such Anglo-Saxon law has a very special characteristic, which many commentators do not agree with. Some argued that in such circumstances the ownership of inheritance should be transferred to a trustee, and therefore the trustee is the legal owner of such property. Some argue that such property falls outside the trustee's jurisdiction, and others argue that the beneficiary is the actual owner. Without having to consider these contradicting opinions, it should be deemed that [the concept of a trust] is a special policy, full of problems, and applicable in the laws of certain countries only. It should not be applied in Thai law as it would only bring about disputes and uncertainties.[39]

[34] Archive of the Office of the Council of State, '(Draft) Number … . President of the People Executive Committee's Message to the Secretary of the Law Drafting Committee' (Document 131/58, Microfilm Roll 19, p.1003 of 2685).

[35] Ibid., 1008.

[36] Ibid., 1005 (Thai language, translation by the first author).

[37] Ibid.

[38] Archive of the Office of the Council of State, 'Minutes of the Meeting of the Drafting Committee on the Draft Civil and Commercial Code Book VI, 25th December B.E.2477' (Document 130/72, Microfilm Roll 19, p.397 of 2685) (Thai language, translation by the first author).

[39] Archive of the Office of the Council of State, 'Draft Civil and Commercial Code Book VI' (Document 131/64 Microfilm Roll 19, p.1009 of 2685) 1092. (Thai language, translation by the first author).

With these consistent reinforcements of partiality with regard to equity and trusts, Siam proceeded with section 1686, which prohibits the legal effects of trusts.

However, it is important to note that the effect of section 1686 is only to invalidate the legal effects of trusts established after the provision came into force, and it was never intended to have the retrospective effect of invalidating trusts established in Siam prior to 1 October 1935. This much is clear from both the position of the Drafting Committee and the subsequent rulings of the Supreme Court. Regarding the Drafting Committee, evidence to support this contention may be found in a report on the revision of Book VI by Mom Rajavong Seni Pramoj and René Cazeau in 1938.[40] On the issue of section 1686, the report shows that a question had been submitted by the British Legation concerning the consequences of the provision: 'it is presumed that Section 1686 was not intended to apply retrospectively',[41] to which the answer was as follows:

> The British legation is right when presuming that it was not intended to apply retrospectively Section 1686 . . . [T]he matter of trust as dealt with in Section 1686 is one of juristic act made contingently by parties and likely to be interpreted by lawyers, who shall take it as unquestionably governed by the legal principles of non-retrospectivity.[42]

To the same outcome, the Supreme Court has consistently held that Section 1686 does not apply retrospectively to invalidate or dissolve trusts established in Siam prior to its coming into force, whether in the case of charitable trusts[43] or private trusts.[44] Indeed, these trusts remain valid and enforced up to the present day, as cases which have reached the Supreme Court as recently as 2012[45] consistently demonstrate the Thai judiciary's willingness to recognise and enforce these common law trusts in accordance with the trust instruments, applying English law to the extent that it is not directly contrary to Thai law.[46]

40 Archive of the Office of the Council of State, 'Revision: Civil and Commercial Code Book VI (1937–1938), Examination by Mom Rajavong Seni and Mr. Cazeau' (Document AC 34, 136, Microfilm Roll 19, p.1886 of 2685).

41 Ibid., 1920.

42 Ibid.

43 In Dika Case 7278-7279/2554 of the year 2011, the Supreme Court ruled that the charitable trust in question was established prior to Section 1686 came into force, and hence would be enforceable in perpetuity, except when all beneficiaries agree to dissolve it. Similarly, in Dika Case 3477/2540 of the year 1997, the Supreme Court stated that trusts established prior to 1 October 1935 remained legally valid at the time of hearing because Section 1686 did not apply retrospectively.

44 In Dika Case 1404-1405/2506 of the year 1963, the Supreme Court held as valid a will that established a private trust of the deceased's estate because it was executed prior to the promulgation of Book VI of the CCC and was not contrary to any law being in force at the time. Similarly, the Supreme Court in Dika Case 136/2481 of the year 1938 clearly stated that trusts established prior to the coming into force of Book VI remained legally valid. Moreover, in Dika Cases 661/2481 of the year 1938 and 871/2478 of the year 1935, the Supreme Court held that trusts established prior to the coming into force of Book VI remained valid and enforceable in accordance with the law which existed prior to Book VI.

45 Dika Case 9757/2555 of the year 2012.

46 According to the ruling of the Dika Case 136/2481 of the year 1938, it was held that the will which established a trust was not barred by Section 1686 as it was executed before the provision came into force. The Court went on to state that prior to Book VI Siam did not have any legislation solely on trusts, thus the country imported English trust law into the legal system. As such, the Court was of the opinion that it may apply English trust law to the extent that was not contrary to public order, and such application of the law formed part of Siamese law (para. 5). In another case, Dika Cases 1404-1405/2506 of the year 1963, the Supreme Court showed willingness to recognise and enforce common law trusts established prior to 1935 as long as they were not contrary to the applicable Thai law at the time.

11.2.3 *Domesticating Trusts: the Roles of the Council of State and Court of Justice*

The historical materials discussed in the preceding sections offer glimpses into the early development of common law trusts in Siam. This section attempts to understand this development in a wider context.

Three reasons may be offered as answers to the questions of how and why 'common law' trusts were established and enforced in Siam. The first avenue by which trusts were introduced onto Siamese soil was through legal necessity. As seen from the above records concerning the British Consulate, trusts were introduced into Siam out of a particular necessity – to manage the estates of British subjects who died in Siam in accordance with one of the prescribed duties of the British consular court, or the HBM Court under Article 4 of the Order in Council which stated:

> Notwithstanding anything contained in Article 3 the Courts established by the Principal Order shall continue to transact all non-contentious business in relation to the probate of wills, and the administration of estates of deceased British subjects who were registered in accordance with Part VIII of the Principal Order at the date of the said Treaty.[47]

Apart from the consular power over the estates of preregistered British subjects residing in Siam at the time of decease, it seems that the British Consulate could also exercise its power over the estates of post-registered and non-registered British subjects, and those who were not residing in Siam at the time of decease, or those who held property in the country but never resided there, for the purpose of protecting the estate.[48] This duty of the British Consulate to protect the estate of British subjects, as well as the interests of the beneficiaries,[49] necessitated the use of trusts, among other legal devices.

The second avenue of reception of English trust law in Siam was the use of *inter-vivos* trusts by British subjects, either for charitable purposes or for personal asset management. Whilst this type of trust instrument remains private and confidential to this day, court disputes have revealed that a good number of these trusts must have been established prior to 1935, such that they led to at least seven disputes concerning trusts expressly established by British subjects that eventually reached the highest court of the land.[50]

The popular use of common law trusts amongst British subjects in Siam was acknowledged, albeit in passing, in a record of the Office of the Council of State. The record concerned the Council of State's answer to the consultation by the Land Registrar regarding the British Consul's request to register a trustee of a piece of cemetery land on the land deed in his capacity as a trustee. In rejecting this request, the record went on to state that: 'Moreover, trust is an English law creation, which at the time [of King Chulalongkorn's

47 Siam Order in Council, 1909 (Statutory Rules and Orders, 1909., No. 754).

48 Thornely, *History of a Transition*, 219.

49 As seen from a British consul's observation that he wished he was as successful in his personal investments as he was in managing estates for the benefit of the deceased's offspring (Wood, *Consul in Paradise*, 37).

50 The trust central to the disputes in three cases (Dika Cases 7278-7279/2554 of the year 2011, 3477/2540 of the year 1997, and 3148/2540 of the year 1997) was settled by Mr Lo Kai Chuy, a British Singaporean. In a further two cases (Dika Cases 1106/2501 of the year 1958 and 1372/2498 of the year 1955), the settlor of a number of trusts was Mr E. H. Joangulia, a British subject residing in Siam. The sixth case is Dika case 1735/2500 of the year 1957, where the settlor was Captain John Bush, a British man who served in the Siamese government. The final case where the settlor was clearly stated in the facts as being British was Dika Case 719/2475 of the year 1932.

Apart from these seven cases, five more may be assumed from the facts to very likely involve British settlors, even though this was not clearly stated. These are Dika Case 871/2478 of the year 1935, 163/2491 of the year 1948, 507-508/2480 of the year 1937, 390/2463 of the year 1920, and 9757/2555 of the year 2012.

reign, 1868–1910,] was not included in Thai law. Afterwards some English subjects had established trusts [in Siam] and hence it was necessary that the courts accepted cases which involved these trusts'.[51]

This record also offers a glimpse into the necessary pragmatic solution of the Thai judiciary in dealing with common law trusts – that the courts had to consider disputes which involved trusts that were established within the jurisdiction.

The third avenue is the spillover popularity of common law trusts from the British expatriate community to the Siamese elite circle. One learns from the facts of a number of Supreme Court cases on private trusts that these cases share similar characteristics: they either involved assets or concerned elite families or highly-ranked officials, or both.[52] Apart from these cases, another indication of the popularity of trusts among the Siamese is the fact that the concept of trust was once officially acknowledged and incorporated into the country's new regime of land law. Section 8 of the Issuance of Land Deed Act Number 2 of 1916, promulgated on 17 September 1916, provided that:

> If someone is a trustee of land which has a map deed, or of land which has investigation receipt or receipt for a deed or a map, that trustee has the right to register his name. And after the name the record must state "On the duty of trustee in such matter". And when all trustees have transferred or revised the registration for the benefit of another person fraudulently or mistakenly, and the transferor or the one who benefits from this does not know of this fraud or mistake, it shall be that the transfer of such benefit is valid in law.[53]

Although this is the only piece of legislation in Siam that officially recognised trusts established in accordance with English law, it demonstrates that by 1916 common law trusts must have been widely used such that they were important enough to be included in the country's new land-registration system.

These three routes to the use of common law trusts in Siam prior to 1935, viewed from the country's socio-economic perspective, stood in contrast to the prevailing view of the executive and legal elites as examined in the previous section. To the expatriates and elite Siamese communities alike, common law trusts were a convenient legal tool for asset management, either for charitable purposes or personal ends. The parties involved, at least as one learns from the facts of these cases, were not hindered by the complexity of equitable principles or the fear that trusts would only be compatible with a common law system.

The fact that there were over forty Supreme Court cases concerning common law trusts established, or purported to be established, in Siam prior to 1935[54] demonstrates that the Thai judiciary seems to have adopted the same pragmatic way of thinking. The courts accepted and adjudicated these disputes, as mentioned above, in accordance with English law, to the extent that it was not directly contrary to Thai law. Their highly practical approach has resulted in a body of trust law jurisprudence in Thailand that is wholly judicially developed,[55] and exists independently from the statutory trust regime that has later been introduced.

[51] Record of the Office of the Council of State entitled 'A request for signing the land deed as trustee which is a problem in relation to section 1686 of the Civil and Commercial Code' (Completed Matter Number 56/2479 of August BE 2479) 2.

[52] See, for instance, Dika Cases 3680/2535 of the year 1992, 1483/2506 of the year 1963, 1041/2484 of the year 1941, 176/2483 of the year 1940, 136/2481 of the year 1938, and 208/2477 of the year 1934.

[53] Government Gazette, vol. 33 p. 136 (17 September B.E. 2459) (Thai language, translation by the first author).

[54] See Surutchada Reekie and Adam Reekie, 'The Surviving Legacy of English Trust Law' in Ying Khai Liew and Matthew Harding (eds.), *Asia-Pacific Trusts Law: Theory and Practice in Context* (London: Hart Publishing, forthcoming 2021).

[55] For further discussion, see ibid.

11.3 TRUST LAW AFTER 2007: THE RISE OF THE REGULATORY STATE

11.3.1 *Trusts As a Regulatory-Instrument Regime*

As mentioned briefly in the introductory section above, trust law was first conceived as means by which Englishmen from the upper echelon of society managed their assets without incurring unnecessary tax liabilities both during life and on death. F. W. Maitland observed that the trust is 'an institute of great elasticity and generality; as elastic, as general as contract'.[56] Most crucially, he pointed out that the trust is one of the most important 'lawyers' devices', used chiefly within the domain of private property transactions and institutions, capable of serving a wide variety of purposes.[57] As a result, trust law is situated firmly within the domain of private law, dealing with the relations between individuals or private entities, rather than relations between private entities and the government. Regulation, on the other hand, aims at either supplementing deficiencies in public administration[58] or correcting incidents of market failures.[59] Unlike private law, which enables two or more private parties to enter into a legal relationship in pursuit of their choices and liberty, regulation is, by its very nature, designed to restrict the very freedom we as free women and men hold most dear, doing so in protection of the public interest.

In contrast to the pragmatic approach to the recognition of common law trusts in Siam as explored in the previous section, the second episode of the journey of trust law through Thai legal history demonstrates both the versatility of trusts as postulated by Maitland and arguably a significant departure from the original inception of the concept, in exchange for utility gained from allowing qualified licence-holders to offer certain financial services or products to the general public. Ultimately, the narratives support the pragmatic approach of integrating trust law into the Thai legal system.

11.3.2 *Opening the Floodgates: the Trusts As Investment Vehicles in the Capital Market*

During the period between the Second World War and the mid-1990s, in which Thailand had undergone a remarkable transformation from an agricultural society to an industry-driven and export-led economy, the liberalisation of the financial sector, especially the capital market, was seen as a crucial engine for growth. The progress, including all major legal reforms, was suddenly halted by the devastating effects of the Asian financial crisis. The reform effort only resumed almost a decade after the crisis when the government adopted the Financial Sector Master Plan Phrase 1 (2004–8), formulated by the Bank of Thailand. With this Plan, the Bank of Thailand effectively announced that the government was willing to equip the financial sector with sufficient resiliency to withstand new competitive forces brought by liberalisation and the appropriation of traditional financial services by new market entrants. Catching this wind of enthusiasm, the Thai Securities and Exchange Commission (SEC) proposed a Bill on Trusts for Transactions in the Capital Market, arguing that trusts

56 F. W. Maitland, *Equity: A Course of Lectures* (A. H. Chaytor and W. J. Whittaker (eds.), 2nd ed., Cambridge: Cambridge University Press, 1936) 23, F. W. Maitland, *Selected Historical Essays* (Cambridge: Cambridge University Press, 1957) at 129.

57 Maitland, *Equity*; Maitland, *Selected Historical Essays*.

58 Julia Black, 'Learning from Regulatory Disasters' (2014) *Law Society and Economy Working Paper Series* 3–4.

59 Daniel P. Kessler, 'Introduction to Regulation v Litigation' in Daniel P. Kessler (ed.), *Regulation v Litigation: Perspective from Economics and Law* (Chicago: The University of Chicago Press, 2011) 1–11 at 1.

would help the Thai capital market remain competitive against growing headwinds from emerging neighboring economies in the Southeast Asian region.[60]

The major legal roadblock, however, was the presence of section 1686 of the TCCC as discussed at length above. During the deliberation of the Council of State (3rd Committee), the reasoning of which has become the official interpretation of the TCCC on this particular issue, the Council stated that the main justification for section 1686 was that trust law was seen by the government at the time as a facilitating instrument that could potentially enable the concentration of wealth among a small selection of wealthy individuals.[61] At the time this section was introduced, Thailand was at the beginning of the longest period of economic growth in her recent economic history. Such a sustained and aggressive economic expansion might have been unnecessarily hampered, should a large number of productive assets, notably land, have been held in trust for the benefit of privileged few. To demonstrate that section 1686 deals primarily with the inter-generational transfer of assets, the Council pointed to the fact that it was included in the TCCC under Title II (Wills) in Book VI (Succession) rather than under Book II, which deals with the law of obligations, Book III on business associations, or Book IV regarding the law of property. In other words, it might arguably be within the bounds of the law to introduce legislation establishing a trust regime specific to the context of the capital market without the need to amend the TCCC. Regardless of the aforementioned reasoning, the Council adopted a strict reading of the TCCC, interpreting section 1686 as a universal prohibition against the creation of trusts for all purposes.[62] As a result, the TCCC was amended such that section 1686 now reads: 'Trusts created whether directly or indirectly by an act *inter vivos* or *mortis causa* shall have no effect whatever, unless arising by virtue of a provision of a law for the establishment of trusts only.'

It was clear at the time that the added phrase was intended merely to allow for very narrow and specific cases using trust law, such as that relating to facilitation of investment activities in the capital market.

11.3.2.1 Scrutinising the 2007 Act

To really understand why the trust regime under the 2007 Act is less about enabling private arrangements and more to do with setting up of a regulatory framework, one should look no further than the texts and provisions of the Act itself. The most blatant signpost of a regulatory regime can be found in Chapter 1 of the Act, entitled 'Supervision of Trust for Transactions in Capital Market'. The SEC has a wide range of powers, including the power to set the scope within which a trust may be created.[63] To this end, the SEC further announced that a trust certificate[64] is a security, effectively bringing the entirety of the trust regime in the 2007 Act

60 Preamble to the Trusts for Transactions in the Capital Market Act B.E. 2550 (2007), ('the 2007 Act').

61 The Council of State (3rd Committee), meeting report of 27 January 2004 (in Thai), on file with the second author.

62 Ibid., Accompanying Note.

63 Section 4 and Section 8(1) empowers the SEC to issue a notification (subsidiary rule) to limit the scope of a trust to the following three transactions:

(1) the issuance of securities under the Securities and Exchange Act;
(2) the securitisation under the Royal Enactment on Special Purpose Juristic Persons for Securitisation;
(3) other transactions which are supportive or beneficial to capital market development.

64 A trust certificate is an instrument that represents the rights of the beneficiary in that particular trust. Under a given trust, there will be a number of trust certificates, each with the same monetary values and beneficial rights (unitisation).

under the regulatory and supervisory authorities of the Securities and Exchange Act B.E. 2535 (1992) (SEA). There are two other unique features of the SEA that may not be found in trusts in common law jurisdictions or even most civil law renditions.

The first set of provisions lays down the supervisory framework for trustees. Contrary to the prevailing principle of trust law which states that a trustee can be drawn from a wide variety of people from all walks of life, the eligible class of trustees under the 2007 Act is extremely narrow. No person is allowed to undertake the role as a trustee without approval from the SEC.[65] To be eligible to apply for approval, the prospective applicant must be either a financial institution already licensed under the Financial Institution Businesses Act B.E. 2551 (2008) or a finance and investment company regulated under the purview of the SEA.[66] Furthermore, since a licensed trustee under the 2007 Act is assigned to manage trust property financed by the investing public, the SEC is also authorised to prescribe the threshold business and operating requirements as well as being endowed with ongoing supervisory power over licensed trustees.[67]

While it may not be as prominent as the SEC's close regulatory and supervisory relationship with licensed trustees, the second distinctive aspect of this trust regime concerns the requirements and other specific rules applicable to the settlor of a 2007 Act trust. Contrary to conventional trust law in most countries, the law imposes a limitation on the eligible class of settlors. Under section 12, a settlor must be either a securities-issuing company under the SEA, an originator under the Emergency Decree on the Special Juristic Person for Securitisation, or other types of juristic person as prescribed by the SEC.[68] Furthermore, while it is perfectly within reason for a settlor under the English law of trusts to create a trust for the benefit of her or himself, the 2007 Act prohibits a settlor or a trustee to be named as a beneficiary unless there is another beneficiary (or other beneficiaries) specified in the trust instrument.[69] When considering the business use case of the 2007 Act trust (most notably Real Estate Investment Trusts – REITs), it is perfectly understandable that the public-policy consideration would move against allowing a large company which raises capital from the public to name itself as sole beneficiary of the scheme.

Having pointed out two primary departures of the trust regime under the 2007 Act from the conventional principles of trusts, there are several other features under the regime that can be mapped out against the four following essential characteristics of a trust as accepted by academic literature and practitioners across various jurisdictions.[70]

Firstly, a trust must set out the basic arrangements regarding the relationship between trustee and trust assets. In gist, the trustee should in theory have powers to manage the property held in trust and to alienate the assets free from the beneficiary's rights. To this end, section 18(2) clearly stipulates that the trustee is the legal owner of trust property[71] and shall

65 Section 54, the 2007 Act.

66 Section 55, the 2007 Act.

67 Sections 56–61, the 2007 Act.

68 The SEC has so far announced two additional classes of settlors, namely, settlors of Sukuk and REIT manager. See the SEC Notification KOR ROR 14/2555 (consolidated version).

69 Section 13, the 2007 Act. The second paragraph of this section states further that 'In cases where the settlor or the trustee, by virtue of beneficiary, receives interest more than the proportion specified in the first paragraph, the interest shall be allocated to another beneficiary or other beneficiaries'.

70 D. J. Hayton, S. C. Kortmann, and H. L. E. Verhagen (eds.), *Principles of European Trust Law* (The Hague: Kluwer Law International, 1999); M. J. de Waal, 'In Search of a Model for the Introduction of the Trust into a Civilian Context' 12 *Stellenbosch Law Review* 63–85 at 67; Lusina Ho, 'Trusts: the essentials' in Smith (ed.), *The Worlds of the Trust* at 3.

71 Either an owner of the property or a person entitled to the right over the property.

have the duty to manage the trust property in accordance with the trust instrument and this Act. Corresponding to the universal principle of trusts in this aspect, the trustee's ownership right is qualified. In other words, he does not have the complete liberty to exercise the ownership right as he pleases. Due to the hybrid personality of the trust,[72] he owes an *in personam* obligation towards the beneficiary to the extent stipulated in the trust instrument and according to the 2007 Act framework.[73] Even though the power to divest or alienate trust assets is not explicitly stipulated in this Act, it could arguably be construed that such power is subsumed in the power to manage the trust property under section 30 and the right of the trustee to assign the management duty to a third party expert under section 37.[74]

Second, one of the most desirable advantages of the trust over other asset-management techniques such as agency or mandate is the ability to ring-fence the trust assets from the claims of third parties, including connected persons and family members of the trustee upon his death, divorce, or bankruptcy. Again, on this point, the 2007 Act is mostly consistent with universal principles. Section 50 is unequivocal in affirming that trust property is not within reach of the trustee's own creditors. Crucially, in cases where a trustee becomes bankrupt, the trust property shall not be deemed part of the trustee's estate. The Act however does not make any specific reference to the right (or lack thereof) of potential family members of the trustee over the trust property since, as stated above, the trustee cannot by law be a natural person. As a result, the possibility of a claim by his family member becomes moot.

Third, the beneficiary ought in theory to be able to enforce certain obligations against the trustee and third parties to protect his interest over the trust property. At the most basic level, the beneficiary is expected to have *in personam* claims against the trustee to make distributions to him according to the terms of the trust instrument. Additionally, there should also be certain mechanisms that allow the beneficiary to protect himself against the unauthorised transfer of trust assets. To address these two issues in reverse, Chapter 4 of the Act deals in an elaborate manner with the beneficiary's rights in the case of an unauthorised transfer and a third party with bad faith.[75] The beneficiary can trace unauthorised transfers in most cases except in the case of a good faith purchaser without notice of the unauthorised transfer.[76] Nevertheless, he can still recover any costs incurred as a result of enforcing such rights regardless of whether the tracing exercise is successful or not.[77] Last but not least, the beneficiary has a *statutory* right to demand the trustee manage the trust property in accordance with the terms, including timely payment of the benefit.[78]

Finally, what all successful trust regimes of the world have in common is a meaningful system of check and balance. Chiefly, there should be a mechanism by which the trustee can be held accountable for his action in breach of his duty to the trust and the beneficiary. In common law jurisdictions, the elements of check and balance are inherent in various duties

72 Jongchul Kim, 'Identity and the Hybridity of Modern Finance: How a Specifically Modern Concept of the Self Underlies the Modern Ownership of Property, Trusts and Finance' (2013) 38(2) *Cambridge Journal of Economics* 425–44.

73 For instance, the duty to carry out one's duty with integrity and prudence as a professional with expertise by providing fair treatment to beneficiaries (section 30), the duty to refrain from any action in conflict with the interest of the trust either for one's own benefit or for the other's (section 31), the duty to prepare an account of trust property separately from any other accounts under its responsibility (section 32).

74 The management of trust is the trustee's personal duty except where the law explicitly allows for assignment of such duty.

75 In particular, sections 44 and 45, the 2007 Act.

76 Paragraphs 2 of section 44 and Section 45, the 2007 Act.

77 Paragraph 3 of section 44, the 2007 Act.

78 Paragraph 1 of section 44, the 2007 Act.

owed to the beneficiary by the trustee. Where needed the court of justice is well equipped to provide clarifications, and make incremental changes, as well as to point out loopholes and deficiencies in the law. Without the same depth and breadth of experience with trust law as in other trailblazing jurisdictions, the 2007 Act consciously and purposefully supplements the internal mode of check and balance with the regulator's sanctioning powers. The SEC is equipped with the authority to issue administrative orders and initiate criminal proceedings.[79]

11.3.2.2 Trust Law in Action

If push comes to shove, the purists among trust-law scholars would possibly be able to make peace with the deployment of trust law in the form of regulated instruments in the capital market. As a matter of fact, the introduction of the 2007 Act represents merely a small carve out that exists only in the highly specialised field of finance and investment. In exchange of intellectual compromise, Thailand has gained significantly in economic terms. The SEC envisaged two possible scenarios. First, a trust may be adopted as a wealth and investment management scheme, the so-called 'active trust' and, secondly, a trust may also help facilitate the settlement of securities traded on the Thai bourse, otherwise referred to as 'passive trust'.[80]

The most popular use of trusts for transactions in the capital market is in the form of REITs. REITs are corporate trusts that invest exclusively in real estate. Typically, the owner of a real estate project or development (under this law, the so-called 'REIT manager') appoints and transfers the legal title to the real estate to a trustee (either a licensed financial institution or a licensed investment firm). The trustee may (and usually does) delegate the management function back to the REIT manager in the case that the latter is professionally capable and experienced in administering the task.[81] For instance, a shopping mall developer can sign a trust deed appointing a bank or subsidiary of a bank with a trustee license to act as a trustee of that shopping mall with a delegation clause in the deed, which effectively reverts the management right to the mall back to the developer, who is more knowledgeable in the retail business sector than the trustee bank or bank subsidiary. Subsequently, the developer/REIT manager will work with a financial advisor in order to undertake the public offering of REIT units. Depending on what is promised in the prospectus, REIT investors (beneficiaries of the trust) generally have a right to a predetermined portion of revenue or profit arising from the management of real estate held in trust. There are currently twenty-three registered

79 Chapter 8 (Sanctions, Statute of Limitation and Settlement Committee), the 2007 Act.

80 Examples of active trusts include institutional investor/high net worth trust funds (II/HNW), exchange traded trusts (ETT), special purpose trusts for securitisation, REITs (Real Estate Investment Trusts), and Sukuk Islamic wealth management trusts while passive trusts can be structured as employee stock ownership programs (ESOP), employee joint investment programs (EJIP), and trusts for derivative warrants, reserve accounts, or sinking funds.

81 Section 37, the 2007 Act:

> Management of trust is a trustee's personal duty. A trustee shall not delegate its duty to other persons except where:
>
> (1) the trust instrument provides otherwise;
> (2) it is a transaction that is not personal in nature and needs no capability of trustee's profession;
> (3) it is a transaction that a reasonable prudent owner of the property of the same characteristics as the trust property, who manages such property with similar objectives to those of the trust, may delegate a third person to manage such property;
> (4) any other cases as specified by the SEC in its notification as delegable matters.
>
> In cases where the trustee contravenes the first paragraph, the management shall bind the trustee personally, and not bind the trust.

REITs traded on the Thai Stock Exchange, raising the total of approximately THB 140 billion (or US$ 4.6 billion).[82] At present, the total REIT market capitalisation is around THB 288 billion (US$ 9.5 billion) accounting for 1.7 per cent of the Thai stock exchange's total market capitalisation.[83] Evidently, REITs still do not represent a sizeable share as compared to other subsectors, but the 2007 Act has given an alternative, more flexible avenue for fundraising for real estate developers and investment opportunities for the public.

11.3.3 *Expanding the Scope of the Regulatory Trust Model: a New Landscape for Personal Wealth Management*

During the Junta Government of General Prayuth Chan O-cha (2014–19), there was a growing concern over the rate at which the well-heeled families and private individuals transferred their investible assets abroad in search of more profitable, tax-efficient asset-management services, particularly to Hong Kong and Singapore.[84] The Ministry of Finance undertook a study of this phenomenon and subsequently identified a lack of effective wealth-management tools as a primary cause of the outflow.[85] As a result, the Personal Asset Management Bill ('the Bill') was proposed and approved by the Cabinet on 10 July 2018 and is at the time of writing under consideration by the Council of State. In gist, the Bill mirrors the structure and operating mechanism of the 2007 Act. In other words, upon coming into force, it will create a regulatory regime for licensed trustees under the supervisory authority of the SEC. Rather than raising funds from the public through sales of trust units, the Bill envisages that a settlor would hire a licensed trustee to manage assets that he would like to put in trust for his, or a designated beneficiary's, benefit. In other words, a trust under the Bill would more closely resemble a traditional common law trust, which is in effect a legal instrument for an individual's asset management.

11.3.4 *A Path Unknown: Lack of Conceptual and Practical Clarity of the Bill*

The major point of departure from the common law trust regime is that the Bill adopts the regulatory trust model first introduced in the 2007 Act. In fact, a significant portion of the draft provisions mirror the language of the 2007 Act verbatim.[86] This results in at least two concerns: one conceptual and another practical.

Firstly, it is arguable whether a general trust law is compatible with the Council of State's interpretation of section 1686 of the TCCC. As explained above, the amendment to section 1686 took place concurrently with the introduction of the 2007 Act. The Council of State at

82 The statistics was compiled by the SEC and the second author's own research from the Stock Exchange of Thailand investment portal www.settrade.com/settrade/ updated as of 1 December 2019.

83 The statistics was compiled by the second author's own research from the Stock Exchange of Thailand investment portal www.settrade.com/settrade/ updated as of 1 December 2019.

84 The issues of capital outflow and promotion of domestic wealth management were cited as two primary reasons for the draft legislation, as proposed by the Ministry of Finance (7 June 2018).

85 On file with the second author. An alternative and more widely shared theory of the outflow is the enforcement of the inheritance tax law which came into force from 1 February 2016.

86 Particularly, the regulatory frameworks of both the 2007 Act and the Bill are exactly the same, word for word, with one exception. Unlike in the 2007 Act, the powers of the SEC under the Bill have been elaborated with additional details, for instance, licence fee, application standards, as well as operation rules. It should be noted too that the Bill will be revised and edited thoroughly before it becomes law, if at all. Therefore, this chapter tries to limit the discussion of the Bill to its core rationale, principles, and important legal mechanisms while minimising the discussion of the specificities of each draft provision to only when necessary.

the time read the original section 1686 as a provision designed to prevent a concentration of wealth among certain classes of rich and powerful individuals. In addition, the learned members of the Council did not see the 2007 Act as being against the aforementioned principle. To the contrary, by providing Thai people, regardless of their wealth or class, with an additional way to invest, the 2007 Act would have helped alleviate the country's economic inequality. Nevertheless, it could very well be argued that a general trust law would come up against the public-policy reason underlying section 1686, since it would effectively encourage the inter-generational transfer of wealth within the same societal class. This point can be illustrated by referring to the draft provisions on the creation of a trust. Unlike the 2007 Act, the Bill allows a trust to be created by trust deed or by will.[87] Furthermore, the draft section 8 states that a trust deed is limited by a statutory period of 100 years. Any trust deed created in perpetuity or with a period of operation longer than 100 years will be invalidated.[88] Worse still, this statutory period may only be as effective as a 'paper tiger' since the beneficial owners of the trust assets can easily re-establish the trust by signing a new deed extending the life of the trust by another century if need be.

Secondly, it is unclear how the regulatory general trust regime would function in practice. Unlike in the narrow context of the Thai capital market, the possible types of asset that may be put in trust is wide-ranging.[89] It is thus entirely plausible that, under the scenario of this Bill, a farmer settlor may decide to put his paddy field in trust and ask for a licensed financial institution or investment firm to manage it. One of the licensed trustees could accept the challenge and provide trust services by delegating the management task to a more capable third party.[90] Additionally, the SEC is a specialist regulator primarily tasked to ensure the orderly and efficient functioning of the financial market, which is a far cry from regulating the administration of various kinds of private property. It remains to be seen whether the SEC will be able to equip itself with necessary resources in time to provide the expected level and quality of supervision for this potentially new industry in time should the Bill come into effect, if at all.

11.4 CONCLUDING REMARKS

The journey to integrate the law of trusts into the Thai legal system is far from its conclusion. If the history thus far has taught us anything, it would be that the pursuit will be highly adaptive to time and context. In the early years of the experiment, the Thai courts and other legal adjudicatory bodies took a highly pragmatic approach by recognising common law trust arrangements, even though they were not founded under Thai law. As soon as Thai legal modernisation caught up with the proliferation of trusts mostly created by foreign individuals and wealthy Siamese, the public-policy rationale and conceptual incompatibility swayed overwhelmingly against any form of trust regime, since it was viewed as a mechanism

87 Draft section 7.

88 The language of this draft provision is still unclear. A trust deed created in violation of this section could either be invalidated all together or capped to 100 years.

89 Under draft section 3, trust fund means any assets specified in the trust deed and encompasses all assets, dividends, debts and liabilities arising from the management of trust according to the trust deed or as prescribed in the Act.

90 Alternatively, licensed trustees may collectively decide to accept only more liquid and investible types of asset in trust but by doing so, they would exclude the vast majority of the population and thereby exacerbate the inequality problem already prevalent in the country.

employed to entrench wealth and prosperity among the rich and powerful section of the population.

The development of trusts was halted and only resumed once the country entered the mid-2000s economic recovery period after the Asian financial crisis. By that time, trust law was seen as a flexible fundraising and asset-management tool. Within the confines of the capital-market governance framework, and under the rigorous supervision of the SEC, a regulatory trust regime was introduced in 2007. Since then, trusts have been utilised to unlock the the economic potential of various real-estate projects, fostering promising yet unproven sectors of the economy, and optimising the operation of the Thai stock exchange.

Due to the relative success of the regulatory trust regime under the 2007 Act, the government is now planning to expand its scope beyond the realm of capital markets into personal asset management, broadly defined. As a result, Thailand is indeed at an important crossroad with regard to its trust law journey. Turning left, the country might choose to keep the regulatory trust regime as a productive tool for an affluent few. Turning right, the new Bill could provide the legal foundation to solve a growing societal concern, namely the fight against deep-rooted social and economic inequality for all.

12

The History of Thai Family Laws

Strong Women and Weak Gender Equality under the Law

Apinop Atipiboonsin

This law seems to treat women like buffalos while treating men just like men. This is truly unjust and thus the law must be repealed.

– King Mongkut[1]

12.1 INTRODUCTION

Thailand is singular in Asia or even in the world with its impressive female representation in the academic and business world: almost half of the Thai chief executives are women and university students are overwhelmingly more women than men.[2] Despite this, gender equality is far from perfect. There is a lack of female representation in politics as well as discrimination against women in both public and private sectors.[3] Also, the prevalence of domestic violence and exploitation in its enormous sex industry only helps highlight the contrast.[4] These statements are simply a restatement of the popular account, mostly from a Western perspective, of how Thai women live in a contradictory space with the coexistence of positive economic female roles and the negative prevalence of sexual abuse.[5] But amidst this puzzling account, the main legal texts in Thailand, on the surface, rarely reflect these outstanding features of the strong and weak aspects of the status of women.

Indeed, the Civil and Commercial Code, the law governing the general private law, shows few distinguishable features that address the issue of gender equality or women's rights in particular. Book V of the Code, which deals specifically with family law including marriage and divorce, does not and cannot accommodate the progressive side of the status of Thai women today. A more perplexing story, however, is the absence of any unique characteristics

1 Act on the Sale of Wives and Children BE 2411 (1868), Preamble.

2 Randy Thanthong-Knight, 'Why Thailand's Women Are So Successful in Business (But Not Politics)', Bloomberg, 2 September 2019 www.bloomberg.com/news/articles/2019–02-25/women-gain-ground-in-thai-c-suites-not-so-much-in-government (accessed 9 September 2019).

3 Paritta Wangkiat, 'Gender Equity Push Must Start in the House', *Bangkok Post*, 3 June 2019 www.bangkokpost.com/opinion/opinion/1688320/gender-equity-push-must-start-in-the-house (accessed 9 September 2019) points out to the recent drop in women's representation in the parliament and the 'glass ceiling' that still exists in the corporate world.

4 Sandra Neuman, 'Female Prostitution in Thailand – Described Through a Victim-Agent Framework' (Bachelor Thesis, Linnaeus University, 2012) 28–30.

5 Darunee Tantiwiramanond and Shashi Pandey, 'The Status and Role of Thai Women in the Pre-Modern Period: A Historical and Cultural Perspective' (1987) 2(1) *Sojourn: Journal of Social Issues in Southeast Asia* 125–49 at 125–6.

of Thai women of the past. Despite the long-established fact that Thai women in old Siam were among those few enjoying the privilege of living in a matrilineal and matrilocal society, Book V, while often considered as reflecting characteristics of past Thai culture, does not show traces of such an outstanding feature. This chapter brings together the old and new problems and tries to solve them at the same time with the assumption that both the past and the current laws are pieces of the same jigsaw puzzle that cannot be solved on its own.

With regard to the literature on the history of Thai family law, there are only a few works which deal directly with the issue. Most studies so far deal with Thailand and its treatment of women by focusing mainly on the influence of Buddhism,[6] although there are studies that adopt a more holistic and broader perspective in terms of factors that might contribute to the status of Thai women.[7] But this research is not legal in its essence; the laws are merely discussed in the background or considered as reflections of the underlying social phenomena. The closest to the scope of this Chapter is a book written by Tamara Loos which tells a story of how family law reform was an integral part of the rise of modern Thailand.[8] Her work, however, focuses mostly on the law on marriage and the dilemma faced by Siam between monogamy and polygamy. In addition, there are outstanding dissertations written in Thai which focus on some parts of family law or some periods of time; these works also provide significant insights here.[9] This chapter thus fills the gap in the literature by looking at Thai family law as a whole from its pre-modern influences to its contemporary application.

The rest of this chapter consists of three parts. Chronologically, the first part captures the pre-modern status of Thai women in the law from the time of the Sukhothai period until the advent of the Civil and Commercial Code, tracing the background of Thai law before the complication of Western influence. Next, the chapter discusses the modernisation of Thai family law since the introduction of new concepts such as monogamy. The story of gradual law reforms in this period will help explain the discrepancies between the law on the books and the salient features of the status of Thai women. Finally, the third part further analyses the causes of the silence on gender issues and presents how the current family law is lagging behind in terms of its scope and objectives.

12.2 STRONG WOMEN OF THE PAST: WOMEN'S RIGHTS BEFORE THE MODERN LEGAL SYSTEM

Thailand, known as Siam before 1939, has always been a country of diversity and plurality in many aspects.[10] This feature, however, is the source of confusion over the exact nature of Thai women's status in the past, including in the relationship between men and women. Hindered by the lack of written records, the accounts of Thai women's status are often based on beliefs

6 For example, Khin Thitsa, *Providence and Prostitution: Image and Reality for Women in Buddhist Thailand* (London: Change International Reports, 1980).

7 Tantiwiramanond and Pandey, 'Status and Role of Thai Women'; Vitit Muntarbhorn, Wimolsiri Jamnarnvej, and Tanawadee Boonlue, *Status of Women: Thailand* (Bangkok: UNESCO, 1990).

8 Tamara Loos, *Subject Siam: Family Law, and Colonial Modernity in Thailand* (Ithaca: Cornell University Press, 2006).

9 See, for example, Boondoen Pairoh, *The Status and Role of Women in Thai Society* (Bangkok: Chulalongkorn University, 1976); Lampan Nuambunlue, *The Rights and Duties of Women According to Thai Laws During the Bangkok Period* (Bangkok: Chulalongkorn University, 1976); Apichai Noyounsen, *Legal Status of Women in Lanna Society between 1838–2442 B.E.: A Study on Marital Relationship* (Bangkok: Thammasat University, 2000).

10 Apinop Atipiboonsin, 'Volcanic Constitution: How is Plurality Turning Against Constitutionalism in Thailand?' in Jaclyn L. Neo and Bui Ngoc Son (eds.), *Pluralist Constitutions in Southeast Asia* (Oxford: Hart Publishing, 2019) 227–30.

or assumptions; extreme portrayals of women range from workers who did all agricultural work by themselves to domestic housewives who never worked a day outside.[11]

To complicate matters, there are many fundamental differences in ethnicity, culture, and language amongst groups of people living in different regions: the Siamese people of the central plains, the Southern Muslims, and the Northern and Northeastern peoples.[12] Scholars as well as Thais in general perceive women from the North and the Northeast, both of which were assimilated as part of Siam later in the twentieth century, as the strongest and most independent in Siam.[13] The most obvious reason for such a reputation is the strong matrilineal and matrilocal nature of its culture, preferring to place women at the centre of society.[14] As shown in the Northern Kingdom of Chiangmai, the scarcity of labour combined with the abundance of irrigated rice land made matrilineal organisation more sustainable as women provided a more available workforce and provided better management of the land.[15] Even in modern Thailand, married couples in the North still 'live initially with their maternal parents-in-law'.[16] However, the prevalence of women there was merely within the confines of economic activity and local ritual;[17] their overall status was better, but not significantly different from their status under the laws of the central plains, as will be discussed in Section 12.2.

Moreover, the predominantly Muslim regions in the southernmost part of Thailand also present another perspective on women's status, influenced by an entirely different set of beliefs and histories. Though the Siamese had already conquered four Muslim provinces (Pattani, Yala, Narathiwat, and Satun) by 1789, the Muslim administrative units in these places retained power over family law and inheritance.[18] Even with the modern Civil and Commercial Code, there is still an exception for Muslims living in these provinces to be able to continue practising religious laws,[19] and the Islamic law accepts certain states of affairs such as polygamous marriage as legal, contrary to the general family law regime.[20] This legal pluralism, which is 'a hallmark of colonial states',[21] shows how the Thai government adopted the practice of the British Empire by applying different laws to parts of the population according to differences in religion.[22]

[11] Alec Gordon and Napat Sirisambhand, 'Evidence for Thailand's Missing Social History: Thai Women in Old Mural Paintings' (2002) 47(2) *International Review of Social History* 261–75 at 261.

[12] David Streckfuss, 'An "Ethnic" Reading of "Thai" History in the Twilight of the Century-Old Official "Thai" National Model' (2012) 20(3) *South East Asia Research* 305–27 at 306–7.

[13] Katherine Bowie, 'Standing in the Shadows: Of Matrilocality and the Role of Women in a Village Election in Northern Thailand' (2008) 35(1) *American Ethnologist* 136–53 at 139–41.

[14] Richard Davis, 'Muang Matrifocality' (1984) 14(4) *Mankind* 263–71; Mary Lim, 'Women of Northeast Thailand: Privilege and Obligation', *Berkeley Center*, 2 December 2011 https://berkleycenter.georgetown.edu/posts/women-of-northeast-thailand-privilege-and-obligation (accessed 19 November 2019).

[15] Andrew Turton, 'Matrilineal Descent Group and Spirit Cults of the Thai-Yuan in Northern Thailand' (1972) 60 (2) *Journal of the Siam Society* 217–56 at 228–31.

[16] Konrad Kingshill, *Ku Daeng-The Red Tomb: A Village Study in Northern Thailand* (Chiang Mai: Prince Royal's College 1960) 47.

[17] Monica Janowski and Fiona Kerlogue (eds.), *Kinship and Food in South East Asia* (Copenhagen: NIAS Press, 2007) 227–9.

[18] Mahamatayuding Samah, Raihanah Abdullah and Nahid Ferdousi, 'Muslim Family Law in Southern Thailand: A Historical Overview' (2017) 37(3) *Journal of Muslim Minority Affairs* 357–70 at 359–60.

[19] Act on Application of Islamic Law in the Provinces of Pattani, Narathiwat, Yala and Satun, BE 2489 (1946).

[20] Pongdej Vanichkittikul, *Handbook of Principles of Islamic Law: Family and Inheritance Law* (Bangkok: Court of Justice of Thailand, 2012) 21.

[21] Loos, *Subject Siam*, 74.

[22] Tamara Loos, 'Competitive Colonialisms: Siam and the Malay Muslim South' in Rachel V. Harrison and Peter A. Jackson (eds.), *The Ambiguous Allure of the West: Traces of the Colonial in Thailand* (Hong Kong: Hong Kong University Press, 2010) 75–92 at 77–9.

With different shades of culture found in each region as illustrated, Siam did not and could not impose its own way from its capital until much later into modernity. While Thai laws may be presented in textbooks as homogeneous since the codification of the Three-Seals Law Code (*kotmai tra sam duang* or KTSD) early in the Rattanakosin Period, it took years for the power of the Siamese administration to reach beyond its centre.[23] The lords of the North, for instance, had full autonomy until after the end of King Mongkut's reign.[24] Siam did not reform its laws and court system until the passage of the Act on Provincial Courts in 1895.[25] By then, modern legal codes had already started to be available; it is safe to assume, accordingly, that until the advent of Book V of the Civil and Commercial Code, there was no uniform set of rules regarding family law for the whole of the territory recognised as Thailand today. Family matters were governed in each region according to the local custom of each.

What is more, the roles of women and the laws imposed upon them were also different depending on the social class of the particular woman. Women of high status might be well-educated but they had to be kept within the strict confines of the palace, while the majority of women who were of low class found themselves in an entirely different world with more freedom.[26] Lower-class women were not 'submissive and domesticated'; they could do as much as their men could, including choosing their own spouse; but they were equal only because they were equally powerless under the social structure of the time.[27] The divergence between women of different classes led to another source of confusion, as one can discover cases of exceptional women who became tax collectors through connections with the upper class, or legendary heroines in Thai history like Queen Suriyothai of Ayutthaya who dressed herself as a soldier to fight a war alongside her King,[28] as a clear evidence of how women succeeded as much as men in political or economic endeavours.[29]

That said, amidst many laws throughout the history of Siam, it was the convergence in economic and political settings that principally defined the role of Siamese women. Under a status system which regularly subjected most men to serve the king or the nobles for up to six months away from home,[30] the matrifocal system became a necessity in order to maintain agriculture essential to the livelihood of the people.[31] Women had to take charge of the economic production as equals among men due to the lack of male labour.[32] Combining this with the belief in ancestral spirits found in many places from the North to the central plains, which requires a woman to stay with the spirits in her dwelling,[33] there was at least the

23 David M. Engel, 'Rights as Wrongs: Legality and Sacrality in Thailand' (2015) 39(1) *Asian Studies Review* 38–52 at 42.

24 Wilai Suthisirikul, *Chiang Mai before 'Municipality' from 1846 to 1899* (Master of Arts thesis, Chulalongkorn University, 1985) 37.

25 Charter of Provincial Courts BE 2438 (1895).

26 Tantiwiramanond and Pandey, 'Status and Role of Thai Women', 136–7.

27 Ibid., 139–40.

28 Amporn Jirattikorn, 'Suriyothai: Hybridizing Thai National Identity Through Film' (2003) 4(2) *Inter-Asia Cultural Studies* 296–308 at 299.

29 Pornpen Huntrakoon, 'Thai Women in Three Seals Law: From Women as Leaders to Women as Buffaloes' (2003) 32 *Journal of Arts, Chulalongkorn University* 246–99, 265–6.

30 Wuttichai Mulsilp, 'Phrai Chooses Nai-as Phrai Likes it, 2411–2442 B.E.' (2012) 37 *Journal of the Royal Institute of Thailand* 271–95, 273–4. However, see Koizumi Junko, 'King's Manpower Constructed: Writing the History of the Conscription of Labour in Siam' (2002) 10(1) *South East Asia Research* 31–61, which argues that the extent to which the conscription of labor was enforced is vague and without enough strong evidence.

31 Tantiwiramanond and Pandey, 'Status and Role of Thai Women', 137–9.

32 Ibid.

33 See, for example, Andrew Walker, 'Matrilineal Spirits, Descent and Territorial Power in Northern Thailand' (2006) 17(2) *The Australian Journal of Anthropology* 196–215.

appearance of a strong female status via the division of labour and control over the management of land. From this impression came the illusion of gender equality in Siam, presenting a uniquely utopian account of a society where women were in power even before the notion of women's rights in modern times.[34] The reality was, of course, disappointingly far away from what one perceives as a perfect equality, as will be shown through the laws and practice of Siam in this first part of the chapter. The account of Siamese men's status during the reign of King Narai the Great in 1688 by Simon de la Loubère gives a clear impression of the relationship between men and women in pre-modern Thailand, hundreds of years before its modern reform:

> They (Siamese men) love their Wives and Children exceedingly, and it appears that they are greatly beloved by them. Whilst the Men acquit themselves of the six months work, which they every one yearly owe to the Prince, it belongs to their Wife, their Mother, or their Children to maintain them . . . He works not at all, when he works not for the King: he walks not abroad; he hunts not: he does nothing almost but continue sitting or lying, eating, playing, smoking and sleeping. His Wife will wake him at 7 a clock in the morning, and will serve him with Rice and Fish: He will fall asleep again hereupon; and at Noon he will eat again, and will sup at the end of the day . . . The Women plough the Land, they sell and buy in the Cities.[35]

12.2.1 *The Earliest Evidence of Family Laws in Siam*

The oldest official account of Thai legal history is the Sukhothai scriptures, which depict the early form of governance just before the arrival of Hindu influence in the palace.[36] In the reign of King Ram Khamhaeng (1279–98), the king was not considered to be a god; this occurred later, in 1374, when King Lithai regarded himself as a divine king.[37] However, the written text of that era already painted a picture of a patriarchal society, by mentioning almost nothing of the significance of women in society and granting male royal family members the exclusive right to rule.[38] That said, there was no authoritative legal text during this era that can inform us of the exact nature of women in the family. The most well-known source of all, the Ramkhamhaeng Inscription, is a source of controversy among historians, who still debate whether the document was written in the reign of King Mongkut, hundreds of years after 1292,

34 See, for example, Solot Sirisai and others, 'Matriarchy, Buddhism, and Food Security in Sanephong, Thailand' (2017) 13 *Maternal and Child Nutrition* e12554, 4–5 ('the matriarchal structure in Sanephong demonstrates that women are both self-reliant and at the centre of economic life in the community. Women own the family property while men provide labour in the wife's home'); also Nibondh Tipsrinimit, 'Thai Women and Leadership Roles in the Modern Society' (2003) 16(1) *Parichart Journal* 78–83, at 79 who cites Kukrit Pramoj, 'Society in Ayutthaya Period' in Faculty of Liberal Arts (ed.), *Textbook for Introduction to Thai Civilisation* (Bangkok: Thammasat University Press, 1979) 177 ('Thai women in Ayutthaya period had more rights than women in other countries from the same time . . . because women had to take on the task of family business out of necessity which is probably why, in practice, women have equal or even more rights than men till today').

35 Simon de La Loubère, *A New Historical Relation of the Kingdom of Siam* (London: Horne, Francis and Saunders, 1693) 50.

36 Prince Damrong Rajanubhab, *Ancient Siamese Administration* (Bangkok: Sophonpiphatthanakorn, 1928) 16–19 (explaining that the Hindu idea of a divine king might exist since the time of Sukhothai Kingdom but the kings preferred to treat their subject as children under a paternal government according to the Thai tradition).

37 Suphawat Kasemsri, 'The Crown and Thailand' in Princess Maha Chakri Sirindhorn Foundation (ed.), *Directory of Thai Kings* (Bangkok: Nanmee Books, 2011).

38 *Collection of Stone Scriptures Volume I* (Bangkok: Fine Arts Department, 1972) 17–18 ('When receiving silver or gold, I brought it to my father. When my father died, I looked after him like I did to my father. Once my brother died, I inherit all my kingdom').

when it was supposedly written.[39] So far, there have only been speculations and assumptions about women in Sukhothai based on the absence of direct content regarding women's status; for instance, because the Nakhon Chum Inscription (from the year 1357, during the reign of King Lithai) prescribed that property should be inherited by children from their fathers,[40] the ambiguity as to the gender of the 'children' could be interpreted as equal treatment for both sons and daughters. But it is more likely that inheritance was patrilineal, especially when considering the content of available inscriptions as a whole.[41] It was believed, however, that women in the Sukhothai era at least had a relatively stronger status in the household, according to an observation in by a Chinese imperial scholar written about Sukhothai: 'Women control expenditure of money as they are intelligent; men who are husbands should listen.'[42]

In order to access initial status of women with more concrete evidence, the *Mangraisat* – a law code derived from the reign of King Mangrai of Chiagmai (1259–1317) around the early years of the Sukhothai era (1238–1438)[43] in a region that is part of Northern Thailand today – may reflect the nature of the relationship between the sexes just before it was fully governed by the more patriarchal vision of the *Dhammasat*. Even though the *Mangraisat* also referred to the *Dhammasat*, its content could be attributed to the adaptation by 'Mon people' with a less Brahmist tone and content which is more in line with Buddhist thinking.[44] Thus, in general, the document may provide a more localised story of ancient Thai people. This goes to the point, claimed by an author, that Lanna society was immensely conservative of its tradition and the Hindu preference of men did not affect the importance of women.[45]

Even though the *Mangraisat* did not value women independently of the men protecting them,[46] many of its provisions were favourable to women. For instance, in settling the inheritance of a parent between several children when the other siblings already had children, the law gave preference to the last-born single daughter, who would receive half of all the estate.[47] Indeed, the youngest daughter, who should get married last, had to take care of the parents and it was thus natural that she should inherit the property in return.[48] Furthermore, the law recognised the need for women to own property in preparation for their future matrifocal family, in which the husband relied on his wife's parents for a home and agricultural supplies.[49] Also, daughters and sons were treated equally for their shares of inheritance, depending on whether the mother or the father died first; for instance, if the mother died before the father, the first daughter would inherit all personal belongings and a quarter of the estate, while the father would inherit the rest.[50]

39 See, for example, Piriya Krairiksh, 'An Epilogue to the Ram Khamhaeng Inscription' in James R. Chamberlain (ed.), *The Ram Khamhaeng Controversy, Collected Papers* (Bangkok: The Siam Society, 1991) 553–65.

40 *Collection of Stone Scriptures*, 13–37.

41 Pornpen Huntrakoon, 'Thai Women in Three Seals Law', 253–4.

42 Pra Jane Jean Aksorn, *Records on the Relationship between Siam and China* (Bangkok: Funeral Memorial Book for Luang Sakkarintara Phakdee, 1962) 10.

43 David K. Wyatt, 'Laws and Social Order in Early Thailand: An Introduction to the Mangraisat' (1984) 15(2) *Journal of Southeast Asian Studies* 245–52.

44 Apichai Noioonsaen, 'Legal Status of Women in Lanna Kingdom' (Thammasat 2000) 10–21.

45 Ibid., 3.

46 Adisorn Saksoong, 'Women in Mangraisat' (2007) 2 *Journal of Social Sciences Taksin University* 76–7. The law categorises twenty kinds of women based on their protectors and even prescribes that indecent acts towards those without a protection do not count as a sinful act.

47 Royal Society of Thailand, *Dhammasatprakorn* (2007) 124–5.

48 Bowie, 'Standing in the Shadows', 140.

49 Ibid.

50 Royal Society of Thailand, *Dhammasatprakorn*, 117–21 (When the mother died, the daughter and the father would inherit the estate; when the father died, the son and the mother would instead inherit all).

The roles of Siamese women then took a downturn during the Ayutthaya era (1350–1767). While the previous laws from the Sukhothai Kingdom might forbid women from adultery without the same provision for men, there was no formal recognition of polygamous practice and social attitudes still reproved adultery by men.[51] However, with the Laws on Husbands and Wives of 1361, the law clearly stipulated that men could have polygamous relationships and went so far as to classify wives into three different classes:[52] Major Wife (*Mea Klang Muang*) who becomes a wife through parental arrangement; Minor Wife (*Mea Klang Nork*) who becomes a wife through the request of a man; and Slave Wife (*Mea Klang Tasi*) who is bought by a man to become his wife.[53] Husbands could also subject their wives into slavery,[54] physically punish them,[55] or demand damages if their wives abandoned the household.[56] Representing the overall attitude of the law towards women in Siam, these laws gave husbands virtually complete control over their wives. These same provisions both in the text and in practice were in force in Siam, in their lesser forms,[57] until the introduction of modern reform in 1935.

In this way, the husband was the head of the household, as authority passes from 'the father-in-law to the son-in-law' in a matrifocal society.[58] It might be true that property devolved matrilineally, but there was not much a women could do given that she was powerless if her husband decided to sell her into slavery.[59] It is worth noting that there are also many provisions in the Law of Husband and Wife dealing with infidelity on the part of the wife, and the law mainly demanded monetary compensation from the man involved but subjected women to various means of public humiliation, from undergoing a public procession to tattooing of the face.[60] Judging from the law texts available, there is little evidence that Siamese women were less gender-oppressed than their contemporaries in other cultures.

In those situations where the law favoured women, it was often based on customary or economic reasons. Starting from the moment of engagement, the 'bride price' or *Sinsod* – which could be seen as a privilege for women as they did earn the gift unilaterally through marriage – was actually a way to compensate the bride's parents, the use of whose property was necessary for the husband's agricultural work.[61] Similarly, though the husband had to move to the bride's land to work on her family's farm, this hardship was negated by the fact that the control over the property was in the hands of the husband as the head of the

51 Dararat Mattariganon, 'Monogamy in Thai Society' (1985) 6 *Silpa-Wattanatham* 1–4.

52 *Kotmai Tra Sam Duang Book II* (Bangkok: Thammasat University Press, 2004) 206.

53 Ibid. There was also another special category of wives called a royal wife (*Mea Pra Rad Cha Tarn*) who was given to a man by the king. They were treated specially, as equal to their husband, with many exceptions from the rules such as having a fair share in inheritance or protected from excessive bodily punishment from the husband. See ibid., 75, 95.

54 Kotmai Tra Sam Duang, Law on Slavery s. 31 and s. 37.

55 ibid., s. 60.

56 ibid., s. 22.

57 See, for example, fn. 59 for a change to the right to sell wives as slaves.

58 Tantiwiramanond and Pandey, 'Status and Role of Thai Women', 137.

59 Until the Act on the Sale of Wives and Children was handed down in 1868 by King Mongkut, men as the heads of households could sell anyone in the family, including his wives, to other persons. The prevalence and frequency of the selling of wives or other family members was also recorded in history with the estimation that as many as a third of the population were slaves. The reason for such occurrence was that slavery turned out to be an effective way of securing a loan in a country without organised law enforcement. See further in Akin Rabibhadana, *The Organisation of Thai Society in the Early Bangkok Period, 1782–873* (Ithaca: Cornell University Press, 1969) 109–11.

60 *Kotmai Tra Sam Duang Book II*, 206–7.

61 Koichi Mizuno, 'Multihousehold Compounds in Northeast Thailand' (1968) 8(10) *Asian Survey* 842–52 at 846.

family.[62] Likewise, the law of inheritance may, on its face, have provided equal shares among sons and daughters,[63] but these shares were insignificant after the marriage due to the fact that whatever the bride might inherit from her family would be part of the matrimonial property which granted all effective control to the husband.[64]

Overall, Thai laws since the earliest recorded times treated women within this framework. The varying degrees of preference towards women from the North to the South, albeit fascinating, rarely mattered to the actual livelihood of women. This is especially true when one considers the expansive influence of Buddhism and Brahmanism that defined Siamese culture until today. The already influential teachings of Buddhism and the full embrace of Brahmanism in the Ayutthaya period might resonate generally,[65] but their presence can be seen especially in family law through the repression of women with few rights and many duties.[66] Whatever local beliefs that might have empowered women in the ancient past had faded away through time, and the emergence of other competing forces opened a space for men to assert their dominance in almost every way.

However, an important question is whether these laws truly represent the real practice of most Thai people at the time; this is especially problematic since it is possible that the law only applied to a selected few in the ancient Siamese kingdoms. As for polygamous relationships, only those in the upper classes who could afford to have multiple wives would be eligible for such practice, not all Thai people.[67] Moreover, the laws of the Ayutthaya period were studied based on the KTSD which was revised in 1804, and there is no feasible way to measure the similarity between the Laws on Husbands and Wives, even though KTSD claims to strictly follow the law as it was given in 1361.[68] Nevertheless, given no major alteration to the relationship between women and men in the entirety of Ayutthaya period, it is unlikely that differences in the law could be significant, except maybe in the causes for divorce, as will be discussed in the following part.

12.2.2 *The First Codification of Law in the History of Siam*

In 1804, during the reign of King Rama I, the founder of Rattanakosin Kingdom and the first monarch of the reigning Chakri dynasty, *Amdaeng Pom* went to the court asking for a divorce from her husband.[69] Even though she did not prove any fault or misconduct on the part of her husband and she herself was allegedly having an affair with one of the judges, the Court granted her a divorce.[70] This case came to the attention of the King, as the husband petitioned to the Royal Palace claiming that the judgment was unfair; however, when the King compared all available editions of the relevant legal provision, they all stated that '[w]hen

62 It is suggested, however, that the presence and support of the father-in-law acted as a check on the power of the husband as initially he had to rely on the land and equipment from his father-in-law and could only take control of the property later when the father-in-law had passed away. Nidhi Eoseewong, *Wrap-around loincloths, female tube skirts, and underwear* (Bangkok: Matichon, 1995) 91–2.

63 Boondoen Pairoh, *Status and Roles of Women*, 67.

64 Ibid., 182–3.

65 Chatsumarn Kabilsingh, *Thai Women in Buddhism* (Berkeley: Parallax, 1991) 3–7.

66 Ibid., 15–17.

67 La Loubère, *New Historical Relation*, 72.

68 *Kotmai Tra Sam Duang Book II*, 205.

69 See generally Chris Baker and Pasuk Phongpaichit, *The Palace Law of Ayutthaya and the Thammasat: Law and Kingship in Siam* (Ithaca: Cornell University Press, 2016).

70 David M. Engel, *Law and Kingship in Thailand during the Reign of King Chulalongkorn* (Ann Arbor: Michigan University Press, 1975) 3–4.

the husband has no fault and the wife asks for a divorce, let the wife have a divorce'.[71] The King deemed the law to be inappropriate as a result of perverted modification by amoral people. He therefore initiated a project to fix the wrongs and codify the laws into one source called the KTSD. How a divorce case gave rise to law reform could be more than just a coincidence. Contrary to the available text of KTSD, which only allowed a divorce when there was fault such as negligence or criminal activities of the husband,[72] the corrupted text might just be the law that had evolved to match with the real practice of the people: an extension of a similar provision in the KTSD itself which gave the husband a right to complete a divorce by simply leaving the house with his belongings and make a cut with a knife on the foundation of the house.[73] But one can never know for certain.

In this connection, as the monarchy earns part of its legitimacy and authority from a virtuous King,[74] the codification of the KTSD not only purified the law but also tried to marginalise all other customary norms (such as those in the North) that did not fall in line with the principles of the KTSD, comparable to the purification of Buddhist practices occurring at about the same time.[75] The Buddhist influence in the KTSD is thus different from that which inspired the *Mangraisat* in the North. That said, while Buddhist teachings were among the sources of the KTSD, the law itself was not a reflection of any direct reference to Buddhism in the area of family law. The effects of Buddhism, however indirect, were fundamental; the way Buddhist teachings generally treat women as always dependent on their relations to others around them gave the impression that women are weak and thus deserve to be protected from harm,[76] like valuable belongings that could cause their family great shame if a woman were led astray.

12.3 WOMEN IN TRANSITION: WOMEN'S RIGHTS UNDER THE REFORMS

As men (parents or husbands) always had the real control over their women as bestowed on them by law,[77] whatever powers and privileges women had in the realm of economic production did not translate into legal rights. This claim is worrying when one considers how the KTSD might be considered the first edition of modern Thai family law, as the very structure of the Law on Husband and Wife in KTSD is still comparable to the provisions of the law today: starting with the forms and requirements of a marital relationship, then setting out the personal and property rights and duties within the couple and between the couple and others, and finally prescribing different ways in which marriage could be terminated. The subsequent history of the development of Thai family law can be thought of as stages of legal progress made from this starting point, for better or for worse. The first and most important stage of progress is the coming into force of Book V of the Civil and Commercial Code which standardised and formulated the old laws within a globally recognisable legal platform, with

[71] Ibid.

[72] Lampan Nuambunlue, *Rights and Duties of Women*, 6–52.

[73] KTSD, Laws on Husbands and Wives s. 51.

[74] See generally Patrick Jory, *Thailand's Theory of Monarchy: The Vessantara Jataka and the Idea of the Perfect Man* (Albany: SUNY Press, 2016) 15–20.

[75] Engel, 'Rights as Wrongs', 43–5.

[76] See, for example, Kajiyama Yuichi, 'Women in Buddhism' (1982) 15(2) *The Eastern Buddhist* 53–70, at 55–6 which discusses the Buddhist axiom 'Three Kinds of Subordination', meaning a woman is always under either her parents, her husband or her eldest son.

[77] Robert Lingat, 1935 *History of Thai Law (Private Law): Private Wrongs* (Bangkok: Thai Wattana Panich, 1935, reprinted 1983), 98–9.

monogamy as the only form of marriage and rational sets of rules following the start of a marriage, dealing with issues ranging from marital property, the personal relationship between spouses, legitimation and the custody of children to divorce.

Before getting to the modern Code, however, there is a force that subtly and gradually began to make a transition between the past and the future of Thai family law, starting from the reign of King Mongkut, the fourth king of Chakri dynasty who reigned from 1851 to 1868. In his reign, more liberal ideals had in effect caused a change in the interpretation of longstanding rules in the KTSD, arising from the influence of Western powers, and inspiring unexpected changes, such as eradicating the practice of selling one's wife into slavery without her consent and granting young women the right to choose their own husband after coming of age.[78] By the time Prince Raphi Phatthanasak – a key figure in Thai legal reform – gave his lecture on what would later become probably the first comprehensive and modern academic treatment of family law in 1889, he observed that the control over women kept 'decreasing these days'.[79]

However, bigger changes came only after the imposition of monogamy in Thai law, as it fundamentally affected the framework of the ancient family law on what was recognised by law as a valid marriage. The magnitude of this development was crucial as it directly challenged the whole conception of the status of wives in Thailand; instead of collecting wives of different categories as property, men had to be satisfied with one wife. Women were not buffaloes under the control their owners anymore, but were suddenly turned into equal partners in a relationship.

It is worth noting here that, although it is easy to conclude that criticisms of polygamy in Siam led to the abolition of polygamy as part of the plan that ultimately led to the end of extraterritoriality,[80] this is questionable in light of the fact that many countries were willing to make an exception to the adoption of modern family law as part of required legal reforms under several trade agreements between Siam and other Western nations.[81] This preservation of polygamous practices shows a global trend of limiting the liberalisation of law to the area outside of family and gender roles, in accordance with the way globalisation of law took place in other parts of the world: this liberalisation only shaped reforms regarding economic activities, stopping short of tearing apart the societal status quo at the cost of retaining inequality and the suppression of women.[82]

More likely, as Loos has suggested, the demise of polygamy in the law was a matter of domestic rather than international circumstances, as the reforms made throughout successive reigns of kings since King Chulalongkorn (1868–1910) resulted diminishing the function of polygyny as a tool both to demonstrate masculine authority and to integrate the kingdom through numerous offspring and relatives, filling the ranks of officers with loyalty guaranteed by blood ties.[83] In effect, 'polygyny's sexual connotations were emphasised, moralised, and politicised while its former role in state affairs was depoliticised, disavowed, or omitted altogether' due to the swift change of circumstances in modernising Siam.[84]

78 Kabilsingh, *Thai Women in Buddhism*, 16.

79 Prince Raphi Phatthanasak, *Unveiling the Statues, Lecture on Land Law and Lecture on Law on Husbands and Wives* (Bangkok: Funeral Memorial Book for His Serene Highness Prince Wimwathit Rapheephat, 1959) 68.

80 On extraterritoriality, see Krisdakorn Wongwuthikun and Naporn Popattanachai, Chapter 15 of this volume.

81 Loos, *Subject Siam*, 106–7.

82 Duncan Kennedy, 'Three Globalisations of Law and Legal Thought' in *The New Law and Economic Development: A Critical Appraisal* (David M. Trubek and Alvaro Santos eds., Cambridge: Cambridge University Press, 2006) 50–2.

83 Loos, *Subject Siam*, 129.

84 Ibid.

On this issue, Prince Svasti Sobhana – a son of King Mongkut and the first Head Minister of the Ministry of Justice – supported monogamy with inspiration from Japanese law at the time, which banned polygamy but still allowed the father of a child born out of wedlock to register the child as legitimate, maintaining indirectly the previous status quo.[85] However, King Vajiravudh did not agree with the recommendation and refrained from changing the law based on the principle that making the law without the means of truly enforcing it would be damaging to the legal system, and that religious and cultural differences between Siam and Europe were too much to be reconciled at the time (1913).[86]

That said, the reformation of the legal system as part of the plan to free Siam from unjust extraterritoriality could not succeed without completing the Civil and Commercial Code. This inevitably forced the government to deal with family law and its place in modern Siam. But it took decades and the revolution to a constitutional monarchy before the promulgation of Book V of the Code in 1935 could finally state that monogamy is the only legalised marital relationship in Thailand.

12.3.1 *Later Legal Reforms*

While legal advisors, both foreign and Thai, strove to transfer the elements of KTSD into the modern law code to the greatest extent possible, the only parts that they truly considered in the drafting were family law and inheritance law.[87] When any reform was made to family law, 'the rhetoric was [that] of protection, rather than of freedom and equality'.[88]

Also, imperial ideologies treated family matters as the foundation of society, as manifested in the way several treaties between Siam and other foreign powers required exceptions regarding family law and inheritance law as part of the judicial reforms.[89] This deference was taken to the extent that the advisors were ready to 'substitute monogamy for polygamy in the draft, if instructed by the government to do so'.[90] This reflected the tension colonialism brought to the debate on polygamy, which turned into a clash between Christianity and Buddhism after 1835 when Dan Beach Bradley, the founder of the first newspaper in Siam, asked King Mongkut to abolish the practice as it was contrary to the will of god.[91]

Even in 1931, less than a decade before the change to monogamy, King Prajadhipok, the last monarch under absolute monarchy, formalised polygamy by amending the KTSD to cover the registration of multiple wives with the state.[92] And in concluding the resolution of his royal counsellors, the King remarked: 'Then, there is no need to feel embarrassed by foreigners because the fact is that all countries which undertake monogamy are not completely monogamy [sic] . . . polygamy is preferred as it is based on reality which will remain as such for a long time'.[93]

85 'The End of "Polygamy": What Thailand Had Been through for Monogamy', *SILPA Magazine*, 25 February 2019 www.silpa-mag.com/history/article_28423 (accessed 27 November 2019).
86 Ibid.
87 Loos, *Subject Siam*, 65.
88 Ibid., 52.
89 Ibid., 105–7.
90 Ibid., 109.
91 Surachet Suklarpkit, 'Before Monogamy: A Brief History of Siamese Family Law B.E. 2410–2478' (2014) *Political Science Journal* 1, 4–5.
92 Ibid., 28.
93 Ibid., 27–8.

However, this did not prevent the Siamese men who supervised the reform from applying Western conceptions in Book V of the Code in 1935, just three years after the democratic revolution. While the members of the legislature debated between monogamy and polygamy with familiar arguments from the past, such as reference to the old Thai tradition for polygamy or to the universal laws of civilised countries prescribing monogamy, many of the arguments were based on practical and moral reasons, such as insufficient resources to raise multiple children and the misery of minor wives who were ignored by their husband.[94]

That said, certain legal terms adopted from the old laws during the drafting of the legal codes carried with them some notions of gender inequality. For example, the Civil and Commercial Code today still retains a provision which deals with secondary wives who acquired their legal status before the enforcement of the Code and provides that they are entitled to inherit one half of the share to which the principal wife is entitled.[95]

However, the Western implant of laws did not truly help raise women's rights and equality either. As may be seen from the first version of the Civil and Commercial Code, in some cases women were deprived of protection provided by the law in an attempt to follow Western laws. For example, sections of Book V of the Code removed an ambiguity in the KTSD which potentially provided some women a right to manage the matrimonial property without the permission of their husband.[96] In this way, rarely found powers of women were erased by the imposition of Westernised family law; outside influences once again affected the status of Thai women.[97]

Another watershed moment for women's rights came with the advent of the 1974 Constitution – a result of the popular uprising in 1973 – which provided an equality clause requiring that men and women should have equal rights under the law. Although the Women Lawyers Association of Thailand, an elite organisation of female lawyers, succeeded in adding a clause on gender equality in the democratically advanced Constitution, the implementation of the clause relied heavily on bureaucrats and specialist committees who left most of the issues originally demanded by the movement unfulfilled.[98] The Code was then amended accordingly in 1976; the law no longer made the husband the head of the family with absolute control over family matters and matrimonial property.[99] Although equality had improved, the reform was by no means perfect, leaving subtle anomalies within the legal system which remain today.[100] One notable example of this is the law on engagement, from Section 1435 to 1447/2 of the Civil and Commercial Code. For modern Thai men, this law grants a windfall for brides-to-be in the forms of a required engagement gift and a recommended bride price to be paid by them. But this law also causes them trouble over estimating the economic value of their brides; men were expected to give publicly as valuable a gift as possible and a bride price reaching a level that would satisfy the bride's family and prevent their embarrassment.[101] While many jurisdictions where there once existed a law on engagement have already

94 Lampan Nuambunlue, *Rights and Duties of Women*, 146–8.

95 Civil and Commercial Code s. 1636.

96 David M. Engel, *Code and Custom in a Thai Provincial Court* (Tucson, University of Arizona Press, 1978) 168–9.

97 Ibid., 169–70.

98 Lampan Nuambunlue, *Rights and Duties of Women*, 178–90. For example, measures and sanctions against bigamy, which was a widespread practice among Thai men, were outright dismissed citing the lack of resources and readiness of the most Thai people as the reasons.

99 Muntarbhorn, Jamnarnvej, and Boonlue, *Status of Women: Thailand*, 35–6.

100 Ibid., 36–7.

101 Monchai Wongkittikraiwan, '*Sinsod*, Economics, Marketing, and the Cost of Love', *The Standard*, 25 January 2018, https://thestandard.co/the-economics-of-dowry-and-bride-price/ (accessed 29 December 2019).

discarded these clauses from the text on account of both the decline in the use of the practice and the unequal nature of the practice,[102] the Thai law retains engagement in the Code.

Until the change of relevant laws in 2007, previous decisions of the Supreme Court regarding Sections 1442 and 1443 of the Civil and Commercial Code, which should each work as a mirror image of the other, meant that the law operated differently depending on one's gender. While Section 1442 deals with the right of a man to terminate the engagement when his fiancée is unsuitable for marriage, Section 1443 deals with the same right for the women but with different application in practice. A line of cases show successful claims of women against men who took another woman to his home and took care of her as if they were married.[103] But for men, in reference to the previous version of Section 1445, they could terminate the engagement based on a single act of sexual intercourse between his fiancée and another man.[104] Textbooks before the reform explained this unequal treatment as part a long standing Thai tradition where having sexual relations or preserving male virginity did not matter in married life and, therefore, the law took this reality into consideration when it gave women an additional duty to save her body only for her future husband.[105]

In this regard, the resistance to alien cultural values and the adoption of Western ideas often resulted in a hybridisation between the Western family model and the local model.[106] In this fashion, women were granted what they never asked for[107] and got rid of rights they never held dear. The whole endeavour of reformation, in effect, means little to the livelihood of women. Given the lack of case law on family matters in the past except in the cases of a few rich and powerful people, one could even doubt that formal law mattered at all for most people in their family life.

12.4 ANALYSIS AND PROGNOSIS

Students of Thai family law learn how women gradually strengthened their place among men until today, from having no place to being equal to their male compatriots. That said, despite all the groundbreaking reforms in family law that have seemingly eliminated all unequal treatment based on gender, the extent to which such a word like '*issraphapi*' (freedom) may cause tangible effects to women seems to be limited.[108] On the contrary, because the law on family and inheritance is among those that reflect the 'allegedly authentic cultural identity of the Siamese',[109] problems may still exist in the system despite the absence of language that evidences inequality.

102 For example, the United States almost completely abolished all actions for breach of promise to marry since the early 1900s as the law adapted to the modern understanding of love and marriage; however, the court enforces cases where men file a complaint for the return of engagement ring from their fiancées, benefitting generally all men in the process. Rebecca Tushnet, 'Rules of Engagement' (1998) 107(8) *Yale Law Journal* 2583–618 at 2583–4.

103 See Supreme Court Case no. 3731/2533 and no. 234/2508.

104 Civil and Commercial Code s. 1445.

105 Natchapong Samran, '*Family Law for Unregistered Couples Part I*' (2017) 9 *Academic Journal of the Faculty of Law, University of the Thai Chamber of Commerce* 122–37, at 128–9.

106 Arland Thornton, *Reading History Sideways: The Fallacy and Enduring Impact of the Developmental Paradigm on Family Life* (Chicago: University of Chicago Press, 2005) 237.

107 See, for example, Tamara Loos, 'The Politics of Women's Suffrage in Thailand' in Louise Edwards and Mina Roces (eds.), *Women's Suffrage in Asia: Gender, Nationalism and Democracy* (London: Routledge, 2004) 170–94 at 179, which shows the lack of women's movement in rallying for changes such as universal suffrage and other gender concerns; for example, polygamy and patriarchal forms of address.

108 Tamara Loos, 'Issaraphap: Limits of Individual Liberty in Thai Jurisprudence' (1998) 12 *Crossroads: An Interdisciplinary Journal of Southeast Asian Studies* 35–75 at 68–9.

109 Loos, *Subject Siam*, 100.

Notably, while the current law has corrected all the patriarchal aspects of engagement such as providing both men and women equal opportunity to file for damages from those infringing the rights of the fiancée,[110] the inherent implication of paying for marriage still exists symbolically. It seems favourable to women that Section 1437 requires an engagement gift, or *khongman*, for an engagement to be valid, and that a promise of bride price, or *sinsod*, is enforceable,[111] providing certainty and property to the bride's family. While this could indicate that Thai law still recognises one of the last effects of matrifocality,[112] enforcing the contract which grants the bride and her family a right to the *sinsod* and *khongman* only helps perpetuate the unequal relationship between the couple, pointing back to the time when men still had control of all matrimonial property. Along this line of thought, the comparison between marriage and other commercial transactions was made in the past to the point that the engagement was considered a down payment anticipating the bride price as full payment for the bride.[113] There is indeed a clash of values between preserving tradition and progressing into the modern concept of marriage; and the result is the inconsistency found in the rest of the family law system.

Furthermore, even when the law was equal on its face and unproblematic, the mere change of wording sometimes did not bring about equality between men and women. This is especially true of legal terminology with a culturally charged meaning. For instance, one of the grounds of action for divorce is through the act of adultery, or '*pen choo*' or '*me choo*'.[114] It is problematic because in order to say the phrase 'commit adultery' in Thai there are two verbs to be used, depending on the gender of the adulterer. The phrase *pen choo* only works in a case where a man forms a sexual relationship with the wife of another; but the same word cannot be used for an unmarried woman who has a single act of sexual intercourse with another woman's husband. On the other hand, the word *me choo* is exclusively employed in describing a situation where a married woman has a sexual relationship with any other man, regardless of his marital status. In effect, the law allows a man to have extramarital relations as long as it is not a regular relationship up to the point of having a mistress,[115] while a woman is strictly prohibited from any act of unfaithfulness. Thus, it is uncontroversial for men to file for a divorce based on a single act of adultery by their wife; as long as the terms involved retain the same meaning, a woman does not have the right to end her marriage based on an unfaithful act on the part of her husband that, if committed by her, would give rise to her husband being able to seek a divorce.

This juxtaposition of the traditional and modern aspects of family law presents problems that are all in need of (more than just legal) reform; attitudes towards women and attitudes of women towards themselves have to be adjusted in order for the legal change to be really transposed into the reality of marital relationships. As discussed, the attempt to fix the problem of unequal grounds for divorce between husbands and wives was a failure simply due to the lack of suitable vocabulary. Thai women may have been long past the point of being compared to buffaloes, but they are still on their way towards being able to claim an equal footing in law.

110 Civil and Commercial Code s. 1445 and s. 1446.

111 Supreme Court Case no. 878/2518.

112 See Section 12.2.1 on *Sinsod*.

113 Prince Raphi Phatthanasak, *Law on Husband and Wives*, 74–5.

114 Civil and Commercial Code s. 1516: 'Grounds of action for divorce are as follows: (1) the husband or the wife has given maintenance to or honored such other as his or her spouse, or has committed adultery, the other spouse may enter a claim for divorce.'

115 See, for example, Supreme Court Case no. 981/2535. In this case, the husband had publicly treated his mistress as a lover and thus the wife had the right for compensation from the mistress.

In conclusion, this chapter questions whether the original 'strong status' of women in the past has anything to do with contemporary family law in Thailand by exploring family laws in history and pointing out certain features in the laws which might explain the discrepancies between the legal text and women's societal status. As it turns out, historical analysis here shows little, if any, female privileges that might reflect the strong status women of the past, or that even women used to be strong in their rights. To the contrary, while the Constitution directly protects gender equality,[116] there is still some unequal treatment of men and women in the contemporary family law system. As discussed through the chapter, Thai women were never wholly independent. They were given economic or political freedom out of necessity and only when it was not too troublesome. True enough, the law sometimes recognises such freedom as shown in the reign of King Mongkut.

There is not one exclusive source of law which is entirely responsible for the state of the law today. Forces such as Buddhism, patriarchal traditions, and economic factors still shape the law on the relationship between men and women as strongly as they have done since pre-modern times. Nevertheless, the perceived state of equality of Thai women somehow overshadows the existing subtle inequality that still persists. This chapter should only be perceived as an early attempt to delve into this hidden issue of gender in Thai law. From the laws governing monks in the law of inheritance, which naturally exclude women from certain legal benefits provided to men, to the downplaying of domestic violence and reproductive rights as part of family law, there is still a myriad of unexplored issues that could produce a whole new literature in the near future.

116 2017 Constitution, s. 27(2): 'Men and women shall enjoy equal rights.'

13

The Origins of Thailand's Bureaucratic State and the Consolidation of Administrative Justice

Peter Leyland

13.1 INTRODUCTION

This chapter explores relationships between present and past in order to investigate the current regime of administrative justice. The objective is not to chart the formal steps towards the present legal set up but rather to present selective related 'histories' which help not only to cast light on the current system but also allow contrasts to be made with other attempts at Thai institution building under successive constitutions. In approaching 'the facts' there is an unending dialogue between the historian and the past. As E. H. Carr famously observed:

> The historian starts with a provisional selection of facts, and a provisional interpretation in the light of which that selection has been made – by others as well as by himself. ... And this reciprocal action also involves a reciprocity between the present and the past as the historian is part of the present and facts belong to the past.[1]

Michel Foucault was repeatedly concerned with what he termed a genealogical question, namely, what kind of political relevance enquiries into our past have in making intelligible the 'objective conditions' of our social present.[2] This study of administrative law in Thailand takes its place in an historical collection, but the objective is not to demonstrate 'how the seamless web of yesteryear leads slowly and inexorably into the present'.[3] Rather, it is to discover how some of the diverse and overlapping mechanisms of power relating to bureaucratic structures and administrative justice have been formed and are now able to function. Chronological narrative linearity is abandoned, as this survey is conducted as a kind of mapping exercise. It presents a series of episodic themes which taken together produce a meta-narrative of administrative justice in Thailand from the late nineteenth century until the present.

This discussion begins by identifying the main features of the system of administrative justice in its contemporary context. Familiarity with the present configuration is the embarkation point for the investigation of a series of genealogical questions relating to the formation of the modern Thai state. The opening section seeks to first particularise the prevailing conditions in nineteenth century Siam for the formation of a nation as a geographical entity. Second, the imposition of a new form of centralised power base of formidable complexity is related to the emergence of the current national bureaucratic polity. Third, with reference to

1 Edward Hallet Carr, *What is History?* (London: Penguin, 1964) 30.
2 Michael Foucault, *Power / Knowledge* (Hemel Hampstead: Harvester Press, 1980) 232.
3 Mark Poster, *Foucault, Marxism and History* (Oxford: Polity Press, 1984) 74.

the Council of State of King Chulalongkorn, it will be suggested that there has been an interrupted (rather than continuous) path to the present as this body has turned out to be only the indirect precursor of the modern council of state, petitioning council, and now administrative courts. The second section discusses the degree of outside influence in fashioning the system of administrative justice, with particular reference to the incorporation of the legal concepts of legitimate expectation and proportionality. The final section turns to focus on the court's role in environmental litigation with particular reference to prominent recent decisions. The objective is to evaluate the present contribution of the administrative courts in upholding rule of law values in Thailand against the backdrop of current inhibitions on political freedom and human rights.

13.2 THE CURRENT PROFILE OF ADMINISTRATIVE JUSTICE

One of the reasons the 1997 Constitution was regarded as an innovatory step in establishing a liberal democratic form of government in Thailand is because it created an institutional legacy of specialist bodies designed to provide executive oversight, eliminate corruption, protect human rights, and provide remedies for the citizen.[4] Prominent among these new institutions was a separate system of administrative courts.[5] In the wake of detailed legislation enacted by the Thai Parliament which set out the legal and procedural framework,[6] the courts opened their doors to litigants in 2001. As we will see later, the national system had obvious affinities with continental European models, first, because it had its own distinct jurisdiction apart from the ordinary courts and Constitutional Court; second, because it consisted of regional courts of first instance (now totalling eleven); third, it had a Supreme Administrative Court at appellate level;[7] fourth, because the procedure adopted is, in common with European systems, inquisitorial.[8] The administrative courts since their inception have been relatively well insulated from the toxic political environment as they have guaranteed funding, a cohort of professionally trained, well remunerated judges recruited to the court on merit,[9] and these judges are also protected from summary dismissal.[10]

The court's institutional independence is reflected in the maintenance of an informative and user-friendly website revealing details of its structure, organisation, and performance.[11] Moreover, administrative courts continue to be recognised as having the powers to adjudicate administrative cases in the 2017 Constitution drafted under the supervision of the ruling military junta.[12] However, in this latest document two brief sections replace the provisions of the 1997 and 2007 Constitutions which set out in more detail the procedure for appointment

4 Constitution of the Kingdom of Thailand 1997. See Andrew Harding and Peter Leyland, *The Constitutional System of Thailand: A Contextual Analysis* (Oxford: Hart Publishing, 2011), chapter 1.

5 Constitution of the Kingdom of Thailand 1997, Section 276.

6 Establishment of Administrative Court and Administrative Procedure Act 1999 (EACAP).

7 Thailand's administrative courts share the same structural layout of European nations such as France, Germany, Italy, Spain, and the Netherlands, with a separate system of administrative courts with a distinct jurisdiction.

8 EACAP, Article 57.

9 Ibid., Articles 13–15, Article 30.

10 Ibid., Article 22. See Peter Leyland, 'Droit Administratif Thai Style: A Comparative Analysis of the Administrative Courts in Thailand' (2006) 8(2) *The Australian Journal of Asian Law* 121, 129–32. The rules for recruitment, dismissal, and disciplinary action for judges were amended under the Act on Establishment of Administrative Courts and Administrative Court Procedure (No 9) 2017.

11 www.admincourt.go.th/admincourt/site/?lang=en&page=03organization_internal. See also Administrative Court booklet available from the court website.

12 Constitution of the Kingdom of Thailand 2017, sections 197 and 198.

and removal from office, the composition of the Judicial Commission, and the requirement for an independent secretariat.[13] In common with the 2007 constitution, the jurisdiction of the court is restricted and 'does not include rulings made by Independent Organs pursuant to the direct exercise of their powers under the Constitution'.[14] This limitation means that their oversight function no longer extends to constitutional watchdog bodies.[15] Nevertheless, the extent to which these courts make a contribution and have emerged as a counterweight to Thailand's bureaucracy can be partly assessed in terms of raw statistics which suggest the workload is increasing. Compared with a volume of 26,689 adjudicated in the first five years of its operation with an average of 5,337 cases a year,[16] the average has risen to 9,963 cases a year between 2012 and 2016. In 2017, the last full year for which there are records, 10,412 cases were adjudicated.[17]

In order to tackle the backlog of cases a series of other measures have been implemented to enhance the performance of the courts. In 2016, forty-two additional qualified judges were appointed, twenty-nine as judges of first instance and thirteen of the Supreme Administrative Court. The procedures have been modified to strengthen case management and to allow a time frame to be set for adjudication.[18] The court is in the process of introducing cutting edge information technology with a shift to paperless e-records, and the court itself is in the process of becoming an e-court and smart court with the introduction of online justice.[19] Finally, although beyond the scope of this chapter, it should be noted that in providing remedies in this field of law the administrative courts work alongside the office of the Thai ombudsman[20] and mechanisms for alternative dispute resolution (ADR).[21]

13.3 DEFINING THE NATION: CENTRALISATION AND BUREAUCRATISATION

How does the current Thai system of administrative justice relate to the earlier configuration of Siam[22] in the latter half of the nineteenth century? The Thai nation encompasses a particular conception of history and culture which is at variance from Western accounts and our discussion calls for an understanding of the history of the origins of aspects of Thai nationhood. The conditions for the practice of administrative law can be linked to the novel acceptance of territoriality and the formation of the state of Siam during the course of the nineteenth century.[23] Viewed from the outside, we observe a tension throughout the

13 Ibid., sections 276–80.

14 Ibid., section 197.

15 For example, the Election Commission (section 222); the Ombudsman (Section 228); the National Anti-Corruption Commission (section 232); State Audit Commission (section 238); National Human Rights Commission (section 246).

16 Statistics supplied by the Administrative Court covering the period from March 2001 until 31 December 2006. See Leyland, 'Droit Administratif Thai Style'.

17 Report on the Work of the Administrative Court given on the Occasion of the Court's 17th Anniversary, *Administrative Court News*, No 17/2018, www.admincourt.go.th/admincourt/upload/webcmsen/Publication/Publication_110418_133851.pdf.

18 This is to meet the requirements of section 258 of the 2017 Constitution that, for example, requires under (D) that the time limits for the justice process are clearly specified.

19 Administrative Court News: Report by President on 16th Anniversary.

20 Peter Leyland, 'The Ombudsman Principle in Thailand' (2007) 2(1) *Journal of Comparative Law* 137.

21 See, for example, The Arbitration Act 2002 (Thai) and the Thai Arbitration Institute. www.thac.or.th/arbitration_menu.

22 Siam changed its name to Thailand in 1939.

23 See Thongchai Winichakul, *Siam Mapped: A History of the Geo-Body of a Nation* (Honolulu: University of Hawai'i Press, 1997).

nineteenth century as the spectre of colonialism confronted the Siamese Chakri dynasty, particularly under Kings Rama IV (Mongkut 1851–68) and Rama V (Chulalongkorn 1868–1910). The survival of the life of the Thai was pitched against that of the European imperial nations. In the context of the region a realm did not exist as a territorial state with frontiers. Almost reminiscent of a feudal system, subjects were bound to a lord rather than to a state. The very idea of mapping in a European sense amounted to new knowledge and became the geographical language through which information originated and the new notion of the realm of Siam was conceived. As Thongchai Winichakul explains, 'the discourse of mapping was the paradigm within which both administrative and military operations worked and served'.[24] Mapping was turned into a necessary device for the reformed administrative mechanisms and for military purposes. The state of Siam was, in effect, created as a geographical entity by the imperialist scramble of the British and the French for territory. The portions that remained after the imperialist land grab could be claimed as Siam. This territory consisted of a 'conglomeration of states and provinces'[25] populated largely with villages which operated as self-governing communities.[26] Before the advent of modern communications and the reforms to its structure, the institution of absolute monarchy was ineffective in exercising power over vassals who simply acknowledged tributes to the throne but were only notionally under its rule.[27]

Glancing within the polity of Siam, the changes in law and administration went a great deal further than drawing lines on a map. The external pressures prompted the foundations of the contemporary bureaucratic state. To establish direct control, Siam was rapidly transformed in a geographical sense from territory without clearly defined boundaries to a compact state with a definite frontier.[28] Not only was it necessary to identify a geographically defined state with borders, but, for the survival of Siam and its monarchy, it was essential to demonstrate that the territory was under the control of a ruler. Siam was of course a Buddhist society with a strictly hierarchical status system ruled under the Three Seals Code of traditional law.[29] At the inception of the Bangkok dynasty in 1782, it already had a complex bureaucracy centred on the Royal Palace corresponding to the cosmological belief system.[30] The structure of government organisation was linked to cosmological architecture and it was based on a complex strictly hierarchical organisation. Fred Riggs observes that: 'A conception of governmental organisation based on cosmological and topographical considerations [it] contrasts strikingly with modern ideas about the place of function, technique, clientele, and territorial jurisdiction as criteria for organisational design.'[31]

As will be explained below the first steps in the modernisation of the machinery of government were launched within the Palace early in the reign of Chulalongkorn (1868–1910). Between 1890 and 1919, under the bureaucratic reform programme, there was a spectacular increase in the number of professional civil servants, from 12,000 to

24 Ibid., 130.

25 Ibid., 146.

26 Fred Warren Riggs, *Thailand: The Modernization of a Bureaucratic Polity* (Honolulu: East West Center Press, 1966) 95.

27 Ibid., 83.

28 Thongchai Winichakul, 142. The French crisis caused by the French blockade of Bangkok in 1893 might be regarded as a pivotal moment.

29 Andrew Huxley, *Thai Law: Buddhist Law: Essays on the Legal History of Thailand, Laos and Burma* (Bangkok: White Orchid Press, 1996) 4ff. See also Tamara Loos, *Subject Siam: Family Law, and Colonial Modernity in Thailand* (Ithaca, NY: Cornell University Press, 2006) 32ff.

30 Riggs, 74ff. The four courts represented the guardian deities and functions were distributed between them.

31 Riggs, 69ff.

80,000.[32] The theme of centralising control is further underlined by these reforms. In order to govern the provinces effectively, the Ministry of the Interior was transformed into its present configuration from 1892 under the direction of Prince Damrong, and it was turned into a functionally specialised department. By 1910 it numbered more than 15,000 salaried employees, with 3,000 officials appointed to the provinces.[33] The revised centralised system of bureaucratic administration was based upon 'the new technology of administrative organisation and procedure' borrowed selectively from the West.[34] Chulalongkorn's first trips abroad in 1871 had been to study British colonial government in Singapore, India, and Burma.[35] In consequence, it is unsurprising that there were structural affinities with the British model. Commissioners backed up by troops were sent to establish direct control and to administer frontier states.[36] John Girling observes that: 'tighter control was imposed through the division of the country into a small number of administrative units (*monthon*), each coordinating several provinces under the supervision of a royal commissioner.'[37] Not only were local lords replaced by a 'new centralised pyramid of bureaucratic administration', termed the *thesaphiban* system, but an intricate apparatus of central control was established. This included judges dispatched from Bangkok to preside over provincial and district courts implementing the new European-style legal codes; provincial finance officers responsible for tax-raising and the disbursement of funds; and the formation of a national police department.[38] It has been argued that certain aspects of the administrative state have evolved, modifying elements of the bureaucratic polity model;[39] however, in regard to the pattern of law and administration, we can see from this brief survey that the essential characteristics of a centralised system of bureaucracy were superimposed over the existing system, and have been carried forward into the present.

From a somewhat different standpoint the emergence of this bureaucracy was geared towards the making and the implementation of laws.[40] It has been pointed out that in the previous reign of Mongkut 'large numbers of decrees and royal proclamations [were issued] which were not administrative orders but statements of principle intended to guide the actions of officials and people – somewhat in the style of Chinese imperial rule'.[41] The revised system was formalised into legislation. In modernising the law Chulalongkorn also recognised the advantage of introducing legal codes.[42] However, the older system did not disappear, but was simply combined with the new, thereby illustrating the capacity of the Siamese to innovate by combining new and old as part of a complex multilayered culture.[43] It will already be apparent that the legal and bureaucratic elements of the state were established, but these developments did not lead directly towards the introduction of a system of administrative justice. The formation of the Council of State by Chulalongkorn in 1873–4

32 Maurizio Peleggi, *Thailand: The Worldly Kingdom* (London: Reaktion Press, 2007) 104.
33 Chris Baker and Pasuk Phongpaichit, *A History of Thailand* (Cambridge: Cambridge University Press, 2005) 54ff.
34 Riggs, 111, 138. This included H. Slade, a British expert from India.
35 Loos, 49.
36 Baker and Pasuk Phongpaichit, *A History of Thailand*, 54.
37 John L. S. Girling, *Thailand: Society and Politics* (Ithaca, NY: Cornell University Press, 1981) 54ff.
38 Riggs, 141ff.
39 James Ockey, 'State, Bureaucracy and Polity in Modern Thai Politics' (2004) 34(2) *Journal of Contemporary Asia* 143, 144.
40 In this volume the origins of royal lawmaking are discussed in Chapter 3.
41 Baker and Pasuk Phongpaichit, *A History of Thailand*, 50.
42 Leyland, 'Droit Administratif Thai Style', 127ff.
43 Baker and Pasuk Phongphaichit, *A History of Thailand*, 77.

serves as a useful starting point, partly because it demonstrates again an interest in modern forms of law and administration inspired by European influence.[44]

Although not dependent on the military in the same way as is currently the case, the attempts to institutionalise a form of Royal government might be viewed as the nineteenth-century precursor to what has been more recently termed 'network monarchy'.[45] The Privy Council and Council of State were formed against a background of factional struggle within the Royal Palace which saw the King, shortly after his accession in 1868, having to deal with opposition from a conservative old guard within the Royal Court. To consolidate his own position, and as a vehicle for reform, Chulalongkorn established a Privy Council with an advisory capacity. This was comprised mainly of brothers and friends, who, once appointed had to swear a personal oath of allegiance.[46] Alongside the Privy Council the Council of State, modelled on the French Conseil d'Etat,[47] was introduced in its embryonic form.[48] It was staffed with a carefully selected group of loyal and progressive (in the sense of outward looking) senior officials of Phraya rank and its task was to assist in the exercise of royal control over prominent ministries and to supervise the drafting of laws and regulations. In parallel with the functional reorganisation of ministries, the trend towards reliance on officials is reflected through their domination of the lawmaking process. Subsequently, under Thailand's many constitutions a parliament has been responsible for passing bills into law, but it is still left to officials to draft laws and to develop the specific procedures and regulations necessary to apply the law.[49] However, notwithstanding the expansion of the executive branch as part of a centralised system of government, the Council of State was temporarily replaced by the Council of Ministers as a consultative forum since it was found to be ineffective in its original form.[50]

After the coup d'état which led to the adoption of first Siamese Constitution in 1932, the Council of State Act 1933 was a limited step in the direction of administrative justice. This is because it identified two distinct roles for a new Council of State and its legally trained officials. Law Councillors were responsible for drafting laws,[51] but petition councillors were to be responsible for adjudicating administrative cases.[52] Thus under this Act the Council of State was recognised as potentially having an adjudicative function,[53] but although Pridi Panyomyong advocated the development of administrative justice, adopting the French model and including administrative courts,[54] it was not until the Council of State Act of

44 David K. Wyatt, *Studies in Thai Law* (Chiang Mai: Silkworm Books, 1994) 268.

45 Duncan McCargo, 'Network Monarchy and Legitimacy Crises in Thailand' (2005) 18(4) *The Pacific Review* 499, 506.

46 Barend Jan Terwiel, *Thailand's Political History: From the 13th Century to Recent Times*, 2nd ed. (Bangkok: River Books, 2011) 186–8.

47 See Sophie Boyron, *The Constitution of France: A Contextual Analysis* (Cambridge, UK: Hart Publishing, 2013) 119ff; N. Brown and J. Bell, *French Administrative Law* 5th ed. (Oxford: Oxford University Press, 1998) 6.

48 David K. Wyatt, *Thailand: A Short History*, 2nd ed. (New Haven: Yale University Press, 2003) 177.

49 Ockey, 148.

50 Bhokin Bhalakula, 'Pridi and the Administrative Court' (Administrative Courts of Thailand, 2001) 6. The Legislative Council command of 1893 repealed the Royal Proclamation that established the Council of State, and the Council of Ministers Act 1893 set up the replacement body.

51 The law drafting department established under King Rama VI to revise Thailand's legal codes was transferred from the Ministry of Justice to the Council of State following the abolition of absolute Monarchy in 1932.

52 See Ackaratorn Chularat (former President of the Supreme Administrative Court), The Administrative Court of Thailand, published by the court, November 2007, 50.

53 Further provisions were included in the Petition Act 1949.

54 Pridi, as well as being active in politics, was one of the founders of Thammasat University and pioneered the teaching of administrative law in Thailand.

1979 that the Council of State routinely accepted petitions from citizens who had a grievance against administrative organs of the state.[55] While petitioning before Law Councillors offered a judicial process applying legal concepts derived mainly from France,[56] there is no method of ascertaining whether the Thai Petition Council made a significant contribution to the improvement of public administration.[57] Certainly, the petitioning procedure lacked essential elements typical of European systems of administrative justice. For instance, Pridi in his lectures had described administrative law as 'the principles and rules concerned with regulations and practices of officials in the executive branch, and concerned with relations between private individuals and officialdom'.[58] It was further recognised by him that: '[the] legislative power and the judicial power should be separate from the executive power, because if they were combined it may lead to injustice. In other words, those adjudicating are applying laws which they themselves legislated.'[59] First, under this system there was no bifurcation into a separate system of administrative justice with dedicated courts and distinct jurisdictional demarcation for administrative law which is now in place in Thailand. Second, there was no clear distinction between executive and judicial power. The decisions of the Petition Council were not legally binding unless receiving the endorsement of the Prime Minister. Furthermore, the provisions relating to procedural defects and bad faith depended on the issuance of ministerial regulations which, in practice, were never forthcoming.[60]

As noted above, the plan to establish administrative courts was included in the 1997 Constitution. At the time of its adoption the 1997 Constitution[61] was widely regarded as a breakthrough in the nation's democratic development.[62] This was partly because it was a bottom-up exercise allowing broader consultation across the wider community prior to its drafting and promulgation, and, as a result of more extensive public involvement, had a claim to legitimacy.[63] In spite of certain shortcomings[64] the text was radical, with both an emphasis on human rights protection and on the inclusion of a series of watchdog bodies intended as oversight mechanisms to promote good governance.[65] Legislation and related regulations were enacted almost immediately by the Thai Parliament, setting out the fundamentals of the new system, and the relevant sections of the 1979 Act were repealed.[66] However, as we have already observed, Thailand's administrative courts, when they were established more than twenty years later, went a great deal further than assuming the adjudicative function of the Petition Council of the Council of State.

55 Bhalakula, 'Pridi and the Administrative Court'.

56 The grounds under the now repealed section 19 of the 1979 Act might be compared with the grounds set out under the Act on the Establishment of the Administrative Court 1999, section 9.

57 No statistical data is available comparable to that published by the current administrative courts.

58 See Chris Baker and Pasuk Phongpaichit (eds.), *Pridi by Pridi: Selected Writings on Life, Politics and Economy* (Chiang Mai: Silkworm Books, 2000) 45.

59 Ibid., 44.

60 See Bhalakula, 24ff.

61 In this volume the backdrop to the 1997 Constitution is discussed in Chapter 17, this volume. See especially the section, 'New Constitutionalism and the DRKH in the 1997 Constitution'.

62 Harding and Leyland, *The Constitutional System of Thailand*, 22.

63 Duncan McCargo, 'Competing Notions of Judicialization in Thailand' (2014) 36(3) *Contemporary South East Asia*, 417, 419.

64 For example, the exposure of the courts to political controversy discussed in the final section.

65 Peter Leyland, 'Thailand's Constitutional Watchdogs: Dobermans, Bloodhounds or Lapdogs?' (2007) 2(2) *Journal of Comparative Law* 151.

66 See EACAP.

13.4 ADMINISTRATIVE JUSTICE: GAUGING EXTERNAL INFLUENCE?

It is widely acknowledged that the creation of Thailand's modern legal system depended greatly on outside influence.[67] This influence is perhaps reflected most obviously in the transplantation of legal codes adopted in Thailand[68] since the late nineteenth century.[69] Thailand relied heavily on expert legal advisers from other nations[70] who worked alongside Siamese lawyers to codify and translate modern penal, civil, and procedural codes. These were based on the codes of foreign countries. Tamara Loos states that: 'As participants in a global circulation of legal reform, Siamese and foreign legal advisers linked Siam to a network of ideas that went beyond national boundaries'.[71] Foreign legal advisers brought with them culturally specific concepts of justice, legal codes, and institutions that circulated throughout Siam.[72]

To evaluate this trend at a technical level in the domain of administrative law, we now focus in more detail on one such transplantation with a European provenance which seeks to restrict bureaucratic power, and, at the same time, re-enforce rule of law values.[73] The Administrative Procedure Act 1996 (APA) was introduced to place constraints on arbitrary conduct by Thai officialdom. Although the terminology is slightly modified,[74] the doctrine of legitimate expectation based on the rule of law and the related doctrine of 'legal certainty' is introduced as part of Thai administrative law.[75] The version adopted is an obvious 'borrowing' as it is clearly derived from the German Law of Administrative Procedure.[76] The principle of legal certainty itself has since been recognised by the Thai Supreme Administrative Court. For example, in a recent case it was stated that 'the Court needs to take into account the principle of legal certainty and the protection of rights of a *bona fide* third person'.[77]

In light of the decision by the drafters of the Thai law to use this German source, it is worth pointing out the implications of selecting a model which incorporates substantive protection of such rights. In a state governed by the rule of law, citizens are entitled to trust that the actions of officialdom are taken in compliance with current applicable laws and that their rights under those laws will be protected. These laws will continue to be recognised by the legal order, along with all of the legal consequences that originally had been tied to such actions. This principle of legitimate expectation, also referred to as legal certainty, would apply in the German system if the lawmaker has enacted a law for a limited period of time

67 Loos, 47ff.

68 For example, in Chapter 9 of this volume there is an in-depth analysis of the origins of the Thai Civil and Commercial Code.

69 Sometimes a literal copying over of texts by teams of scholars and jurists. See, for example, Law of Evidence (1895); First Civil Code (1896); Land Law (1905); Penal Code (1908); Nationality Law (1913); Trademark Law (1914); Revised final version of Civil Code (1935).

70 For example, Belgium (Gustave Rolin-Jaequemyns), Britain (W. A. Graham), France (Georges Padoux and René Guyon), Japan (Tokichi Masao), and the United States (Edward Strobel and Francis B. Sayre).

71 Loos, 65.

72 The process of codification is discussed in Chapter 5, this volume; see particularly notes 84ff.

73 Søren Schønberg, *Legitimate Expectations in Administrative Law* (Oxford: Oxford University Press, 2000) 12ff.

74 Administrative Procedure Act BE 2539 (1996), referred to hereinafter as the APA.

75 See Paiboon Chuwatthanakij, 'The Principle of the Protection of Legitimate Expectation: Analysis of the Adjudications of Thailand Court' (2015) 9(3) *World Academy of Science, Engineering and Technology, International Journal of Law and Political Sciences* 810.

76 See the German Law of Administrative Procedure of 1976, section 48: 'An administrative act which gives rise to a right or an advantage relevant in legal proceedings or confirms such a right or advantage (beneficial administrative act) may only be withdrawn subject to the restrictions of paragraphs 2 to 4.'

77 See *Thawin Piansri* v. *Prime Minister and Merit System Protection Commission* [2014] Black Case 992/2556; Red Case 33/2557.

and, before the deadline has expired, there is an attempt to amend the law. Legitimate expectation under German administrative law places particular emphasis on the protection of monetary benefits. It is not permissible therefore for the state to retroactively strip its citizens of their legal position or to devalue it.[78] German courts, except in exceptional circumstances, recognise administrative discretion only when it is expressly granted.[79] According to the Bundesfassungsgericht, the element relied upon (in the form of a law, regulation, promise, or commitment) was protected both by the principle of 'Rechtsstaat' and by the general principle of freedom of action (Article 2(1), Grundgesetz). It follows that similar and related rules which are now codified in sections 48 and 49 of the Federal and State Administrative Procedure Acts are but 'concretised constitutional law'.[80] The courts in Germany have held that, in principle, actions by a public authority with retroactive effect will be regarded as unconstitutional and impermissible, and it also follows that a public authority cannot depart from a representation, or at a later stage place additional burdens on the claimant.[81]

In Thailand the principle applies to the rule about the revocation of an administrative order or other administrative acts.[82] In general, when changing or cancelling an administrative act the decision-maker needs to show how the public-interest element has subsequently become so pressing as to override the original decision.[83] Sections 51–53 of the APA relate to subsequent actions and the statute imposes stronger legal restraints applicable to the decision-maker and comparable to its German counterpart discussed above. The detrimental reliance (bona fide reliance) element of section 51–53 will apply when a revocation is made.[84]

Underpinning the notion of reliance is the idea that if a person has reason to trust another individual or agency, that individual or agency will be expected to act in accordance with that trust. Applied in an administrative law context, it introduces a sense of responsibility in the use of administrative power. Even though a public authority has been granted a power that may have a public benefit, where a legitimate expectation arises there are limitations preventing an unreasonable interference with the rights of the claimant and/or that he or she suffers financial loss.[85] Put simply, '[t]he reliance theory argues that legitimate expectations should be protected because to do otherwise would inflict harm on individuals who rely upon such expectations'.[86]

Under the Thai APA the situation relating to revocation of a lawful act is clearly delineated where there is detrimental reliance.[87] Such a rule against retroactivity supports one of the

78 Klaus Rennert, 'The Protection of Legitimate Expectations under German Administrative Law', President of the Federal Administrative Court, Association of Councils of State and Supreme Administrative Jurisdictions of the European Union, Vilnius [2016]; paper on file.

79 Georg Nolte, 'General Principles of German and European Administrative Law – A Comparison in Historical Perspective' (1994) 57(2) *Modern Law Review* 191, 196.

80 Ibid., 203.

81 Schønberg, 14ff.

82 Section 49 of the APA refers to 'beneficial administrative act'. Administrative order is defined under Article 5 of the Administrative Procedure Act 1987.

83 APA 1996, Section 53(5): 'it is necessary to prevent or eliminate serious harm to the public interest or individual'.

84 Detrimental reliance is related to estoppel and it applies when the claimant has already acted on the basis of a decision by a public authority, for example, after the grant of planning permission a developer commences clearance only to be informed that planning authority will be withdrawn.

85 See Paiboon Chuwatthanakij, 811.

86 Schønberg, 9.

87 Under the relevant paragraph of the APA Section 53: 'A lawful administrative act giving rise to the payment of money or the transfer of property or an advantage which is severable may be revoked, whether in whole or in part, either retroactively or prospectively or with effect for the future as prescribed, *only when*: (i) there is no implementation or a delay in implementation of the administrative act; (ii) the beneficiary fails to observe or delays to comply with the conditions of the act.'

fundamental values of the rule of law which is here incorporated into Thai administrative law. This part of APA section 53, based as it is on legitimate expectation and legal certainty, might render a change of a decision legally void or, if not, it provides entitlement to financial relief. It does not, however, in itself, guarantee a substantive benefit in the form of particular outcome. This is because there are certain limits restricting the extent to which formal legal constraints might be placed on public authorities changing policy or practice. Certain exceptions are well recognised. While the German Federal Constitutional Court has repeatedly held that any retroactive effect of legislation will be in principle unconstitutional and impermissible,[88] legitimate expectation cannot be relied upon where there is evidence of bad faith by the claimant. A further exception applies if there is a disproportionate impact on the wider public interest. This will be when the balance struck shows that the interest of the public in obtaining a new legal status outweighs the interests of the individual in seeing the previous status continue to apply.

In a similar vein, a proportionality test is employed by the Thai administrative courts in order to determine whether the threshold has been reached for judicial intervention. In particular, under the APA, the Thai court will consider whether '[the action or decision] is necessary to prevent or eliminate serious harm to the public interest or the individual'.[89] This construction confirms that, as a matter of Thai administrative law, the legitimate actions of the administrative body will be weighed against the claimant's rights. The test applies to decide if the revocation of a lawful administrative act is justified. In other words, to establish whether the interference with the claimant's rights was necessary to achieve one or more of the legitimate aims of the State.[90]

In summary, this form of detrimental reliance giving rise to a legitimate expectation imposes legal restriction on the exercise of administrative power, but the recognition of legitimate expectation as an extension of the doctrine of legal certainty does not actually prevent a policy change or guarantee a particular outcome. Rather, a benefit is protected under Thai law because even if the change of a decision is considered by the court to be justified, the claimant will still be entitled to compensation under the APA. Further, given the nature of the general grounds of review, there is also an implicit 'legitimate expectation' to procedural fairness.[91] Naturally, the effectiveness of the law depends upon an accessible means of enforcement. In Thailand, the Act on the Establishment of the Administrative Court 1999 not only sets out in detail the fundamentals of a new dedicated courts system,[92] and clarifies the legal grounds for challenging *ultra vires* decisions,[93] but it also lists the remedies at the disposal of the court.[94]

88 Klaus Rennert, 'The Protection of Legitimate Expectations under German Administrative Law' (paper given at seminar, Association of Councils of State and Supreme Administrative Jurisdictions of the European Union, Vilnius, Lithuania, 21 April 2016) 9.

89 APA, s. 53.

90 Under Section 9 of EACAP (1999), 'causing excessive burden to the public' is interpreted as introducing a proportionality test. This is explained by a judge of the Thai Supreme Administrative court. See Dr Charnchai Sawangsagdi, National Report of Thailand, 'Review of Administrative Decisions of Government by the Administrative Court of Thailand', Report to the 10th Congress of IASAJ, Sydney, March 2010, 70/71.

91 The relevant wording from Article 9 of EACAP states: 'in a manner inconsistent with the law or the form, process or procedure which is the material requirement for such an act or in bad faith or in a manner indicating unfair discrimination'.

92 For example, appointment of judges, procedure for filing cases, secretariat for the court.

93 As stated above, EACAP Article 9 sets out the grounds of review. For further discussion see Leyland, 'Droit Administratif Thai Style', 135ff.

94 EACAP, Article 72.

13.5 THAILAND'S MULTILAYERED LAW

Viewing external influence broadly, since the era of Chulalongkorn the association with other legal systems and the influence of lawyers from Europe,[95] Japan, and the United States has been a prevalent feature.[96] The initial strategic plan of the administrative court introduced by its first President in 2005 emphasised the need to generate academic cooperation on administrative law questions, both domestically and internationally, in order to develop principles of administrative law, codes of practice, and administrative standards. The prime objective here was stated as promoting 'the development of an administrative justice system for Thailand comparable to other countries'.[97] As well as adopting legal principles to include in its codified legal system, this initiative has included forging formal academic links, for example, between Bangkok's prestigious law schools at Thammasat University[98] and Chulalongkorn University and leading law schools in France and Germany.[99] The senior cohort of judges (formerly judges or Petition Councillors) appointed to the Administrative Court were Thammasat LLB graduates, partly educated in civil law countries (mainly France, Italy with some also in the United Kingdom).[100] At the same time the court has a Bureau of Foreign Affairs[101] to establish and maintain links with courts internationally,[102] and it has established an Administrative Judge and Official Training Institute tasked with organising training courses for judges in specialist legal fields in order to sharpen their judicial expertise.[103] There are regular lectures delivered by visiting jurists and academics, and a generous budget is allocated annually to support a range of such activities.[104]

Comparative legal scholars have recognised that there has been a strong propensity towards transplantation between systems;[105] however, any recognition of apparent similarities at surface level should be heavily qualified by observing a much more subtle multilayered cultural dimension. As Professor Andrew Harding observes:

> The extent of legal reception in Southeast Asia is truly staggering. . . . It is appropriate to think of law in South East Asia geologically, as a series of layers each of which overlays the previous

95 See Chapter 8, this volume, which assesses the contribution of four British lawyers on the committee of the Supreme Court between 1910 and 1941.

96 Jean-Michel Galabert, 'The Influence of the Conseil D'Etat Outside France' (2000) 49 *Journal of International and Comparative Law* 700, 705.

97 Prof. Dr Ackaratorn Chularat, President of the Supreme Administrative Court, Strategic Plan of the Administrative Court (2005–8) [2005] 6.

98 For example, Thammasat University has a German Southeast Asian Centre of Excellence for Good Governance and Public Policy.

99 For example, training course for administrative court judges held at the University of Münster in June 2018, supported by the Asian Governance Foundation, Administrative Court of Thailand Quadrimester Newsletter, Vol. 3, June–September 2018.

100 Ibid., 27.

101 www.admincourt.go.th/admincourt/upload/webcmsen/The%20Institution/The_Institution_030614_103339.pdf.

102 Thai Administrative Court hosted the 9th Congress of the International Association of Supreme Administrative Jurisdictions (2007). See *The Nation*, 13 November 2007.

103 For example, training courses organised by the University of Toulouse for 16 Thai administrative court judges. See *Administrative Courts of Thailand Quadrimester Newsletter*, Vol. 3, June–September 2017.

104 For example, *Administrative Courts of Thailand Quadrimester Newsletter*, Vol. 1, October 2017–January 2018 Reports: 'Training, seminars, technical presentations and domestic study visits for Administrative Court judges will be conducted so as to strengthen their expertise in expediting the adjudication and execution of administrative cases, leading to a more standardised jurisprudence.'

105 See, for example, David Nelken, 'Legal Transplants and Beyond: Of Disciplines and Metaphors' in Andrew Harding and Esin Örücü (eds.), *Comparative Law in the 21st Century* (London: Kluwer Law International, 2002) 24ff.

layers without actually replacing them, so that in places, due to tectonic shifts, the lower layers are still visible, although not perfectly distinguishable from each other.[106]

The idea of a multilayered legal order suggests the current workings of the Thai legal system are to varying degrees understood not simply by textual readings of law, but from a combination of cultural, religious, historical, political, and economic factors that lie beyond the surface of the legal text.[107] The law in Thailand might be considered to exist as a series of layers, each one overlaying the previous layers without actually replacing them.

This begs the broader question of how the superimposed layers were received by a relatively uneducated citizenry unfamiliar with such law. To take one example in a speech broadcast in 1936, Pridi Banomyong offered a traditional and emphatically not a legal justification for the new constitutionalism. 'The constitution is the highest dhamma to enable the Siamese people to survive as an independent nation. For those of you who abide by the constitution, who abide by the dhamma good things will result. Dhamma always protects those who practice dhamma'.[108]

The point to stress is that this conception of multilayering does not recognise any simple core or essence for the study of law and legal history, and it assumes that a strict autonomy of disciplines geared towards only looking at formal law is inadequate. Lawyer's law in legal codes, statutes, or case reports is simply one of a series of normative orders which have evolved with society.[109] Rather, recourse to codified law in formal courts reflects what Loos has referred to as 'the hegemonic narrative of Thai national history'. It is a confirmation of the 'perspective if not the ideology of the ruling elite' and, at the same time, it overlooks how the reform process was used by monarchs and the Thai elite to centralise power in their favour by constructing a bureaucratic framework backed up by military force.[110]

A parallel line of sociolegal scholarship indicates that the trend towards liberal legalism in Thailand is by no means one-way traffic. The studies by David and Jaruwan Engel[111] indicate that, at least in the field of tort law, 'there is little evidence that the spirit of legal legalism has expanded and taken root in the consciousness of ordinary people during an era of global change'.[112] In terms of gauging the active role of the administrative courts, the statistics referred to at the outset demonstrate a constant case load and extensive usage across the nation, while a rising throughput of cases appears to provide support for the idea that the administrative courts are, to some degree, satisfying a need for citizen remedies in formal courts to counter a powerful executive. There is no equivalent study of administrative law geared to investigate whether a gulf exists between the codified body of laws and the wider perception of administrative law by the Thai public. Moreover, it will be suggested in the final section of this chapter that from the bottom up it has often been NGOs that have assumed a pivotal role in orchestrating prominent litigation, particularly in the field of environmental law.[113]

106 Andrew Harding, 'Comparative Law and Legal Transplantation in South East Asia' in David Nelken and Johannes Feest (eds.), *Adapting Legal Cultures* (Oxford: Hart Publishing, 2001) 205.

107 Nicholas Bamforth and Peter Leyland, *Public Law in a Multi-Layered Constitution* (Oxford: Hart Publishing, 2003) 5ff.

108 Baker and Pasuk Phongpaichit, *Pridi by Pridi*, 196.

109 John L. S. Girling, *Thailand: Society and Politics* (Ithaca, NY: Cornell University Press, 1981) 25ff.

110 Loos 2006, 15. See earlier discussion in Section 13.4.

111 In Chapter 7, this volume, which explores the multilayered meaning of modernity and legal consciousness against the background of contemporary political conflict.

112 David Engel and Jaruwan Engel, *Tort, Custom and Karma* (Stanford: Stanford University Press, 2010) 7.

113 Naruemon Thabchumpon, 'NGOs and Grassroots Participation in the Political Reform Process' in Duncan McCargo (ed.), *Reforming Thai Politics* (Copenhagen: NIAS Books, 2002).

13.6 ADMINISTRATIVE JUSTICE AND ENVIRONMENTAL ACTIVISM

Our survey of historical episodes relating to administrative law proceeds to consider a little further the gulf between the law as text and the spirit and effectiveness of its application. Examining the history of administrative law from the 1990s, it has been noted how legitimate expectation and proportionality found their way into legislation as concepts adopted from German administrative law, with the objective of consolidating the rule of law by preventing retrospective action by public bodies. This final section focuses on the environmental jurisprudence of the administrative court and it argues that administrative courts, in contrast to other institutional bodies, especially the Constitutional Court, have made and still make a distinctive contribution to the acceptance of important rule of law values in Thailand.

We have observed that the Administrative Courts were established as an independent body under the 1997 Constitution at the same time as the new Constitutional Court as the apex court[114] and a battery other watchdog bodies.[115] Of course, with hindsight both the 1997 and 2007 Constitutions have been regarded as only fleeting and ultimately flawed experiments in democratic constitution-making. These recent constitutions and the 2017 Constitution were drafted on the questionable assumption that a marked increase in the scope for judicial intervention, particularly by the Constitutional Court, would serve as an antidote to Thailand's extreme political volatility.[116] Despite apparently rigorous mechanisms for the appointment of its judges,[117] the Constitutional Court was, in effect, subject to a form of capture by the Thai establishment.[118] We find that this apex court was required to either endorse or disqualify actions of the executive, or take actions against what were regarded as troublesome politicians on behalf of the monarchy, and sometimes to intervene with the encouragement of the former King.[119] For instance, first, under the 1997 Constitution, the Constitutional Court was made responsible for ratifying decisions of other watchdog bodies. This included the decisions of the Electoral Commission. As a result, the Constitutional Court had to finally determine the validity of the outcome of national elections held in 2006.[120] Second, under the 2007 Constitution, the Constitutional Court was required inter alia to rule on the dismissal of the Prime Minister, on the dissolution of mainstream political parties, and on the validity of a key constitutional amendment concerning the composition of the Senate passed by Parliament.[121] These, and other similar cases, illustrate how the Thai Constitutional Court was flung repeatedly into the cauldron of Thai political conflict and,

[114] Andrew Harding and Peter Leyland, 'Indonesia and Thailand: The Constitutional Courts of Thailand and Indonesia: Two Case Studies from SE Asia' in Andrew Harding and Peter Leyland (eds.), *Constitutional Courts: A Comparative Study* (London: Wildy, Simmonds & Hill, 2009) 333ff.

[115] Leyland, 'Thailand's Constitutional Watchdogs', 157ff.

[116] McCargo, 'Competing Notions', 420–1, 434. See also Björn Dressel, 'Thailand: Judicialization of Politics or Politicization of the Judiciary?' in Björn Dressel, *The Judicialization of Politics in Asia* (Abingdon, UK: Routledge, 2012).

[117] The Constitution of the Kingdom of Thailand 1997, section 255; The Constitution of the Kingdom of Thailand 2007, Article 204.

[118] McCargo, 'Competing Notions' at 437, identifies a regressive form of judicialisation manifesting itself in a series of legal decisions, giving the unfortunate impression of a judiciary instrumentalised to oppose the political career of Thaksin Shinawatra and his supporters.

[119] Duncan McCargo and Peeradej Tanruangporn, 'Branding Dissent: Nitirat, Thailand's Enlightened Jurists', *Journal of Contemporary Asia*, published online 16 March 2015, 11.

[120] Harding and Leyland, *The Constitutional System of Thailand*, 182.

[121] See Dressel, 'Thailand: Judicialization of Politics', 85ff; James Wise, *Thailand: History, Politics and the Rule of Law* (Singapore: Marshall Cavendish, 2019), 85.

consequently, how its credibility as an independent judicial body was also called into question.[122]

To some degree the relative success of the Thai administrative courts, in terms of their endurance as a respected judicial institution over such a turbulent period, is partly because these courts perform a different, less overtly controversial type of political role. This perception of administrative justice may also relate to the nature of the caseload and the fact that the court is dealing with narrower questions of legality. For instance, a substantial proportion of cases concern routine issues that arise from the administrative contracts of public functionaries.[123] The introduction of administrative courts coincides with a trend towards more frequent reliance by government on the private sector for policy delivery and the privatisation of state assets.[124] In consequence, a proportion of administrative court litigation has been concerned with regulatory decisions by central and local government and how these impact directly on the activities of private companies.[125] Also, cases might involve challenges to the procedure adopted for the continuation or renewal of licenses issued by central government departments.[126]

At the same time, there has been a non-partisan community-based political dimension to certain types of legal activism in the administrative law domain. The administrative courts have been used by NGOs and the middle-class environmental movement in Thailand with limited resources,[127] but also increasingly by businesses seeking to challenge the power of Thai bureaucracy. '[N]ew strategies, new careers, and unexpectedly, a new personal identity' have been required of lawyers to defend local populations faced with the loss of land, water, air quality or even their livelihood.[128] The mobilisation at a local level has acted as an indirect form of political empowerment from below. NGOs have orchestrated the population at the local level to support campaigns with an environmental objective.[129] The environmental movement emerged as an opposition force in the 1980s in preventing the construction of the Nam Choan Dam,[130] and it has grown steadily to address concerns by the international community about the impact of development affecting valuable natural resources.[131] Moreover, as well as any direct legal outcome from challenging their activities, media exposure generated by such litigation has pressured government and public bodies to justify their actions and provide explanations.[132] Statistical data from the court testifies to a significant case-load in the environmental field. The annual average number of cases before the court ranged between 500 and 900 between 2001 to 2010. This was followed by a surge of

[122] Harding and Leyland, *The Constitutional System of Thailand*, 254.

[123] Bhokin Bhalakula, 'Administrative Contract in the Thai Legal Context', *Office of the Administrative Courts*, March 2003.

[124] See The EGAT Case, Supreme Administrative Court Judgment No D5/2006; Harding and Leyland, *The Constitutional System of Thailand*, 205ff.

[125] Supreme Administrative Court Judgment D118/2007.

[126] See *Chalong Concrete 1999 Co Ltd et al* v. *Ministry of Natural Resources and Environment* Supreme Administrative Court Judgment D33/2553, 21 April 2010.

[127] Naruemon Thabchumpon, 'NGOs and Grassroots Participation', 186.

[128] Frank Munger, Peerawich Thoviriyaveh, and Vorapitchaya Rabiablok, 'An Alternative Path to Rule of Law? Thailand's Twenty-First Century Administrative Courts' (2019) 26(1) *Indiana Journal of Global Studies* 133, 163ff.

[129] See, for example, *Community Committee of Saranrom Village (P)* v. *District Director of Bueng Kum District (D1) and Bangkok Metropolitan Administration (D2)*, Supreme Administrative Court, Judgment No 49/2554, 16 March 2011.

[130] Philip Hirsch, 'The Politics of Environment: Opposition and Legitimacy' in Kevin Hewison (ed.), *Political Change in Thailand: Democracy and Participation* (Abingdon: Routledge, 1997) 179, 188 (NGOs).

[131] Munger, et al., 161.

[132] 'Kudos to the Court for Map Ta Phut Decision', *The Nation*, 4 December 2009. See Munger, et al., 167.

litigation after the environmental division of the administrative court opened its doors in 2011. There were 2,754 cases in 2012. In the year of the 2014 military coup the figure dipped to 697 cases, but it had recovered to 1,397 cases by 2016.[133]

The litigation concerning the environmental consequences of industrial development provides an excellent illustration of the evolving judicial role in overseeing the sensitive policy area of environmental protection.[134] In the latest Map Ta Phut case (*Charoen Detchkum and Kruewan Wongphayak* v. *National Environment Board*), the Supreme Administrative Court had to consider whether in designating a pollution-control area officials acting under the Conservation of National Environmental Quality Act had acted unlawfully by neglecting to perform their duty, or had unreasonably delayed performing their duty. The Map Ta Phut area of Rayong Province is the largest industrial complex in Thailand and it is also the location for a massive petrochemical plant. The case is of particular interest both because of the environmental implications of the decision in such a sensitive location, and because it provides an example of the approach of the Supreme Administrative court in formulating its judgment.

In addition to the statutory framework for regulating pollution, the 1997 constitution is recognised as the ultimate source of legal authority. This is because it sets out a 'precautionary principle' applicable to the environment. The constitution stated that: 'Any project or activity which may seriously affect the quality of the environment shall not be permitted, unless its impacts on the quality of the environment have been studied and evaluated'.[135] In turn, this calls for the commissioning of reputable studies from academic institutions or organisations working in the environmental field. In addition, the court referred to the relationship between domestic law and international law. It was pointed out that this principle of environmental law regarding the precautionary principle had been accepted by Thailand (and by implication included into the 1997 constitution) as it forms part of the Rio Declaration on Environment and Development. Chapter 15 stipulates that, in cases where there are threats of severe and irreparable damage to the environment, the Government in question must adopt a precautionary approach in order to protect the environment and the local community.[136]

The court held that, under the relevant Thai legislation, there are pollution control areas that must be established in order to control, reduce, and eliminate pollution.[137] In view of the extensive scientific evidence that had been provided demonstrating that the facts met the statutory criteria,[138] the National Environment Board (NEB) were ordered to issue a notification under the Act setting up a control area. Further, this would entail preparing an efficient action plan to eliminate the pollution in the pollution control area at the provincial level and require pollution control officials to provide advice and assistance. The lack of definitive scientific evidence could not be relied on by the NEB as the reason

133 Munger, et al., 156.

134 *Charoen Detchkum and Kruewan Wongphayak* v. *National Environment Board*, 18 October 2017, Black Case No 326/2552/Red Case No 921/2560.

135 The Constitution of the Kingdom of Thailand 1997, section 56. Section 67 of the 2007 Constitution, which contains similar provisions, is also referred to in the judgment. Now the requirement of impact assessment is contained in section 58 of the 2017 Constitution.

136 Thailand attended the Conference on Environment and Development, UNCED, in Rio de Janeiro in June 1992.

137 Section 59 of The Enhancement and Conservation of National Environmental Quality Act 1992.

138 The accountancy survey showed the type, origins, and extent of pollution origin, as well as the measures required for its reduction.

for postponing the execution of cost–effective measures to prevent environmental degradation.

In a recent study it is argued that 'the greatest obstacle to independent review of executive authority in Thailand has not been the lack of an independent judiciary but the dominant bureaucratic structure of the Thai state'.[139] The Klity Creek case is used to demonstrate the willingness of the administrative courts to push the law by interpreting general constitutional and statutory principles ignored in practice by the ministries responsible for preventing such threats to the public.[140] The Pollution Control Department (PCD) had failed to respect a ruling requiring it to clean up lead waste which was being discharged into Klity Creek. The Supreme Administrative Court ordered the Lead Concentrate Co to help PCD clean up and to pay 36 million baht in compensation. The Klity Creek litigation indicates that, on the one hand, such decisions can present a potential challenge to bureaucratic inertia and to some extent make up for a lack of direct political accountability in the environmental field, but, on the other hand, it also demonstrates how the process turned into a protracted legal battle against officialdom which did not have an immediate impact.[141] From the standpoint of the preceding discussion such cases illustrate that a continental style system of administrative courts in Thailand, fashioned along the lines envisaged by Pridi and other mainly European legal advisors, currently provides an important legal avenue for seeking redress against a powerful centralised bureaucracy.

13.7 CONCLUSION

This foray into Thailand's legal history has identified a series of themes associated with the cultural layering behind the acquisition of a national system of administrative justice. An account largely based on an observation of landmark reforms would perhaps suggest that the current system of administrative courts, founded on a European continental model, was the culmination of a continuous process set in train by King Chulalongkorn who supported the introduction of a Council of State as a useful component in the consolidation of a centralised state governed by formal law. Despite not taking root, this Council of State initiative was followed up first by the Pridi generation, which predicted the need for administrative courts at the time Siam acquired its first constitution in 1932. Then, under the 1979 legislation, the Petitioning Council provided administrative adjudication for the first time as a counterweight to an already powerful bureaucratic polity. The introduction of European-style administrative courts in 2001 is thus the last stage in the realisation of the objective of Chulalonkorn, Pridi, and other jurists.

Of course, such an approach entirely neglects the autochthonous cultural dimension. Given the incessant rivalry between Thai elites and external threats to the nation, there were instrumental reasons to modernise the legal system on European lines; it was not to establish the rule of law and protect human rights in the manner of many democratic constitutions, but rather to introduce a powerful centralised bureaucratic state capable of implementing law. The administrative courts, when they did eventually appear, resulted from the 1997 constitution backed by an emerging middle-class movement of activists and academics. The textual provisions were conceived to provide effective judicial oversight over an already powerful

139 Munger, et al., 170.
140 Ibid., 162.
141 'Klity Creek villagers win 19-year legal battle', *Bangkok Post*, 11 September 2017.

executive. The national system of administrative courts was equipped with the full conceptual legal toolkit of administrative law, including legitimate expectation and proportionality, discussed above. The case statistics do not reveal either how the availability of a new remedy has been received by Thai citizens in general, nor whether Thai bureaucratic practice has been ameliorated by the prospect of being brought before a court.

The 1997 Constitution project depended to a considerable degree on the assumption that a multiplication of legal institutions and watchdog bodies, with a concomitant intensification of legalism (in the sense of a discretion for judges to intervene), would serve as a solution to Thailand's extreme political instability. In constitutional terms the judicialisation of process not only failed to establish stability, but also the independent status of the courts – particularly of the Constitutional Court – was called into question as they were drawn into many political disputes. The 2014 military coup has resulted in a decisive shift away from liberal-democratic constitutionalism towards an autocratic form of government[142] which stifles overt political challenge to the military and the monarchy. The tentacles of the current ruling elite are maintained through a merry-go-round of patronage dispensed mainly to retired generals and other known supporters of the junta faction. On the other hand, the administrative courts have proved to be relatively well-insulated from vested interests and, to a limited extent, they provide a form of surrogate opposition. Despite the repressive current scenario these courts have continued to operate with a rising caseload. By upholding the rule of law in landmark cases, local populations have enjoyed some protection in the environmental and health fields through the enforcement of legal regulation. However, the capacity of the administrative court system to perform an effective oppositional role should be heavily qualified. In the absence of legal aid, the initiative in such cases has often depended on NGOs rather than from grass-roots activism; even when successful, the enforcement of judgments against government agencies and vested interests may be ineffective; and high profiles challenges to government decision-making are a mere fraction of the claims coming before the administrative court.

142 A. Macgregor Marshall, *A Kingdom in Crisis: Thailand's Struggle for Democracy in the Twenty First Century* (New York: Zed Books, 2015) xi.

14

Siam and the Standard of Civilisation in the Nineteenth Century

Krisdakorn Wongwuthikun and Naporn Popattanachai

14.1 INTRODUCTION

History and development of Siam in international law has not been an easy one. From the late nineteenth century, Siam was seen by the Western powers as a half-civilised and barbaric state. Coupled with threats from the colonialism spreading across Asia, it had no choice but to conclude unfairly disadvantageous treaties with them. Such treaties resulted in an inequality between states and the suspension of the principle of sovereign equality. This was highlighted by the fact that Siam was denied full sovereignty with the establishment of extraterritoriality jurisdiction of the Western powers within its territory. In order to rectify the unfair situation, Siam had to take several steps to regain sovereign equality vis-à-vis the Western powers.

This chapter aims to highlight two factors that brought Siam to be an internationally recognised modern state. First, it illustrates how the unjust and unequal treaties had been used to put pressure on Siam to bring about the country's modernisation. Secondly, it demonstrates the enormous attempts of Siam to upgrade and improve the country through several actions. These included the importing of modern international law into the state in order to raise its profile internationally and harness the benefits of maintaining peaceful international relations, developing its allegedly barbaric law by way of improving and introducing the new legal codes and legal system serving the same standards as their Western counterparts. In addition, Siam's decision to participate and appear in the 1899 and 1907 Hague Conferences and join of the League of Nations as one of the founding members in 1920 had helped to establish Siam on the path towards being a civilised nation with international recognition, and ultimately the revocation of all the unequal treaties by 1983. The role of international law in helping to develop Siam to be a civilised nation will also be seen quite clearly in this chapter.

This chapter begins with a brief discussion on how the Westerns saw Siam at the time and how the sovereign equality among states had diminished through the different versions of civilisation. It goes on to discuss the standard of civilisation in international law during the nineteenth century and then highlight how Siam underwent a legal reconstruction within its legal system and took steps in raising its international profile in order to regain its equality vis-à-vis the Western powers as well as to disable all the unfair treaties concluded between Siam and the Western powers.

14.2 SIAM FROM THE PERSPECTIVE OF THE WESTERN INTERNATIONAL LAWYERS

14.2.1 *Natural Law Approaches to the Notion of Sovereign Equality of States*

The understanding of international law as reflected in the works of early writers on international law had taken a natural law approach. In the early seventeenth century, Hugo Grotius, for instance in his 1624 *De Jure Belli ac Pacis*, when dealing with the issue of sovereignty or the highest authority (*summa potestas*), argued that sovereignty is the power 'whose actions are not subject to the legal control of another, so that they cannot be rendered void by the operation of an another human will'.[1] Similarly, another influential international lawyer, Emerich de Vattle, wrote in his 1758 *Le Droit des Gens* that 'nature has established a perfect equality of rights between independent nations. Consequently, none can naturally pretend to prerogative: their rights to freedom and sovereignty renders them equals'.[2] This notion of a natural law approach prevailed from the beginnings of seventeenth century to the end of eighteenth century, and it may seem that Western international law would be applied universally without making any distinction between civilised and non-civilised nations.[3]

The principle of equality is of particular importance to modern international law applicable to all states whatever size they may be. Oppenheim remarked as follows: 'The equality before International Law of all member States of the Family of Nations is an invariable equality derived from their international personality. Whatever inequality may exist between states as regards their size, power, degree of civilisation, wealth and other qualities, they are nevertheless equal as international persons.'[4] According to these explanations, it seems logical to say that powerful states cannot invoke the degree of civilisation against uncivilised states to hold that they lack qualification to be recognised as international persons.

In Siam, the treaties concluded with the western world from the seventeenth and eighteenth centuries could not be said to embody any discrimination. Nor did provisions of the treaties contain clauses that imposed an inferior status on Siam. For example, the 1687 Treaty of Commerce between France and Siam concluded in Ayutthaya period, or the 1826 Treaty between King of Siam and Great Britain, which was the first modern treaty of friendship between the two states and commerce, signed on the behalf of the Governor-General of British India by Captain Henry Burney (also known as Burney Treaty) did not limit the application of the principle of equality of states and the obligations were imposed upon both parties based on reciprocity on every point.[5] This is evinced by the fanciful text in the final clauses of Article XIV of the Burney Treaty which provides that 'The Siamese and English will form a friendship that shall be perpetuated, that shall know no end or interruptions as

1 Summa autem illa dicitur, cujus actus alterius juri non subsunt ita ut alterius voluntatis humanve arbitrio irriti possint redid.

2 Emerich de Vattle, *The Law of Nations, Or, Principles of the Law of Nature, Applied to the Conduct and Affairs of Nations and Sovereigns, with Three Early Essays on the Origin and Nature of Natural Law and on Luxury* (Indianapolis: Liberty Fund, 2008) 281. He also wrote that 'Since men are by nature equal, and their individual rights and obligations the same, as coming equally from nature, Nations, which are composed of men and may be regarded as so many free persons living together in a state of nature, are by nature equal and hold from nature the same obligations and the same rights. Strength or weakness, in this case, counts for nothing. A dwarf is as much a man as a giant is; a small republic is no less sovereign than the most powerful Kingdom'.

3 Anthony Anghie, 'The Evolution of International Law: Colonial and Postcolonial Realities' (2006) 27 *Third World Quarterly* 739, 740.

4 Lassa Francis Lawrence Oppenheim, *International Law*, (3rd ed. Roxburgh, London: Longmans, 1920) 15.

5 Likhit Dhiravegin, *Siam and Colonism (1855–1909): An Analysis of Diplomatic Relations* (Bangkok: Thai Watana Panich Press, 1974) 10.

long as heaven and earth appear'. This led Sompong to conclude that 'the relations between Siam and Portugal as well as Spain and the Netherlands had always proceeded on the footing of complete equality, based on the treaties of friendship and commerce … without any inconvenience or discrimination of any sort'.[6]

14.2.2 *The Distinction between 'Civilised' and 'Uncivilised': Siam As an Uncivilised State*

Traditionally international law as we know it today has developed from Europe in the seventeenth century. From the conclusion of the 1648 Treaty of Westphalia onward the relationships among the Western nations had to be governed by the principle of equality and the principle that all sovereigns are equal.[7] Although the conception of equality among states spread amongst Western powers, this model did not apply to non-Western governments, thus creating a hierarchy of states. During the nineteenth century, the principle of equality ceased to exist when the Western nations began to pose the threat of colonialism, under which Siam had to accept inequality since it was not regarded as the inheritor of modern Western civilisation.

The emergence of the concept of civilisation in international law can be traced back to the nineteenth century when international lawyers described international law as a production of Europe. J. H. W. Verzijl, for instance, held that the body of international law was developed from 'conscious activity of the Western mind' and Western 'common source of beliefs'.[8] International law was a matter for the civilised states, and the societies of the non-Western world would be excluded from the application of (Western) international law. This notion continued even into the last decades of the nineteenth century.

The non-universality of international law was vigorously asserted by Henry Wheaton, who argued that there is 'no universal, immutable law of nations, binding upon the whole human race … . Hence the international law of the civilized, Christian nations of Europe and America, is one thing; and that which governs the intercourse of the Mohammedan nations of the East with each other, and with Christians, is another and very different thing'.[9]

Siam was considered as a half-civilised nation around the year 1900 as since then it had a different legal conscience compared to the Western understanding.[10] Siamese laws were considered barbaric. John Bowring fiercely commented on Siamese penal law that it was too cruel. He wrote that 'some offences are visited by very barbarous punishments. The penalty for melting an idol of gold or silver, stolen from the temple, is to be burnt alive. Adulterers are punished by marking with hot iron on the cheeks, and the forehead is sometimes branded for other crimes'.[11]

In addition, the Siamese tributary-state relationship with neighbouring countries made Siam barbaric in the eyes of the West. This includes the relationship between Siam and Chao

6 Sompong Sucharitkul, 'Asian Perspectives of the Evolution of International Law: Thailand's Experience at the Threshold of the Third Millennium' (2002) 9 *Chinese Journal of International Law* 527, 540.

7 Ibid., 529.

8 J. H. W Verzijl, *International Law in Historical Perspective*, Vol. I (Leiden: A. W. Sijthoff, 1968) 435–6.

9 H. Wheaton, *Elements of International Law: With a Sketch of the History of the Science* (Philadelphia: Carey, Lea and Blanchard, 1836) 45.

10 Andreas Buss, 'The Preah Vihear Case and Regional Customary Law' (2010) 9 *Chinese Journal of International Law* 111, 114 and see Wilhelm Grewe, *The Epochs of International Law* (Berlin/New York: Walter de Gruyter, 2000), 454.

11 John Bowring, *The Kingdom and People of Siam*, Vol. 1 (London: John W. Parker and Son, 1857) 182.

Kavila which dated back to 1755.[12] The former benefited from the latter's forces to defend the Burmese invasion, whereas Chao Kavila of Lanna gained support from the tributary relationship with Siam to revive its ancient State of Lanna.[13] Not only did the tributary relationship exist between Siam and the northern region, this also happened in the eastern and southern counterparts.[14] The tributary relationship also existed between Siam and Cambodia and between Siam and Malay where evidence can be seen from tributes sent to Siam to safeguard its security from any Siamese military actions.[15] Although these tributary relationships 'seemed willing' and were mutually beneficial, this highlights inequality between states and may not be viewed as civilised from the Western perspective.

The question that needs to be addressed, therefore, is how did the Western international lawyers perceive the legal status of other nations such as those Asian countries? This question was reflected upon in the writing of Alphonse Rivier, a Belgian international lawyer, in his renowned book *Principles du droit des gens* where he wrote that the law of nations can exist only between and for the benefit of nations that shared a common legal conscience. He claimed that there is no existence of international law between nations, nor for nations, in which all legal consciousness is lacking. Also, separation should be made between civilised nations and the nations of medium races, half-civilised, or whose civilisation differs from that of Christian-Western nations. Also, William Hall was of the view that 'international law is a product of the special civilisation of modern Europe and forms a highly artificial system of which the principles cannot be supposed to be understood or recognised by countries differently civilised'.[16] The relationship between Siam and the western world was thus governed by 'the principles of Christianity and a humanitarian attitude' or 'moral precept' rather than the international law concept.[17]

In the nineteenth and early twentieth centuries, international law was brought to Siam by Western diplomats with a view to standardising international behaviour and establishing an institutional framework for international society.[18] The purpose of this was to regulate day-to-day international relations and international politics. The conception of the law of the nations was unknown outside Europe before the nineteenth century. This led Richard S. Horowitz to claim that Siam constructed her relationships with other states 'on the basis of hierarchies of rulers, with more powerful states claiming special rights and responsibilities over lesser ones'.[19] In the case where Siam would like to cultivate relationships with others, Theravada Buddhism was one of the tools that it used to claim higher status over other entities.

14.2.3 *The Standard of Civilisation in International Law in the Nineteenth Century*

As mentioned in the previous section, most of the early publicists recognised that equality can be the rule only among states sharing common standards of civilisation. The question then is, what was the purpose of establishing a Western standard of civilisation? When the Western

12 David K. Wyatt, *Thailand: A Short History* (New Haven: Yale University Press, 1982) 155–6.
13 Ibid.
14 Ibid., 156–7.
15 Ibid., 158–61.
16 William Hall, *A Treatise on International Law* (Oxford: Clarendon Press, 1904), 40.
17 Buss, 'The Preah Vihear Case and Regional Customary Law', 115.
18 Richard S. Horowitz, 'International Law and State Transformation in China, Siam, and the Ottoman Empire during the Nineteenth Century' (2005) 15 *Journal of World History* 445, 448.
19 Ibid., 450.

powers tried to expand themselves to the areas outside Europe which were in large part non-Christian, new universal values had to be created. Civilisation was that value established by international lawyers. Gerrit W. Gong noted that the standard of civilisation served two purposes. Firstly, it emerged as a response to the need to protect certain basic rights of Western nationals (e.g., life, liberty, and property) when they extended their powers to or conducted intercourse with non-Western countries. Secondly, the standard of civilisation can be used as a benchmark for determining legal personality in international law.[20]

In his renowned book, Gerrit W. Gong went on to list five requirements for states to meet the standard of civilisation that had emerged in the nineteenth century. There are two requirements that this chapter uses as a framework to assess the civilisation of Siam. Firstly, a civilised state maintains a domestic system of courts, codes that guarantee legal justice for all within its jurisdiction, foreigners and native citizens alike.[21] States which did not follow this criterion were considered not to be civilised. Moreover, standard of civilisation, according to Gong, required 'a "civilised state" [that] fulfils the obligations of the international system by maintaining adequate and permanent avenues for diplomatic interchange and communication'.[22] He describes this requirement by linking participation at international conferences or international organisations as a way of knowing a civilised nation, since it could communicate with international society.[23]

14.3 SIAM'S ROAD TO MODERNISATION

14.3.1 *Unequal Treaties and Extraterritoriality*

Although Siam has never been colonised, at a time when Siam faced territorial encroachments by Western states it had to endure a semi-colonial environment in order to avoid colonisation. Siam remained independent but it allowed Western powers to exert power and influence within an asymmetrical relationship without succumbing to the colonial domination by them.[24] Thongchai Winichakul writes that '[a]lthough not formally colonised, Siam was under the global influence of Western colonialism'.[25] The implication was that in a semi-colonial environment Siam was forced to sign treaties which tended to favour the Western powers and that were non-reciprocal. As mentioned earlier, international law was Christian in its origins, and Siam, as a non-Christian state, was not considered a participant in international law since its civilisation did not meet the standard of civilisation perceived by international lawyers in the Christian world. The concept of civilisation was the classic justification for the conclusion of unequal treaties with Siam.[26] Therefore, unequal treaties were used by the colonial powers as an instrument to force Siam to modernise and overhaul the country's legal system.

20 Gerrit W. Gong, 'Standards of Civilization Today', in Mehdi Mozaffari (eds.), *Globalization and Civilizations* (Abingdon: Routledge, 2002) 80.

21 Ibid., 80.

22 Gerrit W. Gong, *The Standard of 'Civilisation' in International Society* (Oxford: Oxford University Press, 1984) 15.

23 Ibid., 19.

24 Prabhakar Singh, 'Of International Law, Semi-colonial Thailand, and Imperial Ghosts' (2019) 9 *Asian Journal of International Law* 46, 49.

25 Thongchai Winichakul, 'The Quest for "Siwilai": A Geographical Discourse of Civilization Thinking in the Late Nineteenth and Early Twentieth-Century Siam' (2000) 59 *Journal of Asian Studies* 528.

26 Ingrid Detter defines unequal treaties as those 'which only favour the stronger of the parties, treaties which even sometimes are in conflict with the long-term national interest of the weaker State'. See, Ingrid Detter, 'The Problem of Unequal Treaties' (1966) *International and Comparative Law Quarterly* 1069, 1070.

The term 'unequal treaties' can be used to describe the conclusion of the bilateral treaties in the second half of the nineteenth and beginning of the twentieth centuries, mostly between Western powers on the one hand, and Asian as well as African states on the other.[27] Historically, this reality shows that there was a distinction between the Western and the non-Western states, in which the former were labelled as civilised states and the latter labelled as uncivilised states. In the twentieth century, unequal treaties 'the term was embedded in the context of imperialism, Eurocentrism, and connotes injustice or humiliation'.[28] To ascertain whether or not a treaty is unequal, one needs to consider substantive provisions and the treaty-making process. With regard to substantive inequality, the non-Western states were usually forced to accept treaty obligations that were imbalanced by non-reciprocity, or extreme restriction of the exercise of their sovereignty, including restraint of judicial power, understood as extraterritoriality. Procedurally, unequal treaties may have been made under military, political, or economic coercion, including treaties signed as encroachments on sovereignty.

This kind of treaty had already been concluded by Western powers with Japan and China only a few years earlier, but the Siamese history of unequal treaties with the West began in 1855, when it was forced to sign the Treaty of Friendship and of Commerce between Great Britain and Siam on 18 April 1855 (also known as the 'Bowring Treaty').[29] The United States and nearly all major Western States,[30] such as France, the Netherlands, Belgium, and Japan concluded similar treaties with Siam by using the Bowring Treaty as a model.[31]

The more civilised states would seek to conclude such agreements with less civilised States in order to protect the lives of their nationals in states lacking comparable standards of civilisation. The implication was that the domestic law could not provide guarantees as to the protection of foreigners, so that Siam was hardly to be treated as equal on the international scene.[32] In this sense, Christian states would not admit perfect equality with Siam in so far as its undeveloped legal system was inferior to the civilisation of most European and American States and of Japan.

Auguste Dague, former legal advisor to the Government of Siam, once noted in the 1900 *Journal du Droit International Privé* that: 'L' extraterritorialité a pour but d'assurer aux nationaux de certains Etats une protection qu'ils estiment ne pas pouvoir trouver dans un pays moins civilisé que le leur. Cette raison ne s'applique pas aux sujets d'États qui trouvent au Siam au moins autant de protection légale que dans leur patrie' (translation: 'The purpose of extraterritoriality is to provide the nationals of certain states with protection that they believe cannot be found in a country less civilized than theirs. This reason does not apply to subjects of states who find in Siam at least as much legal protection as in their own country').[33] Given the fact Siam's civilisation was thought to differ considerably from those of civilised ones, its legal capacity to conclude treaties was restricted on the basis of degree and character

27 Anne Peters, 'Treaties, Unequal', *Max Planck Encyclopedias of International Law*, online edition.
28 Ibid.
29 Treaty of Friendship and Commerce between Siam and Great Britain (signed 18 April 1855, entered into force 5 April 1856) and see generally in Francis Bowes Sayre, 'The Passing of Extraterritoriality in Siam' (1928) 22 *American Journal of International Law* 70, 70–88.
30 The treaties were concluded with the United States, France, Denmark, the Hanseatic Republic, Prussia, Sweden and Norway, Belgium, Italy, Austria-Hungary, and Spain.
31 Sompong Sucharitkul, 'Asian Perspectives of the Evolution of International Law: Thailand's Experience at the Threshold of the Third Millennium', 546.
32 Detter, 'The Problem of Unequal Treaties', 1076.
33 Auguste Dague, 'De la condition juridique des étrangers et de l'organisation judiciaire au Siam' (1900) 27 *Journal du Droit International Privé* 461, 466.

of civilisation, including fundamental juridical ideas. As Edwin De Witt Dickinson stated, 'fundamental differences in the character of civilisation have always been the source of important limitations on capacity'[34] and could be considered as 'essential factors in determining status'.[35]

Under the reign of King Mongkut (1851–68), the country was opened to foreign trade with a view to preserving Siam's independence. Realising Siam's weakness and backwardness, he had to conclude an unequal treaty under duress such as the one which was signed with Great Britain in 1855. As Rong Syamananda noted, 'if she did not sign the Treaty, she might be forced to do so, as Bowring had hinted at such a step'.[36] The question is what was this hint? Bowring noted in his book, which could be clearly seen, that he would order the British fleet combined with the French and the Americans to enter Siam's waters if he failed to get the desired result. He wrote that 'If I can get a treaty, well: if not, I will not consent to delay, but shall simply state I cannot give more time to the object, but will return to Siam when I have consulted with my colleagues of French and the United States, and the British admiral'.[37] What Bowring wrote in his book provides evidence that he prepared to launch military troops if his proposal was rejected.

To become a full participant in international society Siam needed to revise its law in accordance with international standards, and also found itself compelled to enter into unequal treaties with more civilised States. The conclusion of unequal treaties paved the way to modernisation, so that Siam could be presumed to be a member of the community of states on the condition that it had to prove itself civilised. The prototype of an unequal treaty that Siam concluded with the western world was the 1855 Bowring Treaty. Article II, paragraph 1 established a regime of extraterritoriality. It stipulated that:

> The interests of all British subjects coming to Siam shall be placed under the regulation and control of a Consul, who will be appointed to reside at Bangkok. He will himself conform to, and will enforce the observance by British subjects of all the provisions of this Treaty, and such of the former Treaty negotiated by Captain Burney in 1826 as shall still remain in operation. He shall also give effect to all rules or regulations that are now or may hereafter be enacted for the government of British subjects in Siam, the conduct of their trade, and for the prevention of violations of the laws of Siam. Any disputes arising between Siamese and British subjects shall be heard and determined by the Consul, in conjunction with the proper Siamese officers; and criminal offences will be punished, in the case of English offenders, by the Consul, according to English laws, and in the case of Siamese offenders, by their own laws, through the Siamese authorities. But the Consul shall not interfere in any matters referring solely to Siamese, neither will the Siamese authorities interfere in questions which only concern the subjects of Her Britannic Majesty.

In the eyes of the Siamese, international treaties represented restrictions on state sovereignty for carrying out international relations. Extraterritoriality, as Likhit noted, 'was a thorn in Siam's flesh'.[38] The question is thus, how could a state become a civilised state in order to be accepted as a member of the international society? The answer given by the Western world was that Siam needed to modernise itself in order to become full standing in the family of

34 Edwin De Witt Dickinson, *The Equality of State in International Law* (Cambridge, Mass.: Harvard University Press, 1920), 224.

35 Ibid., 341.

36 Rong Syamananda, *A History of Thailand* (Bangkok: Kurusapha Ladprao Press, 1971) 127.

37 John Bowring, *The Kingdom and People of Siam*, Vol. 2 (London: John W. Parker and Son, 1857) 283. See also, Likhit Dhiravegin, *Siam and Colonism (1855–1909): An Analysis of Diplomatic Relations*, 16.

38 Ibid., 39.

nations by providing 'evidence that the citizens or subjects of foreign states enjoy within their dominions the rights, privileges, and protection of law accorded in European and American communities'.[39] Thus in the absence of protection of law comparable to Western standards, foreign states would on this principle enjoy the right to protect their citizens and subjects and apply their own law as if their citizen lived within territory under the jurisdiction of the foreign state in question. It can thus be seen that Siam decided to enter into treaty-relationships on the basis of an unequal legal status of states.

The inequality could be seen in the Treaty of 1856, an agreement supplementary to the treaty of 1855, when nationals and subjects of the foreign power were immune from local jurisdiction in criminal and civil matters. They were instead subordinated to the jurisdiction of consuls of their country. It provides that 'all criminal cases in which both parties are British subjects, or in which the defendant is a British subject, shall be tried and determined by the British consul alone'.[40] Siam's unequal status could also be seen from the fact that it agreed the entry of warships into the river[41] and it allowed the importation of opium as well as the limitation of duty.[42] Also, in the Treaty between Great Britain and Siam, for the Prevention of Crime in the Territories of Chiangmai, Lakon, and Lampoonchi, and for the Promotion of Commerce between Burmah and the Territories aforesaid of 3 September 1883, the British Government could also exercise an extensive jurisdiction by interfering in legal proceedings in the case where British subjects, or in which British subjects may be parties as complainants, accused, plaintiffs, or defendants; the consul or vice-consul was be entitled to be present at the trial to make any suggestions to the judge or judges which he might think proper in the interests of justice.[43] This extensive powers conferred by such treaty confirms that the application of Siamese law would not provide appropriate justice to foreigners, and Siamese judges were not equipped with necessary legal knowledge up to the Western standard. Therefore, this was the view by the Western counterparts especially the British that protection of their citizens and legal administration should not be entrusted to the Siamese authorities. The ongoing proceedings might be transferred, at any time, to the British consular court if the consul or vice-consul thought that the interests of justice would not be guaranteed. The prisoner might even be removed to the consular prison if the consul or vice-consul shall think it is necessary to do so.[44] It should be noted that the 1883 Treaty between Great Britain and Siam did not contain renunciation clauses which could have been in force everlastingly. This even highlights the inequality during the negotiation and conclusion of the Treaty which rendered Siam to an inferior legal position.

It could be seen that the improvement of the legal codes and the legal system eventually led to the revocation of unequal treaties. The promulgation of legal codes and the improvement of the standard of justice in Siam during the reign of King Chulalongkorn with a view to paving the way for ending extraterritoriality was one of the processes to transform Siam into a civilised state.[45] The making of a modern Siam through legal reforms was the condition by which extraterritoriality would disappear. In 1898, the Japanese Government, on the occasion

39 Editorial, 'British Extraterritorial Jurisdiction in Siam' (1909) 3 *American Journal of International Law* 954.

40 Article II of the Supplementary Agreement to Treaty of Friendship and Commerce between Siam and Great Britain, 13 May 1856, see British and Foreign State Papers, Vol. 46, p. 146.

41 Ibid., Article VII.

42 Ibid., Article VIII.

43 Article VIII see the text in Francis Taylor Piggott, *Consular Jurisdiction and to Residence in Oriental Countries* (London: William Clowes and Sons, 1892) 230.

44 Ibid.

45 Prachoom Chomchai, *Chulalongkorn the Great* (Tokyo: Centre for East Asian Studies, 1965) 140.

of the negotiations of the new Additional Protocol to the Treaty of Friendship, Commerce and Navigation between Japan and Siam, explicitly established a condition in which the regime of extraterritorial jurisdiction of the consuls would be abolished. The Siamese Government agreed that Japanese consular officials should have jurisdiction over Japanese subjects in Siam until the judicial reforms of Siam had been completed to be 'to be on the par with the Western or "civilized nations"'.[46] Siam had a strong incentive to transform itself and to comply with Western practices with a view to justifying equal treatment. In 1899, the *Notices diverses* section in the *Revue de droit international et de législation comparé* noted that Siam faithfully admitted that Japan was now more advanced than Siam in the path of legislative reform and acknowledged that one could expect from Siam also the promulgation of a set of codes and the institution of a system of judicial organisation, based on the principles applicable in modern states.[47] In addition, as Wyatt notes, it was the desire and 'ability of an absolute, but Westernised monarch' that agreed to and accepted changes through an 'introduction of Westernised institutions and techniques' suggested by numbers of its foreign advisors into Siam.[48] Hence, it can be said that the unequal treaties formed part of the westernisation of economic and political relations that Siam carried through 'in order to retain for Thailand her place among the nations'.[49]

An impetus behind the legal reforms and the changes of Siam into closer conformity with Western states was the strong desire to eliminate such obligations and regain full sovereignty. Siam needed to comply with international obligations set forth in those treaties. Faced with the territorial encroachments of Great Britain and France and the conclusion of a series of unequal treaties with the Western nations, Siam was introduced and forced to accept the values and practices of modern international law opening the doors of the family of civilised nations and escaping the fate of being colonised.[50] Martti Koskenniemi provides a description of the civilising mission showing European attitudes towards non-civilised states that 'Even as international lawyers had no doubt about the superiority of European civilisation over "Orientals", they did stress that the civilising mission needed to be carried out in an orderly fashion, by providing good examples, and not through an unregulated scramble'. The conclusion of unequal treaties in the non-Western world cannot certainly be described as one of the 'civilising missions' in which the Westerns sought to provide a good example so that Siam would become civilised, following the Western path in revising its domestic law along Western lines with a view to meeting the standard of civilisation. The brute colonial civilising mission can be seen from the fact that it was carried out by using extralegal military force such as 1855 the Bowring Treaty in which Siam was coerced by Britain to sign and surrender its sovereignty.[51]

[46] Walter E. J. Tips, *Gustave Rolin-Jaequemyns and the Making of Modern Siam: The Diaries and Letters of King Chulalongkorn's General Adviser* (Bangkok: White Lotus Press, 1996) 41.

[47] 'Théoriquement le gouvernement siamois eût été incontestablement en droit de ne traiter que sous cette dernière condition, qui est la seule conforme au droit commun. Il ne l'a pas fait cependant. Il a loyalement reconnu que le Japon était actuellement plus avancé que le Siam dans la voie des réformes législatives ot'i il s'est engagé depuis trente ans; il a reconnu que l'on pouvait attendre du Siam aussi la promulgation d'un ensemble de codes et l'institution d'un système d'organisation judiciaire, basés sur les principes en vigueur chez les États modernes' (1899) 1 *Revue de droit international et de législation compare* 93, 95.

[48] David K. Wyatt, 'The Politics of Reform in Thailand: Education in the Reign of King Chulalongkorn' cited in Gong, *The Standard of Civilisation in International Society*, 217.

[49] Nicholas Tarling, 'The Mission of Sir John Bowring to Siam' (1962) 50 *Journal of the Siam Society* 91, 92.

[50] Frank C. Darling, 'The Evolution of Law in Thailand' (1970) *The Review of Politics* 197, 204.

[51] Peters, 'Treaties, Unequal'.

In addition, the need to eliminate inequality and extraterritoriality of the Western treaties resulted in another two developments of the Siamese to avoid colonisation brought in the disguise of a 'civilising mission'. Firstly, evidence shows that the Siamese government was urged not only to translate international law textbooks into Thai, but also to have their government officials equipped with international law knowledge. Unfortunately, it seemed that, due to the lack of financial resources, the translation of those international law textbooks has never happened.[52] Another development was an expression of civilisation by advocating Buddhist teachings to the Western counterparts. This is evident by several interesting events. For example, Buddhist teaching was done through the World Parliament of Religions at Chicago in 1893.[53] The Siamese monarch sent Prince Chandradat Chudhadharn to perform the presentation entitled 'Buddhism as it Exists in Siam' where 'the moral system' from Buddhist perspective was introduced to the Western countries.[54] Also, the system of recognition for foreigners who served Buddhism was also established by King Chulalongkorn where the title of 'Officer of the Order of the White Elephant of Siam' was given to Edwin Arnold.[55] These attempts aimed to show that Buddhism is 'spiritual, moral, scriptural, and intellectual' as is Christianity.[56] For this reason, as observed by Jory, the promotion of Buddhist thoughts to the Western counterpart helped eliminate 'Western perceptions of "barbarism" and the lack of "civilisation" in the peoples and religious and philosophical systems of Asia' including the Siamese culture and tradition.[57]

14.3.2 *Civilising Siam through Participation in International Conferences and the League of Nations*

Due to the fact that there is no single body endowed with a legislative power to prescribe international law, international conferences provide an opportunity for states to express their opinion to international society gathered in form of the club of civilised nations. Participation at international conferences can be seen as one way to be recognised by international society as full subjects of international law. Perhaps the 1899 and 1907 Hague Peace Conferences were the first occasions that brought the civilised nations together to talk about peace and a mutually accepted code of the laws of war. A major step towards civilisation was thus Siam's participation in the two Hague Peace Conferences, invited by Tsar Nicholas II who had a good relationship with King Chulalongkorn. In both Conferences, Siam was among the four Asian (China, Japan, Persia, and Siam) that sent delegations to the Conference so that it became involved in international affairs and gradually became a civilised nation.

For regaining judicial independence it was a condition not only that Siam reform its administrative and legal system, but there were also external factors, such as the conclusion of the 1919 Treaty of Versailles,[58] which was signed (amongst others) by the United States, Britain, and France as well as Siam, that would help Siam to end extraterritorial rights. After defeating Germany in the First World War, they continued to renounce extraterritorial rights

52 The Bangkok Reader, 'International Law' (1866) Volume 2 Leaflet No 6, 64–5.

53 Patrick Jory, 'Thai and Western Buddhist Scholarship in the Age of Colonialism: King Chulalongkorn' (2002) 61 (3) *The Journal of Asian Studies* 891, 907.

54 Ibid.

55 Ibid.

56 Ibid.

57 Ibid.

58 Treaty of Peace between the Allied and Associated Powers and Germany (signed 28 June 1919, entered into force 10 January 1920) [1919] 225 CTS 188.

over Siam, since Siam was as one of the victorious states after having intervened on the side of the allies.[59] The defeated countries, notably Germany and Austria-Hungary, also renounced the unequal treaties concluded in the nineteenth century. Most importantly, Siam joined the League of Nations, which was a turning point for Siam to enter civilisation.

The League of Nations was the first fully fledged permanent international organisation founded in 1920 after the end of the First World War with a view ensuring collective security, assuring international cooperation, and executing the mandates of peace treaties. Members of the League were obliged to not resort to war and respect international law, even though as it transpired they failed to do so in practice. The League of Nations was open to all states providing that they fulfilled certain obligations. Interestingly, Siam became a member of the League of the Nations as a founding member during the reign of King Vajiravudh (1910–25).[60] It should be noted that the birth of the League of Nations, as Stefan Hell notes, 'was influence by Western ideologies'.[61] Siam's membership in the League was remarkable in the sense that it was the only independent state from Southeast Asia participating in an important international organisation. Siam's participation in the international arena offered a picture of international recognition and prestige which was a very rare case indeed where a semi-colonised small state negotiated and sat 'eye-to-eye at the same table together with the world's colonial powers'.[62] Being a League member Siam would thus have some leverage to influence the Western powers to negotiate bilateral treaties. More importantly, Siam could as a result reassert its national sovereignty during the first half of the 1920s.[63] In theory, Siam could invoke Article 19 of the Covenant of the League of Nations to reconsider the unequal treaties. It stipulated that 'the Assembly may from time to time advise the reconsideration by Members of the League of treaties which have become inapplicable and the consideration of international conditions whose continuance might endanger the peace of the world'. Nonetheless, practically, this Article has never been used. Siam's unequal treaty regime resembled the regime imposed on Japan. Unequal treaties began to be abolished in 1920 and were fully terminated by 1939.[64]

In addition, the profound impact of becoming a member was the pressure that was put on the Western powers 'to revise outdated treaties and grant Siam full sovereignty'.[65] Using the League as a vehicle for ending the unequal privileges, Siam could maintain and increase its autonomy and reinforce its modernity internationally. Thus, it is important to recognise that sovereign equality was very crucial for small States so that their voices would be heard and treated equally with dignity. Mark Sally noted that, '[t]hey were also seeking a voice in world affairs, and most were much attracted to the principle of the equality of nations'.[66]

Unequal treaties concluded between Siam and Western world would be relinquished if Siam actively cooperated with the League. In order to gain full sovereignty and to be respected as a sovereign state Siam had also to work closely with the League in several immediate international problems. Having made significant contributions to the League's

59 Sompong Sucharitkul, 'Asian Perspectives of the Evolution of International Law: Thailand's Experience at the Threshold of the Third Millennium', 550. The United States signed the Treaty to renounce extraterritoriality in 1920 followed by Japan in 1921.

60 Stephen Hell, *Siam and the League of Nations: Modernisation, Sovereignty and Multilateral Diplomacy, 1920–1940* (Bangkok: River Books, 2010).

61 Ibid., 11.

62 Ibid., 12.

63 Ibid., 16.

64 Anne Peters, 'Treaties, Unequal'.

65 Ibid., 17.

66 Mark Sally, 'The Small States at Geneva' (1995) 157 *World Affairs* 191.

mission, Siam was regarded as an important member, since Siam played an active role in tackling human trafficking, especially of Chinese women who were brought into the country for prostitution. The Siamese government showed its willingness to sign the 1921 International Convention for the Suppression of the Traffic in Woman and Children in order to commit itself as a civilised nation in combating human trafficking. However, Siam did not implement the Convention until six years later, after the League put pressure on Siam and a League of Nations Commission of Inquiry paid a visit to the country, which culminated in promulgation of the Women and Girls Act of 1928, and the amendment of the Penal Code in 1930 raising the age of consent to sexual acts from twelve to eighteen. It can be said that Siam complied with international obligations in order to 'remain a respected member of the international community'.[67]

Although the attendance at international conferences did not fully transform Siam to gain civilised status, it did, to some extent, compel Siam to step out of the dark ages.

14.4 CONCLUSIONS

Before the expansion of the Western powers into the non-Western world in the nineteenth century, Siam was treated as equal or with equal concern. However, in the course of the nineteenth century, the applicability of Western international law seemed to be limited since Siam was labelled as an uncivilised country. The standard of civilisation was introduced and applied throughout the world for the benefit of the Westerns. Those who did not conform to this standard were left outside the civilised world and not recognised as having international status. Unequal treaties were used during this period signifying injustice and impairment of the sovereignty of Siam. The attempt of the Westerns to impose their standard of civilisation on Siam did not demoralise Siam in adapting itself to such standards. The unequal treaties on one hand illustrated their efforts to protect life, liberty, and property of their nationals and subjects; but on the other hand, they forced Siam to change its legal practice. Siam made continuing efforts to become a civilised nation with full international legal personality and to become a real member of international society in many ways. To abrogate extraterritoriality, Siam reformed its judicial system in accordance with that of Western nations in order to guarantee the fundamental rights of the Western nations. Realising an advantage in complying with international law, Siam was accepted to be part of two important international conferences, showing its willingness to comply with international law. Furthermore, by using the League of Nations as an international platform, Siam seized the golden opportunity to gain international respect. It can be concluded that Siam remained independent throughout its history and became increasingly modernised by reforming itself through the acceptance of the standard of civilisation imposed by the Western nations.

[67] Gerrit W. Gong, 'The Standard of "Civilisation" in International Society, 240.

PART III

Constitutional Conflicts 1932–2017

15

The Thai-Style Democracy in Post-1932 Thailand and Its Challenges

A Quest for Nirvana of Constitutional Saṃsāra in Thai Legal History before 1997

Rawin Leelapatana[*]

15.1 INTRODUCTION

In its post-1932 constitutional history, the constitutional stability Thailand has been seeking has been harshly shaken by conflict between the local tradition of authority that underpins the so-called 'Thai-style democracy' (TSD) and increasingly sturdy demands for liberal democracy and constitutionalism, all of which have led to a number of military coups, installing the TSD, and the abolition of electoral politics. The juntas, especially since 1947, normally claimed the need to protect the three pillars of *Nation-Religion-Monarchy* – the idea of a predominantly Buddhist nation-state with the virtuous monarch, or *Dhammaraja*, as its soul – to legitimise military takeovers. By contrast, supporters of liberalism at times placed emphasis largely on the principle of legality, rights, liberties, and social equality, and tended not to accept political compromise with the military. Post-1932 Thailand's constitutional graveyard can then be seen as *constitutional saṃsāra* – the repetitive cycle of coups and emergency powers to overthrow parliamentary democracy considered by the traditional elites and the military as the source of political instability and disunity, the instalment of the TSD, and the restoration of parliamentary democracy.[1] Based on this saṃsāra metaphor, my main concern is the pre-1997 constitutional history of Thailand. In this chapter, I ask: to what extent did the irresistible and continuous rise of liberal demands and the trends of constitutionalism, modernisation, and democratisation in Thai legal history challenge the TSD before 1997? I address this question from the legal perspective.

I begin this chapter by exploring the key features of the traditional Thai notion of political stability or authority – the *Dhammaraja* tradition – which was later coined as the three pillars of *Thai-ness* (Section 15.2), before examining the general ideas of the TSD (Section 15.3). Then, in Section 15.4, I explore the overall picture of the TSD struggling against rising liberal forces between the late 1960s and 1997. Next, in Sections 15.5 to 15.6, I assess the extent to

* This chapter is modified from the second and fourth chapters of Rawin Leelapatana's unpublished doctoral thesis, 'The Kelsen-Schmitt Debate and the Use of Emergency Powers in Political Crises in Thailand', submitted to the Faculty of Social Science and Law, the University of Bristol. I would like to thank Professor Steven Greer and Dr Athanasios (Akis) Psygkas for their kind supervision throughout the whole project.

1 In Buddhism, *Saṃsāra* means the cycle of relentless rebirth. A prominent Thai political scientist, Chaianan, calls this 'the vicious cycle'. See Chaianan Samutwanit, *Thai Young Turks* (Singapore: Institute of Southeast Asian Studies, 1982) 1–5.

which rising liberal forces weakening the anti-liberal, conservative regime itself challenge the recurrence of military coups and the reinstallation of the TSD before 1997, in particular their effects on the roles of legality. Lastly, in Section 15.7, I apply the binary-star-system metaphor to reflect the gravitational pull between authoritarianism and liberalism (or, more precisely, egalitarianism) to conclude the general picture of constitutional saṃsāra in Thailand's constitutional landscape before 1997.

15.2 THE *DHAMMARAJA* TRADITION AS *THAI-NESS*: THE BASIS OF POLITICAL STABILITY AND AUTHORITY IN THAILAND

The traditional view of political stability in Thailand is based on the patrimonial concept of *Dhammaraja* (the Buddhist righteous king), largely shaped by the Indian civilisation.[2] The Thais borrowed from the Cambodians (Khmers) the idea of *Devaraja* (the Godlike king), an incarnation of Hindu deity who stands at the centre of the cosmological order, and is paid tribute by 'lesser divinities'.[3] This tradition has also been endorsed by Theravada Buddhist teaching received from the Mon, making it more compatible with Thai culture.[4] As a result, the Thai monarch even today is generally considered to be the *Dhammaraja*, 'the father of the family-nation', expected to reign in accordance with *Dhamma* (Buddhist teachings).[5] What follows from this is that the *Dhammaraja* is subsequently and presumptively viewed as a good person (*Khon Dee*).[6] The *Dhammaraja* tradition is further based on the fundamental Buddhist teaching of *Karma*, under which past and present intentional actions are presumed to cause future consequences. Notwithstanding our inability to know his personal moral quality, due to his position, the Thai monarch is traditionally presumed to have accumulated the highest degree of good *Karma* and therefore *Bun* (good merits) and *Barami* (transcendental virtue) within the kingdom, while those associated with or working in the name of the king are also supposed to accumulate good *Karma*.[7] Overall, the traditional view of political authority reflects the key characteristic of Max Weber's patrimonialism: that it is a product of a traditional belief in a stratified authority rather than that in individualism and humanism.[8]

During the reign of King Chulalongkorn (1868–1910), Bangkok faced a serious colonial threats as the British and French endeavoured to bring Siam (Thailand's name before 1939) under their control, forcing the king to rapidly modernise the country. Together with the king's successful foreign policy, the modernisation project was key to preventing Thailand from being formally colonised by European powers.[9] Notwithstanding his progressive

[2] However, in modern Thailand, the legal-rational and charismatic types of legitimacy also bolster the monarchy. Andrew Harding, 'Buddhism, Human Rights and Constitutional Reform in Thailand' (2007) 1 *Asian Journal of Comparative Law* 1–25, 2.

[3] Frank Darling and Ann Darling, *Thailand: The Modern Kingdom* (Singapore: Asia Pacific Press, 1971) 82.

[4] David M. Engel, *Law and Kingship in Thailand during the Reign of King Chulalongkorn* (Ann Arbor: Center for South and Southeast Asian Studies, the University of Michigan, 1975) 2–4.

[5] See Chapter 3, this volume; Dhani Nivat (Prince), 'The Old Siamese Conception of the Monarchy' (1947) 36 *Journal of the Siam Society* 91–106, 94–6; Patrick Jory, *Thailand's Theory of Monarchy: The Vessantara Jataka and the Idea of the Perfect Man* (New York: SUNY Press, 2016) 180–2.

[6] Thak Chaloemtiarana, *Thailand: The Politics of Despotic Paternalism* (New York: Southeast Asia Program Publications, Cornell University, 2007) 3.

[7] Ibid., 83; Jack Fong, 'Sacred Nationalism: The Thai Monarchy and Primordial Nation Construction' (2009) 39 *Journal of Contemporary Asia* 673–96, 688.

[8] Anthony T. Kronman, *Max Weber* (Stanford: Stanford University Press, 1983) 44.

[9] See Chapter 14, this volume.

policies, King Chulalongkorn was also a conservative, especially in political matters, who saw excessive adoption of Western culture as a threat to 'Thai identity', including the traditional notion of the monarchy. Thus, to maintain monarchical absoluteness in the era of nation-state formation, he sought to transform the *Dhammaraja* into the embodiment of the modern Thai nation.[10] His son, King Vajiravudh (1910–25), subsequently made the three pillars of *Nation-Religion-Monarchy* into official state ideology, which constituted *Thai-ness* (what is 'being Thai'), political stability and unity.[11] The sacred trinity played a crucial role as an institution in determining the existence of a normal situation by distinguishing 'what is identified as Thai' (the *positive* identification of *Thai-ness*) from 'otherness' (the *negative* counterpart) within the predominantly Buddhist nation-state or *Chat*.[12] Hence, the sacred trinity does not traditionally underline the loyalty to the principle of legality. *Thai-ness*, as I will show, provides an ideological weapon for the post-1932 traditional elites and military officials to establish and maintain the regime of the TSD. In the next section, I seek to describe the key features of the TSD.

15.3 SARIT THANARAT AND THE THAI-STYLE DEMOCRACY

When King Prajadhipok (1925–35) succeeded his elder brother, King Vajiravudh, in 1925, political power in Thailand was still monopolised by the royal clan and some members of top aristocratic families, causing dissatisfaction among the expanding middle-class and culminating in the Revolution of 1932. On 24 June 1932, a group of civilian and military officials, called 'the People's Party', mounted a coup d'état, deposing the absolute monarchy. The civilian wing of the People's Party, led by Pridi Banomyong, aimed to move Thailand forward to greater endorsement of the legal-rational state by adopting the ideas of constitutionalism and meritorious bureaucracy, and sovereign power transferred from the king to the people. Pridi took part in drafting the first three Thai constitutions – the 1932 Interim Constitution promulgated on 27 June 1932, the 1932 Constitution promulgated on 10 December 1932, and the 1946 Constitution promulgated on 10 May 1946. Having advocated the core of liberal constitutionalism, that the constitution is the supreme law, he intended to make it 'a new focus of public loyalty' by vigorously urging every Thai, through radio broadcasting, 'to love the nation and [to] preserve the constitution' since it 'fuses [*everyone*] as one unity'.[13] Given that he wanted every faction to participate in a political life of the state on a formally equal footing, Pridi also advocated a permanent constitution to foster peace and compromise between different interests, in particular, between Thai progressives and royalist-conservatives.[14] However, despite the relatively peaceful takeover in 1932, the traditional elites strove to restore their hegemony in the 1930s, leading to several counter-revolutionary

10 Pavin Chachavalpongpun, 'The Necessity of Enemies in Thailand's Troubled Politics' (2011) 51 *Asian Survey* 1019–41, 1023.

11 Björn Dressel, 'When Notions of Legitimacy Conflict: The Case of Thailand' (2010) 38 *Politics & Policy* 445–69, 454; Eiji Murashima, 'The Origin of Modern Official State Ideology in Thailand' (1988) 19 *Journal of Southeast Asian Studies* 80–96, 92.

12 Thongchai Winichakul, *Siam Mapped: A History of the Geo-Body of a Nation* (Hawaii: University of Hawaii Press, 1994) 5.

13 Chris Baker and Pasuk Phongpaichit, A *History of Thailand*, 3rd ed. (Cambridge: Cambridge University Press, 2014) 123–4; ปรีดี พนมยงค์ [Pridi Banomyong], *จง พิทักษ์ เจตนารมณ์ ประชาธิปไตย สมบูรณ์ ของ วีรชน 14 ตุลาคม* [*Safeguarding the democratic will of the 14 October Heroes*] (Bangkok: Saitarn Press, 2000) 76–7.

14 Federico Ferrara, 'Unfinished Business: The Contagion of Conflict over a Century of Thai Political Development' in Pavin Chachavalpongpun (ed.), *'Good Coup' Gone Bad: Thailand's Political Developments since Thaksin's Downfall* (Singapore: Institute of Southeast Asian Studies, 2014) 17–46, 21.

attempts. For instance, in October 1933, a noble and a military commander, Prince Boworadej, organised a counter-revolutionary force aimed at restoring absolutism. Fierce battles were fought between the prince's troops and the state military led by Field Marshal Plaek Phibunsongkhram ('Phibun'), a key figure of the military clique of the People's Party, before the rebellion was eventually overcome, indicating that without the military faction the People's Party would not have remained in power.[15] In turn, the domination of the military clique put in jeopardy Pridi's constitutional project and his intension to compromise with the royalist-conservatives, as many of the former faction did not share his commitment to constitutionalism, but merely intended to claim its protection to maintain authoritarian practices by stealth. Phibun also indirectly preserved the *Thai-ness* tradition as he exploited it to bolster his fascist rule in the 1940s. The traditional notion of political stability based on *Thai-ness* was successfully restored in the late 1950s with the assistance of Field Marshal Sarit Thanarat, who became the Prime Minister in 1958 through two coups in 1957.

To comprehend the instalment of the TSD, which significantly cultivates constitutional saṃsāra after Sarit's death, I need to first explain elite infighting between the following main factions: (1) Pridi's civilian, pro-democracy wing of the People's Party; (2) the ultra-nationalist military clique of the People's Party led by Phibun; and (3) the royalist-conservative camp led by some old nobles and leading bureaucrats. Such instalment also involves the embracement of right-wing constitutional theory. Then, I explain the key features of the royal authoritarian regime implemented by Sarit.

15.3.1 *The 1947, 1957, and 1958 Coups: Royal Hegemony Restored*

Phibun assumed his premiership in 1938. Inspired by the rise of far-right politics in Europe, he later turned against the liberal contortionism the People's Party sought to promote and presented himself as a charismatic Buddhist leader, uniting every Thai (*Phu Nam* or Führer), and jettisoning the People's Party's aspiration of establishing liberal constitutionalism in Thailand. In this respect, given the long-entrenched *Thai-ness* tradition, the anti-monarchist Phibun did not totally negate the elements of 'nation' and 'religion' (Theravada Buddhism), but sought to replace that of 'the monarchy' with *Phu Nam*. The Asia-Pacific War broke out in 1941, and Phibun allied Thailand with Japan. Pridi dissented and formed a secret alliance with the Allies and the anti-Japanese royalist-conservative groups. Following Japan's defeat, the Allies recognised Pridi's resistance, forcing Phibun to temporarily step down, paving the way for Pridi's premiership and the restoration of liberal democracy in 1946. However, the political crisis deepened when King Ananda (1934–46) was mysteriously found dead in his bedroom in June 1946, and King Bhumibol (1946–2016) succeeded his elder brother. With Phibun's support, the royalists, sceptical of Pridi's leftist ideology, and the growing number of leftist political parties, turned against Pridi, accusing him of planning regicide and forced him to resign.[16] This culminated in a coup in 1947 led by Phibun's military clique and the royalist-conservatives, ousting the succeeding government of Pridi's right-hand man, Thawan Thamrongnawasawat. Pridi went into exile in China, while Phibun reassumed the premiership in 1948.

The 1947 takeover was the first time that the traditional elites/royalists allied themselves with the military to undermine liberal democracy. The junta criticised this regime for having

[15] Chris Baker and Pasuk Phongpaichit, *A History of Thailand*, 123–4.

[16] Thongchai Winichakul, 'Toppling Democracy' (2008) 38 *Journal of Contemporary Asia* 11–37, 15.

bolstered the interests of corrupt politicians and political romanticism, that is, '[endless] discussions, through a struggle between different opinions', on values and ends with no last words among political parties within Parliament on an equal footing.[17] The coup fundamentally altered Thailand's public-law landscape. The gradual restoration of the three pillars of *Nation-Religion-Monarchy* was used by self-proclaimed *Khon Dee*, or men with accumulated good *Karma*, notably some conservative senior bureaucrats and military leaders, to bolster their active role in '[overseeing] the usual political life of the nation deemed as corrupt and partisan'.[18] From 1949 onwards, every Thai constitution has consistently declared that Thailand adopts 'the Democratic Regime with the King as the Head of the State' ('the DRKH'). This provision is a symbol of the aforesaid restoration.

Sarit played a vital role in helping Phibun and the traditional elites topple Pridi and Thawan, and was later appointed as Commander of the Royal Thai Army in 1954. Having been aware of the rising power of the royalist-conservatives, their attempt to institutionalise the DRKH, and Sarit's popularity among many Thais, Phibun relentlessly sought to minimise their role in politics. For example, he strove to reinforce his popularity through liberal democratic means, including by permitting political parties' activities and rigging a general election in February 1957. Phibun won, but this malpractice severely damaged his legitimacy, leading to strong popular disquiet. The conservative elites saw this as an opportunity to overthrow Phibun's government by forming an alliance with Sarit. Backed by the conservative clique, Sarit claimed that the rigged election and the security of the throne justified a military putsch and a declaration of martial law, ousting Phibun on 16 September 1957. Sarit mounted another coup d'état, and declared an emergency on 20 October 1958, which eventually replaced parliamentary democracy with the regime of 'despotic paternalism'.

15.3.2 *The Key Features of the Thai-Style Democracy*

Despotic paternalism defines what is known among scholars as the TSD, which, in turn, signifies the militarisation of the DRKH, by prioritising stability and unity embodied by a strong leader deemed to represent the will of the Thai *demos* (that is why Sarit claimed that his regime was democratic) over pluralism, the protection of human rights, and the principle of legality.[19] To implement the TSD, Sarit later issued the 1959 Constitutional Charter, comprised of merely twenty Sections, subsequently endorsed by the king on his advice on 28 January 1959.[20] The Charter not only abolished the parliamentary system and all political rights, but also included Section 17 ('M-17') which established an emergency regime aimed at protecting national unity under *Thai-ness*. This provided:

> During the application of this Charter, in the case where the Prime Minister contemplates the necessity to prevent or repress any threats to national security or the throne; or other threats which undermine, disturb, or imperil peace either occurring inside or stemming from

17 See Carl Schmitt, 'The guardian of the constitution: Schmitt on pluralism and the president as the guardian of the constitution' in Lars Vinx (ed.)(tr.), *The Guardian of the Constitution: Hans Kelsen and Carl Schmitt on the Limits of Constitutional Law* (Cambridge: Cambridge University Press 2015) 125–73, 131.

18 Andrew Harding and Rawin Leelapatana, 'Constitution-Making in 21st-Century Thailand: The Continuing Search for a Perfect Constitutional Fit' (2019) 7 *The Chinese Journal of Comparative Law* 266–84, 274; Thongchai Winichakul, 'Toppling Democracy', 15, 20, 24.

19 Tyrell Haberkorn, *In Plain Sight: Impunity and Human Rights in Thailand* (Madison: University of Wisconsin Press, 2018) 64.

20 1959 Charter, section 4.

outside the Kingdom, he, through Cabinet resolution, shall hold an authority to issue any order or act whatsoever. Such an order and act are deemed to be lawful . . . (my translation)

In general, it was apparent that the TSD was largely inspired by the rightist ideas of 'collectivism' and 'strong leadership' embraced by Phibun, also highly compatible with the mindset of his new patrons, the traditional elites, that liberal ideas contradict the tradition of a benevolent ruler.[21] His closest advisor, an architect of the TSD and one of Phibun's former confidants, Luang Wichitwathakan ('Wichit'), was critically aware of the modernisation process and therefore recognised that European rightist constitutional theory would be useful and compatible with *Thai-ness*, especially for dealing with 'enemies of the state', particularly the radical leftists.[22] Here, four key features of the TSD can be summarised.

First, just like right-wing constitutional theory in Europe, the true spirit of the constitution, under the TSD, concerns 'a strong state' *qua* the political unity of the (Thai) people. Therefore, as Dressel notes, popular sovereignty '[is] not exercised by the people directly but "realized" through the modernized state'.[23] Put simply, this reflects the parallel between the traditional Thai view and right-wing constitutional theory that a written constitution constitutes merely a set of rules, which even possibly hinder the task of safeguarding national security undertaken by a person of great virtue.[24]

Accordingly, and secondly, the TSD advocates extra-normative authority to distinguish 'friends' from 'enemies' to realise political homogeneity. Sarit applied *Thai-ness* to indicate who and what counted as public enemies. In this fashion, a coup d'état together with a martial law declaration were then justified as acts carried out with good intention or, in the Buddhist term, '*good Karma*'. The TSD, we can conclude, implies two types of political enemy – the *anti-Thai* and the *un-Thai*.[25] The term '*anti-Thai*' signifies a public enemy in an institutional sense, namely any foreign ideologies threatening political unity under *Thai-ness*, in particular, liberalism and parliamentary democracy. The liberal regime is defective because the type of homogeneity it entails, to borrow David Dyzenhaus's words, is that of 'market-oriented egotistic' individuals.[26] Such homogeneity is, accordingly, self-destructive because it results in political romanticism by equating a state's general will with mere competing antagonisms among self-interested individuals entering politics for private gain.[27] At the same time, Sarit also labelled parliamentary democracy as self-contradictory. As the elite infighting in the 1930s illustrated, where liberalism regards autocracy as its opposition, attaching the element of 'political' – the distinction between 'friends' and 'enemies' – to liberal democracy to enable it to assert its own truth contradicts the liberal ethos of compromise and reconciliation.[28] Sarit

21 Frank C. Darling, 'Marshal Sarit and Absolutist Rule in Thailand' (1960) 33 *Pacific Affairs* 347–60, 350–2.

22 Federico Ferrara, *The Political Development of Modern Thailand* (Cambridge: Cambridge University Press, 2015) 111–12, 155; Scott Barmé, *Luang Wichit Wathakan and the Creation of a Thai Identity* (Singapore: Institute of Southeast Asian Studies, 1993) 78.

23 Dressel, 'When Notions of Legitimacy Conflict: The Case of Thailand', 459.

24 Tom Ginsburg, 'Constitutional Afterlife: The Continuing Impact of Thailand's Postpolitical Constitution' (2009) 7 *International Journal of Constitutional Law* 83–105, 88–9.

25 Cf. David Streckfuss, 'The End of the Endless Exception?: Time Catches Up With Dictatorship in Thailand' (*Cultural Anthropology*, 23 September 2014) <www.culanth.org/fieldsights/567-the-end-of-the-endless-exception-time-catches-up-with-dictatorship-in-thailand> accessed 24 December 2018.

26 See Dyzenhaus's comment on the conservative theory of law in David Dyzenhaus, *Legality and Legitimacy: Carl Schmitt, Hans Kelsen and Hermann Heller in Weimar* (Oxford: Oxford University Press, 1997) 38–9.

27 See Carl Schmitt, *The Concept of the Political* (tr. George Schwab) (Chicago: University of Chicago Press, 2007) 69–72.

28 Ibid; Kobkua Suwannathat-Pian, *Kings, Country and Constitutions: Thailand's Political Development 1932–2000* (New York: RoutledgeCurzon, 2003) 9.

and his conservative patrons invoked these two alternatives to discredit the People's Party. Meanwhile, the term '*un-Thai*' connotes a public enemy in a concrete, 'flesh and blood' sense, namely Thais who pose a challenge or repudiate *Thai-ness*. Only Thais who accept or do not outwardly oppose such unity belong to the community, whilst those expressly scepticism about 'sovereign authority' declare themselves to be enemies. In the 1960s, Sarit employed M-17 to detain without trial, and even order the public execution of, his leftist, pro-democracy political rivals, accusing them of potentially instigating political instability and even of being communist.[29]

Nevertheless, Sarit was quite aware of the irreversible process of modernisation in Thailand. Due to the 1932 Revolution, a return to the pre-1932 regime would have meant formally bestowing political power upon mere persons or factions, thus undermining his effort to legitimise the 1957 and 1958 coups through popular acclaim.[30] Meanwhile, given Thailand's sympathy with the Capitalist Bloc during the Cold War, it was almost impossible for the conservative camp to negate liberalism absolutely. Moreover, since the *Thai-ness* tradition was resurrected in the presence of nascent democracy and electoral politics, popular disquiet could be anticipated – protest against Phibun's rigged election in 1957, for example. Recognising these developments, Sarit sought to preserve *Thai-ness* by connecting *Karma* to the increasing disenchantment of the world, particularly the nation-state together with its constitutional order and the existential concept of democracy. This reflects the third and fourth features of the TSD.

With respect to the third feature of the TSD, Thak Chaloemtiarana observes that, by portraying the monarchy as the embodiment of *Thai-ness*, Sarit and his supporters then asked the King for a royal proclamation (though it was Sarit who initially declared an emergency and wielded M-17) to legitimise his authority.[31] In this fashion, a prominent royalist, Thai constitutional scholar Borwornsak Uwanno, then regards the monarch as the sovereign who represents the Thai people.[32] Accordingly, Sarit took the opportunity to assert a *democratic* mandate when a royal proclamation was issued on his advice to the 1957 coup and the instalment of the TSD in 1958–9. At the same time, he portrayed himself as a mini-*Dhammaraja* or *Phor Khun* (a fatherlike ruler).

However, and fourthly, the nascent seed of liberalism forced Sarit to employ the vestige of the liberal technique – the concept of constitutionality – to stabilise his authoritarian rule. Thus, where Pridi sought to implement 'liberal constitutionalism' and 'meritorious bureaucracy' in 1932, Sarit turned a written constitution merely into a formal document for legitimising the traditional view of political stability, hegemony, and his authority.[33] The latter clearly decided to constitutionalise the TSD shortly after his coup, rather than to rule exclusively under coup decrees, through the promulgation of the 1959 Charter. This denotes the importance of a closed and impersonal system of legal norms in rationalising and stabilising *Thai-ness*, and in offering a legal-technical cloak of legitimacy insulating the regime itself and any emergency powers invoked from any legal challenges by liberals.

29 See Baker and Pasuk, *A History of Thailand*, 172–3.
30 Dressel, 'When Notions of Legitimacy Conflict: The Case of Thailand', 458.
31 Thak Chaloemtiarana, *Thailand: The Politics of Despotic Paternalism*, 206.
32 บวรศักดิ์ อุวรรณโณ [Borwornsak Uwanno], *กฎหมายมหาชน เล่ม 2: การแบ่งแยกกฎหมายมหาชน-เอกชน และพัฒนาการกฎหมายมหาชนในประเทศไทย* [*Public law II: the Separation between Public-Private Law and the Development of the Thai Public Law*], 5th ed. (Bangkok: Chulalongkorn University, 2007) 206.
33 See Paul Craig, 'Formal and Substantive Conceptions of the Rule of Law: An Analytical Framework' (1997) *Public Law* 467–87.

Sarit held the office of PM until his death in 1963 and left an important legacy: the revived hegemony of *Thai-ness* which has a significant impact of turning the Thai military into an institution which plays a predominant role in protecting the *Thai-ness* tradition through coups and martial law.[34] Nevertheless, given that the traditional view of political stability was fully restored after 1932, it can no longer resist its democratisation and constitutionalisation. While this section examines the attempt to entrench liberal democracy and constitutionalism and the restoration of *Thai-ness*, the next section is concerned with their contestation in the post-Sarit era with no absolute winner that, in effect, precipitated constitutional saṃsāra.

15.4 THE POLITICS OF GRAVITATIONAL PULL BETWEEN 1968 AND 1997

Due to rising and recurring demands for liberal democracy and majoritarian politics among the rising middle-class, fostered by Sarit's capitalist economic policy, his successors, as illustrated in Table 15.1, were forced politically to acknowledge the legitimacy of electoral politics.[35]

According to Table 15.1, between 1958 and 1997, Thailand oscillated between (1) coups and military dictatorial rule under the TSD (in 1971, 1976, 1977, and 1991); and (2) a multiparty parliamentary democracy. Overall, I argue that the landscape of constitutional saṃsāra in Thai legal history, in particular before 1997, reflects the pull of gravity between liberalism and authoritarianism.

To begin with, before 1997, the traditional elites and the military frequently resorted to coups and martial law to repress what they deemed to be excessive demands for liberal democracy. In this fashion, four coups together with martial-law declarations were imposed in 1971, 1976, 1977, and 1991. They also claimed 'public enemies', notably radical leftists and communists, justified their actions, in particular, by criticising liberal democracy for its inability to address this problem. Meanwhile, rather than choosing to rule through sovereign decisions, they applied written constitutions, both interim (i.e., the Constitutional Charters of 1972, 1976, 1977, and 1991) and permanent ones which outwardly restored weak parliamentary democracy with a civilian coalition government deemed the source of political romanticism (i.e., the 1968, 1976, 1978, and 1991 Constitutions) to stabilise and institutionalise *Thai-ness* hegemony, thus preserving the possibility of a military coup. This attempt to build 'constitutionality' will be more comprehensively analysed later in this article. As in 1958, any successful coup normally led to the banning of political gatherings and political parties and to restrictions upon press freedom.[36] However, greater repression together with the greater process of modernisation precipitated pro-democracy movements, particularly among university students displeased with almost three decades of right-wing military domination.

In 1971, the peculiar event of a self-coup led by Sarit's successor, Thanom Kittikachorn, overthrowing his own elected government, abolishing the 1968 Constitution, and making a return of the TSD, fostered public discontent. This resulted in the mass protest against the junta in October 1973 by university students and many middle-class people, demanding the restoration of liberal constitutionalism and electoral democracy. The political crisis reached

[34] Paul Chambers and Napisa Waitoolkiat, 'The Resilience of Monarchised Military in Thailand' (2016) 46 *Journal of Contemporary Asia* 425–44, 426.

[35] Wyatt regarded this circumstance as 'Sarit's paradox'. David K. Wyatt, *Thailand: A Short History* (New Haven: Yale University Press, 1984) 285.

[36] Revolutionary Council announcement no. 1 on 18 November 1971; National Reform Council Announcement nos. 1 and 5 on 6 October 1976; Revolutionary Council Announcement no 1 on 20 October 1977; National Peace Keeping Council Announcement no 1 on 23 February 1991.

TABLE 15.1 *Coups and the restoration of liberal democracy in Thailand between 1958 and 1997*

Coups and martial law	Coup leader	PM/constitution overthrown	Interim constitution declared	Parliament/constitution restored
1. *The 1958 Coup*	Sarit Thanarat	Thanom Kittikachorn/the 1932 Constitution (amended in 1952)	The 1959 Constitutional Charter	The 1968 Constitution/general election in February 1969
2. *The 1971 coup*	Thanom Kittikachorn	Self-coup/the 1968 Constitution	The 1972 Constitutional Charter	- The 14 October 1973 Uprising led to the promulgation of the 1973 Constitution restoring another experiment for parliamentary democracy in January 1974
3. *The 1976 Coup*	Sangad Chaloryu	Seni Pramoj/the 1973 Constitution	- The 1976 Massacre - The 1976 Constitutional Charter	
4. *The 1977 Coup*	Sangad Chaloryu	Thanin Kraivichien/the 1976 Constitution	The 1977 Constitutional Charter	- Semi-liberal democracy under the 1978 Constitution - Prem Tinsulanonda chosen as PM in 1980 - Fuller liberal democracy restored in July 1988
5. *The 1991 Coup*	Sunthorn Kongsompong	Chatchai Choonhavan/the 1978 Constitution	The 1991 Constitutional Charter	- The 1992 Black May incident - The 1997 Constitution

its zenith on 14 October 1973 when the military used martial law power, sustained since the 1971 coup, to disperse protesters, causing violence, acts of vandalism and deaths. Rather than appeasing the situation, the wielding of martial law in 1973, and the deployment of troops under the justification of the protection of *Thai-ness*, enraged the protesters, resulting in one of the bloodiest conflicts between civilians and military officials in modern Thai history. Tanks, helicopters, and rooftop snipers were sent to massacre protesters, causing more than 36 hours of chaos, whilst the people fought back using guns seized from some officers and ramming buses into the military.[37] The 1973 uprising was the first time 'that the government was overthrown by extra-bureaucratic forces through street politics, and not through clientelistic ties'.[38] This incident made it obvious that permanent military rule no longer enjoyed popular legitimacy, and largely 'shook the structure of relations of power in Thai society'.[39]

However, the heyday of liberal politics between 1973 and 1976, in turn, encouraged some leftist university students and politicians, dissatisfied with social and economic inequality, to agitate for greater political inclusion and democracy, causing protests and instability. Aware of the threat to their hegemonic position, some ultra-rightist conservatives eventually reacted harshly, resulting in the 6 October 1976 massacre. The communist triumph in Laos (May 1975), Cambodia (April 1975), and Vietnam (April 1975) had further heightened their fear that their leftist opponents would overthrow the monarchy. Aimed at antagonising their opponents, some right-wing elites were believed to support Thanom, now ordained as a Buddhist novice, to return to Thailand in 1976, causing thousands of university students to launch another protest. Regarded as '*un-Thais*', these pro-democracy leftists were accused of being communists, and were eventually brutally attacked and killed at Thammasat University at 8.00 a.m. on 6 October 1976 by far-right paramilitaries, using live rounds, bazookas, and rocket launchers, especially Village Scouts and other far-right groups and other state forces, notably the police.[40] This incident paved the way for another coup and a declaration of emergency the same day, claiming the need to protect *Thai-ness*. Approximately thirty-six people were reportedly killed, while more than 3,000 were arrested.[41] After the bloody massacre and an internal conflict within the right-wing government established in 1976, which led to another putsch in 1977, Thailand entered the era of 'semi-liberalism'. By 1978, Thai conservative elites, noticing the decline of the communist threat and realising a growing public appetite for popular democracy, enacted the Constitution of 1978 that established semi-liberal democracy – multiparty liberal democracy under the tutelage of the network of the traditional elites, operating under *Thai-ness* hegemony. The former army chief, Prem Tinsulanonda, was appointed Prime Minister by the King in 1980. Prem initially enjoyed significant support from the bureaucrats, the military, the people, and the palace. Nevertheless, corruption scandals, together with greater demands for fuller democracy, forced Prem to dissolve Parliament in 1988.

After the general election in 1988, a civilian coalition government was formed by Chatchai Choonhavan. Chatchai's attempt to take control of the military made his premiership

37 George N. Katsiaficas, *Asia's Unknown Uprisings: People power in the Philippines, Burma, Tibet, China, Taiwan, Bangladesh, Nepal, Thailand and Indonesia, 1947–2009* (Oakland: PM Press, 2013) 308.

38 James Ockey, 'State, Bureaucracy and Polity in Modern Thai Politics' (2004) 34 *Journal of Contemporary Asia* 143–62, 144.

39 Thongchai Winichakul, 'The Changing Landscape of the Past: New Histories in Thailand Since 1973' (1995) 26 *Journal of Southeast Asian Studies* 99–120, 101.

40 Chapter 18, this volume.

41 Sudarat Musikawong, 'Thai Democracy and the October (1973–1976) Events' (2006) 7 *Inter-Asia Cultural Studies* 713–16, 713.

vulnerable. The military eventually overthrew Chatchai and declared martial law in 1991, citing corruption and threats to *Thai-ness* as justifications.[42] Greater demands for popular sovereignty, democratic constitutionalism, and good governance, supported by globalisation and the end of the Cold War, forced the junta to organise a general election later in March 1992. However, the majority of the new Parliament chose as Prime Minister Suchinda Kraprayoon, the member of the 1991 junta who intended to turn the clock back to semi-authoritarianism, as in the 1980s. In May 1992 public discontent culminated in another mass demonstration in Bangkok, this time a crowd of approximate 200,000 people, and caused another emergency and political crisis.[43] Between 17 and 18 May 1992, Suchinda deployed military forces to disperse protesters, resulting in violence, acts of vandalism and deaths, which enormously decreased the government's legitimacy – 52 were reportedly killed, while 293 went missing, and thousands more were arrested or injured, an incident notoriously known as *Black May*.[44]

The above pull of gravity reveals the graver tension between 'waning but still dominant' authoritarian tradition and 'more legitimate but still weaker' pro-liberal forces with, as yet, no absolute winner. Therefore, the study of their struggle must rigorously take this theoretical premise into account.

15.5 THE THEORETICAL QUESTION FOR THE POST-SARIT IMPLEMENTATION OF THE THAI-STYLE DEMOCRACY RENDERED BY POLITICAL STRUGGLES FOR LIBERALISM

According to Ramraj and Harding, the incidents in 1973 and 1992 highlight the importance of *political struggles* against dictatorship and 'political opinion supporting democratic development, good governance and human rights' among networks of middle-class people, notably civil society organisations, intellectuals, business associations, and opposition activists, who were deprived of a 'democratic voice' in the political arena in transforming the inherent authoritarian culture.[45] The term *political struggle* here connotes what Devyani Prabhat regards as 'legal mobilisation', that is, a circumstance in which political actors purposely invoke legal norms, raise awareness of the importance of liberalism among the public, and make their moves 'out of doors', including in the form of bargaining/lobbying and mass protests, to realise their demands.[46]

The struggle for liberalism in public emergencies, no doubt, contributes towards making such rhetoric a component of political legitimacy against the anti-liberal military regime in the 'real-world' political arena. It apparently led to 'the lock' Tamir Moustafa has observed: 'When social forces engage state institutions from the bottom up, they inevitably transform those institutions in ways that were often not initially intended by central decision makers. As a result, authoritarian leaders frequently find themselves *locked* in conflict with the very

42 Order of the National Peace Keeping Council, No 1.

43 Khīan Thīrawit, *Thailand in Crisis: A Study of the Political Turmoil of May 1992* (Bangkok: Thailand Research Fund, 1997) 24.

44 Ibid., 55.

45 Andrew Harding, 'Emergency Powers with a Moustache: Special Powers, Military Rule and Evolving Constitutionalism in Thailand' in Victor V. Ramraj and Arun K. Thiruvengadam (eds.), *Emergency Powers in Asia: Exploring the Limits of Legality* (Cambridge: Cambridge University Press, 2010) 294–313, 312; Victor V. Ramraj, 'Emergency Powers and Constitutional Theory' (2011) 41 *Hong Kong Law Journal* 165–99, 196.

46 Devyani Prabhat, *Unleashing the Force of Law: Legal Mobilization, National Security, and Basic Freedoms* (London: Palgrave, 2016) 2; Mark Tushnet, 'Popular Constitutionalism as Political Law' (2006) 81 *Chicago Kent Law Review* 991–1006, 994.

institutions that were initially created to advance state interests'.[47] In both incidents, the military leaders had to pay 'a heavy price' for stigmatising the protesters as threats to *Thai-ness* and for employing harsh anti-liberal emergency measures to disperse them, notably the use of deadly force. The political cost raised by the struggle clearly forced 'regime insiders', notably some elites and military leaders, to democratise the governing regime to avert further damage to their image. Thanom and Suchinda were even pressured by the palace to resign – the former even having to flee the country. The 1992 Black May incident also galvanised highly vocal demands for political reforms from civil society, and even among many royalist-conservative elites who were aware of the 'political cost' of the military crackdown to the level that resulted in the draft of the 1997 Constitution, the so-called *People's Constitution*.

As we have seen, due to recurring political struggles for emerging liberal demands, the conservative elites could no longer 'kill off' such demands to ensure the hegemony of *Thai-ness*. It is also interesting to note that a pro-democracy opposition struggling for equal rights and opportunities to the military rule was at times, in particular between the late 1960s and 1992, radical and inclined not to accept political compromise. Subsequently, the challenge against the conservatives is therefore: in a society such as Thailand long dominated by the nationalist-conservative tradition, yet experiencing the processes of democratisation and liberalisation, what means would facilitate the former to preserve its political hegemony? Its answer requires us to consider the development of relevant constitutional provisions drafted in both periods to ensure the hegemony of *Thai-ness*. In doing so, we can then arrive at how the pull of gravity between the two forces affects the roles of legality in the Thai constitutional landscape.

15.6 THE IMPORTANCE OF LEGALITY IN THAI LEGAL HISTORY: PERPETUATING CONSTITUTIONAL SAṂSĀRA

The last two sections reveal the tension between liberal demands and conservative forces in pre-1997 Thailand. This tension indicates that the attempt to maintain *Thai-ness* as the hegemonic political ideology and as the basis for the exercise of state authority arguably could not conceal the fact that it constituted the kind of explicit defiance of liberal ideal formally entrenched after the 1932 Revolution. The more authoritarianism had increasingly co-opted liberal democracy, in particular by 'further [restructuring] or [broadening] the ruling coalition, and possibly [granting] some of the demands of newly mobilised constituencies', the more this increasingly called for *the institutionalisation or constitutionalisation of 'coup mechanisms'*, namely a coup together with subsequent resort to emergency powers themselves and the establishment of the TSD.[48]

I already pointed out that Thai political takeovers, in particular after 1968, typically resulted in the abolition of an incumbent constitution guaranteeing room for electoral politics and the promulgation of an interim constitution anchoring the TSD, and including provisions largely similar to M-17 of the 1959 Charter (with the exception of the 2006 Interim Constitution), granting the Prime Minister extensive emergency powers to repress threats to *Thai-ness*.[49] Thus, where a coup and the following uses of emergency powers in Thailand are normally claimed by the military as the expression of sovereign authority, there is now a constitutional

[47] Tamir Moustafa, *The Struggle for Constitutional Power: Law, Politics, and Economic Development in Egypt* (Cambridge: Cambridge University Press, 2007) 41–2 (emphasis added).

[48] Ferrara, *The Political Development of Modern Thailand*, 279; Harding and Leelapatana, 'Constitution-Making in 21st-Century Thailand', 8.

[49] The Constitutional Charters of 1972 (Section 17), 1976 (Section 21), 1977 (Section 27), 1991 (Section 27).

custom that the military needs to build the constitutionality of the TSD shortly after the period of rule by coup decree.

Nevertheless, the changing circumstance after the mass uprising in 1973 means that an interim constitution and the TSD are expected to be replaced later by a new permanent constitution, which not only outwardly restores electoral politics, parliamentary democracy, and individual rights, but also excludes the 'M-17' clause.[50] According to Tom Ginsburg, growing demands for liberal democracy resulting in the 1973 and 1976 incidents at least fostered 'a constitutional understanding' among different factions within Thai society that a permanent, authoritarian rule under the guise of the TSD might provoke more popular disquiet would further tarnish the military's legitimacy.[51] Notwithstanding the revival of party politics, the drafting of new permanent constitutions was normally initiated and influenced by the junta, thus undoubtedly retaining the hegemony of *Thai-ness*, notably by intentionally creating the system of weak parliamentary coalitions labelled as the source of political romanticism, which in turn harboured the possible instigation of coups. In fact, what coup-makers, struggling with greater liberal movements after Sarit's death, did beyond what Sarit had done previously was to include within the 1972, 1976, and 1977 Constitutional Charters an amnesty clause, declaring the *lawfulness* of a coup and relevant action of the junta and others. This reflected the growing need to accommodate what counts as 'unconstitutional' to growing liberal demands. For instance, Section 21 of the 1972 Constitutional Charter stipulated that: 'Any acts or orders of the coup leader issued or done between the takeover date of 17 November 1971 and the day this Constitutional Charter is promulgated in whatever forms and ... forces ... shall be deemed *lawful*'.[52] This clause held the status of a constitutional provision and was therefore not susceptible to a challenge to its constitutionality. Yet, the term lawfulness still leaves room for challenges against constitutionality of coups and subsequent actions of the junta.[53]

After fourteen years of experience with (semi-)electoral politics, the 1991 coup, though initially popular, had to contend more with liberal demands due to rising political awareness after 1973. A more rigorous technique was accordingly required to build the constitutionality of those acts even after the parliamentary system was restored. The 1991 Constitution then became the first permanent constitution which guaranteed, not just the lawfulness, but also the *constitutionality* of the coup and all related actions, including all emergency orders issued by the military government under the 1991 Constitutional Charter. Section 222 stipulated that: 'All declarations and orders of the National Peace Keeping Council ... or other orders issued under Section 27 of the 1991 Constitutional Charter in whatever forces which are still effective until the day this constitution is promulgated shall be deemed effective and *constitutional* under this constitution' (my translation and emphasis added). This provision, in effect, ensures that despite the abolition of an interim constitution imposing the TSD and the restoration of parliamentary democracy, the constitutionality of the takeover cannot be disputed. The 1991 Constitution also confirmed the superiority of the DRKH over alternative political regimes as it was the first Thai constitution which prohibited a motion for a constitutional amendment having the effect of changing the DRKH.[54]

50 The (permanent) Constitutions of the Kingdom of Thailand of 1974, 1978, 1991.

51 Ginsburg, 'Constitutional Afterlife', 88.

52 Author translation and emphasis added. The same provisions reappeared in the Constitutional Charter of 1976 (Section 29), 1977 (Section 32), and 1991 (Section 27). Apart from constitutionalising the immunity clause, these coups also led to the enactment of Amnesty Acts. Tyrell Haberkorn addresses this issue in Chapter 19 of this volume.

53 The Thai Supreme Court decision no 913/2536 (1993).

54 Section 211(13) of the 1991 Constitution.

Overall, we can see that in pre-1997 Thailand, written constitutions had increasingly become important tools for providing sovereign authority with legal-technical legitimacy. In other words, the Thai experience reveals that the validity and legitimacy of the TSD could no longer be derived exclusively from extralegal forces, but had to consider more and more about legality and legitimacy from the normative-liberal standpoint.[55] Yet, the institutionalisation and constitutionalisation of coup mechanisms oppose understanding legality as *normativism*, that is, as law *qua* a sum of impersonal norms which impose limits on the exercise of state authority.[56] The Thai experience ultimately offers four main ways that 'legality' theoretically institutionalises the hegemony of *Thai-ness* and perpetuates constitutional saṃsāra: stabilisation, condemnation, rationalisation, and insulation.

With regard to stabilisation, rather than seeking permanent rule through coup decrees, the Thai military has come to recognise the importance of re-making a new interim constitution after a successful coup. The status of a written constitution as the supreme law of the land is turned into a mechanism for stabilising the anti-liberal, military regime by granting the 'cloak of constitutionality' to mechanisms such as M-17 applied to purge public enemies, in particular, liberal democracy and its supporters.

Furthermore, as indicated, the constitutional understanding observed by Tom Ginsburg makes permanent military rule under the TSD costly, and therefore forces traditional elites to shift from suppressing liberal constitutionalism to co-opting it. However, as most permanent constitutions initiated after coups deliberately restored weak parliamentary democracy and therefore coalition government, they simultaneously function as a mechanism for condemning the parliamentary regime as the source of political romanticism, thus preserving the hegemonic *Thai-ness* tradition and the possibility of coups and any subsequent use of emergency powers.

Lastly, written constitutions, interim and permanent, then play a role in rationalising the hegemony of *Thai-ness* as what Thongchai Winichakul calls 'a euphemism for royalist dominance over the regular government, be it a democracy or military rule' and insulating a coup leader and his associates from the possible charge of overthrowing a liberal-democratic regime.[57] As we have seen, more sophisticated techniques and more cautious constitution-drafting ensure the impunity, hegemony, and reassertion of the TSD.

Besides, although constitutional provisions are crucial for institutionalising sovereign authority and creating the opportunity for coups, they are merely lifeless texts. The core and hegemony of the conservative model, in practice, benefitted from the Supreme Court's decisions deciding whether the takeover was valid. In the Supreme Court decision no. 45/2496 (1955), the first time the Thai judiciary was asked to decide this question, the judges asserted: 'Given that the junta had successfully seized state power in 1947, it then holds the authority to administer the country ... The 1947 Constitution [promulgated after the successful coup] was then a valid law' (my translation). As Harding observes, the first sentence of this decision followed Hans Kelsen's approach that a successfully committed coup begets the validity and effectiveness of a legal order established afterwards to justify it.[58] However,

55 See Andrew Harding and Rawin Leelapatana, 'Constitution-Making in 21st-Century Thailand', 9–10.

56 Carl Schmitt, *On the Three Types of Juristic Thought* (tr. Joseph W. Bendersky) (Westport: Praeger, 2004) 48, 52; Mariano Croce and Andrea Salvatore, *The Legal Theory of Carl Schmitt* (Oxford: Routledge, 2013) 34–5.

57 Thongchai Winichakul, 'The Monarchy and anti-monarchy: Two elephants in the Room of Thai Politics and the State of Denial' in Pavin Chachavalpongpun (ed.), *"Good Coup"*, 84.

58 Andrew Harding, 'The Eclipse of the Astrologers: King Mongkut, his Successors, and the Reformation of Law in Thailand' in Penelope (Pip) Nicholson and Sarah Biddulph (eds.), *Examining Practice, Interrogating Theory: Comparative Legal Studies in Asia* (Leiden: Martinus Nijhoff, 2008) 305–39, 332.

Harding's observation needs further explanation. The 1947 coup, as I already pointed out, was the attempt to revive the *Thai-ness* establishment and the first coup directed against electoral politics. By accepting the reason propounded by the junta that the coup was necessary to restore peace and public order out of a volatile political situation, the verdict left a lasting precedent, namely the superiority of the DRKH over full-fledged, Western-style liberal democracy and ideals, after implicitly praising the former for helping restore political stability and accusing the latter of precipitating political romanticism and instability.[59] A number of later decisions concerning the validity of a coup and related actions, including the implementation of the TSD and the validity of M-17, followed this decision, despite having been decided after parliamentary democracy was restored.[60]

15.7 CONCLUSION: THE BINARY-STAR-SCENARIO AND A QUEST FOR *CONSTITUTIONAL NIRVANA*?

From the above, I argue that constitutional saṃsāra in Thailand, especially between 1932 and 1997, reflects the so-called binary-star-system – two stars, liberal and nationalist-conservative stars, which orbit around a common centre of gravitation, yet, none of which absolutely dominates the other.[61] Instead, each is subject to the gravitational pull of the other, possibly leading to their collision. From the legal perspective, constitutional saṃsāra challenges the juristic thought of normativism Pridi sought to entrench in post-1932 Thailand, and, in effect, exposes the pull of gravity between two notions of constitutionalism (or two stars) – the liberal and the conservative notions of constitutionalism. On the one hand, political struggles for liberalism before 1997 placed emphasis largely on the principle of legality, rights, liberties, and social equality. By contrast, supporters of its conservative counterpart, which merges with the traditional notion of *Thai-ness*, namely the traditional elites and the military, advocated the existence of 'ultimate value(s) or good(s)', thus seeking to resolve political conflicts through bringing 'human behaviour … into harmony with [such] proper order of values given in the cosmos'.[62]

Their pull of gravity can be generally concluded as follows. Firstly, coups and martial law were convenient means for the traditional elites and the military to parry and resolve what they deemed to be threats to the *Thai-ness* tradition. However, and secondly, the more the military strove to prolong the TSD, the more it had to struggle against mass demands for constitutionalism and liberalisation, and risked further losing their legitimacy. This development forced the conservative camp after 1973 to refrain from maintaining a permanent military rule, and instead to accommodate, or, more precisely, to co-opt a greater space for liberalism. But, despite such demands, liberalism could not absolutely prevail as the norm. This is because of the country's strong tradition of *Thai-ness* which labels party politics in Parliament as the main source of political instability and corruption, making a quest for stable political environment, or the nirvana of constitutional saṃsāra, fictitious.[63] The failure to ensure such nirvana before 1997 also indicates that the conservative elites and the military succeeded in:

59 Chapter 18, this volume.
60 See the Thai Supreme Court decisions no 1512–1515/2497 (1956); no 1662/2505 (1962); no 1243/2523 (1980). The same logic was also rendered to justify M-17 (Decision no 494/2510 (1967).
61 Andrew Harding and Rawin Leelapatana, 'Constitution-Making in 21st-Century Thailand', 270.
62 Bradley E. Starr, 'The Structure of Max Weber's Ethic of Responsibility' (1999) 27 *Religious Ethics* 407–34, 409.
63 In Buddhism, *Nirvana* means the release from the cycle of rebirths.

(1) connecting *Thai-ness* with modern ideologies, in particular the modern state, the notions of constitution-making process, and (identitarian, right-wing) democracy; and
(2) institutionalising *Thai-ness* in the presence of struggles against liberalism. A resort to extra-normative measures guaranteed some level of political stability – at least in the sense that it did not counterproductively precipitate a 'sudden' anti-coup reaction.

The gravitational pull between the two notions ultimately reveals the peculiarity, that in pre-1997 Thailand, liberal constitutionalism outwardly operated as the norm *not* because it facilitated peace and political compromise, but because it was constitutionalised as the source of political romanticism, thus, in turn, justifying the restoration of the TSD through a military coup.[64]

To realise the nirvana of constitutional saṃsāra and dissolve the binary-star-system, the constitutional reform was initiated in the mid-1990s, leading to the promulgation of the 1997 'People's Constitution' which made a firm commitment on liberal constitutionalism, stable politics, and nationwide political participation.[65] This Constitution is largely praised as 'a visible symbol of constitutional progress' and of anti-coup sentiment.[66] Nevertheless, the nirvana of constitutional saṃsāra was merely temporary. The rise of Thaksin Shinawatra's regime of plutocracy under the disguise of parliamentary democracy between 2001 and 2005, facilitated by stable politics and strong economy, exacerbated frustration among the traditional elites and many middle-class people who have regarded such regime as a threat to *Thai-ness*, thus causing the contemporary colour-coded politics, a topic to be discussed in the next chapter.[67]

64 Ferrara, *The Political Development of Modern Thailand*, 271.
65 1997 Constitution, Preamble.
66 Andrew Harding and Peter Leyland, 'The Constitutional Courts of Thailand and Indonesia: Two Case Studies from South East Asia' (2008) 3 *Journal of Comparative Law* 118–37, 119.
67 Chapter 17, this volume.

16

Permutations of the Basic Structure

Thai Constitutionalism and the Democratic Regime with the King as Head

Henning Glaser

Since its beginnings in the 1932 revolution, Thailand's constitutionalism has experienced an unsettled history that can be broadly divided into four larger phases. This chapter primarily adresses at the latest one, initiated by the 1997 Constitution and lasting until today. Characterized by a far more refined form of constitutionalism than the previous ones, its organizing principle is the "Democratic Regime of Government with the King as Head" (DRKH). Deeper entrenched, more pronounced and implemented as a legal doctrine, the DRKH in its new form defined the normative fundament, core and horizon of the new charter. Moreover, it fulfilled this function throughout the entire fourth phase of Thai constitutionalism with its three subsequent constitutions and two interim constitutions respectively, forming a carefully guarded constitutional identity. Some temporary changes to one of its central norms since the 2014 Coup reflect, however, also great volatility and the challenge of deep change at the heart of Thai constitutionalism. No other constitutional principle could be more suitable to discover the deep structure of contemporary Thai constitutionalism and the nature of political volatility, which has accompanied it since the early 2000s.

The emergence and development of the DRKH as the single most important emanation of Thai constitutionalism is the central theme of the present chapter. To approach it, I will distinguish the four phases of Thai constitutionalism to situate the DRKH in the larger historical context and track the evolution of the underlying constitutional thought and practice that eventually led to the axial change of 1997. Then, focus is placed on the normative nature and architecture of the DRKH in its new form and its shaping impact on contemporary Thai constitutionalism. Finally, I will address the further development of the DRKH, especially in the wake of the 2014 Coup that sealed Thailand's years-long divisive conflict and which, however, lingers within the Thai polity since then. While it would be tempting to also include the long history of oppositional and counter-hegemonic constitutional discourses, this would go beyond the scope of this chapter.

16.1 SITUATING THE DRKH IN THE LARGER HISTORICAL CONTEXT

To explore the development of the constitutional thought and practice that eventually manifested as the "new" DRKH, a rough structure of the historical development helps track the development of pre-1997 constitutionalism out of which the new DRKH emerged.

16.1.1 *A Four-Phase Model of Thai Constitutionalism*

Since its beginnings in 1932, Thai constitutionalism emerged in four broad phases. During the first period from 1932 to 1957, constitutionalism was practically weak under difficult political conditions and yet it was formally upheld as the ultimate conceptual yardstick and political rule book for most of the time. Despite a series of increasingly fierce and almost uninterrupted power struggles that started with the first day of constitutional rule, a notion of constitutionalism actually persisted with brief exceptions as a unifying principle among the ruling elites that were split in competing factions.

In its embryonic and groping beginnings, the revolutionary group, conscious of the limitations of its power, sought the embittered King's approval to remain as a constitutional monarch after having disposed him as the absolute, deified ruler through the barrel of the gun. Amid fierce factionalism within the new elite, however, the royalist network had already begun to engage in what would be a lengthy royalist *Reconquista*.[1] While it succeeded briefly in weakening the progressive wing of the new elite under Pridi Banomyong, it eventually paved the way for the populist nationalism under one of the Young Turks' military leaders, the later Field Marshall Phibun Songkhram, with the royal party having been effectively neutralized at the latest by the King's abdication in 1935.

Even during the authoritarian wartime regime dominated by Field Marshall Phibun, the "leader's" soft-fascist style of government remained in large part surprisingly bound to the idea of constitutionalism. Albeit weakened and flawed, constitutional practice was displayed in elections, in limited space for parliamentary opposition, as well as in collective decision making and mutual control among different elite factions in the cabinet. Eventually, the "leader" even resigned from office after a parliamentary defeat in 1944.

The postwar years brought four different constitutions in a short sequence. After a short democratic revival, especially under the 1946 Constitution, and a moderate readmission of the royalists to the constitutional arena after Phibun's demise, a band of army officers in alliance with the royalists emerged as the dominating power in the wake of a Coup in 1947. In the following years, the various progressive forces that dominated under the 1946 Constitution were gradually driven out of the constitutional arena, while tensions with the palace rose again. After its abrogation and the progressives' eventual displacement from official politics, tensions with the palace rose again. Meanwhile, constitutional practice had become more repressive, political violence and exceptions from constitutional rule more widespread without, however, relinquishing the principle.

The end to this period of diluted post-war constitutionalism came when Field Marshal Sarit Thanarat, one of the ruling strongmen, staged a coup against Phibun and his other peer competitors in 1957. In retrospect, this heralded the second phase of Thai constitutionalism marked by the promotion of a more indigenous brand of political rule. Sarit entered a cordial alliance with King Rama IX, re-elevating the monarchy and ushering in a transformative period that was dominated by "Thai-style Governance." Based on the regime's reception of ancient kingship, it combined praetorian rule with the restored customary authority of the monarchy at the almost total expense of constitutionalism: "What Sarit did in effect was to overthrow a whole political system inherited from 1932 and to create one that could be termed more 'Thai' in character."[2] Sarit's "despotic

[1] In a broader sense, this royalist Reconquista has been making constant impacts on Thai constitutionalism over almost the entire course of its development until present time, even if in very different forms.

[2] Chai-Anan Samudavanija, *Thailand: State-Building, Democracy and Globalization* (Bangkok: Institute of Public Policy Studies, 2002) 92. See also Chapter 13 in this volume and Andrew Harding and Rawin Leelapatana,

paternalism"[3] was based on the decisive assumption that Western constitutionalism had to be reversed and largely replaced by his Thai brand of governance. Sarit left neither the principle nor the institutions of democratic constitutionalism with any chance of survival,[4] minimized even any constitutionalism in form, but marshaled the most technically adept administrators available to support his regime.[5] By displaying royal tradition and care for the people, engaging the guiding narratives, and linking the paternalistic-authoritarian rule to the King's dignity, the royalist Reconquista started to continuously gain momentum.

The third phase of Thai constitutionalism from 1973 to 1992 begun with the ouster of Sarit's successors and former lieutenants Field Marshals Thanom Kittikachorn and Praphas Charusathien. After a short progressive revival from 1973 to 1976 was crushed by bloody force, it saw a moderate return of the constitution as an actual rule book of the polity which, however, was dominated by the military's national security agenda on the one hand and a steadily increasing royal authority on the other. While constitutionalism remained more a device of limited value than an acknowledged principle, electoral politics re-emerged since 1977 as an arena to balance competing power groups. Ultimate normative yardstick during the third phase remained the unwritten concept of Thai-style democracy.

The 1997 Constitution marks the beginning of the fourth phase that had started to emerge after 1992 and runs to the present day. It is characterized by a new form of constitutionalism in which the constitution operates as a more *legally* conceived rule book with greater reach and impact than before. At the same time, the polity was ultimately still governed by unwritten normative references as they had taken root since Sarit and which became now acknowledged in the framework of the positively implemented DRKH. This is the constitutional era of the new DRKH which reigns as the constitutional order since then and whose fate reflects those of the hegemonic social contract and the actual status of the political system at large.

These four major phases of Thai constitutionalism were each ushered in by short periods of transition, which were characterized by eventually aborted notions of reorientation, mostly followed by reverse trends. This pertains to King Prajadhipok's reform considerations before the 1932 revolutionary coup, Phibun's attempt to revive democratic processes since 1955[6], the short democratic revival between 1973 and 1976, which was followed by the brief royalist authoritarianism under Thanin Kraivichien until 1977, and the orientation period from 1992 to 1997.

From an overall perspective, the unfolding of these four with all their changes to the constitutional order reflects a notion of "Buddhist" impermanence concerning the written constitution's endurance that corresponds with both culturally derived notions of governance and a recurring dominance of military authoritarianism and coup politics.[7] Most significant, however, is the steadily waxing impact of royalism since the second phase of Thai constitutionalism.

'Constitution-Making in 21st-Century Thailand: The Continuing Search for a Perfect Constitutional Fit' (2019) 7 (2) *Chinese Journal of Comparative Law* 266–84.

3 See the state-of-the-art account by Thak Chaloemtiarana, *Thailand: The Politics of Despotic Paternalism* (Ithaca: Cornell Southeast Asia Program Publications, 2007).

4 See Suchit Bunbongkarn, *State of the Nation: Thailand* (Singapore: Institute of Southeast Asian Studies, 1996).

5 See Frank C. Darling, "Marshal Sarit and Absolutist Rule in Thailand" (1960) 33(4) *Pacific Affairs* 347–60, 353.

6 See Kobkua Suwannathat-Pian, *Thailand's Durable Premier: Phibun through Three Decades 1932–1957* (Oxford: Oxford University Press, 1995) 211.

7 See Chapter 15 in this volume.

16.1.2 *Pre-1997 Constitutional Thought and Practice Since Sarit*

As much as the 1997 redefinition of the DRKH marks a watershed in Thai constitutional history, so, too, does it, after all, epitomize a development that started long before, namely the gradual entrenchment of royalist constitutionalism since the late 1950s when Sarit ushered in the second phase of Thai constitutionalism.

Pre-1997 constitutional thought and practice since Sarit can be divided into praetorian and royally dominated forms of Thai-style governance. The former emerged at the end of the 1950s, the latter unfolded with varying impact since the early 1970s during the third phase of Thai constitutionalism.

16.1.3 *Thai-Style Governance with Pretorian Characteristics*

Following Sarit's rise to power, the influence of the monarchy steadily increased. Sarit's 1958 self-coup not only sought to purge the Thai polity of its nascent and vulnerable notions of Western-style constitutionalism, but also aimed to replace it with an alternative order that redeemed the monarchy whose increasing legitimacy reinforced that of the military leaders. Drawing upon and calibrating aspects of Phibun's erstwhile nationalist discourse, the new order was based on three elements. The trinity of "nation, religion and king" was promoted with new emphasis as state motto, reinforced by reference to a "Cultural Constitution"[8] that was built on the reinvention of a benevolent form of pre-constitutional monarchical rule, and complemented by the propagation of an essentialized notion of "Thainess"[9] as a tool of social regulation. These elements elaborated by intellectuals like Wichit Watthakan and Kukrit Pramoj converged toward an encompassing concept of rule under the label of "Thai-style governance."

Kukrit, an aristocrat and ambitious politician was especially influential. The political reality Kukrit was referring to can be well described in comparison to Walter Bagehot's classic account of the British Constitution. There, Bagehot differentiates between "dignified" and "efficient" parts of the constitution. The "dignified" are those "which excite and preserve the reverence of the population," while the "efficient" are those "by which it, in fact, works and rules."[10] To truly grasp the Thai constitutional order in its evolution since Sarit, I suggest modifying and expanding this dichotomy by distinguishing between an efficient and dignified *center* of the constitution, both representing the basic structure, complemented by the constitution's effective part and its merely ornamental proclamations respectively, thus plain constitutional law of actual and just semantic impact respectively.[11]

Under Sarit, the positive constitutional order appeared to a large extent overwhelmingly dominated only by its two centers: the paternalistic dictator as the actual leader – the efficient center – and the revered King as the representation of sovereignty and national grandeur – the dignified center.[12] While the effective part of the constitutional order was largely limited to the bureaucracy, civil rights and liberties not even formed an ornamental part as they would later.

[8] Nidhi Eosewong, "The Cultural Constitution of Thailand," published 14 August 2014, accessible at www.cultureready.org/blog/cultural-constitution-thailand.

[9] See Chapter 15 in this volume.

[10] See Walter Bagehot, *The English Constitution* [1867], edited and with an introduction by R. H. S. Crossman (London: Collins, 1966) 61.

[11] This normative structure has to be differentiated from the factual balances of power that include the dimension of raw power which interacts with the normative structure without being identical with it. Under Sarit both the normative and the factual power structure were closely related to each other though.

[12] See also Thak, *The Politics of Despotic Paternalism*, 119.

In Kukrit's view, the King, as the undisputed dignified center of the constitution, wielded however also some real influence over the ruler as his customary mandate entitled him to control the government's use of power. The interplay between a government that unified the power of the state without being bothered by Western-like separation-of-power concerns and a King whose role and stature were deeply rooted in history, culture and religion forms the central axis of Kukrit's Thai-style governance. It leaves neither room nor need for legislative or judicial supervision, a rule of law, Western democratic representation or popular participation in governance.[13] Kukrit avoided even the term "democracy" explaining that its use could provoke unwanted debates about the regime's democratic quality and trigger demands for individual rights which "may induce tremendous troubles later on."[14]

Instead, he envisioned this order as animated by "Thainess,"[15] an intensively promoted brand of collective identity, that comprised a corpus of guiding values and epistemic tools prescribed to shape the people's perceptions and behavior. As the unifying link among Thai people, Thainess is first and foremost expressed in this view by loyalty to the King, respect to those higher on the social hierarchy and kindness to those lower than oneself.[16] Central is a "know-thy-place" attitude based on the religiously and metaphysically underpinned assumption that any individual's status follows from karma, putting everyone exactly at that place within the social fabric which the cosmic law of dhamma determined for her.[17]

In sum, Kukrit prominently voiced a deeply entrenched theme of Thai political thought and education that still holds significant sway in Thailand: the idea of a "society without politics." Assuming that electoral democracy and politicians are inherently bad, it suggests the people remain in "political silence,"" leaving it to "good people" to govern the country.[18] In this view, Thais will be satisfied to remain "politically silent" as long as they are governed by a good Thai-style ruler under royal supervision with the King as the nation's embodiment and spiritual center.[19]

16.1.4 *Royally Dominated Thai-Style Governance*

By the end of the second phase, the King already enjoyed a gradually increasing influence also over the polity's efficient center. This development culminated when he intervened in the wake of a bloody government crackdown on protesters in 1973. From this watershed moment, the King emerged as the "ultimate source of power and legitimacy in the country,"[20] a position soon reinforced by Thanin's more authoritarian brand of Buddhist-royalist constitutionalism following the Thammasat massacre of 1976.

13 Kukrit Pramoj, "Nailuang khong prachachon [The People's King]," cited in Sala Likhitkun, *Nailuang kap Kukrit [The King and Kukrit]* (Bangkok: Sapprasart, 2003) 103 f.

14 Saichol Sattayanurak, "The Construction of Mainstream Thought on 'Thainess' and the 'Truth' Constructed by 'Thainess,'" at https://pdfs.semanticscholar.org/9a10/5c84daaca1b2d41b93aaa5885acd18de7b28.pdf; Kukrit Pramoj, "Prachatippatai bap Sukarno nai Indonesia [Sukarno-style democracy in Indonesia]," in *Prachum phongsawadan prachatippatai [Collected Annales of Democracy]* (Bangkok: Bannakhan Press, 1969) 241.

15 See Rawin, Chapter 15 in this volume.

16 See Kukrit Pramoj, "Thai (boran) neramit [(Ancient) Thais Creations]," in *Kukrit thok muangthai [Kukrit discusses Thailand]* (Bangkok: Bannakhan Press, 1971) 266 f.

17 See Kukrit Pramoj, "Rich People, Poor People," in *Keplek pasomnoi [Saving up, Little by little]* (Bangkok: Klangwittaya Press, 1959) 475 ff. See also Andrew J. Harding, "The Politics of Law and Development in Thailand," in Gerald Paul McAlinn and Caslav Pejovic (eds.), *Law and Development in Asia* (London, New York: Routledge, 2012) 109, 119, 130. See also Saichol, "The Construction of Mainstream Thought," 17 f.

18 Saichol, ibid., 24.

19 Ibid., 27, 29.

20 Kobkua Suwannathat-Pian, *Kings, Country and Constitutions: Thailand's Political Development 1932–2000* (New York: Routledge, 2003) 171.

Irrespective of all volatility of the 1970s and the limited impact of democratic governance, under the 1978 Constitution (TC 1978) constitutionalism served increasingly as an actually important, politically conceived rule book for the formal political arena. It featured a Prime Minister who had no parliamentary mandate and struggled to balance the interests of the palace, the military, and the political parties – in this order of priority. With a fragmented House of Representatives and an appointed Senate marked by strong military presence, the Government formed the constitution's effective part. An insignificant Constitutional Tribunal and the near absence of any meaningful mechanisms to protect civil rights reflected the constitutional order's ornamental part.

Meanwhile, the King occupied the position of the dignified center with increasingly efficient impact while the military retained a large autonomous space both within and outside the constitutional arena. Staking out the efficient center, the military deployed a robust national security agenda even as it remained fractured into competing cliques.

Especially under Prem Tinsulanonda, the second Prime Minister under the TC 1978, again a former army commander who soon attained a reputation as a particularly loyal servant of the monarchy, the system matured. Prem largely succeeded in balancing out the competing interests, maintaining a fluid equilibrium among them. While fusing cabinets of ex-soldiers and technocrats from the government bureaucracies with businessmen and professional politicians, he endorsed "the military's unprecedented, systematic and purposeful attempt to legitimize its involvement in politics" as long as it accepted the King's centrality and the power status quo enshrined in the TC 1978.[21]

During the 1980s, the constitutional order managed to successfully integrate the country's increasingly differentiated power structure through an official platform marked by a system of functional separation of powers, the circulation of positions, and rules that regulated power competition. This constitutionalism was, however, still relevant as a mere device that ensured elite cooperation, not as a reference point for national identity or as a decisive normative guide. The parliament, devoid of any ideological discourse, served as a formal trading floor distributing power and influence across the different networks. However, the parliament was neither rooted in an actual notion of popular sovereignty nor expected to provide ultimate legitimacy or even a stable governing majority linking a popular mandate with a stable coalition of political parties carrying the cabinet.

Moreover, the constitution still lacked any aspiration for a legal, or even *legalistic*, mode of constitutional rule, and a transition towards a more Western-like form of democratization was not open for consideration. Discussions about reform focused instead on adjustments that served the competing interests of palace, military and politicians.[22] The constitutional process remained largely untouched by any form of constitutional adjudication or any discourse of truly transformative impact. A high frequency of cabinet turnover, a recourse to coup threats and political violence, including at least four attempts to assassinate Prem during his administration, and two actually attempted coups reflect the limits of the constitutional arena to resolve or sufficiently mitigate diverging elite interests though.

[21] Prudhisan Jumbala, *Nation-Building and Democratization in Thailand: A Political History* (Bangkok: Chulalongkorn University, Social Research Institute, 1992) 92. See also, including for the following, David Morell and Chai-Anan Samudavanija, "Thailand: Meeting the Challenges of the 1980s" (1981) *Southeast Asian Affairs* 309–324; Suchitra Punyaratabandhu-Bhakdi, "Thailand in 1983: Democracy, Thai Style" (1984) 24(2) *Asian Survey* (A Survey of Asia in 1983: Part II) 187–94, 187–91; Suchit, *State of the Nation*, 51.

[22] Controversially discussed were for instance a moderate valuation of the elected House vis-à-vis the appointed Senate, a mandatory electoral mandate of the prime minister and a reform of the election law.

The environment of Thai constitutionalism eventually underwent a transformation at the end of the decade after Thailand had emerged as one of the most rapidly growing economies in the world during the mid-1980s. A changing global and regional context in the aftermath of the Cold War, an increasingly complex set of elite dynamics, and a more dynamic and differentiated society in general favored a trend towards more refined mechanisms of governance and enhanced applications of constitutionalism – even if still more in form than in substance.[23]

While constitutionalism remained a rather fragile set of formal rules regulating a constrained arena of political competition, a richer governance schema thrived beyond the dimensions of formal constitutionalism. Its master narrative found one of its most influential formulations by Seni Pramoj, a brother of Kukrit, founder of the Democrat Party, and three-time Prime Minister. Seni was a warhorse of the royalist *Reconquista* since the 1940s and a major advocate of the unwritten conception of royalist Thai-style democracy until he passed away in 1997.

In his account of a twelfth century stone inscription of King Ramkhamhaeng of Sukhothai – one of the iconic texts of traditionalist constitutionalism in Thailand – he describes a golden age that serves as a prescriptive assessment for the present. Published on the eve of constitutional reforms at the end of the 1980s, Seni juxtaposes the stone inscription as the "first Thai Constitution" and the grand constitutional documents of the West to provide an autochthon model and guideline for modern Thai constitutionalism.[24]

In essence, his vision of good government is one of a benevolent King who rules his subjects like a father does his children, so they can enjoy their life in a freedom that is shaped by political silence. Calls for substantial constitutional reform willingly threaten this peace: "Today, people are loud in their demands for democracy," he claims,[25] but such a democracy is nothing but a fallacy that only invites rule by corrupt politicians: "The duly elected representatives of the people, instead of being their mouths and voices, became their mouths and stomachs."[26] The voters are not better though, just selling their votes: "We, the people, elected them, sometimes merely because they bought us a small drink or a bowl of noodles."[27] Concerning constitutional reform, he expects nothing, at best: "The new Constitution will not change anything [for the better]."[28] Peril is likely to come. After all, the decline of the golden era of Thai democracy in twelfth century Sukothai was not only due to the "abuse of power by the rulers, but also the abuse of liberties by the people .... The democratic people of Sukothai were abusing their rights and liberties." Consequently, they lost it all as: "freedom corrupts; absolute freedom corrupts absolutely."[29] The rule of law, civil rights and representative institutions promise a change to the worse for Seni, who advocates for Thai-style governance instead.

All conservative resistance notwithstanding, a moderate wind of change finally brought some limited constitutional reforms that carefully lifted the stakes of electoral democracy, accompanied, however, by serious doubts of senior politicians. Noteworthy are the remarks of

[23] See Chai-Anan, *Thailand: State-Building*, 94 ff.; Prudhisan, *Nation-Building and Democratization*, 66–89.

[24] Seni Pramoj, "Father King Ram Khamhaeng's Stone Inscriptions: First Constitution of Thailand," in Pinit Ratanakul and U. Kyaw Than (eds.), *Development, Modernization, and Tradition in Southeast Asia: Lessons from Thailand* (Bangkok: Mahidol University, 1990) 18 ff. Seni refers to the Magna Carta, the US Declaration of Independence, the French Declaration of the Rights of Man and Citizen and the UN Charter.

[25] Ibid., 44.

[26] Ibid., 43.

[27] Ibid., 42.

[28] Ibid., 43.

[29] Ibid., 46.

Kasem Sirisamphan, a reputed academic and high-profile politician from Kukrit's Social Action Party. In a 1987 interview, Kasem lucidly warned that the debated introduction of a mandatory popular mandate of the Prime Minister would directly endanger the DRKH.

> If people are elected by popular vote, some are asking if this will affect the DRKH. . . . The prime minister . . ., this elected official, will not be a weak person. He will be very strong. He will have a mandate from the people of the country. Thus, to put it simply, can there be two tigers in the same cave? If we do things in this way, this would definitely affect the DRKH. Do we want that? . . . The king is the country's tutelary spirit. The monarchy is the foundation of the country. Thus, how can we do anything that might affect this institution? I don't understand. I am opposed to this. I don't think that this would work. That is the truth.[30]

Although moderate reforms were not prevented in the end, predominant constitutional thought remained averse to substantial change. In the words of Chai-Anan: "Western-style constitutional government in Thailand has been highly unstable and ineffectual."[31] Moreover, the constitutional form remained carefully distinguished from the substance of Thai-style governance, or, as Tongnoi Tongyai, a then-deputy principal private secretary to King Bhumibol, stated in view of the reform:

> Consider even a lifeless thing like the [written] Thai Constitution. It has been shifted and changed so much within these past fifty-odd years that no-one can say what are its basic tenets. The Thai monarchy on the other hand, is the only thing that remained all the time closely identified with the basic interests of the Thai nation and people, and although highly personalized at any single time, it is the only thing in Thailand which people readily accept as an institution. As such, the Thai monarch stands on a par with, for example, the Constitution in the United States or Marxism in communist countries.[32]

Whereas the unwritten or "Cultural Constitution" is utterly decisive, notably, the written constitution is not only of limited range and impact in this account but also without a true basic structure or "basic tenets." Nidhi described the literally absolute nature of the unwritten autochthon constitution and its center particularly clear: "Whether it is written or not, the king is in a position of revered worship and shall not be violated. If the section in the constitution on the king were totally removed, it would not shake the Thai monarchy at all." While this view represented an almost unchallenged orthodoxy of constitutional thought at the end of the third phase of Thai constitutionalism, shifting balances of power at the eve of the new decade led to a period of severe volatility that finally ushered in a new form of constitutionalism.

16.2 NEW CONSTITUTIONALISM AND THE DRKH IN THE 1997 CONSTITUTION

With the end of the Prem era, the old constitutionalism entered a stage of moderate reform followed by upheaval and eventually a more transformative reform again, finally manifesting

30 See Kasem Sirisamphan, Interview, *Su Anakhot*, 5–11 Aug. 1987. This assessment echoes Prince Damrong's emphatic rejection of the idea to introduce a prime minister as early as 1926 as this could cause trouble if the King would like to discharge a prime minister trusted by the people. Damrong Rajanubhab, "Memorandum 1 August 1926," [1926] in Benjamin A. Batson (ed.), *Siam's Political Future: Documents from the End of the Absolute Monarchy* (Ithaca, NY: Cornell University, 1974) 39.

31 Chai-Anan Samudavanija, "The Bureaucracy," in Somsak Xuto (ed.), *Government and Politics of Thailand* (Singapore: Oxford University Press, 1987) 1, 33.

32 Tongnoi Tongyai, "The Role of Monarchy in Modern Thailand," in Pinit Ratanakul (ed.), *Development, Modernisation, and Tradition in Southeast Asia: Lessons from Thailand* (Bangkok: Mahidol University, 1990) 155.

in the 1997 Constitution. To understand this transition and the DRKH as the new constitution's main feature it is necessary to have a closer look at the first half of the 1990s, focusing on the nature of both the underlying power shifts and doctrinal achievements of this transitional sub-phase ushering in the fourth phase of Thai constitutionalism.

16.2.1 *Power Transitions and Doctrinal Developments toward a New Constitutionalism*

Prem's rule ended in 1988 when he dissolved the House of Representatives to escape a no-confidence motion. After elections, General Chatichai Choonhavan became the first Prime Minister since 1976 who had been elected as a member of parliament. His administration, amid mounting tensions with the military, bureaucracy and palace, implemented a number of ambitious reform policies. In 1991, the military staged a coup under General Suchinda Kraprayoon. Corruption, interference with military promotions, a parliamentary dictatorship, and a threat to the throne were given as his reasons for the ouster.[33]

When a coalition led by the military-controlled party won the post-coup elections of 1992, Suchinda became Prime Minister, contrary to his former promise not to pursue the office, seemingly cementing a long-term dominance of his military faction within the armed forces and the country.[34] In response, Maj.-Gen. Chamlong Srimuang, a confident of Prem, who himself had been appointed to the Royal Privy Council after leaving politics,[35] mobilized fierce civilian resistance leading to a bloody government crackdown until a nationwide televised royal intervention ended both the street protests and Suchinda's prime ministership.

The ruling party coalition went on, however, to elect Suchinda's Deputy Prime Minister, Air Chief Marshal Somboon Rahong, as Interim Prime Minister. In a move "with no [sc. written] constitutional basis whatsoever,"[36] the King appointed Anand Pancharayun instead who had already served as the Interim Prime Minister following the Suchinda coup. This event "seemed to epitomize the rising power of the monarchy" as it reflected both the neutralization of the military as an independent actor in national politics, and "a popular mood of dissatisfaction with political parties and institutions."[37]

Finally, all the different forces had arrived at an unprecedented equilibrium with the King "towering over the military, constitution and parliament"[38] as the single unified center of the formal and informal power structures in both a dignified and an efficient sense.[39] In a polity

33 See Yoshifumi Tamada, *Myth and Realities: The Democratization of Thai Politics* (Kyoto: Trans Pacific Press, 2009); for the reasons, see Thitinan Pongsudhirak, "The Tragedy of the 1997 Constitution," in N. John Funston (ed.), *Divided over Thaksin* (Singapore: Institute of Southeast Asian Studies, 2009) 28.

34 Tamada, *Myth and Realities*, 86 ff. Part of this was his alliance with his military academy classmate and brother-in -law General Issarapong Noonpakdee who succeeded him as army chief.

35 Chamlong served as the Prime Minister's secretary until both fell apart over Prem's support for a law that legalized abortions by rape victims. Chamlong soon entered politics with his Buddhist Phalang Tham Party whose leadership he would pass later to Thaksin Shinawatra. Years later again, Chamlong became a core leader of the anti-Thaksin protest movement.

36 Kobkua, *Kings, Country and Constitutions*, 65. Arguably, the unwritten constitution that manifested in the King's action entailed the prerogative power to do so.

37 Duncan McCargo, "Network Monarchy and Legitimacy Crises in Thailand," (2005) 18(4) *The Pacific Review* 499–519, 508.

38 Kobkua, *Kings, Country and Constitutions*, 65.

39 See Kasian Tejapira, "The Irony of Democratization and the Decline of Royal Hegemony in Thailand," in *Liber amicorum Vishnu Varunyou* (Bangkok: Nititham, 2017) 94–116, 101: "Arguably, in his heyday King Bhumipol became much more powerful in an informal, extra-constitutional sense than some of his absolute predecessors."

that resembled a perfect mandala of power, the politically relevant actors found and accepted their place in an order animated by this brand of royalist constitutionalism. This is a constitutionalism with the King at the center in both a dignified and an efficient sense.

At the same time, the demise of military preponderance allowed an apparent expansion of civilian politics akin to the global zeitgeist of liberal democracy. A more dynamic, diverse and economically booming Thai society of the 1990s sought to align the newly achieved Thai "mandala of power" with a new governance structure that would accommodate, integrate, rationalize and stabilize the new realities. Against this background, widespread reform talk resumed in 1993 until the 1997 Constitution emerged as an entirely new brand of constitutionalism in Thailand.

The reform debates were dominated by leading scholars like Amorn Chantarasomboon, Bowornsak Uwanno and Chai-anan Samudavajiva. The conservative doctrine which they represented was so unassailable and so tightly interwoven with an underpinning political theology that this doctrine formed nothing less than the orthodoxy of Thai constitutionalism. A publicly visible counter-hegemonic discourse begun to emerge since the 2006 Coup. After the 2014 Coup, it needed until 2020 to again reach its full swing with a student-led reform movement challenging the monarchy and referring back to the revolutionary spirit of 1932.

For Amorn, constitutionalism would ensure sufficient leadership and control with regard to an inevitably expanded arena of electoral politics badly in need of meticulous rationalization and control. This echoed an anti-electoral sentiment that overwhelmingly dominated the discourse since progressive voices were muted in the wake of the 1976 massacre. In his authoritative account on constitutionalism, Amorn frequently rejects the coherence of the foundational fiction of Western democracy for the Thai realities: Rather, elected parliamentarians neither represent the people nor exercise supreme power in Amorn's account who further links the elected politicians' inherent defectiveness to coup politics as a response.[40] In place of this flawed Western-style constitutionalism, Amorn invokes ultimate royal sovereignty and the view that the "present King" is the sole actual representative of the Thai people – irrespective of any contra-factual constitutional notion that the parliament would represent the people.[41]

For him, democracy and constitutionalism are two separate conceptions: Constitutionalism is a mere tool for controlling and disciplining electoral democracy, and has nothing resembling a Western-style normative substance *per se*.[42] This notion is also reflected by the way other leading reformers framed civil rights. Rights and liberties hold in fact a similarly low position in the reform debates like electoral democracy, as summed up by Chai-Anan: "The most important aspect of a Thai constitution is not the provision and protection of civil and political liberties, but the extent to which it allows the House of Representatives to participate in the political process."[43]

While Amorn and Chai-Anan focused on the negative, disciplining effect of constitutionalism, describing it as a mere cure against the vagaries of electoral democracy, Bowornsak sounded out the royalist substance of the constitutional order, both written and unwritten. Bowornsak's doctrinal approach can be seen as the master narrative of what became the orthodox doctrine of the DRKH. For him, the televised end of the Suchinda episode exemplified the King's singularity: "The King instructed the Prime Minister and the

[40] See Amorn Chantarasomboon, *Political Reform: Can This Really Happen?* (Bangkok: Thammasat University Press, 1996) 65 ff., 92 f., 112 f. (in Thai).

[41] Ibid., 64–5.

[42] See Amorn Chantarasomboon, *Constitutionalism: Political Reform: The Way Out for Thailand* (Bangkok: Thammasat University Press, 1994) 11 f., 14, 46, 66 f., 86 (in Thai).

[43] Chai-Anan, *Thailand: State-Building*, 104.

protesters like a teacher instructing students."[44] Among the entitled high priests of constitutional law with insight into its esoteric dimensions, Bowornsak stands out as the one who was able and daring enough to provide a comprehensive illumination of the royalists' constitutional orthodoxy with regard to the royal power at its apex.

Bowornsak points out that the sovereign power exercised by the King belongs to King and people in their mutuality.[45] While the sovereign power emanates from the Thai people according to the written constitution, the King is the original and ultimate holder of the sovereign power. He embodies the unwritten, autochthon constitution as the "permanent, unchangeable and immortal" Constitution that cannot be changed or amended by written law.[46] Those drafting a written constitution are just finding and acknowledging this real Constitution.[47] In doing so, however, they can only refer to some of the royal customs established between the King and his people, while others remain unwritten. All unwritten, customary royal powers are, however, legally binding in this account.[48]

An integral part of this conservative doctrine is its account on "coup constitutionalism." Relating to its conception of sovereignty, the term denotes a constitutional framing of coup politics within the unwritten constitution. In parts, it builds on the historic experience that those staging a coup always sought a royal endorsement. The doctrine interprets this as a sort of customary constitutional script having emerged *ab origine* with the 1932 compromise between the King and the revolutionary party.[49] The short-lived compromise is counterfactually depicted as the very foundation of Thai constitutionalism and democracy. Blanking out what has been an audacious power seizure and act of sacrilege from the very same royalist point of view then as now, focus is placed solely on a view of the King as willingly granting the constitution to the Thai people at a time of his own choosing. Conservative doctrine, thus, identifies the origin of constitutionalism in a royal decision rather than in a revolutionary act, thereby laying the ground for the concept of a shared sovereignty of King and People.[50]

In this vein, Bowornsak reiterates that those abolishing a written constitution will return the sovereign power to the King as the ultimate holder of sovereignty.[51] If the junta acts with good

44 Bowornsak Uwanno, 'The King and the People, Characteristics of Thai Democracy," [1993] in Bowornsak Uwanno (ed.), *Law and Solutions of Thai Society* (Bangkok: Nititham, 1996) 27 (in Thai).

45 Bowornsak Uwanno, *Public Law, Vol. 2: Separation of Public and Private Law and the Evolution of Public Law in Thailand* (Bangkok: Chulalongkorn University Press, 2005) 189–90 (in Thai).

46 See Bowornsak Uwanno, 'The King and the People, Characteristics of Thai Democracy," 9 ff., 23 ff., 27 ff.

47 Ibid., 27.

48 Ibid., 22 f.

49 See also Wissanu Krea-ngam, *Constitutional Law* (Bangkok: Thiranusorn, 1979) 20 (in Thai). In his 1979 standard textbook, Wissanu pointed out that every leader of a coup group needed the consent of the King to establish a new Constitution in order to obtain the necessary legitimacy domestically and internationally. Wissanu, another one of the few high priests of Thailand's esoteric constitutionalism, is a cousin of Bowornsak and one of the 2014 Coup group's deputy prime ministers. Since 1991, he has served as deputy secretary general and then secretary general of the cabinet under all subsequent governments before he became a minister under Thaksin when Bowornsak took his position as secretary general of the cabinet. These personal continuities indicate a sort of semi-official acknowledgement of the esoteric dimension of Thai constitutionalism and its entitlements.

50 See for this discourse Henning Glaser, "Constitutional Conflict and Restatement – The Challenge and Transformation of the Hegemonic Basic Consent in Thailand," in Henning Glaser (ed.), *Norms, Interests, and Values: Conflict and Consent in the Constitutional Basic Order* (Baden-Baden: Nomos, 2015) 309–16; Henning Glaser, "Setting the Course for Thailand? – Content, Structure and Impact of the 2016 Constitution Bill" (2016) *European-Asian Journal of Law and Governance* 25–34.

51 Bowornsak, "The King and the People," 29. See also Kittisak Prokati, 'King Rama V and Constitutionalism in Thailand', in Pornsan Watanangura (ed.), *The Visit of King Chulalongkorn to Europe in 1907: Reflecting on Siamese History* (Bangkok: Chulalongkorn University Press, 2009) 114–32. This orthodox view is disputed by dissident progressive scholars. See Piyabutr Saengkanokkul, "Creating a Definition of Constitutional Lawyers under the Royalism," (2016) 1 *Fa Daewgan* 17–29, especially pp. 17 ff. and 23 ff. with extensive reference to Bowornsak (in Thai).

intentions, i.e. not on a self-serving agenda but as true guardians of royalist constitutionalism, it will receive a royal endorsement to create an interim constitution to be given to the people by the King.[52]

This conception implies the distinction between the King as the permanent and de jure owner of sovereign power and a junta as merely a temporary and de facto possessor of supreme power. Thus, the junta remains dependent on the King's endorsement to receive the necessary legitimacy and an amnesty for the violent overthrow of a lawful government of his Majesty.[53] It is for this reason that the King gives a new constitution. With this restoration of legality through the King, the sovereign power is transferred back to the People as the owner of the constituted power to be further exercised by the King under the new constitution.[54]

Crucial here is the notion that the unwritten constitution provides a yardstick and frame for both legitimacy and legality in the context of coup politics. This view discloses an inherent tension and ambiguity regarding the military's role in Thai constitutionalism. Whereas a junta is supposed to situate its action within the boundaries of the unwritten or Cultural Constitution, military groups had effectively often acted as independent power players pursuing their own agenda which, nevertheless, however, had to resonate with the sanctity of the unwritten constitution in the wake of Sarit's restoration of royal authority. This inclination of independent praetorian politics, however, seemed to phase out in the wake of the Suchinda-debacle enabling an increasing alignment of military politics with the demands of the Cultural Constitution over the course of the following years. These reflections on the orthodox constitutional doctrine are leading to the following discussion of the actual reform process and how it manifested in the 1997 Constitution.

16.2.2 *The 1997 Constitution: Co-evolution of Constitutionalism and DRKH*

In 1994, the parliament established a Committee on Developing Democracy (CDD) under the leadership of Prawase Wasi to pave the way for a new constitution and set the tone for the ensuing deliberations. Two assumptions with defining impact on the further direction manifested in the CDD debates: the absolute dominance of the royal position as constitutionally manifested in the DRKH and the conviction that "[electoral] politics is the root of all evil."[55] Based on these axiomatic foundations and Amorn's rehashed and appreciated understanding of constitutionalism as a sophisticated tool, the 1997 Constitution (TC 1997) would eventually emerge as a true watershed in Thai constitutionalism.

Two closely related transformations emerged from this impact. First, the drafters further developed the DRKH as a concept, implementing it as a more pronounced and differentiated constitutional basic structure. Second, the Constitution expanded the realm of electoral politics in scope and political weight, though not in dignity, which induced a strong impulse to tightly control and confine the electoral dynamics as a dialectical response. While it is hard to tell whether one of the two transformations caused the other, both were deeply intertwined concerning their rationale, manifestation and fate.[56]

52 See on Bowornsak's line also Kittisak, "King Rama V and Constitutionalism." Putschists who did not follow this script were Phibun, Kriangsak, Suchinda as well as the Young Turks and their promoters behind the failed and aborted coups against Prem.

53 Bowornsak, *Public Law, Vol.* 2. See also Chapter 18, this volume.

54 Bowornsak, "The King and the People," 29.

55 Tamada, *Myth and Realities*, 119.

56 See also Kasian Tejapira, "The Irony of Democratization and the Decline of Royal Hegemony in Thailand," in *Liber amicorum Vishnu Varunyou* (Bangkok: Nititham, 2017) 102: "Thai democracy and the Thai monarchy thus

16.2.3 *The Dialectics of Democratization and Anti-electoralism*

The most notable expansion of electoral politics was the introduction of a parliamentary responsible government. Without precedent, the TC 1997 required cabinet members to be selected from party-list MPs based on an untested proportional representation election system that featured as a particularity that the whole nation formed the constituency. This made it possible that a Prime Minister with a corresponding mandate could claim to posses a democratic legitimacy as it had never been conveyed before.[57]

In 2001, this possibility became reality when Thaksin Shinawatra crafted an unprecedented electoral platform through a mix of new and old but more forcefully applied tactics such as merger-and-acquisition-style takeovers of other political parties, an unparalleled use of public relations and the concerted resort to the well-established practices of lubricating the political machine with money. Eventually, his CEO-style governance, administrative skills, political instinct and populist politics secured him an absolute majority in the House of Representatives. For the very first time in Thai history, a Prime Minister claimed a sound democratic mandate, served a full term and was reelected. However, when Thaksin was not willing to integrate this stunning mandate into the DRKH's conceptual framework, it caused a chain reaction that divided Thai society over Thaksin's fate, the integrity of the societal consensus and, eventually, the DRKH.

This development was not foreseen by the drafters.[58] They had a strong sense for an abstract danger enshrined in the electoral mechanism but could not expect this outcome. While they envisioned a strong civilian leadership under the DRKH by expanding the realm of electoral politics, the drafting of the Constitution was nevertheless governed by a strong anti-majoritarian tendency to shield the King's centrality. The drafters viewed the electoral mechanism as an inherently ambiguous phenomenon, useful and opportune but inhabited by a dangerous potential to receive an unwarranted popular spin and emancipate from its narrow constitutional constraints.[59] They met this seemingly abstract danger with a forceful application of Amorn's view of constitutionalism as a tool to contain the critical realm of electoral politics.

This inclination directed the largest part of the drafting and was manifested in two ways. First, the Constitution introduced a stunning range of new, or significantly upgraded, institutions as watchdog bodies over electoral politics.[60] Examples are the Senate, the Constitutional Court, the administrative courts and the "independent constitutional organizations" – especially the Election Commission and the Anti-Corruption Commission. Second, both the Constitution and the concretizing organic laws created a differentiated regime of highly rigid anti-electoral regulations that were reinforced by an apparatus of draconic sanctions.

All this induced a tight legalism as the major mode of operations. In consequence, the constitutional arena vastly expanded and transformed, especially turning the formerly predominant political mode of constitutionalism into a decisively legalistic one for the first time

are conditional upon each other, forming an integral whole in which the former is unimaginable without the latter" (in Thai).

57 Yoshifumi Tamada, "Democracy and Populism in Thailand," in Kosuke Mizuno and Pasuk Phongpaichit (eds.), *Populism in Asia* (Singapore/Kyoto: NUS Press, 2009) 104.

58 See also Siripan Nogsuan Sawasdee, *Politics of Electoral Reform in Thailand* (PhD Thesis, Kyoto University, 2014) 30.

59 See Tamada, *Myth and Realities*; Kevin Hewison, "Constitutions, Regimes and Power in Thailand" (2007) 14(5) *Democratisation* 932.

60 See Peter Leyland, "Thailand's Constitutional Watchdogs: Dobermans, Bloodhounds or Lapdogs?" (2008) 2 *Journal of Comparative Law* 151–62.

in Thai constitutional history. Reiterating Amorn, Chai-Anan reflected this shift when he stated that "most significantly, this transition is what I call a 'constitutional transition' rather than a 'democratic transition'."[61]

Most notably, the deeply anti-electoral sentiment that had dominated almost all strands of the visible political discourse since decades, with the military's national security agenda and royalist constitutionalism leading the way, became now legally explicit and institutionally embodied in large parts of the Constitution's effective structure. As a result, public law became much more appreciated than before without, however, transcending the boundaries of a mere legalism in a way similar to Western-style rule of law thought.

16.2.4 *Transformation of the DRKH*

Corresponding with the emphatic entrenchment of anti-electoralism, the Constitution revisited and reshaped another well-established element of Thai constitutionalism, the DRKH. While the DRKH had represented the paramount principle of Thai constitutionalism since at least the 1976 charter,[62] it demarcated a rather vague commitment to the shifting notions of Thai-style democracy. It was, at any rate, not understood to be an expression of a predominantly legal (or legalistic) form of constitutionalism until the TC 1997 transformed its character and meaning and with it the nature of constitutionalism as such.

This shift in how the DRKH was conceived partly responded to the revamped constitutional structure and its new legalism that, for its part, was induced by the aforementioned dialectic of expanding and concurrently containing electoral politics. Notably, this shift reflected the actual balances of power only after the royal hegemony had reached its climax.[63]

Expressions of the DRKH in its already established constitutional form were acknowledged in the preamble, in its explicit adoption at the top of the constitutional text (section 2) and, most noteworthy, in the regulation of the sovereign power (section 3). In this form, it is the King who exercises the sovereign power while "sovereignty" itself belongs to the Thai people. Moreover, the King enjoys a position of revered worship that forbids exposing the King to any sort of accusation or action (section 8). Arguably the acknowledgement of Thailand as one and indivisible kingdom (section 1), is also a part of the classical DRKH.

Based on this foundation, the TC 1997 developed the DRKH significantly further in two ways. First, the drafters accentuated and laid out the DRKH as the constitution's now more legally conceived *basic structure*. Generally, the constitution's basic structure is understood here as any meaningful constitution's normative basis, core and horizon that designates the sphere in which the underlying social contract evolves in constitutional law.[64] The basic structure, if properly pronounced, is that part of the constitution in which constitutional identity manifests most significantly and which forms a higher level of constitutional law that evades amendments. In positive constitutional law, the basic structure can be often derived especially from the *preamble*, the *fundamental principles* of state, provisions exempting parts

61 See Chai-Anan, *Thailand: State-Building*, 207.

62 Michael Kelly Connors, *Democracy and National Identity in Thailand* (Copenhagen: NIAS Press, 2007) 128. While present constitutional jurisdiction traces the DRKH to the beginnings of Thai constitutionalism in 1932 (see for instance Constitutional Court DC 7/2559, 26 October 2059), the terminology rather supports Connors' point. See also Kasian, "The Irony of Democratisation," 138, 145, 155.

63 See Kasian, ibid., 101.

64 See Henning Glaser, "Watchmen With and Without Arms? – Some Remarks on Selected Oversight Bodies Under the 2017 Constitution," in Ingwer Ebsen, Dirk Ehlers, and Henning Glaser (eds.), *Democracy, and Human Rights. Festschrift in Honour of Warawit Kanithasen* (Bangkok: Rabbit, 2017) 448–501, 454 ff.

of the constitution from changes by *amendments* and those provisions seeking to protect certain principles by establishing a form of "*militant constitutionalism*."[65]

In this sense, the TC 1997 acknowledges the DRKH in its preamble and the fundamental principles of the state. Moreover, for the first time, the new Constitution made the DRKH a mandatory yardstick for the internal organization of political parties (section 47 (1) (2)) and set it as a limitation for the exercise of civil rights (section 63 (1)). The DRKH now also became subject to protection by a newly introduced form of militant constitutionalism (section 63 (2)), a mandatory theme of public education (section 81), and exempted it from constitutional amendments (section 323 (2)).[66] This entrenchment and differentiation of the DRKH as the TC 1997's basic structure reflects the transition of the constitution as a rather politically conceived rulebook for the political arena with rather limited scope to a comprehensive supreme law of the land intended to be legally implemented. Furthermore, it implies an unprecedented distinction between a plain and a higher layer of positive constitutional law.[67] Second, through section 7, the TC 1997 added as its most important, and for a long time yet almost unequivocally overlooked innovation, an entirely new dimension to the DRKH.[68] Section 7 reads: "Whenever no provision under this Constitution is applicable to any case, it shall be acted or decided in accordance with the constitutional practice in the democratic regime of government with the King as Head." Section 7 was adopted only in July 1997, at the very end of the drafting process after the public hearings on the draft had ended.[69] Earlier, in June, the drafters had discussed to introduce a provision in the chapter on the Constitutional Court (section 264, later section 265 of the draft) that allowed the Court to decide cases not regulated by the Constitution with regard to "the constitutional practice with the King as Head" to fill gaps in the constitution.[70] Bowornsak, however, pointed out that this could allow the court to unduly expand its jurisdiction and assume too much power.[71] Accordingly, the drafters dropped the proposal in favor of what emerged first as section 6A and eventually became section 7.

At first glance, the nature and meaning of section 7 are not entirely clear. When the TC 1997 was passed, there was not much talk about it. From 2006 to 2014, however, its reference to the unwritten practice of the DRKH has been understood time and again as an

65 These areas reflect the basic structure typically but not necessarily, exclusively or conclusively though. Further helpful to derive the basic structure are doctrinal orthodoxy and the constitutional context including the grand political narratives on the foundation and mission of the constitutional project. As the normative center of the constitutional order, the basic structure, once identified, is offering the single most important heuristic key to analyze the status and development of constitutional politics.

66 Other manifestations of the DRKH as the 1997 Constitution's basic structure are provisions concerning the constitutional duties of the citizens (sect. 66) and the state (sect. 72).

67 This distinction would manifest in several decisions of the Constitutional Court under the 2007 Constitution that invalidated constitutional amendments introduced by the government based on the DRKH. See Decision No. 18–22/2555, 13 July 2555 (2012) and Decision No. 1/2557, 1 January 2557 (2014).

68 See, however, Michael Connors, "Article of Faith, The Failure of Royal Liberalism in Thailand," (2008) 38(1) *Journal of Contemporary Asia* 143–65. Connors was the first who diligently elaborated on sect. 7 of the TC 1997 in English, albeit not in context of the overarching basic structure, the DRKH, or the substantial shift the new DRKH meant for Thai constitutionalism. His article inspired the author to analyze the DRKH as the basic structure of Thai constitutionalism. See Henning Glaser, "Crisis, Conflict and Consensus in the Constitutional Basic Order – An Introduction," in Glaser (ed.), *Norms, Interests, and Values*, 20 f.

69 See the 14th sitting of the CDA on 8 July 1997, https://library2.parliament.go.th/giventake/content_cons40-50/cons2540/14_25400708.pdf, p. 58 ff.

70 See the 24th sitting of the CDA's subcommittee on 24 June 1997, https://library2.parliament.go.th/giventake/content_cons40-50/cons2540/pi400624.pdf, p. 34 ff. The initiative came from Wisut Phothithaen, a former dean of the faculty of political science of Thammasat University.

71 See Bowornsak, CDA sub-committee from 24 June 1997, ibid., 36.

acknowledgment of the King's broad unwritten powers and prerogatives. Another interpretation identified section 7 as a mere reference to constitutional customary law and convention.

It contributed to some confusion that the earlier draft of section 264, which had referred to the unwritten practice of the DRKH in order to allow the Constitutional Court to close eventual gaps, emulated a similar reference that had reoccurred in slightly different forms in a number of previous constitutions. Similarly, the new sections 6A and 7 respectively seemed to refer likewise to customary law. All these former constitutions, the TC 1959, 1972, 1976, 1977 and 1991, were, however, merely interim constitutions that compensated their natural brevity by a reference to the unwritten "constitutional practice," "traditional practice," or "administrative practice" respectively of the "democratic regime" as a sort of constitutional customary law.[72]

A similar reading of section 7 mere as a reference to constitutional customary law in accord with this tradition is, however, highly problematic, as it does obscure the fundamental difference between mere interim and regular constitutions,[73] between the "democratic regime" and the DRKH, the subsidiary nature of customary law and the hierarchy of norms established by the TC 1997.[74]

In particular, the aforementioned interim constitutions referred consistently to the "democratic regime" while only section 7 refers to the unwritten practice of the DRKH, which are two essentially different things in Thai constitutionalism. Moreover, in their reference to unwritten constitutional practice, the said interim constitutions always explicitly stated that decisions based on this unwritten practice were not to contravene the letter or the spirit of prior regular constitutions and, furthermore, subjected to review by the National Assembly.[75] Section 7, on the other hand, does not regulate such a double restriction in substantial and procedural terms. The recourse to the unwritten practice of the DRKH is neither subject to review nor has it to conform with any normative standards. Lastly, the older interim constitutions regulated the reference to the unwritten practice of the democratic regime in one of their very last provisions. Section 7 on the other side concluded the first chapter of the Constitution, which comprised some of the constitutional core provisions constituting the DRKH as indicated above.

Different from the interim constitutions' references to constitutional customary law, section 7 was, in other words, an integral part of the DRKH as the constitutional basic structure. It participated therefore in an even higher level of constitutional law, ranking above not below the plain layer of the written constitution.

It is noteworthy in this context that Connors relates the late introduction of section 7 to the debate on section 3, which regulated the sovereign power under the written constitution.[76] While the principle had been part of previous constitutions, a slight modification of its wording from "the sovereign power derives from the Thai people" to the formulation "the sovereign power belongs to the Thai people" heated up the debate. This caused some discomfort among some of the drafters about a flagging commitment to the royalist cause to which Connors sees section 7 as a response.[77]

[72] See Glaser, "Constitutional Conflict and Restatement," 313 ff.

[73] See also CDA member Somkit Srisangkom at the 14th sitting of the CDA on 8 July 1997, above fn. 69, 58.

[74] See Srisangkom at the 14th sitting of the CDA from 8 July 1997, 59; Sawas Khamprakop, ibid., 62 ff.

[75] See Glaser, "Constitutional Conflict and Restatement," 313 ff., with further references and, as an example, sect. 30, 31 TC 1991.

[76] See Connors, "Article of Faith," 145.

[77] Ibid., 150.

In this sense, section 7 represents an innovation whose nature follows from the norm's reference to the DRKH rather than the "democratic regime," the positioning in the first chapter of the Constitution, the general enhancement of the DRKH in the TC 1997, and the dominating constitutional doctrine, which Bowornsak represented in the Constitution Drafting Committee whose influential secretary-general he was. Section 7 is therefore understood rightly as an acknowledgment of the unwritten dimension of the DRKH that supersedes positive constitutional law. From a Western perspective, the nature of this super-Constitution is ambiguous as far as the powers to which section 7 arguably refers also contain the King's ownership of ultimate sovereignty, while they are rooted in the lofty layers of Buddhist kingship suggesting a discrete, benevolent and, if possible, almost invisible exercise of power.

That section 7 remained somehow opaque although an innovation of greatest significance is explained by this nature of royal power and the fact that it is one of the properties of Thai constitutionalism that questions concerning the King ought to be discussed in inverse proportion to their importance. Correspondingly, the dominant constitutional discourse cloaks core questions in a layer of esoteric knowledge carefully guarded by the adepts of the higher levels of constitutional wisdom. This notion would become all too evident by the resounding silence that occurred when the principle enshrined in section 7 experienced substantial changes in an extended process of reshaping after the 2014 Coup as will be shown below in Section 16.3.

With the introduction of section 7 into the TC 1997, the deep transformation of Thai constitutionalism culminated in this capstone of a constitutional structure defined by a valorized DRKH and the corresponding dialectics of enhanced electoral politics and its constitutional disciplining by means of legal procedures. Ultimately, the formerly loose coexistence of a written constitution of limited scope and impact and Thai-style democracy as a vague governance ideology became replaced with an explicit acknowledgment of a supreme layer of the constitutional order hovering high above the written constitution, which, however, links itself by means of sect. 7 to this super-constitution.

16.3 POST-2014 PERMUTATIONS AT THE CORE OF THAI CONSTITUTIONALISM

The significance of section 7 became evident when, in a series of royalist protests against Thaksin and his successors as Prime Minister and alleged proxies, protesters and academics alike invoked the norm asking the King to discharge the Prime Minister.

Thaksin had been increasingly seen as encroaching on the DRKH's preeminence by turning the Constitution's electoral element into an alternative source of legitimacy and thereby into a weapon directed at the basic structure.[78] While the royalist coup of 2006 aimed at decapitating this challenge to protect the DRKH, it only fanned a fire against it from below. From 2007 onwards, it went on to spread with the Redshirt movement directed against both the societal and the constitutional status quo. After the pro-Thaksin election victories in 2007 and 2011 had repeatedly reinforced this challenge irrespective of a barrage of Constitutional Court decisions fielding the 2007 Constitution's provisions protecting the DRKH, the 2014 Coup ended the chapter with a more forceful action. Part of the larger context preceding the Coup was the deteriorating health of King Bhumipol since 2013 who finally passed away in 2016; a bit just over

[78] See Andrew J. Harding and Peter Leyland, *The Constitutional System of Thailand: A Contextual Analysis* (Oxford: Hart Publishing, 2011) 32; Tamada, *Myth and Realities*, 262; Tamada, "Democracy and Populism," 100 f. and 107.

two years after the military had established its post-coup government. The authoritarian government went to great lengths to root out any challenge against the power structure established and secured by the Coup respectively. At the same time, it saw itself compelled to restate the constitutional basic structure that had depended so much on King Bhumipol.

The latter turned out, however, to be a long journey with many stages. While the coup succeeded in freezing the deep societal conflict over the country's hegemonic social contract, a complex set of interests, challenges and constraints ushered in a period of fearful uncertainty and volatility reflected by successive attempts to restate the constitutional basic structure.

The post-coup Interim Constitution 2014, a 2015 draft and the 2016 bill of the regular constitution as well as the finally adopted 2017 Constitution all represent different, if not diverging notions of the DRKH pointing at tectonic movements at the heart of both the Thai society and its constitutionalism.

All these efforts culminated in repeated attempts to adjust the principle enshrined in the former section 7. A first dramatic shift was the restatement of this principle by the 2014 Interim Constitution (TC 2014), namely in form of its section 5. In a move that would have been unimaginable not long before, and even more unusual for a mere interim constitution, section 5 introduced two major novelties with respect to the former section 7. First, it required that a decision based on the unwritten principles of the DRKH would have to be in accordance with the written constitution. Secondly, the norm designated the actor charged to decide whether such decisions were in accordance with the written constitution. Depending on the type of case, this was either the National Legislative Assembly or the Constitutional.

These modifications turned the normative character of the principle upside down, transforming the acknowledgement of an unwritten "super-constitution" centered at monarchical prerogative into a reference to a merely subsidiary constitutional customary law. In this regard, by reshaping the reference to the DRKH in a way that receded to pre-1997 constitutionalism, the Interim Constitution dismantled the DRKH's most significant manifestation and evolutionary achievement since 1997. To compensate the normative vacuum left by this shift at the very center of the constitutional order, the Interim Constitution resorted to another novelty by granting the military junta an unprecedented status and power. To be read in conjuncture with section 5, section 44 conferred the undivided sovereign power to the chairman of the constitutionally institutionalized junta turning him into a commissarial governor of the sovereign power.

Although both innovations were dramatic, the long search for a permanent solution to redefine ultimate sovereignty did not stop there. Before a regular constitution was eventually promulgated in 2017 to replace the TC 2014, two further attempts to solve the pivotal problem had been made.

A first draft constitution worked out under Bowornsak's chairmanship in 2015 which was rejected in the end, kept section 5 in form of the TC 2014 and introduced as a last-minute change a so-called "crisis committee"[79] with unspecified and unchecked prerogative powers to "commit or suppress any action" in the event of a crisis or conflict in the country. This section 260 resembled a softer form of section 44 TC 2014.[80]

79 The Committee for Reform Strategy and National Reconciliation.

80 This resembled earlier versions of the 2007 Constitution draft that provided two different versions of a softer form of "crisis committee" in times of national crisis (sect. 68, para. 4).

The second draft constitution of 2016, crafted under the chairmanship of Meechai Ruchuphan, transferred the idea of such an unconstrained politburo-like body back to section 5 on the unwritten principles of the DRKH. This new version of section 5 looked entirely different. While it shifted the power to decide or act finally and bindingly on the basis of the unwritten principles of the DRKH to a joint committee consisting of the heads of the constitutional bodies, it no longer required that decisions would have to be made in accordance with the constitution and stipulated no instance for review. The new section 5, thus, combined the idea of a "crisis committee" with the original formulation of the former section 7 of the 1997/2007 Constitution effectively creating an ad hoc supreme leadership committee with comprehensive prerogative powers.

While section 5 restored a power center that operated above the written Constitution, it could only emulate section 7 as it could not fully root the immense powers it conveyed in a similarly tangible layer of normative ordering. The powers of the former section 7 were, after all, intimately linked to a whole body of rules, narratives and historical experiences of kingship that integrated norm, power and actor in a sort of Thai natural law and thus created a continuum of governance based on an elaborated kind of political theology.

This deficit in the new section 5's normative fabric underlines the constructive difficulty that the drafters had to cope with in their attempts to restate the constitutional order from its core while further tightening the anti-electoral screw. This restatement of the basic structure in a long transitional moment of the fading ninth reign seemed to leave the ultimate frame and basis of the constitutional order under a veil of uncertainty until the conditions changed again with the succession of Rama X to the throne in October 2016.

The new King returned the 2016 constitution bill that had already been approved by a national referendum, requesting three changes among which the most significant one was a return of section 5 to the formulation of the former section 7. Once the principle was restored in the form introduced in 1997, the Constitution was promulgated as the current 2017 Constitution.

This corresponded with a significant drive to forcefully bolster the royal position, followed by unprecedentedly challenging demands to reform the royal institution by a new protest movement. With these developments Thai constitutionalism edges at the possibility of the dawn of a fifth phase. The royalist version of it could resemble a return to pre-1932 governance indicated as a possibility by a number of incidents. As an example, in the wake of the first post-coup elections in 2019, the cabinet delivered its oath of office before the King without the constitutionally prescribed commitment to upholding the constitution. Requested to decide about the constitutionality of the omission, the Constitutional Court declined in a unanimous decision to rule on the case declaring the oath to the King was not under its authority to review. The notion that the Constitution could become decoupled from an unwritten layer of order defining an absolute royal position is reinforced by the failure of authorities to convincingly respond to or at least explain the disappearance of historic monuments commemorating the origins of the first phase of constitutionalism and its victory over the absolute monarchy. Ironically, one of the revolutionary memorials having been mysteriously removed became the symbol of the 2020 protests that are demanding a reform of the royal institution and its relation to the constitutional order.

Whereas the 2014 Coup froze the deep divisive conflict of the Thai society, continuing constitutional volatility just started since then. Whether the first paragraph of a fifth chapter of Thai constitutionalism is in the writing remains to be seen as much as the question which direction such a rewriting of constitutional history might take.

17

The 1991–1992 Judicial Crisis

Personalities or Principles?

Duncan McCargo[*]

The so-called 'judicial crisis' of 1991–2 centred on the controversial figure of Pramarn Chansue and conflicts between the judiciary and the two appointed governments of Anand Panyarachun that followed the February 1991 military coup. Claiming that elected politicians had become hopelessly corrupt, a junta known as the National Peace Keeping Council (NPKC) seized control of Thailand. Following a familiar script, the junta promised to reform the Constitution and to restore democracy in short order. However, the military leaders behind the NPKC did not assume executive power themselves. Instead, they appointed the distinguished former diplomat Anand Panyarachun as Prime Minister and gave him free rein to select most of his Cabinet members. Anand presided over a conservative, technocratic, reformist administration with a focus on updating legislation and modernising the bureaucracy. Anand's cabinet was widely praised as among the most competent ministerial teams ever assembled in Thailand. Despite its inauspicious beginnings in a military coup, Anand's first administration proved surprisingly successful. Except, that is, where judges were concerned.

During the crisis, Anand and his justice minister Prapasna Auychai stood accused of political interference in the appointment of senior judges, in a pivotal episode in the recent history of the Thai judiciary. Pramarn eventually emerged triumphant from the crisis and became a very powerful Supreme Court President thereafter: the debacle led directly to the separation of the Office of the Judiciary from the Ministry of Justice a few years later. Yet, many of the issues raised by the crisis continue to be extremely salient: most importantly, how far should Thai judges be permitted to regulate themselves?

Pramarn Chansue was a larger-than-life figure, a career judge with an unusually prominent public profile who served as President of the Supreme Court from 1992 to 1996. Pramarn held a Bachelor in law from Thammasat University and gained American graduate degrees from Yale and Pepperdine Universities. His career included spells as the Chief of Judicial Region 5 (the upper North) and Region 9 (the lower South).[1] The younger brother of former Senate speaker Van Chansue, Pramarn ushered in a new way of working for the Supreme Court. Unlike previous presidents, who had been very concerned to present an image of dignity and neutrality, he enjoyed close relations with top military officers and business tycoons, and held regular meetings with leading

[*] I should like to express my warm appreciation to the Leverhulme Trust for the award of a Major Research Fellowship to work on politics and justice in Thailand; to Andrew Harding, Munin Pongsapan and Khemthong Tonsakulrungruang for their comments and assistance; and to the colleagues and research assistants who contributed to the project in various ways.

[1] See 'Leading Jurist Pramarn, 70, Dies', *The Nation*, 8 February 2007.

politicians including Chatchai Choonavan, Banharn Silpa-archa, Montri Pongphanit, Sanan Kajornprasert and Chavalit Yongchaiyudh.[2] After retiring from the judiciary, he served for a time as an appointed Senator, passing away from a lung infection at the age of seventy.

After he was appointed Prime Minister by the military junta led by General Suchinda Kraprayoon in 1991, Anand made Prapasna Auychai Minister of Justice. Prapasna was an ex-Vice-President of the Supreme Court, who, like Anand, had studied in Britain.[3] Anand assumed that, as a former senior judge, Prapasna would be well qualified for the post: by his own later admission, Anand failed to grasp the extent and the nature of factional infighting inside the Ministry and the judiciary.[4] Prapasna, who was aligned with a rival faction to that of Pramarn Chansue, then the Justice Ministry's Permanent Secretary,[5] nominated another candidate, Sawat Chotipanch, for the position of Supreme Court President coveted by Pramarn, and uproar ensued.

Prior to 1997, the Courts of Justice were overseen by the government of the day, through the Ministry of Justice. Judicial appointments and assignments were in the hands of the Judicial Commission, which also oversaw the conduct of judges. The Judicial Commission comprised twelve members: the President of the Supreme Court, Chief Justice of the Court of Appeal, the most senior Vice-President of the Supreme Court, the Permanent Secretary of the Ministry of Justice and eight judges who were elected by their peers.

According to Article 20 of the Act on Judicial Service of the Courts of Justice (1978), matters concerning the appointment, promotion and transfers of judges originated with the Minister of Justice, who would forward proposals to the Judicial Commission, which in turn had the authority to make decisions on all matters affecting the assignment of judges. After examining the proposals, the Judicial Commission would send its resolutions to the Minister of Justice for implementation. However, if the Minister of Justice disagreed with the Judicial Commission's resolutions, the Minister had the power to veto them within thirty days and to ask the Commission to reconsider. Following any reconsideration, the Judicial Commission's decision would be final: the Minister was no longer empowered to veto the proposal and was obliged to report the Commission's resolution to the Prime Minister. The latter would then forward the Judicial Commission's final list to the King for royal signature, after which the appointments would take effect. From 1983 onwards, a tradition was established that the Judicial Commission would consider all appointments and transfers once a year, every September, and would not make any decisions on these matters except in response to ministerial proposals.[6] The system was a recipe for conflict between the executive and the judiciary.

The judicial crisis first erupted following a development on 19 August 1991: Minister Prapasna abruptly withdrew his own proposal to the Judicial Commission for Pramarn to step down from his post as Permanent Secretary and return to the judiciary. Prapasna had made the proposal in response to a request from Pramarn earlier that month – but then the

[2] See Piyanart Vorasiri and Oueiporn Techutrakul, 'เส้น ทางการ เมือง ของ ประมาณ ชัน ซือ [Pramarn Chansue's Political Direction]' (1995) 18 (2), Issue 993 (76) *Arthit* 20–3.

[3] Prapasana was also a former speaker of the House of Representatives, and a former President of the Thammasat University Council.

[4] For exhaustive details of the judicial crisis during Anand Panyarachun's first administration which inform the first part of this chapter, see Pong Santi (ed.), *บันทึกลับวิกฤตการณ์ตุลาการ* [Secret Notes on the Judicial Crisis] (no publisher or place of publication, 1992).

[5] See Dominic Faulder, *Anand Panyarachun and the Making of Modern Thailand* (Singapore: Editions Didier Millett, 2018) 364.

[6] Pong, *บันทึกลับ*, 463.

minister got wind of a rumour that the Judicial Commission might immediately appoint Pramarn as President of the Supreme Court, thereby upending the judiciary's seniority system.[7] At fifty-five, Pramarn was very young for this promotion, which would have given him a rare five-year term as President. Prapasna declared that he needed more time to consider the request. However, the Judicial Commission, meeting that day, viewed the withdrawal of the proposal as highly irregular and proceeded to consider the issue regardless. The Commission went on to approve Pramarn's transfer back to the judiciary and to appoint him as a Vice-President of the Supreme Court with effect from 2 October, replacing another judge who was retiring at the end of September. The Judicial Commission also asked the minister urgently to submit a list of judges to be appointed to senior posts – including the positions of President and Vice-Presidents of the Supreme Court – otherwise the Commission would proceed to discuss these appointments at its next meeting, without any ministerial input. In the event, Prapasna failed to propose any names for these top positions for the subsequent meetings of the Judicial Commission held on 26 August and 2 September. On 2 September, seven Judicial Commission members (a bare majority) voted to consider these top judicial appointments despite not having received a ministerial proposal, while the remaining five Commission members argued that this procedure was illegitimate and proceeded to walk out. The remaining members invoked Article 40 of the relevant 1978 Act, arguing that this provision granted the Judicial Commission the right to make decisions on certain issues without ministerial approval.

According to the Judicial Commission's minutes for 2 September 1991,[8] the remaining members proceeded to review the potential candidates in order of seniority. They began with Sawat Chotpanich, the most senior candidate, who was ironically one of the members of the Commission who had just walked out. Sawat lacked experience of judging cases, since he had worked mainly in administrative positions and had never served in the Supreme Court. Commission members also expressed concerns about his honesty and financial probity. On this basis, Sawat was not qualified to become President. The second most senior candidate Siang Treewimon was also viewed as unqualified because of an alleged drinking problem. The Judicial Commission also had reservations about the third most senior candidate, Thaworn Tantraporn, arguing that he was not very articulate either orally or in writing: again, they believed he was not qualified to be President. The fourth most senior candidate was Pramarn, who renounced his claim for the post. Accordingly, the Judicial Commission appointed Prawit Khamparat, the fifth most senior candidate, as President of the Supreme Court. The following were appointed as Vice-Presidents (in order of seniority): Pramarn Chansue; Chusak Bunditkul and Kiang Bunperm.

Justice Minister Prapasna rejected the Judicial Commission's resolution as illegal for two main reasons. First, he had not submitted any proposed candidates for the appointments, and so the Commission had no legal authority to come up with its own names. Second, Prawit, Pramarn and Kiang were all among the seven members of the Judicial Commission that had made the appointments – but each judge had left the room when his own case was considered, leaving only six Commission members to make each decision. Seven members had to be present for the meeting to be quorate. Throughout the month of September, Prapasna stalled for time, refusing either to submit his own nominations or to endorse the Judicial Commission's proposal. It was widely understood that he was waiting for the end of

[7] Pong, *บันทึกลับ*, 10–11. For background on the workings of the Thai judiciary, see Duncan McCargo, *Fighting for Virtue: Justice and Politics in Thailand* (Ithaca, NY: Cornell University Press, 2019).

[8] Cited in Pong, *บันทึกลับ*, 40–50.

the month, when the current President Sopon Rattanakorn and two of the Vice-Presidents (who also served on the Judicial Commission) would retire. Prapasna then planned to appoint acting officers to the posts of President, Vice-President and Permanent Secretary, who would vote in favour of Sawat Chotpanich as President. If Prapasna had nominated Sawat in August or September, his nomination would have been rejected by the majority of the Judicial Commission, who would have insisted on appointing Prawit. Although Prapasna could have vetoed their decision, the wording of the 1978 law meant that the Judicial Commission would ultimately have triumphed.

On 28 September, around 500 dissatisfied judges held a gathering at which they formed a group known as the Working Group for the Independence of Judicial Power,[9] with Udom Fuengfong as head and Vicha Mahakun as secretary.[10] The group expressed support for the Judicial Commission's proposed appointments and urged the Minister of Justice to resign, since his inappropriate behaviour was tantamount to interference by the executive branch in the judiciary. Four members of the group later called on Prime Minister Anand Panyarachun at Government House, asking him to dismiss Prapasna – a meeting that, as then Deputy Cabinet Secretary-General Wissanu Krea-ngam drily notes, 'did not help improve the situation in any way'.[11] The working group subsequently went on to declare that if Prapasna made any temporary appointments to replace those key officials who were due to retire at the end of September, they would neither accept nor co-operate with them. However, another clique of around 60 judges declared that the working group was not representative of the judiciary as a whole, and declared their support for Minister Prapasna, who they insisted had acted lawfully and simply tried to follow the traditional seniority system of the judiciary.

At the beginning of October, when three former key members of the Judicial Commission had retired, and Pramarn was no longer serving as Permanent Secretary, Prapasna controversially made a series of temporary appointments: Jaran Hatthakam as Acting Permanent Secretary, Siang Treewimon as Acting President of the Supreme Court, and Thaworn, Chusak, and Pramarn as Acting Vice-Presidents. Crucially, however, Pramarn was not designated the most senior of the three Supreme Court Vice-Presidents, which meant he no longer had a seat on the Judicial Commission – while Jaran and Thaworn now did.

Prapasna proposed to appoint Sawat Chotpanich as President of the Supreme Court, and the following as Vice-Presidents in order of seniority: Thaworn, Chusak and Pramarn. He nominated Prasert Bunsri as Permanent Secretary of the Ministry of Justice, while Prawit Khamparat – who had been proposed as President of the Supreme Court by the old Judicial Commission – would serve as a Chief Justice of the Supreme Court.[12] In the event, Acting President Siang Treewimon recused himself from chairing the first meeting of the new Judicial Commission on 3 October, handing over to Sak Sanongchat, the most senior judge present. The main item on the agenda was the high-level judicial appointments. The Commission endorsed most of the Minister's appointments and even requested the Ministry

9 In Thai, คณะทำงานเพื่อความเป็นอิสระของอำนาจตุลาการ.

10 See Vicha Mahakun, *บันทึกประวัติศาสตร์ 100 ปี กระทรวงยุติธรรม: การต่อสู้เพื่อ ความเป็นอิสระของ อำนาจตุลาการ กรกฎาคม 2534 – มีนาคม 2535* [Historical Record, 100 Years of the Ministry of Justice: The Struggle for the Independence of Judicial Power, July 1991 to March 1992] (Bangkok: Working Group for the Independence of Judicial Power, Group to Protect the Judicial Institution 1992) 50. The first 117 pages of Vicha's book contain his own firsthand account of the initial phase of the judicial crisis from an anti-Prapasna perspective. They are followed by more than 300 pages of invaluable contemporary documents, including meeting transcripts.

11 Wissanu Krea-ngam *เล่าเรื่องผู้นำ* [Stories of Leaders] (2nd ed., Bangkok: Matichon Books, 2012) 97.

12 The impressive sounding post of 'Chief Justice of the Supreme Court' was actually a standard promotion: there were numerous Chief Justices, each of whom simply chaired a group *(ongkhana)* of three judges who worked together reviewing cases.

of Justice to investigate those judges who had instigated protests among the judicial community. However, the Judicial Commission declined to endorse promotions for Pramarn and Prawit, arguing that they had been involved in agitation against the Minister. Wissanu argues that by this point judges were divided into three different factions: those who were effectively supporting Prawit and Pramarn, those who were effectively supporting Sawat, and a third group, whom Wissanu describes as outwardly non-committal, but were actually more 'bewildered' by developments than genuinely neutral.[13]

The Judicial Commission's decision caused uproar and was immediately attacked by the Working Group. Critics argued that the resolution was unlawful because two of those who had taken part in the Commission meeting were not eligible to do so: Pramarn's return to the judiciary had not received the royal signature, so he (and not Jaran) was still technically Permanent Secretary of the Ministry; while Thaworn had only been assigned to work as a Vice- President of the Supreme Court, but not officially appointed as an Acting Vice-President. The Working Group asked the Prime Minister to reject the Commission's decision and not to forward it to the King for approval.

In response, Prapasna insisted that he was legally entitled to move a judge from the Ministry back to the courts without royal approval, since the person concerned already had the status of judge. Royal approval was only required for high-level assignments. In Pramarn's case, he had already been moved back to the courts and so was no longer Permanent Secretary; this meant he was not eligible to serve on the Judicial Commission. Prapasna also argued that as Minister he had a responsibility to make acting appointments to ensure the work of the judiciary could continue after people holding those positions retired; and that those holding acting appointments such as Thaworn and Jaran were entitled to take part in Judicial Commission meetings. Prapasna's actions were clearly designed to block Pramarn from manoeuvring his way into the Supreme Court Presidency.

Concerned that Prapasna was stirring up a hornet's nest that could lead to judicial insurrection, Prime Minister Anand Panyarachun reviewed the issue carefully; finally, the Cabinet asked for advice from the Council of State on the legality of the 3 October Judicial Commission resolution. The idea of consulting the Council of State originated from the distinguished jurist Meechai Ruchuphan, who served as Deputy Prime Minister and one of the government's chief legal advisors, but was regarded by many newspaper columnists as a Pramarn supporter. Deputy Cabinet Secretary-General Wissanu Krea-ngam faced similar perceptions of bias, since one of his relatives was a member of the pro-Pramarn judicial faction.[14] Pramarn also appealed directly to Anand, claiming that Prapasna's order transferring him back to the courts was illegal and could mean he was still technically Permanent Secretary of the Ministry of Justice. Anand duly forwarded Pramarn's complaint to the Council of State. However, the Cabinet decision to involve the Council of State actually worsened the crisis, since critics viewed it as further evidence that the executive was meddling with the judiciary. In practice, however, the Council of State was only empowered to provide non-binding legal opinions to the government of the day: It had no authority to overrule the Judicial Commission. In response, a group of pro-Pramarn judges declared the Cabinet's decision was nullified since it violated the provision of the 1978 Constitution that established the Judicial Commission as the body authorised to decide on judges' appointments and transfers. They asked the Prime Minister to forward the 3 October resolution to the King,

[13] Wissanu, เล่าเรื่องผู้นำ, 98.

[14] Wissanu, เล่าเรื่องผู้นำ, 100.

according to the law. Another group of lawyers asked Anand to remove Meechai from his post as Deputy Prime Minister because of his improperly advising that the Council of State become involved in the issue.

Following the Cabinet decision, the conflict between the two sides became more intense following the leak of a telephone conversation, which had apparently been secretly recorded around the end of September, possibly by the Pramarn faction, between two senior figures, one of whom appeared to be Prapasna. The two men discussed how to prevent their opponents – those who supported Prawit and Pramarn – from successfully appointing their preferred candidate as President of the Supreme Court. During the conversation, Prapasna explained that he had succeeded in persuading Anand to stop supporting Prawit and Pramarn. The apparent willingness of people sympathetic to the Pramarn camp to tap a ministerial telephone line showed just how much was at stake in the struggle. The recording also demonstrated that the conflict was not simply one between the Minister and some members of the judiciary and the Judicial Commission, but had spread to wider elites in Thai society. Even the Privy Council was divided into two groups: Jitti Tingsapat and Atsani Pramoj supported Prapasna, while Sanya Thammasak and Prakorb Hutasing backed the other side.[15] Privy Council President Sanya Thammasak was so preoccupied by the controversy that he asked Wissanu to give him an almost daily personal update at his house.[16]

Around a week before the end of October, the Council of State finally submitted its opinion to the Prime Minister. The majority view of the Council of State was that Pramarn's transfer from the ministry to the courts was not legally complete, since it had not received royal assent. According to this reading, Pramarn was still legally Permanent Secretary and so should have remained a member of the Judicial Commission; while Jaran was not officially acting Permanent Secretary, and should not have attended the Judicial Commission meeting on 3 October. These participatory irregularities invalidated the decisions taken at that meeting.

The Council of State's opinion left Anand on the horns of a dilemma. If he accepted the opinion and declined to forward the Judicial Commission's recommendations to the King, he would stand accused of interfering with the judiciary. This would have entailed a huge loss of face for Prapasna, as the Minister directly responsible. But if Anand decided to ignore the Council of State's advice and forwarded the Judicial Commission's appointments to the King, people would question why the Cabinet had bothered consulting the Council of State in the first place, and why the Prime Minister saw fit to reject its recommendations.

Prime Minister Anand finally broke the impasse by asking Prapasna to submit his concerns over the 3 October resolution for further consideration by the Judicial Commission. Prapasna could not simply veto the whole resolution, since it included various points he had himself requested, notably the appointment of Sawat as President of the Supreme Court. Thus, Prapasna had to ask the Judicial Commission to reconsider whether or not Jaran and Thaworn had been eligible to attend the 3 October Judicial Commission meeting. Prapasna attached the Council of State's dissenting opinion about their eligibility to his request.

The Judicial Commission convened on 4 November to reconsider the issues raised by the Minister. The Commission rejected the Council of State's opinion, arguing that its reasoning was unsound. The Judicial Commission insisted that its own resolution of 19 August was

15 Pong, *บันทึกลับ*, 337–45, 353.
16 Wissanu, เล่าเรื่องผู้นำ, 98.

sufficient to transfer Pramarn back to the courts, despite the lack of a royal signature for this move. The Judicial Commission then went over the decisions it had made on 3 October, including all of the senior appointments, and declared them final. The next step was for the King to approve the appointments.

Unsurprisingly, the Judicial Commission's decision infuriated the anti-Prapasna faction among the judiciary, and a large protest was planned for 9 November. The recently retired President of the Supreme Court Sopon Rattanakorn criticised Anand as an 'untrustworthy person', revealing that Anand had initially accepted Pramarn but then asked Sopon to find a 'less evil' compromise candidate for President of the Supreme Court.[17] Sopon also complained that many people had accused him of appointing Prawit as his interim successor with undue haste, but that he had done so at Anand's request. Later, Anand seemed to change his mind and wanted to find another candidate who was neither Pramarn, Sawat or Prawit, and who was not a party to the ongoing conflict. In response, Sopon told Anand his side was quite flexible and could accept anyone other than Sawat – but Prapasna was only happy with Sawat.[18] The pressure on the Prime Minister increased when academics from the law faculties of Thammasat, Chulalongkorn and Ramkhamhaeng universities petitioned the King, asking him to reject the Prime Minister's proposal and so avert a crisis.

On 6 November, Anand submitted the Judicial Commission's proposed appointments to the King, who signed off on them two days later. Sawat was retrospectively appointed President of the Supreme Court from 1 October. Although the pro-Pramarn judges still gathered as planned on 9 November, instead of continuing their protest they announced their acceptance of the royal approval: A temporary truce ensued. This brief interlude of calm did not last, however. The 3 October Judicial Commission meeting had set up a committee to investigate the judges who had been involved in agitating over the proposed appointments. After an investigation lasting almost four months, the committee produced a report that was extremely critical of the behaviour of many leading figures in the anti-Prapasna faction. Despite pleas to postpone any decision about punishing these judges until the formation of a newly elected Judicial Commission in March 1992, the existing Commission pressed ahead on 17 February, dismissing five judges – including Prawit and Pramarn – from the judiciary without pensions, dismissing six others with pensions, and ordering that two other judges be placed on probation.[19]

In light of strong opposition from the judiciary to these severe punishments (Thai judges are very rarely dismissed, and then only in cases involving serious corruption or abuse of power), Prapasna vetoed the resolution and asked the Judicial Commission to reconsider it. The Judicial Commission agreed to reduce the punishments so that the five judges it had planned to dismiss would be permitted to resign, and so receive their pensions. Again, Anand was obliged to submit this controversial decision to the King for approval – and faced considerable judicial opprobrium for doing so. However, Anand then added his own personal

[17] Wissanu, เล่าเรื่องผู้นำ, 96; Vicha, *บันทึกประวัติศาสตร์*, 36. This English phrase used by Anand (who is virtually bilingual) was widely quoted and caused outrage among judges. But while 'less evil' sounds dreadful when translated into Thai, the original meaning from the colloquial expression 'the lesser of two evils' is much milder.

[18] Pong, *บันทึกลับ*, 514–18.

[19] See 'Panel Confirms Dismissal Order for 11 Judges', *Bangkok Post Weekly Review*, 6 March 1992. The dismissed judges were Pramarn Chansue, Veerachai Sootsuwan, Prawit Khamparat, Udom Fuangfung, Vinai Vimolseth (dismissed without pension); and Manit Chitchanklab, Vicha Mahakun, Kiat Jatanilphan, Pramote Chanphanond, Chanthawat Worathatat and Atthavit Vathanavinij (dismissed with pension). Bandhit Rachatanan and Chuchart Srisaeng were placed on probation.

opinion to the proposal, asking the King to grant clemency to the eleven judges obliged to leave their positions. The judges themselves also submitted two petitions to the palace.

The King decided to accept Anand's advice: The dismissed judges were kept on, but were placed on probation. This made them ineligible for promotion, though they were now eligible to become members of the Judicial Commission. The King was widely praised for resolving the crisis, although the legal basis on which he was able to grant clemency was obscure. Clemency for the rogue judges prefigured King Bhumibol's 20 May 1992 'resolution' of the 'Black May' protests and violence by giving Prime Minister Suchinda Kraprayoon and opposition leader Chamlong Srimuang a televised dressing-down: A royal intervention that strengthened the legitimacy and prestige of the throne, and was later seen as among the King's finest hours.

Anand declared at the time, on his last full working day in office before the 22 March general election:

> I believe all the judicial officials who have been plagued with divisiveness and factionalism will be grateful to His Majesty the King for his mercy, and this will recreate unity in the judiciary as it marks its 100th anniversary on March 25 ... I want to see solidarity and unity in the judiciary so that judicial officials can still have the people's respect.[20]

Alas, Anand spoke too soon: the conflicts inside the judiciary were deep-rooted and about to erupt all over again. Conflicts between the Ministry of Justice and the courts had been in existence long before the Pramarn-centred crisis. According to one senior judge, judges were very unhappy with the actions of the government, especially following orders from the Ministry to cut judges' salaries.[21] As a result, judges were always calling for a separation of powers between the executive and the judiciary.

Sak Sanongchat, the chair of the Judicial Commission, later claimed that the conflict between the pro-Pramarn and pro-Sawat groups stemmed from the Judicial Commission's appointment decisions in September 1990, when Sawat was selected as Chief Justice of the Courts of Appeal, defeating some more senior candidates. As a result, the losing side became determined to have its revenge.[22] Some feared that the appointment of the Supreme Court President would directly influence the outcome of ongoing cases relating to the confiscation of assets belonging to ten former ministers, the so-called 'unusually rich' politicians who had been targeted by the National Peace Keeping Council following the February 1991 military coup.[23] Among these figures were former Prime Minister Chatichai Choonavan and several of Thailand's most prominent politicians. In the event, in March 1993, not long after Pramarn eventually became President, the Supreme Court exonerated all ten of these politicians, and the rulings of the assets examination committee set up by the 1991 junta were declared unconstitutional.[24] While there is no evidence to prove any connection between these developments, some very wealthy and influential people were big Pramarn supporters.

As a result, Thailand's judicial crisis did not quietly end when Pramarn and his associates were restored to their posts. Anand became embroiled in a new round of controversy when he became Prime Minister for a second time in May 1992. A list of judicial appointments, including Pramarn's, which should have been forwarded to the King for approval was still

20 See 'King Pardons Judges Facing Dismissal', *Bangkok Post Weekly Review*, 20 March 1992.

21 Pong, *บันทึกลับ*, 88.

22 Pong, *บันทึกลับ*, 270.

23 Pong, *บันทึกลับ*, 298.

24 Nopporn Wong Anan and Paul M. Sherer, '"Unusually Rich" Ministers Survive Scandal in Thailand', *Wall Street Journal*, 5 December 1996.

languishing in the prime-ministerial in tray, having been passed over by the short-lived Suchinda Kraprayoon government. Frustrated by the byzantine workings of the Judicial Commission, Anand decided to issue a decree that would reconstitute the Commission and include a number of non-judges among its membership. Senior legal minds, including Bowornsak Uwanno (then dean of the Chulalongkorn University Law Faculty), Phongthep Thepkanjana and Anand's own Cabinet Deputy Secretary-General Wissanu Krea-ngam, strongly urged him against it. On 11 September 1992, on what was his government's last effective day in office, Anand issued an executive decree replacing the existing Judicial Commission with a new body comprising twenty-eight members: twenty-two appointees and only six elected by the judiciary.[25] Anand's reform was thrown out by the newly elected Parliament less than a month later.[26]

Soon after Anand stepped down following his second stint as Prime Minister, Pramarn Chansue became President of the Supreme Court, serving an unusually long four-year term of office (1992–6). Suwit Khunkhitti, who became Minister of Justice in the newly elected Chuan Leekpai government, had again tried to block Pramarn's appointment and nominated Thaworn as the next President, but was ultimately thwarted by the Judicial Commission.[27] – A famously independent-minded judge whose motivations were not entirely clear subsequently pursued a criminal case against Anand, accusing him of abuse of power for not having submitted the list of judicial appointments for royal signature. The case dragged on for four years until Anand was finally acquitted. At one point, Sanya Thammasak invited Anand and Pramarn to lunch, hoping to mediate and bring the embarrassing court case to a close. But Pramarn insisted that Anand make him an apology, which Anand refused to do.[28] Many of those judges who had supported Pramarn continued to believe that he was the victim of a political witch-hunt: They insisted they had acted out of principle, rather than because of any personal allegiance.[29] Pramarn's critics, by contrast, believed that his larger-than-life personality and his fondness for socialising with prominent figures made him ill-suited for high judicial office.

In a different decade, Pramarn might have made a successful post-judicial career move into electoral politics, but it was not to be. Before he retired, Pramarn was courted by a number of political parties, and flirted with the idea of running for office. The weekly news magazine *Arthit* ran a flattering cover story portraying Pramarn as a new-style leader who was broad-minded, decisive and charismatic – in sharp contrast to then Prime Minister Chuan Leekpai.[30] After his retirement from the judiciary in 1996, Pramarn actually joined Chavalit Yongchaiyudh's New Aspiration Party, but never won elected office. Pramarn made an unsuccessful, highly controversial attempt in 1997 to become chair of the Counter-Corruption Commission: His nomination was torpedoed by the Senate, which viewed him as too close to then Prime Minister Chavalit.[31] The episode demonstrated that Pramarn – who sent explanatory letters to judges all over the country after his nomination was rejected – was

25 '500 Thai Judges Protest against Judicial Revamp', *The Straits Times*, 15 September 1992.

26 'Thai Lower House Rejects Judiciary Reform Decree', *Xinhua General News Service*, 7 October 1992; Faulder, *Anand*, 366–8.

27 'Dispute over Senior Judicial Posts Settled', *The Straits Times*, 13 November 1992.

28 Duncan McCargo, interview with Anand Panyarachun, 29 September 2018.

29 Interview with former judge Vicha Mahakun, 27 August 2019.

30 Piyanart Vorasiri and Oueiporn Techutrakul, 'เปิดใจ ... ประมาณ ชันซือ "ผมอาจเป็นภาพลวงตาก็ได้" [Revealing Pramarn Chansue "I Might Be a Mirage"]' (1995) 18 (2), Issue 993 (76) *Arthit* 18–24.

31 '250,000 Thais Must Declare Assets Under the New Charter', *The Straits Times*, 18 October 1997.

still eager to deploy his considerable residual influence, but was no longer at the height of his powers.

Ironically, today Praman Chansue is not remembered primarily for his role in the 1991–2 judicial crisis. Fellow judges may like to recall his various achievements as President of the Supreme Court, which include founding the Judicial Training Institute – featuring certificate programmes that allow non-judges to study alongside senior members of the judiciary – and especially his policy change that allowed senior judges to be reappointed to the bench until the age of sixty-five. But among the wider Thai population, Pramarn became best known as the victim of a bizarre failed 1993 murder plot allegedly involving top Bangkok architect Rangsan Torsuwan,[32] who was eventually found guilty in September 2008 and sentenced to twenty-five years in jail, before being acquitted by the Court of Appeal in 2010. Rangsan's purported motives for wanting to murder Pramarn were always rather murky, but Rangsan's wife was a senior judge, and he was a good friend of Pramarn's former rival Sawat.[33] In the event, Pramarn died from natural causes in 2007, the year before Rangsan was convicted.

The 1991–2 judicial crisis led directly to the removal of the Courts of Justice from the supervision of the Ministry of Justice, under the provisions of the 1997 Constitution, a separation maintained under the subsequent 2007 and 2017 Constitutions. Prime Ministers and Ministers of Justice are no longer involved in judicial appointments and promotions: the Thai judiciary has become an essentially self-regulating body. In principle at least, top judicial appointments are based solely on seniority: judges are ranked based on their performance in their original entrance examinations, and carry these numerical rankings throughout their careers.[34] Whoever takes the main entrance examination at age twenty-five and comes out top is in pole position eventually to become President of the Supreme Court.

Most judges will insist that the Anand-era crisis illustrated the importance of judicial independence and the need to prevent politicians or partisan outsiders from interfering in the workings of the courts. For all the merits of this argument, it greatly oversimplifies the murky and ambiguous sequence of events at the time and the complicated issues involved. While neither Prapasna nor Anand covered themselves in glory during the judicial crisis, the internecine conflicts inside the judiciary were not entirely a problem of ministerial making.

Judicial politics at the time closely resembled the factional infighting that characterised the Royal Thai Army during the same period, which saw Suchinda Kraprayoon's Army Cadet School Class 5 stage a coup that reflected a longstanding feud with Class 7, whose 'Young Turk' members included Manoon Roopkajorn and Chamlong Srimuang.[35] Pramarn Chansue was a hugely polarising figure whose assertive personality split the monarchical network – including the Privy Council – down the middle.[36] In many ways, Pramarn's rise prefigured that of controversial Prime Minister Thaksin Shinawatra a decade later: how could the conservative Thai establishment cope with a dominant personality who challenged conventional modes of deference and hierarchy? The elite was torn between embracing and domesticating Pramarn/Thaksin, and trying to expel him from the fold.

32 Kamol Henkietisak, 'Famed Architect Arrested', *Bangkok Post*, 9 June 1993.

33 'Election Commission Candidates', *The Nation*, 6 November 1997.

34 See McCargo, *Fighting for Virtue*, 35.

35 See Duncan McCargo, *Chamlong Srimuang and the New Thai Politics* (London: Hurst 1997) 41–50; 244.

36 On this concept, see Duncan McCargo, 'Network Monarchy and Legitimacy Crises in Thailand' (2005) 18(4) *The Pacific Review* 499–519.

The judiciary has long enjoyed a complicated relationship with unelected governments. As David Streckfuss has demonstrated, the courts have never challenged the right of the army to seize power in a coup, despite the fundamental illegality of such power-grabs.[37] But while elected governments have tiptoed nervously in their dealings with the judiciary, military-appointed regimes have been more willing to take judges in hand. It is debatable whether Prapasna would have dared make such bold interventions in the Judicial Commission's decisions if he had been accountable to an elected Parliament. The judiciary was well aware that the junta was in the process of drafting the new 1991 Constitution, and judges were nervous about any changes to the composition or workings of the Judicial Commission that might increase outside control over their affairs. Judicial concerns about military rule peaked in 2006, when the junta actually briefly abolished the Constitutional Court, and added two externally selected members to the Judicial Commission in the subsequent 2007 Constitution. As during Anand's time, elections to the Judicial Commission continued to be rather problematic: judges readily replicated the negative campaigning behaviour they were so quick to criticise in politicians.[38]

The unusual moral authority of Prime Minister Anand Panyarachun – backed up by his known proximity to King Bhumibol – also provided Prapasna with an unusual degree of cover for his actions. Despite his Cambridge law degree, Anand initially had little idea just what a mess he was getting himself into: he later came to believe the Ministry of Justice was barely functioning during his time as Prime Minister.[39] Reflecting on the episode, Anand later argued that the Thai judiciary was 'a very archaic system' involving 'a lot of inbreeding'.[40] By contrast Vicha Mahakun ended his commentary on the first phase of the judicial crisis on a dramatic note. Invoking the fate of short-lived Prime Minister Suchinda Kraprayoon, who was forced to resign from office after he ordered the shooting dead of innocent protestors in May 1992, Vicha declared: 'Sinners receive inescapable punishments for the sins they have committed. This is an undeniable truth. Thus, those who have wronged the judicial circle shall be given severe and instant punishments.'[41]

Far from being severely punished, Anand was reappointed Prime Minister by the King for a brief second term from June to September 1992. This time, however, Anand did not put Prapasna back in the justice portfolio, having concluded that during the first wave of the judicial crisis his Minister was 'part of the problem, too'.[42] Anand's second term was a rare juncture in Thai politics: his was now effectively a royal government, and Anand was bold enough to use his four months in office to challenge the military elite (who were very unpopular in the wake of the army's shooting dead dozens of unarmed protestors in the events of 'Bloody May'),[43] demoting key army commanders and abolishing the notorious Internal Peacekeeping Command.[44] Anand approached the judiciary in much the same way:

37 David Streckfuss, *Truth on Trial: Defamation, Treason, and Lèse-Majesté* (Abingdon: Routledge, 2011) 118–21. See also Chapter 18, this volume.

38 See Amnat Chotichawaranont, ความคิดเห็นของผู้พิพากษาศาลยุติธรรม ต่อระบบการสรรหา คณะกรรมการตุลาการศาลยุติธรรม (ก.ต.) ตามรัฐธรรมนูญ ฉบับปัจจุบัน พุทธศักราช 2550 [Judges' Opinions on the Selection System of the Judicial Commission According to the Current 2007 Constitution], Paper prepared for the Senior Executives' Training Program [Bo Yo So] Class 12, (College of Justice, Courts of Justice, 2009) 61–5.

39 Faulder, *Anand*, 364–5.

40 Faulder, *Anand*, 364 and 366.

41 Vicha, *บันทึกประวัติศาสตร์*, 117.

42 Faulder, *Anand*, 366.

43 On the May events, see McCargo, *Chamlong Srimuang*, 239–74.

44 Surin Maisrikrod, 'Thailand 1992: Repression and Return of Democracy' in Daljit Singh (ed.), *Southeast Asian Affairs 1993* (Singapore: ISEAS, 1993) 335–6.

exasperated by their shenanigans during his first term, he was intent on reforming the Judicial Commission to prevent any repetition of the Pramarn fiasco. Unfortunately, he reckoned without Pramarn's ability to lobby Parliament and defeat his emergency legislation; he also underestimated the extent to which even jurists who disliked Pramarn could be enlisted to the shared cause of preserving judicial autonomy.

Long after Anand had failed in his attempts to reform the Judicial Commission, judges continued to resist any further changes. Critics had always argued that non-judges, such as senior members of the Bar Council, ought to sit on committees investigating ethical and disciplinary lapses by judges. Judges, however, insisted on the power to regulate themselves and tended to look askance at non-judge appointments. When NIDA professor Medhi Krongkaew was appointed to the Judicial Commission by the National Legislative Assembly following the 2014 military coup, eighteen lawyers sent a letter of protest to Supreme Court President Direk Ingkaninan, who forwarded the petition to the President of the Assembly.[45] The lawyers alleged that Medhi was unqualified, morally unsuitable and was himself facing criminal charges. By appearing to endorse their letter, Direk echoed many judges' unease at the appointment process for external Judicial Commission members. The subtext here was that judges believed only fellow judges were truly qualified to serve on the Commission. In the event, Medhi remained in office.

Following the May 2014 military coup, the first Constitution Drafting Committee, chaired by Bowornsak Uwanno, proposed changes to the composition of the Judicial Commission, which would have increased the number of non-judge members from a fixed number of two, to an ambiguously worded 'not less than 1 in 3' – with the implication that outsiders could even form the majority.[46] The proposal met with fierce resistance from the judiciary, provoking a petition signed by 1,380 judges.[47] The signatories declared that they supported reforms that would bring real benefits to the justice system or the people, but it was important that any changes were not counter-productive. They raised seven objections to the changes proposed in the draft Constitution, which they argued would facilitate political interference and undermine the credibility of the Judicial Commission. While opponents of change argued they were concerned about possible political interference,[48] judges were also extremely resistant to any attempts to increase public scrutiny of their work. The 2015 draft Constitution also proposed that academic or legal experts could be appointed to positions as Supreme Court Judges. In the end, the draft was voted down by the National Reform Council, and these proposals went nowhere.[49] Ironically, Bowornsak was one of those who had counselled Anand against reforming the Judicial Commission in 1992. More than twenty years later, Bowornsak had changed his mind, but his draft Constitution suffered the same fate as Anand's emergency decree: Voted down by an assembly controlled by conservative vested interests.

17.1 CONCLUDING REMARKS

The 1991–2 judicial crisis was partly about interference in the Thai judiciary by politicians. While today's judges have extracted from the story the simple moral that politicians must not

45 See '"กล้านรงค์-เมธี" ได้ปมกต. โร่แจงปธ.ศาลฎีกา ' ['"Klanarong-Medhi" Argue about Judicial Commission Tangle and Rush to Explain to the Supreme Court'], 2 November 2014, www.khaosod.co.th/view_news.php?newsid=TUROdo1ERXdNVEF5TVRFMU53PTo=.

46 See Article 225, 29 March 2015 version, draft Constitution.

47 See จดหมายเปิดผนึก [Open Letter], 17 June 2015, signed by 1,380 judges, including many senior administrators.

48 Duncan McCargo, interview with a judge, 8 July 2015.

49 For a discussion, see Duncan McCargo, 'Peopling Thailand's 2015 Draft Constitution' (2015) 37(3) *Contemporary Southeast Asia* 329–54.

be allowed to meddle in judicial appointments and decisions, there was much more to the crisis than that. The story was also about a prominent judge who became in effect a politician in his own right, polarising the judiciary from within. While the contestation over Pramarn's appointment was generally framed in terms of questions of legality and legitimacy (who exactly had the right to make such decisions?), these were also personality-based struggles, reflecting competing views of Pramarn's *nak leng* (generous tough-guy) style. The crisis would never have arisen, had judges themselves not been divided over Pramarn's domineering personality.

Pramarn Chansue himself is no longer with us, while Anand Panyarachun has now retired from public life. Yet, the issues raised by this troubling episode remain extremely salient. Judges will still fight tooth and nail to prevent outsiders from scrutinising them. Unfortunately, the judiciary remains largely unaccountable to wider society and has yet to convince the public that it can always be trusted to regulate itself. Accordingly, while the social and political context has changed significantly since the Anand era, the possibility of a future judicial crisis cannot be discounted.

18

Without Account

Coups, Amnesties and Justice in Thailand

Tyrell Haberkorn

18.1 INTRODUCTION

Following the end of the absolute monarchy on 24 June 1932, there have been twelve 'successful' – meaning that the coup-makers seized power – coups in Thailand.[1] There is a number of explanations as to how and why the military and other powerful figures involved in fomenting coups have been able to get away with so many of them. Of the available explanations, the one that I take up in this chapter is the role of amnesty laws. Impunity has been secured in eight coups by stand-alone laws, in two coups by articles in post-coup constitutions, in one coup by both a constitutional article and a stand-alone law, and in only one case with no special legal measure promulgated. Each amnesty article or law has retroactively legalised the coup in question and protected the coup-makers from possible prosecution or other sanction. In each instance, the amnesty has turned the illegal act of rebellion into a legal, administrative action. Over time, the repeated amnesties have institutionalised the emptying of democracy and the removal of the role of the people in the Thai polity.

I take the repetition of coup amnesty laws as a point of departure and an invitation to think explicitly about the production of impunity and its undoing. By impunity, I mean the failure to secure accountability for state violence, and in the specific case of coups, for the illegal destruction of the constitutional order. In several cases, prior, simultaneous, or subsequent violence, sometimes given a legal gloss by the resulting regime, is also temporally covered by the amnesty laws, meaning that the laws are written in such a way to extend their coverage to periods both before and after the specific moment of the coup. By the undoing of impunity, I mean the imagination of judicial and legislative actions in the service of accountability, which would make a coup actually an illegal action with consequences for anyone who foments one. My interest in repetition is inspired by Kojin Karatani's view of transformation over time in Japanese history, in which he uses a Marxian lens to examine empire and crisis during the Meiji (1868–1912) and Showa (1926–89) periods to identify hegemonic processes and moments of revolutionary opening. He argues that 'When we say that history repeats itself, what counts is not the events that repeat, but the structure of repetition. Sometimes, the structure of repetition may accompany the event … we must comprehend the structure of

[1] To be clear: 'successful' here means that the officers assumed the seat of the prime minister and never found themselves sleeping behind bars in prison. The experience of the people, particularly those who come to be seen as dissident, has frequently been less pleasant during or in the aftermath of coups.

repetition itself instead of focusing on the similarity of phenomenal events.'[2] Attention to the transformation of the coup amnesty laws over time in Thailand becomes a lens through which to view political history and comprehend the changing stakes of maintaining the ability of the powerful to overturn the system of governance at will. The structure of the repetition here is the 'successful' coup followed by the promulgation of a coup amnesty.

Retrospectively, the history of amnesty laws can seem specific to the coups that generated them and the particular contexts – of struggles over power between different military factions, fear of Communism, fear of Thaksin, and the end of the reign of King Rama IX. But over the past eighty-eight years since Thailand became a constitutional regime, the repeated amnesties have gathered force. Resonant with the increasing use of law to sacralise the king (see Chapter 6, this volume) and the increased dispossession of the people's rights through successive constitutions (see Chapter 17, this volume), each iterative amnesty law draws both epistemologically and politically on prior laws.

In an essay written after the 19 September 2006 coup, Somchai Preechasilpakul argued that the string of amnesty laws, and the foreclosure of even the possibility of prosecution for criminal acts, therefore serve as an incentive for would-be coup-makers.[3] David Streckfuss suggests that the repeated passage of amnesty laws is a process that gathers salience and legitimacy over time and entails the resetting of the political order through violence and sacrifice.[4] While this process acquires a particular meaning within a Thai Theravada Buddhist context which prizes a continual process of purification and the cultivation of virtue, the result is also an explicitly secular one: avoidance of criminal prosecution and sleeping behind bars.

In the remainder of this chapter, I reflect on how the repetition of amnesty laws has foreclosed the possibility of prosecution for criminal acts and consider how this repetition might cease. I proceed in two parts. First, I trace the history of coup amnesty laws and the structure of the repetition of the evasion of accountability contained in the law. Coup amnesty laws in Thailand are short: four articles only. The first article names the law, the second indicates when it goes into force, the third describes who/what/when is covered by it, and the fourth stipulates who is responsible for its enforcement. The critical article is the

2 Kojin Karatani, Lecture at UCLA on ' History and Repetition Today' 5 April 2012, www.kojinkaratani.com/en/talks/history-and-repetition-today.html accessed 30 May 2019. Also see Kojin Karatani, *History and Repetition* (New York: Columbia University Press, 2012).

3 สมชาย ปรีชาศิลปกุล [Somchai Preechasilpakul], 'หลักนิติรัฐประหาร' ['The coup rule of law'] in ธนาพล อิ๋วสกุล [Thanapol Eawsakul] (ed.), *รัฐประหาร 19 กันยา: รัฐประหารเพื่อระบอบประชาธิปไตยอันมีพระมหากษัตริย์ทรงเป็นประมุข*, บรรณาธิการ [*The 19 September Coup: Coup for Democracy with the King as Head of State*] (Bangkok: Fa Diew Kan, 2007), 192. Alongside the amnesty laws, a jurisprudence in support of the legality of fomenting coups has also been developed through a series of Supreme Court decisions (Supreme Court Decision nos. 1874/2492 (1949), 1153–1154/2495 (1952), 45/2496 (1953), 1512–1515/2497 (1954), 1662/2505 (1962), 1234/2523 (1980), 2376/2526 (1983), and 6411/2534 (1991)). See รังสิมันต์ โรม และ ปิยวัฒน์ สัตยพานิช [Rangsiman Rome and Piyawat Satyapanich], 'เมื่อตุลาการเข้าข้างกบฏ: ปัญหาการใช้และตีความกฎหมายอาญามาตรา 113 และ 114 ของศาลไทย' ['When the Judiciary Sides with Rebellion: Problems of Use and Interpretation of Articles 113 and 114 of the Criminal Code by Thai Courts'] (2015) 13(2) *Fa Diew Kan* 117–39. This is then reinforced by how history is taught within the military, as Chanan Yodhong argues in a fascinating article: see ชานันท์ ยอดหงษ์ [Chanan Yodhong], 'ประวัติศาสตร์นิพนธ์และการเรียนประวัติศาสตร์ของทหารกับ การสร้างความชอบธรรมและ 'ชอบทำ' รัฐประหาร' ['Military historiography and study of history and the creation of 'legitimacy' for coups'] (2015) 13(2) *Fa Diew Kan*, 83–115.

4 Streckfuss describes how coups and amnesty laws function politically, and his use of the past tense in his general description also suggests how they serve as the writing of a particular form of history: 'The political order was reset. A new order was established by men of virtue (with guns). Their virtue allowed them to seize power not for themselves, but for the whole social and political order. However, they had to ritually purge themselves of the necessary violence by declaring an amnesty.' David Streckfuss, *Truth on Trial in Thailand: Defamation, Treason, and lèse-majesté* (New York: Routledge, 2011) 122.

third one. Beginning with the amnesty passed by the People's Party that resulted in the transformation from absolute to constitutional monarchy, which occupies an uncertain position with respect to the history of coups as I describe below, the third article undergoes constant transformation and expansion in terms of actions and figures provided with impunity. I offer a brief sketch of how the content of the eight stand-alone amnesty laws and three constitutional provisions have changed over time, with a particular focus on the third articles of the amnesty laws. I also analyse the notes appended to each law explaining its *raison d'être*, which were included beginning with the amnesty for Field Marshal Sarit Thanarat's first coup in 1957 and in which a logic of coups *as necessary* for the maintenance of order, the security of the nation and the preservation of the institution of the monarchy developed. Second, I turn to the most recent coup, that of 22 May 2014, to think through the specific possibilities and challenges of interrupting the repetition of impunity produced through coup amnesty laws. The National Council for Peace and Order (NCPO), which carried out the coup, opted for a constitutional provision rather than a stand-alone law. A civil society group, Resistant Citizen, challenged the legality of the coup in a criminal court case. In a series of decisions, all three criminal courts – first instance, appeal, and supreme – affirmed the legality of the coup.[5] The repetition of coup impunity seems secure. However, a careful reading of Resistant Citizen's challenge and the specific response of the courts provides an invitation to imagine a different outcome perhaps possible in a more democratic political moment.

18.2 A HISTORY OF COUPS AND COUP AMNESTY LAWS

A coup is 'a change of government [that] often issues from the threat or use of force against the incumbent regime'.[6] The series of twelve 'successful' coups and the resultant changes in power are one way to temporally divide the political history of Thailand from the end of absolute monarchy until the present. In doing so, regime change punctuates and breaks the calendar down into relatively short periods between coups. The resulting understanding of Thai political history is that the polity is marked by considerable instability. I instead propose that the series of coups be understood as a reflection of, and primary contributing factor to, enduring stability in the polity. What is stable is the ability of the military and other powerful actors to overturn the existing regime when they choose to do so. This stability is produced and guaranteed by the series of amnesty laws that has followed after each coup.

Although I long assessed the number of 'successful' coups as twelve by excluding the actions by the People's Party to depose the absolute monarchy on 24 June 1932 as a coup, the study of the history amnesty laws forced me to change my assessment to thirteen coups. The Chakri dynasty began ruling what is today Thailand in 1782 with the reign of King Rama I. Rumbling of discontent began in the reign of King Rama VII in the first decades of the twentieth century. United by a desire for increased equality, rights and liberty in Siam, and inspired by transformations both inside and beyond the country, a group of seven students met in Paris in February 1927 and began developing the plans for what would become the People's Party (*khana ratsadorn*). They decided that the overthrow of the absolute monarchy would be necessary to achieve their goals and worked to develop a network to do so upon their

[5] Criminal Court Order, Black Case O. 1805/2558, 29 May 2015; Appeal Court Decision, Black Case No. 2196/2558, Red Case No. 18002/2558, 23 November 2015; Supreme Court, Decision No. 1688/2561, 27 March 2018.

[6] Tayyub Mahmud, 'Jurisprudence of Successful Treason: Coup d'Etat and Common Law' (1994) 27(1) *Cornell International Law Journal* 5 1.

return to Siam. The membership of the People's Party ultimately reached 102 members, with Colonel Phraya Phahon Phonphayuhasena leading the military faction and Pridi Banomyong leading the civilian faction.

In the early morning of 24 June 1932, the military faction seized and neutralised military and key government figures. Pridi and the civilian faction disseminated information to the public calling for a constitutional regime; the manifesto proclaimed that 'The king maintains his power above the law as before. He appoints court relatives and toadies without merit or knowledge to important positions, without listening to the voice of the people.'[7] They allowed the King to remain on the throne as long as he was willing to be placed under a constitution. He quickly assented and no blood was shed. The resulting post-absolutist constitutional regime was what Arjun Subramanyan describes as a democracy in which the very content of democracy remained ambiguous.[8] Pridi Banomyong, the civilian leader of the People's Party which led the transformation, explained that there was no word for 'revolution' in the Thai language in 1932, and so they used the phrase 'a change from the system of government in which the king is above the law to the system of government in which the king is under the law' to describe their actions.[9]

The work by the People's Party to create a system of rule of law which restrained the power of the King, rather than destroy the rule of law, is the reason why I previously did not include the end of the absolute monarchy as part of the totality of coups in Thailand. But in an unexpected and unfortunate turn, the amnesty that the People's Party passed to absolve themselves of the action of deposing the King became the point of departure for coup amnesty laws, including the coup which deposed them less than a year later. For this reason, I changed how I tabulated the number of coups and I begin my brief history of coup amnesty laws with it.

The People's Party placed the King under the law and themselves above it. Passed two days after the King was deposed, Article 3 in the amnesty for the 24 June 1932 transformation from absolute to constitutional monarchy stipulated that, 'The entirety of the actions, regardless of who within the People's Party [carried them out], are not to be considered a violation of any law, at all.'[10] This provision made all of their actions – left entirely unspecified – not illegal. The beginning of the constitutional polity was sealed with an amnesty law. The transformational impulse for the rule of law contained within the events of 24 June 1932 soon began to undergo a process of repression and erasure, and the will to redefine illegal actions as legal has instead become foundational in Thailand through the series of subsequent amnesty laws.

The first coup against the new constitutional regime came less than a year later. On 20 June 1933, Colonel Phraya Phahon Phonphayuhasena carried out a coup against the civilian-led government of Phraya Manopakorn Nititada and replaced the members of the cabinet. His actions were precipitated by the presentation of Pridi's Draft Economic Plan, a democratisation of ownership and the economy, to parliament; the document was attacked as communist and Pridi fled into exile. The amnesty law began by noting that since the coup transpired smoothly and without violence, it was appropriate for those involved to receive

7 Chris Baker and Pasuk Phongpaichit, *A History of Thailand* (Cambridge: Cambridge University Press, 2014) 118.

8 Arjun Subramanyan, 'The Unruly Past: History and Historiography of the 1932 Thai Revolution' (2019) 50(1) *Journal of Contemporary Asia* 78.

9 Pridi Banomyong, *Pridi by Pridi: Selected Writings on Life, Politics, and Economy*, translated by Chris Baker and Pasuk Phongpaichit (Chiang Mai: Silkworm Books, 2000) 124–5.

10 All translations in this chapter are my own. 'พระราชกำหนดนิรโทษกรรมในคราวเปลี่ยนแปลงการปกครองแผ่นดิน พุทธศักราช 2475' ['Royal Amnesty Act on the Occasion of the Transformation of the Country, B.E. 2475'] *Ratchakitchanubeksa*, 26 June 1932, Book 49, 165.

royal grace in response to their actions. Here, violence is described as the absence of physical harm, without recognition of other possible forms of violence or other recipients than individuals. The text of the amnesty law that was passed five days after the coup was very similar to the one that the People's Party had passed a year earlier. Article 3 closely resembled the same article in the previous amnesty and specified that: 'The entirety of the actions, no matter who within the army, navy and civilian factions [carried them out], if they were illegal, are not to at all be considered a violation of the law.'[11] By noting that actions that might be illegal were not to be interpreted as such, the law implicitly acknowledged the illegality of the coup. Although Pridi was soon able to return, briefly, to Siam, the coup and the amnesty signalled the consequences for actions or rule that attempted to clarify the ambiguity of the new democracy or push it too far.

Fourteen years passed before the next coup. On 7 November 1947, a junta calling itself the *khana thahan*, or military group, unambiguously carried out a coup to increase the role of the military in politics and to install a dictatorship. Article 3 in the coup amnesty prescribed that

> The entirety of actions carried out before this law comes into force, as a result of the coup nullifying the 1946 (Interim) Constitution, if they were illegal, the perpetrators who carried them out shall be absolved from guilt and all responsibility. Anything carried out under the various announcements and orders issued during the aforementioned coup are to be considered legal.[12]

This amnesty goes beyond delimiting illegal actions as *not being illegal* to making them *legal* and to protecting perpetrators from prosecution. Further, by making actions that follow from orders and announcements issued by the junta legal, the very meaning of law is transformed to include that which is issued from the barrel of a gun.

The only coup without an accompanying amnesty took place a year later during the 6 April 1948 coup when the *khana thahan* replaced their civilian prime minister, Khuang Aphaiwong, with Field Marshal Phibun Songkhram. Three years later, the *khana thahan* carried out an autocoup against themselves to increase their power. Article 3 in the amnesty for the 29 November 1951 coup used very similar language to that of the amnesty for the 1947 coup and noted that

> The entirety of actions carried out before this law comes into force, as a result of the coup nullifying the 1949 Constitution and bringing back the 1932 Constitution, with the 1939 amendment on the name of the country, and the 1940 transitional provisions, if they were illegal, the perpetrators who carried them out shall be absolved from guilt and all responsibility. Anything carried out under the various announcements and orders issued during this transformation are to be considered legal.[13]

The use of *if* in various amnesties to delimit the actions covered by them functions as the opposite of the usual purpose of the conditional to signal the hypothetical or possible: the actions *were* illegal and that is the very reason why the amnesty law was passed.

11 'พระราชบัญญัตินิรโทษกรรมในการจัดการให้คณะรัฐมนตรีลาออกเพื่อให้มีการเปิดสภาผู้แทนราษฎรตามรัฐธรรมนูญ พ.ศ. 2476' ['Amnesty Act for Arranging the Resignation of the Cabinet to Open Parliament According to the B.E. 2476 Constitution'] *Ratchakitchanubeksa*, 25 June 1933, Book 50, 391.

12 'พระราชบัญญัตินิรโทษกรรมแก่ผู้กระทำรัฐประหาร พ.ศ. 2490' [' Amnesty Act for Those Who Carried Out the Coup B.E. 2490'] *Ratchakitchanubeksa*, 23 December 1947, Book 64, Part 62, 743–4.

13 'พระราชบัญญาตินิรโทษกรรมแก่ผู้ที่ได้นำรัฐธรรมนูญแห่งราชอาณาจักรไทย พุทธศักราช 2475 กลับมาใช้ พ.ศ. 2494' ['Amnesty Act for Those Who Reinstated the B.E. 2475 Constitution B.E. 2494'] *Ratchakitchanubeksa*, 31 December 1951, Book 68, Part 80, 28.

A significant shift in the content of the amnesty law arrived when Field Marshal Sarit Thanarat launched his first coup on 16 September 1957 and ended the 'semi-free, semi-unfree' rule of Field Marshal Phibun Songkhram.[14] Article 3 of the amnesty law stipulated that

> The entirety of actions carried out before this law comes into force, whether by an instigator, supporter, a person acting for another, or a person who was used, in the course of seizing the administrative power of the country on 16 September 1957, and other related actions, no matter how they were done and no matter if they were carried out on the aforementioned day or before or after the aforementioned day, if those actions were illegal, the perpetrators who carried them out shall be absolved from guilt and all responsibility. Anything carried out under the various announcements and orders issued, in whatever form, that are related to the aforementioned actions, whether directly or implicitly, are to be considered legal and in force.[15]

In this law, a wide range of actors is specified – many, not only the high-ranking officers in the junta, are covered by 'instigator, supporter, a person acting for another, or a person who was used'. The time covered is also expanded in this amnesty: on, before, or after the date of the actual coup. In addition, in a note appended to the Act, the first amnesty law to have such a note, it is explained that those who fomented the coup did so 'with the wish to eradicate rotten civil service administration and the unfair exercise of power that causes hardship and fear among the people . . .' and therefore it is appropriate to grant them amnesty.[16] In this note, the legislation of the coup 'for the people' begins.

A year later, on 20 October 1958, Field Marshal Sarit launched an autocoup to consolidate his power. Article 3 prescribed that

> The entirety of actions carried out before this law comes into force, that resulted from the coup on 20 October 1958 and other related affairs, all of the actions of the head of the junta or people delegated by the head of the junta carried out for the order and happiness of the people, including punishment and other administrative actions, no matter how they were done and whether they were carried out by an instigator, supporter, a person acting for another or a person who was used, and no matter if they were carried out on the aforementioned day or before or after the aforementioned day, if those actions were illegal, the perpetrators who carried them out shall be absolved from guilt and all responsibility. All of the announcements and orders of the head of the junta, in whatever form, and whether they have administrative or legislative effect are to be considered legal and in force.[17]

The note appended to the law offered that the coup was carried out 'with the wish for Thailand to have a constitution to rule the kingdom that is appropriate and [so that the country] remains an absolute and more orderly democracy and with a wish to limit the strategic activities of communists to take over the country, which is a very grave danger'.[18]

14 Craig Reynolds, *Thai Radical Discourse: The Real Face of Thai Feudalism* (Ithaca, NY: Southeast Asia Program Publications, 1994) 34.

15 'พระราชบัญญัตินิรโทษกรรมแก่ผู้กระทำการยึดอำนาจการบริหารราชการแผ่นดินเมื่อวันที่ 16 กันยายน พ.ศ. 2500 พ.ศ. 2500' [' Amnesty Act for Those Who Seized the Administrative Power of the Country on 16 September B.E. 2500'] *Ratchakitchanubeksa*, 26 September 1957, Book 74, Part 81, 2–3.

16 Ibid., 3.

17 'พระราชบัญญัตินิรโทษกรรมแก่ผู้กระทำการผฎิวัติเมื่อวันที่ 20 ตุลาคม พ.ศ. 2501 พ.ศ. 2502' ['Amnesty Act for Those Who Carried out the Revolution on 20 October B.E. 2501 B.E. 2502'] *Ratchakitchanubeksa*, 3 April 1959, Book 76, Part 41, 3.

18 Ibid.

A permanent constitution remained a far-off dream until 1974, despite the alleged wishes of the coup-makers.

Reference to the institution of the monarchy enters the picture in the amnesty for the coup that Field Marshal Thanom Kittikachorn, who took over the dictatorship after Sarit's death in 1963, launched against himself to consolidate his power on 17 November 1971. Article 3 noted that

> The entirety of actions before the law enters into force, that were carried out in relation to the coup on 17 November 1971 or related affairs, the entirety of actions of the head of the junta or people delegated by the head of the junta or people ordered by the person delegated by the head of the junta that were carried out for the security of the nation and the Crown, and for the order and happiness of the people, including punishment and other administrative actions, no matter how they were done and whether they were carried out by an instigator, supporter, a person acting for another or a person who was used, and no matter if they were carried out on the aforementioned day or before or after the aforementioned day, if those actions were illegal, the perpetrators who carried them out shall be absolved from guilt and all responsibility.[19]

The 'people' are positioned third here, after the nation and the Crown. The note explains that the junta fomented the coup 'with the wish to resolve the situation dangerous to the nation, the institution of the monarchy, and the people, and to set an administrative structure appropriate for the state of the country, the economic foundation, and the sentiment of the people, in order to create well-being for the Thai people and prosperity for the country'.[20] The coup – which was a coup of Thanom against his own government to further centralise power – in this rendering was allegedly carried out for the happiness of the people and in order to mitigate danger to the institution of the monarchy. What was the precise nature of the danger to the monarchy, who made this assessment, and who called for its insertion into the law? The coup took place during the years of the Cold War in which fears of communism were both real, as prompted by the long-time organisation of the Communist Party of Thailand, and imagined within the heated atmosphere of US-supported counterinsurgency in the region. The institution of the monarchy has remained a frequent feature of amnesty laws since then.

The dictatorship of Field Marshal Thanom Kittikachorn ended on 14 October 1973 after hundreds of thousands of students and citizens took to the streets and demanded a constitution. During the subsequent three years, the most fulsome democracy since 24 June 1932 emerged in Thailand and a wide range of citizens participated in politics, including farmers, workers, teachers, artists and many others. But regional transformations, including transitions to communism in Cambodia, Vietnam and Laos in 1975, and the rising right-wing in Thailand, led to a backlash in the claimed service of protection of the monarchy as well as the nation and the Buddhist religion. This backlash culminated in a massacre of university students at Thammasat University on the morning of 6 October 1976, and a coup that returned the country to dictatorship on the same afternoon.[21] In the amnesty soon

19 'พระราชบัญญัตินิรโทษกรรมแก่ผู้กระทำการปฏิวัติ เมื่อวันที่ 17 พฤศจิกายน พ.ศ. 2514 พ.ศ. 2515' ['Amnesty Act for Those Who Carried out the Revolution on 17 November B.E. 2514 B.E. 2515'] *Ratchakitchanubeksa*, 26 December 1972, Book 79, Part 197, 235–6.

20 Ibid., 237.

21 Puey Ungpakorn, who was Rector of Thammasat University at the time of the massacre, assembled a timeline of events on 6 October 1976; see Puey Ungpakorn, 'Violence and the Military Coup in Thailand' (1977) 9(3) *Bulletin of Concerned Asian Scholars* 4–12. Puey notes that the NARC said that forty-one were killed, several hundred injured and 3,037 arrested, but that 'sources at the Chinese Benevolent Foundation, which transported

promulgated, perpetrators of a wide range of violent actions in addition to the coup itself were absolved of their guilt in the service of the protection of the monarchy. Article 3 of the amnesty passed for the 6 October 1976 coup carried out by the National Administrative Reform Council (NARC) stipulated that

> The entirety of actions taken along with the seizure of the administrative power of the country on 6 October 1976 and the actions of individuals connected with those aforementioned actions were undertaken with the intention of fostering the security of the Kingdom, the Crown and public peace. The entirety of actions of the NARC or the head of the NARC or those who were appointed by the NARC or the head of the NARC, or those who were ordered by someone appointed by the NARC or the head of the NARC that were carried out for the reasons noted above including punishment and the bureaucratic administration of the country, all of the aforementioned actions, irrespective of their legislative, administrative, or judicial validity, irrespective of whether they were carried out by someone in the position of a principal figure, a supporter, a person acting for another, or a person who was used, and irrespective of whether or not they were carried out on the aforementioned day or before or after that day, if the actions were unlawful, the person is absolved from wrongdoing and all responsibility.[22]

An amnesty article was included in the immediate post-coup constitution, but the military was concerned that it was not sufficient, which is why a separate amnesty law was drafted and passed in December 1976. During the drafting process and the debate on the draft in the appointed legislative assembly, the importance of preventing prosecution of grave crimes for *all* involved, including soldiers at the rank of privates and ordinary citizens, not only the officers in the junta, was highlighted. The actions which needed to be amnestied extended beyond the administrative action of the coup that displaced the civilian government. This was an amnesty not only for the coup, but also for the massacre of students at Thammasat University that preceded it and the drafters were confident that that the temporal language in the amnesty made its coverage universal.[23] The reason given for the coup in the note appended to this law was identical to the note for the amnesty for the 1971 coup.[24] But here, brutal and lethal violence against the people was made legal, if not legitimate in a broader sense, as part of the defence of the institution of the monarchy.

However, the far-right regime of Thanon Kraivichien put in place by the 6 October 1976 coup by the NARC did not last long, and a little over a year later, on 20 October 1977, General Kriangsak Chomanand launched another coup. Article 3 of the amnesty for this coup stipulated that

> All of the actions by individuals taken along with the seizure of administrative power of the country on 20 October 1977 and the related actions by individuals that were carried out with the intention to foster the security of the Kingdom and for the happiness of the people, and

and cremated the dead, it was revealed [sic] that they handled "over a hundred corpses" that day'; Puey, 'Violence and the Military Coup', 8.

22 'พระราชบัญญัตินิรโทษกรรมแก่ผู้กระทำการยึดอำนาจการปกครองประเทศ เมื่อวันที่ 6 ตุลาคม พ.ศ. 2519 พ.ศ. 2519' ['Amnesty Act for Those Who Seized the Administrative Power of the Country on 6 October B.E. 2519 B.E. 2519'] *Ratchakitchanubeksa*, 24 December 1976, Book 93, Part 156, 44–5.

23 This cannot be discerned from the text of the law itself, but it is clear in the file from the Office of the Juridical Council file about the drafting process and the minutes from the debate in the assembly. See Tyrell Haberkorn, 'The Hidden Transcript of Amnesty: The 6 October 1976 Massacre and Coup in Thailand' (2015) 47(1) *Critical Asian Studies* 44–68.

24 Ibid., 'Amnesty Act for Those Who Seized the Administrative Power of the Country on 6 October B.E. 2519 B.E. 2519', 45.

> the entirety of the actions taken by the revolutionary council of the head of the revolutionary council, or people received ordered from those who were appointed by the revolutionary council or the head of the revolutionary council, which were done for the aforementioned reasons, including the punishment and bureaucratic administration of the country, all of the aforementioned actions, irrespective of their legislative, administrative, or judicial validity, irrespective of whether they were carried out by someone in the position of a principal figure, a supporter, a person acting for another, or a person who was used, and irrespective of whether or not they were carried out on the aforementioned day or before or after that day, if the actions were unlawful, the person is absolved from wrongdoing and all responsibility.[25]

The text of this law is almost identical to the amnesty from the prior coup. Even though there was no need to apply the broad, universal coverage used for the amnesty for the 6 October 1976 massacre and coup to this coup, which resembled a more typical coup in which the existing government was illegally ousted, the drafters left it in place. The reason given for the coup in the note appended to this amnesty further elaborated an idea of a coup for progress, national unity and happiness, similar to the amnesty for Field Marshal Thanom Kittikachorn's 1971 autocoup. It was appropriate for those who launched the coup to receive an amnesty because they acted

> with an intention for the country to be administered efficiently, able to solve the problems of the country in a timely manner, quickly restore the economy and society, and to improve national unity and peace and order, and to restore international relations. [It was carried out] For the internal and external security of the Kingdom and to foster the happiness of the people and the progress of the country.[26]

Those who carried out the coup were considered to have done so with no desire for personal benefit and were therefore deserving of protection from prosecution. The note seems to suggest that as long as one abrogated the constitution and illegally seized power in a selfless manner, then it was acceptable.

During the waning years of the Cold War, Thailand entered a period without coups and almost fourteen years passed until the next one. On 21 February 1991, General Suchinda Krapayoon and a junta calling itself the National Peace Keeping Council (NPKC) ousted the elected government of Prime Minister Chatichai Choonhaven, which they claimed was corrupt. Article 3 of the amnesty passed for the coup was very similar to that of the 6 October 1976 and 20 October 1977 coups and stipulated that

> The entirety of actions taken along with the seizure and control of the administrative power of the country on 21 February 1991 and the actions of individuals connected with those aforementioned actions and all of the actions of the NPKC or the head of the NPKC or those who were appointed by the NPKC or the head of the NPKC, or those who were ordered by someone appointed by the NPKC or the head of the NPKC that were carried out for the reasons noted above including punishment and the bureaucratic administration of the country, all of the aforementioned actions, irrespective of their legislative, administrative, or judicial validity, irrespective of whether they were carried out by someone in the position of a principal figure, a supporter, a person acting for another, or a person who was used, and irrespective of whether or not they were carried out on the aforementioned day or before or

25 'พระราชบัญญัตินิรโทษกรรมแก่ผู้กระทำการอันเป็นความผิดต่อความมั่นคงของรัฐภายในราชอาณาจักร ระหว่างวันที่ 25 และวันที่ 26 มีนาคม พ.ศ. 2520 พ.ศ. 2520' ['Amnesty Act for Those Who Committed Offences Against State Security Inside the Kingdom Between 25 and 26 March B.E. 2520 B.E. 2520'] *Ratchakitchanubeksa*, 3 December 1977, Book 94, Part 121, 7.

26 Ibid., 8.

> after that day, if the actions were unlawful, the person is absolved from wrongdoing and all responsibility.[27]

The reasons given for this coup in the note appended to the law were more expansive than those given in earlier notes and included 'the wish to resolve the situation dangerous to the nation, institution of the monarchy, and the people, in order to create security for the Kingdom, fairness in rule, unity of those in the country, peace and order, well-being of the Thai people, and prosperity of the country'.[28] Through the series of six notes appended to the amnesty laws, a logic in which coups are cast as a way to protect the nation and the institution of the monarchy, foster economic prosperity, and in this note, fairness and unity, is advanced. But can a coup – the illegal seizure of the authority to govern a country – do any of these things?

The 1991 coup was the last one for which a stand-alone amnesty law was passed. The 19 September 2006 coup that ousted the elected government of Prime Minister Thaksin Shinawatra was addressed by a constitutional article. Section 37 of the 2006 Interim Constitution stipulated that

> All acts done by the Chairman of the Council for Democratic Reform which related to the seizure and control of the State administrative power on 19th September 2006 as well as any act done by persons involved in such seizure or of persons being assigned by the Chairman of the Council for Democratic Reform or of persons being commanded by the Chairman of the Council for Democratic Reform which done for such above act. All these acts, whether done for the enforcement in legislative, executive or judicial force as well as the punishment and other acts on administration of the State affairs whether done as principals, supporters, instigators or persons being commanded to do so and whether done on such date or prior to such date or after such date which if such acts may be unlawful, the actors shall be absolutely exempted from any wrongdoing, responsibility and liabilities.

The form and content of the constitutional provision is nearly identical to the series of Article 3s that began with the amnesty for the 6 October 1976 massacre and coup. The expansive coverage of time and actors provided was in excess of what was needed to protect the instigators of the 1977, 1991 and 2006 coups from prosecution but became a useful foundation for the amnesty for the rule of the National Council for Peace and Order, and the junta that launched the most recent coup on 22 May 2014.

18.3 THE 22 MAY 2014 COUP AND A FUTURE END TO IMPUNITY FOR COUPS

The 19 September 2006 coup began a period of color-coded contention and chaos between the generally royalist-nationalist yellow shirts who called for the coup and the generally democratic-populist red shirts who variously supported the ousted prime minister, opposed the coup, or desired radical democracy that remains unresolved after thirteen years and another coup.[29] Extended protests and public violence became frequent after 2006, including

27 'พระราชบัญญัตินิรโทษกรรมแก่ผู้กระทำการยึดและควบคุมอำนาจการปกครองแผ่นดิน เมื่อวันที่ 23 กุมภาพันธ์ พ.ศ. 2534 พ.ศ. 2534' ['Amnesty Act for Those Who Seized and Controlled the Administrative Power of the Country on 23 February B.E 2534 B.E. 2534'] *Ratchakitchanubeksa*, 3 May 1991, Book 118, Part 79, 2–3.

28 Ibid., 4.

29 See this special issue of the *Journal of Contemporary Asia* about the background and effects of the 19 September 2006 coup: Michael Kelly Connors and Kevin Hewison (eds.), 'Issue 1: Thailand's "Good Coup": The Fall of Thaksin, the Military and Democracy' (2008) 38(1) *Journal of Contemporary Asia*.

a state crackdown on a red shirt demonstration in April–May 2010 which both stands as the greatest loss of life during a protest in Thai history and catalysed a return to building a more democratic polity.[30] But by late 2013, a combination of concern over the critical nature of dissent in the midst of a looming royal transition and anger by yellow shirt conservatives at actions by the government of Prime Minister Yingluck Shinawatra (the younger sister of the exiled former prime minister) began to grow. After six months of protests by a yellow-shirt network called the People's Democratic Reform Committee that aimed to bring about chaos and therefore create an opening for military intervention, a junta calling itself the National Council for Peace and Order (NCPO) launched a coup on 22 May 2014.

The regime of the NCPO is the most repressive since the anti-communist counterinsurgent dictatorships of the late 1950s to the late 1970s. Although a detailed review of the human rights violations is beyond the scope of this chapter, political freedom and freedom of expression have been severely restricted, arbitrary detention and torture of dissidents frequent, and concerning reports of disappearance and death in custody of those seen to be critical of the monarchy have all marked the regime of the NCPO.[31] The manipulation and excessive use of prosecution and the law itself is at the core of the dictatorship of the NCPO; even when extrajudicial violence has taken place under the NCPO, it is frequently in relation to the exercise of law.[32]

The amnesty provision promulgated by the NCPO is very similar to and contains the same universal frame as the earlier amnesty laws beginning with that for the 6 October 1976 massacre and coup. Section 48 of the Interim Constitution of 2014, issued less than two months after the coup by the NCPO, stipulated that

> In regard to all acts which are performed on account of the seizure and control of State governing power on 22 May 2014 by the Head and the National Council for Peace and Order, including all acts of persons incidental to such performance or of persons entrusted by the Head or the National Council for Peace and Order or of persons ordered by persons entrusted by the Head or the National Council for Peace and Order, which have been done for the benefit of the abovementioned performances, irrespective of whether such acts were performed to have constitutional, legislative, executive, or judicial force, including punishments and other official administrative acts, and irrespective of whether the persons performed such acts as a principal, an accomplice, an instigator or an agent and whether those acts have been done on, before or after the aforesaid date, if those acts constitute offences under the laws, the persons who commit those acts shall be entirely discharged from such offences and liabilities.

But will this amnesty hold permanently? On 23 March 2019, the first national election since the coup by the NCPO was held. Despite a grossly uneven electoral field in which campaigning was restricted and the political party affiliated with the NCPO was given a significant leg up on other political parties, a significant number of voters indicated a desire for democracy and for an end to military involvement in politics.[33] The combination

30 See People's Information Center for Those Affected by the Dispersal of Protests in April–May 2010 (PIC). *Truth for Justice: A Fact-finding Report on the April–May 2010 Crackdowns in Bangkok* (Bangkok: PIC, 2017).

31 See the periodic updates and annual reports created by Thai Lawyers for Human Rights, established on the night of the coup to defend those targeted by the NCPO and document human rights abuses, in Thai and English at www.tlhr2014.com (accessed 17 June 2019).

32 'The Miracle of 'Law': The Judiciary and the 22 May 2014 Coup, Three Years of the Coup Regime of the National Council for Peace and Order' Thai Lawyers for Human Rights, 1 August 2017, www.tlhr2014.com/th/?p=4774 (accessed 12 May 2019).

33 Punchada Sirivunnabood, 'Thailand's Puzzling 2019 Election: How the NCPO Junta Has Embedded Itself in Thai Politics' ISEAS Perspective, 29 May 2019, www.iseas.edu.sg/images/pdf/ISEAS_Perspective_2019_44.pdf (accessed 3 June 2019).

of the provisions in the 2017 Constitution that provide for the NCPO's continued involvement in politics, even after the election and their ongoing attempts to discredit progressive political parties, indicate their desire to hold on to power by all means necessary.[34] But why? The significant power and financial benefits one can accrue as a member of a ruling junta provide part of the answer. But I would like to propose that their concerns may be far more direct: the desire to avoid prosecution for the coup and the subsequent human-rights violations and other transgressions of the law carried out by or in relation to the NCPO during their five years of rule. The available evidence suggests that at a minimum, General Prayuth Chan-ocha and the NCPO could be facing allegations of arbitrary detention, torture, disappearance, extrajudicial killing, land grabbing, and corruption, were they to exit power. Even a judiciary sympathetic to coups *qua* coups may not be willing to forgive this range of violations of the law.[35]

Although Thailand has thus far been immune to what Kathryn Sikkink calls the 'justice cascade' that has led to the increase in prosecution of dictators around the world in recent decades, just as many Thai voters selected a change in March 2019, transformation may begin in other arenas as well.[36]

A new jurisprudence – an anti-coup jurisprudence – is needed to begin undoing the legal, political, and social effects of the repetition of amnesty laws over the last eighty-seven years.[37] The seeds of such a jurisprudence can be found in the criminal case referred to above against the NCPO brought by a civil society group, Resistant Citizen. On the one-year anniversary of the coup, fifteen members of the group filed a criminal complaint against General Prayuth and the other four members of the NCPO. Resistant Citizen argued that they should be prosecuted for violation of Articles 113 and 114 of the Criminal Code, which define the crimes and prescribe the punishments for the crimes of rebellion and treason, respectively. The maximum penalty for Article 113 is death or life imprisonment and for Article 114 is three to fifteen years imprisonment. They describe the precise effects of the coup and the subsequent repressive regime on their lives as evidence of the crimes of the NCPO. The complaint is significant because the members of Resistant Citizen frame their argument with a notion of sovereignty in which the people are at the centre of the polity, which is an idea that first entered the polity with the 24 June 1932 end to absolute monarchy but has slowly but steadily lost official credence since then.[38]

The Court of First Instance and the Appeal Court both dismissed Resistant Citizen's complaint without examining it. But the Supreme Court accepted the complaint and ruled on it in March 2018. Like the two lower courts, the Supreme Court dismissed the complaint.

34 Khana Nitirat, 'Declaration of the Khana Nitirat: The Draft Constitution and the Referendum' Prachatai English, 10 June 2016, http://prachatai.org/english/node/6251 (accessed 15 March 2019).

35 On the other hand, the judiciary might. Writing about the bizarre decision of the Criminal Court to dismiss the case against Abhisit Vejjajiva and Suthep Thaugsuban for their role in ordering the crackdown on red shirt protestors during April–May 2010, Nidhi Eoseewong argued that the decision marked a point in modern Thai history when amnesty laws were no longer necessary because the courts were willing to legalize murder. See Nidhi Eoseewong, 'The Past-Present-Future of the Court's Decision' translated by Tyrell Haberkorn, Prachatai, 17 September 2014, www.prachatai.org/english/node/4340 (accessed 10 May 2019).

36 Kathryn Sikkink, *The Justice Cascade: How Human Rights Prosecutions Are Changing World Politics* (New York: W.W. Norton, 2011).

37 This is the context in which the legal challenge brought by Resistant Citizen against General Prayuth and the NCPO for launching the coup and subsequently carrying out rights violations is very significant. Although the Criminal Court did not accept the case, they acknowledged that the plaintiffs had sustained negative effects from the coup. A future of impunity is not a foregone conclusion.

38 In the section, I draw on analysis I wrote for Thai Lawyers for Human Rights: 'The Owners of Sovereignty' Thai Lawyers for Human Rights, 12 March 2019, www.tlhr2014.com/?p=11291&lang=en (accessed 5 June 2019).

Their primary reason for doing so was that Section 48 of the Interim Constitution of 2014 placed the NCPO's actions beyond prosecution. Since decisions refuting challenge to the 1947 and 1958 coups, the Supreme Court has advanced a jurisprudence in line with Hans Kelsen's theory of revolutionary legality: if the coup government can retain power, then it is valid.[39]

On the one hand, then, this decision is in line with previous decisions. But in their short decision, the Supreme Court also inserted a subtle question about the legitimacy of the 22 May 2014 Coup. They wrote that 'The NCPO instead entered to exercise the authority of the sovereign, even though, as the fifteen plaintiffs have claimed, that authority was secured in a manner not in accordance with democracy. Whether or not that power was legitimately obtained is another issue to be discussed elsewhere.'[40]

These two sentences break significant new ground in the jurisprudence of coups. The Supreme Court did not specify where or how this discussion should be taken up, but in raising the question, they cast a shadow over the unchallenged legitimacy of coups and their own role in maintaining it.

Jules Lobel argues that unsuccessful legal battles remain significant in the long-term movement for justice because they create a community of solidarity, memory of struggles, and the aspiration of a different and better society.[41] I would also add that the cases perform the crucial, initial work of describing and making a different and better society imaginable in legal terms. In responding to Resistant Citizen's case, the Supreme Court in Thailand was forced to take a position in response to their articulation of a fundamental contradiction between the text of the law and questions of justice that go beyond the text. Although the Supreme Court adhered to the text of the law in their interpretation, they left the door open for a future reinterpretation. Combined with concerted citizen action, this invitation to a reinterpretation of the legality of the coup is precisely what is needed to interrupt the repetition of coup amnesties, and coups, in Thailand.

39 See Supreme Court decisions 1153–1154/2495 (1952), 45/2496 (1953), 1512–1515/2497 (1954), and 1662/2505 (1962). Many thanks to Rawin Leelapattana for this insight. For a comparative analysis of the application of Kelsen by courts in the aftermath of coups, see Tayyub Mahmud, 'Jurisprudence of Successful Treason'.

40 Supreme Court, Decision No. 1688/2561, 27 March 2018.

41 Jules Lobel, *Success Without Victory: Lost Legal Battles and the Long Road to Justice in America* (New York: New York University Press, 2003).

Glossary

THAI TERM TRANSLATION

Aggañña Sutta Buddhist history and cosmology
Aggati Prejudice
Aiyakan Business of the Lord
Arahat The enlightened one
Barami Transcendental virtue/moral perfection and charismatic authority
Bun Buddhist merit
Chao Phaendin Lord of the Land
Chat Nation
Chonplon Robbery committed by more than ten people
Dassakorachon Robbery with arson
Devaraja God-King
Dhamma Buddhist teaching
Dhammaraja The righteous King
Dhammasattha Traditional law codes in Burma; a Burmese rendering of Dharmasastra
Dhammikkaracha The King who rules in accordance with Dhamma
Dharmasastra / Dhammasastra Traditional law codes from India and their descendents in Southeast Asia
Dumin Insult
Issraphap Freedom
Jataka The Great Births of Buddha
Kha tham khawn Damages paid by an injurer to the victim
Khana Ratsadorn The People's Party
Khaphraphuttachao Slave of your Lordship
Khodecha fulaong thuliphrabatbokklaobokkramom May the power of dust under the dust of the soles of your sacred feet protect the top of my head
Khongman Engage gift
Khwam Dee Ngam Virtue
Khwam Pen Dham Justice
Kinnari A mythical bird-human hybrid
Kod Mai Phra Song Law on monkhood
Kwai Buffalo/dirty and ignorant labourers
Lameut mi dai Inviolable
Maha Sommutiraj The Great Elected
Mahachonnikorn Samoson Sommot Elected by the consensus of all
Mangraisat Lanna's premodern law texts promulgated by King Mangrai
Manudharmmasattham Law of Manu

Mea Klang Muang Major wife
Mea Klang Nork Minor wife
Mea Klang Tasi Slave wife
Minpramat Defame
Monthon Units of subdivision of Thailand
Nititham Rule of law
Parajika Monkhood invalidated
Phithii saab charng Cursing ritual
Phor Khun Father-like ruler
Phra aiyakarn laksana phua mia Royal code concerning husbands and wives
Phra Ayakarn Laksana Bet Set Miscellaneous Law
Phra Mahakasat Thai Nai Rabobprachati pa tai Thai Monarchy in a Democratic System
Phra Phathom Borom Ratcha Ong – kan Initial royal command
Phrachaoyuhua Lord above our heads
Phraratcha Kamnot Royal decree
Phu Nam Leader
Prawatisat Kotmai Thai History of Thai Law
Rachasap Royal language
Rajasat Law made by the King
Sadeng Khwam – a khatamat – rai Threaten
Sakara Sacred
Satsuon Proportionality
Sinsod Bride price
Thammapiban Good governance
Thammasat Traditional law codes in Siam; a Thai rendering of Dharmasastra
Thanong ong at Dare without fear or embarrassment
Thra ayakan luang Section on crimes against the King
Yokkrabat Officers who acted as royal emissaries to the provinces
Yu-ti-tham Justice

Index

For EU product safety concerns, contact us at Calle de José Abascal, 56–1°,
28003 Madrid, Spain or eugpsr@cambridge.org.

www.ingramcontent.com/pod-product-compliance
Ingram Content Group UK Ltd.
Pitfield, Milton Keynes, MK11 3LW, UK
UKHW030903150625
459647UK00022B/2837

* 9 7 8 1 1 0 8 8 2 9 8 6 1 *